MW01194120

God and Wealth

The Rise and Fall of Nations

Nicholas Christos Georgalis

Contents

List of Figures 8
List of Tables 11
Prologue 12
   The Soul of the Soldier 12
   Private Property and the Enforcement of laws and contracts 20
   Obedience to law compelled by fear of God and the sovereign's power
   of eminent domain 21
   Fear of God or Love of Man 22
   Biblical root of freewill 22
   Human Sacrifice and Human Psyche 24
   The existence of God 26
   Rapid increases of productivity and unemployment 27
   Moral Philosophy 28
   Law does not sanction Justice 30
   Equity and Justice conflated 31
   The "Justice" of the French Revolution 31
   Colonization Justified 33
   The morality of slavery 34
   Obligation, Duty and Responsibility 35
   The Golden Rule as a manifestation of self-interest 36
   Charity 37
   Gratitude and Resentment 39
   No Social Contract 40
   Laws equally applicable to all 41
   The Soul of the Soldier, Productivity and Unemployment 42
   God's Law, Sovereign Law, and Natural Law 43
Introduction 45
   Rapid gains in productivity as the source of wealth and war 46
   Fractional banking not a cause of calamity 46
   Calamity is the destruction of private property 56
   Definition of encumbered economy 57
Section 1. Private Property and Free Will 58
   Private Property 58
   Individual liberty 58
   Man's passions and economics 59
   Intelligence manifested in productivity 60
   Intellectual capital and wealth creation 61
   The philosophy of wealth creation 62
   Private Property and Freewill 63
   A man's life is private property 64
   Conception is an act of God not of man 65
   Burdensome laws 66
   Suicide 67

Property right is a misnomer 67
Sovereign's life held in common 68
God created an individual and not "people" 69
Citizens of a nation 69
"War of all against all" 70
The language of sovereignty 71
The Nation 71
Security in exchange for liberty 72
Republic overthrown by civil war, a tyranny or monarchy overthrown
by rebellion 73
The Meaning of Wealth...76
Measurement of Wealth Creation 79
The US Treasury coins money the Federal Reserve Bank prints money
....81
Money is not wealth...85
Distinction between monetary inflation and economic inflation 95
The sovereign burdens wealth creation 97
Subtracting government spending from GDP 108
Total government expenditures 109
Interest rates reflect government burden and interference in the
economy...110
The gold standard imposed fiscal and monetary discipline on the
government 113
Federal Reserve Act Amended by Congress to enable political
accommodation 114
Community Reinvestment Act – an example of regulatory
encumbrance...117
The Actual Burden of Government..119
Laws that mandate terms and conditions in a contract encumber the
economy...122
Abrogation of the Bretton-Woods Agreement 122
The price of gold...125
Returning to the gold standard will result in the creation of wealth ..128
Variation in wealth 129
Absent the fear of God, individual wealth variation engenders envy 131
Measurement of Productivity..132
Private Property and Enforcement of Contract................................136
Characteristics of Private Property...136
The Marriage Contract 136
Conception an Act of God...137
Sovereignty of the Child Bearing Woman...138
Overpopulation is a flawed notion 139
Enclosure laws in England resulted in wealth creation 140
Malthus predicts calamity...142
Fear of God is essential for wealth creation 147

The United States Constitution significance to wealth creation 147
Flawed notions of the nature of man and purpose of government ...148
Private Property is assignable and inheritable.....................................149
A will and a deed impose duty on the Sovereign 149
The Sovereign Power of Eminent Domain 151
Contract cannot exist between the Sovereign and an Individual.......151
The Corporation as Private Property..152
A corporation that does not make profit is unethical 152
No duty to employees...153
Loyalty...154
Loyalty in Rebellion and Civil War..155
Morality and Ethics..155
Is covetousness the ultimate expression of man's self-interest and
Man's freewill? 157
The Soul of a Corporation...157
Labor Contacts are unethical because they are coercive....................158
Individuals must yield some productivity and some liberty for security
....160
Sovereign poses risk to wealth creation in two ways. 162
Sovereignty of multiple elected officials 162
The hypocrisy of the French Revolution..164
Rapid gains in productivity lead to unemployment 165
A sovereign who does not fear God threatens the survival of a nation
....168
The Nation's Wealth...168
Replacement of equipment or structures is not wealth creation 169
The ability to create wealth resides in the intellect of individuals.......169
Sovereign acquires assets by force or threat of force 170
Wealth is the only hedge against calamity. 172
Efficiency of capital and efficiency of labor 172
Sources of inflation 173
Profit is wealth creation and a measure of efficiency 175
Profit is a measure of the satisfaction of consumer needs 176
Sustaining an unprofitable enterprise places a burden on wealth
creation..176
Supply and Demand determine price in an unencumbered economy
....178
In an encumbered economy price is independent of supply and
demand..181
USPS is an example of how government distorts the free market.....184
Inflation similar to income taxes because it affects all goods and
services 189
Government interference in the economy accelerated in the 1970s..191
Prices have no moral or ethical basis in an unencumbered economy193
Usury laws 193

Usury laws is an early example of coercion in an economy 195
Coercion in the economy..197
Are productivity improvements that lead to layoffs ethical and moral?
....201
Low interest rates leads to unemployment..202
All productivity improvements are due to technological advancements
....205
No sovereign encumbrance to Western economies from 17th to 19th
Century..206
Germany's 19th Century social security system encumbered her
economy...207
Private property and all its manifestations is the source of wealth 209
Little civil unrest arising from gains in productivity prior to the 20th
century...210
Universal suffrage engenders wealth destruction 211
Flawed romantic notions of man's nature gave rise to universal
suffrage..213
The alienation of Man from God engenders envy................................216
Rise of labor unions meant the demise of wealth creation.................219
Affirmative action, social and environmental legislation encumber the
economy...224
Causes of Inflation and Deflation 225
"The Moral Equivalence of War"..228
Rapid changes in productivity growth rates cause economic inflation
or deflation 230
Inflation 230
Federal Reserve Bank prints money when it purchases government
debt...235
Federal Reserve Bank intended to support the fractional banking
system..237
Economic inflation is due to changes in supply and demand............245
Relationship between productivity, employment, inflation and union
membership...246
Paradigm shifts in technology during the 1980s.................................250
Government caused the collapse of financial markets in 2008..........251
Clinton – the father of the sub-prime mortgage debacle....................252
Relationship of productivity growth rate and inflation growth rate...253
Variation in inflation rate between labor and capital affects
mechanization. 254
Monetary inflation means that the sovereign does not fear God.......255
Deflation 256
Unions react to the influx of labor from the farm..............................259
Wagner Act and the Glass-Steagall Act encumber economy.............260
Rapid gains in productivity create short-term oversupply of labor....265
Universal suffrage...267

Summary of Section 1..268
Section 2. The Sovereign, the Passions, and God.................................270
Human virtues do not create wealth nor do human vices destroy
wealth 270
The sovereign makes his will known through law 274
The sovereign...276
The sovereign is above all law including Natural Law and God's Law
....278
Taxation is a manifestation of the sovereign power of eminent domain
....279
The head tax is the most equitable of taxes and the most ethical 284
Exchange of property always involves a contract.................................286
Constitutional Laws 287
Duty of sovereign...289
Inflation measures the degree a sovereign encumbers an economy ..292
Man's passions and economics 294
Security in space and in time relies on reason.....................................301
Envy destroys life...302
Encumbering an economy is unethical...305
Gains in productivity are ethical in an unencumbered economy 306
Government infrastructure projects burden wealth creation..............306
Public education burdens wealth creation and is therefore unethical308
Destroying wealth by educating those that cannot be educated........312
Intelligence and Education 318
A nation formed under God is necessary for the survival of the nation
....325
Summary of Section 2..327
Section 3.   The Future of Mankind..328
Ethical and Moral Behavior..328
The individual as an actor in the wealth creating economy................333
Ethical behavior for the individual actor...334
Ethical behavior for the agent..334
Ethical behavior for the sovereign 335
Corruption is particularly insidious unethical behavior......................338
The Wealth Creating Economy – a summary......................................340
Ethical behavior is any behavior that leads to the creation of wealth342
The fear of God distinguishes a wealth creating economy from
capitalism..343
The case for socialism stems from envy and not fear 345
A communist economy relies on envy...349
Truth and Beauty...352
Man can direct his genius to the destruction of wealth......................354
Beauty and wealth 357
Art and Economics 361
The Great Error of Western Philosophy...366

6

Becoming Sovereign 370
God and Sovereignty 372
The future of Mankind..375
The inheritance of intelligence 387
God and Science...394
The destiny of a nation..402
Summary and Conclusion 403
To Critics 405
Appendix 1 406
Determining the Burden of Government 406
Reinvestment of Federal Government Outlays and State and Local
Spending 406
Appendix 2 409
Non-random processes effect on statistical measurements.................409
Bibliography 413
Index...415

List of Figures

Figure 1-Fractional Banking Process..48

Figure 2- Federal Reserve Discount Rate and Percent of Bank Failures .50

Figure 3 – Call Loan Interest Rate and Real S&P 1919-1938 51

Figure 4-Number of IPOs 1973 to 2007...54

Figure 5-Difference between the 12-month moving average change in annualized CPI and the Monthly Prime Interest rate 1950-2012 54

Figure 6 – Price of Cotton per bale 1800 to 1859................................74

Figure 7 –Cotton Production 1000 bales 1800 to 1859 75

Figure 8 – Correlation between US CPI level and Cumulative Monetized debt -1940-2011 82

Figure 9 – Correlation between US CPI level v. US Gross Debt 1900 to 2011 83

Figure 10 – Relative Median Income and Relative Employment Rate – 1967 to 2011 84

Figure 11 – US CPI from 1774 to 2011...85

Figure 12 – Gold net of imports and exports...90

Figure 13 – Agricultural Exports and Imports 1901 to 1935...................92

Figure 14-Relative Changes in M2 Money Supply, Gold Stock and CPI (1914 – 1970)..93

Figure 15 – Ratio of Current Government Transfer Payments to Nominal GDP Personal Expenditures...100

Figure 16 – CPI v. Percent Transfer Payments......................................100

Figure 17-Real GDP in 2009 Chained Dollars.....................................103

Figure 18 – M2 Money Supply v. Ounces of Gold in US Treasury 1914-1970 104

Figure 19-GDP less Government Spending...108

Figure 20-Total Government Outlays 109

Figure 21-Interest Rates and CPI from 1956 to 2012 111

Figure 22 – Difference between level of M2 and level of Gold between 1914 and 1970..112

Figure 23 – Nominal Price of Gold v. CPI..121

Figure 24-Billions ounces of Gold purchasable by the Nominal GDP..121

Figure 25-US Government Debt and Debt Owned by the Public 124

Figure 26-Monthly Prime Interest Rate since 1949 125

Figure 27 – Percent Difference between Annual Average Family Income and Annual Median Family Income (1947-2012)............................131

Figure 28-IBM and AT&T Income Statements-Measure of Productivity 133

Figure 29-GDP per capita v. Real Value Added Output between 1948 and 2010..135

Figure 30-English Agriculture 1250 to 1899...141

Figure 31-Britain's Population 1300 to 1901 142

Figure 32 – Central African Republic per Capita GDP v. Population – 1950 to 2008...144

Figure 33 – Mozambique Per Capita GDP v. Population – 1950-2008.144

Figure 34 – Gabon Per Capita GDP v. Population 1950 to 2008...........145

Figure 35 – Norway Per Capita GDP v. Population 1950 to 2008.........146

Figure 36 – Japan Per Capita GDP v. Population 1950-2008..................146

Figure 37- Federal Government Revenues from 1913 to 1930...............167

Figure 38-Comparison of Growth in average weekly pay, Growth in GDP and Growth in Per Capita GDP for Japan.............................178

Figure 39-Supply and Demand Curve 179

Figure 40-Supplier Revenue and Demand Cost......................................180

Figure 41-Wholesale Food prices v. Number of Farm Tractors............183

Figure 42-USPS Labor Productivity..185

Figure 43-USPS First Class Rates and Revenue Changes 2000 - 2012...187

Figure 44-Correlation between USPS First Class Rates and Revenue after 2000 187

Figure 45-Correlation between USPS First Class Rates and Revenue between 1980 and 2000...188

Figure 46 – Postal Employees and Volume of First Class Mail -1926-2012 189

Figure 47-European Debt 1880-1913..208

Figure 48-GDP Deflator Change in Five-year Moving Average............227

Figure 49 – Treasury yield Curve (April 4, 2014).................................231

Figure 50 – Inverted Treasury Yield Curve..232

Figure 51-Comparison of Monetized Debt, CPI and GDP....................240

Figure 52-Relative Changes in Average Pay times number of employees, Corporate Profits, and GDP since 1994...........................241

Figure 53-Inflation Adjusted Median Income 242

Figure 54-Corporate Profits 243

Figure 55-Real GDP 1994-2012 243

Figure 56-Change in Productivity vs. Change in CPI............................245

Figure 57-Productivity-Employment-Inflation-Union Membership 246

Figure 58-Productivity-Employment-Inflation Instantaneous Rate of Change 248

Figure 59-Instantaneous Rate of Change of Real GDP from 1947........248

Figure 60-Union Membership 1964-2012...250

Figure 61-Prime Interest Rates, CPI and DJIA......................................262

Figure 62-Federal Outlays v. CPI Index between 1948 and 2008...........281

Figure 63-Federal Outlays v. CPI between 1920 and 1939 282

Figure 64-Federal Outlays v. CPI 2008-2012 283

Figure 65-India per Capita GDP from 1884 to 1960..............................291

Figure 66- India's Famine Relief in British Pounds................................291

Figure 67-India change in per capita tax to GDP ratio...........................292

Figure 68 – Relative CPI and Per Capita GDP – benchmark 1890 – 1948 to 2010 293

Figure 69 – Labor Participation Rate of White Women Actual and
    Projected from 1960 to 2008..312
Figure 70 – Total Education Spending in 2005 Dollars – 1929 to 2011 314
Figure 71 – Per Capita Spending on Education - 1929 to 2011 314
Figure 72 – Education expenditures v. Population 1900 to 1965 315
Figure 73 – Education Expenditures v. Population 1966-2012 Actual v.
    Projected..316
Figure 74 – Percent of total school enrollment in private schools 1969 to
    1988 317
Figure 75 – Percent Change in Japan's GDP – 1953 to 2011..................378
Figure 76-Japan's GDP 1964 to 1995......................................379
Figure 77 – Japan's GDP 1996 to 2011....................................379
Figure 78 – Japan population v. per capita GDP 1964 to 1995.............380
Figure 79 – Japan's population versus per capita GDP 1996 to 2011....380
Figure 80 Distribution of normal random variable...................410
Figure 81 Underlying deterministic process...........................411
Figure 82 Distribution with underlying deterministic process...............411

List of Tables

Table 1 – US 2012 GDP Major Components 80
Table 2 – Share of consumer expenditures on food in the Middle East 102
Table 3 - Comparison of the 2000-2007 Economy with the 2008-2012 Economy 117
Table 4 - Productivity measures used by economists 134
Table 5-Example of Net Cash Flow Analysis...203
Table 6 – Black and White Average IQ and Standard Deviation derived from State of Ohio Math Proficiency Testing 321
Table 7 – State of Ohio 12th Grade Math Proficiency test results...........323
Table 8 – Relative Negroid occupation representation based on minimum IQ of occupation – sorted by percent overrepresented.................384
Table 9 – Relative Negroid occupation representation based on minimum IQ of occupation – sorted by percent overrepresented.................385
Table 10 – Occupations under represented by the Negroid based on IQ 386
Table 11 – Occupations significantly over represented by the Negroid based on IQ...386
Table 12 – Mixing of two populations with the same average and different variances 388
Table 13 – Standard deviation assumptions for specific ranges of IQ ...393
Table 14 – Projected Change in World average IQ and population 393

God and Wealth

Prologue

The Soul of the Soldier

The idea for this book stems from two basic questions that have vexed me for many years. The first question concerned the soldier's soul. This question concerned me ever since I was a youth and faced the prospect of going to war. The war that I speak of is the Vietnam War. Specifically the question concerns the disposition of the soul of a soldier who kills his enemy in light of God's prohibition on killing. Is the killing of a man who is the enemy right or wrong in God's eyes? By the soul, I mean the soul of a man in the Christian Tradition, i.e. as a separate entity apart from the corporal and carnal body. The soul is the incorporeal essence of man that remains after his corporal death. It is the soul saved from condemnation by the Grace of God but only if man obeys the Commandments of God and commits no mortal sin as is murder or is envy. The question of the killing of a man who is the enemy is a moral question, i.e. a question of right and wrong in an absolute sense because the Commandments of God are absolutes, i.e. God's Commandments are the same for all men and apply to all men whether men acknowledge them or not. By this statement, I mean violating God's Commandments has irrevocable consequences for a man's soul apart from any spiritual redemption brought upon a man's life through God's mercy and as manifested in the Christian Tradition. The disposition of the soul of the soldier who kills his enemy depends on the answer to this question. If it is morally wrong for the soldier to kill a man who is the enemy, then God condemns the soul of the soldier as God condemns the soul of any other man because that man violated God's Commandment proscribing the killing of another man. An enemy soldier is a man who seeks or whose goal is to take life and property from another man against his will and under the auspices and sanctions of another nation that is the enemy. A nation exists to secure and protect the private property of those who are its citizens. I will have more to say about the purpose and reason for the existence of nations later in this book. I will also discuss why a single world nation or some would say a single world government is not possible.

An enemy is distinguished from a criminal whose acts are not sanctioned by any nation but instead violate the laws of the nation that exists to protect his victim as well as himself. The enemy is not subject to the protection of the nation that he opposes because he is not bearing the burden of the sovereign whom he opposes. In this sense, any man who does not support the burden of the sovereign is an enemy of the nation. The killing of a man who is the enemy is an act committed solely because he is the enemy and for no other reason. If there is another reason for the killing then with certainty it is a violation of God's Commandment. It makes no difference to the disposition of the soldier's soul if the soldier is the defender of his homeland or the aggressor. If the aggressor, then the soldier is acting on behalf of his nation and if God condemns the soul of the aggressor then God condemns the soul of the defender as well.

Murder is the taking of an innocent man's life whereas killing is the taking of any man's life for any reason or for no reason. Murder is an immoral or sinful act because it violates God's Commandment, i.e. God's law. It is a criminal act because it violates man's law. Murder is a criminal and immoral act, whereas killing a declared enemy or killing in self-defense or in defense of another are not criminal acts, i.e. illegal acts. However, are these immoral acts? In other words, is killing in self-defense or in defense of another still a violation of God's Commandment? God's Commandment is *"Thou shalt not kill"* or from the Greek "ου φονεύσεις" which more literally translated is *"Thou shalt not murder"*. The Greek word for kill is "σκοτονω" which literally means to bring darkness or to take the light away and therefore it is a broader term as it applies to all living animals as well as to man. Thus in the Greek version of the Ten Commandments God proscribes murder but not killing. Why the English Biblical translation, The King James Version (KJV), is *"Thou shalt not kill"* rather than *"Thou shalt not murder"* is a subject for another time. Indeed, the more recent New International Version (2011) of the Bible the Commandment is *"You Shall not Murder"*. (Exodus 20:14)

Philosophers and theologians have agreed with the Greek version of the Ten Commandments and argued that God specifically proscribes the taking of an innocent man's life, which is murder (φονευω) but not necessarily the taking of a man's life, which is killing (σκοτονω). The consensus among moral and legal philosophers and theologians is that killing a man in self-defense, or to protect another man, is a legal and moral act not punishable by Man or God.

The concept that the taking of one individual's life by another is justified in absolute moral terms, i.e. apart from any legal or even moral standard such as God's Commandments, has roots in primitive times when human blood sacrifice or the killing of a person appeased or attempted to appease the gods. Individuals believed, and many still believe, that the appeasement of the gods was, and is, necessary to receive the favor of the gods or to atone for sinning against the gods thereby redeeming oneself of sin or redeeming a nation of sin and thus avoiding the wrath of the gods. To sacrifice is to give up something of value or something held dear in return for the god's favor knowing that the god may or may not grant the favor. In other words, the sacrifice must be painful to the supplicant in one way or another. The ritual killing of a man who is the enemy is not a sacrifice to the gods since the enemy is by

13

definition not one of value to the supplicant undertaking or ordering the ritual killing.   Keep in mind that when I speak of the taking of a man's life I mean the taking of one man's life by another regardless of the circumstances, i.e. whether or not it is justified in a moral or legal sense. Specifically I am concerned here with the soul of the king, soldier or public executioner performing or ordering the act.   To the ancients human sacrifice was neither immoral nor illegal but rather a necessary act called for by the god from whom the supplicant seeks favor or protection. The great significance of the Old Testament is the replacement of human sacrifice by the ritual of circumcision as the sign of the covenant between God and the progeny of Abraham, i.e. God's Chosen People.   Thus, the rabbi who performs the ritual of circumcision escapes the condemnation of God and the wrath of those who did not submit to the rationale for the blood sacrifice of a particular individual.   Such an event happened as told by Homer in the Iliad, when Agamemnon sacrificed his daughter, Iphigenia to the goddess Artemis to dispel the calm and enable the Greeks to sail to Troy.   Agamemnon's wife Clytemnestra, who opposed this deed, avenged the sacrifice of their daughter ten years later after Agamemnon returned from Troy when she and her lover murdered Agamemnon in his bath.   Thus, Agamemnon won a shallow victory at Troy for himself.   He gained nothing from the sacrifice of his daughter, as he condemned himself the moment he sacrificed her.   The lesson of course is that there is always a high personal price to pay for the favor of the gods.   This was also true of Abel, the son of Adam and Eve in the Biblical account of Creation.   Abel won God's favor through his burnt offering of a lamb thereby engendering the envy of his brother Cain, who failed to win God's favor for his burnt offering of grain.   Abel suffered death at the hands of his brother, Cain and in consequence of God's favor.   Abel paid the ultimate price for winning God's favor.   Cain killed his brother not to take from him God's favor, which he could not do, but to deny Abel God's favor, i.e. God's blessing that is the source of wealth and of life.   Cain thus killed Abel to spite God.   Thus, a man's envy is the passion, that in the end, does not seek the possessions or attributes of another man per se, rather envy is only satiated when the other man is denied the envied possessions or attributes.   It is irrelevant to the passion whether the possessions or attributes of the one envied redounds to the one who envies.   Envy seeks only to deny the coveted possessions or attributes to the man who possesses them.   One way that the passion is satiated is through murder or the death of the one envied as happened in Cain's envy of his brother.   Another way to satiate envy is to take the coveted possessions by force of arms and destroy them or redistribute them, which is the same thing.   Envy is the human passion that gives rise to socialism and communism, which are economic systems based on denial to others the fruits of their labor and the fruits of their genius, i.e. their wealth, and to deny it to their seed or posterity as well.

Envy, more than any other human passions, seeks not only the denial of possessions or of God's blessings to the one envied, but also the denial of possessions or of God's blessings to the progeny of the one envied. Envy seeks the destruction of the wealth of its object in all its forms. Note that after Man's disobedience of God, the second sin against God that Man committed was the envy of his brother. Man's disobedience to God gave rise to all the passions including envy. Envy therefore arises in Man as God's punishment for Man's disobedience and his seeking to be God. The temporal mechanism God manifests to punish man for his sins and in particular the sin of unbelief, is envy. When man does not fear God then envy is unleashed and calamity in the form of wealth destruction ensues. All evil that man perpetrates arises out of envy. Envy threatens mankind's survival that God ordained to be immortal. It is the reason for God's Commandment. Thus, envy is Man's inherent source of evil as ordained by God and the reason evil exists. While God resides without Man, Satan resides within Man and because of Man.

The significance of monotheism to the ancient Hebrew world is the end of human sacrifice, supplanted by circumcision, a much less morally and less psychologically troublesome ritual. Accordingly, circumcision is a more practical ritual acceptable to God in securing His Covenant to His chosen people. (See Genesis 17) God's Covenant manifests in the protection of His chosen people from their enemies, who envied them. In return for God's protection, His people must obey His Commandments, place no other gods before Him, and keep the Sabbath. Thus, the ancient Hebrews had no king but God. Since God was their protector, there was no need for a king. The ancient Hebrews under God's Covenant no longer sacrificed their progeny to the gods for favor or as tribute, as did others. The references in the Old Testament to Moloch and Baal were to gods to whom others still sacrificed their progeny whether within the womb or born, an abomination to the now monotheistic Hebrews. The last minute substitution of Abraham's son, Isaac by a ram at the sacrificial altar in Genesis 22 was the mark of the Old Testament Covenant between God and Man after Noah. This manifested later in Exodus as the Ten Commandments through Moses. God's Covenant was to protect His chosen people from their enemies as long as they obey His Commandments. Note that unlike those that believed in other gods, the ancient Hebrews did not believe that God protected Man from the vicissitudes of nature. Famine and other natural calamities still befell the ancient Hebrews and the wrath of God often manifested in natural forces, as was the case with Noah. Rather God's covenant was to protect the Hebrews from other men and primarily the envy of other men. Thus, the manna that God bestowed on the Hebrews to feed them in the forty years of their Exodus out of Egypt did not arise from any act of nature but from the acts of men. The unjust enslavement of the Hebrews by the Egyptians arose out of envy of the economic success of the Hebrews by the Egyptians. This was the reason for the Exodus and the reason that the Hebrews hungered and thirst as they wandered the desert. At times when the Jews strayed from the Word of God, God delivered them to their enemies as, for example, when they were captive in Babylon. Hence, God's Covenant with the Hebrews depended on their obedience or disobedience to God.

The fact that Abraham was willing to sacrifice his progeny, Isaac, to God without protest by Abraham points to the early pervasiveness of the practice of human sacrifice even amongst the ancient Hebrews going back to the time of Noah. The prevalence of human sacrifice, as well as the accompanying cannibalism, caused God to destroy his Creation through the Flood. The fact that human sacrifice and cannibalism existed in the ancient world manifests in the Words of God to Noah after the Flood. Among the first Words of God to Noah after the waters recede are in Genesis 9:4-6: *"But flesh with the life (soul) (ψυχων) thereof, which is the blood thereof, shall ye not eat. ⁵And surely your blood of your lives (souls)(ψυχων) will I require; at the hand of every beast (savage)(θηριων) will I require it, and at the hand of man; at the hand of every man's brother will I require the life (soul)(ψυχων) of man. ⁶Whoso sheddeth man's blood; by man shall his blood be shed: for in the image of God made he man."* There are two misinterpretations of the Greek in the King James Version thereby confounding the Words of God to Noah. The first misinterpretation is the translation of ψυχων more accurately translated as soul rather than as life. The second is the translation of the word θηριων more accurately translated as savage rather than as beast or animal. The use of the word "hand" is inconsistent with the translation θηριων as animal, but it makes sense when the word θηριων translates to savage, which is another translation of the same Greek word, and a translation consistent with the context. A beast or an animal does not have hands nor does it have a soul but a savage, i.e. a cannibal or one who sacrifices humans and feeds upon them as he would an animal, has hands and a soul. The meaning therefore of Genesis 9:4 is that man shall not eat man. Thus, God's admonishment to Noah refers to human sacrifice and cannibalism as the cause of the Flood, which was to cleanse man of these sins. Genesis 9:6 anticipates the proscription of murder in the Ten Commandments of Exodus. Extending this view to Genesis 9:2 wherein God tells Noah *"And the fear of you and the dread of you shall be upon every beast (savage) of the earth, and upon every fowl of the air, upon all that moveth upon the earth, and upon all the fishes of the sea; into your hand are they delivered".* God tells Noah that if Noah's descendants, i.e. the descendants of man, become savage, i.e. cannibals, God will deliver them into the hand of Noah, i.e. the hand of Man: *⁶Whoso sheddeth man's blood, by man shall his blood be shed: for in the image of God made he man."* In other words, if a man sacrifice another man and consume him then Man will kill him, because God made Man in His image. Thus, God authorizes man to kill savages and cannibals.

16

Savages and cannibals are men who sacrifice men and consume the sacrifice.

It was not until 97AD that the Romans forbade human sacrifice in the Roman Empire. Prior to 97AD, many peoples in the known world except for the Hebrews since the time of Noah practiced human sacrifice. The Carthaginians were one such people, and their sacrificial altar resembled the ancient Old Testament god, Moloch with the head of a bull and the body of a man. The Romans vanquished forever the Carthaginians in the Punic Wars. The great irony of course is that after the Roman Republic and well into the Roman Empire, the pagan Romans drew great pleasure in sacrificing humans for sport.

In Euripides' version of the story of the sacrifice of Iphigenia by her father, Agamemnon, the goddess Artemis replaces Iphigenia by a deer at the altar at the last moment of the sacrificial act. Thus in both the Hebrew and Greek traditions there are references to the sacrifice of man's progeny, whether within the womb or born. With such sacrifice being contrary to God's will, and contrary to nature as represented by Artemis, and manifested in both traditions by the miraculous replacement of the progeny with an animal at the sacrificial altar.

The great significance of the New Testament is the New Covenant with God, which supplants the circumcision or any sort of human blood sacrifice to secure the New Covenant with God and replaces it with the baptism. Both circumcision and baptism stem from sacrificial rites as both rituals secure God's blessings on the soul of the supplicant. In the case of circumcision, the supplicant is a group, the chosen people of the Old Testament. God's blessing therefore redounds to the group and is to protect the group from their temporal enemies. Thus, only the son undergoes the ritual and not the daughter since it is the son through whom the Lord God works to protect the Hebrew from their enemies. In the case of the baptism, the supplicants are the individual parents of the child baptized and not any group. The baptism is atonement for original sin and is for the sake of the parents not the child as commonly believed. As it was in the days when the ancients sacrificed their progeny to appease the gods to win favor and for atonement, it was for the benefit of the parents, i.e. the supplicants not their progeny. Thus, the baptism of the child is the same. The Baptism is an act of free will by the parents that acknowledges the existence and authority of God by the parents. The Baptism is for the sake of the parent's soul, and is to secure the parents the New Covenant with God. The New Covenant is with the individual parents and it is to secure the soul of the individual parents. It is not to cleanse the sin of the child, because a child has no sin. Under the New Covenant, a sin is an act of freewill that a newly born child cannot perform. The purpose of the baptism is to cleanse the original sin of the parents and to secure God's New Covenant, which is God's promise to secure the immortal soul. It

17

was the knowledge of good and evil that gave rise to the child, and man acquired this original knowledge as well as his passions in his disobedience to God. Thus, man became as God who has inherited the knowledge and acquires naturally the passion to create man in his image but at the cost of man's immortality. Yet God created man to be immortal and obedient to Him. Marriage is the means by which Man achieves the immortality as ordained by God in Genesis, but lost by Man's disobedience to God. The baptism of his progeny is the atonement for the original sin of disobedience by Man. The original sin of disobedience to God therefore falls on the parents not the child when the parents fail to baptize the child, as baptism is an act of freewill on the part of the parent not the child. A child or man who self baptizes without the assent of the parents does not cleanse the sin of the parents. Such an act is meaningless signifying nothing unless performed by the disciples of Jesus who themselves were baptized, or in other words, who themselves were anointed, by Jesus. The baptism of Jesus was a symbolic act meant to teach and legitimize the ritual among the Jews and later the Gentiles as His earthly parents were without sin by the Grace of God. Thus, the significance of John the Baptist's words to Jesus "…*I have need to be baptized of thee, and comest thou to me?*" The words of John the Baptist mean to signify the divinity of Jesus to the world, i.e. the He was at once and everywhere Man and God, as well as supplicant and the one sacrificed. Note that despite the words of John the Baptist, Jesus did not perform the baptism upon him nor did Jesus baptize anyone save his disciples.

The act of baptism by John foreshadows the Crucifixion. The One to whom man's progeny was once sacrificed, i.e. God, is the One whose Son, i.e. God's progeny is sacrificed on the cross. Baptism is thus a sacrificial ritual, i.e. a sacrament. While still practiced by the people of the Old Testament, circumcision under the New Covenant fails to atone of the sin of the parents. Indeed Judaism recognizes no original sin. The New Covenant does not promise protection or deliverance of the followers of Christ from their earthly enemies, as did the Covenant of the Old Testament promise the Hebrews protection from their enemies. Rather the New Covenant is the promise to secure an individual man's soul from damnation as long a man obeys the Commandments of his own freewill. Christianity thus speaks to the individual while Judaism speaks to the group.

Note that the baptism is a ritual, as is the circumcision, and as is all human blood sacrifice. A ritual is a process performed by a third party such as a priest, rabbi or shaman and accompanied by prayers. The process depends on the religious tradition whose tenets its subscribers recognize as valid, i.e. true. Religion in general is not only a set of beliefs about how man relates to God but also a set of rituals by which that relationship manifests or becomes known. The appointment

18

of the priest, rabbi or shaman, i.e. clergy, is not a matter of any consensus or plebiscite such as is the appointment of the sovereign in a free nation. The appointment of clergy is more akin to the imposition of a sovereign through force, i.e. the adherents to the faith usually have little say about who is going to be their priest or who can become priest.   In the Christian tradition, there is even a question about the need for priests or even an organized religion.   This really extends to all religions except Judaism by which God ordained a priestly class, the Levites.
Accordingly, any third party can perform the act of baptism since it does not involve a cutting of the flesh as circumcision does.   Unlike Judaism, which treats man as a group, i.e. the chosen people, and establishes the relationship between God, the protector, and the group, Christianity is the religion of the individual.   Christianity establishes and defines the relationship between God and the individual.   Judaism is a religion of a group and the group precedes the individual in all matters.   The inability or refusal of the Jews to accept Jesus as the Christ is because he spoke about and to the individual, and not about or to the group.
Circumcision is a rite enabling the physical and unimpeachable identification of a man as a member of the group.   No such physical identification is called for under the New Covenant and baptism does not bestow such physical identification.   Thus, Christianity is an individual religion requiring no formal organizing principal or organized church. As long as each individual man fears God then each man is a church undo himself.   Indeed Christianity probably has more individual sects than any major religion thereby attesting to its inherent individualism. In this sense, Christianity comports well with a wealth creating economy because in both outlooks the individual's life and individual self-interest precede the life of the group, and the interests of the group, thereby enabling the survival and prosperity of the group, i.e. the nation. Whereas Judaism is more comfortable in a socialist or communist economy, which explains its relative inability to be the dominant religion of Western Civilization that Christianity is, despite the propensity of its individuals to create wealth.   It is this accommodation with socialism and communism inherent in Judaism, which is and has been the undoing of the modern Jew.

The ordained and foretold sacrifice of God's own Son, Jesus, who was at the same moment the offering to God, the priest or rabbi making the offering to God, and the One to whom the offering is made, marked the end of God's temporal Covenant with man as manifested in the Old Testament.   God is no longer the protector of man from man. However, it did not mark the end of God's spiritual Covenant as otherwise manifested in the Ten Commandments.   The resurrection of the Christ fulfilled prophesy, secured His divinity before all men, confirmed the existence and immortality of man's soul, and marked the beginning of God's New Covenant with Man.   The resurrection also affirmed God's power to dispose of the soul and thus instilled the fear of God in Man. Thus, the chosen people are no longer subject to the temporal protection of God as there is now a New Covenant. The Jewish Diaspora within two generations after the Crucifixion is the sign of God's withdrawal from His original Covenant as God, now under the New Covenant, no longer was the Jew's protector from his earthly enemies. Through the sacrifice of his Son, God freed all man from the Original Sin, i.e. his inherent disobedience to God. Under the Old Testament Covenant, circumcision is the ceremonial sacrifice of man's male progeny, which secures and perpetuates God's Covenant. Baptism, which includes both the male and female progeny, secures and perpetuates the New Covenant. The baptism acknowledges that God created both man and woman to be immortal. Before man's fall from Grace, God created woman as man's companion or helper not the bearer of his progeny. (Genesis 2:18)

Under the New Covenant, the disposition of Man's soul is in the hands of Man himself. No longer are there a chosen people or group who are under God's spiritual and temporal protection but individuals who themselves by an act of freewill chose to fall under God's spiritual protection, i.e. the security of their soul. Redemption and forgiveness are individual acts of freewill. The admonitions enshrined in the Ten Commandments take on a new meaning under the New Covenant in both a temporal and spiritual sense. In particular, the proscriptions against murder and envy are now not only essential for the disposition of the soul as the spiritual sense, but also essential for the creation of wealth, and the survival of the individual and the nation as the temporal sense. Thus, while under the Old Covenant, God protected the ancient Hebrews against their temporal enemies and the creation of wealth secured the Hebrews against the calamities of nature, under the New Covenant the creation of wealth protects an individual against calamities both manmade and natural. As the creation of wealth enables the survival of mankind, and thereby secures his immortality, as God ordained, then the creation of wealth is a blessing from God and the sole obligation of Man to God and of Man to himself. I will address these themes in more detail.

Private Property and the Enforcement of laws and contracts

Then what of war and the soul of the soldier or more broadly the soul of the king who is the appointed protector of a nation? Does the soldier commit mortal sin, i.e. violate God's Commandment when he kills a man in war and if not why not? Similarly, does the king commit a mortal sin when he executes a man or has a man executed, thus taking a man's life?

The concern with the soldier's soul may raise a question in the mind of the reader regarding the relationship between the soul of the soldier and the subject of this book that is God and wealth. The relationship is indeed there, and rests with the sole and true purposes of government, i.e. the protection of private property and the enforcement of contracts. Government manifests in the laws it creates, enforces, and adjudicates. Government has a single power to protect private property, and enforce contracts, the sovereign power of eminent domain. Eminent domain is the power to take a man's private property in all its forms including his life with no recourse for the man whose life and property the sovereign takes. Under all law, a man's life is his private property, i.e. it belongs to him and owned by him alone, and accordingly the sovereign power of eminent domain is the power to take a man's life as well as the fruits of a man's life, which is his property. Therein lays the connection with the soul of the king and by extension the soul of a soldier who serves the king. It is one reason that a nation under God, i.e. a nation whose citizens fear God, survives and prospers. Without the fear of God compelling man's obedience to God's Commandments, a nation cannot create wealth and survive calamities because in the absence of the fear of God and obedience to God's Commandments there is no bound to the king's (the sovereign's) power of eminent domain other than what the king sets for himself. Also without the fear of God in the heart of man there is no bound to envy which is the only human passion proscribed by God by His Ten Commandments. As I demonstrate later in this book, envy is the most destructive of the passions whereas greed is the most fruitful of the passions in terms of wealth creation. Unlike envy, God's Commandments do not proscribe greed because, unlike envy, greed is self-regulating as one man's greed controls another man's greed through competition. There is no such temporal control mechanism for envy.

Obedience to law compelled by fear of God and the sovereign's power of eminent domain

There exists two forces compelling man's obedience to laws and to the fulfillment of contracts and these forces are the sovereign's power of eminent domain and the fear of God. The sovereign power of eminent domain maintains the temporal peace by protecting and securing private property, and the fear of God suppresses notions of rebellion or civil war through the proscription against envy. Both these forces must exist in the minds and hearts of individual men for man to survive and prosper. These forces must exist in fact and in law in order that a nation prosper i.e. create wealth to survive.

Besides the protection and securing of private property, the only other valid purpose of government is to enforce laws and contracts. Contracts are agreements between persons, either individuals or organized groups of individuals such as corporations, made and executed of their own individual freewill. Given the sovereign power of eminent domain, the king or sovereign, who is the government, ensures the fulfillment of contracts, or the promises among and between individuals. This enables commerce and with commerce comes a prosperous economy and the creation of wealth. Individual freewill is essential for the creation of wealth and the survival of a nation. The degree a government limits or abrogates individual freewill, then to the same degree the creation of wealth is also limited or abrogated, and the survival of a nation less certain. The creation of wealth is man's only hedge against calamity.

Fear of God or Love of Man

While some may argue that man's goodwill compels his actions or at least his obedience in a civilized society or that love of man is more compelling of men's actions than fear of God, yet this is clearly not the history of man nor can it be. In fact, where those seeking to overthrow sovereignty profess love of man the results are always calamitous and murderous and thus destructive of wealth as in the case of the French Revolution and its aftermath. I will address the causes and aftermath of the French Revolution in more detail later. Without the fear of God, man succumbs to envy, which is destructive of wealth. Without the sovereign's power of eminent domain to enforce contracts, man succumbs to the temptation to cheat his fellow man destroying commerce and thereby destroying wealth creation. Man's goodwill only arises out of the spiritual fear of God and temporal fear of the sovereign. Absent these forces then there is no bound to inhumanity as man's passions always trump his reason from the time of Cain and Abel, despite the Stoic's claims to the contrary. I will also discuss Stoicism and its handmaiden atheism later.

Biblical root of freewill

Man's individual freewill has Biblical roots. The fact that the wealthiest nations historically are also Christian nations is no coincidence. Man's freewill becomes manifest through the suicide death of Judas Iscariot. Judas, a disciple of Jesus, fulfilled the ancient prophesy of the Christ as foretold in the Old Testament, accordingly he did not act and could not act of his own freewill. Rather he acted according to the will of God, as did all generations of the Old Covenant preceding the coming of the Christ. Consequently, Judas did not betray Jesus rather he fulfilled the will of God made known by ancient prophesy; *"Even my close friend, in whom I trusted, who ate my bread, has lifted up his heel against me." (Psalm 41:9)*; *"For it is not an enemy who reproaches me, Then I could bear it; Nor is it one who hates me who has exalted himself against me, Then I could hide myself from him. But it is you, a man my equal, My companion and my familiar friend."* (Psalm 55:12-13). Indeed, in the Greek language Jesus called the act that Judas committed παραδιδοσθαι, which means to deliver to another's hands or to surrender to another, and not προδώστε, which means betrayal. Jesus

22

himself never refers to Judas as a traitor.   In the Greek, the only reference to Judas as a traitor was by Luke in Luke 6:16 and not by the words of Jesus although in the KJV there are several references to Judas as a betrayer.   Even at the Last Supper, Jesus said that "καὶ ἐσθιόντων αὐτῶν εἶπεν ἀμὴν λέγω ὑμῖν ὅτι εἷς ἐξ ὑμῶν <u>παραδώσει</u> με" which means that "And as they did eat, he said, 'Verily I say unto you, that one of you shall <u>deliver me to the hands of another</u>.'"   Although this has been translated in the English KJV to mean "*And as they did eat, he said, Verily I say unto you, that one of you shall betray me*". (Matthew 26:21)   Jesus never used the word betrayal to describe Judas's act in the Greek translation. The word betrayal entered into Jesus' lexicon only through the translators from the Greek to English.   The difference between "delivering to another's hands" and "betrayal" is subtle but significant.   The latter is bearing false witness, which is a mortal sin, whereas the former could be an act of love.   Delivering an abandoned child to the hands of another for care is an act of compassion or love and not an act betrayal.

Biblically, Judas's suicide death was Man's first act of freewill, as nowhere in the Old Testament was his suicide death foretold.   Thus, despite his own words in Mathew 27:3, Judas sinned not because he delivered Jesus to others as prophesy and God bound and ordained Judas to do but because he killed himself of his own volition and in violation of God's Commandment.   Note that betrayal is not a mortal sin per se however bearing false witness is a mortal sin and betrayal requires that a man lie about his loyalty to his sovereign or protector.   This Judas did not do.   Jesus knew Judas as the one who must fulfill prophesy and Judas never denied this other than to question Jesus about his assertion. In Matthew 26:25, Judas replies to Jesus "*Then Judas, the one who would betray him, said, "Surely you don't mean me, Rabbi?"*   Jesus answered, "*You have said so.*"   It is of interest to note that Peter on whom Jesus said he was going to build his church lied when he three times denied that he knew Jesus.   Thus, Peter, the staunchest of Jesus' Disciples betrayed his faith in Jesus but Judas did not betray Jesus.   Rather Judas delivered him to others to fulfill prophesy and the will of God.   Indeed the Biblical account of Peter's denial of his knowledge of Jesus was prophetic in the sense that the Church has often acted to appease envy rather than as the teacher and standard-bearer of the Christian faith.

One of the consequences of the New Covenant and the Resurrection therefore is that the disposition of man's soul is now in the hands of man himself and not in the hands of God.   There no longer is a people chosen by God for whom God predetermined the disposition of their souls, but all individuals, both Hebrews and Gentiles, of their own freewill thus determine the disposition of their individual soul.   Man, under the New Covenant, rather than predestined by God or Providence, now determines his own individual temporal destiny as well as the fate of his soul, i.e. his incorporeal destiny.   It is through the spread of

23

Christianity with the notion of each man's freewill engendered by Christianity that eventually led Western Civilization out of the Dark Ages. However, a man's freewill bears fruit only among men who have the intellectual capital to create wealth and thus overcome calamity. The exercise of individual freewill among men lacking the intellectual capital, i.e. a low average IQ, is much less fruitful and in fact counterproductive in most cases. It is the reason that not all nations are prosperous and that some nations are little more than large primitive tribal villages with their single chief despite their professed adherence to Christianity or fear of God. Nations whose individuals lack the intellect to create wealth also lack the individual discipline to obey God's Commandments thus such nations succumb to envy and become tyrannical socialist or communist economies eventually collapsing in terms of their ability to sustain their populations. The same is true of nations whose individuals possess the intellect to create wealth but who do not fear God.

Hence, there are three preconditions necessary for the creation of wealth and the survival of a nation. The first two are the intellectual capacity of the populace, i.e. the average IQ of the population, and the fear of God. The third precondition is the burden of the sovereign who limits man's freewill, and who protects private property and enforces contracts. In this book, I will address these preconditions in more detail and explain their import for the creation of wealth and the survival of nations.

Human Sacrifice and Human Psyche

I would like to return for a moment to the act of human sacrifice and its significance to the human psyche particularly where the sacrifice of progeny is concerned. There is a seeming contradiction or paradox between the desire to procreate, an innate drive to further the human species and thereby the immortality of man as God intended and ordained, and the act of killing one's progeny whether in the womb or born. The paradox is easily resolved when one considers it a form of population control particularly in a primitive agrarian economy with its high variance in the production of food. Although, some misguided individuals still use the idea of population control to justify the current tendency to sacrifice progeny within the womb in much the way that the ancients sacrificed their progeny outside the womb. These individuals do not differ from the primitives in this regard and admittedly so. In other words, there is very little change in the primitive aspects of human nature as manifested after Man's fall from Grace and since the time of the beginnings of agriculture or even before. The high variability in the early agrarian economy created over-production in some years and low yields in other years. The story of Joseph in the Old Testament (Genesis 37-50) wherein Joseph interpreted the dream of the Pharaoh of Egypt as seven years of plenty followed by seven years of famine points to the vicissitude of the ancient agrarian economy. The Pharaoh ordered the storage of grain or in other words, a store of wealth in anticipation of the calamity that indeed followed. Thus, Egypt survived the calamity and was able to feed the rest of the world as well while growing even wealthier in the process. Lacking the ability of Joseph to foretell the future, there was accordingly the tendency by men to produce progeny in years of plenty that resulted in suffering and death in years of famine. Limiting the size of the local population served the purpose of minimizing the suffering and death in the years of famine.

The ancient Greeks created city-states known as polis that were deliberately limited in the size of their population. Whenever the local population exceeded a certain level as determined by the ability of the land to sustain the local population under worst-case scenarios, then migration occurred in search of new opportunities and new city-states formed. As these new poleis where established in areas where the land was more suited to a different crop or use, then the spread of the polis engendered trade and commerce thus creating wealth. This did not altogether preclude human sacrifice or infanticide as a means to control population although it minimized the practice. The ancient Spartans for instance exposed any newborn that had any apparent physical defect. The practice of the sacrifice of progeny appears in myth repeatedly. The myth of the Minotaur of Ancient Crete is another example of such myths. The Minotaur was a monster with the head of a bull and the torso of a man that could only be satiated by human blood. It was the mythical offspring of a human, Pasiphae, the wife of King Minos and a sacred white bull intended as a sacrifice to Poseidon, god of the sea. The Minoan Cretans forced the Athenians to send seven young men and seven young women annually to sacrifice to the Minotaur as tribute after Crete defeated Athens. The Cretans fought Athens to avenge the killing of King Minos' son, Androgeus, by the Athenians as the Athenians envied his victory at the Panathenaea Festival. The Minotaur is a similar creature in appearance to Baal or Moloch of the Old Testament and of which I spoke earlier. The Minotaur ate the victims in much the same way that Moloch devoured his and thus, the reference to cannibalism in both the Greek and Hebrew traditions. Considering that the Minotaur was half man speaks to the fact that the ancient Greeks knew of cannibalism. He was a θηρίων. Clearly human sacrifice was often associated with cannibalism in the ancient world. The Greeks and Hebrews depicted the god to whom they sacrificed their progeny as a creature with the head of a bull and the torso of a man and who called for the sacrifice of man's progeny. The bull therefore in both the Hebrew and Greek traditions is both a sacrificial animal, i.e. the sacrificial bullock of the Old Testament and the godlike bullock to which the ancients sacrificed their progeny. In both cases, the end of the sacrifice was a feast of the sacrificial offering. In general, there appears to be a primitive psychological principle at work here wherein man conceives of a single entity as both the entity sacrificed and the object or motive of the sacrifice. The principle seems to be constant in the high psyche of the Caucasian or Western Man. Thus, Jesus was both the sacrifice for the atonement of Man's sins but also God or the Son of God, i.e. God's progeny, to whom Man in the past sacrificed his progeny, and therein lays Jesus' dual nature and the purpose of His dual nature. The Eucharist is the body and blood of Christ by His own words and so completes full circle human sacrifice in the same fashion as animal sacrifice carried out, i.e. with a feasting of the sacrificial animal. Christ's resurrection marked the immortality of the soul and the final human blood sacrifice to God in all its manifestations other than symbolically and ritualistically for the atonement of sin.

There may also be a deeper and more primal source of this principle, which rests with the need to kill an animal for food and the abhorrence of cannibalism at least in the more intelligent Caucasian psyche. The animal served as a store of energy between harvests and helped to sustain an agrarian population during years of poor harvests. In pre-agrarian times, the animal was the only source of food year round. Thus, a domesticated or wild animal is a hedge against calamity in the ancient world and this explains God favoring Abel's animal burnt offering over Cain's grain offering in Genesis.

The existence of God

A cogent argument for the existence of God is that the vicissitudes of an ancient agrarian economy and the necessity of population control evoked in the human psyche the means to resolve the paradox of human life, i.e. the sacrifice of one's progeny whether within the womb or born. Given the prevalence of the sacrifice of progeny in the ancient world there is no mystery to the depiction of the Cherubim as a babe with angel wings and traditionally the spirit proximate to God. In Greek Mythology, the daughter of Agamemnon whom he sacrificed becomes the goddess Hecate – the Mother of Angels. God takes the soul of children as his own and they are all in heaven with Him and closest to Him. Thus, the paradox of sacrificing one's progeny whether within the womb or born and who are a hedge against calamity, i.e. wealth, is resolved through the existence of God. So also resolved is the disposition of the soul of the one who makes the sacrifice, i.e. the supplicant. As it is against God's will from the time of Abraham and as manifested in the replacement of Isaac with a ram, then the one who sacrifices his progeny born or within the womb and whether a sovereign or not is committing a mortal sin and damns his body and soul before Man and God. King Agamemnon, who was sovereign, his fate is a testament to the damnation of his body, and God's Commandment proscribing murder a testament to the damnation of the soul. In a sense, the resurrection of Jesus, the Son of God, is the resurrection of all the sons and daughters sacrificed to Baal.

Rapid increases of productivity and unemployment

The second question that has vexed me is more prosaic and it concerns productivity improvements and the effect of rapid gains in productivity on employment. This question concerned me as I was conducting economic studies to justify investments to improve productivity for the Ohio Bell Telephone Company during the 1980's. These economic studies justified capital investments in computer-based technology to make telephone company operations more efficient. The recovery of the investment in the technology depended solely on labor savings. In an expanding and unencumbered economy, labor savings result from hiring avoidance. In other words, productivity gains in an expanding market or growing economy do not result in layoffs but lead to greater profits and greater wealth creation. A growing market means greater revenue and if the cost to produce the product or service rises less than the rate of revenue growth then this improves profit, which is the creation of wealth. These greater profits also lead to higher wages and salaries, as greater skills are invariably required to operate in a highly productive and efficient company and economy in general. Wealth creation in an unencumbered economy in turn leads to greater employment opportunities and increased employment as investment in the economy generates more wealth and further secures the nation against calamity. However, in a mature market or an encumbered economy where corporate revenue is stable, shrinking or even growing very slowly the hiring avoidances become layoffs and thus unemployment increases. The layoffs from gains in productivity pay for the investment plus the return on investment that in turn creates greater wealth; i.e. profit. An encumbered economy is a taxed, regulated and coerced economy whereby the government abridges the freedom to contract through the law in ways that I will discuss in this book.

In the case with Ohio Bell and AT&T in general, productivity gains resulted in the loss of thousands of jobs. AT&T held all of Ohio Bell's stock at the time. By the 1990's the total number of employees at Ohio Bell went from its peak of 30,000 in 1974 to 3,000 twenty years later. At the same time, the value of AT&T's, i.e. Ameritech's stock increased ten times (AT&T became Ameritech and six other companies as a result of the Federally mandated divestiture of AT&T in 1984). The layoffs that occurred over that period affected both management and non-management employees so the effect of introducing productivity improving technology was widespread and pervasive. However, these layoffs did not affect total US unemployment because the economy was growing at the time and the economy was creating new opportunities particularly in the digital communication field to which AT&T's

technology had much to contribute.   In other words, the same technology effecting productivity gains in the telephone industry also spawned a new telecommunications industry.   Additionally the economy was not as encumbered in the 1980's and early 1990s as it is currently although it was still more encumbered than at the beginning of the twentieth century, thus more of the productivity improvements went toward wealth creation during the 1980's and 1990's than it does currently. The introduction of means to improve productivity and reduce labor costs continues to this day in the general economy.   In this current time (2008-2014), the rapid gains in productivity are increasing the number of unemployed but only because increasing regulation, taxation, the printing and spending of money by government, as well as the embedded unionization all encumber the economy thus preventing it from growing. It is the large number of layoffs in a short time and the civil disruptive effects of such layoffs that raised the second moral question that I now address in this book.   The question is – Are the improvements made to productivity that knowingly result in a large number of layoffs ethical? In other words is there, and should there be, an ethical component to decisions to improve productivity knowing that such improvements will lead to layoffs.   Note that I use the word ethical and not moral as the characterization of the motives for economic acts.   Nevertheless, there is a moral dimension to the motives for economic acts but the moral dimension arises only in an encumbered economy, as I will explain in the course of this book.

Moral Philosophy

          Whether the motive for an act or the act itself is morally right or wrong is a question of moral philosophy and at the heart of any moral philosophy is not only the question of right and wrong but also the question of truth and falsehood, and the question of beauty and ugliness. In other words, what is truth and what is beauty.   I define an economic act as any act that generates a profit or intends to generate a profit. Thus making an investment in labor savings machinery or entering into a contract to provide goods and services are economic acts because the actors intend to generate a profit, i.e. create wealth.   An economic act also includes hiring and firing employees since the hiring and firing of employees is for generating a profit.   All moral philosophy distinguishes between acts that are right and acts that are wrong in light of moral standards.   In other words, a moral philosophy answers the questions about what is right, and what is wrong and why some acts are right and some wrong.   In so doing, a moral philosophy must first establish standards against which a judge, whomever that may be, determines right and wrong.   A moral philosophy also answers the questions about what is truth and what is beauty, as measured against these same moral standards.   Thus, once moral standards exist in the minds of men those

28

same moral standards determine truth and beauty as well as right and wrong. Moral standards exist apart from any other beliefs of the individuals comprising a nation and so are absolutes. A moral standard is from God and not from man. The single and only moral standard that secures the survival of the individual and the nation embodies in God's Ten Commandments, which incorporates not only the Golden Rule but is also consistent with Natural Law. Natural Law is the law of self-interest or self-preservation and includes the law of self-perpetuation, and it is the most basic of temporal laws as all temporal law derives from Natural Law. When a sovereign through his laws subverts truth and beauty and instead attempts to redefine these terms in a strange image or a strange standard, it also redefines what actions are right and wrong as well as why some actions are right and some actions wrong. With the redefining of truth and beauty away from Natural Law and from the Commandments of God, a sovereign undermines the nation's capacity to create wealth and survive calamity, as truth and beauty inextricably bind with right and wrong and the creation of wealth. The redefining of truth and beauty is through law enacted by the sovereign. Laws that promote falsehoods and ugliness burden the creation of wealth as they steer men away from the unencumbered pursuit of self-interest and self-perpetuation, which only absolute truth and absolute beauty must guide. Thus, laws that interfere with or corrupt the natural relationships and God's ordained relationships between individuals are destructive of wealth creation. The natural relationships are those that promote the creation of wealth such as the freedom to contract and the creation of progeny. Laws that interfere with or proscribe unnatural relationships and acts or relationships abhorrent to God serve to promote wealth creation and are laws that a sovereign must enact and enforce. Thus, laws proscribing miscegenation and homosexual behavior serve to secure private property, perpetuate the inherent genius of the Caucasian Race, and promote wealth creation. Where such laws do not exist there is the destruction of wealth and a decline in a nation's ability to withstand calamity. As a nation's laws and institutions turn men's hearts away from absolute truth and absolute beauty, i.e. turn away from God's laws and from Natural Law, then the nation's laws and institutions corrupt the mind of man turning him away from God's laws and from Natural Law.

Truth and beauty as manifested in art and culture relate strongly to the creation of wealth as the hedge against calamity particularly in a capitalist or wealth creating economy. The appearance of such non-sense concepts as "black is beautiful", "all cultures are equal", abstract art, atonal and so-called "hip-hop" music, all serve to undermine and corrupt the concept of beauty and with it the concept of truth. The juxtaposition of beautiful blond Caucasian women with the primitive Negro male in news shows, advertisements, movies and television shows are other attempts at the corruption of beauty and truth in insidious attempts to promote the wealth destructive mixing of the races through the media. So are the not-so-subtle attempts by the atheists in the media, educational system, and government to undermine Christianity and the fear of God. This is true despite the trivial and corrupt claims of inclusiveness as the motive for such displays and attempts. I will have more to say about these concepts and their wealth destruction throughout man's history and in man's future later in this book.

Law does not sanction Justice

I do not include the idea of justice as an element of moral philosophy. The reason for this is that the idea of justice conflates with the idea of vengeance to such an extent that it is inseparable in the mind or in the act. One man's justice is always another's vengeance. By its nature, vengeance is morally wrong because it arises from envy and God proscribes envy. Envy is the most destructive human passion. Envy is a force that a nation and a nation's economy must continuously overcome in order that the nation prosper and survive. In any case, the concept of justice is problematic as a moral precept. The term is also a misnomer when applied to the actions of the king. A king does not mete out justice rather he protects private property that includes the protection of life and enforces laws and contracts. His acts are, and ought to be, only for these purposes. To act otherwise, i.e. to act in accordance with so-called justice or vengeance, endangers the king's soul before God and invites rebellion before Man. The king's execution of a murderer is not a matter of justice or vengeance but a matter of law. It cannot be otherwise or else a nation will succumb to calamity arising from nature or in the form of rebellion or civil war. Law dictates the actions of a sovereign and when a law calls for the execution of a murderer then the law is sanctioning through due process the taking of a man's life, i.e. the life of the murderer, by the sovereign under the sovereign's power of eminent domain as sanctioned by Man and God. Just as God ordained that Judas fulfill prophesy, i.e. the law then God also ordains the king to fulfill Man's law through the divine right of king. Indeed the law may not sanction the taking of a man's life for committing the act of murder and some may argue that the law is unjust. However, the argument is specious since justice or vengeance is not the intent of the law but rather the intent of the law is the protection of private property, which includes the protection of life, through the sovereign exercise of the power of eminent domain. Note that while the sovereign is above the law, the law nevertheless governs his actions. Thus, the sovereign does not commit murder when he executes a man in accordance with the law. However if he kills a man outside of the law he cannot be punished as the sovereign cannot punish himself unless he chooses to punish himself. Rather a sovereign who acts outside of the law that he enacts invites rebellion and subjects his soul to damnation.

30

To the extent that no rebellion occurs then a sovereign remains immune to corporal punishment. He nonetheless jeopardizes his soul before God as he has usurped the divine right of king, which comes only from God. The divine right of king presupposes the king fears God and acts in accordance with the law the king himself enacts and in accordance with God's law. This is true whether the person or persons of sovereignty acknowledge it or not as it cannot be otherwise for a nation to create wealth and survive calamity. The king who does not fear God will destroy wealth and thus his kingdom along with himself.

Equity and Justice conflated

The law does not, nor can it sanction justice or vengeance but it does sanction and it must sanction equity. Equity under law exists only in the instance of contract enforcement and not in instances where the taking of private property or the taking of life by the sovereign is concerned. The sovereign taking of private property from a criminal or taking the life of a criminal is to punish the criminal for violating the law. Nor is punishment intended as a deterrent to others nor as rehabilitation. Punishment is the wages of sin and nothing more and nothing less. It is not to make the victim of the criminal or the nation in any way whole. The latter is a common misconception, that conflates equity and justice and this misconception often justifies vengeance bred of envy. When I speak of equity I do not mean justice, rather I mean equity in the enforcement of contract as I have said. I will not use the term justice because it conflates with vengeance although I will use the term justification to mean a reason other than vengeance for an action.

The "Justice" of the French Revolution

There is no better example of the conflation of justice and vengeance bred of envy than the French Revolution and its aftermath. I will discuss the true causes of the French Revolution in more detail later because it is a profound turning point in political and economic history. For the present, I use it to illustrate how godlessness unleashes envy to bring about so-called "justice". To bring about their revolution, the leaders of the French Revolution had first to deny God's existence. This was easy for them as the revolutionaries were very much a product of the Enlightenment. Voltaire one of the more influential philosophers of the so-called Enlightenment, dismissed and mocked the existence of God, calling the belief in God mere superstition and non-sense. Jean-Jacques Rousseau is another of the influential philosophers and atheists of the time who argued that the sovereign power rested with the people and not the government and that there was no divine right of kings. Instead, there was the divine right of the people. His arguments as well as the arguments of Voltaire unleashed the horrors of the Reign of Terror, as there was now no fear of God and thus no compelling limit to the sovereign's power of eminent domain.   As long as the "people" authorized an act, it made no difference what the act was.   In other words, any act sanctioned by the "people" in a plebiscite was legal, moral and ethical as the "people" and not God was the final and only arbiter of all law and morality.   Rousseau was in this sense one of the first relativist. Democracy in the hands and minds of these atheists, and all atheists since the French Revolution, is not only a political system, i.e. a manner of selecting the sovereign, it becomes a moral system as well.   Thus, the killing of innocent men, women and children was justified as long as it was in the name of the "people" and sanctioned by the "people", notwithstanding God's proscription against murder or envy since God does not exist.   The aim of the Enlightenment as an intellectual movement was to reform the nation through reason and to challenge ideas grounded in tradition and faith while advancing knowledge through the scientific method.   To reform the nation means to overthrow the existing sovereignty and enact laws advantages, and acceptable to the proponents of the Enlightenment.   The overthrow of the existing sovereignty is necessarily a violent act and if the majority deems the act legal and moral then the act is "justified" temporally and incorporeally in the minds of the actors.   The Enlightenment was a set of beliefs that relied on the false idea that man precedes God and therefore God is a mere construct of man's imagination.   It was a revival of the ancient philosophy of the Stoics who taught that man's reason through his will controls his passions therefore there is no need for God's Commandments, as man through his reason and the force of his will can rein in his passions and thus survive.   Thus, the Enlightenment was above all an atheistic movement, and accordingly it led to the murder and the destruction of wealth, as all atheistic movements must do, and apart from the mere act of rebellion.   The French Revolutionaries engendered in the French hoi polloi the envy of the aristocracy, as the fear of God no longer reined in that passion either in the new sovereignty, so-called republic, or in the populace.   The French Revolution ended in "justice" with the gruesome murder of 50,000 individuals including young children and infants, and the taking of the private property of many worthy individuals by those generally unworthy in ability or intellect to manage properly.   The so-called "justice" of the French Revolution manifested itself in vengeance bred of the envy of the life and property of innocent individuals in much the same way that Cain's envy of God's favor led to the murder of his brother Abel.   The murder of Abel also halted the generations of Abel thus Cain's envy changed the course of Biblical history and of man's history.   It mattered little that the property of those murdered did not redound to the benefit of the murders, as it did not matter to Cain that God's favor did not redound to him on the murder of his brother.   It was enough to satiate envy that the envied aristocracy no longer had their property including their lives and the lives of their progeny, i.e. their wealth.   The murder of the French aristocracy was as much to spite their wealth, as it was to take their wealth.   It was also to spite God.   So too the murder of Abel by his brother Cain was to spite God's favor.   The mark of Cain remains on the French as it does on the Russians, Germans and others who performed similar acts of murder and stealing bred of envy one century after the French Revolution in order to establish their communist and national socialist utopian "paradise on earth".   Thus, the idea of justice is not part of my moral philosophy nor can justice be part of any wealth creating economy.

Colonization Justified

At this point, some misguided readers may argue that the colonization of other lands by the Europeans that took place in the centuries before the French Revolution and during the 19th Century also involved murder of innocents and stealing of their property. Consequently, colonizing of other lands is to be as much condemned as the French Revolution for this reason.   However, unlike the impetus for the French Revolution, the impetus for colonization was not envy but rather it was greed and God does not proscribe greed but He does proscribe envy.   This alone justifies colonization apart from the fact that the colonized nations failed to create sufficient wealth to prevent the calamity that befell them, i.e. the European armies and navies.   A European power undertook colonization of remote lands for profit in competition with other powers.   The competition limited any misuse of the colonized lands or of the population of these lands since misuse or abuse enabled another power to supplant the entrenched power or to provoke rebellion in the colonized lands as indeed happened in the case of the American Colonies.   This is an argument against a single world nation.   Such a nation would enslave the populace since it would have no competition but rebellion.   Thus, the mark of Cain is not on the colonizing nations for the desire to create wealth, as these nations acted in accordance with God's admonishment to go forth and prosper and in accordance with Natural Law.   However, the mark of Cain is on those nations whose sovereign engendered envy in their population leading to the suppression of wealth creation as happened in the nations previously cited.

The difference also between the French Revolution, driven by envy, and the process of colonization, driven by greed, is that the former destroyed wealth while the latter created wealth.   While instances of abuse did occur, colonization by the Western Christian nations generally improved the lives of the subjugated populations in relative terms.   All colonies were generally better off after they became colonies than they were before they became colonies.   India is one example that I will discuss in more detail later.

The morality of slavery

To the extent that slavery was a factor in colonization then an argument may exist about the morality of colonization. Slavery is the taking of a man's time on earth against his will. The taking of one man's time on earth by another against his will is akin to theft, thus slavery is immoral as God's Commandments proscribe theft. However, the taking of a man's time on earth by the sovereign or protector through the sovereign power of eminent domain and in accordance with due process is not slavery as it is not and cannot be theft. A sovereign may possess slaves as long as he does so in accordance with the law that the sovereign enacts and invokes to protect private property and enforce laws and contracts. Indeed taxation laws that result in the taking of property from individuals, subject individuals to a form of slavery as are laws that mandate conscription in service to the nation. An individual who is a citizen of the nation cannot possess slaves as such possession is theft of the life of the slave and therefore immoral. If a man is willing to be enslaved then this is moral because a man of his own freewill can give himself to another in exchange for his care and keeping. Indeed many slaves freed by the result of the War Between the States did not want to be free. They were better off as slaves and desired to remain effectively as such. A nation that colonizes another nation effectively imposes its sovereignty on the colonized nation through force or by agreement. The sovereign nation is the protector of the colonized nation and if the law allows then the sovereign can possess slaves. Therefore, it is moral for the sovereign under the divine right of king to possess slaves but immoral for individuals to possess slaves. However, since the sovereign cannot create wealth and everything possessed by the sovereign is commonly held, then the sovereign's possession of slaves, while moral and legal, is not ethical unless it is for the purpose of protecting private property and enforcing laws and contracts. Sovereign laws sanctioning the ownership of slaves by individuals are themselves immoral as they contradict God's laws and the law of nature. Thus, a nation with such laws does not fear God, thereby encumbering its economy, and thus failing to create wealth it will eventually succumb to calamity.

Note that I use the term sovereign in place of king at times. To be sovereign means to be independent of the law and above the law. One who is sovereign can do no wrong and is beyond reproach ethically, morally and legally. The divine right of the kings comes from God and falls to the sovereign. The king cannot and does not jeopardize his soul before God when he exercises the sovereign power of eminent domain. Therein is the divine right of kings, i.e. to take a man's life and/or property with no consequence to the king's person or soul. The sovereign power of eminent domain therefore is a divine right and an absolute right. It is the only right of the king in that it comes from God, but only as long as the king fears God, for should the king not fear God then his nation, i.e. his life, will succumb to calamity and his soul damned. Under a godless sovereign, as in the case of the French Republic, the nation does not create wealth, envy prevails, and the nation becomes vulnerable to calamity, i.e. the loss of private property in all its forms including life. This happens in all the atheistic economies, as are the socialist and communist economies that arose in Europe and Asia after the French Revolution to the present time, and which drew inspiration from it and from the Stoicism and atheism of the Enlightenment.

Obligation, Duty and Responsibility

Another commonly held moral precept is obligation, or duty or responsibility. Obligation is a relative concept, i.e. obligation does not exist nor can it exist apart from any reason to compel the obligation. Self-interest motivates man in accordance with Natural Law, and a man's self-interest is the most accurate predictor of his behavior, the most compelling reason for his behavior, and the only justification for his behavior. Self-interest manifested in greed is the motivating force of wealth creation and thus greed insures man's survival. Obligation apart from any motivating force is akin to altruism, i.e. the irrational desire to do good expecting nothing in return. Altruism is destructive of life and of wealth creation, as it undermines and is contrary to self-interest or greed. To the extent that obligation is an absolute then the only moral obligation that a man has is the creation and preservation of wealth, i.e. the only moral obligation that a man has is protecting and securing himself and perpetuating himself. Bringing forth children is wealth creation because children are a hedge against calamity. Therefore, a man has an obligation toward his children not for altruistic reasons but because of self-interest as children hedge calamity, and secures the future of the individual and of man in general. Thus, a man loves his children as he must love all wealth because they are a hedge against calamity and security for the future. A man must love his wife because she is one with him and he must love himself, as it is his obligation to follow Natural Law. Love is a manifestation of greed whereas hate is a manifestation of envy. Note that God does not explicitly proscribe hate other than hate born of envy. Thus, murder arising out of love is just as immoral or sinful as murder arising out of hate or envy. There is no inherent obligation or duty to obey man's law or God's law. Fear of the sovereign's power of eminent domain compels Man's obedience to the law, and the fear of God, not the love of man, reins in man's envy. Similarly, it is fear of the future that compels the creation of wealth as the hedge against calamity. Thus, fear obligates an individual only to himself, which includes his wife and progeny and in accordance with Natural Law. There is no inherent duty or obligation to others, nor can there be other than by contract. Only the sovereign and by extension the soldier has an inherent duty and inherent obligation to others, but only to the extent necessary to secure private property and enforce laws and contracts. The sovereign has no inherent duty to care for the poor, the orphan, the widow, or the indigent To the extent that the sovereign undertakes such duty under the law then it is to this extent that he encumbers the creation of wealth and weakens the nation's ability to withstand calamity. Similarly, to the extent that charity undertakes the care of the poor, the orphan, the widow or the indigent then to this extent charity encumbers the creation of wealth.

The Golden Rule as a manifestation of self-interest

Self-interest gives rise to the love of another. *"Love your neighbor as you love yourself"* or *"do unto others as you would have them do unto you"* as a statement of the Golden Rule is an appeal to self-interest not to altruism, nor does the Golden Rule appeal explicitly to any spiritual or temporal obligation or duty. If it were not an appeal to self-interest then there would not be a reason to follow the Golden Rule. The Golden Rule does not apply in war so why should it apply in any other context absent self-interest. Indeed war is the suspension of self-interest and the ultimate expression of altruism since its goal is the same, i.e. the destruction of wealth and life, not its creation. The moral code can be *"Love your neighbor's property as you love your property"* or *"Protect your neighbor's property as you would protect your property"*. Therefore, saving a drowning man is not for altruistic reasons but rather for self-interest, i.e. the fear of God. In such situations, God and man accord the individual the divine right of king. He becomes for the moment the protector of private property. That is he can do no wrong in a legal or moral sense while engaged in the saving of the life of another man or in the saving of his own life. As sovereign for the moment, a man engaged in saving the life of another or saving his own life is not compelled to follow man's law or God's law but rather Natural law, which is the law of self-interest. If in the process of saving another man, a man gives up his life then he has committed suicide, and if he were not sovereign and shielded for the moment under the divine right of king then he would have committed a mortal sin. However, since he was acting for the moment as sovereign then his soul is secure as he acts under the divine right of king, and accordingly he can do no wrong in God's eyes. This is apart from his original motivation, which could be love of man but is actually the fear of God. This concept extends to the soldier who is in service to a nation except the soldier is sovereign in all matters at all times. The Golden Rule manifests in the Ten Commandments. The proscription of murder for instance, as restated in terms of the Golden Rule is *"Love life of another as you love your own life"*. Therefore, the proscription of murder is an appeal to self-interest, i.e. love of oneself, and not to altruism. The Golden Rule is from God and its violation is a mortal sin. Its violation is also a violation of Natural Law. Envy's proscription is also in terms

36

of the Golden Rule, i.e. thou shalt not covet thy neighbor's things, applies to both you and your neighbor. While atheists and humanists argue the Golden Rule as a moral code exists apart from God because it does not invoke God expressly, these pseudo intellectuals fail to realize that the Golden Rule is from God as it is in every sense a restatement of the Ten Commandments written in stone by the hand of God. Accordingly, the true motivation to obey the Golden Rule rests with the disposition of the soul and thus the fear of God, i.e. self-interest, as well as with corporal self-interest through fear of the sovereign's power of eminent domain. The violation of the Golden Rule in all its forms is a violation of the Commandments of God, a violation of Natural Law, and violation of man's law, and therefore punishable by God and by Man. To think or do otherwise is to deny reality and to promulgate atheism and thus the destruction of wealth.

The rationale for saving of a drowning man extends to the preservation of wealth creation or the ability to create wealth. Individual wealth creation is for the benefit of all as it secures the entire nation against calamity and gives rise to greater wealth creation eventually encompassing all others who engage to satisfy their individual self-interests. A man acting in his self-interest is acting ethically in the temporal sense and morally in the spiritual sense. He is acting out of love of himself, and by application of the Golden Rule, he acts out of love for his fellow man. He is acting ethically in a temporal sense because he is protecting private property and creating wealth thus ensuring temporal survival, and he is acting morally in a spiritual sense as he secures his soul before God. The creation of wealth both materially and through man's progeny secure man's immortality as ordained by God and it is the purpose of man's Creation and the reason for his Creation.

Charity

The act of charity is a manifestation of the Golden Rule, i.e. do undo others that which you would have others do unto you. Just as obedience to the Golden Rule rests with the disposition of the soul arising from the fear of God and self-interest, i.e. the fear of the future, or the fear of the sovereign's power of eminent domain, so too self-interest motivates the act of charity. Thus, charity is not an altruistic act but an act of self-interest in every sense of the word. Since self-interest motivates charity then charity is an act of individual freewill. It cannot be an act of the sovereign or the state. Self-interest or freewill cannot motivate the sovereign or else he risks rebellion and jeopardizes his soul. Hence, a sovereign cannot be charitable. The sovereign acts only in the interest of the individuals comprising the nation, and acts only to protect their property and enforce their contracts in accordance with the law that he enacts. To the extent that charity is an act of the sovereign then it further burdens wealth creation thus making a nation more susceptible to calamity.   In the Christian Tradition, charity is an act of the individual in accordance with individual freewill not an act of the sovereign or in other words not an act of the state.   The state or the sovereign cannot provide charity because doing so burdens the creation of wealth and reduces the nation's ability to survive calamity.

Furthermore, the act of charity only consummates by freely giving something of one's own possessions to the object of the charity. The sovereign has nothing of his own to give as everything the sovereign has, including his life, is commonly held, and disposed according to law, and only for protecting private property and enforcement of laws and contracts.

While charity is an act of individual freewill, it nevertheless does not create wealth, as charity does not provide an economic return for the money given.   Individuals who give to charity rather than invest in an economy are destroying wealth and therefore make an economy more susceptible to calamity and in fact create greater need for charity rather than alleviate the reason for the charity.   To the extent that the sovereign rewards individuals or institutions for giving to charity through the tax laws then individual freewill is not the motivator and so charity is not an act of compassion but rather an economic act, i.e. an act of self-interest, used to reduce the burden of taxation.   In so doing the sovereign, through the tax laws promotes the poverty that gives rise to charity and wealth destruction.   Compassion, self-interest, and individual freewill motivate charity in an unencumbered economy and less so in an encumbered economy but the act is nevertheless destructive of wealth creation.   Thus, compassion is a passion that must be limited through a man's freewill and his self-interest in an unencumbered economy, as it leads to even greater poverty than the poverty the misguided compassion intends to alleviate.   Economic considerations more than compassion motivate charity in an encumbered environment.   Regardless of the motivation, charity is destructive of wealth creation.

Charity if given must be humbly given and if taken must be humbly taken as both the benefactor and the recipient have no reason to be proud of the wealth that they are destroying.   If compassion motivated everyone then there would be no wealth created, thus compassion, as a human passion is naturally self-limiting.

Some argue the Christian Tradition teaches it is not enough for salvation merely to be good one must also be charitable, or do a good. Satisfying ones self-interest and creating wealth is doing the good because wealth secures man's immortality as God ordained.   While charity may satisfy one's ego and vanity, it does not create wealth.   Therefore, salvation only manifests in the creation of wealth not in charity since the creation of wealth is doing good and charity is not wealth creation but wealth destruction.

Many critics of wealth, point to Jesus' Words in Matthew 19:24

"Again I tell you, it is easier for a camel to go through the eye of a needle than for someone who is rich to enter the kingdom of God." These critics thus justify the belief that wealth is evil and that a wealthy man cannot enter the Kingdom of Heaven.   Yet these same critics fail to mention Matthew 19:26 *"Jesus looked at them and said, "With man this is impossible, but with God all things are possible."*   In other words, while men may desire to believe the former the truth is the latter.

In any transaction between individuals there must exist an exchange of tangible private property.   The tangible private property can be a man's time in the form of labor for money, which is another form of tangible property when converted to cash.   The transaction would not take place unless there is some material benefit to both parties.   A charitable transaction is by definition a transaction in which one party willingly relinquishes private property such as cash while ostensibly expecting or obtaining nothing tangible in return.   Such a transaction if truly charitable is destructive of wealth and therefore unethical.   Those that give to charity are engaging in the destruction of wealth and weakening their ability and the nation's ability to survive calamity   The argument that charity brings man closer to God has some validity in the sense that it makes his physical demise more likely as it reduces his ability to survive calamity.   In this sense, charity is immoral as well as unethical. A man's soul is secure before God only when man creates wealth as wealth ensures Man's immortality as ordained by God at Creation.   The creation of wealth is the means by which Man fulfills the will of God and not charity.   Referring to the problem of a drowning man, which I discussed earlier, whosoever saves the drowning man does not perform an act of charity but rather he is securing private property.   For the moment, the savior of the drowning man is sovereign and accorded the divine right of king.   Thus insofar as the act is concerned it neither secures nor condemns the savior's soul before God.   Failure to act however condemns the soul as the failure to act results in the loss of private property, i.e. the ability to create wealth.   Failure to act is the abrogation of duty as sovereign and thus condemned by God as if he committed murder.   Thus, the fear of God compels a man to act to save another who is drowning and in the process, the savior is sovereign and can do no wrong.

Gratitude and Resentment

Linked to charity are the passions of gratitude and resentment. Given that each man has freewill then the manifestation of charity by the recipient are unpredictable.   It is just as likely that the immediate response of the beneficiary to an act of charity will be resentment as it will be gratitude.   If the beneficiary fears God then he is naturally grateful.   If the recipient does not fear God then the long-term response is always resentment.   Thus, charity and altruism always engender envy in the heart of the godless.   Beneficiaries of charity must fear God or else charity will engender envy and with envy comes socialism and the destruction of wealth compounded.   This is true whether the benefactor is the sovereign or an individual.

No Social Contract

Unlike the word justice, however, I will use the words obligation and duty in this book in two senses.   The first sense is obligation and/or duty arising through contracts exercised according to individual freewill and directed toward individual self-interest.   The second sense is the duty and obligation of the sovereign to the nation.   Philosophers have used the term "social contract" to describe the perceived agreement that exists between the sovereign and the individuals whom the sovereign protects and secures.   This perceived agreement involves an exchange of liberty for security.   In other words, individuals comprising a nation agree to relinquish some liberties in exchange for a measure of security.   There are two problems with this concept.

One problem is that there can be no explicit or implicit contract, social or otherwise with the sovereign.   One cannot contract with himself because such a contract is unenforceable, and a so-called social contract is a contract with oneself.   A government comes into existence to satisfy the need for security of private property and enforcement of laws and the contracts between individuals.   The perceived "social contract" is a misnomer in the sense that if the sovereign fails to protect private property and enforce contracts the individual cannot sue the sovereign without his permission.   Thus, the relationship between the government and the governed is not contractual but imposed through force manifested in the sovereign's power of eminent domain.   I will not reference any social contract since none exists nor can it exist.   There is no such thing as a contract between an individual and society implied or otherwise.   First, because the term "society" as a political term is an inherently corrupt concept invoked only to justify altruism and thus for inherently destructive ends.   Second, a contract by definition can only exist between individuals or entities such as corporations that are legally, and ethically individual persons.   Society is not a legal entity, nor is it a political entity, as it is insubstantial, i.e. no one exists or can exist to represent society before the law or as a party to a contract.   A prosecutor in a criminal proceeding, for instance, represents the sovereign or the nation not so-called society.   The sovereign can make no laws to govern or regulate society in any general way.   The sovereign's laws are to govern the conduct of individuals that include corporations and only to the extent as these laws protect and secure private property and enable the enforcement of contracts.   The king or sovereign does not represent a society in any legal or even moral sense; he only exists to protect private property and enforce laws and contracts.   An ambassador or minister appointed by the sovereign only represents the sovereign to the nation or to other nations in his duty to protect the individual private property and enforce the individual contracts of his nation.

The second problem with the concept of a "social contract" i.e. the exchange of liberty for security is that not all the individuals comprising a nation agree to every exchange. In the absence of the agreement of all parties to a contract, there can be no contract.

Laws equally applicable to all

Implicit in any law is that the law applies equally to all individuals in a nation. Laws singling out individuals or groups, whether to benefit or to punish are the most burdensome and most destructive of wealth creation thus exposing the nation to calamity. The US Constitution explicitly prohibits laws that punish particular individuals or groups. Article 1 Section 9 paragraph 3 states, *"No Bill of Attainder or ex post facto Law shall be passed"*. Article 1 Section 10 applies the same prohibition to the States. Note that the same paragraph also prohibits laws that apply to past events. The Constitution permits the levying of tariffs to raise revenue for the nation. However, Congress must apply the tariffs equally to all products and services. Article 1 Section 8 of the Constitution states *"The Congress shall have Power To lay and collect Taxes, Duties, Imposts and Excises, to pay the Debts and provide for the common Defence*(sic) *and general Welfare of the United States; but all Duties, Imposts and Excises shall be uniform throughout the United States;…"*. Laws that benefit particular groups, individuals and companies also engender envy in those that do not fear God and set the stage for rebellion. A sovereign who desires to impose a socialist or communist economy, i.e. an economy whereby the sovereign owns the means of production, must first engender envy by removing God from the public discourse and then enacting laws that benefit one group at the expense of another. This was the strategy of the French revolutionaries as well as the German National Socialists, aka NAZI. Such a sovereign becomes himself the calamity originally appointed by the individuals of the nation to prevent, and thus he is ripe for rebellion.

Note that Article 1 Section 8 explicitly states that the purpose of taxes is to provide for the Common Defense, which refers to the protection of private property and for the general Welfare of the United States as a nation and not for the general Welfare of the individuals comprising the nation. The general Welfare of a nation manifests only in the wealth of a nation and the Framers wrote the Constitution to secure the creation of wealth by limiting the sovereign power of eminent domain and no other reason.

41

The Soul of the Soldier, Productivity and Unemployment

It is my intention through this book to resolve the two problems that I first posed. The first is the moral problem that is the disposition of the soul of a soldier and by extension the soul of the king. The second is the ethical problem that is the unemployment engendered by rapid gains in productivity in an unencumbered economy. Note that I make a distinction between a moral problem and an ethical problem. A moral problem concerns the disposition of the soul, which is a matter for God. An ethical problem concerns the survival of the individual or the nation, i.e. a matter of wealth and wealth creation. A moral problem may or may not be a legal problem. For instance, murder is both a violation of man's law, i.e. illegal and a violation of God's law, i.e. immoral. Since murder is a destruction of private property, i.e. the life of a man, then murder is also unethical. Income taxes are a destruction of wealth creation hence income taxes are unethical but are moral. The sovereign undertakes taxation hence it is not theft as the sovereign can do no wrong. The sin of envy is a moral concern but it is not a legal or ethical concern. However, to the extent that envy results in the destruction of wealth creation it becomes an ethical concern as well as a moral concern. To the extent that envy results in the destruction of private property or life then it becomes a legal concern as well. Cain's envy of God's favor of Abel damned Cain's soul, as envy is immoral. Cain's murder of his brother Abel condemned his body and his soul therefore his act was illegal in the eyes of man, as well as immoral. As Cain murdered his brother, he also dishonored his parents and violated God's admonition to honor thy father and thy mother. Cain's envy of Abel drove him to murder his brother, Abel, and by doing so dishonored his parents compounding his sin. Cain then lied to God when God asked Cain the whereabouts of his brother. The murder of Abel was an unethical act as well because Abel created wealth and his murder was the destruction of wealth creation.

A company that does not make a profit for example is an ethical problem however it is not a legal or moral problem in an unencumbered economy. The failure to make a profit in an unencumbered economy is due to the inability to supply goods and services efficiently, i.e. profitably. This failure leads to unemployment and a destruction of wealth. An unencumbered economy is able to absorb the layoffs and ensuing destruction of wealth thus there are no moral issues that need to be resolved. A company that fails to make a profit in an encumbered economy results in unemployment and destruction of wealth the economy cannot absorb, thus moral issues arise that now must be resolved. When the resolution is through some form of government assistance the sovereign's encumbrance of the economy increases thus creating more failures. Therein is the moral issue, to wit the taking of wealth by the sovereign now becomes theft since the taking is not to protect private property or enforce of contracts. The failure of one company results in the failure of others through acts of the sovereign. Only a godless sovereign undertakes the redistribution of wealth. This is the situation currently faced in Japan, as I will discuss later. The United States is also facing the same situation as the government is financially supporting many unprofitable and inefficient companies at the expense of profitable and efficient companies.

God's Law, Sovereign Law, and Natural Law

I make a distinction between three types of laws. Sovereign laws should be toward the protection of private property and the enforcement of contract. God's laws are the Ten Commandments directed to the disposition of a man's soul. These are the moral laws. Natural Law, directed to the preservation and perpetuation of one's own life and property, these are the ethical laws. Suicide for instance is a violation of Natural Law and God's Law but not the sovereign's laws. In other words, under sovereign law a sane and rational man may chose of his own volition to destroy his own property, e.g. take his own life, but not the property of others. However, God condemns his soul as he violated the Commandment proscribing murder. That is, the act of suicide is immoral, and unethical, but it is legal. Note that throughout this book I assume that man is both sane and rational and the exercise of individual freewill is on this basis. I will use the term intellectual capital to refer to the intelligence of the nation's populace as measured by the average IQ. In general, history, common sense, reason, and the current evidence has shown that a nation whose population has an average IQ of 100 with one standard deviation of 15 is a nation that will prosper given that the nation is under God, i.e. its populace fears God, and the economy is unencumbered. Nations with populations significantly lower than an average IQ of 100 and/or a smaller standard deviation will not be prosperous and will more likely be under a tyrannical or semi-tyrannical sovereign with an encumbered economy. These nations will not benefit from an unencumbered economy nor will the fear of God assuage the envy of the populace. Such nations will fail and have failed with either the more intellectually capable nations colonizing these nations or the individuals live in perpetual poverty and misery, as this is their inherent destiny. Thus, the moral philosophy that I herein present applies only to those nations that possess within the populace the intellectual capital, i.e. a high average IQ, to create wealth.

In the process of solving the two problems that I posed, I provide and have provided novel and basic insights into the nature of God, economics, the purpose of government, and the nature and purpose of wealth. These insights will bring to light and put to the lie much of modern media's propaganda and the self-serving and ultimately destructive godless pabulum taught today in most of the schools and universities.

Introduction

Engineers are often engaged in implementing technologies to improve productivity in manufacturing, services, and infrastructure industries. Besides creating wealth, the gains in productivity also have ethical and moral consequences in terms of employment. This book addresses these ethical and moral consequences. This book draws in part on my experience as a staff manager and engineer with the Ohio Bell Telephone Company, which became Ameritech and is now AT&T. As a staff manager, I conducted economic studies to improve productivity. The result of my economic studies as well as the economic studies of other managers was a tremendous and rapid gain in productivity in the telecommunications company and in the telecommunications industry in general. In the case of Ohio Bell, which was a subsidiary of AT&T (later Ameritech) at the time, the number of employees decreased from a peak of 30,000 in 1974 to about 3,000 twenty years later. During the same period, the number of telephone lines installed and managed by Ohio Bell increased from 20 million to 30 million. As a manager with the company, I was directly responsible for the elimination of a large number of jobs including my own as the gains in productivity affected both labor and management jobs. Accordingly, I have first hand experience with the disruptive consequences of rapid gains in productivity since I was both a promoter and a casualty of efficiency. The gains in efficiency or productivity resulted in Ameritech's stock increasing about 10 times over the same period. Similar gains in productivity have been occurring throughout the service industry during the last 50 years. The gains in productivity in the service industry mirrored the gains in productivity in manufacturing that occurred in the middle part of the twentieth century and the rapid productivity gains in agriculture in the first part of the twentieth century in the Western nations. In all these cases, the result over time was a tremendous gain in wealth and a higher standard of living in the Western nations. This gain in wealth was despite two historically destructive wars and the relentless encumbrance of the economy by government. The gain in wealth is a testament to the power of productivity that in turn is a product of individual human genius and creativity. Yet the gain in wealth is much smaller by at least 80 times than it would have been without government interference in the economy beginning in 1930. In other words even though the United States created great wealth since 1930 the amount of wealth created was 1/80th of the amount that could have been created .(See Appendix 1) Government interference in the economy began in earnest in 1930. However, the stage was set almost 20 years earlier under Woodrow Wilson. Wilson and the Democrats pushed through radical changes to the Constitution and Federal Law that permanently and negatively altered the course of wealth creation in the United States.

The changes with the most impact on wealth creation included the income tax amendment to the Constitution (16th Amendment), the passage of the Clayton Anti-Trust Act, the popular election of Senators under the 17th Amendment, the creation of the Federal Reserve Bank in 1913, and the enactment of universal suffrage in 1920 (19th Amendment). These laws more than anything else enabled a massive redistribution of wealth and a reduction in the creation of wealth beginning in 1930 and extending to the present time with a brief but significant respite in the decade of the 1980s.

Rapid gains in productivity as the source of wealth and war

Rapid gains in productivity, the source of wealth creation, have also resulted in the most devastating wars and the greatest number of human deaths ever recorded in human history arising solely from conflict. The later part of the nineteenth century and the entire twentieth century are the productivity centuries because of the exponential rise in human output. When I speak of productivity, I mean the efficiency of production in terms of the ratio between output and input, i.e. percent profit. I do not mean the level of production or the amount of goods and services produced. Although the level of production has also increased greatly since the beginning of the 19th Century, it is due to the gain in productivity, which gave rise to increasing investment. The gain in productivity thus ushered in new products and services that eased the burden of life contributing to significant gains in life expectancy and improvements in the quality of life in the Western Nations along with and not despite increases in population.

It is no coincidence that during the same period history has witnessed the most devastating and murderous wars in human history. The correlation between rapid gains in productivity, or efficiency, and civil unrest is deterministic in an encumbered economy. In other words, civil unrest is inevitable and unavoidable but only in a taxed, highly regulated and otherwise coercive economy, which is an encumbered economy. An unencumbered economy or an economy free of government taxation, regulation and coercion witnesses little or no civil unrest arising from rapid gains in productivity. This is critical to understand, because throughout modern history (since 1800) government, through taxation, regulation and coercion, is the great destroyer of wealth and therefore the great purveyor of poverty, war and death. The encumbering of economy by government is the sole reason for so-called business cycles, depression, unemployment, poverty, civil unrest, and war since the later part of the 19th Century.

Fractional banking not a cause of calamity

Although others have ascribed business cycles to fractional banking methods such methods do not exist apart and in isolation from the economy in general or more importantly from government regulation, taxation and coercion.   Government efforts to regulate and tax the banking industry undermine the fractional banking system, and create the disruptions and upheavals in the general economy.   Fractional banking is the lending of a large proportion of depositor's money to individuals who promise to pay it back with interest.   The bank accounts for the depositor's cash as if all the cash is in the bank's vault.   This creates a problem whenever depositors demand more of their money than the bank has in the vault.   When this happens, it is a run on the bank and the bank fails with depositors possibly loosing their money.   On the other hand, it is the only way that a bank can pay interest to the depositors, make a profit, and create wealth.   Figure 1 is a spreadsheet illustrating fractional banking.   In this example, the reserve rate is 20%. Each bank must keep 20% of the physical money deposits in reserve for the demand deposits but it shows or accounts 100% of the deposit as an asset.   The balance of the physical money on deposit is on loan to individuals who are paying back the loan.   The loans are contracts enforceable by the sovereign.   Thus, the sovereign secures bank deposits through the enforcement of contracts.   An individual makes an initial deposit in bank 1 of $1000 and the bank holds $200.00 in reserve.   The $1000 deposit is a liability to the bank and an asset to the depositor. The bank loans the balance of $800 to someone else.   The loan is a contract that is an asset to the bank, who is the creditor, and a liability to the individual who is the debtor.   The debtor uses the $800 to buy property such as a capital tool from a third party by which the debtor will earn the money needed to pay back the original loan.   The third party who is the owner of the property, i.e. the capital tool, exchanges his property for the $800 and deposits this money in a second bank.   The original $1000 shows up as an asset of the first bank and the $800 shows up as an asset in the second bank.   In terms of total wealth there is now $1800 in assets where before there was $1000 although the total money is still $1000.   This process continues as the second bank now loans $640 and this amount appears in a third bank as a new deposit thus creating total cash deposits of $2440 and the process is repeated.   Note that each step in the process there is a promise made to pay back the loan and in order for the debtor to pay back the loan he must create or provide something of value to others.   In other words, the debtor or debtors must satisfy consumer needs in order to create wealth.   The rate of wealth creation must exceed the interest rate of the loan in order that the debtor profit or create wealth.

Reserve rate	0.2	Amount loaned	Amount reserved
Bank1	$1,000.00	$800.00	$200.00
Bank2	$800.00	$640.00	$160.00
Bank3	$640.00	$512.00	$128.00
Bank4	$512.00	$409.60	$102.40
Bank5	$409.60	$327.68	$81.92
Bank6	$327.68	$262.14	$65.54
Bank7	$262.14	$209.72	$52.43
Bank8	$209.72	$167.77	$41.94
Bank9	$167.77	$134.22	$33.55
Bank10	$134.22	$107.37	$26.84
Bank11	$107.37	$85.90	$21.47
Bank12	$85.90	$68.72	$17.18
Bank13	$68.72	$54.98	$13.74
Bank14	$54.98	$43.98	$11.00
Bank15	$43.98	$35.18	$8.80
Bank16	$35.18	$28.15	$7.04
Bank17	$28.15	$22.52	$5.63
Bank18	$22.52	$18.01	$4.50
Bank19	$18.01	$14.41	$3.60
Bank20	$14.41	$11.53	$2.88
Bank21	$11.53	$9.22	$2.31
Bank22	$9.22	$7.38	$1.84
Bank23	$7.38	$5.90	$1.48
Bank24	$5.90	$4.72	$1.18
Bank25	$4.72	$3.78	$0.94
Bank26	$3.78	$3.02	$0.76
Bank27	$3.02	$2.42	$0.60
Bank28	$2.42	$1.93	$0.48
Bank29	$1.93	$1.55	$0.39
Bank30	$1.55	$1.24	$0.31
Bank31	$1.24	$0.99	$0.25
Bank32	$0.99	$0.79	$0.20
Bank33	$0.79	$0.63	$0.16
Total	$4,996.83	$3,997.46	$999.37

Figure 1-Fractional Banking Process

Fractional banking rests on the notion that the depositors will probably not need their deposits all at the same time and that the interest on the deposits serves as a sufficient incentive for the depositors to keep their money in the bank rather than use it for other purposes.   It is a statistically efficient means of creating wealth but the system contains risks because it relies in part on the confidence of the depositors that their savings are secure and therefore will not demand all their deposits at the same time.   It also depends on the fact that debtors return all the money loaned and with interest as promised.   As the debt is paid back additional money becomes available, which can also be loaned out. Consequently, there is a moral as well as a legal component to the loaning of money in the sense that the debtor must be truthful about his intent and the value of his assets that are the collateral to the loan.   Keep in mind that a debt is a contract that is enforceable by the sovereign.   That is, the sovereign's power of eminent domain can take asset or property from the debtor to satisfy the debt and the interest on the debt in the event that the debtor does not perform on his contract, i.e. does not pay his debt. This is a critical element to the operation of a fractional banking system. If events occur that shake confidence then depositors will demand all their money, and they will not be able to get it. Thus, the bank fails and money is lost and wealth destroyed despite of the sovereign's power to take the property of debtors. Such situations have occurred from time to time for a variety of economic reasons and due in large part to government interference in the economy beyond the enforcement of the loan contract. For example, the bank failures that occurred in the later part of the 1920's and early 1930's were in large part due to the existence of the Federal Reserve Bank, which controlled to a large degree the interest rates that banks could charge. Prior to the establishment of the Federal Reserve Bank in 1913, interest rates were set by the market for debt, i.e. supply and demand. The original purpose of a central bank such as the Federal Reserve Bank was to serve as a bank of last resort in a fractional banking system. In the event a large number of an individual member bank's depositors demanded their money, the central bank provided the necessary liquidity needed to avoid the collapse of the bank. It did this by serving as a bank for banks and loaning money to its member banks. Member banks funded the Federal Reserve Bank by depositing a portion of their deposits with the bank. The Federal Reserve Bank was also authorized by the Federal government to print money or add to the money supply as demand for money increased with a growing economy. The amount of gold held by the US Treasury limited the amount of money printed by the Federal Reserve Bank prior to 1970. Thus, a bank that was imprudent in its loans needed to borrow money from the Federal Reserve Bank to pay depositors and the interest on the Federal Reserve Bank loan reduced the bank's profit. The bank's shareholders thus paid a price for the imprudence of the bank's management.

The operational assumption in a fractional banking system is that debtors will pay back all loans. Accordingly, bankers created central banks and deposited a certain proportion of their reserves in the central bank to guard against runs on the member bank and not to guard against loan defaults although such defaults occur they must be generally few, and far between in order for the fractional banking system to remain viable. While this is the theory, in actual practice, the operation of the Federal Reserve Bank nevertheless depends on the ability of its management to respond properly to events. The weakness in the system showed itself early in its history when large numbers of banks started to fail because large numbers of debtors were defaulting in the 1920s and early 1930s. These debtors were farmers who had borrowed money to expand their farms only to have farm prices drop quickly due to over production. The central bank, i.e. the Federal Reserve Bank, tried to rescue banks by removing liquidity through increases in interest rates in order to reduce the number of new loans.   That is instead of loaning money to the troubled banks at low interest rates, the Federal Reserve made it difficult for the troubled banks to borrow money by raising the discount rate.   Rather than adding liquidity to the financial system as banks began to fail, which should have been the response, the Federal Reserve Bank instead increased interest rates causing the banks to call in low interest loans and forcing bankruptcies to occur.   The bank failures caused a run on the banks as depositors became concerned about their savings.   See Figure 2 below.

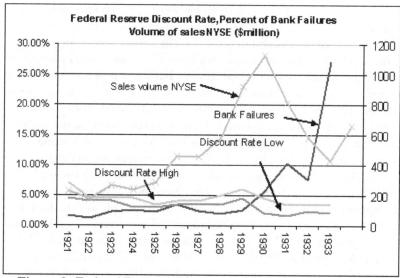

Figure 2- Federal Reserve Discount Rate and Percent of Bank Failures

Note that the Federal Reserve Discount Rate, i.e. the high and low range, was increasing as bank failures were increasing in 1928 and into 1929.   It was only after bank failures started to accelerate in 1929 that the Federal Reserve Bank dropped interest rates to record lows.   This was insufficient to stem the tide of bank failures.   Investors sold stocks to cover the bank losses as reflected in the increase in NYSE sales volume as bank failures increase and in the face of increasing interest rates.   Had interest rates been determined by the market prior to the bank failures, rather than by the Federal Reserve Bank, then interest rates would have risen much sooner as loan demand rose and not remained artificially low while farm prices were dropping at the time due to overproduction on the farm.   Thus, banks would not have made loans or made much fewer loans to farmers at the time of falling prices, and there would have been a slowdown in farm production and stable or increasing farm prices.

Clearly, the central bank failed to play its proper role after the bank failures occurred, which was to provide liquidity when a run on the banks occurred due to a lack of confidence in the banking system. In other words, the Federal Reserve Bank acted too late with the increase in interest rates causing the opposite of its intended reaction. As is always the case with any central planning, the planners always make the wrong decisions in reaction to the problem.

It is instructive to compare the interest rates in the free market with the interest rates as determined by the Federal Reserve Bank during the 1920s and 1930s. I will use the call interest on equities for this comparison. The call interest is the interest on money loaned by brokers and others to buy stocks. Borrowing money to buy stocks is buying on margin. Figure 3 shows the relationship between the call interest on equities and the Real S&P between 1919 and 1938.

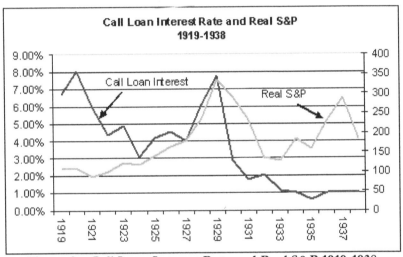

Figure 3 – Call Loan Interest Rate and Real S&P 1919-1938

Note that the call interest rate declined between 1920 and 1925 as the demand measured in the level of the real S&P increased. Conversely as the level of real S&P increased so did the call interest. The unprecedented number of bank failures led to the collapse of the real S&P otherwise the high call rates would have merely stemmed the rapid rise in the real S&P and not cause its rapid decline. The collapse of the S&P was due in large part to margin calls as brokers and banks called in loans whose underlying collateral, i.e. the price of a stock started to drop below the value of the loan thus forcing the sale of stocks. Bank failures occurred due to the lack of confidence resulting from the high number of defaulting loans. Yet even if the Federal Reserve Bank provided the necessary liquidity, it may not have been able to stem the tide of loan defaults. The gold standard regulated the amount of currency in circulation at the time so the government could not simply print more money and shore up the banks with new capital. Had this not been the case then the injection of capital into the banking system at the time may have unleashed inflation causing an even greater economic calamity than the depression. Recall at the time that Germany was undergoing tremendous inflation due to reparations imposed on that nation by the Allies at the Treaty of Versailles. Germany was paying reparations by massively devaluing its currency thus causing crushing inflation in Germany. Germany's inflation eventually brought down the German government, giving rise to a socialist state under the National Socialists. This was undoubtedly the fear that existed at the time in the United States as well. So rather than leave the gold standard and unleash inflation the US government instead reverted to a sort of mercantilism by taking all private holdings of gold and after doing so increasing its official price. This allowed it to print more dollars in an attempt to prop up farm prices. This failed and farm prices remained low and bank failures continued to occur well into the 1930's. The reason the government's attempt to prop up farm prices failed is that farm productivity continued to grow. Farm production continued to increase as farmers and bankers believed that prices would rise because the government was attempting to keep the prices high first by imposing the Smoot-Hawley Tariff, then through the confiscation of gold. It was the assurances by the government that it could overcome the increasing production and thus increase prices that caused farmers to continue producing in the face of falling prices. FDR's radio broadcasts and his famous fireside chats merely served to encourage farmers to plant even more thus compounding the problem and destroying the lives of many people in the process. The government under FDR multiplied the deflationary problem and caused the second downturn in the stock market in 1935 and with it unemployment going to over 20%.

With prudent bank management in an unencumbered economy, i.e. an economy without the Federal Reserve Bank, the loss to depositors should be a rare occurrence since the marketplace always imposes discipline on management. Loans to farmers as occurred during a time of declining farm prices in the 1920s would not have occurred had not bank managers believed that the Federal Reserve Bank would bail them out. In other words if the Federal Reserve Bank did not exist as the bank of last resort for depositors, then the Great Depression would not have been great and neither would there have been as many loans defaulting as there were. The lesson here is that there is very little that a banking system or monetary system can do in the face of rapid gains in productivity as occurred in the farm sector. Nevertheless, had banks been managed more prudently and loans to expand farm production not been given in the face of declining food prices due to overproduction in the first place, then bank failures would not have occurred and food prices would have stabilized. The Federal Reserve Banks existence was the monetary as well as ethical cause of the depression, and the Federal Government simply prolonged the depression through its fiscal policy, i.e. taxation and regulation. The consequence was great destruction of wealth and much poverty and misery, which did not have to happen.

A similar situation existed some 60 years latter with a different set of government regulations. This time it was the Federal Deposit Insurance Corporation (FDIC) laws. These laws, passed as an aftermath of the bank losses during FDR's depression, insure deposits using taxpayer dollars thereby taking the burden of prudence once again off the shoulders of bank management and placing it on the shoulders of taxpayer. As with loans to farmers during the 1920s, bank managers of savings and loans companies during the 1980s and 1990s were more willing to take greater risk when shielded by the taxpayer than they would otherwise, consequently increasing the possibility of losses. Indeed this happened during the 1990s leading to the failure of 747 out of the 3,234 Savings and Loans Associations in the United States. This was in spite of the existence of the Glass-Steagall Act of 1933, another FDR boondoggle, which ostensibly regulated the investments that a bank can make. Congress effectively repealed the Glass-Steagall Act in 1999 and after the bank failures occurred.

Just like the 1920s, the 1980s and 1990s were decades of tremendous gains in productivity with the serious and ubiquitous introduction of the computer in the workplace, the introduction of the cell phone and the internet. Also helping productivity growth during the 1980s and 1990s was the rapid decline in unionized labor, the North American Free Trade Agreement, significant reductions in the corporate tax rate and reduction in the tax rate on capital gains. The resulting gains in productivity led to a rising stock market with real wealth creation and much investment in new technologies such as fiber optics that set the stage for even greater gains in productivity in the following decade. The increase in investment as well as the effect of reducing encumbrance on the economy through lower corporate and capital gains taxes is evident from the number of IPOs or initial public offerings that occurred during this period. The following chart shows IPO activity during the 1980's and 1990's. This was a period of relatively low taxes, declining unions, and increasing productivity.

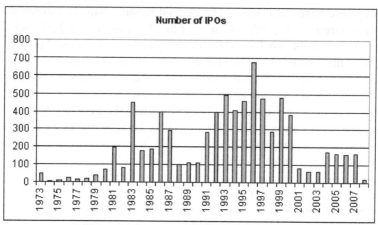

Figure 4-Number of IPOs 1973 to 2007

Prices were stable or dropping causing inflation to be at relatively low levels during this period, yet the interest rates remained relatively high in comparison to the inflation rate due once again to the Federal Reserve Bank's general ineptitude and particularly the utter incompetence of its Chairman, Alan Greenspan.   Figure 5 below illustrates the historically large difference between the inflation rate and the Prime Interest Rate beginning in 1982 and lasting until 2000.   This large difference was the reason that real estate values fell during this period.

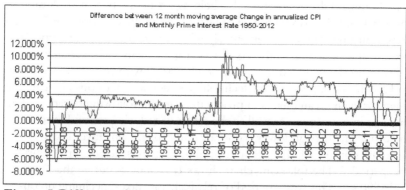

Figure 5-Difference between the 12-month moving average change in annualized CPI and the Monthly Prime Interest rate 1950-2012

Unlike the 1920s where market forces would have driven interest rates higher as loan demand increased and farm prices declined, the artificially higher interest rates during the 1990s made it difficult for savings & loan companies to make loans while at the same time paying high yields to attract depositors.   Bank managers were looking for other means to increase their margins in the face of higher costs driven by regulation and the Federal Reserve Bank's high discount rate.   As a result, they made increasingly risky investments, particularly in commercial real estate, knowing that the FDIC would bail them out if the returns on the investments did not materialize. The investments in commercial real estate created a boom in building during the 1990s leading to an oversupply of commercial real estate and a drop in the value of the commercial real estate loans held by many banks. The result was bank failures and a bail out by the FDIC. Again, the supply of commercial real estate increased beyond the demand because the Federal Reserve Bank continued to hold interest rates high despite many years of low inflation and no inflation on the horizon due to high productivity growth. Just as in the 1920s when overproduction on the farm funded in large part by bank loans led to bank failures, so too in the 1990s overproduction of commercial real estate funded in large part by bank investments in commercial real estate also led to bank failures. In the 1920's and 1930's, the Federal Reserve Bank's interference in the economy caused the bank failures while in the 1980's and 1990's it was the FDIC in combination with the Federal Reserve Bank's unrealistically high interest policy that effectively caused the bank failures. The FDIC laws introduced an ethical hazard into the banking business by shielding management from the consequences of their decisions and in the process costing the taxpayers billions of dollars. Similarly, the Federal Reserve Act of 1913 introduced ethical hazard into the banking business by shielding bank management from the consequences of their decisions. The only difference is that in the case of the Federal Reserve Bank in the 1920s and 1930s they failed to do what everyone expected them to do and that was to pump liquidity into the system. If the Federal Reserve Bank was not a product of government but rather was a product of the free market, i.e. independent of political considerations and manipulation then there would not have been a Great Depression and the number of bank failures due to loan defaults would have been minimal. Better yet if the Federal Reserve Bank did not come into existence in the first place then there would not have been a Great Depression, or the inflation of the 1970's, or the S&L crises in the 1980s and 1990s, and the economy would have created much wealth and prosperity.

In general, the fractional banking system when left unencumbered and in an unencumbered economy free from taxes and regulations is a source of wealth creation because it relies on and consequently promotes improvements and growth in productivity.

Rapid gain in productivity is a direct consequence of free enterprise. Free enterprise has fulfilled and continues to fulfill its promise to provide the greatest good for the greatest number. However, the rapid gains in productivity also led to periods of civil unrest primarily from disruptions in employment exacerbated by government taxation, regulation and coercion. The ethical question concerning implementing technologies and methods for improving productivity arises from the resulting disruptions in employment and the ensuing civil unrest. Should productivity improvements be undertaken knowing that these improvements will result in unemployment particularly in an encumbered economy? This question presumes that individuals have the ability to decide on the improvements in productivity. This is not always the case. Where corporations are concerned, many proposed improvements in productivity are discretionary but others are not. In the case of the farmers of the 1920's there was no way they could control productivity improvements other than the free market causing prices to drop. Nevertheless, I will answer the question in terms of the maximization of wealth creation, which is the ultimate result of rapid gains in productivity.

Wealth creation is the hedge against calamity, yet the rapid creation of wealth may also lead to calamity particularly in an encumbered economy. This is the example of the 1920s with the rapid gains in farm productivity while the Federal Reserve Bank encumbered the economy by mismanaging interest rates. An encumbered economy cannot absorb the resulting displacement of individuals from the rapid gains in productivity. Such displacements do not occur in a growing unencumbered economy or if they occur they are short lived. As I come to show government taxation, borrowing, and regulation slows the growth of the economy leading to unemployment as gains in productivity occur. This is not the case in an unencumbered or laissez faire economy and in a nation under God. This last phrase, i.e. "a nation under God" is significant in the understanding because government is simply the means to the destruction of wealth it is not the motivating force. The motivating force is envy and only God proscribes envy. Envy is the source of government interference in the economy. A nation whose sovereign, and whose individuals have no fear of God, is on a path of self-destruction and the government, intended as the protector of private property, becomes instead the means to its end. I will have more to say about the fear of God and its relevance to the creation of wealth shortly.

Calamity is the destruction of private property

Calamity is the destruction of private property, which is the destruction of wealth brought on by man or nature. Wealth creation depends on the security of private property and the enforcement of contracts that are the only purposes of government. At the same time, the drive for security has risks that lead to civil unrest, which threatens private property and the creation of wealth. The risks are a consequence of the burden on the economy imposed by the sovereign as necessary to protect and secure private property and enforce laws and contracts. The criteria about whether any act by the sovereign is ethically right or wrong will be whether the ultimate end of the act increases the security of private property or increases the ability to enforce contracts. Similarly the criteria about whether any act by an individual other than the sovereign is ethically right or wrong is whether the act increases the ability to create wealth or creates wealth. In this book, I will also address the inevitability of civil unrest in an encumbered economy and the role of the sovereign in exacerbating the consequences of rapid gains in productivity and the ensuing civil unrest.

Referring back to my comments about human sacrifice as a means of population control in ancient agrarian economies, we see the connection between progeny and rapid gains of productivity as both progeny and productivity are wealth and security against calamity. The connection is that both progeny and rapid gains in productivity may also cause calamity. In ancient times, the vicissitudes of nature often laid waste men's fields and prompted human sacrifice to secure the present moment, while in modern times government encumbrance of an economy lays waste to productivity and gives rise to unemployment, which is the modern industrial state's version of human sacrifice. As I will show, government encumbrance of an economy beyond the burden necessary for the protection of private property and the enforcement of laws and contracts comes from envy. A nation whose populace fears God inoculates itself against envy. Therefore, only a nation under God, i.e. a nation whose populace fears God can create wealth, prosper and overcome calamity whether caused by man or nature.

Definition of encumbered economy

When I speak of an encumbered economy, I mean an economy burdened by the sovereign beyond the burden necessary for the protection of private property and the enforcement of contracts. This begs the question, which is at what point is the sovereign overbearing? Government overburdens an economy when it undertakes and finances functions not directly related to the protection of private property and the enforcement of contracts. Some of the functions that are currently overburdening the economy because they are unrelated to protecting private property and enforcing contracts include welfare, social security, Medicare, Medicaid, public education, environmental regulation, public housing, environmental protection, and the enforcement of union contracts, affirmative action requirements, public parks, etc. All of these functions, which manifest in law, are undermining wealth creation, impoverishing the nation, and subjecting the nation to calamity.

Section 1. Private Property and Free Will

Private Property

I will now discuss private property and its significance in the creation of wealth and its role in ethical, legal, and moral considerations. Along with private property is the individual exercise of freewill that engenders the exchange of private property through contract thus giving rise to commerce. I will discuss the nature and purpose of wealth and its relationship to ethics, to law, and to morals. The creation of wealth is essential for survival as it is the only hedge against calamity. I define ethical behavior as behavior directed to the creation of wealth or profit. Gain in productivity, which is the efficient production of goods and services, or in other words, increasing profit, creates wealth. Productivity or profit in the economic actions of individuals and companies is essential to the survival of an economy and of a nation. At the same time, a rapid rise in productivity or a rapid rise in the efficient production of goods and services is civilly disruptive because it engenders unemployment particularly in any economy encumbered by the sovereign. Since the sovereign encumbers all economies then a rapid gain in productivity is always disruptive in terms of employment and in terms of the peace and survival of a nation. The extent of the unemployment arising from rapid gains in productivity is a function of the degree of encumbrance. The higher the taxes, the more onerous the regulations, and the more unionized an economy then the greater the unemployment with gains in productivity. Nevertheless, despite the increase in unemployment due mainly to the excessive burden of government, making a profit or in other words increasing productivity is ethical behavior because it creates wealth.

Individual liberty

Individuals can only undertake a contract of their own freewill and this is a basis of wealth creation. Freewill exists under liberty. Liberty means freedom from government intrusion or interference in contracting. Liberty does not mean freedom in all behavior. The freedom to create a labor union for example is not a liberty sanctioned under common law when the purpose of the union is to coerce management into a labor contract. Common law is law established by judicial precedence and it ensures equal outcomes for similar disputes. Accordingly, the sovereign must suppress this so-called freedom to create labor unions as it interferes with the freedom to contract, which is paramount to wealth creation. The freedom to contract in accordance with freewill is the definition of free enterprise. Government through the laws it enacts is a coercive force essential for the securing of private property and the enforcement of laws and contracts. Government is at the same time a burden on wealth creation and as such, government may act, and at times does act, to reduce rather than increase the security of private property and thereby reduce the ability to create wealth. Government that reduces the security of private property or the freedom to contract invites rebellion or civil war, and destruction of an entire nation. Government through the law restricts the exercise of individual freewill, i.e. the government restricts liberty, which undermines contracting and encumbers commerce thus reducing the ability or capacity of an economy to create wealth. A government also undermines wealth creation by failing to secure private property including life leaving a nation susceptible to calamity.

The freedom to contract in the case of the United States embodies in the Constitution both implicitly and explicitly. Article 1, Section 10 states in part, that *"No State shall…pass any Bill of Attainder, ex post facto Law, or Law impairing the Obligation of Contracts…"* Note that this law explicitly limits the laws of the States. Since the US Constitution is a document of enumerated laws, i.e. explicit laws, and since it does not explicitly give authority to the Federal Government to pass laws that interfere with individual freewill, contract formation or execution, then such interference, if it occurs, would be unconstitutional and unenforceable. Laws such as the Wagner Act of 1935 aka the National Labor Relations Act is such a law. This law essentially grants authority to the Federal Government to employ the sovereign power of eminent domain to enforce labor contracts executed against the will of the company, a party to the contract. Notwithstanding the Supreme Court's decisions otherwise, this law is unconstitutional as well as unethical. The National Labor Relations Act is unethical because it destroys wealth. Furthermore, the enforcement of laws and contracts falls to the States and not the Federal Government under the Tenth Amendment of the Constitution. The Tenth Amendment states, *"The powers not delegated to the United States by the Constitution, nor prohibited by it to the States, are reserved to the States respectively, or to the people"*. Even contracts that involve interstate commerce nevertheless adjudicate under the laws of the State specified in the contract.

Similarly, laws that require the paying of a minimum wage or prevailing wage are also unethical and illegal because they interfere with employment at will. Employment at will is the freedom for an employee to sell his labor at the market price and for an employer to pay the market price. Minimum wage and prevailing wage laws destroy wealth because they rob freedom to contract at will. Minimum wage laws and prevailing wage laws are therefore unconstitutional.

Man's passions and economics

In any consideration of economics, human emotions or passions as opposed to reason play a major role. Economic activity, as well as acts of the sovereign, therefore has irrational components. The study of macroeconomics in particular is a study of the aggregate behavior of individuals and human passions to a large degree play a role in human behavior. The human passions apart from human reason therefore are a contributing and determining factor to economic activity and to ethical and moral behavior. Indeed one can say that economics is the measurement of aggregate human passion. For example, if the aggregate human passion is greed in an unencumbered economy then the economy creates wealth – this is capitalism or a wealth creating economy. If the aggregate human passion is envy then the economy consumes wealth – this is socialism or communism. A nation whose king or sovereign and whose culture engenders greed and the fear of God in the populace is a nation that creates wealth. Such a nation was the United States at the beginning of the 20th Century. Since greed engenders wealth, it is rational and managed rationally through the mechanism of competition. Envy is irrational and not manageable by reason acting through the will. A nation whose king or sovereign and whose culture engenders godlessness and envy is a nation that destroys wealth. Such a nation was the old Soviet Union, France at the time of French Revolution, Germany after the fall of the Weimar Republic, and the United States after the first decade of the 21st Century.

The basic human passions affecting economic decisions and influencing ethical behavior are fear, greed, envy, empathy, happiness, vanity, love and hate. I will touch upon these passions in terms of their effect on economics and ethical behavior. I will also show how competition and self-interest serve to regulate and limit the expression of all passions save the passion of envy. Envy, the most destructive human passion as ordained by God, is not self-regulating and proscribed only through the fear of God. Indeed, unlike the other Commandments of God, which govern man's conduct, the proscription of envy in the Tenth Commandment governs this single passion. It is a mortal sin to envy whether envy manifests itself as some act or not. I will show how competition regulates the other passions, particularly greed, and how competition is the engine of wealth creation. Further, I will show how envy is the source of the destruction of wealth by man that has occurred throughout modern history and into the present times.

Intelligence manifested in productivity

Of course, other individual human characteristics affect an economy in general. These include determination, persistence, and intelligence, which is the ability to reason and adapt to an environment and the ability to acquire and use knowledge. These characteristics manifest themselves in productivity and I will account for them in part in this manner.

Intellectual capital and wealth creation

Besides the fear of God and the burden of the sovereign, one additional and critical factor remains that determines whether a nation or a civilization can create wealth and survive a calamity. This factor is the store of intellectual capital that resides within the nation's population as measured by its average intelligence or IQ and the distribution of the intelligence as measured by the standard deviation (SD). The creation of wealth relates directly to the productivity of the individuals comprising a nation and productivity in turn relates directly to intellectual ability as measured by the average IQ of the population. A population that tends to produce men of genius, i.e. men with IQs greater than 140, is more productive than a population that fails to produce men of genius. Genius as an individual human trait enables adaptation to the environment through its attention to detail, and therefore such a population is more likely to create wealth and survive calamities. The decline of past civilizations and nations is the result of a decline in the ability of the population to produce men of genius in sufficient numbers to sustain the civilization and nation. The collapse of the Roman Empire for example was due to a decline in the ability of the Romans to create men of genius necessary for the administration and expansion of their empire. This led to the Dark Ages with little human intellectual progress and little creation of wealth. The tendency of the men of a conquering nation such as Rome to mix with those it has conquered or colonized accounts for the decline in its ability to sustain its dominance. This is how the conquering nation becomes the fatherland. Those that were conquered were obviously less intellectually capable, or else the Romans would not have subjugated them. Otherwise, they would have overcome the calamity that befell them, i.e. the Roman Army, through their creation of wealth. Thus, we have the rise and fall of empires corresponding with the general appearance of the population, i.e. from blond and fair skin, as were the early Romans to the darker, curly haired and darker skin of the present day Italians. It was not until the fall of the Roman Empire halted the admixture with the less intelligent dark races that the new blonde and blue-eyed conquerors from the North introduced inheritable genius back into the general European population thus ending the aptly named Dark Ages and ushering in the Renaissance. Without the intellectual capital inherent in a population, the idea of private property and liberty is meaningless since without the ability to create men of genius there is little creation of wealth despite the private property and liberty. Without the creation of wealth, a population will succumb to calamity regardless of the form of government or the burdening of its economy by the sovereign or even its fear of God. This is an important point since it limits the idea and benefits of private property and the freedom to contract only to those nations whose citizens are intellectually capable of taking advantage of these ideas with an economy built around these ideas. To argue that the idea of private property and freedom to contract as the means to wealth creation is universally applicable is to diminish its significance and its result. I address this book therefore to nations that have the intellectual capital in the general population necessary to create wealth. Nations whose populations are inherently incapable of managing their affairs because they fail to produce men of genius in sufficient numbers will not benefit from free enterprise and consequently they will fail to create wealth and will succumb to calamity. Wealthy nations will dominate and have dominated these nations through colonization while exploiting them accordingly and appropriately.

This raises the question of obligation of the wealth creating nations to those nations who fail to create wealth. The obligation only exists to the extent that the wealthy nations colonize the poor nations for profit and accordingly it is an ethical obligation not a moral or legal obligation. Otherwise, without profit then there is no moral or ethical obligation and if such obligation is undertaken regardless of profit, then it serves only to undermine wealth creation and expose the benefactor nation to calamity. Even if a benefactor nation with the wherewithal to create wealth undertook this obligation, it would be unethical and immoral because it would nevertheless weaken the benefactor's ability to overcome calamity. Natural Law therefore proscribes any perceived obligation by wealthy nations to nations that fail to create wealth unless the obligation serves the economic interest of the benefactor nation through the proper and profitable exploitation of the subjugated populations. The obligation therefore is to the benefactor's self-interest in accordance with Natural Law with any emotional reaction as to the misguided morality and to the contrary notwithstanding.

The philosophy of wealth creation

The philosophy of wealth creation is the view that the purpose or aim of human activity is to secure private property and create wealth. To the extent that individuals acting of their own freewill create wealth, then to the same extent mankind secures his future survival and improving condition. In other words, the best predictor of the future of mankind or the future of a nation is the amount of wealth created and the rate of wealth creation. When there is little wealth created then the future of mankind is less secure with poverty, misery, and war more likely. A wealth creating economy is an unencumbered economy existing in a nation under God, i.e. a nation whose populace and whose sovereign fear God. Although capitalism or free enterprise is the most closely aligned with wealth creation, it does not easily account by itself for the effects of rapid gains in productivity and the disposition of the soul of the king or sovereign. In other words, capitalism by itself does not answer the question of what happens when productivity increases too quickly or what happens to the soul of the king or soldier?   A godless capitalism succumbs to envy and this leads to socialism or communism, which are in themselves calamities since these economic systems destroy wealth and create no wealth.   Rapid gain in productivity is a source of civil unrest in a godless capitalist economy encumbered by the sovereign.   Without the fear of God to rein in envy, and with a burdensome sovereign a nation with a capitalist economy will eventually succumb to socialism or communism, which are wealth destroying and self-immolating economies.

To distinguish my philosophy from others I will refer to my philosophy as the philosophy of wealth creation, and to the economics arising out of this philosophy as wealth creating economics.

Private Property and Freewill

Private property is essential for the creation of wealth.   Private property is the basis of all ethical and moral behavior, or in other words behavior that is ethically and morally right or wrong.   When God created Man, he created private property.   The creation of man was as much an ethical, moral, and legal act by God as it was an act of physical creation.   The fall of man from God's Grace gave rise to Natural Law, i.e. the law of self-interest, self-preservation and self-perpetuation.   A statement of Natural Law is that Man always directs his thoughts, and acts to self-preservation and self-perpetuation, thus self-interest always directs and informs Man's thoughts and acts.   A corollary of Natural Law is that Man is innately incapable of acts that are altruistic or even of empathizing with others.   Man is innately incapable of charity.   A man can only undertake altruistic acts with an act of will, as all such self-destructive behavior must overcome man's natural tendency toward self-preservation and self-interest.   If it were true that Man were innately capable of altruistic behavior, then there would not be a need for the Ten Commandments or for that matter the existence of God.   Because the Ten Commandments came into being is a sign from God that while He Created Man to be an altruistic being, i.e. in God's image, man's Fall from Grace gave rise to Natural Law.   The Ten Commandments were necessary to regulate man's behavior through the disposition of his soul but not to change man's nature as determined after the Fall.   Thus, altruism and empathy are characteristics of an immortal man as God originally intended and ordained man to be, absent man's fall from Grace. However, to populate the earth with immortal men would mean that the process of Creation must continue.   Yet God only created Adam and Eve and they sinned by disobeying God and sought to be God, so now man creates man in the image of God.   Since the individual man is mortal and not God, then altruism and empathy are not man's natural characteristics and can only manifest with an act of will contrary to Natural Law, i.e. contrary to self-interest and self-perpetuation.   To be clear, sacrificing oneself to save the life of another is not an altruistic act

63

rather it is an act in defense of private property, i.e. the act of a sovereign. An altruistic act is one in which there is no profit or benefit to the one performing the act. It is the reason there is no profit that makes the altruistic act unethical and destructive of wealth. Only God is altruistic, empathetic, and charitable and He is immortal.

The Biblical account of Creation is as much a prescription for the law as it is the manifestation of man and of all things. Therefore, private property and ultimately God's Law and Natural Law are inviolable and inalienable. Private property did not exist prior to the Creation of Man. This statement is more profound than it may sound. It means that the elimination of private property or the denial of its existence by Man is the elimination or the denial of Man himself by himself. When one considers the fate of nations that denied or continue to deny the existence of private property, and where all property is common, including the life of the individuals comprising the nation, then the statement becomes profoundly significant. Communist and socialist nations that by definition hold all or most property in common invariably fail resulting in the ultimate demise of the population. Given that such nations must also deny the existence of God as they must deny God's creation, i.e. private property, then it is inevitable that nations who deny God, and therefore do not fear God, will fail to create wealth and will fail to survive calamity as indeed they have in the past. The old Soviet Union is the archetypical nation comprising of a highly intelligent populace that denied the existence of God and failed to secure private property even denying the very existence of private property. The Soviet Union no longer exists and ceased to exist in the span of four generations. The nations that emerged from the old Soviet Union are now increasingly Christian Nations, whose sovereigns and populace increasingly fear God and are creating wealth. Russia however remains a socialist nation despite the revival of the fear of God in certain of its populace and limited tolerance of private property. As long as Russia remains a socialist nation, it is a threat to its neighbors because eventually it must go after its neighbors' wealth to sustain itself and the military that it is continuously building. The correlation between the fear of God as manifested by the prominence of the Christian Church and the creation of wealth is indeed striking throughout Western history.

A man's life is private property

By wealth, I mean the ability or capacity to overcome calamity. The building of a shelter for example, is wealth creation because it secures the individual against the calamitous elements of nature and thereby insures his survival. Therein lays the value of the shelter. Private real property is a prerequisite for the building of shelter. Private property in general can be tangible or intangible. Examples of intangible private property include an idea for an invention, and other

64

products of human thought such as a composition of music or a work of literature as well as plans for a building wherein the private property is in the expression and not in the material used to convey the expression such as a book, drawing or CD. Without means to secure an idea someone else easily takes the idea, and uses it as if it were his own. The same is true of tangible private property. That is, all private property is subject to taking by others if not secured by force or the threat of force. The threat of force can be corporal, incorporeal, or both. The taking of private property against the will of the possessor or owner is an unethical and immoral act condemned by all religions. Therein lays the incorporeal force. Thou, shalt not steal is a Commandment of God and thereby a thief's soul is condemned by God as stealing is a mortal sin. God's stealing proscription is akin to God's murder proscription as a man's life is his property just as his material possessions are his property. Stealing and murder, i.e. the taking of life, are illegal acts punishable by man's law. Securing private property, which includes securing life, from others taking it, is the foundation of all criminal law and moral codes. A person's life is private property owned or possessed by that person. A person's soul however belongs to God. Accordingly, a soul is not private property as it is the property of God. A soul is disposed at the will of God whereas man or nature disposes a man's life and property. The taking of a life is akin to the taking of private property against the will of the owner. The taking of the life of another man is killing, while the taking of innocent life is murder. Taking of all other property against the will of the owner is theft. This includes taking another man's wife, which is adultery. Adultery and rape is trespass, which is a taking of another's private property against his will and for one's own use. A man's life, as private property under the law, is the basis of ethics and is the subject of economics, i.e. the nature of property determines the economic system. In an economy where the sovereign holds all or most property in common, then the economy is socialistic or communistic in nature. In such economies, the sovereign also holds a man's life in common. In an economy where the individuals hold property then the economy is capitalistic, free enterprise or wealth creating. In such an economy, a title or deed secures private property and a patent, copyright, or trademark secures intellectual property before the law. No such documents exist in a communist economy and a birth certificate becomes the title of a life transferred to the sovereign by the parents.

Conception is an act of God not of man
I would like to make one more point here and that is the difference between the taking of private property and the taking of a man's life. Stolen property is restorable by man whereas a man's life once taken is lost for eternity. While the life of a man is not restorable, the soul, which is God's creation and belongs to God is indestructible

and exists for eternity.   It is no coincidence that the term conception defines the beginning of a human life in the womb as well as an idea. An idea must exist in some mind as it cannot exist without a mind.   The beginning of a human life is an idea or concept that exists in the mind of God, and therein is its immortality that is the soul.   As the soul is a conception in the mind of God it belongs to God and God disposes the soul.   Therefore, the act of conception is an act of God and not of man as the act of conception creates a soul at the instance of conception. God inspires each individual mind and an individual is himself a conception existing in the mind of God.   Without God, there cannot be man but without man, there is still God.

Burdensome laws

In an operational sense, private property is anything relinquished or given up by a person in whose possession it is either through force or by the exercise of freewill.   The relinquishing of private property against the will of the owner or legal possessor is necessarily only through the exercise of force.   Therefore, a characteristic of private property is that it is anything violable either through a taking by another or by trespass by another.   Trespass is a theft and therefore a mortal sin.   As murder or killing is a taking of a life against the will of the owner, rape is a trespass on the life of the God ordained possessor of that life.   Adultery is a trespass on the marriage unit, which is private property that exists apart from the individual husband and wife.   As trespass is theft and a mortal sin then so rape and adultery is theft and mortal sins.   Rape is a violent act as it is through force as is any taking of private property.   Patent infringement is trespassing on or theft of a person's secured invention or idea.   Plagiarism is taking of intellectual property against the will of the owner.   In the sense that trespass is already punishable by law, then environmental laws are laws that ostensibly protect and secure private property, but they are unnecessary, redundant, burdensome, and therefore unethical.   The spoiling of a stream for instance violates the private property of the owner of the land downstream and thus the spoiling of a stream is trespassing or theft in both a legal and moral sense. Accordingly, existing sovereign and moral laws proscribing trespass or theft are the only laws necessary to enforce the spoiling of the environment as long as all property is in the possession of individuals, and not held in common by the sovereign.   Environmental laws in a free economy are therefore redundant and unnecessary and as such, environmental laws burden the creation of wealth without adding to the security of private property or even to the quality of the environment. The less property that is held in common or owned by the sovereign then the less there is a need for environmental laws.   Recall that a sovereign is above the law but he must act in accordance with the law or else he risks rebellion and jeopardizes his soul.   Accordingly, for the property held in common then environmental laws serve to regulate the behavior of the sovereign since a sovereign cannot trespass on property held by him or in other words property held in common. Thus, an encumbered economy requires environmental laws to regulate the acts of the sovereign. However, if such laws are necessary then the economy is not creating wealth because too much property is in common. Environmental laws further encumber an already encumbered economy and make a nation more susceptible to calamity because these laws undermine the creation of wealth.

The forced taking, by other than the sovereign, of a human life is a violation of God's law and man's law, as is the forced taking or trespass of any person's possession including his life, i.e. his wealth and his means to create wealth.

Suicide

Suicide, or the taking of one's own life of one's freewill, is a mortal sin because it violates God's Commandment proscribing killing. In the eyes of God, killing oneself is not different from killing another individual. *"Thou shalt not kill"* does not merely mean thou shalt not kill another individual. Famously the ancient Greek Philosopher Socrates killed himself by drinking hemlock on the orders of the Athenian Counsel, as the Athenians found him guilty of corrupting the youth. This act was not suicide since he took the hemlock against his will, i.e. he did not want to die. The sovereign in the persons of the Counsel through the sovereign power of eminent domain took the life of Socrates in a manner specified by law. It is the reason that Socrates did not flee his punishment as he could have, as his punishment was in accordance with the law. Thus, his act served as his final lesson to his pupils and indeed to posterity.

Property right is a misnomer

I am deliberately not using the term property right. Property right is a misnomer as it implies that the nation or the sovereign precedes the individual. In fact and in truth, the individual precedes the nation and the sovereign in all matters. That is, the individual creates or gives rise to the nation and the sovereign. The nation or the sovereign does not create or give rise to the individual. The term property right implies that the sovereign, who comes into existence by an act of the individual, grants rights to the individual or indeed grants life to the individual. It implies that man in a legal and moral sense created himself. This notion is absurd on its face and therefore I will not use the term "property right". Rather I will use the term private property or simply property to describe something tangible or intangible owned and/or possessed by an individual including the individual's life.

When a nation imposes its sovereign on another nation by force or by guile then the sovereign owns all property including the life of the subdued individuals.   In this case, property rights come into existence, as the sovereign owns all that was conquered.   In such a situation, the sovereign of the conquering nation disposes of all property including the life of the conquered, since the conquered nation failed to protect private property thus enabling their calamity.   The sovereign thus grants property rights or individual rights to the conquered to the extent such rights benefit the conquering nation.   The term property right therefore applies to a conquered nation or people and not to a wealth creating economy that is secure from such calamity.   When a liberal politician or other such demagogue speaks to you of granting rights, he is implying your subjugation by him.   Thus, Rome extended property rights to the Jews whom the Romans conquered, and protected these rights by force of arms.   These rights were lost when the Jews rebelled and failed in their rebellion in 70AD.   The inability of the Jews to create sufficient wealth to defend themselves, led to their subjugation and to the eventual expulsion from the land of their fathers for two millennia.

Sovereign's life held in common
          Private property implies a separation from the property of others in a manner recognized and honored by others and with boundaries secured by the chosen or imposed protector, who is sovereign.   Property held in common or held by the sovereign is property held only to the extent employed to protect private property or the property not held in common.   Property held in common is unproductive property and therefore detrimental or anathema to wealth creation.   From an economic, legal, moral, and ethical perspective, a person's life is private property while the life of the sovereign and the life of a soldier in service to the nation is property held in common just as is any tangible or intangible property held in common.   The life of the sovereign or the soldier therefore is in the possession of the nation or held in common by the individuals comprising the nation.   Consequently, the life of the sovereign is, as is the life of a soldier, unproductive property.   Since the sustenance due the sovereign and the soldier is from productive or wealth producing property, then both the sovereign and the soldier burden wealth creation.   An individual who chooses to be sovereign or chooses to be a soldier willingly agrees to convert private property, which is his life, to property held in common, i.e. property in service to the nation and owned by the nation.   A person conscripted during a time of war forfeits a portion of his life taken against his will through the sovereign's power of eminent domain.   In return for his service, the sovereign compensates him and/or his family in accordance with the law.
However, if the law calls for no compensation then none is given.   Any property in service to the nation is property held in common; accordingly, it is not productive and is a burden or tax on wealth creation.   As such,

property held in common must be minimal and used solely for the two purposes of government, i.e. securing of private property and the enforcement of laws and contracts. The sovereign taking more than minimal property necessary for the efficient protection of private property and enforcement of laws and contracts unnecessarily increases the burden on wealth creation, and thereby weakens a nation's ability to withstand calamity threatening the survival of a nation. When I speak of property, I mean to include everything owned by the individual, including his life, and cash in the bank as well as tangible property such as real property, and intangible property such as creative works or intellectual property. I also include the marriage unit and progeny as they are private property. Taxation is in general a taking of an individual's cash or earnings, which becomes cash. Taxation is the sovereign act of taking private property through the law, i.e. due process. Taxation is thus a manifestation of the sovereign power of eminent domain.

God created an individual and not "people"

Note I do not the use the term "people" to characterize those that comprise a nation, and appoint or elect a sovereign. The term "people" implies individuals in common which is equivalent to property held in common and thereby unproductive and a burden on wealth creation. Rather I use the term individuals to emphasize the primacy of the freewill of the individual to contract, and not the will of the people, as the means to wealth creation. Historically, the term "will of the people" often justifies a sovereign's acts and laws that are beyond the legitimate scope of the sovereign as I have explained that scope. Actions or laws enacted in the name of "the will of the people" or in the name of the "common good" are necessarily actions that reduce liberty and wealth creation beyond the point required merely for the protection of private property and enforcement of laws and contracts. Historically this has been the case as this phrase is often associated with laws and in justification of laws that reduce freedom of contract, increase taxation and introduce regulation thereby encumbering an economy. God did not create people he created an individual man in His Image and ordained man's immortality through man's soul. This alone is enough reason to forgo the term "people" when discussing a nation or an economy.

Citizens of a nation

The individuals that comprise a nation are citizens of the nation. Citizens of a nation are those individuals whose labor and wealth bear the sovereign's burden and for whose life and property the citizens appointed or elected the sovereign to protect. Those individuals who do not bear the burden of the sovereign are not ethically entitled to the protection of the sovereign. To the extent that such individuals receive protection of the sovereign, then the greater is the burden on the creation of wealth and the more susceptible the nation is to calamity.

Whenever the sovereign performs acts or enacts laws that burden the wealth creation of a nation beyond the burden necessary for the protection of private property and the enforcement of contracts or fails to protect private property and enforce contracts, then that sovereign risks rebellion and jeopardizes his soul before God.

"War of all against all"

In the absence of law and a common means to protect private property and enforce contracts, the individual, when alone, must himself secure his private property and thus his life with force or the threat of force. Under these primitive conditions, individual freewill or liberty is at a maximum, and all property including life goes to the strongest and the most capable. Thomas Hobbes in Leviathan wrote in 1651 that man in such a primitive state of nature is in a state of, *"Bellum omnium contra omnes"* or *"the war of all against all"*. The time and effort spent by the individual in securing his property under such primitive conditions precludes the creation and accumulation of wealth. This makes the individual susceptible to calamity or to forces that the individual by himself cannot overcome and to which he must succumb. Thomas Hobbes, again from Leviathan , wrote, *"In such condition there is no place for industry, because the fruit thereof is uncertain, and consequently, not culture of the earth, no navigation, nor the use of commodities that may be imported by sea, no commodious building, no instruments of moving and removing such things as require much force, no knowledge of the face of the earth, no account of time, no arts, no letters, no society, and which is worst of all, continual fear and danger of violent death, and the life of man, solitary, poor, nasty, brutish, and short."* In other words, there is a physical or practical limit to an individual's ability to secure his private property including his life absent the Grace of God, which Man abrogated through his disobedience. In order to increase their ability and thereby the likelihood to withstand calamity, individuals organize themselves in such a manner as to appoint or to elect a protector who is sustained by the individuals, and whose sole purposes are the securing of private property and enforcement of contracts. The protector is sovereign or in other words, he can do no wrong in a legal, ethical, or moral sense and therefore is beyond reproach in the carrying out of his appointed purpose to secure and protect private property and enforce contracts. He must only act according to the law, which he creates, invokes, and adjudicates. This poses a moral dilemma vis-à-vis the soul of the protector that I spoke of earlier. The moral dilemma of the soul of the king is resolved through the doctrine of the divine right of kings. Under this doctrine, the king can do no wrong and God secures his soul.

The language of sovereignty

Sovereignty is enshrined in the words characterizing the actions of a sovereign, which are different from the words characterizing the same actions of the individuals who appointed or elected the sovereign. For instance, the sovereign cannot commit murder or kill a man. He instead executes a man. However, he can only execute a man in accordance with due process or laws that the sovereign himself enacts and invokes. A sovereign does not steal property instead he takes property in accordance with due process and only to the purpose of his appointment in the first place, i.e. to secure private property and enforce laws and contracts. In a monarchy, the sovereign is the king and accorded the power of eminent domain. The functions of the sovereign are to legislate, to adjudicate, and to execute. Note that these are not powers but functions. There is only one power that any sovereign has and that is the power of eminent domain. The sovereign cannot give he can only take. The sovereign has nothing of his own to give as all held by the sovereign is in common with the nation including the life of the sovereign. Accordingly, a sovereign cannot show mercy as mercy is a quality of the individual whose life is in his possession, and not of one whose life is in common, as the nation holds the life of the sovereign in common. Instead the sovereign acts and he must act, only in accordance with the law, which he enacts. When the sovereign shows mercy, he needlessly burdens the creation of wealth and thus risks rebellion and jeopardizes his soul before God. The quality of mercy in a sovereign strains the creation of wealth.

In a monarchy, the function to legislate, to adjudicate, and to execute reside with the person of the king. In a constitutional republic, these functions rest with different elected persons and not a single person. In any case, the sole purpose of the sovereign is the efficient securing of private property and the enforcement of contracts in order to enable and to promote the creation of wealth or store. Wealth is the hedge against future calamity, hence the sovereign secures not only against present dangers but against future calamity as well.

The Nation

The organization of individuals for securing private property and life is a nation. The number and intelligence of individuals who subscribe to the protection the nation offers, i.e. its citizens, determines the military and economic strength of a nation. The more efficient and effective a nation's government is in protecting and securing private property and enforcing laws and contracts, then the greater the wealth of the nation becomes and the more likely it will survive a calamity. The less efficient the government of a nation then the less capable it is of protecting private property and enforcing laws and contracts and as a consequence the less likely it is that the nation will create wealth and survive a calamity.   No better example of his principle exists than the contrast between the Japanese ability to survive a devastating calamity that was the 2011 earthquake and tsunami and the Haitian ability to survive a similar catastrophe in 2010.   The Japanese who are wealthier than are the Haitians because of their inherently higher intelligence and concomitant ability to create wealth, recovered much faster from their calamity than did the Haitians whose government is notorious for its inefficiency and inability to protect life and property.   Apart from the fact that Haitians are naturally and inherently intellectually incapable of managing their affairs, nevertheless the inability of the government to protect private property is one reason that there is little wealth creation in Haiti.   Accordingly, the Haitians were incapable on their own of overcoming the calamity that befell them. Even with the unrequited and generous charity of other nations, Haiti still was unable to recover from this calamity.   On the other hand, the Japanese government is efficient in the protection of private property and as a result, the Japanese are able to take advantage of their natural and inherent high intelligence to create wealth thus easily overcoming a calamity similar or even more devastating than the calamity that befell Haiti.

Security in exchange for liberty

The sovereign, through his laws, by necessity limits the freewill or liberty to contract of the individual.   As individuals must sustain the sovereign then there is a burden or tax placed on the creation of wealth and in this sense the sovereign poses a risk to the nation.   However, as long as the burden is significantly less than it would be in a primitive state of nature then the nation benefits from its protector whether that protector is a king or a constitutional republic.   The risk to private property and to the creation of wealth is a protector whose burden or tax is so great that it begins to undermine private property and thus the creation of wealth.   Under these conditions the nation becomes susceptible to calamity and the protector threatens the survival of the property of those that he was appointed to secure and to protect.   These conditions give rise to rebellion or civil war.   A rebellion or a civil war is a return to Hobbes primitive state wherein there is *"Bellum omnium contra omnes"* or *"the war of all against all"*.   This is an unstable state of being and it is usually resolved quickly with the appointment of a new protector. Thus, a nation collapses into rebellion or civil war when the sovereign fails to secure private property or enforce contracts and laws efficiently, i.e. with minimum burden on wealth creation.

The securing of private property including life involves a relinquishing of some liberty or some restriction of freewill to contract. In other words, the individuals comprising the nation must willingly, or through force, relinquish a portion of their liberty to achieve a measure of security.   The answer to the question how much liberty to relinquish to provide the necessary security determines the form of government, i.e. tyranny, republic, or democracy, and the limits to the power of eminent domain placed on the sovereign by himself absent rebellion.   The extent of the liberty lost to achieve security also determines the extent of wealth creation lost and wealth is a measure of the ability of the nation to survive calamity.   The limits to the sovereign power of eminent domain manifest in the laws enacted by the sovereign.   In other words, a sovereign is the only one that can place limits on his sovereignty.   A sovereign with no limits is a tyrant and if a tyrant fails to secure private property and enforce laws and contracts then he risks his soul and the nation's individuals will rebel appointing a different sovereign.   The English monarch King Charles I was a monarch who turned tyrannical as he levied taxes without the consent of Parliament thus angering the population, who rose up against him, overthrew him and executed him. In his place, England forged a short-lived republic.   A tyrant, who knows no limit to his power of eminent domain because he does not fear God, is not subject to the divine right of kings, and by definition, a tyrant is godless.   Thus, the soul of a godless tyrant who fails to protect private property and enforce laws and contracts is damned because the nation fails to create wealth.

Republic overthrown by civil war, a tyranny or monarchy overthrown by rebellion

One difference between a tyranny or monarchy and a constitutional republic is that the failure of a tyranny or monarchy to secure private property is usually resolved with acts of violence whereas the failure of a constitutional republic to secure private property is generally resolved at the ballot box.   However, the constitutional republic or a representative democracy is also susceptible to civil war and more so than is a monarchy.   Generally, a civil war is more devastating to life and property than is a rebellion.   Thus, there is an inherently greater risk in a constitutional republic than in a monarchy.   This is because the sovereign's power of eminent domain disperses amongst the representatives of the individuals in a constitutional republic or a representative democracy.   A constitutional republic or representative democracy will fall into civil war when half the individuals of the nation employ the sovereign's power of eminent domain as manifested in the law to subjugate in some fashion the other half.   This happens when individuals succeed in voting benefits for themselves thus burdening those who create wealth by unequally distributing the tax burden.

The American War between the States is an example of a civil war that arose in large part out of the protective tariffs on imported goods imposed by the Northern States to protect their nascent manufacturing and mining industries at the expense of the less populous Southern States who relied on the importation of low priced

manufactured goods.   The election of Abraham Lincoln in 1860, and
who supported the proposed Morrill Tariff resulted in the War Between
the States.   The Morrill Tariff, passed in 1861 after the Southern States
seceded from the Union, significantly increased the price of manufactured
goods in order to support the emerging industries of the Northern States.
The increase in the cost of manufactured goods occurred at the same
time that the unit price of cotton was near historical lows.   Thus, the
South was paying more for manufactured goods while earning less per
bale of cotton.   Cotton was the main export product of the South at the
time and the source of its wealth.   The decline in the price of cotton was
due primarily from competition from India, which was becoming an
increasingly important market for Britain, the main importer of cotton.
Unlike the American Colonies, India did not rebel against the British
Sovereign and remained a part of the British Empire or British
Commonwealth until the middle of the twentieth century.   Figure 6
illustrates the price of a bale of cotton from 1800 to 1859.

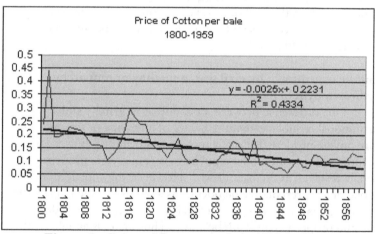

Figure 6 – Price of Cotton per bale 1800 to 1859

In order to make up for the declining price per bale and partly in
anticipation of secession Southern planters ramped up production of
cotton tremendously thus becoming even more dependent on their slaves
than in the past.   Figure 7 shows the increase in cotton production
leading up to the War Between the States.   This was necessary to store
wealth in anticipation of the calamity that was to befall the nation.   The
declining price of cotton would have eventually led the South to switch to
other less labor-intensive crops and slavery would have disappeared of its
own accord as it was in other parts of the world.   The North's constant
pressure to increase tariffs on manufactured goods during the 1820's and
1830's combined with the self-righteous and envious abolitionist
movement was rightly seen by the South as a threat to its survival and its

reaction was to break all ties with the Union.   In this way as a separate nation, it could engage in trade without tariffs, and thus sustain and improve its economy and in the process, slavery would end of its own accord.

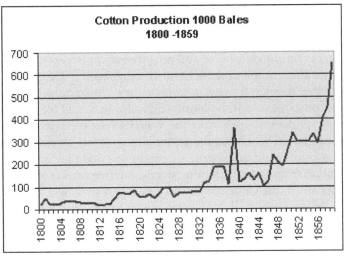

Figure 7 –Cotton Production 1000 bales 1800 to 1859

The War Between the States occurred because the government encumbered the economy through unequal taxation, i.e. a selective tariff. The <u>Address of South Carolina to Slaveholding States Convention of South Carolina, December 25, 1860</u> stated in part *"…And so with the Southern States, towards the Northern States, in the vital matter of taxation.   They are in a minority in Congress.   Their representation in Congress, is useless to protect them against unjust taxation; and they are taxed by the people of the North for their benefit, exactly as the people of Great Britain taxed our ancestors in the British parliament for their benefit.   For the last forty years, the taxes laid by the Congress of the United States have been laid with a view of subserving the interests of the North. The people of the South have been taxed by duties on imports, not for revenue, but for an object inconsistent with revenue— to promote, by prohibitions, Northern interests in the productions of their mines and manufactures…."*

Thus, the Federal Government used its sovereign power of eminent domain invoked by the more populous North to take the productive capacity of the less populous South through tariff-inflated prices not for revenue for the government but in order to benefit the North's industries.   The fact that the North won the War Between the States gave legitimacy in the minds of many to the actions of the North in utilizing the sovereign power of eminent domain to benefit itself at the expense of the South.   The North's perversion of the original US Constitution manifested itself once again some fifty years later under the Wilson Administration with the income tax amendment (16th

Amendment) and the election of senators by plebiscite rather than the appointment of senators by the State legislatures (17th Amendment), and with universal suffrage (19th Amendment). The result was the Great Depression some 20 years later or within one generation. The Federal Government has undermined the creation of wealth ever since that time.

The only way to prevent a collapse of a constitutional republic, or even a monarchy, is through each individual contributing the same amount of tax to the government or in other words, the burden of the sovereign is equally distributed and no government largess accrues to some individuals at the expense of other individuals. This is true of all laws whether they are for raising revenue for the government or restrict liberty in other ways. If the North had not won its call for protective tariffs during the years preceding the War Between the States, the South would not have rebelled and the institution of slavery would have died out of its own accord as the price of cotton was declining quickly due to competition from India. In other words, the free market would have ended slavery in the United States because it was no longer profitable.

In a monarchy, the sovereign power of eminent domain is only in the person of the monarch and all servants to the king owe their allegiance only and directly to the king and not to the individuals comprising the nation. Therefore, a civil war is less likely under an absolute monarchy as the monarch has less of an incentive to burden or tax his subjects unequally. A constitutional republic or a monarchy becomes a tyranny when the tax burden increases to the point where the individuals comprising the nations resist the collection of taxes. Under these conditions, the sovereign uses his power of eminent domain to enforce the collection of taxes and rebellion in the case of a monarchy or civil war in the case of a republic ensues.

The other difference between a monarchy and a constitutional republic therefore is in the manner of the resolution of the government's failure to protect and secure private property, i.e. rebellion as opposed to civil war. A monarchy is subject to rebellion whereas a constitutional republic is subject to civil war as means to remove and replace the sovereign.

The Meaning of Wealth

The greater the individual's liberty to contract in a nation that efficiently protects private property and enforces contracts the greater the wealth created. I have spoken of wealth creation in terms that may not be familiar to the reader. Therefore, I will take a few paragraphs here to expand and clarify what I mean by wealth, the creation of wealth, as well as the purpose of wealth. The idea of wealth derives from the idea of store or savings. In turn, the idea of store is from an agrarian economy but it is equally applicable to an industrial economy. Storing grain or food is an investment in the next year's crop and as the hedge against a poor harvest in the next year.   This is security against some future calamity.   Store or wealth therefore arises from the inherent inability to predict or foretell the future that is fear of the future.   In a sense, wealth is a measure of the human passion of fear.   The more a man saves the less certain or the greater fear that the man has of the future.   In the absence of a calamity then sufficient storage will require less planting in the subsequent year and so store or wealth reduces the effort or burden of planting in the subsequent years.   In other words in the absence of calamity then store or wealth eases the burden of life.   At the very least, therefore wealth frees the individual from the necessity to plant as much in subsequent years.

In this sense, wealth or store engenders the expression of man's freewill, which manifests in commerce or contracting.   Surplus is wealth. Surplus is the result of overproduction, i.e. production in excess of that needed to survive the current and near future conditions as an individual expects them.   In this sense, surplus is profit.   When a farmer produces more than he needs to survive and for storage against the next years' crop then the farmer can exchange the excess or the surplus with others. This is the essence of commerce.   The creation of wealth or store therefore engenders commerce.   Commerce gives rise to contracts. Contracts are means to secure or make more predictable the future.   To secure their future and overcome their fear individuals must continuously create surplus or wealth.   I will address the wealth of nations later, but for now, I want to emphasize that wealth in this context is the hedge against future calamity.   In the absence of calamity, wealth eases the burden of life and engenders the exercise of individual freewill, i.e. commerce or investment and the profit thereof, thus leading to greater wealth creation.   This process, i.e. the creation of wealth, which includes the bringing forth of progeny, must continue ad infinitum in order that the individual and the nation survive.   God ordained man's immortality and the creation of wealth is the means toward that end.

What is true for an agrarian economy is also true of an industrial economy.   In an industrial economy, as in an agrarian economy, wealth resides in the stock of the nation.   The stock of a nation includes the buildings, factories, houses, as well as in the equity market and the cash accounts in the banks.   Note that money is not wealth.   Money is a means of exchange whose purpose is to facilitate commerce or the free exchange of private property.   Liquidity is the property or attribute of stock that enables its rapid conversion to money.   Cash is the most liquid of stock as it most readily converts to money.   This distinction is important in understanding the nature of wealth in an agrarian or an industrial economy.   The totality of stock or store of individual wealth is the nation's hedge against calamity.   A nation's infrastructure most of which is funded by taxes, such as its roads and ports are not part of a nation's wealth they are a product of its wealth.   Insofar as taxes pay for the construction then roads, ports and other such infrastructure are a burden on wealth creation. Tax supported infrastructure exists solely to facilitate the protection of private property. The facilitation of wealth creation is collateral or incidental use of infrastructure not its primary purpose. There is no return on investment expected or calculated when the government using tax revenue undertakes the construction of infrastructure. Thus, there is no expectation of wealth creation and there can be none. The United States Interstate Highway System for example began in 1955 under the Eisenhower Administration and was infrastructure built in response to the Cold War. The Federal Government built the system to enable rapid evacuation from cities in the event of a nuclear attack or natural disaster. It was justified for national security reasons, i.e. the protection of private property – the life of the individuals comprising the nation. The building of the Interstate Highway System consumed wealth it did not create wealth. Prior to the construction of the tax funded and supported Interstate Highway System, the states were engaged in the construction of toll roads to connect major cities. Toll roads are user supported and not supported by taxation of the general populace. Thus, toll roads are less of a burden on an economy than are freeways built by taxing the general population. Although taxes on gasoline, which is currently the main means of funding the construction and maintenance of the Interstate Highway System is less burdensome than is an income tax or other more general tax for the same purpose. The sale of revenue bonds funded toll road construction with the revenue going towards debt service and maintenance. In some cases, the state government may have insured the bonds as in the case of some railroad construction in the 19th century. In my view, this too is beyond the scope of government unless driven by the legitimate need to protect private property. Ultimately, the securing of private bonds by the government remains a burden on wealth creation because it puts tax dollars at unnecessary risk.

A nation's infrastructure is property held in common and by definition and in fact, property held in common is unproductive. In the absence of a calamity, the nation's private stock eases the burden of life and creates more wealth through investment in private property whether tangible such as buildings and structures or intangible as in patents, books, movies, etc. The accumulation of wealth is only through individuals acting on their own freewill, with no coercion in contracting, and under the nation's protection of private property, and under the nation's enforcement of laws and contracts. The nation acts through the sovereign as manifested in the laws the sovereign enacts. The less taxed, regulated or otherwise encumbered the economy by the sovereign or in other words the greater the individual liberty or freedom to contract, the greater the wealth created, and the more likely the economy and the nation will survive a calamity. In the absence of calamity, wealth eases the burden of life for the individuals comprising the nation.

Measurement of Wealth Creation

The Gross Domestic Product or GDP is the modern measure of wealth creation. Note that it is a measure of wealth creation and not wealth. Wealth is in the value of the total accumulated stock of a nation as I had described earlier. Recent estimates (2014) place the total private wealth, i.e. private stock of the United States at approximately $70 trillion. The GDP is the total annual value of the goods and services produced and consumed by labor and capital as measured by individuals purchasing those goods and services plus the expenditures by the government. The GDP consists of four major components.

(1) Personal Income and Outlays
(2) Gross Private Domestic Investment
(3) Net of Imports and Exports
(4) Government Purchases or more accurately Government Spending.

The Gross Private Domestic Investment component of the GDP less capital depreciation represents the annual addition to the nation's stock or store of wealth. This is the Net Private Domestic Investment found in the National Income and Product Accounts maintained by the Bureau of Economics Analysis. The inclusion of government spending distorts the GDP because the government does not produce goods and services that create profit or wealth. Whereas the other components of the GDP arise from the effort on the part of individuals and companies to produce goods and services, government spending arises not from the creation of goods and services but from taxing goods and services created by the private sector. Thus, government spending does not and cannot contribute in any way to the creation of wealth since the government produces nothing of value in exchange for the revenue it receives, i.e. the government does not create profit. Personal income and outlays arise from the productivity of individuals. The greater the productivity of individuals then the greater is the personal income in the absence of inflation. Individuals must produce a good or service in order to acquire the ability or money to make the expenditures reflected in the Personal Income and Outlays component of the GDP, that is at least to the extent that the expenditures are not the result of government transfer payments. This is the same with the other two components of the GDP, i.e. Gross Private Domestic Investment, and the Net of Imports and Exports. Table 1 is the US GDP at the end of 2012 in terms of the four major components:

	2012
Gross domestic product	$16,244.6
Personal consumption expenditures	$11,149.6
Gross private domestic investment	$2,475.2
Net exports of goods and services	-$547.2
Government consumption expenditures and gross investment	$3,167.0

Table 1 – US 2012 GDP Major Components

The dollar amounts are in nominal dollars.   Nominal dollars are dollars
not adjusted for inflation.   The US GDP in 2012 was over $16.2 trillion.
Note that the Personal consumption expenditure is the largest
component making up almost 70% of the total GDP.   The Gross
Private Domestic investment component includes replacement costs.   In
order to determine the amount of wealth added to the stock of the nation
we must subtract the Capital Consumption Allowance (CCA) from the
Gross Domestic Investment.   This amount was $1.2 trillion in 2012.
Therefore, the total nominal wealth added to the stock of the nation in
2012 is $1.28 trillion.   The Net of Exports of Goods and Services was a
negative amount in 2012.   This means that the nation imported more
than it exported in 2012 and therefore it is running a trade deficit.
Under the gold standard, the trade deficit balances by moving gold to the
nations with whom the trade deficit exists.   In turn, interest rates would
decline in the nation with the deficit and increase in the nation with the
surplus.   In this way, exchange rates remain constant.

However, under a floating exchange rate, the value of the dollar
in terms of foreign currencies affects the Net of Exports of Goods and
Services.   If the value of the dollar is strong in relation to a major
trading partner such as China or Japan then the price of imports
decreases and the price of exports increases.   For instance if a car from
Japan costs 2,000,000 yen and the dollar can buy 105 yen then the
Japanese car costs $19,048.   If the dollar strengthens against the yen so
that it can buy 110 yen then the car now costs $18,182.   This has a
tendency to increase total imports.   On the other hand, the stronger
dollar makes exports more expensive and this has a tendency to decrease
total exports.   Generally, a stronger dollar vis-à-vis the currency of the
trading partner leads to a larger trade deficit.   This was the case in 2012
as shown in Table 1 and the effect is to reduce the overall GDP.   The
Government Consumption Expenditures in 2012 was almost $3.2 trillion.
This includes Federal, state and local government expenditures, and it
comprises almost 20% of the GDP.   These expenditures are the result
of government tax receipts and borrowing.   As I will show later this is
not the total of government expenditures because it does not include
interest payments on debt and Federal transfer payments, i.e. money
taken from the taxpayer or borrowed and given to the non-taxpayer or
rather the non-producer with nothing in return.   The latter amounts

appear in the Personal Consumption Expenditures and makeup over 20% of this component.

Despite its flaws, I will use the GDP as a measure of the wealth creation of an economy because it enables comparisons with other nations as well as with the past.

The US Treasury coins money the Federal Reserve Bank prints money

The government acquires money from tax revenue, borrowing, and/or printing of money. Strictly speaking, the US government, through the Department of the Treasury coins money it does not print money. Demand from the nation's banks determines the amount of money coined by the Treasury based in turn on the demand of business and individuals for liquidity. The demand for liquidity, i.e. money, increases as the productive capacity of the nation increases. Demand for liquidity arising out of increases in production or productivity is not inflationary. The Federal Reserve Bank on the other hand, which is a privately owned entity ostensibly independent of the Federal Government, prints money under the authority of the Federal Government, and uses the money it prints to buy government debt through the Federal Open Market Committee (FOMC). It also loans new capital to member banks to shore up their capital reserves in the event that excessive loan losses occur or there is excessive withdrawal of deposits. In this manner, the Federal Reserve Bank mitigates bank failures and maintains confidence in the banking system although it does this at the risk of inflating the currency. Bank failures have the effect of undermining confidence in the banking system and confidence in the banking system is essential to its existence. Member banks pay a price for infusion of capital by the Federal Reserve Bank in terms of their profitability because the member banks must pay back the loans with interest. Through this process, the Federal Reserve Bank evens out the occasional fluctuations in the economy, in theory preventing isolated events, i.e. bank failures from having a domino effect, but it does so at the risk of sparking inflation. Of course, if the economy in general begins to suffer significant losses then the Federal Reserve Bank may exacerbate the losses and indeed this has been its history since its founding. The Congress created the Federal Reserve Bank in 1913 through enactment of the Federal Reserve Act and ever since then the existence of the Federal Reserve Bank has created more problems than its existence was intended to prevent.

When the Federal Reserve Bank loans money to the Federal Government by printing the money and buying government bonds the expectation is the Federal Government will honor the debt through tax revenue. Oftentimes this does not happen. Instead, the Federal Reserve Bank forgives the debt and simply hands the bonds back to the Federal Government when they become due. This process is monetizing debt.   Monetizing the debt effectively injects unearned dollars into the economy thus increasing the supply of money without adding to the things that the money can buy.   This is the definition of inflation.   This is unlike the process of coining money, which the Federal Government does in response to the increases in the quantity or quality of goods and services produced and which is non-inflationary. Thus, monetizing the debt always leads to inflation and it is one reason that inflation has been a part of the US economy since the creation of the Federal Reserve Bank.   The gold standard served as a brake to the printing of money until 1970 when the Federal government decided to abrogate the Bretton-Woods Agreement and leave the gold standard.   I will discuss the gold standard and the Bretton-Woods Agreement later. The other reason for inflation is the Federal debt itself apart from the printing of money to purchase it.   Figure 8 shows the high correlation between the cumulative monetization of the debt and the CPI level since the beginning of this policy of monetizing the debt in 1940.   The CPI level is the measure of inflation in goods and services.

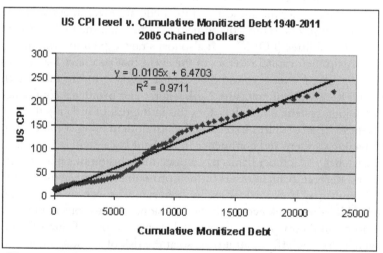

Figure 8 – Correlation between US CPI level and Cumulative Monetized debt -1940-2011

Figure 9 illustrates the correlation between the United States CPI and US Government debt from 1900 to 2011.

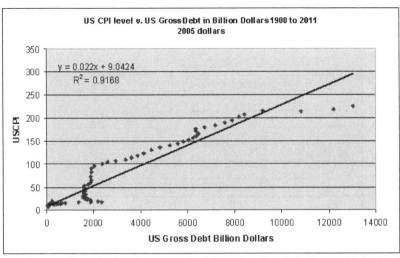

Figure 9 – Correlation between US CPI level v. US Gross Debt 1900 to 2011

The high correlation coefficient between the CPI level and the gross debt establishes the certainty that greater government debt engenders inflation. This is regardless of the manner of funding the debt, i.e. whether through public purchase or by purchases by the Federal Reserve Bank. An interesting feature of this chart is the apparent reduction in the rate the CPI grows and the growth of debt that occurred when the debt exceeded $10 trillion. This occurred in 2009. The departure of the gains in inflation from the gains in government debt is attributable to rapid increases in the productivity growth rate as reflected in the decline in the number of employed individuals and the decline in median income. The decline in the number of employed individuals and the decline in median income are the result of gains in productivity, which offsets the inflation rate. Figure 10 illustrates the gains in productivity beginning in 2008 as reflected in the accelerated decline in the relative employment rate and the relative median income. The relative employment rate is the number of employed individuals compared to the number of employable individuals. These factors contributed to the increase in corporate earnings in the face of very low revenue growth thus sustaining the increasing valuation in the equities market fueled by the unprecedented influx of fiat money, i.e. money printed by the Federal Reserve Bank beginning in 2009 and from the Federal Reserve's Quantitative Easing policy.

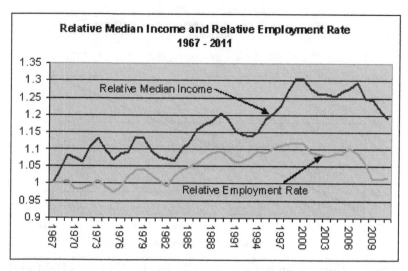

Figure 10 – Relative Median Income and Relative Employment Rate – 1967 to 2011

Contributing to the general gains in productivity are imports from China and other low cost manufacturing nations.   Annual nominal imports from China for example have increased at an exponential rate since the 1980s from $8.5 billion in 1985 to $440 billion in 2013.   This has helped to keep United States inflation low and it has contributed to unemployment as well.

Although some inflation existed before the creation of the Federal Reserve Bank, this institution is the main reason for inflation since its creation in 1913.   Prior to the creation of the Federal Reserve Bank, government created inflation by debasing the currency.   Debasing the currency involved printing or otherwise creating more currency or species than the gold or silver backing the face value of the currency. Although this is a different process than the Federal Reserve and other central banks now use to support governments, the effect is the same, i.e. inflation and the undermining of wealth creation or productivity. Figure 11 illustrates the level of CPI from 1774 to 2012.

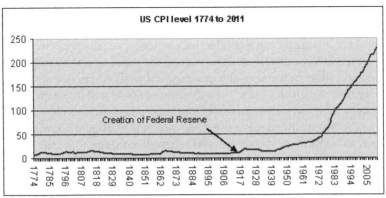

Figure 11 – US CPI from 1774 to 2011

Note that the CPI level was relatively stable before the creation of the Federal Reserve Bank and there was enormous wealth created prior to the creation of the Federal Reserve Bank. Most of the productivity growth prior to 1913 went into creating wealth. Much of the productivity growth after 1913 went into offsetting inflation engendered by government spending. Although the economy created wealth after 1913, if measured since 1929 the amount of wealth created would have been 80 times greater had it not been for the inflation engendered by government taxation, spending, and debt. Under the section entitled "The Actual Burden of Government", I will explain how I arrived at this figure. (See Appendix 1)

Money is not wealth

Money is not wealth it is a means of exchange. In historic terms, money enables a trilateral exchange as opposed to bartering which is a bilateral exchange. Rather than barter one good or service for another good or service, there is an exchange of a good or service for common specie, whose value or purchasing power does not change over time. This facilitates commerce because it solves the problem of finding bartering partners. Specie also promotes savings since the value of the specie does not decrease over time then there is no need to exchange it immediately for goods or services. Thus, specie is a store of wealth. For the common specie to be acceptable in trade, it must have an inherent and consistent value to ensure its use in the future. Gold and silver are such specie as well as are bronze and copper. Gold is particularly useful as specie since it is an inert metal and holds its weight and luster. Nations and individuals have used these metals as money throughout the ages. One of the problems with gold and silver is that the quantity is naturally limited at any point in time, and so in a rapidly growing economy, i.e. an economy where increasing quantities of goods and services are supplied and demanded, a shortage of acceptable specie

85

can restrict commerce and thereby restrict the creation of wealth. Just like any other commodity, the value of gold and silver increases as the demand for it increases so a productive economy, i.e. an efficient economy, will have the effect of increasing the value or purchasing power of gold and silver in terms of the quantity and quality of goods and services that the species buys. As the value of gold and silver increases, the mining of these metals increases and this adds to the supply. As long as the supply increases at the same rate as the demand increases then the unit value of these metals remains relatively constant in a free and unencumbered market. The key point is that there is always a time lag between supply and demand and this is the cause of price fluctuations unless the price is constant by law. This is the meaning of the gold standard. In this case, increasing productivity increases the purchasing power of gold. When the supply of species becomes limited then those individuals that hold gold or silver become wealthier in terms of purchasing power. Those individuals that do not hold these metals must improve their productivity in order to acquire the metal in exchange for their goods and services or they can resort to bartering which would tend to reduce the demand for specie thereby lowering its value or purchasing power. On the other hand, if the supply of gold or silver increases more rapidly than the goods or services supplied by the economy then there is economic inflation, i.e. the value or purchasing power of the gold or silver decreases. This has happened at times. One example is during the California Gold Rush with the discovery of large quantities of gold, prices in terms of gold increased. The CPI increased from 7.65 in 1848 to 8.46 in 1857 or 10.6% dropping slightly again before the beginning of the War Between the States. In this case, those holding cash or gold lost purchasing power and had to increase investment in the provision of goods and services in order to acquire a return, which is more cash. In other words, the increasing supply of gold increased productivity and created wealth. Investments in goods and services result in competition and prices drop as a result. Indeed the California gold rush did lead to investments in railroads, the telegraph, steel manufacturing, farm mechanization, and similar technologies that enabled the creation of great wealth. There is no better symbol of the private investments spawned by the California gold rush than the Golden Spike used ceremoniously to complete the first US Transcontinental Railroad between Omaha, Nebraska and Sacramento, California in 1869. The discovery of gold in California created wealth manifested through increased investment in the private stock of the nation. Note that the sale of private bonds, i.e. private credit funded the 19th and early 20th Century railroads. Government had little to do with financing the railroads other than providing security during the construction and some of the land through eminent domain.

    In an unencumbered economy fluctuations in the supply of

specie is self-correcting but there are short-term disruptions in prices nonetheless due to a lack of specie. Since even before the Roman Empire the coinage of money was a function of government although this is not an inherent function of government, and that is why I do not list it along with the protection of private property and enforcement of laws and contracts. That is, individuals do not originally appoint or elect a sovereign or protector to coin money. There is a persuasive argument for the use of bank notes or government backed notes as legal tender instead of gold and silver with the bank notes or government-backed notes exchangeable at any time for the equivalent gold or silver. The use of gold backed paper instead of gold creates a buffer between the supply of gold, which depends on the uncertainty of locating and mining gold and a growing economy, which demands more gold as specie for exchange. Indeed this is the basis of fractional banking which I discussed earlier whereby an initial amount of gold deposited in a bank leads to notes issued which are promises, i.e. contracts to redeem the gold with interest to the holder of the note. The note holder can deposit his note in another bank, which also issues its promise, i.e. contract to return the note with interest to the holder. In both the first case and the second case each of the banks then loan the money to someone who issues a personal note, i.e. contract to the bank promising to return the money with interest. This process continues and as long as the borrowers create something of value to enable them to return money with interest, then the process creates wealth. The government's role in this process is to enforce the contracts, i.e. the notes, and secure the private property of those engaging in the commerce. The government provides neither the gold nor the notes to start and sustain the process. In the United States, the government coined money as governments have done from the dawn of history and private banks issued bank notes backed by the gold, i.e. the coined money in their vaults. The establishment of a central national bank was controversial because this meant that the United States government would not only coin money but also enable the government to issue bank notes, which made it easy for the government to debase the currency and control interest rates. Recall the sovereign cannot sue himself nor can anyone sue the sovereign without his permission so there is no way to secure a contract, i.e. a bank note with the sovereign. Debasing the currency and controlling interest rates is a burden on wealth creation and a means to subjugate the population to the will of the sovereign. After the American Revolutionary War, there was little appetite in the United States to cede the power to debase currency to the sovereign. This was the reason the American Colonists fought the war in the first place. It is also the reason that the United States created as much wealth as it did during the 19th Century and early 20th Century. During the first half of the eighteenth century, a central national bank came and went twice before permanently established in 1862 during the War Between the States thus enabling the government to print money to fight the war. The Legal Tender Act of 1862 allowed the issue of $150 million in national notes known as greenbacks and mandated by law the issuance and acceptance of paper money in lieu of gold and silver coins. Congress increased the $150 million limit to $450 million in 1863. The Confederate States did the same thing and they too printed money. This increase in the money supply caused prices to increase 90% between 1860 and 1864 or almost doubling within a span of 5 years. The result was a rapid increase in interest rates after the war as the government stopped the printing of money to stem the tide of inflation. The increase in interest rates then lead to bank failures, and a great depression beginning in 1873 and lasting to 1879. Had the government increased taxes to fight the War Between the States instead of printing money there would not have been the depression of 1873. In all likelihood, the war would have been short lived had the taxpayers in both the North and the South bore war's pain as equally as the men that fought and died. Thus, a lot less men would have died and the results would have been the same and Lincoln would not have been so great. Note that the value of greenbacks as well as Confederate notes issued during the war plummeted after the war as people refused to accept paper currency.

Paper currency began in widespread use with the English in the 18th Century and it began to replace gold and silver as money. The Bank of England was a private company until 1946 when the British government nationalized it. William III first gave the Bank of England a royal charter to print paper currency in 1694. A royal charter is an agreement between the sovereign and a citizen that says that the sovereign will use the power of eminent domain to prevent others from engaging in the same economic activity as the recipient of the charter. A royal charter creates an inviolable monopoly. This is the only true meaning of monopoly, i.e. an enterprise secured from competition by the government. It is a misapplication of the term when used to describe a large dominant corporation such as in the case of John D. Rockefeller's Standard Oil Company. Capitalism does not create monopolies only governments create monopolies by law. Gold backed all paper currency in the major world economies under the gold standard until 1970 except for interruptions during the two World Wars where the belligerents resorted to inflating their currencies to fund the wars rather than raise taxes. Just as in the case of the War Between the States the pain of war was not felt by the taxpayer which otherwise would have shortened wars. Instead, the printing of money led to the needless death of hundreds of thousands of men. The flower of Europe perished on the government printing presses in World War I. Despite returning to the gold standard after both the War Between the States and World War I, there was damage done to the idea of a gold standard in the minds of many politicians because of the temptation to print money to achieve political ends without raising taxes. The sovereign printing of money created a problem for future sovereigns but secured the position of the current sovereign by enabling promises of government largess without raising taxes. Britain only reluctantly returned to the gold standard after the First World War largely through the efforts of Winston Churchill who was Britain's Chancellor of the Exchequer between 1924 and 1929. The English socialists vilified Churchill for his success in restoring Britain to the gold standard after World War I. It is one reason that he was defeated as Prime Minister after World War II despite his practically single-handed defeat of the National Socialists. Godless socialists are enamored with the printing of money because it is an effective means of surreptitiously achieving their atheistic wealth destroying agenda thus satiating their envy.

The Bretton-Woods Agreement enacted after World War II effectively restored the gold standard but it only lasted about 23 years. While it was in force, the gold standard facilitated trade between nations each of whom had various currencies and various productive capacities. The value of gold determined the value of one currency vs. another currency. Nations fixed the value of an ounce of gold in their respective currency by law so that exporters and importers could calculate an exchange rate from these values. The United States fixed the value of gold at $20.67 until 1934 when the US Government arbitrarily raised the value to $35.00 after the government made the holding of gold illegal and confiscated all monetary gold in private hands. The increase in the official price of gold enabled the legal printing of more money by the Treasury. This move also increased the world price of gold causing foreign holders of gold to sell gold for dollars and using the dollars to buy foreign currency thus making an immediate profit in terms of the foreign currency. United States gold imports went from a net outflow of -173.5 million dollars (-8.4 million ounces) in 1934 to an inflow 4.744 billion dollars (135.6 million ounces) by 1940. Figure 12 shows the net flow of gold between 1915 and 1970.

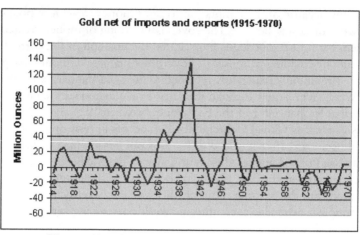

Figure 12 – Gold net of imports and exports

The money supply as measured by M2 increased by almost 45% between 1934 and 1940. This was the deliberate and failed attempt to inflate prices by the FDR Administration and thus end the depression by applying the flawed ideas of Keynesian economics. The increase in the quantity of gold held by the US government was one reason that Japan attacked the United States and Hitler declared war on the United States. It was also the reason that the United States felt financially comfortable entering the war. The socialist states of Japan and Germany lusted after the gold and they warred to get it. Thus, FDR's misguided attempts to salvage farm prices in the United States led to World War II and the death of millions of people.

Fluctuations in the market price of gold in terms of the respective currency resulted in the movement of gold between nations to maintain the price of gold at or near the official level. The relative productivity of nations determined the price of gold and the resulting amount of gold moved between nations. For example, assume that productivity gains in one nation result in a drop in the price of goods and services. This increases the value of gold in that nation thus the price of gold goes up in terms of the currency of the nation. The lower prices in terms of gold increase the quantity export of goods and services, and reduce their quantity imports. The importing nations now have a deficit in their balance of payments and the exporting nation enjoys a surplus. This caused the movement of gold from the nation with the trade deficit to the nation with the trade surplus thus increasing the supply of gold in the nation with the trade surplus introducing more money into its economy causing inflation in prices and bringing prices back to normal including the price of gold. To facilitate the outflow of gold the central bank in the nation with the trade deficit suffered deflation and thus was obligated to lower its interest rates while the nation with the trade surplus suffered inflation was obligated to increase its interest rates. A productive nation, i.e. a nation whose rate of productivity is increasing would end up accumulating gold while a less productive nation would loose gold. A productive nation would also end up with higher interest rates, which would slow productivity growth, and cause prices to rise. In this way, the exchange rates between different currencies stayed relatively stable and so did prices. The only thing that fluctuated was the interest rates in the different nations and the amount of gold held by the different nations. This system helped to prevent trade wars, which under mercantilism led to war between nations. The gold standard maintained monetary discipline and promoted productivity growth in all the nations that subscribed to it and these nations created great wealth until World War I. Note that if the sovereign did not coin the money and trade between nations was by bank notes backed by gold or gold used as the specie there would be no need to regulate exchange rates. The need to regulate exchange rates arises from the sovereign coining of money. World War I saw nations leave the gold standard and start inflating their currencies in order to fight the war. Despite efforts of some nations to return to the gold standard after the war, most notably Great Britain as I mentioned, the fact is that the monetary system could not bring back the price stability that existed prior to the war. Price inflation continued immediately after the war as food prices increased in the US. The increase in food prices happened primarily because the US was feeding the world at the time since European agriculture was struggling due to the devastation and destruction of wealth brought on by the war. This was economic inflation because it was due to increased demand and decrease in supply and not monetary inflation caused by government monetary and fiscal policy. German government monetary and fiscal policy led to World War I in the first place, as I will come to show. I will discuss the difference between economic and monetary inflation later in the book. Economic inflation always adjusts itself and this is what happened once European agriculture recovered. Food prices increased 120% from 1913 to 1919 and then dropped 78% from 1919 to 1921. The increasing prices in the US prior to 1920 also stimulated US food imports and the competition caused prices to drop thereby reducing the value of both imports and exports. Figure 13 shows that the value of agricultural exports also increased 244% from 1915 to 1920 and then dropped quickly by 60% between 1920 and 1922. The demand for food after the war contributed to the increasing prices in food prior to 1920.

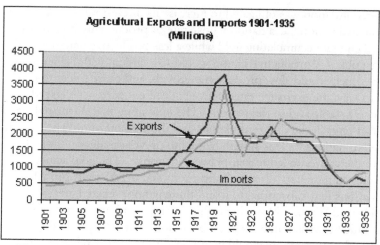

Figure 13 – Agricultural Exports and Imports 1901 to 1935

The high volume of lower priced agricultural imports resulted in the Smoot-Hawley Tariff. It was his promise to enact the tariff that got Herbert Hoover elected in 1928. It was much like the promise to enact the Morrill Tariff that got Lincoln elected in 1860 thus engendering the War Between the States. The increasing US food prices prior to 1920 resulted in farmers mortgaging their land to buy more land in order to increase production, as demand appeared to be increasing. At the same time, the farmers started to invest in tractors, which improved their productivity tremendously. Annual farm mortgage loans increased from $5.8 billion in 1916 to $10.8 billion in 1923 in nominal dollars almost doubling and stayed close to this level through 1930 despite the fact that farm prices fell 78% between 1919 and 1921 as European agriculture recovered from the devastation of the war. The real S&P dropped 21% over the same period. The need to pay off the mortgage loans put more land into production and the tractor made it possible to do this with a lot less labor. Prices remained stable as consumption matched demand rather than increase as would be necessary to pay off the loans. Then Prohibition became law in 1920 at the same time that universal suffrage also became law. Prohibition reduced the market for grains used to produce alcoholic beverages further reducing demand for farm produce thus driving prices lower. The production of beer alone for example went from 60.8 million gallons annually in 1917 to 4.9 million gallons annually by 1924 or a reduction of 92%. This reduced consumption of the grains that went into the manufacture of beer placing additional downward pressure on farm prices. Following the drop in farm prices, the number of bank failures went from 63 in 1919 to 505 in 1921. This resulted in the S&P dropping by 21%. Bank failures totaled 5882 between 1919 and 1930 when food prices collapsed along with the stock market. The total number of banks fell 22% between the peak of 1921 and 1930.

   Despite the obvious inability of farmers to pay back loans, the banks continued to loan them money and the result was the aforementioned bank failures.   This was due in large part to the Agricultural Credits Act of 1923 establishing a network of twelve Federal Intermediate Credit Banks in different regions of the country (corresponding to the twelve regional banks in the Federal Reserve System), each capitalized at $5 million.   The Act authorized these Banks to lend more money to farm cooperative associations, which then lent it to farmers.   The passage of this act continued the lending to farmers while their productivity continued to increase keeping farm prices low and ushering in the call for greater tariffs and the election of Herbert Hoover.   The irony here is that despite the obvious failure of the Agricultural Credits Act of 1923, the Federal Government passed the Federal Deposit Insurance Corporation Act one decade later, which even now posses a continuous threat to the banking system.   Thus, the government once again interfered in the economy resulting in the collapse of farm prices leading to acceleration in bank failures along with a collapse in the value of all other assets.   The government made every attempt to inflate food prices between 1923 and 1934 and each attempt resulted in even greater production thereby negating the government efforts and leading to such calamities as the Dust Bowl and the Great Depression.   The Dust Bowl was the direct result of farmers over plowing sensitive prairie lands in an attempt to save their farms and homes from foreclosures on the flawed promises by President Roosevelt that prosperity, i.e. higher farm prices, was just around the corner. Figure 14 shows how the Federal government tried to inflate prices after 1930 by printing more money.

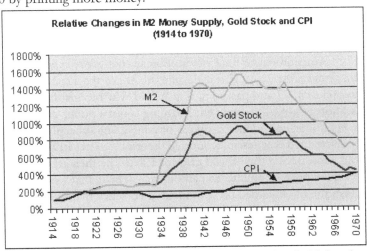

Figure 14-Relative Changes in M2 Money Supply, Gold Stock and CPI (1914 – 1970)

Note that even though the money supply as measured by M2 expanded with respect to the amount of gold in the US Treasury between 1930 and 1938 yet the CPI declined during the same time. It was not until after World War II that the full affect of maintaining the large spread between the supply of gold and M2 started to show up as inflation or a rising CPI. This was due to a slow down in farm productivity and a shift to a heavily unionized manufacturing based economy that had not yet undergone the kind of productivity gains that the farm sector had seen in the decades prior.

The worldwide depression that followed the European, Japanese and United States increasing government interference in their respective economies in the 1920s and 1930s culminated in the Second World War with even greater wealth destruction than engendered by the government induced depression. If governments did not interfere in their economies such events would not occur and while there may be short-term disruptions in employment and some temporary civil unrest from the rapid gains in productivity, an unencumbered economy would recover and create more wealth. The human spirit in an intelligent populace would overcome adversity and adapt to the adversity if left unhampered by taxation, regulation and other coercions foisted upon it by law and by those who they ostensibly appointed solely to secure and protect private property and enforce the law and contracts but act otherwise.

Figure 14 also illustrates that the gold standard was effective in regulating the money supply as the M2 money supply followed the gold stock. The separation in the ratio between the gold stock and the money supply occurred in 1934 when FDR declared the private holding of gold illegal in 1933 to prevent so-called "hoarding". What made FDR think that whoever was hoarding gold would not hoard the money the government paid for the gold is a mystery that can only be resolved by saying that FDR used this as an excuse to take private property. Private property is anathema to those wishing to rule rather than govern. The Fifth Amendment of the Constitution states, *"nor shall private property be taken for public use...."* This is despite the use of the Trading with the Enemy Act of 1917 and passed during World War I to justify the confiscation of gold. To prevent hoarding is not a public use and it is not an economic consideration unless of course one subscribes to the widely discredited Keynesian economic theories. After FDR confiscated the gold while paying the official price of $20.67, he then arbitrarily increased the price of gold to $35 an ounce. Those that were forced to relinquish their gold ended up with inflated currency that was worth less than if they held on to the gold. The inflated currency increased costs of almost everything except food prices, which continued to be subject to overproduction thanks to the Smoot-Haley Tariff and promises by the government that prices would increase. The result was another downturn in the economy in 1936 when unemployment hit almost 20%

and the DJIA dropped 33%. All this was due solely to the actions of FDR and the Democrats at the time. Had FDR not interfered in the economy, and had instead lowered taxes, and repealed the Smoot-Haley Tariff there would not have been a Great Depression, nor a Dust Bowl, and instead great wealth created. Also given the fact that the actions of FDR had significant effects on world trade and the economies of other nations it is likely that Germany would have recovered from its inflation and Hitler not have come into power.

An interesting aspect of FDR's executive action to confiscate gold was that it excluded gold contained in jewelry and ornaments and FDR gave plenty of time to those people that had large amounts of gold to move it overseas to avoid the confiscation. Thus, the order did not affect most of FDR's wealthy friends, and Hollywood people, who supported the progressive agenda of Wilson and FDR. Indeed these individuals profited from FDR's policy because now their gold was worth $35.00 an ounce and not $20.67 an ounce. However, those that were simply saving small amounts of gold to cover a rainy day lost their money. Such is the hypocrisy of the left.

It is little wonder that Hollywood, radio, and the print media treated FDR with such reverence in movies, radio programs, and all print media at the time and even to this day. He made them wealthy at the expense of the economy and the lives of farmers and laborers and Hollywood is grateful to him and the Democrat Party to this day.

Distinction between monetary inflation and economic inflation

I will make a distinction in this book between monetary inflation -the debasement of the currency- from economic inflation- an increase in prices due to increased demand or decreased supply of goods and services. Historically monetary inflation has also occurred with species. The difference between the cost of producing coinage and the value of the coinage is seigniorage, and governments have often used seigniorage to raise revenue by not raising taxes. It is for this reason that governments assume, or rather take the responsibility of coining money rather than leave it to the banks. For example during the reigns of Henry VIII and then his son Edward VI the debasement of coinage occurred when the English Crown replaced to a significant degree the gold or silver content of coinage with a baser metal such as copper. By reducing the value of gold or silver content relative to the face value of its coins, the English Crown extracted usable revenue from domestic money stocks since each coin was worth less in terms of its precious metal content while the face value of the coin remained the same. This allowed the English Crown to mint more money for itself and thereby add to its treasury without openly having to tax the population and risk their ire. The value of the silver content of the coin was 25 percent of its face value within 10 years. This action led to inflation as the debased currency was worth less and it was a form of taxation without the need to obtain Parliament's approval. The high rate of productivity growth of the English kept inflation at a relatively low level until 1544 when inflation increased considerably. Nevertheless, there was little civil unrest arising from the debasement. Indeed the only significant civil unrest was due instead to the laws enacted by Parliament and Henry VIII related to establishing and securing the Church of England with Henry VIII as its head. This civil unrest speaks to the seriousness that men took their belief in God at the time. The fear of God kept the passions at bay and England created great wealth despite the debasing of the currency. As I will show later, the high rate of productivity growth of the English was due solely to the enclosure of land resulting from the Enclosure Laws, and the creation of private property. This in large part accounts for the fact that there was little unrest due to the inflation of the currency. Queen Elizabeth I retired the debased currency beginning in 1561 but in the meantime, England was creating great wealth despite the debasement. That is, despite the debasement of the money, the English farmers and manufacturers were able to produce goods and services at increasingly lower unit cost with greater profits offsetting the debasement of the currency but at the cost of less wealth creation than had the debasement not occurred. This became apparent as the wealth created by the English manifested itself during the Elizabethan Age and after Queen Elizabeth restored the metal in the currency to equal its face value. The Elizabethan Age is the golden age in English history when the English produced great works of genius and created great wealth. The debasement of the currency prevented this wealth creation from manifesting earlier as the productivity gains went toward offsetting the debasement instead of towards the creation of wealth. Henry VII is a hero to the socialist despite the execution of his wives. He printed money and used it to aggrandize himself. This is the goal of all socialists.

The rise in productivity used to offset the debasement of Henry VIII was due in large part to the Enclosure Laws, which allowed individuals to purchase and own the property they farmed. Nevertheless, there was a reduction in wealth creation that otherwise would not have occurred had the debasement of the coinage not occurred. The resulting revenues to the Crown from the debasement led to the building of a great navy that enabled England to defeat the Spanish Armada in 1588 and to create and sustain a vast and highly productive empire. Thus in this instance the debasement of the currency with the resulting reduction of wealth creation in England prior to the reign of Queen Elizabeth I was offset by the high productivity of the resulting English Colonies and the securing and protection of trade routes during her reign. The question is could England have been able to build a great navy if the debasement of the currency did not occur? My answer to this is that England could have still been able to build a great navy because England was creating great wealth at the time the currency was debased and had the debasement not occurred England would not only have had a great navy but much greater wealth as well. Nevertheless, had England failed to secure its colonies and make them productive then there is no doubt the English Crown would have ceased to exist and we would have an altogether different and probably poorer world. As it was, English genius created much wealth worldwide. Thus, the creation of the British Empire was justified in these terms alone and despite the debasement of the currency under Henry III and his son Edward VI.

The sovereign burdens wealth creation

While money is not wealth, cash is wealth. Cash is money held in an account that earns interest. Cash has the potential of investment for productive ends i.e. the creation of wealth. Cash is also money stock when held for long periods such as in certificate of deposits or other long-term accounts. The tax revenue of the government is cash, or in other words productive potential, taken out of the productive economy by the sovereign. In an agricultural economy, the sovereign takes grain from the farmer and consumes it in order to sustain himself and his soldiers. This allows less for the farmer to plant in the subsequent year or as surplus to engender commerce. In return, the sovereign protects the farmer's private property and enforces his contracts. Nevertheless, the sovereign reduces the wealth of the farmer, and reduces the ability of the farmer to create wealth. The sovereign also reduces the volume of commerce as there is less left for the farmer to exchange. Thus, it is not only the farmer whose ability to create wealth is impaired but also the ability of those with whom the farmer would have engaged in commerce. Taxation therefore has a ripple effect throughout the economy because it impairs commerce as well as impairing the wealth creation of the individual specifically taxed. As I will demonstrate later, the ripple effect on the economy is much more significant than it seems simply from the tax on an individual producer. The ripple effect arises from the action of compound interest, as I will demonstrate later when I calculate the true burden of government. Recall that the sovereign has the power of eminent domain, which is the ability or means to take all that the farmer produces. If the sovereign takes so much from the farmer so that there will not be enough to plant the next year this reduces the amount of grain produced the next year. If an ensuing calamity occurs and the crop fails there is starvation and death, and the sovereign suffers as much as the farmer as there will be rebellion. In an industrial economy, liquidating stock i.e. liquidating cash or other assets pays the sovereign's tax burden. This is a reduction of wealth and of the ability to create wealth. It is also a reduction in commerce. Cash withdrawn from the bank and converted to money is a reduction in wealth. Remember money is not wealth so when an asset converts to money it is a reduction in wealth.

Money taken by government as taxes and deposited in its account is cash that now becomes property held in common by the sovereign. The sovereign has taken private property, i.e. cash and made it property held by the sovereign, i.e. property held in common or common property. Since common property is unproductive, a corresponding and significant reduction in the ability of the nation to create wealth results from the taking. Government cash is unproductive because while it may earn interest sitting in the bank it has lost the potential to create wealth, as it is no longer in the productive economy. The government takes the money and provides nothing tangible in return to ease the burden of life. There is no incentive for the government to invest the money in order to make a profit. In fact, the incentive is just the opposite, which is to spend the money to secure private property and enforce the law and contracts. This spending provides no cash return. Neither does the government spending the money on anything other than securing private property and enforcing laws and contracts provide any return. Programs, which manifest as laws such as welfare, public education, infrastructure, unemployment, social security, medical care, job training, environmental protection or any of the other myriad programs of the sovereign do not and cannot provide a cash return and consequently these programs burden the economy and undermine wealth creation. Government cannot invest taxpayer money it can only spend taxpayer money. Cash earning interest is not wealth creation rather it is wealth preservation until invested in enterprise but only if held by individuals and not by the sovereign. The reason that interest on money is not wealth creation is due to inflation caused by the government taking of private property. When government takes private property, it reduces the supply of private property in this case cash and this increases the price, which is interest on the cash. Wars, famine and pestilence for instance lead to the loss of life, which is private property and this in turn reduces the pool of labor causing the price of labor to increase until men create private property i.e. more men. The price of labor will decrease as the supply increases assuming there is no growth in the economy or the government encumbers the economy. Government encumbering an economy is equivalent to an economy not growing, i.e. not generating wealth. Money spent for purposes that do not provide a return greater than the interest on the equivalent cash results in loss or reduction of wealth due to the inflation caused by the burden of government. Since all spending by government generates no cash return, i.e. no profit, then a reduction of the ability to create wealth results when cash becomes property of the government or in other words property held in common.

The government relies on the wealth created by the other components of the GDP since the government cannot create wealth, since this is not the reason for its existence or its purpose nor can it be. The greater the government spending component of the GDP the less the real wealth created and the more that is destroyed. The destruction of wealth manifests in the reduction in commerce engendered by the taking of private property, i.e. cash by the government. Thus, government expenditures should subtract from the other components of the GDP rather than added to the other components of the GDP. If we subtract the government-spending component from the GDP, then the real GDP is obviously less than currently portrayed.

Note that the government-spending component of the GDP does not include all government spending. Total spending by government is much larger than the spending included in the GDP. "Current expenditures" is the term used to measure all spending by the government. As defined by the US Bureau of Economic Analysis (BEA) "current expenditures" measures all spending by government on current-period activities. It consists of government consumption expenditures and current transfer payments, interest payments, and subsidies (and removes wage accruals less disbursements). The US Bureau of Economic Analysis (BEA) excludes payments such as transfer payments and interest payments from the calculation of GDP because these payments do not represent government purchases of goods and services, though income from transfer and interest payments may fund consumption expenditures or investment in other sectors of the economy. Thus, a portion of the personal income and outlays component of the GDP is actually unproductive or unearned income transferred from the taxpayer to the non-taxpayer. Therefore, in order to determine the true wealth creation we must subtract transfer payments from the personal income and outlays component of the GDP in addition to subtracting the government-spending component. In 2012, government transfer payments were almost 22% of the nominal GDP personal income expenditures. Thus, almost 22% of the personal expenditures in 2012 were from unearned income. Figure 15 illustrates the increasing proportion of current government transfer payments to the nominal GDP personal expenditures. This proportion is growing at an average rate of 0.24% per year as shown by the trend line. Figure 16 correlates the CPI level with the ratio of transfer payments to the GDP personal expenditures. The inflationary effect of government transfer payments appears in Figure 16. Note the inflation level as measured by the CPI grows exponentially with the ratio of transfer payments to GDP personal expenditures. Thus while the annual increase in the ratio is small the effect on inflation is exponential. This is an unsustainable course and unless brought under control the result will soon be hyperinflation with rapidly rising interest rates and a collapse in equity values, in other words a great destruction in wealth.

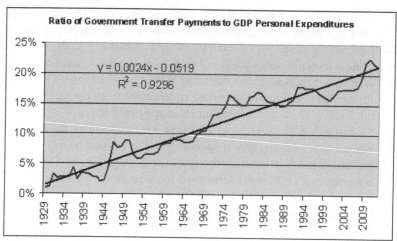

Figure 15 – Ratio of Current Government Transfer Payments to Nominal GDP Personal Expenditures

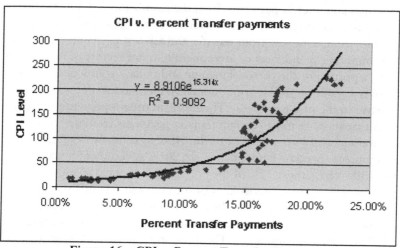

Figure 16 – CPI v. Percent Transfer Payments

A great irony in the US tax code is that money earned through capital gains, dividends or interest is "unearned income" whereas payments to individuals by government such as welfare, food stamps, unemployment and even government salaries is earned income. The truth is just the opposite.

Borrowing of money by the government is a burden on future tax revenue. In this regard, government borrowing is more insidious than current taxes because it burdens future wealth creation and jeopardizes the well-being of a nation's posterity. Since the future generations are themselves wealth, as children are also a hedge against calamity, government borrowing puts at risk the survival of the nation's posterity and thus the nation. The printing of money by the government is always inflationary because the government produces no goods and services for profit. It increases the supply of money without adding to the things that money can buy. Increasing the supply of money without creating something purchasable with the money is the classic definition of inflation, i.e. too much money chasing too few goods. Inflation robs productivity and is itself a form of taxation that further reduces wealth creation. The reason inflation may not appear in an economy despite the printing of money or the debasement of the currency is that the rate of productivity growth exceeds the rate of the printing of money or the rate of debasement of the currency. While there is no inflation, there is nevertheless a loss of wealth creation as inflation offsets productivity. This was the case with England during the reign of Henry VIII as previously mentioned and it is the case currently.

The historical inclusion of government spending in the GDP, as well as government transfer-payments to non-taxpayers makes it easier for the government to claim that the economy is growing when in fact the real economy may not be growing. It is a form of subterfuge foisted on the nation by those who seek to rule rather than to provide security and to enforce laws and contracts, as is the true and only purpose of government. Government simply borrows or prints money and then spends the money or sends it to non-taxpayers as transfer payments to make it appear the GDP is growing in order to claim its wealth destroying policies instead create wealth thereby furthering the subterfuge. In truth, the government borrowing and printing of money undermines wealth creation by inflating the currency thereby exposing the economy and the nation to calamity. By inflating the currency, I do not mean necessarily in relation to other currencies but rather in terms of the quantity and quality of goods and services that the currency can buy. An inflated dollar causes the value of the dollar to decline in terms of other currencies thus making exports less expensive and increasing the number but not necessarily the value of exports while making imports more expensive. Artificially inflating a nation's currency in terms of other currencies is equivalent to establishing a tariff against all imported goods and services. Trading nations retaliate by then inflating their currency to reduce the price of their exports. Such behavior further reduces wealth creation in nations thus creating civil unrest and instability. The gold standard prevents this kind of instability. Since 1970, i.e. after the abrogation of the Bretton-Woods Agreement, the US dollar has acted as a de facto standard because it is the world's reserve currency. International transactions are in dollars and as long as the United States economy is growing and productive then the dollar is relatively stable in terms of the other currencies. However, in attempting to overcome the 2008 collapse in the financial markets and restore asset values the Federal

Reserve Bank injected unprecedented liquidity into the United States economy. Productivity gains in the US since 2008 have offset the unprecedented liquidity thus holding US inflation somewhat at bay. Nevertheless, the effects of the influx of fiat dollars caused inflation to appear in the less wealthy and less productive nations such as those in the Middle East and China. China in particular has maintained a weak yuan. With the weak yuan, the costs of Chinese imports have been low and this has helped to hold US inflation low. This is at a cost to Chinese productivity which up until recently has held Chinese inflation down. However, this is changing as productivity declines in China and inflation is starting to increase in China as of the writing of this book. Productivity declines in China manifest in calls for higher wages. Unless China increases interest rates to strengthen the yuan against the dollar, it faces civil unrest. The effect of a stronger yuan will be to increase inflation in the United States. We see civil unrest in the Middle East where productivity growth is significantly less than it is in China primarily due to the lack of intellectual capital inherent in the Middle East as opposed to China. The lower productivity growth in the less intellectually capable Middle Eastern countries is the reason inflation exists in those countries, while it is more subdued in the more intellectually capable China. Although the Chinese communists are still capable of engendering inflation in that economy as it is inevitable that a godless and centrally planned economy will eventually collapse regardless of the store of intellectual capital. The inflation in the Middle East manifests itself most insidiously in the price of food and it is the reason for the continued instability in that part of the world where individuals spend a larger proportion of their income on food than in the Western Nations. Table 2 lists the percentage of consumer expenditures on food by Middle East country. For the United States, the percentage of consumer expenditures that go to food is 6.6%. For Israel, it is 15.9%

Share of consumer expenditures on Food	
Country/Territory	Percent
Bahrain	13.94%
United Arab Emirates	14.26%
Kuwait	18.56%
Turkey	22.17%
Saudi Arabia	25.84%
Jordan	32.20%
Morocco	40.45%
Egypt	42.72%

Table 2 – Share of consumer expenditures on food in the Middle East

Accordingly, increases in the price of food have a much larger impact on these nations than in the United States and Europe. This accounts for the civil unrest in many of these nations.

It is instructive to note that the GDP came into being under FDR in the 1930's, which was the time when Keynesian economics was taking hold among progressive politicians such as FDR. Keynesian economics is the flawed notion that government spending aides an economy. Keynes essentially intellectualized the printing of money or the debasement of currency as the means to create wealth. The envious sovereign quickly adopted Keynes' ideas to justify its ruinous actions and thus impose socialism on the economy to perpetuate himself. Keynes notion politically and intellectually justified the further burdening of the economy by the sovereign, i.e. FDR and the Congress, through taxation, increased regulation, and government borrowing as well as transfer payments to non-productive ends thereby causing the depression to last much longer than it otherwise would have. The facts bear out this analysis. The result was the election of FDR for an unprecedented and disastrous four terms. Fortunately, FDR died before he could complete his fourth term thus halting the United States' march to socialism until the 1960s when it resumed once again.

Figure 17 below is a chart of the real GDP using 2009-chained dollars from 1929 to the present (2013).

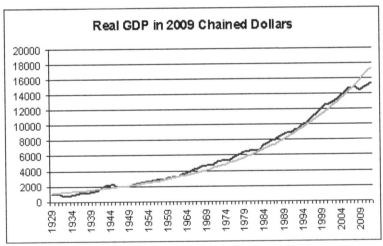

Figure 17-Real GDP in 2009 Chained Dollars

This chart shows the rise of the United States Real Gross Domestic Product in chained dollars since 1929. It includes changes to the calculation of the GDP enacted July 2013. These changes included adding intellectual property product expenditures to the Gross Private Domestic Investment category, and accounting for employer payments to defined benefit pension plans as wages on an accrual basis. Intellectual property product expenditures include expenditures on R&D as well as the production of movies and music. The effect of these changes is a higher level of GDP than previously reported in each year from 1929 to the present.   There is no actual GDP data prior to 1929 although there are derived estimates made by various economists that I will reference later in the book.   The GDP is a commonly accepted measure of the annual wealth created in the United States as well as all other nations. Keep in mind that wealth, as I have defined it, embodies in the stock of the nation and not all of the GDP goes toward building up the stock of the nation.   Nevertheless, it is a rough practical measure of wealth creation and it enables comparisons with other economies as well as with the past so it is useful in this sense.   Chained dollars are dollars adjusted for inflation.   One problem with the use of chained dollars is that prior to 1971, the US was on a de facto gold standard and after 1971 there came the introduction of the fiat currency which allowed all the free nations' currencies to float relative to each other although the US dollar remained the world's reserve currency.   In other words, most international transactions are in US dollars.   This was the beginning of significant monetary inflation in the US because the government could now print money at will, i.e. without any regard to a legal limit as existed under the de facto gold standard known as the Bretton-Woods Agreement.   Figure 18 shows the high correlation between the money supply as measured by M2 and the amount of gold in ounces in the US Treasury from 1914 to 1970, which marked the end of the gold standard. The gold standard effectively limited the money supply and thus inflation during this period.

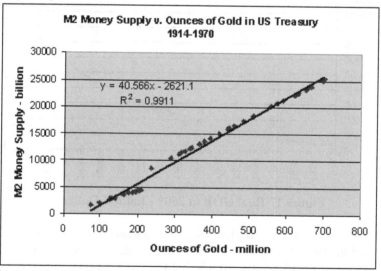

Figure 18 – M2 Money Supply v. Ounces of Gold in US Treasury 1914-1970

The CPI over this same period increased 301% or at an annual compound rate of 2.43% correlated at 0.87.   After 1970 the CPI grew at an annual compound rate of 4.72% correlated at 0.93. The relatively low correlation of the actual CPI with its annual compound growth rate before 1970 is due primarily to the inflation engendered by the high food prices following World War I and the deflation due to relentless and government supported overproduction in the farm that led to the Depression. This was economic inflation due to increasing demand and economic deflation engendered by the fall in food prices due to overproduction in the farm sector but aggravated by the Federal Government attempts to inflate food prices. The inflation after 1970 was due primarily to the printing of fiat money or monetary inflation thus the relatively higher correlation between the derived inflation compound rate and the actual inflation rate after 1970, i.e. 0.87 before 1970 vs. 0.93 after 1970.

The US debt ceiling is ostensibly a legal limit to the printing of money but the government has managed to find ways around this legal limit. The purchase of mortgage backed securities (MBS) by the Federal Reserve Bank at the rate of $42 billion a month from Fannie Mae and Freddie Mac, both being government entities, is one way that the Federal Reserve Bank pumped its fiat currency into the economy in a process known as Quantitative Easing 3 or QE3. Neither Fannie Mae nor Freddie Mac are members of the Federal Reserve System nor are they federal agencies under the Federal Reserve Act. The purchase of their assets by the Federal Reserve is a violation of the Federal Reserve Act and thus illegal. The questionably legal method used by the Federal Reserve Bank to enable its purchases was to establish private limited liability companies (Maiden Lane LLC) and loan these shell companies with the money to purchase the toxic assets from Freddie Mac and Fannie Mae. Toxic assets are non-performing mortgage loans. Purchasing these assets from Freddie Mac and Fannie Mae enabled these GSE's to appear solvent when in fact they were insolvent. The fact that Maiden Lane LLC is a limited liability company means that its legal liability is limited to the assets it owns. The assets that it owns are the non-performing subprime loans. These assets are worth a fraction of the amount paid for them. Therefore, the Federal Reserve Bank will never recover the money that it loaned Maiden Lane, LLC to purchase these loans and everyone knows this. The result is a monetizing of the debt and fiat dollars inserted into the economy placing additional burden on wealth creation.

Prior to 1971, the value of and amount of gold held by a government was the legal limit to the money supply, i.e. the amount of money in circulation and in demand deposits, which are the most liquid assets. Therefore, the use of chained dollars prior to 1971 gives a somewhat biased view of wealth creation in the sense that there was probably more wealth created than the chained numbers show particularly during the period between World War II and 1970. That is, economic inflation drove the CPI more than monetary inflation prior to 1970 or at least until 1966 when the so-called War on Poverty and Civil Rights legislation started to take their toll on the economy.   Unlike monetary inflation, economic inflation is self regulating and less onerous to the creation of wealth in an unencumbered economy.   More about this later but for now I will use the US Bureau of Economic Analysis (BEA) numbers as the measure of inflation during the entire period of the GDP.   Referring back to Figure 17, note the sharp decline in the real GDP that took place between 2007 and 2009.   This decline was 3.1%. The last significant decline, after the 26.3% decline between 1929 and 1933, took place in the aftermath of World War II between 1944 and 1947 where the real gross domestic product declined by 13.4%.   This is attributable to the drastic reduction in the government-spending component following the war.   Heavy borrowing by the government to sustain the war effort accounted for the large government-spending component during the war.   The relatively large government-spending component of the GDP made it appear the economy created wealth during World War II when in fact there was very little wealth created during this period.   The US government never paid back all the money it borrowed from the Federal Reserve Bank to fight World War II.   The government relied on the Federal Reserve Bank to buy debt during the war because the sale to the public was insufficient and there were few other sources available to buy US debt at the time.   The Federal Reserve Bank purchased about 11% of the total debt issued between 1940 and 1947 and at the same time, it started to monetize the debt it owned. Monetizing the debt means that the Federal Reserve Bank simply handed the bonds back to the Treasury when they became due so the government did not have to pay back the money it had borrowed from the Federal Reserve bank during the 1930's.   In so doing, this effectively erased a portion of the national debt without the government having to raise revenue and actually pay back the debt.   The total monetized debt during this period was $832 billion in 2005-chained dollars.   This increased the money supply but it did not contribute much to inflation as the gold supply was sufficient to sustain the additional dollars and thus maintain foreign exchange parity, and also because there was high productivity growth during the war years.   A large part of the productivity growth went towards keeping inflation down rather than creating wealth.   The productivity growth was due primarily to the large number of women who entered the work force and who were willing to accept significantly lower pay than their male counterparts who were now at war.

Although the GDP showed wealth creation between 1942 and 1945 there really was none.   Most of the productive capacity of the nation was going toward the production of war related material.   War related materials are not investments, as they serve no other purpose than for the annihilation and defeat of the enemy, i.e. greater destruction of wealth. There is no macro-economic return on investment in the manufacture of a bomb, nor of any other war expenditure. Although a political argument exists which is that the destruction of the enemy is the return on investment, however in economic terms the destruction of another nation or individual is a reduction in wealth and not a return on investment. The object of war is to prevent the enemy from being able to wage war and this necessarily means destruction of the enemy's wealth creating ability. Note that the real GDP has been on an exponential upward course since 1929 despite the US fighting two major wars and two minor wars over that time as well as having to deal with the rise of worldwide godless communism and its threat to private property during the same period. The latter became the cold war, which the United States won under the brilliant and wise leadership of President Ronald Reagan.

If we were to use the GDP in 1929, which was $1055.6 billion in chained dollars and compound it at a rate of 3.44% we would get the smooth curve shown on the chart in Figure 17 above. The correlation between the actual real GDP and the compounded 1929 value is 0.986. This means that the 3.44% compounded growth rate is almost a perfect representation of real GDP growth since 1929. I refer to the 3.44% growth rate as the real structural growth rate of the US economy. A dollar invested in the US economy in 1928 would be worth about $17.17 in real dollars in 2012 based on the structural growth rate. In other words, that dollar would buy 17 times more and higher quality things today than in 1928. The reason that this happened is due solely to the productivity gains taking place in the economy as reflected in the higher standard of living today, i.e. an easing of life's burden that is the object of wealth creation. The structural growth rate includes the effect of an economy encumbered by taxation and regulation. The growth rate would have been much greater if there were no government interference in the economy. This is apart from the government-spending component, which is a manifestation of the taxation and regulation of the other components. Later I will discuss the burden that the sovereign imposes on wealth creation in terms of the money the government takes from the economy. I will put a number to the government's burden on the economy and show how government spending since 1929 has reduced the nation's ability to survive calamity and the degree to which it has actually impoverished the nation. In other words, despite our current high standard of living, our standard of living relative to 1929 would be 80 times higher except for government greatly encumbering the economy since 1929. (See Appendix 1)

Subtracting government spending from GDP

Earlier I mentioned that a more realistic measure of the wealth creating capability of a nation is to subtract the government-spending component from the sum of the other three components. This takes into considerations the reality that government income comes from the other three components through taxation and therefore is a burden to the other components of the economy and a burden to wealth creation. It also takes into account the fact that government produces or creates nothing for the money it forcibly takes and then spends. In other words, the government does not create profit, which is wealth. Figure 19 below shows the real GDP with government spending subtracted from the other three components.

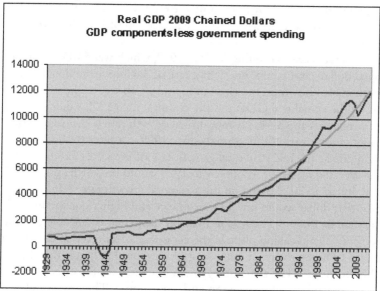

Figure 19-GDP less Government Spending

When we subtract government spending from the other components, it becomes clear that World War II actually resulted in the destruction of wealth as the GDP now becomes negative during the war years. This is reflective of reality and consistent with common sense rather than the idea that the destruction engendered by World War II somehow helped the economy, which it did not. Nevertheless, the government and many economists and historians who earn their living from government largess continue to espouse the flawed idea that World War II brought the United States out of the depression. Many Keynesians continue to espouse this notion arguing that only a world war on the scale of World War II will get us out of the current economic malaise. This illustrates the vacuous mentality of the Keynesians and their leftist adherents. When viewed in this manner, i.e. with government spending a burden on the economy, then the structural growth rate of the US economy since 1929 is 3.36% rather than 3.44%. The other three components of the GDP, i.e. personal consumption, investment spending and net of imports and exports grew at a compound rate of 3.47%. Thus, government spending actually reduced the compounded rate of growth of the economy by at least 0.11 percentage points which is the difference between the growth of the private sector and the growth of the private sector less government spending. During the same time-period, the spending of government rose at the structural rate of 3.89% or much faster than the growth in the other components of the GDP. This had the effect of further burdening the economy and destroying wealth creation by siphoning off cash from the productive sector faster than the growth of the productive sector. The difference between the higher structural growth rate of government and the private economy manifests in the inflation rate. Government spending is the main contributing factor to total inflation and the reason that we must use real dollars rather than nominal dollars to analyze an economy.

Total government expenditures

As I have said, the government-spending component of the GDP does not represent all government spending. It does not include interest payments on debt and Federal transfer payments, i.e. money taken from the taxpayer or borrowed and given to the non-taxpayer or rather the non-producer with nothing in return. Transfer payments include social security, Medicare, and welfare payments. The following chart compares the Federal government-spending component of GDP with total Federal government spending as well as total government outlays, which includes state and local governments since 1995. The comparisons are in chained 2005 dollars

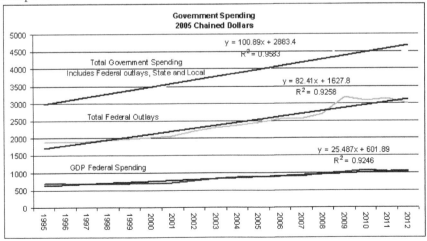

Figure 20-Total Government Outlays

Figure 20 shows that since 1995 total federal government outlays have grown much faster than the federal government-spending part of the GDP. On a linear trend line basis the rate of growth of total federal government outlays is about 3.23 times faster than the rate of growth of the GDP government-spending component since 1995. I calculate this using the ratio of the x-coefficients in the trend line equations, which is the slope of the trend lines. In other words since 1995 the federal government's total outlays increased at the average rate of about $82.4 billion per year whereas the government spending reported as part of the GDP increased at an average rate of about $25.5 billion per year. Total government spending in 2012 including Federal outlays and State and Local government, was almost $4.5 trillion dollars in an $11.1 trillion dollars private economy. In order to sustain this level of spending, the government (federal, state and local) must take 40% of the productivity, and therefore the wealth creating ability, of the nation. Government and in particular the Federal government does this in two ways first by taxation and second by inflating the currency. This of course means there is 40% less wealth or surplus available for commerce. Just as in the case where the feudal lord takes the surplus of the serf's labor and leaves little for the next year planting, or for trade, the reduction in the wealth created lowers the ability of the nation to withstand calamity as well as increasing the burden on individuals. This burden eventually leads to civil unrest as it threatens the survival of individuals because calamity is inevitable.

Interest rates reflect government burden and interference in the economy

After 1971, interest rates as well as inflation more directly relate to government interference in the economy as that was the year that the United States abrogated the Bretton-Woods agreement, and the fiat currency was born. Nineteen seventy-one was the year when inflation began to grow at an unprecedented rate for the United States. Figure 21 compares the bank prime interest rate between 1956 and 2012 with the interest rate on Moody's AAA corporate bonds, and CPI.

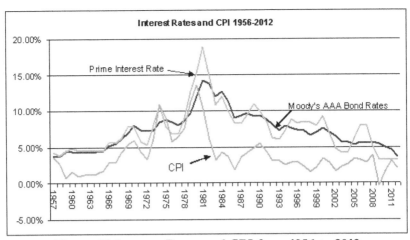

Figure 21-Interest Rates and CPI from 1956 to 2012

Note that the CPI is the primary driver of interest rates, and the CPI is a function of government interference, and coercion in the form of union demands. The Federal Government negated common law by sanctioning union contracts under the Wagner Act. I will discuss the Wagner Act in more detail later. Interest rates have historically been greater than inflation except for a brief period in the high inflation years during the 1970s and after the abrogation of the Bretton-Woods agreement. US inflation was growing at the fastest rate in modern history during this period.

Despite the Bretton-Woods agreement, governments continued to print money at a faster rate than justified by the value and quantity of gold in the world and some monetary inflation existed prior to 1971, nevertheless the Bretton-Woods agreement served as a nominal limit to the amount of money printed. As seen in Figure 22 the difference in the relative level of M2 and the relative level of gold in the US Treasury has fluctuated. The difference increased after 1934 continuing to increase until 1940 during the government's failed attempt to inflate the currency to overcome the decline in food prices.

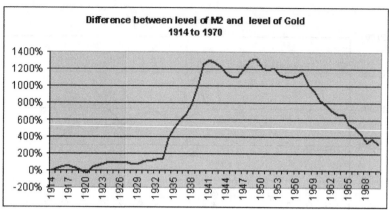

Figure 22 – Difference between level of M2 and level of Gold between 1914 and 1970

Note how the difference between M2 and the level of gold held by the US Treasury started to decline in 1960 as the United States tried to maintain the world's exchange rates by selling gold as Federal spending accelerated during the 1960's. The function of the US Treasury prior to 1971 and under Bretton-Woods was to increase or decrease the money supply to maintain the constant market value of gold at $35.00 an ounce and in the process maintain a constant foreign exchange value of all currencies tied to the dollar. Thus if the price of gold were to go up the US Treasury would sell gold to drive its price back to the $35.00 level and increase the money supply. If the demand for gold decreased and its price dropped then the Treasury would buy gold and thereby decrease the money supply. This was equivalent to maintaining trade balances during the time that gold was the reserve currency. Thus, the money supply fluctuated under the gold standard but it fluctuated for different reason than it does now. The problem that occurred in the 1960's that forced the US to abrogate the Bretton-Woods agreement was mainly the radical increases in government spending primarily for burdensome social programs enacted under the law, which are beyond the original scope of government as I have presented it here. This government spending was for Lyndon Johnson's Great Society Programs like the failed so-called War on Poverty, Civil Rights legislation, as well as the escalating cost of the Vietnam War with the former two much more of a factor than the latter. The United States had to sell gold in order to counter the decline in the value of the dollar reflected in upward pressure on gold prices. The decline in the value of the dollar was due to the inefficiencies introduced into the economy by the government through higher taxes, increased regulation as well as aggressive union demands for more benefits and higher wages during the 1960's and 1970's. The Treasury was quickly running out of gold to sell and so the price of gold was set to skyrocket thereby collapsing the economy. At the time, politicians obviously thought that this was a worst scenario than abrogating the Bretton-Woods agreement and creating the fiat currency. Despite the abrogation of the Bretton-Woods agreement, the price of gold did increase and inflation did emerge with the US suffering its worst inflation in history during the 1970's. The nominal market price of an ounce of gold went from $36.02 in 1970 to $615.00 ten years later. Once again, as was the case during the 1930s, the Keynesians thought they could manage the economy but they were wrong and all they did was to destroy wealth. The point however is had the United States not undertaken the profligate social spending and unprecedented regulation and encumbering of the economy during the Johnson administration followed by even more interference in the economy by the Carter administration, the nation would not have suffered as it did and the economy would have created much wealth despite the Vietnam War. Indeed the United States would have won the Viet Nam War and in all likelihood, there would not have been a Pol-Pot and the murder of millions of Cambodians. The Soviet Union would have collapsed much sooner as well. Labor union coercion of companies for more benefits and higher wages unjustified by their productivity during the 1960s and 1970s added to the collapse of the economy by further fueling inflation. Democrat administrations, which have supported and promoted the interference of the government in the economy since the beginning of the twentieth century, have undermined wealth creation, robbed individuals and corporations of their productivity with no corresponding increase in the protection of private property or the proper enforcement of contracts. The Democrats have impoverished the nation. The question is how did it happen that the Democrats achieved the political power to effectively destroy a great nation. The answer is universal suffrage, and the engendering of godlessness in law and in culture giving rise to envy as the fear of God dissipated in the populace. Envy manifested in demands for more benefits from the government through universal suffrage, and greater wages from companies through the enforcement of union contracts and not justified by their productivity. The passion of envy only satiates when the object envied no longer exists and this is the objective of the godless socialists and the unionists. Thus, the aim of envy is the destruction of the wealth of others to spite them and not simply the taking of their wealth. The envious Democrats and godless liberals did indeed destroy wealth during the late 1960's and 1970's and the nation continues to suffer as a result. I will have more to say about this later in the book.

The gold standard imposed fiscal and monetary discipline on the government

Under a gold standard, the value of the currency is a function of the productive capacity of the economy. It is a measure of wealth creation.   Hence, as the currency remains more or less constant in value then the more money the greater the wealth and the amount of money in the economy is then a measure of wealth creation.   In an inflationary economy, more money does not correspond to more wealth.   An ounce of gold whose value did not fluctuate bought more goods and services as more and different types of goods and services became available, and therein is the correlation between wealth creation and money as the means of exchange.   The source of all goods and services is the human intellect manifested in the exercise of freewill.   In other words, the source of goods and services or the source of wealth is free enterprise. Thus, under Bretton-Woods the money supply reflected to a large degree the creation of wealth and not inflation.   The gold standard effectively imposed fiscal and monetary discipline on the government.   The abrogation of the Bretton-Woods agreement unleashed a much more rapid increase in the money supply and inflation because there were no limits on the money supply other than that which the Federal Reserve Bank decided by fiat.   Congress further politicized the Federal Reserve Bank on November 16, 1977, when it amended the Federal Reserve Act to require the Board and the FOMC *"to promote effectively the goals of maximum employment, stable prices, and moderate long-term interest rates."*   This amendment effectively opened the money-printing spigot and the money has been pouring out ever since as reflected in the unprecedented increase in the price of gold over this time and to the present day.

Federal Reserve Act Amended by Congress to enable political accommodation

The Federal Reserve Bank increasingly based its decisions on political rather than economic considerations.   Following the abrogation of the Bretton-Woods Agreement, Congress amended the Federal Reserve Act beginning in 1977 to enable the Federal Reserve Bank to respond to political pressure.   Specifically as I indicated it added 12 USC 225a directing the Federal Reserve Bank to *"...maintain long run growth of the monetary and credit aggregates commensurate with the economy's long run potential to increase production, so as to promote effectively the goals of maximum employment, stable prices, and moderate long-term interest rates...".* [1] The Federal Reserve turned its attention to regulating the economy through manipulation of interest rates as well as manipulating the money supply, and it was encouraged to do this by politicians who benefitted from government largess.   Now the government has a license to spend money by borrowing it from the Federal Reserve Bank.   Since government

---

[1] Dec. 23, 1913, ch. 6, §2A, as added Pub. L. 95–188, title II, §202, Nov. 16, 1977, 91 Stat. 1387; amended Pub. L. 95–523, title I, §108(a), Oct. 27, 1978, 92 Stat. 1897; Pub. L. 100–418, title III, §3005(c), Aug. 23, 1988, 102 Stat. 1375; Pub. L. 106–569, title X, §1003(a), Dec. 27, 2000, 114 Stat. 3028.

spending is unproductive, it results in inflation.   The Federal Reserve Bank accommodates government spending by setting an inflation target heretofore unannounced.   In 2012 for the first time, the Federal Reserve publically announced that its inflationary target was between 1.7% and 2%.   The actual compound inflation rate in terms of the CPI between 1971 and 2012 is 4.73% with a correlation coefficient of 0.93.   Thus, the current inflationary target as announced by the Federal Reserve Bank is much less than its historical result since after 1971 or after the abrogation of the Bretton-Woods agreement.   Prior to 1971, the compound inflation rate from 1930 to 1971 was 1.73% with a correlation coefficient 0.94.   This was primarily economic inflation.   In other words after the United States left the gold standard in 1971, the compound rate of inflation was 2.7 times greater in the subsequent 40-year period vs. the prior 40 year period.   It is the height of irony that the Federal Reserve would announce a target inflation range in 2012 corresponding to the inflation range when the nation was on the gold standard thus effectively returning to the gold standard.   This is an admission of the failure of fiat money and a vindication of the gold standard.   There is no assurance that the Federal Reserve Bank will maintain this target since there is no law to regulate the money supply, and the Federal Reserve Bank has already violated its charter by buying non-performing mortgage backed securities through QE3.   Consequently, the Federal Reserve Bank remains a risk to the economy and to the ability to create wealth despite its lofty pronouncements about the economy and its inflation "targets".

     There is no better example of the ability of productivity growth to overcome inflation than in the years after the collapse of the financial equity markets in 2008.   At that time, the DJIA lost over 50% of its value between October of 2007 and March of 2009.   The bank losses alone in the US and Europe were estimated at about $2.8 trillion.   This does not include the loss in value of all the other tangible assets such as homes, and commercial real estate.   It took over 4 years for the DJIA to recover its lost value.   During this period, the Federal Reserve Bank added over $2 trillions to its reserve.   The Federal Reserve Bank has thus far printed $2.8 trillion that went toward the purchase of US Treasury debt and toward the purchase of so-called toxic assets, which were underperforming mortgages or defaulted mortgages thus inserting unearned or fiat dollars into the banking system (see Federal Reserve Table FRB-H41 available on-line).   The Federal Reserve Bank continued this policy with no end in sight as of the end of 2013 and into 2014. This money indirectly and directly enabled the stock market to recover its losses from the financial crises.   However, the general economy did not grow fast enough to sustain the vaulted equity market, i.e. there was little real revenue growth for most companies during this period.   This was due in large part to the government's continued interference in the economy through high levels of spending, low interest rates, increasing

taxes, and onerous regulations.   Comparing the stock market
performance and GDP growth between 2008 and 2012 the GDP grew
4.3% whereas the DJIA grew over 100%, i.e. recovered its level from its
collapse in 2008.   This is not real growth in wealth.   It is simply the
restoring of asset values to previous levels.   Between 2000 and 2007, the
GDP grew 18% while the DJIA grew about 25%. Thus during the latest
period, i.e. 2008 and 2012 the DJIA grew out of all proportion to the
growth of the GDP.   A growing GDP means revenue growth for
corporations.   Corporate profits between 2008 and 2012 grew 61% or
on the average 15% a year and between 2000 and 2007 corporate profits
grew 110% or on the average about 15% a year as well.   Thus, despite
the slow growth in the economy, which translates to low real revenue
growth for corporations, corporate earnings, for the most part, were able
to sustain the increase valuation brought about by the printing of money
by the Federal Reserve Bank.   Corporate profits reflect this somewhat in
the average one-year earnings Price/Earning ratios.   The average S&P
P/E for corporations was 21.5 between 2008 and 2012 and 26.8 between
2000 and 2007.   This indicates that earnings were more than adequate to
sustain the elevated asset valuations in the later period despite the 1%
average annual growth rate of the economy in general.   Some of the gain
in P/E is also due to about 20% of the S&P companies using their
earnings to purchase their own stock increasing the per share earnings.
Thus, rather than invest in growing the company, which would create
jobs and opportunities, corporate earnings went to maintaining asset
valuations.

Since the earnings did not come from a growing economy, i.e.
revenue growth, then they must have come from productivity gains that
in turn led to reductions in employment.   The reductions in employment
were significant during the interval between 2007-2012 with the level of
able-bodied individuals employed dropping 2.45% or at an average annual
rate of -0.05%.   On the other hand, between 2000 and 2007
employment grew 8.25% or at an average annual rate of 1.18%.   This
represented a 142% increase in the annual rate of job loss from 2007 to
2012 than from 2000 to 2007 and it accounts for the increase in corporate
earnings in the absence of growth in the economy during the period after
the collapse of the financial markets.   The Federal Reserve Bank
effectively injected money into the equity markets increasing equity prices
and managing to make up for the monetary losses incurred from the
financial crises.   The price that the economy paid was the loss of a
significant number of jobs and a significant increase in the number of
unemployed individuals.   It was not the number of jobs that was the
only casualty of the Federal Reserve Bank's action but also the median
household income, which declined by 4.17% since the Federal Reserve
Bank's actions in 2009.   Since the collapse in the financial markets in
2008 and until 2012, the drop in real median household income was

116

8.20%. Table 3 summarizes the pre-collapse and post collapse economies.

Economic Factor	2000-2007	2007-2012
	Pre collapse	Post collapse
Gain in DJIA	25%	100%
Average annual gain in GDP	4.3%	1%
Gain in Federal Reserve Assets	$0.16 Trillion (EOY 2002- EOY 2007)	$2.95 Trillion (EOY 2007- Nov 2013)
Value of Bank Assets Lost		$2.8 Trillion (Europe and US Banks)
Percent change employed individuals	8.25%	-2.45%
Percent change in median income	-0.8%	-8.20%

Table 3 - Comparison of the 2000-2007 Economy with the 2008-2012 Economy

The combined loss in the level of employment and the decline in the real medium income accounts for the apparent lack of any significant inflation since 2008. In other words, productivity gains during this period manifested in two ways. One way was through a reduction in the quantity of physical labor required to perform a unit of work, which translated into fewer paid employees in the workforce. The other way was a significant reduction in median income.

Community Reinvestment Act – an example of regulatory encumbrance

No better example exists of regulatory encumbrance of an economy with the subsequent destruction of wealth by government regulation and taxation than the 1978 Community Reinvestment Act (CRA) and the collapse of the financial sector of the economy in 2008 that it engendered. The federal government interference in the economy through the aggressive enforcement of the CRA of 1978 by Clinton during the 1990s created the subprime mortgage market. This is what Clinton meant when he said he was going to end welfare "as we know it". Individuals formerly on welfare acquired subprime loans with no down payment required, and little, if any verification of the ability to pay. The Federal government under Clinton and Attorney General Janet Reno coerced lending institutions through threats of prosecution under the CRA into entering the sub-prime market and approving these loans. This enabled Clinton and the Democrat Party to maintain and support an important constituency, i.e. the former welfare recipients. Lenders responded to this unprecedented coercion by their government by creating new financial instruments called Collaterized Debt Obligations or CDOs. The word "collaterized" did not even exist in the English language prior to the sub-prime market. These CDOs were bundles of performing mortgages combined with subprime mortgages creating a return on investment predicated on a certain percentage of defaults expected to occur. Nevertheless, the relatively high mortgage rates at the time provided a competitive return to investors despite the small percentage of losses expected to occur. Increasingly the CDO became more complex in terms of which mortgages were performing and which were not performing or underperforming. To protect investments in the face of the uncertainty in CDOs a new market emerged to insure the CDO and large insurers such as AIG underwrote the CDO. In order to enable sub-prime (read unqualified) borrowers to afford the mortgages many of the mortgages sold were adjustable rate, or ARM and balloon type mortgages. These types of mortgages came into existence due to the government-induced inflation of the 1970's and were popular in the relatively high interest rates existing in the 1980s and 1990s. Once again interference in the economy by the Federal Reserve Bank emerged in 2000 when the then Chairman Alan Greenspan unjustifiably raised interest rates to stem the rising stock market. Greenspan's flawed idea was that rising asset values such as were occurring would engender inflation despite no empirical or theoretical evidence that this would happen, and yet he set about to undermine equity prices by rapidly increasing interest rates. In fact, the rise in the equity markets, after the collapse in 2008 with no inflation is evidence as to how wrong Greenspan really was at the time. The effect of rapidly rising interest rates was to crash the market rather than slowing its rise as he expected. A now obviously panicky Greenspan turned quickly to lowering interest rates to unprecedented low rates and this spurred more ARMs and balloon loans to subprime borrowers. The demand for housing increased and housing prices increased rapidly as interest rates fell to historic lows, thus creating a building boom in residential housing that was to come to a disastrous and sudden end in 2008.

When interest rates started to rise in the middle of the 2000 decade, many of the subprime ARMs and balloon mortgages started to default jeopardizing investments in CDOs causing insurers such as AIG to fill the gap. In the end, the losses were greater than the insurance companies could handle and the financial markets collapsed as companies sold stocks to make up the difference. This was similar to 1929 where the inability to pay on loan contracts also brought down the market in 1929. The sub-prime market led directly to the collapse of the financial system and the destruction of trillions of dollars in wealth. Yet despite this the government through pressure on the Federal Reserve Bank continued to interfere in the economy in the aftermath of the financial collapse by forcing interest rates once again to historically low levels through the injection of trillions of dollars into the economy. The injection of trillions of fiat dollars into a highly productive economy resulted in historically high unemployment bringing on poverty and the inevitable even greater destruction of wealth. Again, the similarity between the mortgage crises in 2008 to the events leading to the Great Depression is remarkable. In both cases, the government inflated the currency in an environment of rapid productivity growth, and in both cases, this led to great unemployment and the destruction of wealth as productivity gains offset the underlying inflation rather than create wealth. The Democrats even had the audacity to pass legislation that placed even greater regulation on the banks thus further encumbering the economy and effectively adding to the destruction of wealth and unemployment. The Dodd-Frank Act made it even more difficult and expensive for banks to conduct their business.   Thus, even in a historically low interest environment the banks could not, or would not, give loans even to otherwise qualified borrowers.   It appears now that the Federal Government has abandoned its only legitimate purpose and is now on the path toward destroying life and property that individuals originally created government to secure and protect.   Accordingly, this government is ripe for rebellion.

The Actual Burden of Government

      I will now set upon determining the actual burden of total government spending including Federal, state and local government on the US economy.   I will do this by using two scenarios.   The first scenario assumes no government spending or that government spending was zero since 1929.   I will thereby assume that government did not exist and determine the potential wealth creation.   Under this first scenario, I invested all government receipts since 1929 in 10-year corporate Aaa bonds in each year of the receipts at the average interest rate for that year.   The average interest rate is as determined by Moody's Aaa 10 year corporate bond rate in each year.   After 10 years, I reinvest the principle and interest at the average interest rate for the year that the 10-year bond expired or became due, repeating this process for each year since 1929.   I also assume there was no World War II and indeed, if there were no government, there would not have been a war.   I took all the government receipts for the war and invested it in the economy instead.   This did not include money that the Federal Government borrowed to help finance the war.   I use constant 1929 dollars to conduct the analysis.   I determined 1929 constant dollars by taking the nominal value of each year's outlays and discounting it at the GDP price deflators (2009 =1) to 1929 and applying it to government receipts.   To determine the discount factor I took the ratio of the GDP price deflator in 1929, which was 0.0991 and divided it by the GDP price deflator for each of the years after 1929.   This eliminated inflation and all dollars are 1929 constant dollars.   It assumes inflation is entirely due to government interference in the economy, which I have indicated is a reasonable assumption.   I invested each year's expenditure in the 10-year Aaa corporate bonds in the manner described above.   The actual values that I used along with an explanation are in Appendix 1.   The result of investing all government receipts in the private economy is a total return of $166 trillion in 2012 in 1929 constant dollars. The GDP in 2012 in 1929 constant dollars is $1.6 trillion. In other words with no local, state or federal government and all tax revenue invested in the private economy since 1929 the nation would be over 100 times wealthier than it is now. This wealth would have eliminated all poverty, pollution and crime. Instead, we have much poverty, pollution and crime because of government. This is the true burden of government.

However, we do need government to protect private property and enforce contracts. In our second scenario, we assume that the government was able to operate effectively in 1929 with the revenue it received at that time. Obviously, the government was able to perform at least these two functions in 1929 with revenue of $10.4 billion in constant 1929 dollars, so it is reasonable that this amount is all the government needs to provide these functions. Any amount greater than $10.4 billion is overburdening the economy beyond its basic functions and therefore unnecessarily reducing the amount of wealth created. Assuming that all the revenue between 1941 and 1945 went to fighting World War II, then maintaining government spending at 1929 levels would have resulted in a total return of $124 trillion in 2012 in constant 1929 dollars. This means that the nation would be 80 times wealthier than it is now and the government would have protected private property and enforced contracts.

Another way to place the actual burden of government into perspective is to determine how many ounces of gold the nominal GDP will buy at the nominal price of gold. This effectively eliminates the effects of monetary inflation, since the price of gold is more tied to monetary inflation than it is to economic inflation. Figure 23 shows the relationship between the CPI level and the nominal price of gold from 1929 to 2012. Note that prior to 1970 the price of gold was independent of the CPI and that after 1970 at the time the United States went off the gold standard the price of gold increased with the CPI. This was monetary inflation during a time of low productivity arising from government interference in the economy during the late 1960s and the 1970s. The relationship between the CPI and the price of gold lasted until 1981. Between 1981 and 2004 there was little monetary inflation hence the price of gold was independent of the CPI and productivity went toward creating wealth. After 2004, the relationship once again emerged as the government started to print more money and productivity went toward offsetting inflation rather than creating wealth.

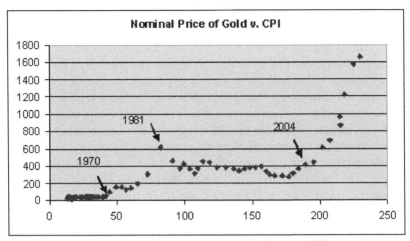

Figure 23 – Nominal Price of Gold v. CPI

Figure 24 shows that the amount of gold purchased by the GDP has fallen precipitously since 2001. The current level is the same as it was in 1950.

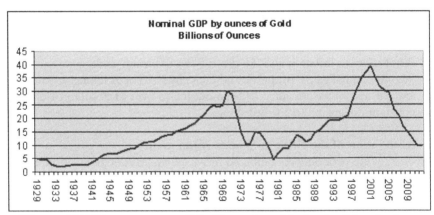

Figure 24-Billions ounces of Gold purchasable by the Nominal GDP

Note that the amount of gold purchased by the GDP in nominal terms is approaching the value that existed in 1950. This means that we are now close to the position that we were in 1950 in terms of wealth. The reason for this is the burden of government whose purpose was to protect private property and enforce contracts. Instead, the government has effectively consumed almost all wealth created since 1950 and the private economy has been left with the crumbs off the table. This is a calamity of unprecedented proportions brought upon the nation by its government.

Laws that mandate terms and conditions in a contract encumber the economy

Laws requiring terms and conditions be added to a contract encumber an economy because they go against the freewill of the parties to the contract. In many cases, such laws prevent the formation of contracts and agreements that would otherwise lead to wealth creation. Environmental law for example operates to reduce the expected return on an investment, and in the case of a marginal investment, the reduction in the expected return may prevent the investment from even consummating. The aggregate effect is such as to reduce significantly the potential for wealth creation. Other laws of this kind include but are not limited to the Wagner Act of 1935 aka the National Labor Relations Act, the Civil Rights Act of 1964, Affirmative Action Executive Order in 1961, The Community Reinvestment Act of 1977, The Endangered Species Act, OSHA, and tariffs. Encumbering laws also include sales taxes, minimum wage or prevailing wage laws, and indirect subsidies to unproductive industries such as the so-called green technology industries. These specific laws and similar laws that introduce terms and conditions into a contract against the freewill of the parties to the contract result in the prices for goods and services to be independent of supply and demand thus encumbering the economy. By assuming zero inflation in my previous analysis on the burden of government, I am also taking into account the absence of these laws because these laws contribute as much if not more to inflation and the destruction of wealth as do taxes on income, capital gains, property, and dividends. The resulting inflation and the loss of wealth since 1929 amounted to over $120 trillion 1929 constant dollars in 2013 GDP alone.

Abrogation of the Bretton-Woods Agreement

An economy encumbered by excessive taxation, regulation, and labor unions creates little or no wealth and such an economy and the nation is vulnerable to calamity. Such calamities have occurred. For instance, the bankruptcy of the steel, rubber, and automobile companies and the collapse of these industries were a direct result of the Wagner Act of 1935, which empowered the government to enforce labor contracts executed against the will of the employer. The collapse of these once great wealth- creating industries manifests in the utter destruction of once great cities as Detroit, Youngstown, and Akron.

A calamity also occurred in 2008 when the economy was unable to absorb the relentless governmental interference and regulation of the financial sector brought upon in large part by the Community Reinvestment Act of 1978 and its subsequent revisions resulting in the eventual collapse of this most important sector of the economy. Therefore, government encumbrances on an economy are unethical. For the United States economy, since 1929, such encumbrances have been profound reducing wealth creation to one eightieth of that which it might have been.

Apart from the laws, regulations, and taxes that have encumbered the United States economy since 1929 there is also the inflationary effect of the fiat currency. As you will recall, the fiat currency came into existence in 1971 when President Nixon took the United States off the de-jure gold standard known as the Bretton-Woods agreement signed toward the end of World War II by all the free nations in 1944. The Bretton-Woods agreement essentially fixed the price of gold at $35.00 an ounce. The unprecedented expansion of government under the disastrous and failed Johnson administration during the 1960s caused a drain on the US gold reserves as the US tried to maintain dollar parity with gold in accordance with the Bretton-Woods agreement. The government printed money, i.e. went into debt rather than raise taxes significantly to finance the expansion of government that took place under Johnson. Note that raising taxes and printing money have the same negative effect on the economy. The only difference is that there is a short-term political price for raising taxes while printing money is a much more subtle and less politically liable way to take wealth from the population. Indeed inflationary pressures in the United States due primarily to the implementation of Johnson's and the Democrats' disastrous social programs, as well as the expansion of existing New Deal social programs such as Social Security in the 1960s began to take hold by the 1970s. The decline in the gold reserves at the time threatened an even greater inflation rate unless the government took action. However as we saw earlier there is no action that a government can take to undo its damage to the economy other than through repeal of what it has done. Nonetheless, the government took action. It was the wrong action as it was not the repeal of the inflationary laws, and which predictably only made matters worse. The action that it took was to refuse to exchange US dollars for gold thereby unilaterally abrogating the Bretton-Woods Agreement and effectively removing the dollar and thus the rest of the world's currencies from the gold standard. Nixon also implemented a disastrous short-term attempt at price controls to counter the resulting inflation that also predictably failed to curtail inflation and resulted in shortages of various commodities including food. Currencies now floated in value relative to each other. This abrogation of the Bretton-Woods agreement gave license to the printing of money by the Federal Reserve Bank and other central banks as well. The printing of money manifested itself through the purchases of the securities or the debt issued by the US Treasury. Normally the public purchases the securities offered by the Treasury for sale at competitive interest rates. That is the US Treasury competes with other issuers of debt such as corporations and municipalities, and the interest rates are set by the market for debt. From the end of World War II until the middle 1960's, the public purchased between 80% and 90% of government debt at competitive interest rates. This served as a loose control over the printing of money, because as demand for credit increased so did the interest rates and the higher interest rates discouraged debt. Beginning in the late 1960's the Federal Reserve Bank was buying between 25% and 30% of government debt. Figure 24 illustrates the growth of US government debt and the proportion owned by the public. The difference is the printing of money by the Federal Reserve Bank to purchase the debt not purchased by the public. The result of the Federal Reserves Bank's actions is to hold interest rates artificially low by adding significantly to the supply of creditors to the market. As the supply of creditors increase the price of the commodity supplied, i.e. interest rate goes down.

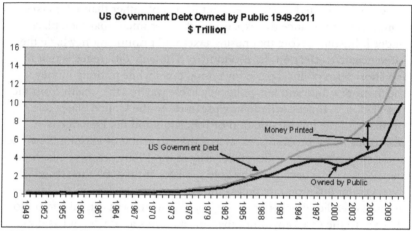

Figure 25-US Government Debt and Debt Owned by the Public

Figure 26 is the average monthly prime interest rates over this same period. Note the decline in interest rates beginning in the early 1970s as the amount of debt owned by the Federal Reserve Bank increased. The printing of money by the Federal Reserve Bank reduced interest rates, but higher inflation was the price paid. This translated to historically high interest rates in the late 1970s. Interest rates dropped when the Federal Reserve Bank stopped printing money in the early 1980's. Interest rates have remained relatively low through the present time, i.e. from 2008 to 2014 despite increasing government debt. This is due to accelerating productivity gains that began in the 1980s and continue to this day.

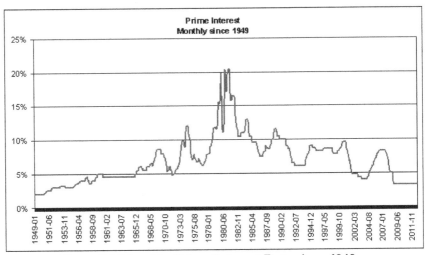

Figure 26-Monthly Prime Interest Rate since 1949

The price of gold

Since 1971, the market price of gold has fluctuated depending on the rate of inflation. That is, the price of gold is a good barometer of the underlying inflation rate of an economy. Converting the GDP to the ounces of gold that the GDP can buy at any point in time effectively removes the effects of inflation, and provides a measure of the wealth that the economy is creating in absolute or, in other words, real terms.

Referring back to Figure 24, note the decline in wealth in terms of gold occurring in the decade following the stock market crash of 1929. Much of this decline is attributable to the actions of the Federal Government at the time including, increases in corporate taxes, increased tariffs on imported products competing with the overly productive farm sector, and increasing unionization. The economy started to recover by the beginning of World War II with the effective repeal of the Smoot-Hawley Tariff in 1934, and a more passive union appeased with the enactment of the Wagner Act, and as World War II loomed. There was no new wealth created during the war years as the productive capacity during the war years went to overcoming the inflation engendered by the calamity of war. This accounts for the flat portion of the GDP-gold curve during the war years. After the war, the economy created increasing wealth despite relatively high tax rates and increased unionization and active unions. The high productivity during the post war years is attributable to the fact that most of the other major world economies were completely devastated during the war. As a result, the US had virtual monopoly pricing power in a large number of industries during this period. The lack of foreign competition eventually led to inefficiencies in the form of increasing demands by unions and increasing regulation by the Federal government during the 1960s, which protected the politically favored industries from competition. The inefficiencies fully manifested in the inflation of 1970's. Once the rest of the industrialized nations recovered from the war and competition emerged in industries such as the automobile, steel, rubber, and electronic manufacturing industries then the years of regulations and unionization caught up with the US economy. This is exactly the pattern occurring after World War I that affected mainly agriculture. This time the effect of increasing foreign competition was in the manufacturing industries, and occurred about 20 years after the Second World War or in the span of one generation. This was also the time that much of the political hubris arising from almost uninterrupted growth after World War II manifested itself in social legislation and regulations favoring vocal and economically unproductive political constituencies with total disregard of the effects of this political legislation and regulation on the economy as a whole. The favored political constituencies include the unionists, environmentalist, the Negroid, and the spinster, i.e. feminist, who together contribute very little to the burden of the sovereign or the creation of wealth yet expect and demand special benefits and special protections from the sovereign. Lurking behind much of the wealth destroying legislation and regulation foisted on the US economy were the socialists and atheists who populated much of academia, the media, and the highest level of government including the judiciary. Thus while the motivation of the aforementioned political groups may have appeared economic, the real driver for social and environmental legislation was envy of the wealthy. The combination of high taxes, increased government regulation mainly in the form of the aforementioned social legislation, and regulations came to a head with the abrogation of the Bretton-Woods Agreement in 1971 bringing about a significant decline in the creation of wealth as shown in Figure 24 above. It is no coincidence, that two years later in 1973 the Supreme Court ruled in Roe v. Wade that no law can bar abortion. Eleven years earlier the Supreme Court also ruled against prayer in public school in a case bought before the court by an atheist. Universal suffrage enabled the institutionalization of atheism and Stoicism in the nation and with it, envy was unleashed leading to the social legislation of the 1960's, the fiat currency and human sacrifice, i.e. abortion. Atheism, Stoicism, and their handmaiden envy has been gnawing away at wealth creation and steering the nation toward socialism ever since but for a brief and significant respite during the 1980s.

At the beginning of the 1980s the economy once again began to create wealth at rates higher than ever before with the lower taxes, industry deregulation, declining unions and tepid enforcement of the burdensome social legislation enacted during the failed Johnson and Carter Administrations. These were the hallmarks of President Reagan's immensely successful administration during the 1980s. President Reagan's administration proved to a candid world the utter bankruptcy of the socialist and leftist ideology. This increasing wealth creation continued until the year 2000, where once again the government driven by the envious in the manner of the Federal Reserve Bank interfered in the economy by causing interest rates to spike during that year when there was little inflation or unemployment to justify such interference. This time the Federal Reserve Bank under Alan Greenspan exceeded its legal authority when it decided to undermine the rapid increase in asset valuations occurring in the last part of the 1990s, ostensibly fearing that such a rapid increase would cause inflation like the 1970s. This was probably the biggest mistake ever made by the bungling Federal Reserve Bank up to that point. Although in retrospect, it may not have been a mistake but rather a deliberate act to satiate the envy of those well placed and not benefiting from the wealth creation engendered by the productivity gains at the time. The irony is the printing of money by the Federal Reserve Bank caused inflation during the 1970's with little increase in asset valuations. The increase of asset valuations occurred independent of monetary infusions by the Federal Reserve Bank during the late 1980s and the 1990s. In other words, unlike the current environment, where the Federal Reserve Bank is printing money to prop up equities, the stock market in the 1990s was rising because of individuals investing in new technology and the resulting gains in productivity. By contrast, the Federal Reserve Bank has been printing money to prop up stock prices since 2008 yet there is little inflation from the rise of the stock market. Nevertheless, in 1999 the sudden and unjustified rise in interest rates engendered by the Federal Reserve Bank had the effect of reducing the wealth creating capacity of the nation causing the stock market to loose 50% of its value in about one year. Greenspan saw his great error, panicked and overcorrected when he began to reduce interest rates every month to the lowest levels in history at the time. The subsequent rapid reduction in interest rates set the stage for the collapse of the financial sector in 2008 thus accelerating the decline in the ability of the economy to create wealth in terms of the amount of gold the economy can buy. As the above Figure 24 shows, the level of wealth creation is now approaching the level that existed in 1950. The interference in the economy by the sovereign, i.e. the Federal government was to effectively erase the accumulated wealth of over 60 years and make the nation increasingly susceptible to calamity. As atheism and Stoicism as driven by the government, the educational establishment, and the media has become increasingly prevalent and entrenched in the national psyche envy has taken root. The death of God brings envy and mendacity to life. Envy of those benefiting from gains in productivity and manifested in universal suffrage drove a large part of the destruction of wealth that occurred in 2000 and then in 2008.

Returning to the gold standard will result in the creation of wealth

Clearly, the way to increase the rate of wealth creation and return to prosperity, and therefore secure the future of the United States is for the government to reestablish the gold standard, and repeal the Federal Reserve Act of 1913 in total.   The Federal government must return to coining money consistent with productivity and not printing money to satiate envy and sovereign greed.   These acts would introduce monetary and fiscal discipline in both the banking system and the Federal government.   Such discipline is necessary to rein in envy's effect and for the creation of wealth.   The government must sell all government assets and land not directly engaged in the protection of private property using the proceeds to pay off the debt.   This includes land designated as monuments.   The government must also privatize all other functions such as Social Security, Medicare and other programs, i.e. laws that take money from one group of people and giving it to another.   Privatization of these programs would enable economic decisions regarding the funding and operation of these programs independent of political considerations.   Revenue used to fund these programs would not fund other programs and the private sector would invest the money in productive enterprises instead.   The nation must repeal the 16th Amendment to the Constitution, which authorized the income tax, and return to a head tax to finance the protection of private property and the enforcement of contracts.   This will more palatable if the sale of assets pays off the debt.   It must also repeal the 17th Amendment that enabled the election of senators and return sovereignty to the States.   Prior to the 17th Amendment, the state legislatures selected senators.   The direct election of senators undermines the bicameral legislature intended to filter house bills and serve as a check on the Executive.   The Senate is now more like the House rather than the direct representative of the independent and sovereign States.   The 17th Amendment effectively relegated the States to second-class sovereigns and it is a direct attack on the sovereignty of the States.   The nation should also repeal the Fourteenth Amendment and Nineteenth Amendments, as they too are an attack on State sovereignty.   These latter laws serve to corrupt the political process and enable government encumbrance of the economy by enabling universal suffrage and interference of the Federal government in the affairs of the States.   Universal suffrage in combination with godlessness or atheism is the bane of wealth creation.   Universal suffrage is an experiment that has failed and it threatens the survival of a nation as it enables those that do not contribute to the sovereign's sustenance to tyrannize those that do.   In other words, universal suffrage enables through the sovereign's power of eminent domain the godless and unproductive envious to destroy the object of their envy who are the nation's productive individuals.   Suffrage should be restricted to those Caucasoid males who fear God, procreate in the name of God, pay taxes, and own property and to no one else.   This will eliminate the temptation to use government's power of eminent domain to satiate the envy of unproductive and godless individuals and thus preserve the creation of wealth and the perpetuation of the race as ordained by God. All these acts would begin to restore the fear of God and free the economy from the encumbrance of government and the grip of the envious and godless.

Variation in wealth

If all the individuals comprising a nation were each equally capable of satisfying all their needs and the future was predictable with accuracy then there would not be a reason to protect private property and secure contracts.   Thus, there would be economic equality and no need for a sovereign or protector.   Nor would God or the fear of God exist. However, this is not reality.   Variations in the fecundity of the land, the intellectual capital embodied in individuals, i.e. the IQ of individuals, and the basic resources at hand as well as uncertainty in the future, and the likelihood of calamity make it necessary to build store or in other words to create individual wealth and to fear God.   The fact that there is a variation in the fecundity of the land, the intellectual capital of the individuals, and the basic resources at hand is what gives rise to wealth and to variation in wealth creation.   However if the variation in wealth among individuals and nations is too great then there is the potential for civil unrest arising from envy and provoked by the godless who will always be amongst us.   The greater the variation in wealth the greater the demands of the sovereign for a greater proportion of individual wealth in order to protect private property, and the more willing the individuals who comprise the nation to acquiesce to the demands of the sovereign.   The demand for a greater proportion of individual wealth arises as a sort of ransom in the form of wealth transfer to subdue civil unrest due to the variation in wealth and engendered by envy.   However, if the demands of the sovereign are so great that they undermine the creation of wealth and liberty, i.e. the freedom to form contracts, then the nation becomes susceptible to calamity.   The calamity may take the form of tyranny, or it may be a calamity of nature, or through aggression of other nations seeking the store or wealth of the weakened nation.   The variation in individual wealth is at the same time an engine of wealth creation and a source of civil unrest.   Economic growth is the means to overcome the civil unrest arising from variations in individual wealth. Economic growth is the result of continuous wealth creation and continuous wealth creation occurs only in an unencumbered economy. In other words, coercive forces that limit the exercise of freewill in the formation of contracts engender the civil unrest arising from variation in individual wealth.   A highly unionized, regulated and taxed economy aggravates the civil unrest arising from variation in individual wealth because such an encumbered economy places barriers to competition in the labor and capital markets thereby burdening wealth creation and indeed exacerbating the variation in wealth. Removing these barriers and burdens, i.e. freeing an economy, will result in economic growth thereby suppressing or muting the civil unrest arising from variation in individual wealth by reducing the variation. At the very least, freeing an economy creates real opportunity for mobility between economic strata.

Indeed the period between 1951 and 1970 saw relatively low taxation, little regulation, high productivity and economic growth due primarily to the dominant industrial and agricultural position of the United States following World War II and facilitated by a laissez-faire economy and the fear of God. The percent of families in the upper annual income bracket ($15,000 or greater in 1967 dollars) increased from 2.3% in 1951 to 18% by 1970. The percent of families in the lowest annual income bracket ($3000 or less) decreased from 25.7% to 11.4% over the same period. Median income as measured in constant 2009 dollars also increased over this period from an annual $3,709 dollars in 1951 to an annual $9,867 in 1970 or by 166%.

Another measure of an unencumbered economy is the difference between the family mean income and the family median income. In a totally, unencumbered economy incomes are randomly distributed and symmetrical about the mean and the mean income equals the median income. The greater the difference between the mean and the median income the more skewed the distribution and the less random the distribution. Non-random factors cause a skewed distribution about the median, and in the case of the economy, these factors include government taxation and regulation as well as unionization.(See Appendix 2) It also includes interference in the economy by the Federal Reserve Bank through control of interest rates. Figure 27 below shows the percent difference between the annual average family income and annual median family income between 1947 and 2012. Note that the difference between the average and median income starts to accelerate after the 1970s as the Federal Reserve Bank increasingly interfered in the economy by manipulating interest rates and the money supply to satisfy political rather than economic objectives. Thus, since 1970 there is an increasing disparity between those in the upper income brackets and those in the lower income brackets as reflected by the rising slope of the curve. As this disparity continues, there is increasing civil unrest and greater demands by the envious majority of the electorate for even more interference in the economy to remedy or to relieve this disparity. The rising crescendo of these demands is a result of the secularization of the nation. The more secular the nation the less the fear of God subdues envy. Envy drives the call for economic equality and universal suffrage sanctions the sovereign's actions to bring it about through socialist redistribution laws and unequal taxation. As we see, instead of reducing the disparity these calls for the sovereign to remedy the disparity followed by the sovereign's attempts at remedy merely increases the disparity. As is always the case government interference in the economy has the opposite of its intended results.

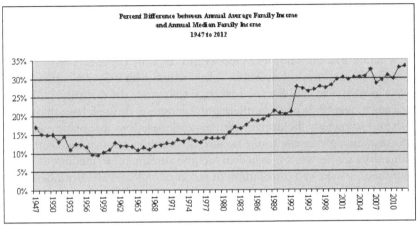

Figure 27 – Percent Difference between Annual Average Family Income and Annual Median Family Income (1947-2012)

Absent the fear of God, individual wealth variation engenders envy
As we have seen, an encumbered economy generates a large disparity in wealth while concentrating wealth in the few hands favored by the sovereign.   An unencumbered economy has a more statistically normal distribution of incomes with less concentration of wealth.   In an unencumbered economy, i.e. a normal distribution in incomes, the greater variation of individual wealth the greater the incentive becomes to create more wealth.   However, in an encumbered economy, i.e. an economy with skewed income distribution, the greater variation in the distribution of wealth the greater the potential to engender envy in a nation where there is no fear of God.   Accordingly, there will be civil unrest and calls for increased government interference in the economy to remedy the disparities.   Since these calls to remedy the disparities arise from envy, the only remedy that satiates the envy is to bring down the so-called rich not to elevate the poor.   The sovereign cannot elevate the poor he can only bring down the rich.   A sovereign who does not fear God will engender envy in the populace of a nation in order to take private property and redistribute it for his own aggrandizement further encumbering the economy of the nation thus undermining the creation of wealth.   Such a sovereign then becomes that which the individuals first appointed the sovereign to protect against, i.e. the enemies of the nation, as he is undermining the creation of wealth and reducing the nation's ability to overcome calamity or to withstand calamity.
To summarize, a normal distribution of incomes indicates an

unencumbered economy where random processes are at work and individuals have opportunity. In an unencumbered economy the greater that the standard deviation is, or in other words the greater the disparity in income, the more wealth that is created because the combination of opportunity and wealth disparity creates incentives to acquire wealth. An unencumbered economy creates opportunity that together with the fear of God suppress envy. Thus, there is little civil unrest engendered in an unencumbered economy or wealth creating economy. However, in a nation that does not fear God wealth disparity engenders envy despite the opportunity available. In a nation with universal suffrage, envy gives rise to calls for the sovereign to remedy the disparity. The sovereign responds by encumbering the economy through laws that attempt to remedy the disparity but instead these laws invariably increase the disparity, giving rise to the skewed distribution of incomes, i.e. the large distance between the median income and the mean income, as we now see. A skewed distribution of incomes indicates an encumbered economy wherein there are deterministic processes at work. Deterministic processes arise from government interference in contract formation as I have already discussed. In such an economy the greater the variation in wealth the less national wealth created and the more concentrated the wealth becomes. As long as the populace does not fear God then a deterministic, i.e. an encumbered economy, will destroy wealth and wealth creation thus weakening the nation and subjecting it to calamity. Calamity can take the form of tyranny, an act of God, or an act of men such as war, rebellion or civil war.

Measurement of Productivity

Productivity is economic efficiency. Economic efficiency is the ratio between economic system outputs and economic system inputs. Economic inputs and outputs are monetary measures. Given this definition then one measure of productivity is the ratio of revenue to net income or percent profit. Note that net income or profit measures a company's output and thus productivity requires an output to exist. If a company produces no profit then it is unproductive and therefore has zero efficiency. A company with zero efficiency consumes wealth. If a company suffers losses, it is inefficient and destructive of wealth. The higher the productivity, i.e. the more revenue that a company converts to net income then the more efficient is the company and the greater wealth that the company creates. Figure 28 is the income statement of IBM and of AT&T and it illustrates this concept of productivity for these two companies. Note that while the latest year's revenue for AT&T is over 20% greater than the revenue of IBM, the productivity of AT&T is about 30% of the productivity of IBM in 2011 and 2012. Even though AT&T has more revenue in comparison to IBM, IBM is more efficient in converting revenue to net income, and therefore creates more wealth than AT&T.   The wealth created by each company redounds to the benefit of the stockholders of each company.   The benefit to the stockholders is an increase in their wealth and their ability to survive calamity.   Note also the income tax expense of each company.   IBM for instance paid about $5.3 billion in taxes in 2012.   This money is unproductive and a reduction in wealth creation accordingly it is a reduction in the ability of the company and the shareholders of the company to survive calamity.   If IBM did not have to pay this tax, the money would go toward creating more wealth as the company would invest it or pay more dividends to the stockholders who in turn would invest it to create more wealth.

IBM Income Statement				AT&T Income Statement			
Period Ending	31-Dec-12	31-Dec-11	31-Dec-10	Period Ending	31-Dec-12	31-Dec-11	31-Dec-10
Total Revenue	104,507,000	106,916,000	99,870,000	Total Revenue	127,434,000	126,723,000	124,280,000
Cost of Revenue	54,209,000	56,778,000	53,857,000	Cost of Revenue	55,215,000	54,836,000	50,257,000
Gross Profit	50,298,000	50,138,000	46,014,000	Gross Profit	72,219,000	71,887,000	74,023,000
Operating Expenses				Operating Expenses			
Research Development	6,302,000	6,258,000	6,026,000	Research Development	-	-	-
Selling General and Administrative	22,479,000	22,486,000	20,683,000	Selling General and Administrative	41,079,000	41,382,000	34,986,000
Non Recurring	-	-	-	Non Recurring	-	2,910,000	85,000
Others	-	-	-	Others	18,143,000	18,377,000	19,379,000
Total Operating Expenses	-	-	-	Total Operating Expenses	-		
Operating Income or Loss	21,517,000	21,394,000	19,305,000	Operating Income or Loss	12,997,000	9,218,000	19,573,000
Income from Continuing Operations				Income from Continuing Operations			
Total Other Income/Expenses Net	843,000	20,000	787,000	Total Other Income/Expenses Net	134,000	249,000	897,000
Earnings Before Interest And Taxes	22,361,000	21,414,000	20,091,000	Earnings Before Interest And Taxes	13,883,000	10,251,000	21,232,000
Interest Expense	459,000	411,000	368,000	Interest Expense	3,444,000	3,535,000	2,994,000
Income Before Tax	21,902,000	21,003,000	19,723,000	Income Before Tax	10,439,000	6,716,000	18,238,000
Income Tax Expense	5,298,000	5,148,000	4,890,000	Income Tax Expense	2,900,000	2,532,000	-1,162,000
Minority Interest	-	-	-	Minority Interest	-275,000	-240,000	-315,000
Net Income From Continuing Ops	16,604,000	15,855,000	14,833,000	Net Income From Continuing Ops	7,539,000	4,184,000	19,400,000
				Discontinued Operations			779,000
Net Income	16,604,000	15,855,000	14,833,000	Net Income	7,264,000	3,944,000	19,864,000
Productivity	15.89%	14.83%	14.85%		5.70%	3.11%	15.98%

Figure 28-IBM and AT&T Income Statements-Measure of Productivity

The same is true for other economic units, such as an individual where the wages or salary is the input and the savings or investments made by the individual is the output.   The more an individual saves or invests in proportion to his income then the greater is the efficiency of the individual in creating wealth.   An individual that does not save or invest consumes everything he earns and creates no wealth.   Such an individual will succumb to calamity.   A nation of efficient individuals and companies creates wealth and the nation is able to withstand calamities.   A nation whose individuals consume all they produce does not create wealth and consequently such a nation is unable to withstand calamities.   A government always reduces the ability of a nation to create wealth and it has happened that the government was the source of calamity and the destruction of the nation as witnessed by the fate of the old Soviet Union.   Thus, in order for a nation to survive, it must continuously create wealth and the government must efficiently and effectively secure private property and enforce contracts.

Besides the ratio of revenue to net income, there are also other measures of productivity.   The United States Bureau of Labor Statistics has developed three different measures of productivity.   These are labor

133

productivity, which takes into account only labor inputs, multifactor productivity (MFP) which takes into account both labor and capital inputs, and KLEMS (capital, labor, energy, materials, and services) a form of MFP which takes into account labor, capital, energy and other intermediate goods and services as inputs.   Table 4 lists the most commonly used productivity measures by economists.

Type of output measure	Type of input measure			
	Labour	Capital	Capital and labour	Capital, labour and intermediate inputs (energy, materials, services)
Gross output	Labour productivity (based on gross output)	Capital productivity (based on gross output)	Capital-labour MFP (based on gross output)	KLEMS multifactor productivity
Value added	Labour productivity (based on value added)	Capital productivity (based on value added)	Capital-labour MFP (based on value added)	-
	Single factor productivity measures		Multifactor productivity (MFP) measures	

Table 4 - Productivity measures used by economists

I will primarily use the capital-labor MFP based on value added output, which is one of the measurements used by the US Bureau of Labor Statistics.   I will also rely on per capita GDP in terms of PPP (Purchasing Power Parity) dollars, which is a broader measure of productivity.   There is a high correlation between capital-labor MFP and per capita GDP PPP dollars so either measure is useful for drawing conclusions about the relationship between inflation, deflation and productivity.   Figure 29 is a scatter chart of US per capita GDP as measured in Purchasing Power Parity (PPP) Dollars and Real Value Added Output.   The latter is as determined by the US Bureau of Labor Statistics between 1948 and 2010.   The correlation coefficient is 0.9845 indicates both variables measure the same thing, which is productivity.   I will use the per capita GDP as a general productivity measure when I speak about nations other than the United States or when I compare other nations with the United States.   I will use the Real Value Added Output as the measure of United States productivity.

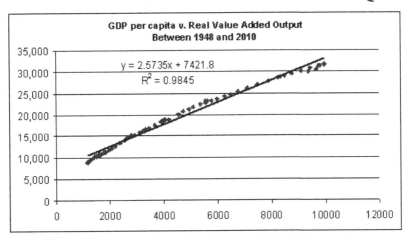

Figure 29-GDP per capita v. Real Value Added Output between 1948 and 2010

Private Property and Enforcement of Contract

Characteristics of Private Property

All human economic activity consists of the exchange of private property in some form. Accordingly, private property has characteristics definable by the exchange that takes place. One characteristic of private property is change of ownership. When I speak of private property, I am speaking in the broadest sense of the term including one's life as private property. An individual's life is property owned by the individual. An exchange of money for service, for example is an exchange of a portion of an individual's life, i.e. time on earth for consideration. Private property bought and sold by the owner of the property constitutes an obvious exchange of private property and is the result of individuals engaging in an agreement or a contract made of their own freewill whether the contract is oral or written.

A second characteristic of private property is private property can be combined or merged. Private property combined or merged with other private property creates new private property in accordance with an agreement or contract and secured by the agreement or contract, and enforceable by the sovereign. Marriage of a man and a woman is the merger of private properties to form a new and independent unit of private property, i.e. the marriage unit.

A third characteristic of private property is it has economic value, i.e. others are willing to exchange either their labor or some possession for it, and because it has value, it is an asset. An asset is collateral against debt.

A fourth characteristic is that private property is violable. In other words, it is liable to forced taking or to trespass by others. A civil tort is harm done to private property including life either through negligence, as in an accident, or deliberately as in defamation, liable or slander. The harm done is manifest in a reduction in value, which is equivalent to a taking of private property. A civil tort is therefore a taking of private property whether intentional or unintentional.

A fifth characteristic is that private property including a man's life is subject to a taking under the sovereign's power of eminent domain and in accordance with due process, i.e. the law as enacted by the sovereign.

The Marriage Contract

Marriage is a contract that merges the lives of a man and a woman into a single unit. Just like any other contract, a marriage is enforceable by the sovereign. Violating the marriage vows is legal grounds for dissolution of the contract and with penalties determined by the sovereign and as embodied into any written agreement. As marriage is an oath taken before God whether explicitly or implicitly by agreement between the man and woman, then violating the marriage vows is also a sin to which the soul must answer to God. In religious terms, the man and woman become as one when married, i.e. when joined together by agreement. This single unit is a new creation or a new person under law, and before God, that exists apart from the component individuals. This new person, i.e. the marriage unit is private property as ordained by God and Man. Thus, a wife cannot testify against her husband since a person cannot incriminate himself under law, and a marriage is a single person under man's law and under God. Since marriage creates a new person under law it speaks as one voice politically, thus the marriage act must abrogate the suffrage of the wife assuming that universal suffrage exists. The abrogation of the wife's suffrage is because the husband is the protector and becomes sovereign over the wife under the marriage vow whether explicit or implicit before God and Man. As the marriage unit is private property then the act of adultery is trespass and a taking of property, i.e. theft, punishable under both man's law and God's Commandments. The individual who forms the marriage unit, aka the spouse, and who commits adultery is trespassing on the marriage unit. The marriage unit is private property that exists legally, ethically and morally apart from the man and the woman. The marriage also results in wealth creation since its sole moral, ethical and legal purpose is the creation of progeny as a hedge against calamity. This is the reason that the marriage or the joining of individuals who cannot, or fail to create progeny is a burden on the nation's wealth and a threat to its survival. Unlike the joining or merger of other types of private property, a marriage between a man and a woman involves the joining of souls as explicitly or implicitly blessed by God, but only if consummated to bring forth progeny. The blessing is because the marriage intention is to give rise to other souls, vis-à-vis the progeny who exist for the Glory of God and are themselves a hedge against calamity as God ordained them to be. Marriage is the means that assures man's immortality following his fall from Grace as God intended, willed, and ordained when God created Man.

Conception an Act of God

Accordingly, conception is an act of God and not an act of man and therefore subject to God's law and not man's law. The woman that carries the child is for the period sovereign over the child and endowed by God under the divine right of king with the sovereign's power of eminent domain over the new and independent private property that is the child and soul in the womb, and at the instant of conception. However, a sovereign has no freewill but only duty to protect private property and enforce contracts. A woman with a child in her womb must act in accordance with God's law or jeopardize and damn her soul. She has no freewill and cannot have freewill, as she is sovereign. In the act of conception, the law is not that of her sovereign, i.e. civil or criminal law, but of God's law as conception is an act of God because it gives rise to a soul.   God's law is clear – Thou shalt not kill.   Accordingly, the sovereign whether the mother carrying the child or the king cannot make laws that conflict with God's law, as king or the mother would forfeit the divine right of king.   Thus members of an assembly in general who act as the legislature or the judiciary, or in other words the nation's sovereign subject their souls to damnation when the legislative bodies enact laws or judicial bodies adjudicate laws that contradict God's laws.   Without the fear of God a man always acts to damn his soul, whether he acknowledges this fact or not.   Thus, an atheist is one whom by his nature and by his freewill acts to damn his soul otherwise he would not profess atheism.   Laws that fail to punish abortion therefore are laws that damn the soul of the sovereign who enacts and enforces these laws. Abortion is human blood sacrifice and thus an act against God as it violates God's Covenant and Commandment, and an act against the Laws of Nature.   If abortion is not an act against the sovereign because the sovereign failed to enact law criminalizing abortion then the sovereign has abrogated the divine right of king and thus damns his soul.

Sovereignty of the Child Bearing Woman

As the woman is for the period of gestation sovereign in the instance of the child in the womb and since Man abrogated his immortality through the original sin of disobedience to God, thus giving rise to Natural Law, then the woman, i.e. a pregnant woman, as sovereign is subject to Natural Law as well as God's law.   Preservation of the woman's life or physical self-preservation due to accidents of man or nature comes into conflict at times with God's proscription against the taking of a life, and the woman or her appointed guardian under God, who is her husband and the father, assumes the role of sovereign.   It is then through divine right of king, i.e. the absolution from sin, that a decision is undertaken.   No such absolution is possible in the instance of out of wedlock conceptions, as God has not blessed these acts and they are acts of man and not of God although conception takes place in the mind and in the sight of God as a new soul comes into existence.   Thus without the blessing of God undertaken under the marriage vow, a woman is not or cannot be sovereign whether she acts in self-defense or not as the reason for aborting the child.   She thus commits sin and is condemned regardless.   However, the doctor or third party who acts on his own volition to save the mother's life is also for the moment sovereign therefore he commits no sin to save the life of the mother and loose the child.   Considering no baptism occurs and cannot occur without the marriage blessed by God either explicitly or implicitly then the unwed parents remain with the mark of original sin, and their souls judged accordingly– not the soul of the child as the child is without sin.

In this case, absolution of original sin is by God through prayer and forgiveness. Considering God also ordained freewill under the New Testament then all who are born determine by themselves the destiny of their lives and the fate of their souls when they succumb to their passions.

A failure to procreate is a failure to create wealth and therefore a reduction in the ability of the nation to survive a calamity. A marriage that fails to brings forth progeny or is incapable of bringing forth progeny is therefore a burden on wealth creation and thereby an abomination before man, and an abomination before God. Those that do not wed and do not bring forth progeny are as seeds fallen on arid ground, a burden on wealth creation, and jeopardize the immortality of man as ordained by God. Those who are physically or emotionally incapable of procreation are equally a burden on wealth creation. The care of orphans falls upon those that fail to procreate, and it is the only redemption of the soul possible and consistent with God's will that Man be immortal.

Overpopulation is a flawed notion

The flawed notion of overpopulation as a calamity in itself is analogous to the notion of a rapid rise in productivity and its affect on unemployment. The notion of overpopulation is often presented to justify all sorts of corrupt and wealth destroying governmental laws and individual action. Overpopulation is an economic issue only in an encumbered economy, i.e. an economy over taxed and over regulated by the sovereign, consequently a sovereign violates God's law and further encumbers an economy when he prevents or restricts procreation by promoting through his law otherwise unfruitful marriages. The concepts of over-taxation and over-regulation exist and are real because they are manifest through the destruction of wealth but there is no such concept as "overpopulation". The control of a population by any means is to destroy wealth creation, therefore when a sovereign undertakes population control through the laws he enacts or fails to enact then he is abrogating the divine right of king and thus acting unethically and immorally.

The sovereign who encumbers an economy must undertake measures to control population as the encumbered economy fails to create wealth to sustain the population. In doing so, the sovereign adds to the burden on wealth and in this way, the economy and the nation eventually fall to calamity. Such a sovereign abrogates the divine right of king, i.e. God disposes the soul of the sovereign in accordance with his acts as an individual and not as sovereign. Thus, when such a sovereign executes a man he condemns his soul when he has abrogated the divine right of king regardless of due process.

Enclosure laws in England resulted in wealth creation

There is no clearer example of the failure of the notion that overpopulation is itself a calamity and of the significance of private property to the creation of wealth than the effect of the Enclosure Laws in England. These laws began to take broad effect in the 16th century in the general population of England. Enclosure was the privatization of land first enacted under the English Statues in 1235 AD and applicable to the barons under Henry III but expanded to the general population beginning in the 16th century. From the first century AD to the 16th century, England had a feudal system where all land was in common and cultivated by peasants or serfs who where subjects to a sovereign lord who oversaw but did not own the land. The sovereign lord arbitrarily extracted as much of the peasants' production as he saw fit in exchange for providing the peasants security. The peasants or serfs did not own the land they cultivated so there was no incentive to produce any more than at a level of sustenance since the sovereign lord took the surplus. This is akin to communism or socialism whereby the government owns the means of production, i.e. the land and there is no private property. Thus, communism and socialism are nothing more than feudalism under a different name and absent the fear of God. In the sense that life is private property, the government or the sovereign also owns the life of the peasants. The difference between feudalism and slavery is that peasants were not chattel property, i.e. the feudal lord could not buy and sell his peasants because they affixed to the land. That is, if the land transferred through warfare, inheritance, or otherwise the serfs went with the land. As long as the sovereign provided for his security, then the feudal peasant lacked fear of the future and had no incentive on this basis to create surplus or store. Without surplus there was little commerce or trade. This is a historic and stark example of the sovereign undermining or encumbering the creation of wealth. Predictably, population in England remained at a relatively constant level or grew very slowly under the feudal system, as did the creation of wealth. After privatization of property resulting from the Enclosure Laws, the peasants who bought property and owned it in fee simple caused agricultural production to increase exponentially. This enabled agricultural output to support a much larger population than when the land was common to all as was the case under feudalism. After general privatization, which occurred over about 200 years, agricultural innovations started to accelerate thus further increasing the productivity of the land arising from privatization alone. Thus, privatization and ownership of land or property enabled both high productivity and innovation amongst a people with an inherently and natural high level of intellectual capital, i.e. high average IQ. The agricultural yield in terms of bushels per acre increased by over three fold as private property became the norm in England. Figure 30 shows the increase in the yield in terms for wheat, rye, barley, oats, peas and beans beginning in the late 16th century until the end of the 19th century. This increase in productivity is almost solely due to English farmland transforming from land held in common to land owned by those farming the land, i.e. private property, and not to any radical improvements in farm technology although such improvements and innovations did occur. These improvements and innovations were also the product of the privatization that was taking place and the desire by the new property owners to increase their individual wealth by increasing their productivity and their production. Along with enclosure and private property came an increase in population and an overall increase in wealth. The more people that England had the more it could feed and the richer it became. This example alone debunks the idea that so-called "overpopulation" causes poverty and starvation. Apart from the fact that the term "overpopulation" is meaningless since there is no standard to judge what the population should be. The cause of poverty and starvation is not "overpopulation" but the lack of private property and too much property held in common. Along with the lack of private property as the cause of poverty and starvation are a lack of intellectual capital, a lack of the efficient and effective means to secure and protect private property, and an absence of the fear of God. An inefficient and ineffective government and a population with a low level of intellectual capital, i.e. a low average IQ, without the fear of God is the cause of poverty and starvation and not "overpopulation".

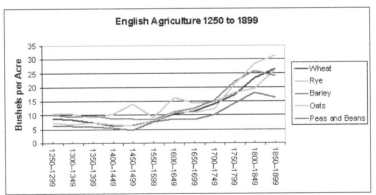

Figure 30-English Agriculture 1250 to 1899

Figure 31 is a chart of Britain's population from 1300AD until the end of the 19th century. Population before 1700 is an estimate. The rapid decline in the population after 1350AD was due to the Black Death.

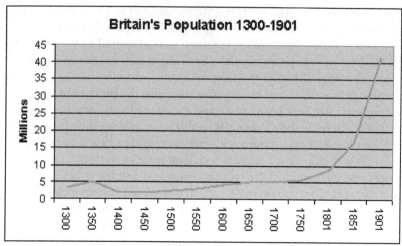

Figure 31-Britain's Population 1300 to 1901

Note that because there was little wealth created, i.e. progeny as well as store during this period, the Black Death calamity reduced the population by about 60%. With the significant decline in population, resulting from the Black Death there was a shortage of labor. Peasants now demanded wages in addition to mere sustenance for their labor. The more successful peasant families were able to buy and hold land as the land once held in common became, under the Enclosure Laws, to be enclosed or privately held. England's population began to increase beginning in the 17th century corresponding to the privatization of property in England, and while the crop yields increased three fold, the population increased nine fold. In other words, food production per unit area was increasing at a linear rate while population was increasing at an exponential rate. Bringing greater amounts of arable land into production more than made up the difference and in the absence of mechanization, greater population was required to achieve the increased production. Demand for labor increased with increased productivity and consequently there was no unemployment and much wealth creation in the process.

Even William Shakespeare took advantage of the Enclosure Laws when in the early part of the 17th Century Shakespeare joined a group of Warwickshire landowners in a profitable scheme for enclosing the common lands at Welcombe[2].

Malthus predicts calamity

Despite the creation of wealth engendered by the increase in population and the privatization of the land, the difference between the

---

[2] A History of English Literature, Peter Quennell, 1973; page 58

population growth rate and the unit rate of food production gave rise to the Malthusian economic theory of calamity.   Thomas Robert Malthus (1766-1834) an English economist theorized that population growth will outstrip the ability of agriculture to sustain the population for the reasons I cited, i.e. unit food production naturally growing linearly and population naturally growing exponentially.   This idea has informed many of the flawed notions of economics, science, and government since the 19th century.   As shown in Figures 30 and 31, population growth follows the growth in agriculture and not the other way around.   In other words in an environment where there is an abundance of intellectual capital as exists in the Caucasian Race, which is the dominant race of Europe and all of Western Civilization, then population growth follows the productivity gains in agriculture.   Highly intelligent individuals in general do not have children they cannot support, and that is the case with Western Man and in Western nations whose populace fears God.

Where Malthus' economic theory does apply, however, is in places like Sub-Sahara Africa.   The inherent lack of intellectual capital, i.e. low IQ in Sub-Sahara Africa has always resulted in rising populations outstripping the ability of the land to support these populations at least prior to the colonization of this land by the Europeans in the 18th and 19th centuries and up to the recent decolonization.   Malthus' prescience is only manifest when tempered by the intellectual capital of the population to which it is applied.   This is the reason that the calamity that it portends will never materialize in Western nations as long as the West preserves its store of intellectual capital.   However, Malthus' dire prediction becomes increasingly more likely with the admixture of the Caucasoid with the Negroid, and with mixed race peoples.   This admixture results in a loss of the ability to generate sufficient intellectual capital, i.e. men of genius to sustain and grow an advanced civilization. The admixture of the Caucasoid with the Negroid and mixed races is the greatest single threat to the long-term survival of the human race in general.   Such admixture reduces greatly the likelihood of men of genius among the progeny as well as reducing the average intelligence, i.e. IQ of the national population.   This admixture caused the collapse of the Roman Empire as the Romans mixed with their dark and semi-dark slaves.   After several generations of mixing with those they conquered, the Romans were unable to produce sufficient numbers of male progeny of genius to sustain their Empire.   Thus, the aptly named Dark Ages emerged during which little material advancement took place.   It took hundreds of years for sufficient numbers of individuals of genius to reappear in the Caucasian Race manifesting in the Renaissance and the Age of Discovery.

A comparison of the per capita GDP versus population growth for various nations bears out the dependence of the Malthusian calamity on the average intelligence of the population.   I have selected three Sub-

143

Saharan nations with relatively homogeneous Negroid population and with average IQ's credibly determined by Richard Lynn and Tatu Vanhanen[3]. The three nations are The Central African Republic with average IQ of 64 and 98% Negroid, Mozambique with average IQ of 64 and 98% Negroid, and Gabon with average IQ 64 and 92% Negroid. Figures 32 through 34 are scatter charts comparing the per capita GDP with the population for each of these nations from 1950 to 2008.

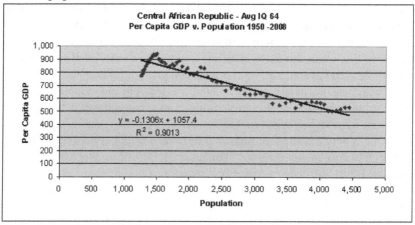

Figure 32 – Central African Republic per Capita GDP v. Population – 1950 to 2008

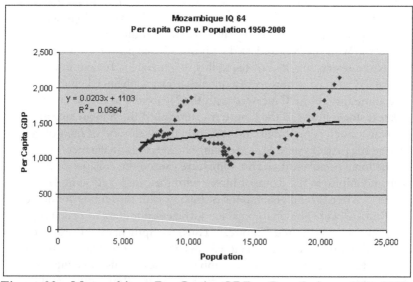

Figure 33 – Mozambique Per Capita GDP v. Population – 1950-2008

[3] IQ and Global Inequality, Richard Lynn and Tatu Vanhanen, 2006   Table 4.3

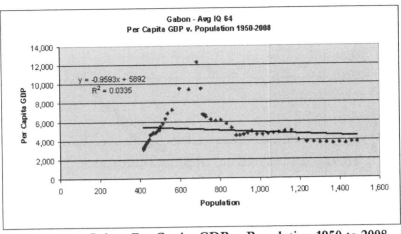

Figure 34 – Gabon Per Capita GDP v. Population 1950 to 2008

Note that the Central African Republic (Figure 32) has a negative correlation (determined by the coefficient of x) between the per capita GDP and population growth with the correlation coefficient (R^2) of 0.90. This indicates that the higher the Central African Republic population grows the poorer the nation becomes in direct proportion. This is the Malthusian calamity. In the case of Mozambique (Figure 33) and Gabon (Figure 34), the correlation coefficients (R^2) are very low indicating that there are random factors affecting the amount of wealth created. In other words, there is great uncertainty in the security and survivability of the individuals in these nations. Typically, these latter two nations are dependent on the exploitation and exportation of natural resources such as oil or minerals to survive, and the discovery and exploitation of these resources is random and unsustainable. In the case of the Central African Republic, the Malthusian calamity is clearly manifesting itself. The greater the population the less the population is able to survive. Clearly, the Central African Republic has few mineral resources worthy of exploitation and it relies on the ability of the population to sustain itself as a nation, which it is failing to do. Given its low average IQ, this nation is deterministically succumbing to the Malthusian calamity. The average IQ of the population is the single most reliable determinant of the fate of a nation apart from the burden of the sovereign and the fear of God.

If we examine a nation such as Norway, whose population is mainly Caucasoid, and whose population has an average IQ of 100 we see a completely different picture. A similar picture to Norway emerges with a nation such as Japan whose population is mainly Mongoloid and whose population has an average IQ of 105. Figures 35 and 36 chart the relationship between population and per capita GDP for Norway and Japan respectively.

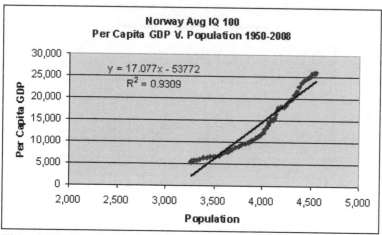

Figure 35 – Norway Per Capita GDP v. Population 1950 to 2008

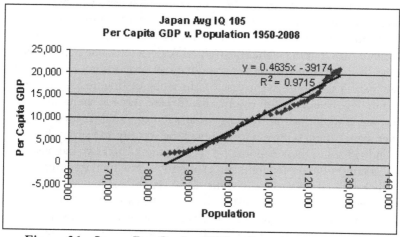

Figure 36 – Japan Per Capita GDP v. Population 1950-2008

Both Norway and Japan have a large positive correlation between per capita GDP and population.   In other words, the greater the population of either of these two nations becomes, then the wealthier these nations become, which is the opposite of Malthus' theory.

The one thing to note is that in the case of the high IQ nations a decline in population generally means a decline in individual wealth, whereas in the case of the low IQ nations a decline in population may or may not mean a gain in individual wealth.   Attempts at population control should be limited to low IQ nations where the smaller populations may, but not necessarily, result in slightly higher individual wealth.   One thing is clear however and that is the only way for the Sub-Sahara African Negroid to survive is to re-colonize him because clearly the Negroid is intellectually incapable of managing himself.

Fear of God is essential for wealth creation

Private property secured by the sovereign is one necessary element for wealth creation the other is the fear of God. The Enclosure Laws that took effect in Britain beginning in the 16th century were under a cultural and political environment where man feared God and followed His Commandments. The religious wars during the 16th and 17th are a testament to the seriousness that the European populations regarded God's Word and thus the disposition of man's soul. Although some atheistic historians characterize these wars as politically motivated, this ignores the seriousness of the Reformation and Counter Reformation in the minds of men. Accordingly, man's envy remained in check through the fear of God and man's envy played little role in the lives of the men until the time of the so-called Enlightenment in the 18th Century. Thus, the wealth and prosperity of one man did not engender envy in the heart of another man, as God proscribed envy and man feared God. Rather the wealth of other men engendered a desire to emulate and follow the man who created wealth. Private property and the end of the feudal system created opportunity and as long as a man had opportunity, it mattered little what other men did or what other men had. When men lack opportunity to acquire private property and the sovereign encumbers individual freewill to contract, and there is no fear of God, then envy takes hold in the hearts of men. Envy brings with it the end of private property, the end of commerce, and ultimately the end of the nation through the hand of its sovereign.

The United States Constitution significance to wealth creation

The securing of private property and the creation of opportunity through liberty to contract was the basis for the United States Constitution, which placed the individual above the state by limiting the sovereign's power of eminent domain and equally allocating that power to three branches of government. Above all the United States Constitution valued private property, individual liberty, and equality under the law, i.e. the equal application of the law including laws of taxation to all individual citizens regardless of wealth or status, and these ideas served as its foundation enabling the creation of great wealth. Thus, the original Constitution sanctioned only a head tax, which is a tax that is the same amount for each citizen not a percentage of wealth or income. Article 1 Section 2 states in part "… *direct Taxes shall be apportioned among the several States which may be included within this Union, according to their respective Numbers, which shall be determined by adding to the whole Number of free Persons, including those bound to Service for a Term of Years, and excluding Indians not taxed, three fifths of all other Persons.*" Article 1 Section 8 states in part "*…No Capitation, or other direct, Tax shall be laid, unless in Proportion to the Census of Enumeration herein before directed to be taken….*" In other words the original

Constitution, prior to the 16th Amendment, required that a direct tax be determined by taking the total outstanding expenses and debt of the Federal Government and dividing it by the total number of people as counted by the census and apportioned among the States. Thus, each individual in a particular State paid the same amount of tax except for the non-free Negro, which according to the Constitution would pay only three fifths of the tax, or have the tax paid on his behalf. Thomas Jefferson abolished the direct tax in effect at the time in 1802 and Congress never again imposed the direct tax. Any individual taxes passed to fight the War of 1812 and the Civil War, Congress quickly repealed after those conflicts were over. Men are not predisposed to paying taxes directly to the government, and they never will be so predisposed. This is obvious throughout the 19th Century. Most revenue collected by the Federal Government during the 19th Century was through high custom duties, i.e. indirectly, and the sale of public lands as the West was rapidly expanding during this time. The Federal Government by law initially owned all land through the sovereign power of eminent domain and just like their progenitors, the English, the Americans wisely embarked on enclosure and privatization of all lands.

The privatization of all property in the United States incentivized the Europeans, especially the highly intelligent and industrious German-speaking people, to come in large numbers to settle the land thereby creating great wealth. The large numbers of German-speaking individuals immigrating to the United States threatened the creation of wealth in Germany as populations depleted in the still largely feudal kingdoms of Central and Eastern Europe. This large migration of German-speaking people to the United States set the stage for WWI, as I will discuss shortly. The lack of interference in the general economy by the United States Government resulted in the creation of great wealth that quickly rivaled and eventually exceeded the wealth of Europe, which took centuries to build, propelling the United States to a world power by the beginning of the 20th Century or within 100 years of its independence from England.

Flawed notions of the nature of man and purpose of government

Had the United States continued on the wealth-creating trajectory begun in the 19th Century then the misery and suffering of the first half of the twentieth century would not have happened. However, the trajectory changed in a destructive way. The change in trajectory was due to the following factors:

(1) Flawed progressive ideological notions of the nature of man, i.e. as an egalitarian, social and communal being rather than as a free and independent individual being;

(2) The flawed notion that overpopulation was itself a calamity;

(3) The purpose of government as benefactor rather than as

protector;

(4) The God is dead notion on the part of many philosophers. These were the principles of the Enlightenment now taking hold in the United States or 100 years after the French Revolution and the result was the same. The result was widespread death, poverty and misery where before there was life, general prosperity, and happiness.

The 16th and 17th Amendments to the Constitution, which enabled the income tax and the direct election of Senators respectively, and universal suffrage as embodied in the 19th Amendment were the manifestations of these progressive notions. So too was the Federal Reserve Act of 1913. These changes to the US Constitution and to the banking law undermined wealth creation and ushered in great misery and poverty for most of the twentieth century. If there is one lesson from the events of the twentieth century it is the Framers of the Constitution were much wiser and more intelligent than those who came later and who envied the Framers. These individuals were the so-called progressives who espoused the atheism and Stoicism of the Enlightenment, and acting on their envy these progressives and modern day liberals forcibly and tragically changed and continue to change the wealth-creating trajectory of the nation steering it deliberately and wantonly toward calamity.

Private Property is assignable and inheritable

Returning to the notion of private property, private property a sixth characteristic is that private property is assignable. This means that the owner or possessor can willingly give it to another. A human life is assignable to others through employment or contract. An employee is assigning his life, i.e. his private property, to the employer for consideration of wages paid. The employer is assigning his life and his investment or wealth to his customers for consideration as well. Customers do business with an enterprise that eases their burden through the purchased goods or services. An individual life itself has a limited time over which it is productive and as such, it has an economic value insofar as it is productive in creating wealth and progeny.

The seventh characteristic of private property is that private property is inheritable. Inheritance is an assignment of a human life or the possessions thereof by the owner to future generations through the will.

A will and a deed impose duty on the Sovereign

Unless the sovereign enacts laws to impose such duty on his own self, the sovereign has no duty to enforce any other contract made with the sovereign other than the will and deed. In other words, a sovereign is able to abrogate any contract made with the sovereign other than a will or a deed. This is because a sovereign cannot be both judge and plaintiff or defendant unless he grants himself that role under law. A deed is a contract with the sovereign that bestows ownership of tangible or intangible property to an individual or corporation after the passing of the owner. This includes title to land. A patent, copyright, or trademark is each a deed to intangible, i.e. intellectual property. The will is a contract with the sovereign that extends a man's life, which is private property beyond the grave. The will is analogous to title to land. A title bestows to an individual ownership to land and sets forth the boundary and conditions of ownership of real property. The sovereign's purpose and duty is to secure and protect the title to land, which is the deed to the land. The sovereign deeds title to land in accordance with the will of the owner of the land and in so doing promises to protect the land from encroachment by others. Thus, the deed to land is a promise made by the sovereign to the owner of the land to secure the land. The sovereign has a duty to honor a will, as it is a contract between the past, i.e. an individual's expired life, and the future. The will is the only contract with the sovereign that the sovereign has a duty to enforce even in the absence of any law that imposes such a duty. The will is a manifestation of an individual man's immortality as ordained by God. Accordingly, the sovereign's duty to enforce the will of a man comes from God, as this duty is the divine right of king. Note here that I use the term duty. Duty is a moral precept only as it concerns the sovereign because the life of the sovereign is common to the nation. As I stated earlier, a sovereign relinquishes his freewill when he becomes sovereign and must act according to the laws he enacts. This is his duty. A sovereign who violates his duty risks rebellion and jeopardizes his soul. Individuals on the other hand only have a moral duty to themselves and not to others except when they are for the moment sovereign as in saving a drowning man or a childbearing woman. Contracts impose an ethical duty on individuals but not a moral duty. Inserting terms into a will by the sovereign through law or by fiat is coercion as it goes against the will of the individual and therefore an encumbrance to an economy. Such coercion undermines wealth creation and the perpetuation of the individual's life as ordained by God. When the sovereign abrogates the will of an individual to meet any perceived social or political end, then the sovereign becomes a tyrant and he is ripe for rebellion. This is also true of a deed where the sovereign cannot impose conditions other than insuring that the boundaries set forth in the application for title do not interfere or impinge on others. This is his duty to protect private property. The sovereign has no freewill and therefore he cannot negotiate a will or deed or insert terms and conditions into a will or a deed beyond the securing of private property. Doing so encumbers the economy, undermines wealth creation, and damns the soul of the sovereign before God.

150

The Sovereign Power of Eminent Domain

The sovereign power of eminent domain is a power given to the protector or sovereign by the individuals of the nation to enable the protector to fulfill his only and sole purposes and duties that are the protection of private property and the enforcement of contracts. The exercise of the sovereign power of eminent domain is only under due process of law. In other words, the sovereign imposes the sovereign power of eminent domain only through laws created by the sovereign and not arbitrarily or ex post facto. In a constitutional republic, the sovereign's power of eminent domain divides between the three functions of the sovereign, i.e. the executive, the legislative and the judicial. The legislative function sets forth the conditions and boundaries of the exercise of the sovereign power of eminent domain by the executive function. This is the sovereign law. Thus, the law governs and limits the application of the sovereign power of eminent domain. The taking of a life by the sovereign is an act of the sovereign power of eminent domain carried out under the executive function. The taking of a life is only through due process as enacted by the legislature or legislative function of the sovereign. The taking of all other individual private property, which is akin to the taking of a life through the exercise of the sovereign power of eminent domain, must involve due process and the taking may or may not include consideration or compensation for the value of the property taken.

Contract cannot exist between the Sovereign and an Individual

In all economic activity there must exist an exchange of things of value or in other words an exchange of private property except in the case where the sovereign takes an individual's life or an individual's property. The sovereign power of eminent domain is absolute and it is only through the action of the sovereign himself that compensation for a taking may exist. In this sense there can exist no contract between the individual and the sovereign or the nation other than the will and the deed. As I indicated earlier, an exchange of private property between the parties is willing or unwilling. Where the exchange is willing it involves contracts, where the exchange is unwilling it involves the use of force. The sovereign's purpose or the purpose of government is to protect against the unwilling taking of private property and in carrying out this purpose, the sovereign uses force or the threat of force to take life or property as punishment. Note that the sovereign power of eminent domain is not for the restoration of losses arising from violations of law. It is only to punish the criminal in accordance with the law, not to make the victim whole or to satiate the desire for vengeance. Nor is it a function of government to rehabilitate a criminal. Therefore, any contract with the sovereign is only through duress and by definition unenforceable. In other words while it is possible to enter into a contract with the sovereign there is no way to force the sovereign to fulfill his end of the bargain absent permission of the sovereign as dictated by the sovereign's own law. If the sovereign decides not to fulfill the terms of a contract, or unilaterally, arbitrarily, or capriciously change the terms of a contract, the other party to the contract has no legal recourse unless the sovereign has enacted laws allowing such recourse.

The Corporation as Private Property

A corporation is also private property and just as in the case of an individual, a corporation has a life, although the corporation does not have a soul in an incorporeal sense. The term life as I use it in this book means the quality of a creation or conception to grow economically, i.e. in terms of creating wealth and to propagate into the future. The individual owns his life and that life must create wealth in order to secure itself against calamity. The life of a corporation belongs to other individuals or corporations in addition to the corporation owning its life. Shares of a corporation are shares in the life of a corporation and the fruits of that life as manifested in earnings or profit, which is the creation of wealth. These shares can belong to other individuals or corporations or to the corporation itself. The formation of a corporation is analogous in an economic and ethical sense to a marriage between a woman and a man. In both instances, a new and independent unit of private property forms from its components. In the case of marriage, the future secures through procreation, which is wealth creation. For a corporation, the future secures through the continuous creation of material wealth or profit. A marriage and a corporation are attempts to extend the individual's life or the individual's will beyond the time that he has on earth. This is the ultimate expression of individual self-interest, and the object of God's Creation, i.e. the immortality of Man. Notice that I did not use the conventional definition of a corporation, which is in legal terms. The conventional definition is a legal entity formed to limit liability to shareholders, which in turn enables them to take a measure of risk and in the process create wealth for themselves. The corporation therefore is a person not only in a legal sense but also in an ethical sense as well. As a person who has a life owned by others a corporation's ethical aspects arise from its purpose, which is the creation of wealth for the owners. As a person in a legal sense, a corporation is a political entity as well. A corporation through its CEO has a say in the selection of the sovereign or influence the laws that a sovereign enacts just like an individual citizen.

A corporation that does not make profit is unethical

A corporation formed for a purpose other than the creation of wealth while legal is unethical. A so-called non-profit corporation is

152

unethical since it arises explicitly for purposes other than profit or the creation of wealth. The creation of wealth is not only essential for the survival of the corporation but also essential to the well being and survival of the individual owners of the corporation and ultimately the nation that protects and secures the corporation. A corporation's ethical purpose, i.e. the creation of wealth redounds to the owners of the corporation not to the employees of a corporation. A so-called non-profit corporation implies that a company exists which provides no return to the investors for the money they invested. The concepts non-profit and corporation are mutually exclusive, thus the term non-profit corporation is an oxymoron or irrational. In general, irrational ideas are always unethical because they never result in the creation of wealth. Therefore, the idea of a non-profit corporation is akin to socialism and to communism, which are irrational ideas since they arise out of envy and envy is always irrational. So-called non-profit corporations are unethical economic units because they create no wealth and instead consume wealth. Non-profit corporations should not exist. Either a corporation is profitable or not. A corporation that is not profitable must dissolve in order to reduce the consumption of wealth or its losses.

No duty to employees

There exists on the part of the corporation, the officers of the corporation or the shareholders of corporation no moral, legal or ethical duty or obligation to the employees of a corporation. This is consistent with the moral philosophy that I am outlining here as duty or obligation is not an element in my moral philosophy insofar as individuals are concerned, apart from their moral duty and obligation to themselves and their progeny who are extensions of themselves. A sovereign on the other hand has a moral duty and obligation to the nation. Duty and obligation to another individual or individuals are moral precepts applicable to the sovereign alone as duty and obligation to the citizens of the nation in the protection of private property and the enforcement of laws and contracts. An ethical duty and obligation also fall upon officers of a corporation. Officers of a corporation have a fiduciary duty to the shareholders of the corporation, and in this sense, they are akin to sovereigns. The ethical duty and obligation of officers of a corporation are as agents and secured by contract.

While duty and obligation are not moral precepts for the individual apart from duty and obligation to himself, duty and obligation are nevertheless ethical precepts in that they arise in matters of contract enforceable by the sovereign under civil code in a court of equity. In other words, a duty or obligation to another only arises through the exercise of freewill in contract. Thus there is no moral or ethical duty or obligation owed "society" unless by contract and since "society" is not a legal entity there can be no contract. An employee of a corporation exchanges his life for money or other consideration of his own free will. This is an ethical matter and not a moral matter. Employment is an exchange of private property and it therefore involves a contract. The terms and conditions of employment exist under common law and there is generally no written contract. This is termed "employment at will" which means an employee has no legal, i.e. contractual or moral obligation to remain an employee and the corporation has no legal or moral obligation to keep an employee. An employee uses his earnings for which he exchanges a portion of his life to create wealth and secure his future and the future of his progeny. The corporation exists to benefit its own self only, i.e. its individual self-interest, and thereby benefit the owners of the corporation. An unencumbered economy accords an employee the same freedom to contract as accorded the corporation. The employee exchanges a portion of his life or labor solely for his benefit and the corporation exchanges the investment of its shareholders, which is a manifestation of their lives, for its benefit and thus the benefit of its shareholders. To the extent that this exchange creates wealth for both the employee and the corporation, and its shareholders then it continues in an economic and thus an ethical sense. In an unencumbered economy, an employee is free to sell his labor at market rates, and employment is at the discretion and discrimination of both the corporation and the employee. In other words, a corporation or, for that matter, any employer has no ethical, moral, or legal duty to maintain a level of employment, or to pay any wage that is higher than the market for labor determines, or to hire anybody for reasons other than to enable the creation of wealth, i.e. serve his self-interest. Nor does an employee have a legal, moral, or ethical duty to continue in his employment when his employment fails to create individual wealth or in other words serve his self-interest.

Loyalty

Loyalty of an employee to an employer or of an employer to an employee has no moral or ethical basis. Loyalty is akin to altruism and as I have shown altruism is inconsistent with self-interest and therefore destructive of wealth creation. Loyalty to a nation manifests itself as volunteering to be soldier or to be king, thereby relinquishing private property, i.e. one's life and becoming property held in common. Property held in common is by definition and in fact unproductive and therefore a burden on the creation of wealth as is altruism in any form. On the other hand, a soldier's or a king's loyalty to a nation is a moral duty as it presumes truthfulness on the part of the soldier or sovereign. In other words, loyalty only manifests when an individual either through force, i.e. by conscription, or voluntarily relinquishes his private property, i.e. his life, to be property held in common, i.e. soldier or king. Betrayal or treason is the abrogation of loyalty to a nation by the soldier or the king.   Betrayal or treason is a moral failure since it involves deception and thus bearing false witness.   Betrayal or treason is thus punishable by God and Man.   When an individual who is not a soldier or the sovereign engages the enemy, he becomes sovereign for the moment.   Accordingly, he has a moral duty to the nation, i.e. he must be loyal to the nation of which he is a part at that moment.   Staying employed in a corporation or continuing the employment of individuals by a corporation solely for the reason of loyalty is self-destructive and thus destructive of wealth creation.   Loyalty of the king and soldier to the nation is a moral obligation as is the loyalty of the individual citizen to the sovereign and to the nation.   Loyalty of an employee to his employer or of an employer to his employee is contrary to self-interest, thus inimical to the creation of wealth and consequently unethical.

Loyalty in Rebellion and Civil War

When the sovereign fails in his duty to protect private property or secure contracts then he subjects himself to rebellion or to civil war.   As I stated earlier a monarchy is subject to overthrow by rebellion and a republic is subject to overthrow by civil war.   The sovereign is subject to rebellion or civil war if he overburdens the nation and undermines wealth creation.   Envy of the sovereign also engenders his overthrow.   Individuals who seek to be sovereign over others may undertake rebellion or civil war to assume the sovereignty.   Envy manifests only in the godless or those who do not fear God.   Those engaging in rebellion or civil war motivated by envy are not under the divine right of king since they do not seek to protect private property or enforce contracts but rather to take from the sovereign that which God ordained the sovereign to have, the power of eminent domain.   Thus, rebellion or civil war by the envious damns their souls before God.   The French Revolution and the Russian Revolution are two examples of rebellion and civil war engendered by the envy of the godless.   In both instances, the rebels paid a high price for their godlessness.   In the case of the French Revolution, there emerged the tyranny of Napoleon with the subsequent death of hundreds of thousands of men in the Napoleonic Wars and the decline of France as a world power.   In the case of Russia, the resulting Soviet Union was a land of poverty and misery.   Russia continues to this day to be more like a third world country than the wealthy nation the high average IQ of its population would otherwise have created.

Morality and Ethics

On occasion, it may appear that I use the terms moral and ethical interchangeably but there is a difference in the terms.   Moral acts are acts that are in keeping with God's Commandments.   An immoral act is one punishable by God through the disposition of the soul.   God's Ten Commandments are for man to live a long and prosperous life and for his soul to enter the Kingdom of Heaven.   The first nine Commandments relate to man's actions.   The last of the Commandments is the proscription against envy.   It is the only human passion proscribed by God and written in stone.   The individual himself knows his heart and if envy is in his heart then he will commit other sins.   Indeed envy is the source of all evil bestowed on man by man.   A man's covetousness of another man's possessions or gifts leads inexorably to adultery, murder, lying and stealing.   Envy is the motivating passion behind socialism and communism as these ideologies rely on envy to justify civil laws taking one man's private property against his will and to give it to another favored by the sovereign or places it in common.   That the ideologies of communism and socialism arose parallel to advances in transportation and communications is not a coincidence.   As men become increasingly aware of the wealth of other men, and as governments have encumbered economies that restrict the exercise of freewill in contracting, and burden opportunity, and as the fear of God evaporates from the hearts of men then envy takes root.   Envy engenders the godless and ultimately ruinous ideologies of socialism and communism.   It is critical to the survival of a nation that the sovereign and the citizen fear God, whose Commandment proscribes envy.   It is also critical to the survival of an economy that the sovereign not encumber the economy so the economy creates wealth and thus ensures opportunity, which overcomes or at least suppresses the temptation of envy.

    Ethical acts are acts that are in accordance with a man's self-interest.   That is ethical acts are acts in accordance with the Law of Nature.   The Law of Nature is common to all men independent of nation or religion.   Every man has the inalienable duty and obligation to self-preservation, to protect and propagate his life and property, and to pursue his self-interest, i.e. exercise his freewill to contract.   The creation of wealth is a manifestation of the Law of Nature.   It redounds to man's self-interest to create wealth and therefore the creation of wealth is ethical as well as moral.   Laws that encumber an individual's freewill or that encumber his ability to create wealth are unethical laws since they conflict with the Law of Nature.   Unethical laws inevitably lead to rebellion or civil war as they threaten the survival of the individual, his property, and his posterity.   Thus, laws that appease or engender envy are not only immoral but unethical as well.   Laws that appease and engender envy include laws that take wealth from one individual against his will and give it to another individual or held in common.   Laws that foreclose on a man's ability to create wealth are similarly laws that appease and engender envy.   So-called environmental laws or zoning laws or regulations restricting or placing barriers to competition in various industries are such laws.   The problems that such laws attempt to solve are more efficiently and less burdensomely resolved with existing laws protecting all private property and through the enforcement of contracts.   It is only in the absence of the fear of God that laws appeasing and engendering the envy in man arise, thus enabling a socialist or communist state and the resulting destruction of private property, which is the destruction of life.

The sovereign who fears God will not enact laws that engender envy in man or appease the envy of men. If the sovereign does not fear God and enacts laws that subjugate men by engendering or appeasing envy, then the sovereign abrogates the divine right of king and becomes a tyrant ripe for rebellion. This is socialism and communism.

Is covetousness the ultimate expression of man's self-interest and Man's freewill?

The reader may well ask the question, are not covetousness and the acts arising from covetousness the ultimate expression of man's self-interest and man's freewill? The answer is yes they are. It is the reason that in a primitive state of nature men exist in a state of war with each other or in Thomas Hobbes words *"Bellum omnium contra omnes"* or *"the war of all against all"*. Such a state is unstable and eventually would end in the extinction of man if continued. God created man to be immortal thus the extinction of man by his own hand is against the will of God. The instability is resolved through the fear of God who proscribes envy, and through the establishment of a nation under a sovereign protector. Natural law therefore confirms the existence of God and gives rise to the sovereign protector, as both are essential for the survival of man. Once a man denies the existence of God who is the Creator of Man, he necessarily dooms himself as he subjects himself to the passion of envy, which no man can control absent the fear of God. It follows that when a nation through its sovereign and its institutions denies the existence of God it eventually succumbs to the passion of envy, the ultimate expression of self-interest. It thereby dooms itself and damns its posterity. The now defunct Soviet Union was such a nation.

The Soul of a Corporation

In the case of a corporation, it acts ethically when it creates wealth and unethically when it does not create wealth. A corporation cannot act immorally or morally since it does not have a soul in the sense that I have defined the soul, i.e. as the incorporeal essence of man owned by God. By its nature, a corporation lives forever so it requires no soul, as it is immortal as long as it behaves ethically, i.e. creates profit, which is wealth. Man exists forever only through his soul. As God created Man, and Man gave rise to the soul by his disobedience of God, then God is the judge of a man's actions and thereby a man's acts judged by God as moral or immoral, i.e. pure or sinful. Had man obeyed God then he would not have a soul, since he would be immortal. Since man creates a corporation then man judges a corporation as ethical or unethical. If it creates wealth, it is behaving ethically and its existence continues.   If the corporation fails to create wealth, it is behaving unethically and it eventually ceases to exist.   Thus, the "soul" of a corporation manifests in profit or the creation of wealth.

Labor Contacts are unethical because they are coercive

A labor contract executed under threat of a strike or under threat of financial harm, as all labor contracts are, is unenforceable since it is signed under duress and therefore against the will of the corporation as embodied by the officers of the corporation.   The officer of a corporation is akin to a sovereign in the sense that he must protect the life of a corporation whose purpose is to create wealth or profit.   He has therefore a fiduciary or ethical and legally enforceable duty to the owners of the corporation.   This duty arises out of self-interest and is contractual not altruistic.   It is not a duty arising from compassion or loyalty for the owners of a corporation although such passions may be present, and laid claim to, the passions cannot be controlling to the point where they operate against the self-interest of the officer.   The sovereign of a nation also has a fiduciary as well as a moral duty to the individuals or the citizens of the nation.   The sovereign must be loyal to the nation as his life is common to the nation or owned by the nation, and he is the nation so he must be loyal to himself in accordance with Natural Law. The sovereign of a nation has a moral duty to the nation wherein he places his soul in jeopardy before God, and his life in jeopardy before Man, should he fail in his moral duty.   The manager of a corporation has an ethical duty to the owners of the corporation and places his position in jeopardy should he fail in his ethical duty.   A manager has no moral duty to the owners and so does not jeopardize his soul if he acts unethically, i.e. fails to make a profit or create wealth.   On the other hand, a manager or employee who embezzles or otherwise steals from a company is committing an immoral and an illegal act but he does not, nor can he, act disloyally.   Loyalty therefore is a moral precept and ethical precept only applicable to the sovereign and neither an ethical, or a moral precept applicable to the officer or employee of a corporation.

Every man is sovereign unto himself.   Every individual owes loyalty only to himself and to his wife, under the marriage vow before God, and his children who are physical and moral extensions of himself. He owes loyalty since he is sovereign over them, and he owes loyalty to no one else, i.e. he jeopardizes his soul before God in failing to act out of loyalty to his marriage vows.   Loyalty means to act against self-interest where necessary to preserve the marriage or for the well-being of the child apart from protecting him from harm, which is a separate duty and not one of loyalty.   Thus, loyalty is a moral precept as well as an ethical precept applicable to the marriage unit.   Loyalty stems from the presumption of truth, i.e. bearing witness.   Disloyalty is bearing false witness hence disloyalty is a sin.   Loyalty is not altruism, which is acting against self-interest by one's volition.   There is no loyalty owed a stepchild or adopted by a stepparent or adoptive parent, but rather a legal duty and not a moral duty.   The stepparent's or adoptive parent's moral duty is to protect the child from harm and he is thus sovereign over the stepchild at the moment the child is exposed to harm, as any individual would be as in the case of saving a drowning man.   Neglecting his legal duty and endangering the life or well-being of the stepchild is an abrogation of his sovereignty and thus he is liable under man's law and his soul is liable under God's law.   A stepparent or adoptive parent cannot be disloyal only unfaithful to his legal duty.   Thus, abandoning an adoptive or stepchild is a violation of man's law but as long as the abandonment does not harm the child, it is not a violation of God's Law. Abandoning your own child is a violation of sovereign law, God's law, and Natural Law because a man must be loyal to himself and his child is an extension of himself.   The distinction is important because it speaks to the disposition of the soul.

A sovereign who enacts laws that enforce a contract that an individual or a company executed under duress, i.e. under threat of financial harm, as union contracts are, is violating his duty to the individuals that comprise the nation and betraying his loyalty to the nation's citizens.   Such a sovereign is subjecting the nation to an additional, unnecessary and unethical burden on wealth creation by encumbering commerce.   The encumbrance to commerce arises from the distortion to the market price for labor introduced by coercive labor contracts and offshoots, which include minimum wage laws and prevailing wage laws.   In other words, the sovereign is undermining the ability of the nation to survive a calamity when he enforces contracts exercised under duress or against the will of any of the parties.   As I have shown, ethical behavior is any act resulting in the creation of wealth because it increases the ability of a nation to survive a calamity and eases the burden of life consistent with Natural Law.   The aim or goal of ethical behavior is therefore the creation of wealth and the easing of the burden of life.   One can say that the goal of ethical behavior is happiness as Aristotle had said, as wealth and an easier life are the sources of happiness.   To the degree that wealth and the resulting ease gives rise to pleasure then the goal of ethical behavior is also pleasure as the Epicureans opined.   Thus, the source of happiness and pleasure is wealth.   The sovereign is acting unethically when he uses the state's power of eminent domain to enforce labor contracts.   He is also acting immorally since he is betraying his loyalty to the nation and therefore his loyalty to himself, as he is the nation.   As I indicated above, loyalty is to be true to others and to oneself.   Betrayal is bearing false witness and therein is its immorality.   Labor unions that engage in collective bargaining are unethical entities because they introduce coercion in an otherwise unencumbered economy and as such they undermine the creation of wealth. An economy where union contracts exist is an encumbered economy that fails to create wealth, and such an economy is less able to withstand a calamity. Ultimately, such an economy will indeed succumb to calamity. The disastrous financial state of once great cities like Detroit, Akron and Youngstown among others, where unrepentant unions dominated the local economies, is the face of such calamity.

However, the sovereign can do no wrong and he is beyond reproach so how then can he behave unethically or even immorally? The sovereign is beyond reproach only when he is engaging in the protection of private property and enforcing contracts. Contracts are by definition acts of freewill. Therefore, a sovereign fails in his ethical and moral duty to protect private property when he enforces the unenforceable and he now becomes a threat to wealth creation. Such a sovereign is ripe for rebellion and replacement because he is no longer protecting private property and he has undermined the liberty to contract. In the process, he has undermined the ability of an economy to withstand a calamity. The divine right of king comes from God and it is the right to take life and property without jeopardizing the soul of the sovereign king. The sovereign jeopardizes his soul as he willingly abrogates the divine right of king as accorded by God when he fails to protect private property and enacts laws enforcing contracts made against the will of one of the parties.

The nation is an organization of individuals established to secure private property and enforce contracts. As I mentioned earlier individuals in a primitive state of nature spend all their allotted time on earth securing their private property against calamity. This affords individuals little time to create wealth or store and it makes them susceptible to calamity. Calamity can be manmade such as wars and attacks on property or natural such as floods, drought, and disease all of which threaten life and property. A sovereign is the protector of the nation as selected by the individuals comprising the nation. The sovereign is dedicated to protecting the nation's private property and the enforcement of contracts. He does not and cannot engage in the creation of wealth. A sovereign becomes corrupt when he engages in actions or enacts laws not directed to the purpose of his appointment or election. Accordingly, he must endure the wrath of man through rebellion or civil war and the wrath of God through the disposition of his soul.

Individuals must yield some productivity and some liberty for security

In order to organize and to sustain a nation the individuals comprising the nation must yield a portion of their productivity or wealth creating ability to the sovereign as well as a portion of their liberty, i.e.

freedom to contract.   Freed of the burden of protecting and securing their private property the individuals comprising the nation can more fully engage their time in creating wealth and thereby secure themselves and the nation against calamity.   However, the wealthier or the greater the store accumulated by the nation the greater the demands made upon wealth by the sovereign in order to secure the wealth.   In the absence of calamity, the wealth of the nation grows continuously.   The wealthier the nation becomes the more it has to loose and the greater the proportion of wealth demanded by the sovereign to secure the private property of the individuals and the more willing the individuals are to tolerate the additional demands.   Thus, the sovereign places an increasing burden on the wealth creation of the nation as the wealth or store of the nation increases.   The increasing burden eventually diminishes the ability of the nation to create wealth and survive a calamity while increasing the power of the sovereign over the nation.   The power of the sovereign is the power to take life and property without fear of corporal or incorporeal punishment or retribution on the person or soul of the sovereign.   The United States created great wealth during the 19th Century and along with the creation of wealth came a powerful navy and army propelling the United States to a world power militarily in a very short time.   This was necessary to protect the worldwide trading and economic interests of United States individuals and corporations that were the source of the wealth.   The increasing demands on the government to protect and secure private property led to the 16th Amendment imposing an income tax with very little outcry from the wealthy at the time as they sought greater security from the sovereign and were willing to pay for it up to a point.   Most individuals impacted by the income tax at the time moved their incomes overseas to avoid the tax as it became more onerous under Woodrow Wilson.   The 16th Amendment ceded great power to the sovereign in terms of what the sovereign could take from individuals and corporations.   Following the 16th Amendment was the 19th Amendment, which gave rise to universal suffrage about six years later in 1920.   These two amendments set the stage for the calamities that followed during the balance of the twentieth century.   Thus, increasing wealth contained within it the seeds of its destruction as it sought greater security at the expense of liberty and productivity, i.e. at the expense of the ability to create wealth.   By the end of the 1930's the nation lost much wealth and much liberty.   Indeed, by the 1930s such destruction of wealth occurred as to set back significantly the ability of a nation to survive future calamities.   By 1933, the real GDP had dropped to the same level as it was 10 years earlier.   It took about three more years before the economy was back to a GDP that exceeded the previous peak in 1929.   By 1937, the economy was producing goods and services at a level greater than in 1929 thus resuming the growth cut short due primarily to rapid increases in productivity in the agricultural sector of the economy but made much worse by the government's interference in the economy.

Sovereign poses risk to wealth creation in two ways.

A sovereign through the exercise of his power of eminent domain therefore poses a risk to wealth-creation in two ways, first through the demand for a greater proportion of the wealth created by the nation, and then through increasing limits to the exercise of freewill. The latter becomes limits to liberty in the execution of contracts. For a nation to sustain itself therefore, the sovereign must limit his power of eminent domain by reducing the burden on the economy both in terms of taxation, i.e. the taking of private property, and in terms of liberty to contract. Envy manifested through universal suffrage engenders a godless sovereign's demand for a greater proportion of wealth and the encumbering of the economy. Thus, envy leads to the destruction of wealth through the sovereign power of eminent domain. This of course requires a sovereign who does not fear God or Man. Such a sovereign is ripe for rebellion or civil war because the sovereign has abrogated the divine right of king accorded by God for the perpetuation of Man as ordained by God then God disposes of his soul accordingly.

Sovereignty of multiple elected officials

Unlike a monarchy, the limit to the sovereign's power of eminent domain in a constitutional republic manifests in the allocation of the power of eminent domain to multiple individuals and the constitution. The limit to the sovereign's power of eminent domain embodies in a constitution created by the Framers, as in the case of the US Constitution, amendable by the legislative branch and the sovereign states by plebiscite, and adjudicated by the judicial branch of government. The election of several individuals to represent the populace for the protection of private property and the enforcement of contracts characterizes a constitutional republic. In a monarchy, there is no written constitution as the king is the constitution and the parliament is the legislature. The king rules according to the law as enacted by parliament and his expenditures are a matter of law, i.e. determined by the parliament. Unlike a constitutional republic, there are no limits to the king's power of eminent domain other than those specifically set forth by the parliament. These limits can easily change from parliament to parliament. In a constitutional republic, the limits to the sovereign's power of eminent domain change only by plebiscite, i.e. through amendment to the constitution. A constitutional republic places direct limits on all functions of the sovereign by plebiscite through amendment, a plebiscite imposes no such direct limits to a monarchy.

Unlike a direct democracy, both a constitutional republic and a monarchy limit the ability of the majority to suppress or oppress the minority. Yet such oppression can and does occur. The American War between the States is an example of the result of the majority North imposing tariffs on manufactured goods needed by the minority South against the will of the South. The French revolution is another example where the French Republic led by the majority by plebiscite dispatched by the guillotine 50,000 of the minority aristocracy.

In any representative government, each elected official is subject to the divine right of king individually and collectively while in office. Other than through periodic plebiscites, the peaceful removal of any seated elected official is by one of two ways impeachment or recall. Impeachment is from within government and recall is through extra-governmental act of the citizens. Violent rebellion or a coup d'état is also a method of removing seated elected officials or monarchs from office. In a pure monarchy or tyranny, the limit to a sovereign's actions, is only by the threat of rebellion or by rebellion.

The divine right of king secures the soul of all who are sovereign as it does all who are soldiers. That is while sovereign or soldier an individual can do no wrong morally, legally or ethically as long as he acts in accordance with due process or in accordance with the law, which the sovereign himself enacts. Even if acting outside the law the sovereign goes unpunished unless he chooses to punish himself or provokes rebellion or civil war. Those individuals who as sovereign succeed in overburdening the economy and undermining wealth creation jeopardize their souls before God and subject the nation to calamity. Such individuals risk rebellion before man. Those individuals as sovereign who resist overburdening the economy, and thereby promote wealth creation secure their souls before God and secure the nation from calamity. Those individuals who would be sovereign by appealing to envy abrogate the divine right of king jeopardize their soul and invite rebellion or civil war. Abraham Lincoln appealed to the envy of the North for Southern wealth by supporting the Morrill Tariff whose intent was the destruction of the wealth of the South. This was the cause of the War Between the States. Thus, Abraham Lincoln and the Northern legislators abrogated the divine right of king as they satiated the North's envy of the South by enacting the Morrill Tariff and thus condemned their souls by provoking civil war.

Universal suffrage and the secularization of its institutions is the bane of a constitutional republic because it leads to a sovereign who overburdens the economy and undermine wealth creation. Universal suffrage and absence of the fear of God will eventually cause a constitutional republic to revert to tyranny, which is the only form of government spawned by economic socialism and communism. Economic socialism and communism are the economic systems of envy and altruism and only exist and can exist under godless tyrannical rule.

The hypocrisy of the French Revolution

One cause of the French Revolution, for example, was the inflation in the price of food brought upon by the sovereign's taking of the fruits of labor of the feudal peasants to finance foreign adventures that provided little return to the nation in terms of security or wealth. Unlike Britain, which implemented a system of enclosure beginning in the 16th Century, thus enabling private property to take hold on a general basis and larger scale within 200 years, France remained a feudal economy through the 17th and late 18th Century with no general system of private property. The king and the landed aristocracy owned the property and France had no enclosure laws, which provided the legal means of dividing and selling property. Thus, the sovereign and the landed aristocracy held most land in common. The French Revolution accomplished in a violent and destructive fashion the privatization that the British had centuries earlier implemented with the Enclosure Statues. The elimination of the feudal system with the establishment of private property became manifest in the French Declaration of the Rights of Man. The inviolability of private property appeared in two Articles of the Declaration. Article 2 states *"The aim of all political association is the preservation of the natural and imprescriptible rights of man. These rights are liberty, property, security, and resistance to oppression."* Article 17 states *"Property being an inviolable and sacred right, no one can be deprived of it, unless demanded by public necessity, legally constituted, explicitly demands it, and under the condition of a just and prior indemnity."* The great hypocrisy is that the French Revolution while espousing the inviolability of life and property resulted in the murder of 50,000 people who had their property stolen, divided, and given to someone else. In the case of the so-called Declaration of the Rights of Man, it only applied to those who were willing to commit murder and steal from others. The important and pivotal question is where was the fear of God during the French Revolution? Unlike the United States Declaration of Independence, which relied on God as Lawgiver and Creator, the Rights of Man had no reference to God. A nation that does not fear God will soon consume itself and France became such a nation in the early 19th century, first under the Reign of Terror, and then as a generation of young men, Frenchmen as well as many other Europeans, perished under the egomaniac and the godless Napoleon Bonaparte. Also unlike the Americans who eschewed the atheism of the Enlightenment, the French embraced the Enlightenment's so-called humanism and atheism. Napoleon crowning himself emperor was the symbolic act, otherwise performed by the Church's bishop, legitimizing to the French and the world the final break with God's Commandments. The French paid a high and terrible price for their apostasy as they succumbed to envy engendered by the godlessness of the Enlightenment. The price for their folly was the loss of their wealth as embodied in their sons sacrificed by Napoleon on the altar of envy. Thus was France, once a great power, weakened and never recovered her ability to defend herself relying instead on the God fearing nations to come to her aide in time of war even until this day.

Rapid gains in productivity lead to unemployment

As I have said, rapid gains in productivity result in short-term disruption in employment leading to civil unrest. If left to its own devices, i.e. the free market, an unencumbered economy will naturally overcome the unemployment as it enters a new phase of growth spurred on by the gains in productivity and the subsequent wealth creation. However, demands for greater security arising from the civil unrest leads to increasing demands on wealth creation by the sovereign unless resisted by the nation. The sovereign's demand on wealth creation manifests itself in increased regulations and greater taxes, which encumber an economy. By increased regulations, I mean laws that interfere with the formation of contracts by legally mandating terms and conditions otherwise not included by any of the parties to the contract. This has the effect of further reducing the wealth of a nation and increasing the risk to the security of private property and the exercise of freewill in contracting. An encumbered economy exacerbates unemployment, thereby fomenting rather than reducing civil unrest.

The optimal action on the part of the sovereign when calls for increased security arise from rapid gains in productivity is to reduce the burden of government by reducing taxation and regulation. Reducing the burden of the government enables economic growth, which mitigates the civil unrest arising from the rapid gains in productivity. Logically and historically, this has proven to be the best response. For example, the depression that occurred from 1920 to 1921 recovered with no interference by government and a reduction in taxes. This depression was due primarily to the collapse of farm prices after the overproduction following World War I as I will discuss later and I show in Figure 41 below. The government took no action under Republican Warren Harding's laissez-faire policies. In fact, Harding cut government spending and reduced taxes thereby ending the depression and ushering in the real boom of the 1920s. Government spending went from $18.5 billion nominal dollars in 1919 to $3.3 billion in 1922 a reduction of 82%. Harding reduced the public debt by 2.5% between 1919 and 1921. He cut the individual tax rates by half at the lowest bracket going from 6% to 3%. He reduced income tax rates from 77% to 56% at the top bracket. He reduced corporate rates by 11.2% going from 12% in 1918 to 10% from 1919 to 1921. He also eliminated the "excess profits tax" of as much as 60% in 1922. The Wilson Administration enacted the "excess profit tax" to punish companies that made a profit from Wilson's unjust and unnecessary war. There was no intervention by the Federal Reserve

Bank to "stimulate the economy" and interest rates were set by the market during this period. The Harding/Coolidge administration cut individual taxes even further while corporate rates were once again increased averaging 11.9% during the decade. Due to the greatly reduced interference in the economy and despite the Fordney–McCumber Tariff, the economy grew at an unprecedented rate from 1922 to 1928. Unlike the Smoot-Hawley Tariff, which emerged a decade later, the Fordney–McCumber Tariff was primarily a defensive ad valorem based tariff, as the gold standard was not yet stabilizing exchange rates after its collapse from the war years. An ad valorem tariff adds a percentage to the value of the imported good. A fixed price tariff specifies the price of an imported good. The latter is much more harmful to the economy than the former. The later Smoot-Hawley Tariff was primarily a fixed price tariff. The lack of a gold standard led to inflating of currencies, which drove foreign prices lower in terms of the US dollar. Thus, the Fordney–McCumber Tariff was a de facto gold standard for the United States economy. Figure 37 illustrates that Federal revenues increased significantly during the Harding/Coolidge Administrations in comparison to the two previous decades and even after the passage of the 16th Amendment authorizing the income tax and the implementation of the "excess profit" war tax. Despite the lowering of the tax rates and the elimination of the "excess profit" war tax, Federal revenues increased during the Harding/Coolidge Administration from an average of about $26 billion annually between 1913 and 1920 to about $43 billion annually between 1921 and 1930. This was due in large part to the repatriation of wealth held overseas to avoid the increasing income taxes under Wilson. This helps explain the lack of outcry from many of the wealthy at the time of the enactment of the 16th Amendment. They simply moved their money and their incomes overseas to avoid the tax.

The immensely successful Harding died within 2 years of his election under mysterious circumstances in California. There is no doubt in my mind that his successful undoing of Wilson's progressive and atheistic agenda had much to do with his early death probably at the hands of the atheists and progressives. Revisionist historians have gone to great lengths to besmirch Harding and his administration. This alone is reason to know that he was highly successful and effective.

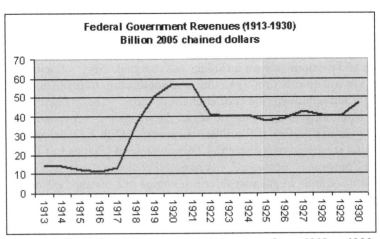

Figure 37- Federal Government Revenues from 1913 to 1930

Contrast Harding's administration with the actions that the Democrats and FDR, i.e. the so-called progressives and liberals, took in response to the depression of 1929-1931, which lasted 11 years, and characterized by unprecedented government interference in the economy. Had Warren Harding been president instead of FDR there would not have been a depression and the economy would have created great wealth. I even argue that there would not have been a Dust Bowl or World War II because the effect of the prolonged depression along with tariffs and the mercantile accumulation of gold by FDR helped to impoverish a fragile German economy leading to political upheaval and the rise of Hitler and German socialism. It also led to Japan's invasion of China as the Japanese economy also suffered from the trade barriers erected by the United States. Although Japan's socialist government would eventually have led to the invasion of China, the United States trade barriers probably accelerated the timing of the invasion as well as precipitating the Japanese attack on Pearl Harbor. Whether or not the United States would have gone to war with Japan had the trade barriers not been erected remains problematic considering the socialist ambitions of the Japanese and their lust and envy of their neighbor's wealth. Just as the Japan socialists invaded China, the current Chinese communists will one day invade Japan as well as South Korea, because they need Japan's and South Korea's wealth to sustain their socialist economy. The reason the communist Chinese continue to prop up the North Korean economy and military is that one day they will rely on the North Koreans to do their part in stealing the wealth of their neighbors.

A sovereign who does not fear God threatens the survival of a nation

The sovereign who does not fear God is susceptible to the foibles and passions of man including and especially envy. Such a sovereign will quickly turn to tyranny and subjugation to maintain his absolute and unlimited power of eminent domain. This is regardless of any constitutional limits to the power of the sovereign. A constitution does not limit a godless and ruthless sovereign. Only by rebellion is a tyrannical sovereign overthrown. This was true of Charles I of England whom I previously mentioned. A nation therefore in order to sustain itself and continue to grow wealth must engage in constant vigilance of the sovereign to prevent the usurpation of private property and the liberty to contract regardless of the form of government. Failure to exercise such vigilance will result in the collapse of the nation as the sovereign continues to demand more of the fruits of labor and capital ostensibly to secure private property but in reality to enrich or further empower his own self as such a sovereign does not fear God. A godless sovereign who envies the nation who appointed or elected him to protect is as much a threat to the creation of wealth and the survival of the nation as is an envious enemy nation or an envious populace.

The Nation's Wealth

The totality of the stock of the nation's individuals comprises the wealth of a nation. The stock of a nation includes the buildings, factories, homes, land, as well as equity and cash in the bank possessed by the individuals of the nation. The measure of wealth is monetary it is not money. In other words, the measure of wealth is in terms of money. Money by itself is a means of exchange. Money is not wealth. The accumulation of stock that is land, buildings, shares, and cash is wealth, which is the hedge against calamity. Money is not cash. Cash is what shows up in a bank account statement. Liquidity is the ability to turn stock into money or the means of exchange i.e. paper money or checks. Cash is the most liquid of stock. The inability to turn cash into money leads to civil unrest because it means that banks holding the cash are unable to convert it into money on demand or to honor checks. This has occurred from time to time, and it has usually led to laws and regulations that encumber an economy resulting in more bank failures after the government enacts these laws and regulations. The Federal Insurance Deposit Corporation (FDIC) law is an example of such laws as I discussed earlier. While the government intended the FDIC to protect and secure depositor's cash the actual result is an increase in the number of bank failures and a greater burden on the taxpayer leading to a reduction in wealth creation as occurred in the 1990's with the Savings and Loan scandal that ensnared many prominent Democrats.

Replacement of equipment or structures is not wealth creation

The simple replacement of worn or damaged equipment or structures does not result in an increase in wealth. Planning or accounting for the expected eventual replacement of worn or damaged equipment or property is depreciation. At a national level, depreciation is Capital Consumption Allowance (CCA) and it diminishes the capital stock or wealth of the nation over time. Failure to replenish capital stock results in a loss of wealth over time. Planning or accounting for unexpected replacement of equipment or property is insurance which is analogous to depreciation. When property damage occurs because of a natural calamity or when equipment wears out, for instance, this reduces the value of that property. This is a reduction in wealth, i.e. a reduction in the ability to withstand future calamity. Restoration merely restores the original value of the property. Therefore, despite the labor and energy that goes into the restoration or replacement there is no increase in wealth. Hence, individuals expend scarce resources without creating wealth. A calamity by definition is the destruction of wealth. As long as the calamity does not destroy the ability to create wealth then wealth is restorable. However if the calamity destroys the ability to create wealth then there is no restoring of wealth and the calamity is total destruction. The ability to create wealth embodies in the intelligence of the population. Such destruction has occurred in the past and I will discuss this in more detail shortly. The inability to create wealth is the reason mankind has been on the precipice of extinction.

A similar argument exists following a sharp reduction in equity prices. A drop in the price of a share of stock is due to some calamity that befell the stock. The restoration of the price to its former level is not wealth creation despite the fact that someone may have gained from the increase in price. Wealth creation only occurs when the price of the stock continues to increase because of increasing earnings.

The argument made by some that a calamity is an opportunity is specious. A calamity is never an opportunity. A calamity is a destruction of wealth that a nation or individual must overcome in order for a nation or individual to survive. The process of overcoming a calamity utilizes resources including labor that otherwise would have gone to the creation of wealth.

The ability to create wealth resides in the intellect of individuals

The ability to create wealth resides in the intellect of the individuals comprising the nation. This is the intellectual capital or intellectual store of the nation as measured by the average IQ of the population. The greater the intellectual capital or the greater the average IQ of the population, then the more likely the nation overcomes a calamity once it occurs. The destruction of intellectual capital will cause the nation to perish because its economy will be unable to create wealth. The destruction of intellectual capital can occur and has occurred and it is the reason that civilizations have disappeared in the past as I have alluded to earlier. The intellectual capacity, i.e. the average IQ of the population of a nation is the single greatest determining factor in the wealth creating ability of a nation that in turn determines the survival of a nation. Apart from this, the fear of God and the burden of the sovereign are the other great determinants of the wealth of a nation and its ability to survive calamity.

The wealth of a nation is the sum total of the wealth held by the individuals comprising the nation and it is the product of the intellectual capital of the nation. A wealthy nation has a great store of intellectual capital and is able to survive and overcome a calamity whereas a nation with a lesser store of intellectual capital is less able to survive or overcome a calamity. Assets including intellectual capital owned by the sovereign or the state are unproductive and so contribute nothing to the wealth of a nation or to wealth creation. Therefore, assets including intellectual assets, i.e. intelligent individuals, owned or employed by the state should be only those assets necessary to fulfill its primary purpose that is the securing of private property and the enforcement of contracts.

Sovereign acquires assets by force or threat of force

The only way for a sovereign to acquire assets is to take them by force from others who may be its citizens or through war from its neighbors. While individuals may vote to tax themselves, it has never happened that all the individuals of a nation agree to the taxation. Rebellion or the threat of rebellion and the fear of God, limits the ability and propensity for a sovereign to take assets from its citizens. The less homogeneous in terms of culture and assimilation a nation then the more likely a godless sovereign will avoid rebellion when taking the assets of selected and easily identifiable minorities. The more homogeneous the nation in terms of culture and assimilation the less success the sovereign will have in taking the assets of its citizens and the more likely it will go to war with its neighbors. Germany during the 1930's is an example of a nation whose godless sovereign took the assets of an identifiable and enviable minority to sustain the sovereign and the socialist state that he created, and to which the majority of the population acquiesced. The persecution of the Jews by the German government was to take their property and wealth so that the nation could recover from the inflation engendered by the payment of reparations under the Treaty of Versailles ending World War I. Those Jews with a great deal of assets relinquished their assets and generally survived. These Jews were able to flee Germany. While Jews with fewer assets lost everything including their lives. The loss of their lives was necessary to avoid supporting them once the state took their wealth and to avoid future reprisals. The assets taken by the government were to increase government spending for a war infrastructure in order to create employment, and maintain a social welfare system for the remaining majority German people. As long as the sovereign engendered envy of the Jewish minority, and the social welfare system served the majority, then there was no outcry and a blind eye turned to the death and destruction of the German Jew. The assets the German government took from the Jews destroyed wealth, i.e. the lives and property of the Jews. There was little wealth creation in Germany during the 1930's as government spending increased and Germany's wealth-creating productivity went toward building armaments and maintaining a social welfare state, and not toward creating wealth. Armaments are not wealth because there is no return on investment. They are implements to destroy wealth, i.e. they are instruments of calamity. Thus while ostensibly the Jews were victimized as a people, the real reason for their fate was for the sovereign to take the wealth of an easily identifiable minority group to sustain a socialist state for the approving majority. Unlike popular notions that anti-Semitism sprang from religious bigotry, which it did not, anti-Semitism is nothing more than a manifestation of envy and envy arises in the atheist since the godless has no compunction against envy or bearing false witness. Nor is an atheist compelled to follow God's Commandments. As was the case of the leaders of the French Revolution, German leaders in the 1930s fomented envy among a cynical and economically suffering populace conditioned not to fear God by the events and atheistic ideas leading up to, and following, World War I. The idea that "God is dead" drew great media attention and through the works of such German philosophers as Friedrich Nietzsche and G. W. F. Hegel. These philosophers as well as other atheists served the purposes of the German socialists as they engendered and fomented envy of the Jew who was a very successful and wealthy minority in Germany. The fate of the German Jews was akin to the fate of the French aristocrats of the French Revolution also persecuted from the envy engendered by the godless socialists of the time. The excuse of anti-Semitism therefore is an invention of the socialists to blame religion or race for their murderous acts arising in fact out of godlessness and atheism, and not from the fear of God but rather to spite God.

On the other hand, the Japanese whose culture was much more homogeneous did not victimize any of its citizens. Instead, the Japanese socialists sought to take the wealth and resources of its neighbor China to sustain its social welfare system and military state. Thus, Japan occupied Manchuria in 1931 and began a full-scale invasion in 1937 to acquire riches and resources needed to sustain their socialism, while the Germans embarked on the isolation and taking of the property and life of the Jew in Germany for the same purpose. Yet this was not enough to satisfy the German leviathan and like the Japanese, the Germans ultimately looked to their neighbors to rob them of their wealth and in the process destroyed themselves as well as much of Europe.

Wealth is the only hedge against calamity.

An example of what I mean by wealth is a house. A house is shelter against the elements or against nature. Nature is a source of calamity, which is the destruction of wealth. The value of the house is as a hedge against calamity therefore the house comprises wealth. This is apart from what another individual may value the house. In other words, wealth is an absolute measure of the hedge against calamity. The stronger the house the greater the store of wealth since it is more likely to survive a calamity. Thus, a well-built house is not expensive because it costs more to build but because it better withstands calamity. The more opulent the house also the greater the store of wealth since opulence eases the burden of life in the absence of calamity. The price of the house depends on the willingness of another to exchange his labor as store, i.e. as accumulated savings for the house. If there is competition for the house then the price of the house increases in terms of the amount of labor as store needed to buy the house. The final price of the house is independent of the cost to build the house or in other words, the final price of the house is independent of the cost of labor expended in its construction, the cost of materials used in its construction, and the interest on the money used to finance its construction. This is true of all prices in general. In other words, the price of a good or service is only a function of supply and demand and not on the cost to manufacture the good or the cost to provide a service. Thus a good or service can bring a price less than its cost of production in which case there is a loss of wealth. However, the loss of wealth is limited to the labor and capital that went into the production of the good or service. On the other hand, the gain in wealth is practically unlimited as the demand for the good or service has no upper limit other than that set by the price and competition. This is the fundamental tenet of a free enterprise economy and the reason that it is always successful, i.e. generates wealth, if left unencumbered. In other words, in a free enterprise and unencumbered economy, losses are limited to the resources expended but gains have no real limit. This is the reason for the material advancement of mankind and in particular Western Civilization.

Efficiency of capital and efficiency of labor

Productivity of an enterprise is a measure of the efficiency of the enterprise. Efficiency in general is the ratio of money output to money input. There are two types of efficiencies in any enterprise. There is an efficiency associated with the investment needed to create, build or grow the enterprise and an efficiency associated with the operation of the enterprise. The input associated with the investment is the capital or cash required to create, build or grow the enterprise and the output is the average profit or average net income over time. This is capital efficiency or the return on investment. The input associated with the operation of the enterprise is the revenue generated and the output is the immediate profit or net income. This is the operational efficiency or the return on labor. Note that the return on investment or return on capital is over a long time, which is generally more than one year, whereas the return on operations or labor is over a short time, which is generally quarterly. Both capital productivity and operational or labor productivity are subject to continuous improvement in efficiency. As we will see, continuous improvement in efficiency is essential to wealth creation and to the survival of the enterprise. Continuous improvement in efficiency translates into a rate over time of gains in productivity that manifests as increasing profit or profit growth in a non-inflationary or unencumbered economy. The rate of gain in productivity is necessary to overcome increasing economic inflation arising from scarcity and resulting in increases in the cost of raw material and the cost of labor. It is also necessary in overcoming monetary inflation in an encumbered economy, which is the result of government monetary and fiscal policy as well as government taxation, regulation and union coercion. Wealth creation occurs when the rate of productivity growth exceeds the rate of inflation and the prevailing interest rate.

Sources of inflation

As I alluded to, there are two sources of inflation and these two sources give rise to two types of inflation. Increasing scarcity arising from increasing demand and/or decreasing supply is one source of inflation, which I call economic inflation. That is, as demand for a good or service increases, then the price of the good or service also increases. Similarly, if the supply of a good or service decreases then the price of the good or service increases. Economic inflation is attributable to changes in the supply and demand of goods and services not to a decrease in the value of money. Economic inflation is an increase in the price of specific goods and services. Government monetary and fiscal policy is the other source of inflation, which I call monetary inflation and is a decrease in the value of money. Monetary inflation is an increase in the price of all goods and services. Improvements in the efficiency of providing specific goods and services offset monetary inflation. Thus while monetary inflation reduces the value of money, its effect on specific prices is a function of efficiency. The overall rate of inflation is the sum of the average economic inflation and monetary inflation. The overall rate of inflation ultimately determines the prevailing interest rates, which is the price of debt. Generally, the higher the rate of inflation is then the higher the interest rates become. Figure 21 above illustrates where the CPI has been for the most part, below the prime interest rates since 1956.

Perceived risk in the economy also affects interest rates, as does the supply and demand for debt. Interest is the cost of debt and debt is one means to finance the growth or the efficiency of an enterprise. The other means to finance the growth or efficiency of an enterprise is through equity. The legal, ethical and moral difference between debt financing and equity financing is that debt is a contractual obligation and it has no claim on the profits of an enterprise. Equity financing is ownership of an enterprise and with ownership come a share in the profits. Debt financing also has first claim on the assets of an enterprise after taxes in the event of bankruptcy. Equity in a bankruptcy has a claim on the assets after debt and taxes are paid. The creation of wealth occurs when the rate of productivity growth exceeds the cost of borrowing, which is the cost of debt. In other words, wealth creation occurs when the return on an investment, i.e. the cost of equity, and the return on labor, exceeds the cost of borrowing money and the rate of inflation. A prudent creditor, who seeks to preserve his principle, will only lend money to a debtor who has assets, or collateral, whose value far exceeds the value of the debt. This enables the recovery of debt in the event of the inability of the debtor to pay back the debt and/or the loss of the value of the asset, which is collateral. The value of assets grows in two ways. The first way is through profit reinvested in new assets increasing the book value of the assets or in other words as the enterprise grows. The second way is through demand for the assets by investors seeking a greater return through future increase in share price and dividends than the return provided by interest on debt. In other words, a rational investor always seeks the greatest return with the lowest risk. Generally, economic inflation affects more the long-term, i.e. greater than one year return on investment, while monetary inflation affects more the short-term return on labor or the return on operating costs.

To the extent that operating costs include depreciation then monetary inflation also affects the long-term return on investment. To illustrate this point suppose that a company purchases a stamping machine for $100,000 and the stamping machine lasts 20 years with zero net salvage value. The company must replace the stamping machine after 20 years so that the company remains in business, although the money can go back to the investor as a return of his capital. The sum of the return of capital and the return on capital is the total return to the investor. This total return must be higher than the prevailing interest rate on the same investment in order to attract the investment, mitigate risk and to create wealth. On a straight-line basis, the cost to the company for the machine is $5000 annually. Inflation reduces the value of the return of capital. To maintain a total return greater than the prevailing interest rate the return on investment or in other words the rate of profit growth must exceed the rate of inflation. If after 20 years the cost of replacing the machine is $150,000 then the depreciation, which amounts to a use of revenue for replacing the machine is insufficient for this purpose. The company must now either borrow or invest the difference in order to remain in business. Thus, the increase in the cost of the stamping machine without any concomitant improvement or operational advantage jeopardizes the survival of the company and in turn jeopardizes the creation of wealth.

Profit is wealth creation and a measure of efficiency

The profit an enterprise earns in an unencumbered economy is a measure of capital and operational efficiency or productivity. Productivity is not the same as production. Production is the level of production, i.e. the quantity or dollar amount that an enterprise generates. Productivity is the efficiency of production or the rate of production in terms of the capital and labor inputs to the enterprise and the net income, which is the output. In mathematical terms, the instantaneous rate of productivity growth is the derivative over time of the productivity, which is the ratio of output to input. As I indicated earlier, an unencumbered economy is an economy free of taxation, regulation, and coercion in which each individual acts in accordance with his freewill to contract. An unencumbered economy is an economy where contracts do not include mandated requirements established by the government, and there is equal taxation of all, and an absolute minimum level of taxation. By equal taxation, I mean a tax in absolute terms or in other words, a head tax not an income tax based on a percentage of income or a percentage of wealth. In other words not a tithe. In such an economy, the profit of an enterprise is a direct measure of the degree to which the enterprise satisfies the needs or demands of consumers. Profit is a measure of wealth creation. The greater the profit of an enterprise is then the greater the wealth that is created by the enterprise. The creation of wealth engenders greater opportunity for more wealth resulting in investments, which increase employment thus mitigating the potential for civil unrest. In this regard, wealth-creation fulfills its purpose, as civil unrest is a harbinger of calamity.

The hedge against calamity in an agrarian economy is the surplus created and the store arising from the surplus. Whereas in an agrarian economy the measure of wealth or store is in bales of hay or tons of wheat, the measure of wealth in an industrial or so-called post-industrial economy is monetary. Carrying the equivalence or analogy a step further, in an agrarian economy the input is the seed and the output is seed as well. Each plant produces a surplus of seeds. So from a single seed come multiple seeds. The number of seeds that come from a single or unit plant is the productivity of the plant. Analogously, in an industrial economy, the seed is money. The plant is the investment and the product or the output is profit measured in money. Money and not the product or service is a measure of the productivity of the investment just like the seed produced is a measure of the productivity of a plant. The profit is the surplus created by the enterprise. Profit is the money that remains after payment of all the expenses of the enterprise including the capital recovery expense. Profit is the net income of the enterprise and is private property subject to the protection of the sovereign. It is wealth creation and it is the reason that the enterprise exists. The more productive the enterprise or in other words the more efficiently it operates the greater the profit, the greater the wealth created, and the more secure is the enterprise and the nation against calamity.

Profit is a measure of the satisfaction of consumer needs

An enterprise therefore creates wealth when its products or services efficiently satisfy a need or demand of consumers in an unencumbered economy. The level of profit is the measure of how well an enterprise meets the needs of consumers in an unencumbered economy. A profitable enterprise therefore is an ethical venture as it creates wealth thereby securing the enterprise and the nation against calamity. An enterprise that does not create profit is unethical and unless it is sustained or subsidized by the sovereign, it will eventually succumb under its own weight, as it should. The reason an enterprise fails in an unencumbered economy is that its products or services do not satisfy the demands or needs of consumers or it does so inefficiently and the price is higher than is its competitor prices. The act of sustaining or subsidizing of an unprofitable enterprise by the sovereign is itself unethical and a corruption of the sovereign since such acts burden wealth creation, and jeopardize the protection of private property and undermine the enforcement of contracts.

Sustaining an unprofitable enterprise places a burden on wealth creation.

The sovereign sustaining an unprofitable enterprise places a burden on wealth creation and therein lays its immorality as well as its mortality. The sovereign jeopardizes the disposition of his soul, risks rebellion, invasion by envious nations, or succumbing to natural calamity, whenever he risks the security of the nation by sustaining unprofitable enterprises. Yet this is what the Japanese economy has undergone since the 1990's. Prior to the 1990's the Japanese economy was one of the fastest growing in the world. The chart of Figure 38 below compares the growth in the average weekly pay of the Japanese worker from 1952 with the growth in GDP and per capita GDP over the same period. Also shown are the corresponding trend lines and correlation coefficient. The slope of the trend line is the coefficient of the independent variable. Note that the average weekly pay for the average worker grew at a rate of 0.54% per year whereas the growth in per capita GDP grew at a rate of 0.16% per year. While the Japanese are very productive individuals due to their high level of intellect, management nevertheless also overcompensate their workers at a rate that is 3.5 times greater than justified by their productivity. In order to sustain this disparity between productivity and compensation the Japanese started printing money and reduced interest rates during the early 1980's. They did this partly in an attempt to overcome a slowdown in growth that occurred during the 1970's and arising from increasing interference by the government in the Japanese economy as well as the abrogation of the Bretton-Woods agreement by the United States and the engendering of the fiat currency. The result was an asset bubble bursting in 1991 and engineered primarily by the government of Japan through increasing taxation, borrowing and printing of money. The Nikkei 225 index fell 41% from its high in 1989 of 39,000 to 23,000 by the end of 1991. This foreshadowed the collapse of the Dow in 2008, as these same socialist and progressive forces were at work in the Japanese economy as in the US economy and begun under Clinton. The Japanese economy has remained stagnant ever since with practically no growth and now with the average weekly pay starting to drop. The Japanese have effectively stopped creating wealth and are living on the wealth created prior to the 1990s. The Japanese government effectively subsidized unproductive industry by printing and borrowing money thus allowing the overcompensation of employees to continue and this is the reason that the economy of Japan is no longer growing. Japan now is more susceptible to calamity than in the past. Indeed Japan has had some difficulty recovering from the tsunami and earthquake that struck its northeastern shore in 2011 although not nearly the difficulty that Haiti has had recovering from its 2010 earthquake. Japan will have a difficult time defending itself against China or North Korea in the event these nations decide to attack Japan and take its remaining wealth. In order for Japan to escape its economic malaise it must allow individuals and companies to fail, it must bring compensation of employees closer to their productivity, and it must eliminate government taxation, spending on social programs, cut taxes and regulation, stop borrowing money, and stop printing money.

Note that the separation between the percent growth in average weekly pay, growth in per capita GDP and growth in GDP for Japan began in 1970 or at the same time that the fiat currency came into existence. Had the United States not embarked on its wealth destroying laws and remained on the gold standard then the Japanese economy would have produced much greater wealth and it would not be in decline as it is currently.

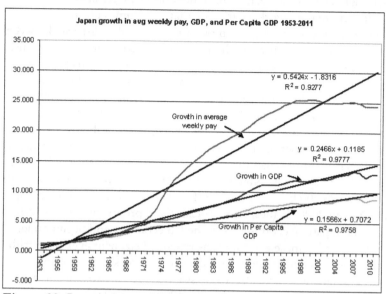

Figure 38-Comparison of Growth in average weekly pay, Growth in GDP and Growth in Per Capita GDP for Japan

Supply and Demand determine price in an unencumbered economy

The supply of a good or service and the demand for the good or service determines the price of the good or service in an unencumbered economy. In an unencumbered economy, the price of a good or service remains stable over time because changes in supply and demand move freely. That is, an increase in the supply of a good or service occurs through additional suppliers of the good or service or increased production of the good or service. This will cause the price of the good or service to decline given a constant demand. In an expanding unencumbered economy a decline in price will cause demand to go up and the price will reach an equilibrium that is close to the previous price. The familiar supply-demand curve shown in Figure 39 illustrates the equilibrium between supply and demand, which is the market price.

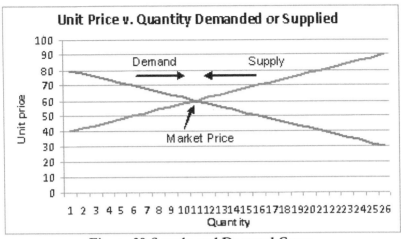

Figure 39-Supply and Demand Curve

Figure 39 shows that as the unit price of a good or service decreases the demand for the good or service increases. The line with the negative slope in the graph represents the demand curve. At the same time, the supply of the good or service decreases. The equation for the demand curve in this case is D=-aQ+b and for the supply curve S=dQ+c. The market unit price of the good or service occurs at the point where D=S or D-S=0. When the demand of the good or service meets the supply of the good or service an equilibrium or market unit price is established. The constant "b" in the demand equation is the unit price that represents zero demand, i.e. Q=0, which is the y-intercept. The constant "b" is the unit price where no sales occur as extrapolated from actual sales at the market price. The quantity coefficient "a" is the strength of the demand. The steeper the slope of the demand curve then the less the quantity bought for an increase in the unit price. The product of the quantity bought and the unit price is the revenue to the supplier. For a constant coefficient "a" the greater the value of "b" is then the greater the demand for a given unit price. As the value of "b" increases or in other words as the demand curve moves to the right, the revenue to the supplier increases assuming that the supply curve does not move. The increase in revenue is exponential while the increase in demand is linear. On the other hand, as the value of "b" decreases, i.e. as demand decreases, the revenue to the supplier decreases exponentially. Increasing demand for a product or service creates a stream of revenue analogous to compound interest. Figure 40 is the integral of the demand and supply curves and it shows the exponential nature of the revenue to the supplier and costs to the consumer.

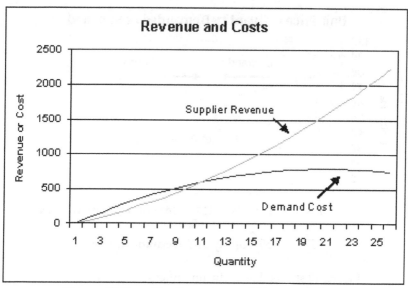

Figure 40-Supplier Revenue and Demand Cost

The demand curve of Figure 39 moving to the right represents an increase in demand. If the supply stays the same then the increased demand will cause the price to go up reaching a new equilibrium point, which is the market price. The increase in the market price will cause an increase in supply moving the supply curve to the left and thereby yielding a lower price and a new equilibrium. The new price equilibrium or market price will be the same as the original, thus over time the price of a good or service remains stable but only in an unencumbered economy. While the unit price remains the same the number of goods or services sold increases, thus the individual supplier enjoys greater revenue while the individual consumer enjoys a constant price. Thus, in an unencumbered economy inflation or deflation of prices are short term phenomena, as changes in supply and demand offset each other.

The underlying assumption that supply and demand is the ultimate determinant of price is that individuals will behave rationally. It is essential that individuals behave rationally in order for an economy to create wealth. In other words, when the nominal price of something increases then consumers will reduce their purchases and suppliers will increase their production. The price of every good or service does not necessarily respond linearly to changes in supply and demand. Similarly, a change in the quantity supplied or demanded of a good or service does not necessarily respond linearly to changes in prices. The degree to which the price responds to changes in supply and demand is price elasticity. However, it is true on a macro economic basis or generally, that changes in the quantity of a good or services supplied and demanded

180

cause changes in the price

When economic decisions rely on factors other than price and cost there is a reduction in the creation of wealth. In other words when individuals behave with total irrationality, then there is no wealth created. Neither is wealth created when altruism is the dominating motivating passion of individuals rather than greed. Altruistic behavior is by definition irrational whereas behavior based on greed is rational, with the former passion destroying wealth and the latter passion creating wealth. Envy is irrational as well and an economy encumbered by envy results in socialism and communism, which destroy wealth. Envy and altruism are manifestation of the same irrational passion. Of course, behaving rationally requires a minimum level of intelligence and I will address this point later when I discuss the intellectual capital of nations.

In an encumbered economy price is independent of supply and demand

In an encumbered economy, the price of a good or service is independent of supply and demand and such an economy creates no wealth. Thus, an encumbered economy is irrational. Referring to the supply and demand curve, the price of a good or service in an encumbered economy will occur at a point where the supply and demand curves do not intersect. This is due to taxes and regulations that in turn increase inflation. An example of the distortion introduced into the economy by government is the sales tax. The sales tax adds to the price of an item independent of supply and demand relative to an unencumbered economy. The added price causes the demand to decline. An illustration of this occurs each time a local or state government decides to offer a holiday from sales taxes. Invariably when this happens sales increase tremendously. Thus, the underlying potential of the supply and demand for a product or service is always greater in an encumbered economy. An encumbered economy therefore creates pent up demand for goods and services. The degree of the pent up demand is the degree that the sovereign encumbers the economy. There is no pent up demand in an unencumbered economy. Un-encumbering an economy always leads to greater wealth creation because it releases pent up demand. This was true during the Harding/Coolidge Administration, the Eisenhower Administration, the Reagan Administration, and the George W. Bush Administrations. Although in the latter case the holdovers from the Clinton Administration, the Democrat Congress, and their shills in the media did their best to sabotage the economy during George W. Bush's administration, a task in which they unfortunately succeeded, and which I will have something more to say later.

If the price of a good or service is higher than it would be under an unencumbered economy then supply will increase while demand decreases and much waste generated or in other words the economy expends scarce resources with no creation in wealth. This happens whenever the government subsidizes a particular industry through tariffs or through targeted tax credits. The Smoot-Hawley Tariff on imported farm products enacted in 1930 propped up farm prices temporarily and it falsely held out the promise of higher prices. As I stated earlier unlike the Fordney–McCumber Tariff, which was primarily an ad valorem tax and therefore defensive tariff, the Smoot-Hawley Tariff was an offensive tariff that placed specific prices on imported goods regardless, or independent, of the supply or demand for the goods. In this sense, it was akin to the USSR's central planning that fixed prices and wages, which resulted in little wealth creation and made the USSR susceptible to Germany's aggression. The Smooth-Hawley Tariff made it economically impossible to import the targeted goods and it bought all international trade to a practical standstill as the other nations responded with offensive tariffs of their own. The tariff did not just affect United States trade but trade amongst and between other nations as well. The Smoot-Hawley Tariff was the failed political solution to an economic problem. Political solutions to economic problems always fail. Gains in farm productivity brought about mainly by the introduction of the internal combustion engine in farm implements, particularly the tractor caused over production resulting in a steep drop in farm prices in the 1920s compared to the post war prices prior to the 1920's. As shown in Figure 41 below, the wholesale price of farm products dropped by almost 70% between 1919 and 1932 as the number of farm tractors increased from about 158,000 in 1919 to over 1 million by 1932, an increase of almost 550%. The agrarian economy was almost 30% of the US economy during the first third of the twentieth century in terms of the number of individuals employed on farms versus the total number of employed individuals. The result was the Great Depression as the drop in farm prices caused farm losses leading to defaults on loans, foreclosures, and bank failures. Note that after 1929, the number of tractors remained constant due to the low prices for farm products and the inability of farmers to obtain credit thus slowing productivity growth, and farm prices started to rise. The rise in farm prices was also due in part to the Smoot-Hawley tariff that effectively eliminated foreign competition in farm products. The rise in farm prices spurred the purchase of more tractors that led to another drop in farm prices in 1935, resulting in more bank failures, a 30% drop in stock prices, and a rise in unemployment to 20%. Fueling the drop in farm prices was a drop in farm exports as other nations retaliated to the Smoot-Hawley tariff by imposing their own tariffs on US farm products as well as some manufacturing goods. By 1935, the government effectively repealed the Smoot-Hawley tariff and increasing demand arising out of World War II and then the Korean War drove prices much higher by the 1950's. This maintained farm productivity gains, which now began to include consolidation of farms and the taking of land out of production. This increased the purchase of tractors until the mid 1950s when the price of farm products dropped thereby flattening out the number of farm tractors sold. After the 1950's farm production, i.e. supply, essentially kept pace with demand and farm prices stabilized as productivity growth went toward offsetting the inflation of the late 1960s rather than creating wealth, which would have been the effect, had government not interfered in the economy through radically increased levels of social spending. Between 1965 and 1968, the total Federal outlays increased over 38% going from 729.4 billion in 1965 to over $1 trillion in 1968 in 2005-chained dollars. Keep in mind that prior to 1970 the US dollar was fixed in terms of the amount of gold it could buy but inflation was occurring as union demands for increased wages in light of foreign competition, and increased government spending was making it difficult for the Federal Reserve Bank to maintain the value of the dollar. This was its legal mandate. Foreign competition in manufacturing started to emerge once again as the Western European and Japanese industrial economies recovered from the devastation of World War II. Despite the tremendous accumulation of gold prior to World War II, the US was running out of gold to sell in order to maintain the value of the dollar and there was a danger the dollar would collapse thus putting trade to a standstill and causing the price of gold to soar and inflation to soar as well. This is the reason the US abrogated the Bretton-Woods agreement thus creating the fiat currency and the floating exchange rates. Despite this action, the dollar still lost considerable value with inflation accelerating through the 1970s reaching a record annual rate of 13.5% in 1980. Ever since 1970 Federal outlays have continued to rise unabated and the Federal debt has increased in almost every year except for a brief respite between 1998 and 2001.

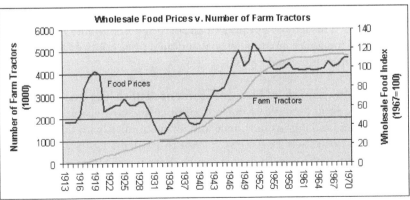

Figure 41-Wholesale Food prices v. Number of Farm Tractors

Had the government not undertaken the social spending and

expansion of welfare spending and other non-defense related government programs, not increased taxes, and regulations on business, and repealed the Wagner Act, which would have effectively ended union contracts and collective bargaining, then there would have been no inflation and much wealth created during the 1970's.   Instead, there was much poverty and misery during the 1970's and the creation of wealth did not resume until the 1980s when the government reduced tax rates, broadened the tax base, and reduced and eliminated regulations, and only tepidly enforced union contracts, and Civil Rights laws, i.e. when the government reduced its burden on the economy.   Innovation and invention also accelerated during the 1980's with the introduction of the personal computer and useful software applications like LOTUS 123, WORD PERFECT and other useful computer programs into the workplace thus accelerating the rate of productivity growth particularly in the service sector.   The 1980's also saw the beginning of the internet, cellular telephones and fiber optics. These innovations were possible because the government reduced its burden on the economy due solely to the politically motivated social legislation, onerous regulations, and taxes of the 1960's and 1970's.   The period of the 1980s and early 1990s was analogous to the enactment of the enclosure laws in England, which increased private property, eliminated feudalism, restored the fear of God and creating much wealth in the process.

If government forces the price of a good or service lower than it would be under an unencumbered economy then demand will increase and supply will decrease and this will lead to forced rationing.   This occurs whenever the government imposes price controls through fiat. These are economically unstable conditions and the longer they persist then the greater the waste of scarce resources and the greater the reduction in wealth creation.   The government tried price controls for a short time after the abrogation of the Bretton-Woods Agreement in a disastrous attempt to stem the tide of inflation unleashed by the new fiat currency.   This led to shortages of all sorts of commodities including food, and the government quickly abandoned price controls at which point inflation increased rapidly.

USPS is an example of how government distorts the free market

A good example of the kind of price and cost distortions that government and unions introduce into an economy is with the economics of the US Postal Service (USPS).   Prior to 1970, the USPS was a department of the government and subsidized by taxpayers.   The USPS was a union operation in one form or another through about half of its history but it was not until 1971 that the Federal government sanctioned collective bargaining after a prolonged strike by postal workers. This strike followed on the heels of much labor unrest during the 1960's and 1970's as unions saw the threat of foreign competition and forced companies to enter into unsustainable contracts. This was with the blessing of the Democrats in power during this time both at the local, state and Federal level. After 1970, the USPS ostensibly became a self-supporting independent agency however, it never become wholly self-supporting requiring taxpayer subsidies every few years. The most current loss (2012) of almost $16 billion is the largest single year loss in the history of the Post Office. This loss comes on the heels of an additional accumulated loss of over $25 billion since 2007. These losses expected to continue threaten the USPS's existence or at least its existence in its current form.

The volume of first class mail grew at an average linear rate of 1.54 billion pieces of mail per year from 1948 until it peaked in 2001. Postal rates on an inflation-adjusted basis remained relatively stable from about 1980 and revenue followed the increase in volume also rising linearly. Expenses however were increasing exponentially at a compound rate of 5.5% per year. The expenses started to accelerate after 1970 as the unions acquired more power in determining their pay and benefits. At this rate, expenses per employee were doubling every 13 years. After 2001, the volume of first class mail began to decline as the number of personal computers increased and individuals started to use email and the Internet instead of the USPS to save time and money and accomplish the same goals. Between 2001 and 2012, the average rate of decline in first class volume was 3.2 billion pieces of mail per year or twice the average rate of increase prior to 2001. The rapidly declining volume caused the expenses per employee to exceed the revenue per employee for the first time in 2010 and continuing on this trend through 2012 resulting in the $16 billion dollar deficit in 2012. This happened despite increases in the postal rates. See Figure 42.

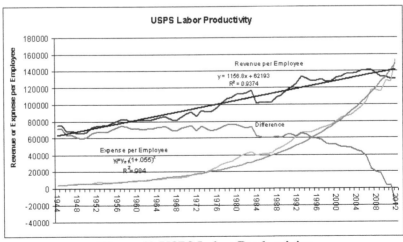

Figure 42-USPS Labor Productivity

Since 2000, the USPS has increased its nominal first class postage rates by over 36% and at the same time its revenue declined by almost 33%. The higher the nominal unit price of first class mail, the lower the total revenue received after 2000. Rather than decreasing unit cost in order to stimulate demand and meet competition from the Internet, the USPS increased prices in the face of declining demand, which it helped to cause by relentlessly increasing nominal rates and thus accelerating the decline in revenue. Shown in Figure 43 is the annual first class mail rates as a percent of the rate in 2001 as compared to first class mail revenues as a percent of the revenue in 2001. Note that revenue started to decline in 2002 while rates were constant and until 2004. After 2004, the USPS started increasing rates aggressively attempting in vain to make up for the lost revenue resulting from the decline in volume. However this time rising rates had the opposite effect and revenue started to decline as quickly as rates increased. The difference in the revenue changes between increasing rates before 2001 and after 2001 is that after 2001 there was competition in the form of emails and the Internet. After the 2008 financial crises, corporations aggressively cut expenses in order to increase earnings in the face of a significant decline in revenues in general thus rapidly improving their productivity partly at the expense of the USPS. Increases in the price of equities between 2008 and 2012 resulting from the unprecedented infusion of liquidity and historically low interest rates by the Federal Reserve Bank in the face of a government induced stagnant economy forced companies to increase productivity, i.e. earnings. They did this by aggressively cutting expenses in order to maintain P/E ratios at historical levels, and mailing expenses were a major expense for many companies. The low interest rates enabled companies to borrow money and invest in technology that offered alternatives to the USPS. The rapid gains in productivity continue as companies and individuals look for alternatives to first class mail in order to save money. Nevertheless, despite the declining mail volume the USPS continues to increase rates, which had the effect of stimulating consumers to look for more alternatives to first class mail thus accelerating the decline in volume and in revenue. In other words, the higher the postal rates the quicker that the USPS loses money in a competitive economy. The USPS is now in the throes of a death spiral.

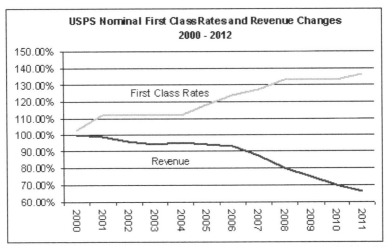

Figure 43-USPS First Class Rates and Revenue Changes 2000 - 2012

Figure 44 below shows the correlation between USPS first class postal rates and revenue after 2000 when it was facing increasing competition from email and the Internet. Note the negative correlation. Figure 45 shows the correlation between USPS first class postal rates and revenue before 2000 when the USPS had a virtual monopoly on first class mail. The effect of competition was to change the pricing dynamic and in the case of the USPS, a government sanctioned monopoly, the failure or inability to respond to competition and to the law of supply and demand by cutting its costs will be its ultimate demise.

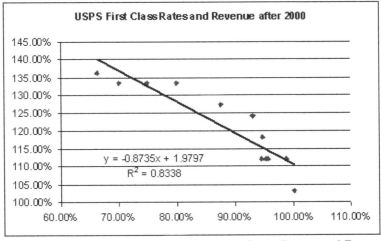

Figure 44-Correlation between USPS First Class Rates and Revenue after 2000

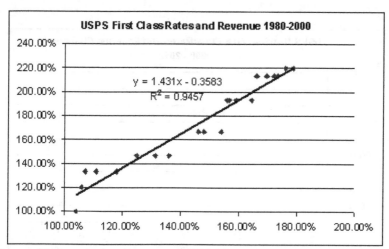

Figure 45-Correlation between USPS First Class Rates and Revenue between 1980 and 2000

Had the USPS maintained a cost structure where the expense per employee less the revenue per employee was a constant level, then the USPS would have at least been able to remain viable in the face of competition. However, even as competition began to take hold, rather than reduce expenses the USPS did, what it traditionally has always done, which is to raise rates. Given that management and the unions knew that the USPS could always go back to the government to bail it out, management had little incentive to fight union demands for more pay and benefits during the monopoly years prior to 2000, and greedy unions had little incentive to stop demanding more. This attitude on the part of USPS management is no different to the attitude that exists now among bank management and their reliance on the FDIC as it arises out of government interference in the economy. The problem of course is that the government itself is now running out of money or has in fact run out of money. Government distorted the market for first class mail by eliminating incentives to control labor costs and by sanctioning collective bargaining at the same time that it made the USPS an independent self-supporting agency. In other words, the union ran the USPS not management and the sole shareholder, i.e. the government, allowed it to happen. Consequently, and predictably it ends up as a failure and a great burden on the economy.

It is interesting to note that the USPS has also invested considerably in technology beginning in the 1980s in order to improve their productivity however, these investments failed to provide a return because in spite of the considerable investments the USPS kept adding employees at a rate faster than the growth in mail volume. (See Figure 46) It was as if the postal union was singlehandedly trying to offset the decline in union membership in the economy in general by adding unionized employees to its payroll during the 1980s. The depreciation of this considerable new investment added to the expense rather than offsetting expenses as expected in a well-managed operation. This accelerated the losses as mail volume declined after 2000.

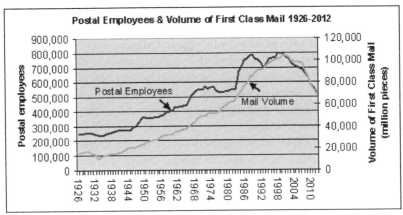

Figure 46 – Postal Employees and Volume of First Class Mail - 1926-2012

In many ways, the USPS is a microcosm of a socialist state where the "workers", i.e. proletariat, manage themselves in a "workers paradise" and its fate is the same, i.e. failure and poverty. There is of course one way the USPS could survive and that way is for the government to eliminate its competition. This is the typical course of action for any tyranny. In other words, if the facts fail to fit the theory then change the facts. At one point, there was a proposal by a Berkley California City Councilman to tax every email to support the Postal Service. This is akin to the demands of farmers for tariffs in the 1920's. Government eventually responded to these demands by the farmers and the result was great poverty, misery, war, and death. Government must resist these demands and stay with its original purpose, i.e. the protection of private property and the enforcement of contracts, if the nation is to survive.

Inflation similar to income taxes because it affects all goods and services

Unlike tariffs and price controls, which tend to affect specific goods and services, monetary inflation is similar to income taxes as it affects all goods and services. With productivity growth constant, then as the value of money decreases this increases the nominal price of a good or service creating a supply side physical surplus amid a declining physical demand. Thus, suppliers expend scarce resources but do not create wealth they instead simply build inventory. In the case of monetary deflation with productivity growth held constant, then as the value of money increases the nominal price of a good or service decreases creating increasing demand with no corresponding increase in supply as suppliers now have lower margins. Monetary deflation leads to shortages. Monetary deflation is by price controls or rationing. In an inflationary or deflationary economy driven by monetary and fiscal policy, there is no wealth created and a nation faces increased risk of succumbing to a calamity. The more rapid the change in the monetary inflation rate or monetary deflation rate the greater the imbalances between the cost of various types of labor and the cost of various materials. While monetary inflation and deflation are ubiquitous in an economy, the effects of rapid monetary inflation or rapid monetary deflation do not evenly distribute. Thus, the rate of inflation of the price of goods and services may exceed the rate of inflation of wages. This creates imbalances in the economy that cause a draw down in savings and a reduction in investments further undermining wealth creation and destroying wealth. A rapid rate of deflation of the price of goods and services may exceed the rate of deflation of wages causing lower profit margins also reducing wealth creation and increasing unemployment.

Unlike economic inflation and deflation that only affect the price of a specific good or service and are due to short-term fluctuations in the quantity supplied or demanded, monetary inflation and deflation also affect the price of money, which is the interest rate on debt or the return on investment. During times of monetary inflation caused by government fiscal or monetary policy the interest rates will tend to rise if left to the free market thus further encumbering the economy over and above the government's fiscal or monetary policy intentions. The price of money, i.e. the interest rate, is a function of supply and demand for money in an unencumbered economy. However, when the government interferes in the market for money, which it has continuously done since the abrogation of the Bretton-Woods agreement in 1970, then interest rates become independent of the supply and demand for credit. The government interferes in the market for money by issuing large amounts of debt to enable its profligate spending, and forcing the Federal Reserve Bank by law to buy the debt at lower interest than free market rates. The law requires the Federal Reserve Bank to buy US Government debt when an insufficient number of private or foreign sovereign creditors buy the debt at the interest rate offered by the US Treasury. The result is two fold, an artificial rise in the value of equities and other assets as lower interest rates tend to push capital to equities, and an underlying inflation rate that suppliers and consumers must offset through increases in productivity. The increases in productivity that would otherwise go toward the creation of greater wealth and manifest in a growing economy as measured by the GDP, instead now go toward keeping inflation at bay with no growth and a flat or even declining GDP. As equities and other assets increase in their nominal value due to the low interest rates, and the unearned increases in the money supply in a no-growth economy, the productivity gains result in rising unemployment. In other words, productivity gains go toward converting the unearned dollars in the money supply to earned dollars instead of to increased wealth, i.e. new dollars. As unemployment increases so does the risk of calamity in the form of civil unrest. To offset the underlying civil unrest the government must increase spending on social programs such as unemployment compensation, welfare, food stamps and other unproductive spending. This adds to the national debt and thus government creates a downward spiral that can only end with rebellion or civil war. Continuous increase in the price of assets is only possible with the assumption that the rate of productivity gains is sustainable during and beyond the time government undertakes to interfere in the economy. If productivity gains cease or slow, then prices for goods and services will rise to sustain company earnings in the face of vaunted asset valuations. The resulting economic inflation will cause interest rates to rise rapidly leading to a flight from the equity to the debt markets and a resulting collapse of the equity markets. A flight from equity to debt occurred in 2000 when the Federal Reserve Bank increased interest rates for no other reason than to stem a legitimate bull market in equities. Unlike the bull market following the collapse of the financial sector in 2008, and driven by productivity growth, revenue growth from new products and services drove the bull market during the 1980s and 1990s as evidenced by the record number of IPOs introduced during this time. Actually, the rise in equities since the 2008 collapse was not strictly speaking a bull market because it did not create wealth. Rather it was a restoration of the wealth destroyed by the government but at the expense of employment and a decline in median income. As I will discuss later, the rapid and irrational increase in interest rates by the Federal Reserve Bank and the resulting massive flight from equity caused the collapse of the equity markets in 2000. Its effects are still reverberating to this day.

Government interference in the economy accelerated in the 1970s

While the government laid the legal groundwork for massive government interference in the economy in the 1960s under Johnson, and added to it in the 1970s under Carter, government interference in the economy began in earnest in the 1970's, and the immediate aftermath was a historically rapid increase in the inflation rate that devastated the economy until the 1980's. After 1980, the government under President Reagan undertook a less burdensome path. The productivity gains in the form of computerization increased the mechanization of manufacturing, the deregulation of major industries as well as the decline of unions, and the reduction of government's interference in the economy during the 1980s, led to an exponential rise in the creation of wealth significantly offsetting the underlying monetary inflation. The pace of technological innovation increased in the 1990's with the introduction of the cell phone, fiber optics, and the internet as well as even broader applications of the computer, particularly in the service industry. The computer along with fiber optic technology enabled innovations in the service industry such as intelligent point of sale terminals, just in time inventory control, on-line retailing, remote call centers, work at home, and other such improvements in productivity. These improvements in productivity offset increasingly aggressive government interference in the economy during the 1990s until the productivity gains could no longer withstand the government interference in the economy through the Federal Reserve Bank. This interference culminated in the collapse of the stock market in 2000. I argue that envy of the innovators who emerged during the 1980s and 1990s and helped propel the NASDAQ to 5048 in March 2000 drove the godless Alan Greenspan, Chairman of the Federal Reserve at the time to bring them down. Greenspan's relentless increases in interest rates caused the NASDAQ to drop to 1423 by September of 2001 for a loss of 72%. This collapse ushered in the sub-prime mortgage market as the Federal Reserve Bank rapidly dropped interest rates to the lowest level in history in an attempt to recover from the debacle it had created by increasing interest rates for no good reason but Greenspan's envy. Greenspan undertook the lowering of interest rates in almost every month in 2001 in an unprecedented and failed attempt to undo the damage his envy had done to the economy. The discount rate went from 6% at the beginning of 2001 to 1.25% by the end of 2001. In January of 2001, Greenspan on his own and without consultation from the other members of the Federal Reserve Bank lowered interest rates three times. The discount rate dropped to a record low at the time of 0.75% by the end of 2002. The low interest rates and the resulting subprime mortgage market led to the even greater collapse of the equities market in 2008. Thus, there are limits to the degree that productivity gains can offset relentless government interference in the economy, and eventually there will be dire and irreversible economic and political consequences that threaten the survival of private property and with that the survival of the nation.

In the 1920s and 1930s, the government failed to support farm prices in the face of rapid gains in farm productivity because the gold standard tied the government's hands. Had the government not imposed the Smoot-Hawley Tariff, increase corporate taxes and government spending farm prices would have recovered on their own. On the other hand, the fiat currency is a new paradigm and it changes the game. Now, the government holds all the cards and it can actually bring down an economy not merely prolong a depression. In other words, once the government knows it can bring down the economy of the nation it was supposed to protect and secure then in the absence of the fear of God, it will do just that. An absence in the fear of God exists in those imbued with the propaganda of the Enlightenment. The so-called Enlightenment taught that scientific reason can and must replace faith and the established tradition and experience in the governing of a nation. This describes the political left in the United States in general and the Democrat Party in particular since the beginning of the twentieth century. Given the unprecedented interference in the economy through the addition of over $3 trillion in fiat currency by the Federal Reserve Bank, and the increased taxation and regulation of business since 2008, it is inevitable that another collapse in the equities market will occur in the near future. This collapse will be due either to rapid increases in interest rates as productivity gains can no longer hold inflation at bay or through civil unrest as the poverty and misery engendered by unemployment spread in the general economy.

Prices have no moral or ethical basis in an unencumbered economy

In an unencumbered economy, the price of a good or service is independent of ethical considerations. There exists no moral or ethical code to invoke justifying the price of a good or service one way or another in an unencumbered economy. However, there is an ethical issue with prices in an economy where regulation, taxation, and coercion in contract formation exist. In such an economy, the price and profit of a good or service is independent of supply and demand, as I have earlier indicated. To the extent that the price of a product or service is independent of free market supply and demand, then the wealth creating capacity of an economy diminishes, and such an economy becomes susceptible to calamity. Government interference in the economy is therefore unethical since it always results in a decline of wealth creation. Thus, the price of a good or service in an economy encumbered by the government has moral and ethical consequences because it results in lower profits reducing wealth creation. The reduced wealth creation makes a nation susceptible to calamity and therein is the ethical and moral consequence of prices in an encumbered economy.

Usury laws

The earliest form of government coercion or regulation in the market place occurred in the marketplace for money or debt. Interest charged on money loaned always existed in one form or another throughout the ages. Where interest charged on money existed, there was a general increase in the wealth of nations. The interest rate charged was determined on a competitive basis, i.e. supply and demand for credit. Since the value of money remained generally fixed then the quantity of money remained primarily a function of the productive capacity of the nation coining the money. That is, as productivity increased so did the level of production, which increased the number and quality of goods and services available for purchase. With the value of money fixed then the supply of money increased to enable the exchange of money for the greater quantity of goods and services available. When gold could buy more things then the supply of gold increased as productivity increased. The high level of productivity of the European nations gave rise to the Age of Discovery. The Age of Discovery meant the Age of Discovery of gold and silver. European nations sought gold and silver to increase the supply of money needed to keep pace with the innovations leading to the increasingly efficient production of goods and services as well as the production of new goods and services, and the increasing demand for these goods and services. These goods and services were a hedge against calamity and in the absence of calamity they eased the burden of life and therein the reason for the demand. The measure of money's value is in how much or what the money can buy both in goods and in labor.

Interest rates during the Roman times were around 2% to 4%. After the fall of Rome and the rise of the Church as the protector of Western Civilization, usury laws, which arose primarily on religious grounds, prohibited the charging of interest for money loaned. The basis of these laws was an obvious misunderstanding of the function of money and the purpose of wealth creation. Unfortunately, this misunderstanding persists even today and it is one reason that socialism persists as a viable economic system in the minds of many people. Usury laws, which prevent or severely restrict the charging of interest on money loaned, are coercive whether based on religious or secular reasoning. Accordingly, usury laws place an encumbrance on free enterprise, i.e. usury laws place an encumbrance on debt contracts and on contract formation, and thus restrict and limit the creation of wealth. The usury laws implemented and enforced during the Middle Ages is the major economic reason that there was little human progress or wealth creation in Western nations during those times despite the fear of God. The other reason was the lack of laws securing and protecting private property. In many respects, there is a similarity to the laws against usury and the socialist or feudal idea of common property. The flawed idea that money and property belong in common or to the sovereign, and that the sovereign owns everything including the lives of his subjects, gives rise to secular laws against usury and a feudal economic system that fails to create wealth. Although parenthetically it was the destruction of intellectual capital that occurred during Roman times that was the main physical cause leading to the lack of understanding of the function of money and the purpose of wealth creation. It was not until the reemergence of intellectual capital as manifested in the Renaissance in the European population that credit at competitive interest rates resumed and Western Civilization reemerged to dominate the world as it did during early and middle Roman times, i.e. prior to the decline in the average IQ of the Roman population. The coercion and limitations to liberty introduced into the marketplace by socialism and communism and their handmaiden, the welfare state, once again threaten to plunge humanity into an economic dark age, or a type of feudalism, with very little real wealth creation, and all productivity consumed and none stored. Coercion within an economy or in other words the absence of freewill or liberty to contract therefore poses an ethical and a moral problem in an economy because it threatens the survival of the economy, the nation, and of the individuals comprising the nation. Usury laws were such coercion in the distant past and the taxes, business regulations, union contracts, and environmental laws are such coercion now.

Usury laws is an early example of coercion in an economy

Usury laws whose source was the religious prohibition against interest charged on money loaned is also the source of the flawed notion that profit is unethical or some misguided individuals would even say immoral. The religious idea behind usury laws is that money is inanimate and therefore incapable of breeding itself, thus usury is against the will of God. This idea is a result of Aristotle's influence on Christian Theology as expounded by Thomas Aquinas. It is the intellectual basis of the labor theory of value. The labor theory of value is the flawed notion that the value of a commodity or the value of anything that is produced rests only in the labor used to produce it. Any value beyond the value of the labor is the same as usury, or as some would say thievery. To those that hold these misguided views, profit is not a measure of the degree an enterprise satisfies the needs of consumers but rather profit is simply a legal form of stealing. According to this laughable notion profit is the same as usury as understood by the Church in the Middle Ages, and therefore unethical and immoral. The usury laws with their legal and moral prohibition against interest charged on money loaned suppressed the creation of wealth and population growth in Europe during the period from the fall of the Roman Empire until the Renaissance. The suppression of the creation of wealth and slow population growth weakened Europe militarily and made Europe susceptible to calamity, and calamity did indeed come during the Middle Ages. The weakened condition of the European nations during this period enabled the rise of the Muslim Moors in Western Europe and the invasion of the Muslim Ottomans from the East. Although the Muslim religion. Islam, also prohibits the charging of interest, Muslims largely ignored this prohibition. This allowed the mixed-race Moors and Ottomans to build wealth that rivaled the wealth of the Europeans at the time, despite the lower average intelligence of these groups thus enabling their ability to insert themselves into the European territory of the Caucasoid. Had the usury laws not existed, the Semite Arabs would not have occupied Europe, and Europe would have created great wealth and a greater population. As it was, the Europeans had to suffer the mixed race Moors and Ottomans until the Caucasoid Europeans recovered their intellectual capital through lack of mixing with these and other non-Caucasian peoples thereby giving rise to the Renaissance and the creation of great wealth.   While the rise of Christianity had the effect of introducing usury laws into the economics of Europe during the Middle Ages, the religious restrictions against marrying outside the Caucasian Race prevented mixing with the less intelligent Moor thus enabling the reemergence of a high level of intellectual capital that is the hallmark of the Caucasian Race.   This was particularly true of the Northern Europeans while less so with the Southern Europeans who had undergone considerable mixing with the Negroid slaves and mixed race populations of Northern Africa and the Middle East during Roman times. Shakespeare's Othello is the quintessential Spanish Moor (in Greek the word "moor" means dim, i.e. dim witted) easily outwitted by the more intelligent and much more clever Caucasoid Iago.   Thus, the lesson of the play is the dim-witted Moor despite his rank easily outdone by the more intelligent Caucasoid Iago as indeed was the historical case.   Along with the rise of intellectual capital came a break with the religious restrictions against usury and interest charged for money loaned, and the ability to create wealth.   Nevertheless, it took until the beginning of the twentieth century finally to expel the Turk from the lands of Southern Europe and the Turk left his mark as the southern European nations extending from Portugal, Southern Spain, Southern Italy, and Greece bear the relatively low average intellect and darker physical characteristics of the Moor and Turk.   The low average intellect along with increasing secularization is the primary reason that these nations are having great difficulty in managing themselves under the European Union.   Ironically, it is the existence of usury, i.e. sovereign debt, weakening these nations rather than its absence.   If the religious prohibition against usury, i.e. neither lend nor borrow, applied only to the sovereign then the aforementioned nations would not be on the verge of calamity.   Usury laws are a stark example of the results of coercion and regulation in an economy and it is a lesson for today, as the Turk and the Moor is now amongst us once more.

As I mentioned earlier the labor theory of value is a form of the misguided idea that usury is immoral.   That is any value obtained for a good or service greater than the value of the labor that produced the good or service is akin to usury, i.e. interest charged on money.   The labor theory of value is a tenet of Marxism and it perpetuates the flawed notion that profit is unethical or even immoral.   One can say that the labor theory of value is the secular equivalent to the religious idea that usury is immoral.   Marxism is very much a product of the Enlightenment in that it eschews the belief in God.   Yet it is a great irony of Marxism to have as a basic tenet the religious prohibition of usury, i.e. the idea that profit is immoral.   Marxism as the philosophical underpinning of communism and socialism has led to the destruction of much wealth in the world and it continues to pose a threat to mankind in general. The view of making a profit and of charging interest as unethical, or worse immoral, is one of the greatest intellectual errors that Western Man has made and continues to make. Marxism is a perpetuation of this error and it is one reason that nations that organize for the protection of private property and enforcement of contracts must devote a greater part of their wealth or productivity to secure their life and property against this existential threat.

It is clear that profit is ethical as well as moral because it is wealth creation and wealth creation is essential for the survival of the individual, the survival of the nation and the survival and perpetuation of mankind as ordained by God. Inflation and deflation greatly affect profit and the creation of wealth. Inflation and deflation are themselves a product both of government and of nature. Before I discuss inflation and deflation in more detail, I would like to address the question of coercion in an economy. Coercion is the encumbrance of freewill in contracting through the law and the sovereign's power of eminent domain.

Coercion in the economy

The question of coercion is from two perspectives. One perspective is that of the investor or the entrepreneur, which is to say the owner of property, and the other perspective is the wage earner or laborer. By laborer, I mean someone who exchanges his time, which is also his private property as a life manifests in time, for a fixed wage or salary in order to secure his existence and to accumulate wealth. By investor, I mean someone who risks his store or his wealth in order to secure his existence and to accumulate wealth. Both the laborer and investor are engaged in the exchange of private property, that is to say commerce. The laborer exchanges a portion of his life that is private property for money, which becomes cash or an asset when saved and therefore wealth. The more productive the laborer then the greater surplus he creates and the greater become his cash savings and other investments, which together comprise his wealth and his hedge against calamity. The investor exchanges his private property, i.e. his wealth or his store for the services of the laborer. Thus, the investor risks his wealth that is his hedge against calamity in order to acquire more wealth. Where the exchange leads to greater wealth then the exchange is profitable for both the investor and laborer and therefore ethical. Note that both individuals each have the same economic goal, i.e. the creation and accumulation of wealth and both can be one in the same, i.e. both laborer and investor. This common economic goal is essential for survival in the event of a calamity. Given that all individuals possess a common goal then based on this goal any human action or organization is either, ethical or unethical, i.e. either right or wrong in an economic sense. In other words, a system of ethics or behaviors agreeable to all men exists, because the goal of all of man's activity is the creation of wealth or store as a hedge against calamity. Accordingly, the desire to create wealth is an immutable Law of Nature because it attaches to self-interest and self-preservation. So too is envy common to all men and in the absence of the fear of God envy emerges to destroy wealth. Envy is the temporal mechanism through which God punishes atheism and it is the reason man acquired this passion when he disobeyed God to become god. In this sense, i.e. as destroyers of wealth, envy, altruism and war are very much akin to each other.

Prosaically the distinction between the investor and the laborer is between thinking and doing or between the mind and the body. In recent history, there has been a sympathetic view of the laborer as the underdog in an economy. A common misconception is that the laborer toiled day and night for subsistence wages in order that the rich could become richer while the poor became poorer. This parochial and simplistic view of labor is at the core of the labor theory of value and it appears repeatedly in left-leaning and atheistic history tomes. As I mentioned, the labor theory of value is the flawed notion that the value of a commodity or the value of anything that is produced rests only in the labor used to produce or mine it. The argument that the value of a good rests only in the labor used to produce it has religious and agrarian antecedents. Essentially the argument is that the earth's bounty already exists, i.e. earth's bounty comes from God. Man's labor clears the fields, plants the seed and harvests the grain. Grain has zero inherent monetary value since the seed comes from God and it is through God's Grace that the seed exists. The argument is analogous to the argument against usury but only in reverse. That is money is inanimate and therefore incapable of breeding itself, thus usury is against the will of God. Money is not seed so it has no inherent ability to propagate i.e. create itself through interest. Had Man not fallen from God's Grace through his disobedience then the earth would bring forth the seed without man's labor. However, Man sinned by disobeying God, and God condemned man to labor for his sustenance for all his life. In Genesis 3:19 God says to Man, "*In the sweat of thy face shalt thou eat bread, till thou return unto the ground; for out of it wast thou taken: for dust thou art, and unto dust shalt thou return.* Neither God's covenant with Noah after the Flood, or the renewal of His covenant with Abraham, and God's New Covenant changes the fact that God ordained man to work and to toil for his food by the sweat of his brow. Accordingly, the value of the grain that a man takes from the earth is only in the labor that he uses to bring forth the grain. An atheist makes a similar argument but atheists do not invoke God as the source of the seed. Rather it is nature herself who by evolution or some similar fantasy-like-mechanism makes the seed and the grain available at no cost to man other than the labor to plant and harvest it. A man selling the grain for more than the labor used to produce it, i.e. for profit, is engaging in usury, and is stealing and therefore he is violating God's law. From the point of view of the atheist, such a man is also stealing and worst yet he is becoming richer at the expense of others to whom he sells the grain and who he is making poorer. In other words, a man who profits from his labor is disrupting the "balance of nature" which calls for economic equality among the hoi polloi and engendered by a universal altruism. Hence, to an atheist the sovereign must enjoin a man from making a profit, and it is the purpose of the sovereign to enjoin him. One way is to tax him, and then take the money as retribution and return it to those that paid the man's profit. Thus, to the atheist the sovereign now becomes "holy" as he restored the "balance of nature" through the taking of profit and returning it to those that unjustly paid it.

The labor theory of value presumes a coercive economy, and it must give rise to a coercive economy in order to validate its conclusions and accomplish its ends. To restrict the price of a good or service to no more than the labor to produce the good or service goes against freewill in contracting and violates Natural Law, and thus requires the force of man's law, i.e. the sovereign's power of eminent domain, to overcome the natural desire to profit, i.e. create wealth. The atheistic version of the labor theory of value as opposed to the theistic version is particularly destructive of private property and of wealth creation and it is the version that most readily gives rise to socialism and communism. The labor theory of value is economically irrational regardless of its supposed religious or atheistic underpinnings. It goes contrary to human nature, i.e. Natural Law, and when embraced politically and economically the labor theory of value is ultimately destructive of life and property and thus against the will of God. Apart from the simple logic required to predict the failure of coercive economies, history is also replete with examples of failed coercive economies. This bespeaks to the extent that this notion has fooled otherwise intelligent individuals and it bespeaks to its dangers as well. The old godless USSR is the quintessential coercive economy, and its inevitable failure occurred within a span of about 70 years or about three generations. The German nation after Bismarck, i.e. about 1885, and leading up to World War I is another example of the demise of a coercive economy where social welfare and unionization led to greater power ceded to the Kaiser. Kaiser Wilhelm II driven by the need for greater state revenues to sustain his military, the German social welfare state, and unionization, imposed high tariffs and looked toward his neighbors rather than his citizens for that revenue. The result was a set of alliances that led to a devastating World War that saw Germany loose over 2 million of its sons and another 500,000 of its civilian population. There are no historical examples of failed God fearing, free enterprise economies. A nation fails only when it becomes secular, thus engendering envy and through envy, giving rise to a socialist or communist economy, i.e. the calamity that wealth seeks to hedge. The secularization of a nation correlates with a decline in the ability of a nation to generate genius. In other words, a decline in the average IQ of the nation leads inevitability to secularization, decline in wealth creation and increased susceptibility to calamity. The decline in IQ arising from racial miscegenation is the reason for the appeal of the simplistic labor theory of value. Interest and profit require mathematical ability to understand and miscegenation reduces mathematical ability. The same is true with the fear of God. Individuals with low IQ's are incapable of conceiving of anyone greater than they are and thus they tend to be atheists.

In reality, the value or the price of a good or service in an unencumbered economy rests solely with the market demand for the good or service and the supply of the good or service. The price is a measure of the demand for the good or services and the supply of the good or service. In other words, in an unencumbered or laissez faire economy the price or value of a good or service is independent of the labor and investment used to produce the good or service. Thus in an unencumbered economy it is possible for a good or service to have a price less than the cost of labor to produce it or to have a price much greater than the cost of labor to produce it. In the former case, the enterprise loses its investment and loses the value of the labor and energy expended thereby destroying wealth. In the latter case, the enterprise prospers and creates wealth. The destruction of wealth is harmful to a nation and threatens its survival, hence greater wealth creation is necessary in the successful enterprises. Historically, free enterprise economies engender many more successful enterprises than unsuccessful enterprises, and the net effect has been an increase in aggregate wealth in the Western Nations. This is the essence of capitalism or more accurately free enterprise.

Given therefore the wealth destroying effect of coercion, the ethical question is whether coercion in an economy is ethical or even moral. Narrowing the question further, it is whether, or not, government regulation, taxation, and enforcement of labor contracts are ethical since these are forms and sources of coercion. The answer is that government taxation and regulation are ethical actions of government insofar as the actions are under due process, protect private property, and do minimal harm to the creation of wealth. However, the enforcement of labor contracts is unethical regardless of the invocation of due process. In other words, laws that permit the enforcement of labor contracts are unethical because these laws serve to undermine the creation of wealth by hindering freewill in contracting, and thus hindering commerce and decreasing the security of private property. When the sovereign writes such laws, he is abrogating his duty to adjudicate contracts between individuals and he is guilty of jeopardizing the well-being of the nation he is to protect. Such a sovereign forfeits the divine rights accorded him by God and stands ripe for rebellion while jeopardizing his soul. In the United States, the Wagner Act of 1935 aka The National Labor Relations Act, which negates common law and authorizes the Federal Government to enforce labor union contracts and thus collective bargaining, is an example of a law that undermines wealth creation by hindering commerce and threatening the survival of the nation. Indeed this law has done at least as much harm to the US economy as taxation or government regulations since Democrats enacted it in 1935. This is evident from the flight of the major manufacturing industries from the United States since the end of World War II and the concomitant plight of cities such as Detroit, Youngstown, and Akron among others. Thus, those Democrats that enacted and justified this law have jeopardized their souls before God because they threatened the survival of the very nation that entrusted them to protect and secure from calamity.

Are productivity improvements that lead to layoffs ethical and moral?

The second ethical and moral question I set upon to answer concerns unemployment. The first ethical and moral question was the disposition of the soul of a soldier and I said the soul of the soldier is secure under the divine right of king. Hence, a soldier does not condemn his soul when he kills the enemy nor does the king condemn his soul when he executes a man in accordance with due process or takes property under due process. Concerning the second question, specifically, should an enterprise make improvements in productivity knowing that the improvements result in labor surpluses. Are such productivity improvements ethical or even moral? A significant source of unemployment is rapid gain in productivity. Another source is a lack of economic growth and investment. The former is wealth creation and the latter is due solely to government interference in the economy. I will focus for now on rapid gains in productivity. When the gains in productivity are concentrated in specific industries the effect on general employment is modest because dislocations in one industry are absorbed in other industries or in new industries that emerge because of technological progress. Technological progress is the application of intellectual capital to problems of production. Technological progress enables gains in productivity. In other words, unevenly distributed productivity gains in a growing and unencumbered economy cause very little disruptions in the labor force and contribute little if anything to unemployment. Once again, I emphasize an unencumbered economy because in a highly regulated, taxed and unionized economy and where there is coercion in contract formation, productivity gains in one industry lead to significant disruptions in employment in general. Wages cannot freely fall in an encumbered economy because labor contracts as well as minimum wage laws, and prevailing wage laws fix wages. Consequently, unemployment results as industry accelerates investment in labor saving machines and methods. The investment in labor saving machines becomes increasingly economical in terms of return on investment as labor costs increase. Investment in labor saving machines also becomes economical as interest rates fall because companies often use debt to finance labor saving machines. Thus, a falling interest rate in an encumbered economy often leads to rapid increases in productivity and increasing unemployment. The Federal Reserve Bank repeatedly claims to meet its political goal of low unemployment by reducing interest rates, yet just the opposite occurs. Unemployment increases as interest rate drop in an encumbered economy as low cost debt finances productivity gains and not expansion or growth, which would have the effect of increasing employment. Let us examine the effect of low interest rates on unemployment in an encumbered economy.

Low interest rates leads to unemployment

Assume a factory assembly line currently employs ten men to operate the line and assume the hourly wage is $25.00 an hour or $1,000 per week under union contract. The union contract is the encumbrance. The current annual expense of operation is therefore $520,000. This is the cost used in year zero of the study of a proposal to invest in labor saving machines and thus save either all or a portion of this expense. Assume that the collective bargaining agreement calls for an annual increase of 2% in the subsequent 5 years. The present operating expense in year zero ($520,000) combined with the annual labor contract increase is the expense of the present method of operation or PMO. Assume that automating the operation will cost $1,000,000 and it will require only two union employees at an annual labor cost of $104,000 with a 2% increase each year to do the same assembly job as the 10 union employees currently do. The current interest rate is 2%. The investment in automating the operation with the fewer employees is the alternative cost to the cost of the PMO. Table 5 illustrates a net cash flow (NCF) analysis for justifying an investment in the automation of the given industrial operation. The NCF analysis time is 5 years and the investment is debt financed at the 2% interest rate. Either the investment in automation pays for itself in less than 5 years or the company makes no investment and the PMO continues.

		0	1	2	3	4	5
Labor inflation	0.02						
Interest Rates	**0.02**						
Tax rate	0.3						
PMO		0	1	2	3	4	5
Hourly rate	$25		$530,400	$541,008	$551,828	$562,865	$574,122
Hours/week	40						
Employees	10						
Annual labor	$520,000						
Alternative							
Capital	$1,000,000	$1,000,000	$106,080	$108,202	$110,366	$112,573	$114,824
Hourly rate	$25						
Hours/week	40						
Employees	2						
Annual labor	$104,000						
PMO-Alternative							
NCF		$1,248,000	$424,320	$432,806	$441,463	$450,292	$459,298
After tax NCF		$1,164,800	$297,024	$302,964	$309,024	$315,204	$321,508
NPV		**$1,080,000**					
After tax NPV		**$456,000**					

		0	1	2	3	4	5
Labor inflation	0.02						
Interest Rates	**0.05**						
PMO		0	1	2	3	4	5
Hourly rate	$25		$530,400	$541,008	$551,828	$562,865	$574,122
Hours/week	40						
Employees	10						
Annual labor	$520,000						
Alternative							
Capital	$1,000,000	$1,000,000	$106,080	$108,202	$110,366	$112,573	$114,824
Hourly rate	$25						
Hours/week	40						
Employees	2						
Annual labor	$104,000						
PMO-Alternative							
NCF		$1,178,034	$424,320	$432,806	$441,463	$450,292	$459,298
NPV		**$908,362**					

Table 5-Example of Net Cash Flow Analysis

This analysis shows that under the given economic conditions, the debt financed $1,000,000 capital investment in automation will reduce employment by eight men without affecting physical output, and at the same time, it will yield a positive Net Present Value (NPV) of $1,080,000. Table 5 shows the NCF over five years for the PMO and the alternative to the PMO with two different interest rates of 2% and 5%. The difference between the NCF is the PMO-Alternative row in each of the two interest rate scenarios. In the case where the interest rate is 2%, the company will have saved $1,245,000 on an NPV basis to recover its $1,000,000 investment within 3 years (NCF yr1-$454,320 + yr2- $432,806 + yr3- $441,463). In addition, the company will realize an additional gain of 1,080,000 under the 2% scenario. Thus the investment in the automation under scenario one will increase the company's profits by

$1,080,000 over the 5 years with no projected increase in revenue, i.e. a no growth economy. This additional margin also makes the company more competitive because the company can reduce prices to meet competition and still make a profit. In addition, if labor costs, material costs, or even taxes increase faster than anticipated the company will be able to absorb a large part of these costs without affecting current margins.

Increasing the interest rate to 5% reduces the NPV to $908,362 and while the investment is still attractive, it is about 16% less attractive than when interest rates were lower. Thus, the lower the interest rate the more attractive that debt financed labor saving investments become. In this example, it is easy to see rather than increasing employment lower interest rates reduce employment because the low rates make it more economically attractive to invest in automation in a no growth economy. If the economy were growing then the investment would fund additional sources of revenue instead of reductions in expenses. This is contrary to the belief of many economists, and in particular, the Keynesians, who believe that lowering interest rates increases employment. This is the case only in an unencumbered economy and growing economy. However, the fact that Keynesians also believe that government spending money stimulates the economy then the result of lower interest rates is just the opposite, which is to decrease employment. The path to wealth creation in a growing or unencumbered economy is lower interest rates because lower interest rates improve capital productivity. The path to wealth creation in a no-growth economy is also lower interest rates but through increases in labor productivity, i.e. greater unemployment. The cause of an economy's growth or lack of growth is government interference in the economy. The greater the government interference the slower the growth and therefore the greater the unemployment when interest rates are kept artificially low.

Note also in the example the labor rate is $25 per hour and it includes a 2% annual growth under the collective bargaining agreement. The labor contract fixes the increase in labor costs over the contract term thereby eliminating any uncertainty in the return on investment. This means investors are more likely to make an investment in the automation of the operation rather than in a similar valued investment with riskier albeit higher return. Labor contracts reduce the risk in labor savings investments and accelerate productivity improvements with the resulting unemployment. An interesting question is what would the labor rate have to be in order to make the investment unattractive, i.e. an NPV of zero or less than zero? The answer is $15 per hour. In other words at the rate of $15 per hour with a 2% annual increase the investment would have to be less than $1,000,000 to provide a return on the automation of the operation. Thus, automating the operation at a cost of $1,000,000 would not provide a sufficient return on investment and the automation of the operation would be uneconomical and not undertaken so there would be nobody laid off as a result. Thus, the combination of high union wages and low interest rates leads to unemployment.

Corporations perform a similar analysis when considering relocation to lower wage areas or lower taxing districts. If the cost to relocate to a lower wage area provides a positive return then a company will relocate. Low interest rates and high union wages therefore promote the relocation of companies to foreign countries in a no growth or encumbered economy, which unions and government create.

All productivity improvements are due to technological advancements

All gains in productivity in a wealth creating economy result from technological improvements in one form or another. Apart from the Enclosure Laws in England that created private real property in England and eventually elsewhere, throughout history technology is the driving force behind the creation of wealth. The Enclosure Laws and the idea of private property stimulated technology to improve productivity. Technology is the general term that means ways of making things, i.e. by machines, and doing things, i.e. by processes. The invention of the eyeglasses in the 13th Century for instance extended the productive capacity of Western Man because it enabled him to remain productive for a longer period during his life. The discovery of sperm whale oil as an effective lighting source during the 18th and early 19th Century extended the workday particularly in Northern Europe where darkness came early in the winter months. The extension of the workday had the effect of improving the productivity and the production of a very productive and intellectually capable populace, i.e. a populace with a high average IQ. The less expensive kerosene derived from petroleum eventually replaced sperm whale oil as the price of whale oil increased with decreasing supply, and the price of kerosene decreased as its supply increased.
The price of whale oil was:

1831	$0.30	1/2 gallon
1843	$0.63	1/2 gallon
1854	$1.92	1/2 gallon
1866	$1.28	1/2 gallon

The price of kerosene was about $0.30 per gallon in 1861 dropping to $.08 a gallon by the 1880s as John D. Rockefeller's Standard Oil Company improved the efficiency of its production and distribution. Note the decline of the price of whale oil in 1866 was because of the competition from kerosene, which became increasingly available during the 1860's. Although improvements in the technology of whaling contributed to gains in productivity thus reducing costs and the price of whale oil, it was not enough to sustain the whaling industry in the wake of the less expensive kerosene. The discovery of whale oil as a source of light and the high demand and cost stimulated the search for alternatives thus the discovery of kerosene. This is an example of the cascading effect of technology. One invention or discovery always stimulates other inventions and discoveries thus continuously increasing productivity and in the process continuously creating wealth. A capitalist economy facilitates, promotes and accelerates this process through the profits arising from the inventions and discoveries as private property secured by the sovereign through the patent process.

The invention of the eyeglasses and the discovery of an inexpensive and effective light source represented paradigm shifts in technology in general that in the first case helped to usher in the Renaissance and in the second case enabled the industrial revolution during the second half of the 19th Century. Compared to the periods before the Industrial Revolution there was tremendous increase in the wealth of Western Man, who emerged from the Dark Ages as a Caucasoid uncorrupted by Negroid or mixed race blood, and whose genius invented and discovered these and other technological improvements and innovations. The Caucasoid male uncorrupted by the blood of the dark and mixed race peoples created the ancient and the modern world.

No sovereign encumbrance to Western economies from 17th to 19th Century

The increase in wealth arising from productivity gains beginning in the 17th Century in Western Nations occurred in unencumbered economies where governments did not interfere with the economy through regulations, and taxes were relatively low. Less clear or obvious is the civil unrest that technological advances and rapid productivity gains have had on nations during the 17th, 18th, and 19th centuries. There are two reasons for this. First, as I stated the economies of Western nations during these periods were relatively unencumbered. There was very little taxation, regulation and coercion in Western economies during this period so gains in productivity did not lead to unemployment and civil unrest despite rapid increases in population. Indeed, the Enclosure Laws in England during this period increased the amount of private property thereby reducing a significant encumbrance to the economy, which was the lack of private property that existed during feudal times in England. The English sovereigns of the time were engaged primarily in the protection of private property and the enforcement of laws and contracts and everyone understood this to be their only function and purpose. That is the sovereign did not concern himself with the state of the poor, the condition of the laborer, or the education of the hoi polloi.

The sovereign also benefited from the increase in commerce that technology and productivity engendered. In fact, where the sovereign attempted to tax or overtaxed the nation there was rebellion. The American Revolution and the French Revolution are two examples where the individuals comprising a nation rose up against their sovereign when taxation became too burdensome and reduced the ability to create wealth. In the case of the French, the burden of the sovereign resulted in higher food prices in addition to higher taxes as the French sovereign embarked on expensive foreign adventures with no return on the expense during the 17th and 18th Centuries. These revolutions set the stage for greater economic growth as they served as a warning to other sovereigns about encumbering an economy through taxation at least through the 19th Century. However, by the end of the 19th Century, governments once again began to encumber their economies with taxation and regulation. This time, however, rather than undertake exploitive colonization , which characterized European powers between from the 16th to the 19th centuries, governments started flirting with socialism to appease their populations. Thus, we see no revolutions after mid-19th century in Europe but we do see great militarization particularly in Germany. The socialism eventually led instead to wars between nations. During the 20th Century, the result of governmental interference in economies was high unemployment and two of the most devastating wars in human history.

Germany's 19th Century social security system encumbered her economy

Germany in the later part of the 19th Century is an example of a sovereignty encumbering an economy by way of tariffs, the protection of cartels such as labor unions from competition, and increased taxation to support social welfare programs. By the time of World War I, almost 20% of German government spending went to social welfare programs including old age pensions and unemployment compensation. German debt increased four fold from 1880 to 1913 going from 5 billion marks to 20 billion marks during that period. Considering that over the same period, the debt of the United Kingdom (0.765 billion pounds in 1880 to 0.706 billion pounds in 1913) and France (24 billion francs in 1880 to 33 billion francs in 1913) remained almost flat, as they did not embark on the kind of ambitious social welfare spending as did Germany. (See Figure 47) In the case of the United Kingdom, social welfare manifested as greater freedom to employees to leave their employment for better wages. Unlike Germany, which employed socialist principles of high taxation and centralized control to deal with civil unrest in the form of government social welfare spending, the United Kingdom relied on freedom to contract and employment at will to deal with civil unrest arising out of low wages or unemployment. It is little wonder then that

Germany would initiate a war on any pretext in the belief that she could extract tribute from her neighbors upon victory to pay her debts, and sustain her social welfare system without further burdening her population by increasing their taxes and thus provoke rebellion. On the other hand, the government of the United Kingdom had no such ambition or need. Had Germany not embarked on a socialist course and thereby encumber her economy it would have created much wealth and there would not have been a World War I. Unfortunately, the French Revolution taught the other monarchies of Europe that unless they appeased the envy of their subjects they would meet the same fate as the French monarchy. This was the beginning of the decline in European world dominance and the new standard-bearer of Western Civilization was now the God fearing United States.

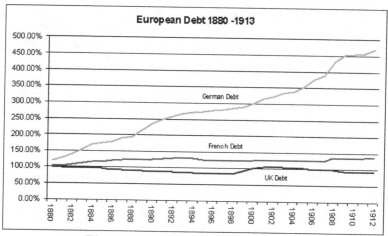

Figure 47-European Debt 1880-1913

The second reason that civil unrest arising from technological progress was not as clear during the 17th, 18th, and 19th centuries as it is in the 20th Century, is a matter of records and the tendency of historians to view history in political rather than economic terms. In other words political history makes for a more interesting read and appeals to the less mathematically inclined of whom there are many, particularly in academia, whereas economic history, which is the reason and motivation for the events in history, is not as interesting to a broad audience. Although the Luddites and the so-called rebellions of the 1830s and 1840s were reactions by employees to technological progress in industry, the results of these rebellions were of no great consequence other than in the mind of revisionist historians. Unemployment was not a serious problem during the 19th Century as the demand for labor was so great that factories in Europe and the United States at the time employed children seven years old. Despite the many romantic notions about the working conditions and treatment of employees at the time, the facts are that conditions of life improved for the vast majority of the Western populations with no unions, no regulations on industry, relatively low taxation of industry, and the freedom to contract.   There were growing economies with wealth creation by a large proportion of Western Man and life expectancy was rapidly improving during the 19th century as technological progress eased the burden of life and reduced the effects of calamities.   Another type of private property, the patent became increasingly important during the 19th and 20th Centuries, and it helped forge the technological progress of Western nations.   Just as the Enclosure Laws did in England several centuries earlier, the patent laws and later the copyright laws particularly in England, and later in the United States in the 19th Century, served to accelerate the development of technological innovations that in turn accelerated the creation of wealth. Thus when the sovereign is engaged only in the protection of private property there is much wealth created in a nation whose populace has a high average IQ and fears God.

Private property and all its manifestations is the source of wealth
        The economic progress of Western Civilization following the Middle Ages or from about 1100 AD is directly attributable to the general emergence of private property as tangible property such as real property with title to land or deeds recorded and secured by the sovereign becoming the basis of common law.   As the wealth engendered by the ownership of real property materialized there came the need to secure and protect intangible property such as inventions and written works. Thus, there emerged the first patents beginning in the 15th Century in England, which roughly coincided with the issuance of deeds to property and laws securing private real property under the Enclosure Laws. Copyrights first issued in the early 18th Century in England.   The English were the first to secure private property in all its manifestations and they became the wealthiest and most powerful nation in the world beginning from the 14th Century and extending into the 20th Century. English common law based on the securing of private property and the enforcement of contracts became the model for the legal systems in all the free Western Nations as well as in India and Hong Kong.   These nations prospered as a result.   Those nations where private property was not secured or protected by the sovereign as in the old Soviet Union, the Eastern Bloc nations, and Communist China, created little wealth. These nations suffered greatly as calamities such as war, drought, famine, and disease took their toll.   Although they possessed the intellectual capital to create wealth, the communist and socialist nations of the twentieth century did not secure private property and did not fear God. Consequently, government institutionalized envy, and envy manifested in the population, thereby preventing the creation of wealth.   It is no

coincidence that the Russian Orthodox Church is now more prominent in Russia than in the old Soviet Union and that Russia is becoming more prosperous and creating wealth as a result. Although Russia has yet to purge the godless communists and their ideas from its population and given increasing wealth disparity, Russia can easily lapse into its former state. The great irony and soon to be great tragedy is that Western Europeans and the United States populace are forsaking God and His Commandments in their public discourse and in their hearts. Thus, the sovereign elected through universal suffrage engenders envy in these nations as they become more like the old Soviet Union creating little wealth. It will be no surprise if Russia overtakes Western Europe militarily as the Russians are deploying a powerful military whereas socialism and the protection of the United States military since World War II lulled the Western Europeans into effectively disarming. The fact that Western Europe spends little of its GDP on its defense relying instead on the United States military is the reason that their socialism and atheism has not yet caused their economies to collapse. Although given the amount of sovereign debt in many of the European Nations, even the lack of military spending will not be able to sustain the economies of many of the European Union nations. When the United States can or will no longer defend Western Europe, then they will become part of the new Russian Empire and pay tribute to the new Czar or there will be nuclear war. Either submission or nuclear war is the only recourse when there is no conventional military to stop or prevent the spread of a militarily powerful socialist state such as Russia seeking the wealth of her neighbors, as she must to survive.

Little civil unrest arising from gains in productivity prior to the 20th century

Little civil unrest arising from gains in productivity existed in the centuries prior to the twentieth century. However, the pace of technological innovation increased exponentially beginning in the later part of the 19th Century. A measure of technological innovation is the number of US patents issued during the 19th century as compared to the twentieth century. From 1836 to 1900 the US issued about 0.65 million patents. The US patents issued from 1900 to 1964 were about 2.5 million, or almost four times more in the same number of years. By 2011, the number of additional patents issued was about 4.7 million or almost twice the number issued as in the first half of the twentieth century. The United States per capita GDP in terms of purchasing power (PPP) as a measure of productivity increased from an estimated $1,588 in 1840 to $4,091 in 1900 and then again to $12,773 in 1964 and $31,357 in 2008. Thus despite the increase in the United States population from 15 million in 1840 to over 300 million in 2008 the rate of increase in productivity was so great that the 300 million people of today are on the average 20 times wealthier than the 15 million people of 1840. Once again the Malthusian idea that population increases engenders poverty is proven false at least in the case of Western Civilization under a free enterprise and relatively unencumbered economy and in the God fearing nations. Although despite the relatively high standard of living currently enjoyed by the United States, the nation could be 80 times wealthier in real dollars if it were not for government profoundly interfering in the economy since the 1930s. (See Appendix 1)

Universal suffrage engenders wealth destruction

The history of the twentieth century offers a clearer connection between rapid advances in technology with the resulting rapid gains in productivity and civil unrest. I will discuss this more as I introduce and define the economics of inflation and deflation in detail. The clear connection between rapid advances in technology, productivity and unemployment is not simply because historians recorded the civil unrest engendered by unemployment. Rather it was because sovereigns undertook to taxing and to regulating their economies thus encumbering their economies and setting the stage for civil unrest arising from rapid gains in productivity. This drive for sovereigns to encumber their economies arose from several sources. These sources included flawed notions of the purpose of government arising from universal suffrage, the ambitions of the sovereign, desire for power over others, and the need for more government revenue to pay for social welfare programs without adding more tax burden on the citizens of the nation and provoking rebellion. Apart from these mundane motives, the sovereign's great motivator for burdening his economy is the need to satiate the envy of the sovereign and of the populace. Envy arises from atheism since only the fear of God proscribes envy. As atheism became a growing movement on the European Continent led by French and German philosophers, envy also began to manifest itself in the form of calls by the hoi polloi for bringing down the aristocracy and the rich. The resulting social welfare programs intended more to deprive the rich their wealth rather than to redistribute their wealth were all the result of universal suffrage.

Universal suffrage changed the relationship between the government and the individuals comprising a nation, as it is nothing more than the institutionalization of envy made manifest by godlessness. Prior to universal suffrage, male property owners appointed or elected the sovereign in Western Nations for the most part. This was true regardless of the form of government or even of the economic system, i.e. feudal or private property based. There was a practical and economic reason for this manner of selecting the sovereign. The male property owners fought the wars to defend their property and the nation, and they had the most to loose should enemy invaders outside the nation-state

211

prevail or should domestic enemies or criminals steal their property. Their choice of sovereign was effectively their choice of a general in time of war and protector of their property in times of peace. The property owner also paid the tax burden to sustain the sovereign. The form of tax is important here because when the populace deems a tax unfair, i.e. when it applies more to one man than another, then it is the law that is also unfair, i.e. it applies differently from one man to the next. This is the reason for rebellion as occurred in the American British Colonies as the English King taxed the Colonies differently and at higher rates than he taxed their English brethren apart even from the fact that it cost more to protect the colonies. A woman or widow who may have acquired property was still liable for the tax on the property and entitled to the income from that property but since a woman is incapable physically, emotionally, or otherwise to engage an enemy in battle then she cannot decide morally or intellectually the man who will lead others in battle. This is as true today as it was at the dawn of history. Accordingly, the election or appointment of the sovereign is only for the individual male property owners of the nation-state and as long as the law distributes the burden of the sovereign equally amongst the owners whose properties the sovereign is to secure and protect then there is no reason for rebellion and the nation creates wealth. The creation of individual wealth always redounds to the benefit of all because it creates more wealth.

The idea of universal suffrage stems from greatly flawed atheistic and romantic notions of man engendered by the Age of Enlightenment. Prior to 1790, intellectual tradition concerned the male property owner as the object of philosophical discourse. When John Locke for instance spoke of Man, he had in mind the white male property owner and not Man in general, i.e. Man including woman, or non-whites or even non-property owners. Thus, the phrase "*All men are created equal…*" in the United States Declaration of Independence, which drew its inspiration from Locke, refers only to white male property owners who the nation also called upon in time of war. It did not and could not have referred to slaves, women or non-property owners because these individuals were never historical antecedents to the word "man" in any prior philosophical, legal or theological discourse of any import. The same is true here. To claim the term "man" to mean "humankind" is a distortion of the true meaning of "man", a distortion of the meaning of the Declaration of Independence, and a betrayal of the covenant with posterity as embodied in this document. Furthermore, the reference in the Declaration to equality is to equality under the law since the Declaration of Independence is a legal document and not a mere commentary on the nature of man, or of mankind as many misguided historians and legal scholars assume or wish to presume. The Declaration of Independence set forth in detail the reason that the American Colonies no longer wished to have the English King as their protector and enforcer of contracts.   The basic reason was that the English King cost too much and the Americans thought they could do it cheaper and better. Equality as referenced in the Declaration of Independence does not mean, and cannot mean equality in intellect, ability or outcomes.

Unlike most of the Enlightenment philosophers such as Voltaire, Rousseau, and John Stuart Mill who were atheist and espoused atheism and Stoicism, both John Locke and Adam Smith feared God.   Thus, it is no surprise that the Declaration of Independence and the US Constitution drew inspiration from the latter two and not the former.   It is also no surprise that the United States and Britain created great wealth and were peaceful nations through the 19th and into the 20th Century. France, Germany, Russia, and the nations who took inspiration from the former created considerably less wealth and were aggressors and warlike through the 19th and into the 20th Century.   The godless always suffer in the end because they succumb to their envy and the aforementioned nations are examples.

Flawed romantic notions of man's nature gave rise to universal suffrage

Romantic distortions about the nature of man emerged due in large part to emotional reaction to the Enlightenment as it unfolded and beginning about 1790.   Two of the most influential men during this time were Voltaire and Rousseau.   Voltaire attacked religion as mere superstition and argued instead for the human virtues of reason, tolerance, and justice as the means to govern man's behavior and not the fear of God.   This was merely a revival of the ancient and flawed Stoic idea that man's reason acting through his will can control his passions and therefore to the ancient Stoics and to the modern Stoics there is no need for God.   Jean-Jacques Rousseau in his infamous work, *The Social Contract,* captured the revolutionary spirit of the age by fusing morality and politics.   The title to Rousseau's book belies its utter absurdity because there is no such thing as a "Social Contract", there is only a protector of private property appointed by the individuals whose property he secures, and who enforces contracts.   As avowed atheists, Voltaire and Rousseau sought to replace the fear of God with the fear of the state or rather with man's reason, which is the same idea.   They succeeded in this, as their distortions about the nature of man and idealized arguments for the egalitarian nature of man enabled the justification of the horrors of the French Revolution and the Reign of Terror.   If all men are equal then the only way that some men are wealthier than others is because they stole to achieve their wealth so they deserve their fate at the hands of those from whom they stole.   The French Revolution was nothing more than a murderous stealing spree carried on by a group of envious, degenerate, self-aggrandizing, and worthless atheists including the aforementioned Voltaire and Rousseau, who in the end destroyed themselves along with many innocent and productive individuals while not advancing man's material condition by one iota.   Unfortunately, their romantic and idealized notions about the nature of man as embodied in a radical egalitarianism survived their demise as it appealed to the less intellectually capable, the less enterprising individuals, and the envious comprising the nation.   This radical egalitarianism, as well as the flawed labor theory of value in the philosophies of Marx and Engels, formed the basis of arguments for universal suffrage in the second half of the eighteenth century.   Thus the French Revolution more than any other event in the past 300 years ushered in the idea of a secular state and with it socialism and communism or in other words the "modern" godless feudal states. Unlike capitalism, which arose naturally and peaceably from feudalism through the division of land and the sovereign's security of title to land, i.e. the acquisition of private property, the return to feudalism is, and will be, a much bloodier affair because it requires the taking of that private property.   Since a man's life is private property then the return to feudalism, i.e. socialism and communism, requires the sovereign taking of a man's life, and this is easier and much bloodier when the sovereign does not fear God.   Universal suffrage enables a sovereign who does not fear God to satiate the envy of the populace and thus destroy wealth and the ability to create wealth in all its forms.

Universal suffrage whereby all males after a certain age and regardless of property could vote first took hold in France in 1792 at the beginning of the French Revolution and then spread to Germany in 1871, or about 80 years later.   It is no coincidence that France's Reign of Terror followed universal suffrage in 1793 as the once God proscribed envy of the aristocracy was unleashed culminating in 1799 with the murder of 50,000 individuals.   Even this blood did not quench the envy of those less capable than those who they murdered in France.   The need for more wealth to sustain the new French socialism after the destruction of wealth that took place gave rise to the godless Napoleon. The ensuing Napoleonic wars exported the death and destruction of French socialism to the rest of Europe and into Asia.

The Stoic idea that man's reason and will could replace the fear of God was a necessary precondition to the unleashing of envy thereby enabling the State, built on universal suffrage, to take the life and redistribute the property of innocent and productive individuals.   The connection between envy and murder first manifested in Genesis as it was envy of God's favor that led to Cain's murder of his brother Abel. The philosophers of the Enlightenment believed that reason is the path to paradise on earth, and they refused to believe that God created man and that He alone judges the fate of a man's soul.   The Enlightenment was nothing more than a revival of the ancient Greek Stoicism, which argued that man's reason and the power of his will could overcome his passions. This is Nietzsche's "Will to Power". It took the aftermath of the French Revolution to show that this is not true, yet there are individuals that continue to believe this. It is these individuals, i.e. the atheist and the godless, acting on this flawed notion who tempt the rest of mankind with the promise to satiate their envy that cause the destruction of wealth. These same atheists continue to threaten the survival of mankind.

Unlike France, German universal suffrage did not lead to civil unrest or rebellion, as the Prussian military was too powerful, highly disciplined, and too dedicated to the Kaiser to tolerate the kind of civil unrest and rebellion that took place in France. Instead, Germany embarked on a socialist course in order to insure the survival and perpetuation of the existing governing elite. Within about 10 years of universal suffrage, Germany passed social welfare laws and went into debt to pay for the benefits. Germany then went to war in 1913 in a failed attempt to pay for the social spending by taking wealth from her neighbors only to loose even more and increase the suffering of her citizens. After World War I, the inevitable occurred as the Kaiser was overthrown and a new Republic formed in Germany. It is my contention that if France and Germany had not adopted universal suffrage, the world would not have seen the Reign of Terror, the devastation of the Napoleonic Wars, and World War I. Without World War I, there would have been no World War II and the Western Nations would have created much greater wealth. As history turned out, these two wars destroyed much wealth and many lives lost on the atheistic altar of envy, as envy engendered these wars. Envy could only take root in a godless populace. This is the environment existing during the later half of the nineteenth century. The rise of the intellectual doctrines of Darwinism and Marxism on the heels of the so-called Enlightenment served to alienate the populace from God and thus fertilize the ground for envy to take root. The philosophies of Nietzsche, Schopenhauer, Kant, Rousseau, John Stuart Mill and others at the time coupled with the general rise in wealth, and the resulting materialism further alienated man from God. Hence, the fear of God did not exist in the mind and heart of men so envy took root. Although Mill argued for individual liberty over state control, his principle that a man can behave any way he pleases as long as *"one does no harm to others"* lacks substance or motivation. Mill offers no compelling reason for a man to obey such a dictum other than the implied power of the state, i.e. the sovereign's power of eminent domain. Thus, the British Mill was no different in outlook from the French and German atheists including Marx. As far as the sovereign is concerned, Mill's dictum is meaningless. That is, without the fear of God there is nothing, short of rebellion, to compel the sovereign to behave in such a manner as to do no harm to others. Thus, Mill essentially espoused an atheistic philosophy to engender envy. He compounded the destructive manifestations of envy by also espousing universal suffrage. It is this alienation and the denial of God and God's Commandments, and the ensuing universal suffrage that gave rise to the socialism in Germany at the time thus leading to the wars, deaths and devastation in the first half of the twentieth century.

The great lesson from the story of Cain and Abel is that envy will overcome the love of one brother for another. Indeed when one examines the nationality of the soldiers of the United States who fought in both wars, the majority of the combatants were Germans whose ancestors arrived in the United States one, two or three generations earlier. Eisenhower the Supreme Allied Commander during World War II was a German. Thus, the tragedy of Cain and Abel was writ large on the bloody fields of Europe in two World Wars. This is the essential naïveté and danger embodied in atheism or the replacement of the fear of God with man's reason and will, thus giving rise to universal suffrage, and leading always to socialism then war and man's destruction.

The alienation of Man from God engenders envy

Besides the desire to appease the envious through universal suffrage, the drive for Western sovereigns to encumber their economies during the twentieth century also arose from the rapid increase in the wealth of Western nations and the resulting materialism. The materialism arising from the rapid creation of wealth helped to alienate man from God. The increase in the level of wealth leads to demands for greater security by the rich, and calls by the envious for greater redistribution to enable the destruction of individual wealth. It is these demands that engendered the welfare state through the mechanism of universal suffrage. The demands for greater security by the rich gives rise to increase militarization. The welfare or socialist state as engendered by its envious populace then employees its military to steal from its neighbors rather than increase taxes and thus provoke rebellion. The formation of the German nation in the 19th Century is an example of this process. As long as an individual and his sovereign fear God, there is no passion for the creation of a socialist state as God proscribes man's envy and the passion remains at bay. When the nation's populace does not fear God then it will become a socialist state as its wealth increases. A socialist state does not create wealth because the sovereign encumbers the economy through taxation and regulation. In order to sustain itself it must either take more from the productivity of its citizens or attack its neighbors to take their wealth. This is what Germany attempted to do in starting World War I and what Napoleon attempted to do a century earlier.

The period from about 1860 to the beginning of World War I in 1913 saw the rise of the German nation in parallel with the great technological progress that took place during that time. The innovations in transportation and communications, which included the railroad, the steamship and the telegraph, as well as the technology of steel making, saw a rapid increase in wealth in all the Western Nations. While Germany may have been a follower of Great Britain in terms of innovations and inventions in the first half of the 19th Century, it was leading the way by the second half.   This was due in part to the increased protection of private property in all its forms by the now unified and more efficiently governed Germany with its powerful Prussian military tradition.   During this period, German GDP went from $59 billion to $237 billion in PPP (purchasing power parity) dollars, which was a compounded real growth rate of 2.514% while the population grew linearly averaging about 600,000 people a year.   A measure of productivity growth is the per capita GDP.   The higher rate of growth in the GDP than the rate of growth in population resulted in a net increase in per capita GDP at a compound rate of 1.4%.   This means that the productivity of the German people increased faster than the population.   This once again puts to the lie the Malthusian idea that population growth in general is the cause of poverty.   Yet it is an idea that persists but it does not derive from Western nations, which are the domain of the Caucasian Race as history shows.   Rather this notion is more applicable to those areas of the Earth populated by less intellectually capable individuals, i.e. low average IQ, and primarily those areas where the previously colonized Negroid dominates.   This is an important distinction because the notion of liberty in contracting and free enterprise presumes a certain level of intellectual capital, i.e. a population with a high average IQ.   In other words, private property, liberty and free enterprise only bear fruit in a nation where there is an abundance of intellectual capital, i.e. a high average IQ.   The lack of intellectual capital in nations or groups of individuals severely hampers their ability to create wealth and survive a calamity.   Much of sub-Sahara Africa falls in this category.   While population growth in Western Nations dominated by the Caucasoid translates to increasing wealth it is much less the case for nations dominated by the Negroid or by individuals of mixed race.   The situation with the Caucasoid is the same with the Mongoloid, the third great race of Man.   The Mongoloid also has a high degree of intellectual capital and population growth results in increasing levels of wealth creation as well.   Despite one of the highest population densities on earth, Japan is also one of the richest in per capita GDP. I will have more to say about the relative average level of intelligence among nations later.

The other great power in 1860, which was Great Britain, had a higher absolute per capita GDP at $2,830 vs. Germany at $1,639 or by a factor of 1.75.   However, by the beginning of World War I, Great Britain had a per capita GDP of $4,921 vs. $3,468 for Germany or 1.35 times greater.   The relatively rapid rate of growth in Germany's per capita GDP led to increasing demands for security by the German population, which led to a rise in militarization and the world's first social security system reluctantly implemented in the 1880's by Otto von Bismarck at the direction of Kaiser Wilhelm II.   Kaiser Wilhelm II promoted the idea of an old age pension system or social security system. One reason for the German social security system was to prevent young men from immigrating to the United States where wages were higher but there were no benefits, so that Germany might continue its wealth creation as well as its militarization thereby preserving and growing the nation.   The promise of lifetime care for workers had its intended effect. The rate of population growth in Germany more than doubled between the 1880's and the beginning of World War I in comparison to the decades before 1880, thus stemming the tide of migration but setting the stage for conflict.   Within thirty years of the implementation of its social programs, Germany went to war consuming much of its stored wealth including many of the progeny of those benefiting from the social programs implemented a generation earlier.   The great tragedy here is that many of the sons of the generation benefiting from German social security paid the ultimate price for the socialism, atheism, and radical egalitarianism of their fathers.   Just as in the case of Agamemnon, a sovereign king, sacrificing his progeny for the favor of the gods only to seal his fate so did the German nation pay the price for compelling the favor of their sovereign.   It is my contention that World War I would not have occurred had Germany not embarked on the social legislation of the 1880's and the accompanying need for greater government revenues, which Germany could only obtain by conquering and absorbing its neighbors without provoking rebellion.   The social legislation in turn was a direct result of universal suffrage manifested by the envy of the godless.

In other words, when individuals realize that they can vote benefits for themselves then that marks the end of capitalism and the end of private property, and the beginning of a national socialism, i.e. the NAZI.   The end of private property is also the end of life.   This is the inherent and tragic flaw in universal suffrage although the atheist and the environmentalist, who is simply one embodiment of the atheist, argue that the end of the lives of the hoi polloi is a desirable outcome and not something to mourn.   However, the lesson here is not simply that individuals are naturally lazy and seek to enrich themselves by electing a sovereign who will use the power of eminent domain to take from the rich and give to everyone else.   The lesson of the envy of man's fellow man is much more sinister and evil.   Just as in the story of Cain and Abel, Cain did not seek God's favor when he killed Abel and he knew God's favor was lost to him forever, yet he still killed his brother.   He did it to deprive Abel of God's blessing, and the wealth that God's blessing would bestow on him and his progeny, and not because he thought God's favor would redound to him.   Thus, Cain did not kill

Abel to benefit himself because this was something he knew would not occur, but rather to prevent Abel from benefiting from God's favor. Similarly, universal suffrage always seeks a sovereign to deny the rich their wealth to satiate envy, and not to enrich the poor from the charity of the sovereign. The sovereign is incapable of enriching the poor but is capable of creating more poor and this is the object of the envious. The result of universal suffrage is always a weakened nation increasingly susceptible to calamity.

Rise of labor unions meant the demise of wealth creation

The twentieth century also saw the rise of the labor unions that further encumbered economies. The labor union is also a manifestation of envy. If man feared God then there would not be labor unions. The atheism of the later part of the 19th century and early part of the 20th century helped to spawn the union movement. During the latter half of the nineteenth century and the beginning of the twentieth century, the labor unions were relatively ineffective. Under all common law, a contract is enforceable by the sovereign only if exercised through an act of freewill by the parties to the contract. A contract is unenforceable by the sovereign under common law and Natural Law when executed by one or more of the parties under coercion or under duress. A labor contract is such a contract. A company always enters into a labor contract under threat of financial loss to the employer or even the ruin of the employer. Accordingly, prior to the 1940's, no law ever sanctioned attempts at forcing employers to enter into labor contracts with their employees or enforce any contract that is entered under duress. In fact, the Sherman Anti-Trust Act of 1890 merely reinforced the freedom to contract in accordance with freewill and it was the intention of the Act to control union organizing which created labor cartels also known as guilds in restraint of trade, i.e. encumbering the economy. It was not the intention of the Sherman Anti-Trust Act to undermine the efficiency of corporations or to encumber the creation of wealth. Indeed the government and weak competitors of successful enterprises have used the Sherman Anti-Trust Act to undermine successful enterprises after Congress rewrote the Act during the Woodrow Wilson Administration. Thus, the idea of coercive collective bargaining leading to a labor contract with a union did not exist under law prior to the Wilson Administration. Hence, any attempts at unionization were properly illegal and attempts to enforce union contracts invariably failed in court and under common law. With the election of the liberal progressive, Woodrow Wilson, the Democrats in Congress modified the Sherman Act through the Clayton Antitrust Act of 1914. This gave license to unions to conduct boycotts, peaceful strikes, peaceful picketing, and collective bargaining, as these acts the Sherman Act did not explicitly regulate or allow, but were now implicitly sanctioned under the Clayton Antitrust Act as long as no property damage was involved.   In other words, judges could issue injunctions against union actions to settle labor disputes only when property damage was threatened.   The irony here is that union labor contracts do just that, i.e. damage property, because unions force labor contracts upon the company against the will of the company.   The property damaged is the profit of the corporation or in other words, the damage is to the wealth created which is the property of the corporation. The fact that Congress and the courts either were blind to this property damage, or ignored it is a testament to the corruption of the intellect by progressive ideas.   Progressive ideas that arose in the United States and Britain as well as Germany at the turn of the twentieth century were nothing more than a rehash of the failed ideas of the Enlightenment that corrupted the French intellectuals one-hundred years earlier and gave rise to much death and destruction of wealth.   It was the same tired ideas about egalitarianism, atheism, and the flawed Stoic notion that scientific knowledge and reason acting through the will (i.e. in Nietzsche's words *"The Will to Power")* can be used to control and manipulate national economies and thereby the control and manipulation of the many, i.e. the hoi polloi, by the few.   Not surprisingly and predictably, these notions once again led to even more death and destruction in the twentieth century just as they did in the previous century.   Congress passed, and FDR signed, the Wagner Act, aka the National Relations Act, in 1935, which enabled the Federal Government to enforce labor contracts regardless that they were contracts enacted under threats and intimidation by the unions against their employers.   Unions started to gain strength and members after this point.   Although individuals and companies challenged the constitutionality of the Wagner Act in court, the Supreme Court ruled it constitutional on the flawed basis of the right of the people to assemble clause of Amendment 1.   Amendment 1 states in part *"Congress shall make no law…abridging…. the right of the people to assemble, and to petition the Government for a redress of grievances."*   Clearly, the first Amendment refers to the right of the people to assemble, and to petition the government.   Amendment 1 intended to limit the power of government not to limit the exercise of freewill in contracting.   This has nothing to do with so-called free association and the term "free association" exists nowhere in the Constitution yet it was this flawed notion of "free association" that justified the enforcement of coercive labor contracts under Amendment 1 of the Constitution thus negating common law.   Moreover, the idea of assembling or for that matter even the erroneously derivative idea of "free association" in no way justifies the government enforcement of contracts made against the will of one of the parties.   This is one of the many fabricated and bizarre concepts introduced into the law by liberal progressive judges in order to justify burdening the nation and undermining the creation of wealth, which they see as anathema to achieving their godless socialist utopia for themselves and not for the hoi polloi. The Wagner Act is clearly unconstitutional as it violates the Tenth Amendment, which is to say it abrogates the power and right of the individuals or corporations as legal persons to engage in contracts of their own freewill and without coercion. The Wagner Act was the beginning of the decline in US manufacturing which culminated thirty years later or within two generations in the 1970s with high unemployment and rampant inflation. The increase cost of labor engendered by the labor unions gave rise to the rapid mechanization of industrial processes and outsourcing at a rate faster than would otherwise have been the case.

This was true in my case as I said in the introduction to this book. I conducted engineering economic studies directed to the mechanization of various manual, i.e. labor intensive, operations of the Ohio Bell Telephone Company, a heavily unionized company. The mechanization involved significant investments in expensive computer equipment at the time, which was the 1980s. The fact there existed union agreements, which fixed labor costs and specified increases in labor costs in future years, enabled me to specify the labor savings and the resulting net present value with great certainty. The certainty in the return on investment and the high return on investment made the investments in computer technology very attractive to management who ultimately approved the investments leading to the elimination of hundreds of union jobs. Had there been no union contract and had labor cost more closely aligned to market labor rates, the mechanization of operations would have been more difficult to justify economically at the time. Although the economy was growing at the time and revenue increases were projected that may have justified the investments in terms of hiring avoidances rather than job elimination, yet the rate of wages increases embedded in the union agreements exceeded the rate of increases in revenue. The implementation of these computer systems, nevertheless, did occur, and the result was the loss of hundreds of jobs as the rate of productivity gains exceeded the rate of the company's revenue growth. The loss of jobs paid for the computers plus a return on the investment. The breakup of AT&T in 1984 along with deregulation of the operating companies at the state level, introduced more competition into the telecommunications industry and this accelerated the rate of job loss as well as the rate of innovation as the phone companies introduced the cell phone, and fiber optics and the internet to the telephone plant. Besides maintaining price stability, competition also stimulates innovation and in the process creates new industries and the introduction of competition into the telecommunications industry did just that. The fact that the Reagan Administration was in office at the time and promoted and implemented deregulation also reducing the tax burdens on corporations accelerated the decline in the unions and promoted the creation of great wealth. The same administration also tepidly enforced labor contracts to the point of effectively nullifying them. The productivity gains in the telecommunications industry set the stage for rapid gains in productivity in other industries as well and for the creation of great wealth and ultimately greater job creation. The wealth creation during the 1980s and into the 1990s was ultimately due to an economy less encumbered during the 1980s and early 1990s than in the immediate decades previous or since. This was an oasis during a time of an increasing socialistic government and encumbered US economy that once again started its march under Clinton and then Obama after it stalled under President George W. Bush.

Unions however did not sit idly by as their numbers declined through gains in productivity and the reluctance to enforce labor contracts by the Federal Government during the 1980s and early 1990s. This reluctance to enforce union contracts by Reagan's Administration at the time was fully justified considering that labor contracts existed against the will of the employer. The unions responded to the investments in productivity improvement tools and processes with attempts to prevent reductions in members by introducing counter productive, burdensome work rules, and greater numbers of job titles into labor contracts. This tactic was particularly successful in the automobile manufacturing industry where there were few layoffs due to mechanization of operations where the mechanization required layoffs to pay for the investments. The result was increasing cost of motor vehicles in the US thus inviting foreign competition seeking higher margins with their lower labor costs. Foreign competition did not have the embedded high labor costs and work rules that were a hallmark of the US auto industry consequently they were able to compete on price as well as quality. Eventually this led to the bankruptcy of General Motor and Chrysler. Although GM did not legally go into bankruptcy because the government bailed them out under the Obama Administration using taxpayer money and by abrogating bond holder's legal rights placing the unions in front of the bond holders in the sale of assets, contrary to established bankruptcy law. The fact that there was no outrage expressed by the mainstream media at this taking of the private property of the creditors is a testament to the corruption of the media and its complicity in the destruction of wealth and the weakening of the nation. Thus, the taxpayer unjustly and at great cost saved the unions from the consequences of their profligate greed thanks to the Democrat Party and a compliant and self-serving media, which is also highly unionized. This resulted in a loss of wealth thus making the nation more susceptible to calamity. The greed of unions is an example of uncontrollable greed because the National Labor Relations Act essentially eliminates competition in the market for labor by forcing companies to negotiate with unions rather than go to the free market and hire labor at market rates. Unlike corporate greed, which is regulated by competition, union greed is a manifestation of envy, and envy always leads to the destruction of wealth in the form of reduced productivity and reduced profitability. Union greed therefore is unethical and immoral and the government makes it as such because it eliminates competition in the labor market by law. Union greed is unethical because it destroys wealth creation and it is immoral because it is a manifestation of envy. Corporate greed on the other hand is ethical and moral because it exists in light of competition. The struggling and nearly bankrupt USPS, which I discussed earlier, is another example of an industry where unions undermined and controlled productivity gains with now obviously disastrous results.

Unions always result in greater expense to the unionized companies, and to industry in general resulting from both the need to recover investment in mechanization foreclosed by union work rules, and the greater cost of labor, thus significantly reducing efficiency and productivity and increasing prices of unionized goods and services. With the reduction in productivity come lower profits despite the inflating of prices thus reducing the creation of wealth. Ultimately, this leads to less investment in new plants and less job creation within the state or nation that enforced labor contracts. Thus, investments in new plant and the creation of jobs moved across state boundaries or national boundaries as investors sought greater return in places where they were not forced into labor contracts against their will.

The steel industry is another example of the destruction of wealth by unions. After World War II, the United States had a virtual monopoly on the manufacture of steel. Accordingly, it created much wealth. The United States produced over 63% of the world's steel production in 1945[4]. By 1969, the US was producing 22% of the world's production of steel, and by 2012, the US was producing only 5.75% of the world's production of steel. The collapse of the steel industry in the US is due solely to the unions. All the resources necessary to make steel, i.e. iron ore, coke, and water are still readily available and at low cost, yet the US makes very little steel compared to the rest of the world. The only variable limiting the manufacture of steel in the US is the price of labor and the work rules embedded in the union contracts.

While unions and the high cost of labor are the main reasons the United States is not producing steel anymore, I cannot dismiss the burdensome environmental laws that have added costs to almost every step in the manufacturing of steel. From the mining of coal and iron ore, to the smelting process, environmental regulations have introduced onerous and unjustifiable costs to the manufacture of steel thus reducing the profit from its manufacture in the United States. While pollution was a problem in some areas, existing laws against trespass could have

---

[4] US Statistical Abstract 1970 table 1152

addressed the specific issues rather than broad and general federal laws that affected all manufacturers equally regardless of any specific trespass. Such laws had little to do with the environment and more to do with satiating the envy of the godless thus accomplishing their destructive ends.

The idea that anybody is motivated more by interest in preserving the so-called environment than by envy or greed is absurd on its face. Environmentalism is simply a façade for envy and nothing more.

Affirmative action, social and environmental legislation encumber the economy

The Federal Government greatly encumbered the economy during the 1960's with the enactment of Executive Order 10925 known as Affirmative Action in 1961, and with social and environmental legislation that increased regulations and taxes on corporations and businesses in general. The final blow to the economy was the unilateral decision by the United States to abandon the de facto gold standard in 1971 thus creating the fiat currency essentially freeing nations including the United States to print money to pay off their debt. The combination of union demands for more wages and benefits, high taxes, regulations, affirmative action, and the abandonment of the gold standard led to the great inflation of the 1970's. The artificial reduction in the supply of oil brought upon by the Arab oil embargo in 1973 and then in 1979 with the energy crises brought on by the Iranian Revolution engendered by the weak and feckless Carter Administration, further exacerbated inflation. The oil embargo as well as the energy crises were caused by the abrogation of the Bretton-Woods agreement as the price of oil was based on the dollar and the dollar started to loose its value due to the US government's profligate spending on social programs. OPEC responded to the weakened dollar by withholding oil from the market thereby causing the price of oil to skyrocket. By the end of the 1970s, unemployment had reached 10% and inflation was over 13%. This situation was counter to the conventional Keynesian economic wisdom at the time, which called for an inverse relationship between employment and inflation, yet both inflation and unemployment increased simultaneously. The simultaneous rise in inflation and unemployment introduced a new word into the lexicon of economists - stagflation. Stagflation was a direct consequence of increasing government spending facilitated by the fiat currency. Stagflation was the undoing of Keynesian economics at the time. However, in order for the government to continue its march toward socialism it relied on Keynesian economics to satiate envy so it revived again after the government induced collapse of the financial markets in 2008.

The stagflation led to civil unrest in the United States manifested by revolution at the voting booth with Democrats deservedly thrown out of office with a landslide victory for the Republicans in the 1980 elections. The 1980s then saw an accelerated decline of unions, which continues even today, albeit at a slower pace, along with unprecedented wealth creation.   The wealth created during the 1980s and the focus of the national government on the protection of private property rather than on wasteful and non-essential social spending sustained a military build up by the United States that brought the Soviet Union to its knees and vanquished that godless communist empire from within and without a war.   The rapid political and economic collapse of the Soviet Union was laughable in light of the propaganda fed the American public by a liberal and sympathetic press about how progressive, enlightened and wealthy the godless Soviet Union was in the decades since the 1930s.   It also is a cautionary tale about much of the so-called reporting of news events by the economically unsophisticated and godless media.

The enforcement of labor contracts by the sovereign that are otherwise unenforceable under common law, precipitated and continues to precipitate civil unrest resulting from rapid gains in productivity engendering unemployment.   The repeal of the Wagner Act, the executive orders imposing Affirmative Action on industry and government, the executive order granting bargaining rights to federal employees, many if not all of the so-called environmental and OSHA laws, and the Civil Rights Act will restore the freedom to contract and the creation of wealth will resume.

Causes of Inflation and Deflation

Inflation is a general rise in the price of goods and services whereas deflation is a general decline in the price of goods and services. There are two causes of inflation and deflation.   One cause is monetary and the other economic.   Government monetary and fiscal policy causes monetary inflation and monetary deflation.   Monetary policy is under control of the Federal Reserve System in the United States.   Monetary policy manifests itself by interest rates such as the discount rate, which is the rate that the Federal Reserve Bank loans money to member banks. The Federal Reserve Bank also controls interest rates by purchasing and holding government bonds.   By law, the Federal Reserve Bank actually purchases government debt through the Federal Reserve Open Market Committee (FOMC) and from private brokers to whom the US Treasury offers and sells its debt.   The effect on interest rates is the same as if the Federal Reserve Bank purchased the bonds directly, but at least the public has an opportunity to purchase the debt as well.   Monetary policy also manifests itself by changes to the money supply also controlled by the Federal Reserve Bank.   The Federal Reserve Bank has the power to add or subtract the amount of money in circulation by controlling commercial bank reserves.   Another way to control money supply is by buying and selling US Treasury Bonds.   The Federal Reserve Bank reduces the money supply by selling bonds that it owns thus taking money out of circulation. When the Federal Reserve Bank sells government bonds, the result is an increase in interest rates since it is increasing the supply of debt thus dropping the price of the bond and increasing its yield, i.e. the interest rate. If the Federal Reserve Bank wants to increase the money supply it buys government bonds thus adding to the supply of money, causing the price of bonds to go up and decreasing interest rates. The interesting aspect of this method of controlling the money supply is that the Federal Reserve Bank must have government debt to buy and sell in the first place. Without government debt, the Federal Reserve is less able to control the money supply, and the money supply aligns more closely with economic growth. In other words with no government debt money is coined and not printed. Money coined is the result of demand by the economy resulting from increasing commerce, i.e. growth. Money printed is fiat money unrelated to the demand for money by the economy. Fiat money is inflationary, coined money is not inflationary. In this sense, there is a symbiotic relationship between the Federal Reserve Bank and the US Treasury, which essentially promotes deficit spending by the Federal government placing a constant pressure on wealth creation by perpetually inflating the currency. The results are unnecessary and disastrous fluctuations in the economy resulting in periodic destruction of wealth. The disastrous deflation of the Great Depression, the disastrous inflation of the 1970's, the collapse of the stock market in 2000, and the collapse of the financial sector and stock market in 2008 are all the result of government interference in the economy directly through the Federal Reserve Bank and indirectly through burdensome laws and regulations. None of these events had to happen. These events only occurred because there are a lot of otherwise intelligent people that do not have a clue, or have some romantic notion (which is the same thing) about how an economy works, the purpose of government, the role of private property, the purpose of wealth, and who do not fear God. God proscribes envy, and it is this passion driving a godless sovereign elected through universal suffrage to interfere in the economy and thus satiate envy.

Fiscal policy is under the control of Congress in the United States, which determines tax rates, and levels of government debt as well as the level and direction of government spending. Thus, Congress and in particular a Democrat controlled Congress is the source of the burden on the nation's economy and the source of its encumbrance and undoing.

Both monetary inflation and monetary deflation is independent of the supply and demand for goods and services but it affects the supply and demand for goods and services and therefore the creation of wealth.

The second cause of inflation and deflation is economic. Economic inflation and deflation is due to rapid changes in the supply of goods and services or in the demand for goods and services. These

226

changes are typically short term in nature and result from either a shortage or surplus in supply or a decrease or increase in demand for a particular good or service.   Unlike monetary inflation and deflation, economic inflation or deflation applies to specific goods and services. Economic inflation and deflation therefore are average measures, whereas monetary inflation and deflation are broad measures.   In an unencumbered economy, supply and demand are self-correcting thus maintaining market price stability for the specific good and service. Consequently, economic inflation is never a factor in reducing wealth creation in an unencumbered economy.   However, in an encumbered economy economic inflation also takes a toll on productivity, as was the case with the Arab oil embargo in 1973.   Even after the supply of oil returned to normal the price of oil never returned to what it was before the embargo as the previously cited Federal Government actions irreversibly encumbered the economy during the 1970s.   Rising prices and wages independent of supply and demand is a result of an encumbered economy and this was clear in the 1970s.

Figure 48 illustrates the relationship between inflation and deflation and major United States historic events since 1795.

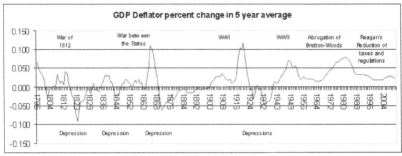

Figure 48-GDP Deflator Change in Five-year Moving Average

The chart of Figure 48 shows the change in inflation on a moving average over a 5-year period.   The five year period was selected to smooth out the rapid fluctuations in changes to the inflation rate and because most wars and other calamities since the 18th century were about five years in length.   Note that the five-year average level of inflation increased during times of war followed by a period of deflation, which occurs during a depression or recession and is the cause of depression or recession.   The deflation is due to oversupply of goods and services arising from the war economy and this oversupply leads to lower prices or a recession for a short period.   A depression is a prolonged period of no wealth creation, which is a negative GDP growth.   A recession is a shorter period of negative GDP growth.   This pattern was true until the end of World War II.   There was no depression or in other words no deflation in the United States after World War II, although there was a dip in the average level of inflation, instead the nation created real wealth and prosperity extending to 1970 when general inflation started to increase at a faster rate once more. Inflation was subdued after World War II because productivity increased at a rate faster than the underlying inflation rate. Low wages and the introduction of many labor saving innovations developed prior to World War II and during the war years contributed to the high rate of productivity growth that occurred after the war. The influx of many women into the work force during the war years and their willingness to work for relatively low wages in increasingly automated factories contributed to the high productivity growth rate and thus helped to hold inflation at bay after the war. Similar gains in productivity after the War of 1812, the Civil War and World War I contributed to the decline in prices or the deflation following these events. In the case of World War II, the cost of the war was so great, and the way the government financed and managed it was so poor, the inflation the war engendered prevented the improvements in productivity from overcoming the underlying inflation completely thus the lack of deflation following World War II. Also beginning in 1940 the Federal Reserve Bank monetized the debt, which means that it effectively forgave the Federal Government debt accumulated in the decades prior to 1940. This added to the inflationary pressure although selling of gold by the Federal Government offset somewhat the inflationary pressure thus maintaining the value of the dollar. The selling of Treasury held gold continued until 1970 with the abrogation of the Bretton-Woods agreement. Add to this the increasing encumbrance of the government on the economy in the years prior to the war, one should not be surprised that prices continued to increase after World War II, albeit at a slower pace, rather than decline as in the period after past conflicts. The government's profligate prewar spending, the inefficient spending during the war and the enormous increase in social program spending in the 1960s set the nation's economy on a different and ultimately destructive path culminating with the collapse of the economy in the 1970s.

"The Moral Equivalence of War"

Although the United States was engaged in a protracted and poorly managed war with Vietnam during the 1960's and into the 1970's primarily due to the incompetence and stupidity of Lyndon Johnson, the scale of the war was not at all like the scale of World War II. Yet it is clear from the chart that the rate of inflation during the 1970's was much higher than even the inflation rate during World War II. The relatively low inflation rate during World War II war was partly due to rationing and it led to shortages in the rationed items. After the war, inflation reemerged and continued at a moderate pace until 1970. This inflation was due mainly to increases in union wages unjustified by productivity. The reason for the high inflation during the 1970s is as I have already mentioned, i.e. the abrogation of the Bretton-Woods agreement in 1971, which introduced the fiat currency, plus the high level of unionized labor, high corporate taxes, environmental regulations, and affirmative action policies all reduced productivity growth by introducing economic inefficiency into the economy. Affirmative action in particular resulted in a large influx of unproductive blacks and woman into the workforce at the expense of the more productive white male, reducing corporate profits and wealth creation. With the introduction of currency floating exchange rates, real oil prices started to drop as the value of the dollar declined primarily from the excessive printing of money by the Federal Reserve Bank to purchase government debt, and the concurrent decline in US productivity from the aforementioned government actions and union demands. Since the price of oil is in terms of dollars, the decline of the dollar in the early 1970s caused the effective price of oil to decline. This affected the value of the revenue of the oil producing countries (OPEC) precipitating the Arab Oil Embargo in 1973 creating an artificial shortage, which led to increased oil prices thus causing economic inflation which added to the monetary inflation engendered by the government. In other words, government interference in the economy gave rise to monetary inflation, precipitating the oil embargo and resulting in economic inflation from the shortage of oil thus compounding the monetary inflation. These factors combined to create a war-like economy in terms of inflation during the decade of the 1970's. In fact, President Carter in an April 18, 1977 speech referred to the fight against inflation as the *"moral equivalence of war".* He obviously failed to understand what he meant and unfortunately, he had no clue how to fight this war and neither did the Democrats. The electorate made the decision for him by electing Ronald Reagan, the man who knew what to do, and did it. The great irony is that it was people who thought like Carter i.e., liberals, Democrats, and Keynesians, who gave rise to inflation in the first place and they essentially admitted through Carter's speech, they didn't know what to do about it and they still don't. Unfortunately, this lesson has failed to penetrate the thick heads and envious hearts of liberals and progressives who continue to espouse Keynesian economics despite its repeated and obvious failures. Clearly, it is their envy arising from godlessness and not reason which drives these individuals. Although they unabashedly profess otherwise, falling back to the Stoic notion, which is that their reason and their will controls their envy, and their desire is to help mankind. Yet neither is manifestly true i.e. reason cannot control envy because envy is irrational and atheists desire the destruction of mankind not its perpetuation or worse yet its growth.

Rapid changes in productivity growth rates cause economic inflation or deflation

Apart from fluctuations in the supply and demand of goods and services, another cause of economic inflation or economic deflation is rapid change in productivity growth rates. Rapid decreases in productivity growth rates lead to economic inflation while rapid increases in the productivity growth rates lead to economic deflation. The reason for this is that it takes time to respond to rapid changes in productivity thus there emerges changes in price levels as well as changes in employment. In an unencumbered economy, the changes in price levels and employment are temporary, localized to a particular industry, and short-lived, and the economy continues to create wealth with stable prices and full employment.

Economic deflation arises generally from rapid advances in technology that engenders rapid gains in productivity. Economic inflation on the other hand is the result of some calamity such as war or natural disaster that directly affects supply and demand for goods and services. Rapid advances in technology lead to deflation because rapid advances in productivity create an increase in profits that in an unencumbered economy spur competition which tends to reduce prices. It is not high prices spurring competition but high profit margins. However, in an encumbered economy, rapid increases in productivity always lead to disruption in the work force and the resulting unemployment can and often does lead to civil unrest. The civil unrest only arises in an encumbered economy, i.e. an economy with high levels of taxation, regulation and unionization. Both monetary inflation and long-term unemployment are the result of an encumbered economy. In an unencumbered economy, the rapid rise in productivity would result in downward pressure on wages as well as prices that in turn would increase employment, as the lower wages would spur investment and risk taking among investors. A rapid rise in productivity eventually leads to a general rise in wealth and a growing economy, and in an unencumbered and growing economy, the general rise in wealth quickly absorbs the surplus labor created by the rapid rise in productivity as we saw starting in the 1980s and up until 2008.

Inflation

General inflation reduces the value of cash savings as well as the value of other stores of wealth such as stocks, buildings and land. General inflation reduces the purchasing power of money and accordingly it reduces wealth and increases man's burden while also creating uncertainty for investors. By general inflation, I mean inflation in the price of goods and services as well as inflation in wages and salaries. In other words, it requires more money or cash at the current time to purchase the same goods and services, pay for the same labor or purchase the same assets than in a previous time. General inflation affects investment decisions through demands for greater return on investment and demands for greater interest on debt. Inflation is a burden on creditors because it reduces the value of existing debt. It is the reason that long-term debt generally has higher interest rates than short-term debt although on occasion this situation has reversed. The yield curve is a graph of the interest rate as a function of the time to maturity of the bond. Figure 49 is an example of a treasury yield curve.

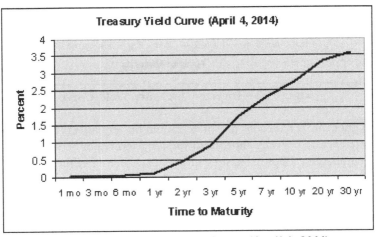

Figure 49 – Treasury yield Curve (April 4, 2014)

When the yield curve inverts, i.e. short-term rates become greater than long-term rates then it portends problems in the bond markets. It means that investors are unwilling to purchase short- term debt because they think interest rates will rise quickly so the price of the short-term bond goes down and its yield goes up. This usually leads to a prolonged drop in the equity markets because short-term debt is analogous to equity. The return on equity in the short term is generally greater than the interest on short-term debt and that is the reason that investors prefer equity to short-term debt despite the relatively higher risk in equities. Thus, when short-term interest rates are greater than long-term interest rates investors sell equities to purchase short-term debt causing a fall in equity prices. Figure 50 is an example of an inverted yield curve. The inverted yield curve remained until May of 2007 and in six months, the 50% decline in the DJIA began.

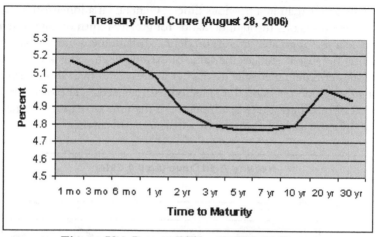

Figure 50 – Inverted Treasury Yield Curve

In an unencumbered economy, there should be very little difference in the interest rate between short-term and long-term debt because an unencumbered economy has little inflation and therefore the price of equities are a measure of wealth creation and not a barometer of inflation as is the case in an encumbered economy. Thus, the slope of the yield curve is a measure of the degree of encumbrance of an economy. The steeper the yield curve the more encumbered the economy. Figure 49 above shows a highly encumbered economy, as short-term interest rates are much lower than long-term rates due to the Federal Reserve Banks purchases of over $3 trillion of US debt since 2008. This is the reason that the equities markets have increased in valuation by over 100% since their trough at the beginning of 2009 while the GDP has remained stagnant during that time. Note that the increase in equity prices since 2009 was not an increase in wealth. Equity prices merely regained their value from the destruction of wealth that occurred in 2008. The recovery in equity prices was at the cost of employment and lower median income. The high unemployment and an 8% drop in median income sustained the earnings of companies to justify the high valuations. Thus, the artificially low interest rates have enabled companies to invest in improvements in productivity through debt financing resulting in layoffs in the encumbered economy. These investments include low interest rate debt financing of dividend payments, building factories overseas, as well as increasing mechanization of domestic and foreign operations.

General or monetary inflation is a boon for debtors because it reduces the value of payments on existing debt. General or monetary inflation means that wages and salaries increase as well as the cost of goods and services. Inflation increases risk tolerance so investors demand greater profits to offset the decline in the value of the currency. In other words, inflation has a tendency to increase riskier investments in order to obtain higher returns.   Accordingly, a higher percentage of failures and destruction of wealth occurs during times of high inflation. The ensuing loss of capital further weakens an economy and the nation becomes increasingly susceptible to calamity.   Inflation is a form of taxation and just as in the case of taxation it is a burden on productivity growth and therefore on wealth creation.   Inflation reduces the ability of a nation to withstand calamity because it reduces the rate of productivity growth and with it the rate of wealth creation or store.   Under inflation, investment capital and productivity growth goes toward overcoming the decline in the value of the currency in terms of what the currency can buy and in relation to other currencies rather than into creating more wealth.

As I mentioned earlier inflation is of two types.   There is monetary inflation and economic inflation.   Monetary inflation is a general increase in prices that is independent of supply and demand for goods and services.   Monetary inflation is due to government actions including taxation, regulation, government debt, the subsidies of unproductive industries, and war.   War is an act of the sovereign and it engenders inflation as scarcity increases during times of war.   Forced rationing is the means that a government uses to control some prices during wartime but this simply creates even more scarcity and so is counterproductive.   Allowing prices to rise in accordance with the free market would accomplish the same thing in terms of rationing but there would be less scarcity.   Everything would simply be more expensive, i.e. inflated in cost.   Taxation includes tariffs, which amount to a subsidy of unproductive industries.   Where tariffs subsidize productive industries, they contribute to deflation, as we shall see later.   Tariffs increase the price of targeted imported goods and services.   This has the effect of eliminating foreign competition in the targeted industries causing prices to rise but not necessarily profit margins.   Invariably the higher prices are necessary to sustain uncompetitive higher embedded labor costs, which is typically the reason for the tariffs in the first place.   As long as there is diminished industry competition, and the higher prices offset higher labor costs, there is little incentive to improve productivity either through investment or through competition for labor, thus undermining wealth creation.   In the meantime, there is diminished demand due to the higher prices of the targeted goods and services in comparison to the prices of non-targeted goods and services.   This creates great imbalances in an economy in terms of the supply and demand of goods and services that eventually leads to higher unemployment and inflation.

Income taxes reduce productivity because they reduce profits or the return on investment and consequently tend to discourage equity investment to improve productivity or to grow an enterprise. Regulations of business and industry increase operating expenses thus also reducing profits and contributing to inflation. In addition to increasing costs to comply with regulations, that in turn reduce profit or wealth creation, regulation also places barriers to competition in both the labor and capital markets thus causing prices to rise. Regulatory and legal barriers to competition increase the prices of goods and services independent of supply and demand, i.e. in comparison to an unencumbered economy. Government debt reduces the value of the dollar with respect to other currencies and with respect to its purchasing power because it places a burden on future earnings through higher taxes. Government debt requires increased taxation to pay back the debt plus the interest on the debt further burdening productivity and wealth creation. The reduction of the value of the dollar in terms of the goods and services that the dollar buys increases the price of scarce resources independent of supply and demand of these resources. In addition to tariffs causing monetary inflation, monetary inflation also occurs due to subsidies to unproductive industries through government grants or through the tax code as "incentives" or credits for favored behaviors or favored industries or businesses. Monetary inflation would not occur if it were not for the fiat currency i.e. currency whose absolute and relative value and supply is independent of a legal standard such as gold. Such a standard reigns in government borrowing, spending and taxation by law. It is the reason that socialist leaning sovereigns oppose the gold standard. Without the ability to print money at will, a godless sovereign cannot satiate the envy of those that placed him in office. Without the ability to satiate envy, he risks rebellion and his overthrow.

The absolute value of money is the quantity or quality of goods and services purchased by the money in hand. The relative value of money is the amount of foreign money purchased by the money in hand. When I discuss the value of money, I am referring to the absolute value and not the relative value of money unless I specify otherwise.

The elimination of the gold standard enables socialist leaning governments to take on debt and to print money to satisfy that debt. By doing this, the government is effectively taxing the economy without having to ask permission of the individual taxpayers. In the United States, the raising of the debt ceiling results in the printing of money by the Federal Reserve Bank who ends up purchasing much of the debt in order to keep interest rates low. Without the Federal Reserve Bank doing much of the purchasing of government debt, then the interest on the debt issued by the government would be much higher because as more debt competes for scarce creditor money the interest rates, i.e. the price of debt, must rise. The Federal Reserve Bank is currently the largest holder of United States debt in the world. The Federal Reserve Bank also began purchasing non-performing mortgage- backed securities (MBS) from the Federal Home Loan Mortgage Corporation (Freddie Mac) and the Federal National Mortgage Association (Fannie Mae) beginning in 2009 in an attempt to recapitalize these government sponsored entities or GSEs using fiat money in the wake of the collapse of financial markets.   Since the Federal Government took over the GSEs after the collapse of the mortgage market in 2009, this strategy on the part of the Federal Reserve Bank allowed more fiat money to flow to the US Treasury without legally having to raise the debt ceiling thus bypassing Congress.   The strategy known innocuously as QE3 or Quantitative Easing 3 eventually became an open-ended purchase of government bonds and mortgage-backed securities in 2012.   Congress also agreed to forego any decision on the debt ceiling until September 2013 while permitting the continued sale of US bonds.   As a result, the Federal Reserve Bank injected over $3 trillion in fiat currency into the US economy between 2009 and 2013 thus keeping interest rates at historically low levels for a historically prolonged period.   In the absence of printing money, interest rates would rise dramatically because of the competition for creditors in the debt market as well as the reluctance to lend money following the government induced mortgage market debacle.

Federal Reserve Bank prints money when it purchases government debt

The printing of money occurs whenever the Federal Reserve Bank purchases US Treasury bills, notes and bonds under a mechanism called Federal Open Market Committee (FOMC).   It also occurs when the Federal Reserve Bank loans money at the discount rate to member banks in order to recapitalize them.   Member banks use the loaned money to buy US Treasuries, which pay a higher interest than the discount rate.   The difference between the discount rate and the interest rate on the US Treasuries is profit or new money for the bank resulting in gains in the value of bank equity and assets or in the payment of dividends to the banks' shareholders.   This new money is fiat money and not money earned by the productive economy.   The strategy to borrow money at the discount rate and use the money to buy US Treasuries at the higher interest rate is the main reason that major banks can claim to make a profit since the collapse of the financial markets in 2008.   It is also the reason that bankers and other large creditors do not oppose government spending or government debt.   The Federal Reserve Bank undertaking the destruction of the equities market in 2000 when the US Treasury was enjoying three consecutive years of significant surpluses is not a coincidence.   The decline in the US deficit beginning in 1997 and the resulting multiyear surpluses was the direct result of a Republican controlled Congress that took office in 1996.   Without government debt, banks and other investors either had to take on riskier credit or purchase equities.   In other words, they had to earn their profit. This explains the rapid rise in the stock market during the late 1990s. Large banks lost an important source of income, which was the difference between the discount rate and the interest on US debt. Thus the Federal Reserve Bank under Greenspan violated the law and set upon destroying the equities market by increasing interest rates in the face of no inflation in the economy but simply because the stock market was rising too rapidly. This had the desired effect, which was to return the Federal government to deficit spending in 2002 and never again to see a surplus. The banks began to buy increasing amounts of Federal debt and in effect rely on the US taxpayer for their solvency. After the government induced collapse of the financial markets in 2008 the amount of US debt held by the commercial banks increased by over 300% from 2007 to 2014. Thus, the banks have become increasingly dependent on Federal debt to remain solvent. This portends a calamity in the making as gains in productivity slow and inflation accelerates the value of the low interest bonds held by commercial banks will drop and banks as well as sovereign holders of debt such as China and Japan will sell their debt to preserve their principle. The sudden appearance of large amounts of debt will cause interest rates to rise very quickly. This will draw money out of the equities market and cause a collapse in stocks. The collapse in the stock market will bring all investment to a halt and cause great unemployment and poverty. The result will be civil unrest and the inability to secure private property.

In a fractional banking system such as exists in the developed world, banks loan depositor's money and keep a small reserve in their vaults to meet demands from depositors. Both the loans and the reserves are assets and the deposits are liabilities on the bank's balance sheet. The interest on the loans is the income to the bank. Loans are contracts that are legally enforceable by the sovereign and thus considered secured assets. This is the reason that in a bankruptcy it is the creditors, which include banks who are first to receive any proceeds from the liquidation of the debtor's assets after taxes are paid. Note that in a bankruptcy the debtor must pay the taxes owed the government before the creditors receive any of the money owed to them. The possibility that a creditor will not get all his money back because of taxes owed by the debtor at a time of bankruptcy is one factor that drives interest rates higher. With that in mind, the interest rates on loans are higher than they would be otherwise, i.e. without taxes. The higher the general tax burden then the greater the interest rates on loans for this reason as well as for reasons due to other government interference in the economy as I discussed previously. The tax deductibility of mortgage interest payments, for instance, offsets the higher interest due to the priority of taxes in a bankruptcy proceeding. This of course only makes other interest rates such as interest on business loans higher than they would be otherwise. There is no real escaping the profound harm done to the economy by the income tax in terms of undermining wealth creation, either directly through the taking of profit, and indirectly through higher interest rates. In the absence of the income tax, interest rates would be much lower, and profits much higher with full employment and great wealth created. With the income tax, we have higher interest rates, lower profits, high unemployment, and much poverty. When I use the term income tax, I am including all taxes based on a percentage of income and this includes besides the Federal income tax, the FICA tax, Medicare tax, State income taxes and local income taxes. In a nation with universal suffrage the high unemployment and poverty results in a downward spiral of greater government spending, increased taxation and inflation and even more unemployment and poverty as individuals learn and are encouraged to vote benefits for themselves. The promotion of godlessness by the media and by the sovereign engenders the envy that contributes to the voting of benefits to the hoi polloi by the hoi polloi. The result is economic collapse, the destruction of wealth, and the demise of the nation's economy as the nation succumbs to its enemies and to the forces of nature.

Federal Reserve Bank intended to support the fractional banking system.

In order to fulfill their contractual obligations to depositors, banks must maintain a percentage of cash available as money to give to depositors on demand in a fractional banking system. As long as the depositors do not demand their money simultaneously then the fractional banking system remains viable. If the economy is growing then the demand for money by depositors is relatively stable and a fractional banking system aids economic growth or wealth creation by making money available to enable wealth creation, i.e. profit in excess of interest. However if the economy is not growing or worse if it is shrinking, i.e. there is no wealth created, then the depositor's demand for his money increases with no supply of new money becoming available through increased deposits engendered by wealth creation. Thus, the probability increases that a bank will not be able to pay depositors their money as obliged under the depositor's contract with the bank. The Federal Reserve Bank and other central banks came into existence ostensibly to avoid this situation, which was occurring frequently as the US economy grew rapidly and unevenly following the War Between the States. The catalyst for the legal formation of the Federal Reserve Bank was the bank panic of 1907 ostensibly due to a failed attempt to corner the market on the stock of United Cooper Company by squeezing the short sellers of the stock. The result was large losses to the banks that financed the attempt. This led to a run on these banks by the depositors worried about the security of their savings. The loss in the value of bank stocks led to a general 50% drop in equity prices. In the end, the financier J.P. Morgan bailed out the banks and stemmed the tide of withdrawals at a loss of at least $25 million to J.P. Morgan, who was not involved in the attempt to corner the stock.   Morgan undoubtedly feared that the loss of confidence would eventually spread to his bank and that is the reason he acted as he did.   Also helping to stem the tide of withdrawals was the US Treasury depositing money in some of the affected banks.   This undoubtedly sparked the idea of the Federal government having a role in the banking system.   The member banks initially capitalized the Federal Reserve Bank.   That is, the member banks agreed to have a portion of their reserves held by the Federal Reserve Bank.   Thus, the Federal Reserve Bank would serve the same function as J.P. Morgan did in the event of another panic but this time it would be the Federal government, i.e. the taxpayers that would assume the responsibility for providing liquidity and the loss would be borne by the taxpayers and not the bankers.   The Federal government pushed through the 16th Amendment authorizing the income tax in the same year that Congress enacted the Federal Reserve Act of 1913 creating the Federal Reserve Bank.   This was not a coincidence.   Deposits to the member banks included deposits by the US Treasury and this provided the ethical link between the Federal Government and the Federal Reserve Bank, which ultimately determined the subsequent disastrous fate and destiny of the US economy.   It is for this reason that the US President appoints the Federal Reserve Bank's Chairman, i.e. the Federal government is the largest depositor and the biggest client.   In other words, the US Government unfortunately for the first time now has a stake and an enormous influence on the US Financial System and the economy in general.   Regarding the 16th Amendment, questions remain to this day about the legitimacy of the ratification of the 16th Amendment by the State legislatures.   Given the atheist Progressives were in charge at the time and given their overwhelming desire to remake the world it is little wonder that the 16th Amendment would pass no matter the vote by the State legislatures.

The Federal Reserve Bank makes loans available at a relatively very low interest to member banks in order to make sure that these banks have enough liquidity to meet demand.   The discount rate is the interest rate charged to the banks for these loans.   Thus if a member bank finds itself in a position where an unexpected demand for cash occurs the bank can borrow money from the Federal Reserve Bank to meet the demand. The price the member bank pays for not anticipating the increased demand for depositor's money or in other words, for insufficient capital reserves is a reduction in their profit by the discount rate.   On the other hand, if the bank has made too many bad loans and it must right down assets then it must raise more equity or attract more depositors to make up the difference.   If the bank cannot do this then the bank fails and if this happens then depositors may loose their money, the Federal Deposit Insurance Corporation notwithstanding.   Banks may also call in loans to prevent depositors from loosing their deposits although generally loans are performing assets and sold to other banks instead.   The proceeds from the sale of assets such as loans secure deposits, and minimize any possible losses to depositors. Effectively the depositors of a bank are loaning their money to the bank in return for a certain interest rate. Since a deposit of money in a bank is a loan to the bank, the banks have a contractual and legally enforceable obligation to pay the depositors on demand and with interest.

The Federal Reserve Act of 1913, which created the Federal Reserve Bank, also authorized the printing of money on behalf of the Federal government by the same Bank. In the absence of growth in the economy, the printing of money by the Federal Reserve Bank reduces the value of the currency because the supply of money increases at a rate faster than justified by increases in the goods and services that the money can buy. More of the dollars are now required to buy goods and services since there is a larger amount of currency now in the marketplace with the same number of goods and services and prices rise. When the supply of dollars increases but the things that it can buy does not because the government does not produce anything that it can sell for the money it prints or has printed then prices increase. However, if the supply of goods and services increases then the printing of money is not inflationary but instead it facilitates commerce. In other words, productivity growth in the economy converts fiat money to coined money. If the printing of money is at a faster rate than necessary to facilitate commerce then gains in productivity serve to offset the resulting cheapening of the currency that is inflation. The extent to which productivity gains offset inflation then it is to this extent that the productivity gains do not contribute to wealth creation. Inflation therefore reduces the ability of an economy and of a nation to survive a calamity. If the rate of gain in productivity slows and the printing of money continues then prices will increase ushering in higher inflation. Thus in order to survive in an encumbered economy the rate of productivity growth must continuously increase in the face of increases in the money supply. As long as this continues, then an encumbered economy will survive, i.e. prices will remain stable but there will be little wealth created and until a calamity occurs. In the meantime, employment and innovation declines as unemployment and the profit associated with innovation go increasingly toward offsetting the underlying inflation rate. Civil unrest eventually ensues from the increasing unemployment. This creates an opportunity for atheism to take hold and engender envy in the populace thus destroying the nation from within. This is the current state of many of the European Nations as well as Japan and it is the present path of the United States economy.

One argument in support of the Federal Reserve Bank printing money and purchasing US debt is that since the Federal Reserve Bank expects the government to pay the money back from future tax revenue then buying US debt is not immediately inflationary. However, this argument ignores the fact that taxes themselves cause inflation by reducing productivity growth. This argument also assumes that the Federal Reserve Bank does not forgive the debt, which is what typically happens since 1940. When the debt becomes due, the Federal Reserve Bank simply hands back the notes to the government thereby forgiving the debt. The term used to describe the process is "monetizing debt" because now the money created to buy the original debt adds to the money supply with no increase in the things the money can buy. Figure 51 shows the annual amount of debt monetized by the Federal Reserve as a proportion of the GDP since 1994. This is money that the Federal Government has borrowed from the Federal Reserve Bank but will never pay back.

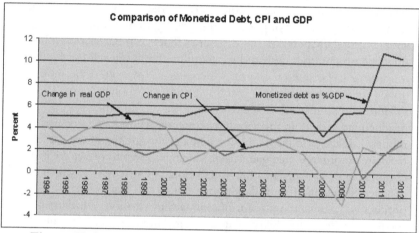

Figure 51-Comparison of Monetized Debt, CPI and GDP

This is additional unearned money inserted into the economy by the Federal Reserve Bank every year. Note the large spike in debt monetization that occurred after 2009. In the absence of productivity gains, the additional money would have caused inflation at the rate that the unearned money entered the economy but instead inflation grew at a lower rate. I overlaid the percent change in the CPI and the percent change in the GDP since 1994. Note that the CPI has been lower than the rate of monetization of the government debt. This is due to gains in productivity in the general economy. The gains in productivity have gone toward offsetting the monetization of the debt instead of creating wealth as the rate of growth in GDP has been under 4% since 1994 and well below the rate of monetization of the debt. The extent to which productivity gains fail to offset the monetization of the debt is the inflation rate. Thus, productivity gains have gone to growing government rather than grow individual wealth since the monetization of the debt has benefitted the government at the expense of national wealth.

In other words, the government primarily through its social spending and transfer payments is effectively eating and destroying the wealth created through the industry and genius of individuals. Since the government and those who feed off the government only defecate after eating, and defecation is not wealth creation by any measure, the nation is increasingly susceptible to calamity. The economy is literally drowning in the defecation engendered by government.

Productivity gains always lead to increased profit. In a growing and unencumbered economy, increasing revenues, i.e. growing markets, provide the increase in profit arising from productivity gains. However, in a no growth or low growth economy, i.e. an encumbered economy, increasing profits arise from reduction in expenses, and the largest expense in most industry is labor. Two factors affect labor costs, the number of employees and the amount paid to the employees, which includes benefits. Thus for a company to continue building profits or creating wealth in a no growth or low growth economy, i.e. a government encumbered economy, it must either reduce the number of employees or reduce the amount paid to employees or both. This is what has happened since 2008. Figure 52 compares the change in average pay multiplied by the total number of employed persons with the change in corporate profits and the change in GDP since 1994.

Note that changes in corporate profits track directly with changes in the GDP and inversely with changes in the average pay multiplied by the number of employees in the economy. Corporate profits tend to decrease following increases in average pay multiplied by the number of employees.

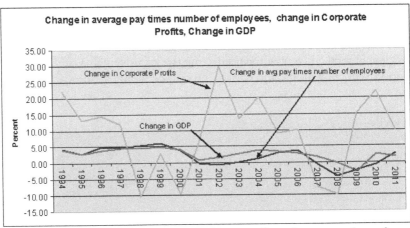

Figure 52-Relative Changes in Average Pay times number of employees, Corporate Profits, and GDP since 1994

The effect of productivity gains in a low growth or no growth economy also manifests in the median income of employees. Figure 53 shows the median income since 1994.   Note that since its inflation adjusted peak of $54,932 in 2000 median income has declined to $50,020 by 2012 with a brief uptick just prior to the collapse of the financial industry in 2008.   If it were not for the government-induced collapse of the financial industry that began in 1999 under Clinton's threats and intimidation of the banks culminating in the collapse of the financial markets in 2008, then real median income would have continued to grow as the economy grew. Real median income declined 8.9% between 2000 and 2012 while corporate profits continued to grow with most of the decline in median income occurring after 2007.   Between 2007 and 2012, real median income declined 8.2%.

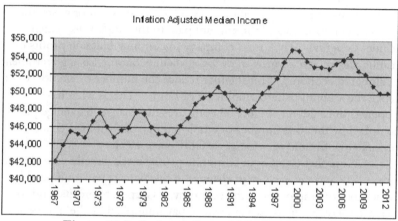

Figure 53-Inflation Adjusted Median Income

During the same time, corporate profits grew over 200% as shown in Figure 54.   While the increase in corporate profits also occurred with the GDP growing before 2007, after 2007 corporate profits grew with a decline in median income thus reflecting the improvements of productivity in a no-growth or slow growth economy as shown in Figure 55.

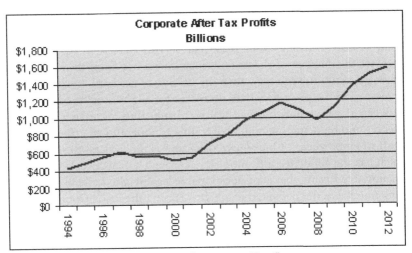

Figure 54-Corporate Profits

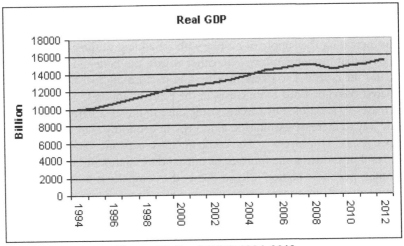

Figure 55-Real GDP 1994-2012

Nevertheless, the fact remains that the Federal Reserve Bank has injected money into the economy without producing anything for the money to buy whether it is loaning the money it prints or just simply printing it and adding it to the money supply through its toxic asset purchases aka QE3. This is the classic definition of inflation, i.e. too much money chasing too few goods.

One can characterize the cause of the collapse of the financial markets in 2008 and 2009 in the following manner. The government forces a bank under the Community Reinvestment Act (CRA) to give loans to people who cannot pay the loans back. The loans go into default and the bank looses the money. The money lost is depositor's money. The bank must make up the difference from bank profits. If the losses are large enough it must increase its reserves in order to be able to meet depositor's demands for their money. The bank can either sell equity or borrow money to increase its reserves. If it sells equity, it then increases the number of shares and since the money from the sale of the shares goes into the reserves, then the liability of the bank to shareholders increases and the price per share decreases for all the stockholders. The bank can also merge with other healthier banks thus increasing its reserves and reducing operating costs through operational efficiencies, i.e. layoff of employees. One source of money is the Federal Reserve Bank, which has the ability to print money. Through a process called Quantitative Easing that is of questionable legality, the Federal Reserve Bank purchases the defaulted loans thus erasing the loans from the bank's accounts and replenishing its capital reserves. The Federal Reserve Bank now holds the nonperforming assets on its books and as a privately held bank, it must be able to overcome the non-performing assets though earnings. The source of earnings is the interest on government debt that it purchases or through money that it prints. By printing money, the Federal Reserve Bank erases the liability for the loans. However, in the meantime it has introduced unearned or fiat money into the economy thus increasing the supply of money without adding to the goods or services that money can buy. In other words, the Federal Reserve Bank inflates the currency to overcome the non-performing loans. The inflated currency leads to increases in the price of equities, which increases P/E ratios thus forcing companies to increase earnings and the only way to increase earnings in a no-growth economy is to reduce expenses, i.e. employees. The company uses its profits to buy back shares thus reducing the number of outstanding shares and driving the earnings per share higher. In so doing, the company is not investing in new plant and equipment or growing but merely sustaining its asset valuation for existing shareholders. This is how the fiat money is absorbed into the economy with minimal inflation. At some point the rate of productivity improvements begin to slow and greater demands for wages and salaries as well as for higher earnings will drive prices higher. This is when monetary inflation takes off and interest rates rise bringing down equity prices in the process.

In addition, payment on the interest on government debt is through higher taxation. This also adds to inflationary pressures. Rapid gains in productivity overcomes this inflationary pressure, which translates into a spiral of massive layoffs, unemployment, poverty, a decline in incomes and a wider stratification of incomes. This also explains why stock prices have increased while real estate prices have remained relatively stagnant since 2009 failing to recover their pre-2008 value. Unlike real estate, which relies on rents as the basic determinant of value, corporations have more ability to improve their return on investment by improving productivity and this is what they did after the market collapsed in 2008.

Economic inflation is due to changes in supply and demand

Unlike monetary inflation, economic inflation is due to supply interruptions or to increases in demand and is self-regulating and short-lived because as the price of a resource increases demand will decrease and the price will fall in an unencumbered economy. Economic inflation is also due to sudden increases in demand, which also leads to an increase in price thereby stimulating additional supply and stabilizing price. Economic inflation is as much a burden on productivity as is monetary inflation. Increasing productivity overcomes or suppresses all inflation whether monetary or economic. Figure 56 illustrates the relationship between inflation and productivity in the US economy between 1947 and 2011. Inflation is in terms of 10-year moving average change in the CPI. Productivity is in terms of 10-year moving average change to the productivity index generated by the US Bureau of Labor Statistics (BLS).

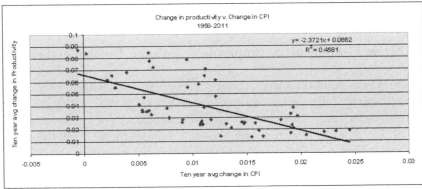

Figure 56-Change in Productivity vs. Change in CPI

Figure 56 shows that in general the greater the change in productivity over this period the lower the change in inflation on a 10-year moving average basis. Thus, productivity growth offsets the growth in inflation. The United States economy has been able to absorb the inflation created by the government encumbrance of the economy through increases in productivity. However, this has come at a steep price, which is a significant reduction in wealth creation manifested in high unemployment and lower median incomes. As I show later, if it were not for the inflation engendered by the government encumbering of the economy since 1929 the annual GDP would be today 80 times larger than it is, and the United States would be 80 times wealthier. (See Appendix 1) Although the economy created wealth since 1929, the amount of wealth created was much less, than the gains in productivity could have generated had the economy not been encumbered by government taxation, regulation, borrowing, printing of money, and spending as well as unionization.

Relationship between productivity, employment, inflation and union membership

Figure 57 is a chart of the annual productivity index, employment index, inflation index and an index of union membership between 1947 and 2012.

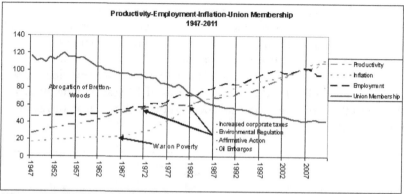

Figure 57-Productivity-Employment-Inflation-Union Membership

This chart shows the actual relationship between employment, productivity, inflation and union membership, since 1947.   The chart is from index data prepared by the United States Bureau of Labor Statistics (BLS).   The union membership data is from both the BLS and from the Census Bureau.   The union membership index is mine and uses 1964 as 100.   The union membership index is in terms of percentage of workforce.   In 1964, 28.9% of the US workforce was unionized and it is set to 100 as the base of the index.   Inflation is in terms of the GDP deflator as determined by the BLS.

I have indicated some significant governmental actions since the 1970s that encumbered the economy causing an increase in the inflation index.   The first event was several pieces of legislation including the so-called War on Poverty legislation, Civil Rights Legislation, Environmental Legislation, Social Security Expansion, Medicare, and the Executive Order calling for Affirmative Action all enacted in the middle 1960s, and coupled economically with the Vietnam War.   The second event was the abrogation of the Bretton-Woods accords in 1971.   As I previously mentioned this action effectively removed the dollar from the gold standard and it gave carte blanche to the central banks and in particular to the Federal Reserve Bank to print money.   This is one reason that inflation started to accelerate during the 1970s with the acceleration in inflation as measured in the increase slope of the inflation index curve.

The other reasons for the acceleration in inflation included increased taxation on corporations in the later part of the 1960's, the onset of efficiency destroying and profit destroying environmental regulations, the aggressive government enforcement of affirmative action executive orders, and the artificial shortage of oil initiated during the Arab oil embargo in 1973 and the manufactured oil shortage in 1978. There was an unfortunate rise in union membership as a percentage of the workforce between 1977 and 1982 during the Carter Administration, which went counter to the general declining trend in union membership since 1947. This too contributed to the high inflation as unions aggressively sought and received large and competitively unjustified increases in wages and benefits. The Vietnam War and the social welfare spending programs of President Johnson euphemistically referred to as the War on Poverty, which is actually a War on Wealth, as well as so-called Civil Rights legislation helped to fuel inflation just prior to 1970. These events all took their toll on the rate of productivity growth and as a result, productivity growth or wealth creation was relatively flat during the period from 1971 to 1982 thus leading to acceleration in the inflation rate. The increasing employment arose partly from the legal requirements imposed on private businesses by government regulations most notably affirmative action, consequently, there was much hiring of relatively unproductive Negro workers combined with an influx of women into the work force further reducing productivity and adding to inflation. The rise in union membership during this period was in large part due to keeping the Negro and women from entering the union trades, i.e. as a reaction to affirmative action. It was essentially the same reason that union membership increased during the 1930s, which was in response to the migration of the Negro to northern cities as the more agricultural South started to succumb to the increase in farm productivity. Environmental regulation also reduced the rate of productivity growth thus fueling inflation. After 1982, productivity began to rise again due primarily to reduction in capital gain taxes, a reduction in the top corporate tax rate, which went from 48% in the 1970's to 34% by 1988 and a broadening of the tax base that made for a more equitable distribution of the tax burden. The deregulation during the 1980s of many industries such as the trucking industry, telecommunications industry, airline industry, financial industry, as well as the deregulation of the electric and gas utilities also reduced the inflationary pressures. Less aggressive and more intelligent enforcement of affirmative action, the burdensome environmental regulations, and the stifling banking regulations also contributed to the increased rate of growth in productivity. The nominal repeal of the Glass–Steagall Act through lax enforcement during this time effectively reduced bank regulations allowing freedom of action in capital markets. The reduction in the slope of the inflation curve after 1982 is the reduction in the rate of inflation growth while the increase in the slope of the productivity curve is an increase in the rate of productivity growth.

The instantaneous changes in the rate of growth of productivity, employment, and inflation are the curves in Figure 58. I obtained the curves of Figure 58 by fitting six-degree polynomials over the productivity, employment and inflation curves of Figure 57 and then differentiating the curves over time. The six-degree polynomials had the highest correlation coefficient for each of the curves and this enabled the differentiation of the curves to derive the instantaneous changes in each of these factors.

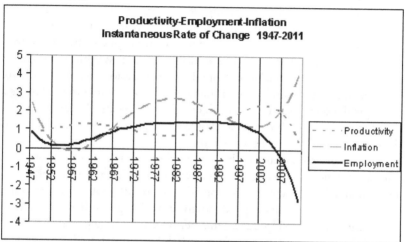

Figure 58-Productivity-Employment-Inflation Instantaneous Rate of Change

Figure 59 is a chart of the instantaneous change in the real GPD from 1947 using the same technique of curve fitting.

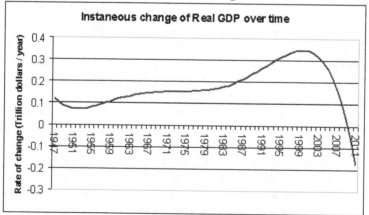

Figure 59-Instantaneous Rate of Change of Real GDP from 1947

Many conclusions are possible from these curves.   For now, however note the relationship between the instantaneous rate of change of productivity and inflation in Figure 58.   As the rate of productivity growth increases, the inflation growth rate declines.   The employment growth rate before 1970 pushed the inflation growth rate higher because the productivity growth rate started to decline.   In other words, less productive employees were entering the work force.   The increasing inflation rate combined with the low productivity growth rate after 1970 resulted in almost no change in the rate of employment growth. Although there was job creation during this time, the rate of growth was essentially flat.   Increasing productivity growth rate after 1982 brought down inflation while employment growth rate remained relatively constant.   The inflation growth rate started to increase after 2002, and the productivity growth rate started to decrease.   The result was a sharp decline in the employment growth rate as the rate of economic growth started to decline (see Figure 59) due to increasing government interference in the economy.   After 2007, the productivity growth rate accelerated its decline and inflation growth accelerated with its assent indicating significant encumbrances on the economy by the government leading to the financial collapse in 2008.   The result was a negative growth rate in employment and thus a rapid increase in unemployment. The significance is that it is the first time in the last 60 years that the employment growth rate turned negative and remaining negative for at least 4 years.   The negative employment growth rate is occurring at the same time as the inflation growth rate has reached record levels.   Not even in the high inflation years of the 1970's did this situation exist. Figure 59 shows that the instantaneous growth rate of the real GDP has also been falling from its peak in 2000 turning negative for the first time in 60 years in 2009 and continuing on a negative growth rate course through 2012.   This is a destruction of the nation's ability to create wealth.   These charts indicate that the economy has now lost the ability to create real wealth and it is relying on its store of wealth to sustain itself. Were it not for the great store of real wealth accumulated between 1982 and 2002, inflation and unemployment would be much worse and the nation would be on the verge of civil collapse manifested by food riots and armed rebellion.   Nevertheless, the current situation is a new paradigm, as the nation is consuming its store of wealth, creating no real wealth, and losing the ability to create wealth as government increasingly encumbers the economy through taxation, regulation, money printing and unbridled spending.   This paradigm portends significant and continued destruction of wealth with a coming calamity in terms of civil unrest of biblical proportions.   At this point, it is impossible to predict the form that the civil unrest will take but the fact of its occurrence is inevitable.

The government's easing and pulling back on the encumbrances to the economy between 1982 and 2000 led to a general increase in wealth creation extending until the collapse of the financial sector in 2008 due solely to interference in the mortgage markets by the government. The previously mentioned action of the Federal Reserve Bank along with the failure to rein in the Government Sponsored Enterprise (GSEs) by Clinton and the Democrats during the 1990's and the Democrats in Congress after 2000 led directly to the collapse of the financial sector.

The historical decline in union membership continued after 1982 and accelerated during this period. (See Figure 60)

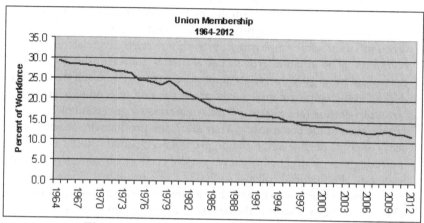

Figure 60-Union Membership 1964-2012

This is obvious from the increase in the negative slope of the union membership curve that occurred after 1982. Although the decline in union membership also contributed to the sharp increase in productivity and wealth creation, there was nevertheless upward pressure on wages and salaries during this period arising mainly from the gains in productivity, which were non-inflationary and from fear of unionization, which was inflationary. This upward pressure on wages and salaries due to the fear of unionization was a contributing factor to the upward movement in the rate of inflation as was the continued printing of money by the Federal Reserve Bank. Productivity gains kept pace with inflation after 1982 as shown in Figure 58 resulting in wealth creation. Increasing employment as well as increasing wages arising from the creation of wealth and the resulting investment continued for the most part unabated until 2008 when the financial sector collapsed due to government interference in the mortgage market that started under Clinton.

Paradigm shifts in technology during the 1980s

The increase in productivity during the period from 1982 to 2008 was not only due to a relatively significant reduction in the encumbrance of the economy by the government through lower taxes and deregulation but also to paradigm shifts in technology. The paradigm shifts in technology during this period mirrored the paradigm shift in technology that occurred in the 1920's and 1930's with the introduction of the tractor on the farm, electrification, telephony and the automobile. The 1980's and 1990's saw the introduction of the personal computer with accompanying software and the Internet into the work place. The development and wide deployment of fiber optic networks and the cell phone also occurred during this period. In addition, there came an increasing emphasis on quality improvement in the workplace, which focused on a reduction in waste and greater precision in manufactured goods. As these technological and management innovations became ubiquitous they had a profound effect on productivity in the service and manufacturing industries and they continue to do so. Were it not for these technologies, the rate of productivity growth would have been much slower since the 1980's and the economy would not have been able to absorb the growing work force as it did during that period. Nor would the economy have been able to generate the wealth now necessary to sustain the United States and world through the economic calamity of 2008, which was the government-induced collapse of the financial markets.

Government caused the collapse of financial markets in 2008

Unlike most previous calamities in which the government only made matters worse, the collapse of the financial markets was due solely to the government and the Federal Reserve Bank interfering with the economy beginning in 1979 with the Community Reinvestment Act (CRA). Wisely, the CRA was not widely enforced by Ronald Reagan or H.W. Bush but unfortunately aggressively enforced by Clinton who was a non-majority president, i.e. he won by less than 50% of the vote. The deliberate and calculated failure on the part of Clinton and his administration to regulate the government-sponsored entities (GSE) Freddie Mac (Federal Home Loan Mortgage Corporation) and Fannie Mae (Federal National Mortgage Association) caused the collapse of the financial markets. The Federal Reserve Bank made its contribution to the calamity under its Chairman, Alan Greenspan, and a Democrat, who professed free market principles but acted otherwise. The Federal Reserve Bank Chairman first raised interest rates beginning in 2000 deliberately and admittedly to undermine the stock market in his flawed belief that rising asset values portended inflation. He forced already high prime interest rates from 7.99% to 9.23% or by almost 16% within one year despite the fact that there was no inflation to justify such an increase. In other words, he was acting outside the scope of his legal mandate, which was the Federal Reserve Act of 1913 and its amendments. He thus succeeded driving the DJIA down over 30% and the NASDAQ dropped 84%. Surprised by the collapse of the equity markets, and in a panic, Greenspan then lowered the discount rate almost monthly in 2001 resulting in a prime rate of 4.12% or by over 55% within one year paving the way for the sub-prime mortgage market and thus setting the stage for the collapse of the financial sector about 6 years later. A great irony is that unlike Greenspan, the man that followed him, Chairman Ben Bernanke saw no problem with a rapidly rising stock market that occurred after 2009 and did not try to fight the market like Greenspan. This illustrates the utter incompetence of many so-called economists who end up on the national stage because their thinking supports those in power and not because of their competence. That is anybody that defends the printing of money, i.e. a Keynesian, is a good candidate for Federal Reserve Chairman especially to Democrat administrations. The difference between the stock market gains of the 1990's and the gains after 2009 of course is the stock market gains in the 1990's were in spite of Federal Reserve Bank policy, i.e. high interest rates, whereas the gains in the stock market since 2009 were the result of Federal Reserve Bank policy, i.e. low interest rates. In the first instance, the stock market gains created great opportunities, increasing employment and great wealth with the stock markets reaching new highs on a regular basis. In the second instance, the stock market merely recovered from the government-induced calamity and created less opportunity, decreasing employment, and very little wealth. These so-called economists have even now failed to learn any lessons in the events of the past 100 years.

Clinton – the father of the sub-prime mortgage debacle

Clinton and his feckless and incompetent Attorney General Janet Reno aided Greenspan in destroying the US economy by effectively creating the subprime market through the aggressive enforcement of the Community Reinvestment Act (CRA) of 1979. Presidents Reagan and H.W. Bush largely ignored the CRA but when the Republican Congress forced the Democrat Clinton to sign welfare reform in 1996, he had to get even with them and to protect his political constituency by aggressively enforcing the CRA. Welfare reform negatively affected the Negroid who was Clinton's and the Democrat's biggest single and most loyal constituency so he needed to make it up to him. Without the vote of the Negro, there would never be a Democrat or other liberal elected to public office. Clinton and Reno did this by forcing the banks to give mortgages to his constituents and voters, who were mainly the Negroid by threatening prosecution under the CRA. The low interest rates instituted by the Federal Reserve Bank under Greenspan and the introduction of such financing instruments as ARMs, and balloon mortgages during the disastrous Carter years helped Clinton and Reno get what they wanted from the banks. Mortgages with no down payment and the deliberately lax investigation of the borrower's ability to pay the loan back characterized the sub-prime market, as did the large number of unqualified Negro borrowers who were the former welfare recipients.

Mortgages with no down payment effectively eliminated competition in the mortgage market, which led to rapidly rising home valuations and an artificial and unsustainable building boom in residential construction. Individuals once on welfare now lived in mansions that they could not pay for. This stealing from the banks at gunpoint by the government helped to get enough Democrats elected in 2006 to enable them to control the House of Representatives and further undermine the economy by thwarting President Bush's repeated attempts to bring sanity to the mortgage markets. President Bush called for halting or severely restricting all the purchasing of mortgages by Federal Home Loan Mortgage Corporation (Freddie Mac), and Federal National Mortgage Association (Fannie Mae) since his election in 2000. A Democrat Congressman from Massachusetts named Barney Frank thwarted all attempts by President Bush to regulate these GSEs. Franks was an admitted godless homosexual who was on the House Financial Services Committee and later headed that Committee whose responsibility was to oversee the Freddie Mac and Fannie Mae. As a godless homosexual, Barney Frank did not fear God and he had no compunction about lying and distorting the truth and this is exactly what he did. Knowing the danger to the financial markets, Franks nonetheless defended the subprime lending, and Fannie Mae and Freddie Macs role as buyers of last resort for mortgage instruments. All this ended in 2008 with the collapse of the financial industry. Thus, we see that a godless sovereign in the person of a homosexual Congressman and who, driven by envy, facilitates the destruction of a prosperous economy.

Relationship of productivity growth rate and inflation growth rate
Referring back to Figure 58, from 1947 to about 1970 there was a steady increase in the employment growth rate as well as an increase in productivity growth rate with a declining union membership rate, and the inflation index was relatively constant so inflation was not a significant factor during this period. The increase in productivity growth rate created wealth that in turn resulted in greater employment with relatively low inflation during this period. After 1980, the decline in union membership continued, particularly in the automobile manufacturing sector with the introduction of foreign enterprises building non-union factories in the United States. The off-shoring and foreign outsourcing of manufacturing in general also contributed to the improvement in productivity and the low inflation rate. Median income during this period, i.e. 1983 to 1989 went from an inflation adjusted $44,823 to $50,624 or an increase of 13% as employment also increased. The employed people increase by 18% over the same period. The decline in unions, the outsourcing of manufacturing, the deregulation of many key industries, the reduction in corporate taxes, and the more equitable distribution of taxes, all of these actions led to a significant increase in the

real median income and employment. Imagine the increase in the median income and employment if the nation eliminates unions, eliminates all corporate taxes, evenly distributes taxes, and deregulates all industry. In fact, I have made this analysis in Appendix 1 and the United States would be 80 times wealthier. Thus, the relationship between the inflation growth rate and productivity growth rate determines the amount of wealth created by the economy and thereby its ability to survive calamity. Attempts by the government to "stimulate" an economy by taking on more debt and printing money to hold interest rates low invariably lead to greater unemployment and destruction of wealth, which is just the opposite of the purported and intended outcome. If one desired to destroy an economy and a nation, there would be no better way to do it than driving it into debt and then monetizing the debt at a sustained rate faster than the rate of productivity growth and let nature or rather mathematics take its course. This would quickly drain the store of wealth and subject the nation to calamity as indeed it has occurred in Germany after World War I and lately in the case of the US economy.

Variation in inflation rate between labor and capital affects mechanization.

The variation in inflation rate between labor and capital is a significant factor in industries where capital replaces labor. Such variations inevitably occur, as they are the result of man's constant search for machines and processes to make his work or his burden easier. Inflation in the cost of capital arises from the cost of equity and from the cost of debt. In an environment where taxes are low and government debt is a small proportion of the GDP or in other words in a relatively unencumbered economy there is low inflation in the cost of labor. The cost of labor includes hourly cost and the cost of benefits. Whenever these costs are low and stable then there is little inflationary pressure. Mechanization or the replacement of labor with machines occurs whenever the rate of inflation of labor exceeds the rate of inflation of capital, i.e. equipment and machines used to replace labor. Gains in productivity offset both economic and monetary inflation. As long as the rate of productivity growth exceeds the rate of taxation plus the rate of monetary growth and the rate of scarcity, then the net inflation is zero. However if the rate of productivity gains slows then the combined effects of taxation, monetary growth, and increased scarcity will lead to inflation with a decline in wealth and a decrease in the ability of a nation to survive a calamity.

The historically high level of inflation during the 1970s resulted in historically high interest rates, which meant that the Federal Reserve Bank stopped printing money effectively removing itself from the credit markets. Thus during the 1980's under President Reagan the government assumed its proper role as protector of private property and enforcer of contracts while reducing the encumbrances imposed by decades of over regulation and unionization. This was analogous to Elizabeth I restoring the value of the currency debased by Henry VIII, and Edward VI setting England on a wealth-creating course for the centuries to come. In doing this, President Reagan created unprecedented rates of growth in the nation's wealth as reflected in the surge in the US Gross Domestic Product that extended until 2008. The US GDP in constant dollars grew by 36% during that period. This outpaced population growth resulting in an unprecedented creation of wealth. In 2008 the increasing and relentless government coercion and regulation of the economy, particularly of the financial markets that began in the late 1990's under Clinton, reemerged and manifested itself in the collapse of the financial markets in that year. There is no better evidence of the power of the government to destroy the wealth of the nation it meant to protect than occurred during the Clinton administration. In addition, there is no better evidence of the power of the government to prevent wealth creation and make the nation more vulnerable to calamity than during the current period, i.e. 2008 to the present.

In an unencumbered economy, i.e. an economy free of regulation, taxation and other forms of coercion, and in which the currency has a fixed value, inflation is a function of supply and demand for specific goods and services. Accordingly this economic inflation is local and not general, thus its value is an average of the inflation of the price all goods and services. Generally, on a macro basis economic inflation tends to be close to zero as the prices of some goods and services increase the prices of others decrease. In such an economy, inflation has no moral or ethical component as it arises of natural and random processes i.e. specific supply shortages or increases in demand for specific goods and services. These natural and random processes manifest in a general average rise in prices that in turn result in increasing supply and decreasing demand for goods and services. As long as the currency has a fixed value, the prices will reach equilibrium close to the prices prior to the changes in supply and demand for specific goods and services. Therefore, economic inflation is amoral and ethically neutral. Gains in productivity or the rate of output overcomes any long-term economic inflation and creates wealth in an unencumbered economy.

Monetary inflation means that the sovereign does not fear God

Monetary inflation arising from government interference in the economy through regulation, taxation, enforcement of coercive contracts such as labor contracts, and printing of money is unethical and immoral. As I have defined ethical behavior as behavior directed toward the creation or wealth or profit then monetary inflation is unethical.

Monetary inflation is unethical because it is deliberate, unnecessary, and a destruction of wealth that does not have to happen and is preventable. Monetary inflation is a measure of the incompetence and mischief of government. The mischief of government arises from envy engendered by those in public office who do not fear God or in other words envy engendered by a sovereign who does not fear God. In this sense, monetary inflation is also immoral as it arises out of envy. The undermining of productivity gains and the concomitant reduction in wealth creation renders an economy susceptible to calamity. Such a calamity could include disasters such as wide spread drought, floods, wars, disease or other affliction. Calamities lead to economic inflation. Monetary inflation amplifies economic inflation thereby making it even more difficult for an economy to recover its ability to create wealth after a calamity. By debasing the currency of the nation, the sovereign destroys the value of private property, which is equivalent to destroying the private property that the nation appointed the sovereign to protect in the first place. Monetary inflation is due to the actions of men and not of God, whereas economic inflation is due to acts of God. Monetary inflation is a form of rape or trespass on the life of the individual arising out of envy because it is a forced taking of the fruits of his property and labor. As long as the rate of productivity growth exceeds the rate of scarcity arising from government regulation and taxation then inflation is in check. However, because inflation effectively nullifies growth in productivity there is no wealth creation, and this compromises the ability for an economy to survive a future calamity. When this occurs then government has reached a point of diminishing returns because now it is taking for itself that for which its establishment was to secure for the nation, i.e. life and property. Hence, those to whom the nation entrusts its sovereignty and who promote and enact laws that undermine the creation of wealth jeopardize their souls before God. A sovereign such as this is himself susceptible to rebellion or civil war.

Deflation

Deflation is a general reduction in prices. Like inflation, deflation has both a monetary and an economic cause. Monetary deflation is independent of supply and demand for goods and services and is due to government policies encumbering an economy. Government promotes and maintains deflation by tax subsidies to productive industries either through tariffs or through direct tax subsidies. Such tax subsidies prevent businesses within an industry from consolidating to reduce the supply of goods and services and allow prices to rise or remain stable instead of fall. During the Great Depression, for instance, the Smoot-Hawley tariff subsidized agricultural products in an industry that saw tremendous gains in productivity arising primarily from the application of the internal combustion engine to farming over the previous 20 years.   Thus, the Smoot-Hawley tariff served to prolong high production in agriculture and slowed the consolidation and reduction in the number of farms that would have otherwise occurred with the economy left unencumbered.   The artificially high prices and the expectation of high prices by individual farmers brought upon by the tariff resulted in even greater production.   This led to a total and general collapse of farm prices and land values thus increasing farm foreclosures and resulting in more bank failures prolonging the depression.   Congress passed the Smoot-Hawley tariff in 1930 and the number of bank failures went to over 9000 by 1933.   These were mainly rural banks, which loaned money to the farmer.   At the start of the depression, the price of milk declined by 28% going from 28.2 cents per half gallon in 1931 to 20.4 cents a gallon in 1933.   The price of milk was so low in comparison to its cost of production, and due to over production, that dairymen were spilling milk on the road rather than selling it for a loss.   The price of milk remained below 28 cents a gallon until 1942.   Despite the implementation of the Smoot-Hawley tariff the price of food continued to decline as overproduction in anticipation of higher prices took hold. This encumbered the rapid consolidation of farms, which would have occurred otherwise.   If Congress did not enact the Smoot-Hawley tariff, then the decline in farm prices would have quickly led to farm consolidations and reductions in the number of farms in anticipation of foreign competition and in anticipation of lower prices.   This would have ended the depression much sooner and the bank losses would have been much less.   Again, this was no small thing since agriculture comprised over 30% of the US economy at the time in terms of the number of people in the farm economy compared to the total employment.

Economic deflation as opposed to monetary deflation results from rapid changes in supply and demand of goods and services.   These rapid changes are due to radical new technology or technologies that cause paradigm shifts in the efficiency of production of goods and services.   The resulting rapid gains in productivity increase the supply of goods and services resulting in lower prices.   It also leads to increased unemployment in the short term.   The introduction of the internal combustion engine to the farm created unemployment in the farm sector causing people in large numbers to move to the cities where industry was expanding.   In 1880, the farm labor force was 49% of the total labor force declining to 21% by 1930.   This is despite the fact that the US population grew by 2.5 times during the same period creating greater demand for food and other farm products.   This is a tribute to the tremendous growth in farm productivity during this period brought on mainly by the introduction of the tractor to the farm sector between 1915 and 1920.   The total farm population was about 46% of the population in 1880 declining to less than 25% by 1930.   Thus, there was a tremendous migration to the cities during this period.   High levels of immigration primarily from Eastern and Southern Europe compounded the growth of the cities.   Despite the large number of people moving to the cities, unemployment was not a concern until 1930.   In 1920, the unemployment rate was 5.2%.   The unemployment rate was 4.2% in 1928 and it went up to 8.7% by 1930.   In 1932, unemployment went to 23.6%.   Despite the high unemployment rate, FDR increased taxes on corporations by 36%; increased government spending; aggressively enforced the Smoot-Hawley tariff; and robbed people of their gold. Under FDR, unemployment remained around 20% during the 1930s. Had it not been for the increased taxation of industry to pay for FDR's self-aggrandizing and self-serving social programs, the enactment of the Smoot-Hawley Tariff, and the confiscation of gold, the unemployed would have been absorbed and the Great Depression would not have been great.   Thus, the improvement in productivity in the farm sector during the 15 years before 1930 led to declining food prices, and caused the collapse of a significant number of banks between 1929 and 1932 and this was the cause of the depression.   The government made things worse through increased taxation, regulation and spending on unproductive and wasteful programs.   In other words, the depression was inevitable because improvements in productivity are inevitable and are the result of natural processes arising out of man's genius. Government attempts to remedy the natural progress of human genius exacerbate economic downturns and mitigate economic upturns. Nonetheless, herein lies the ethical question, i.e. should enterprises make improvements in productivity if these improvements lead to a rise in the general unemployment rate?   Before answering this question, it is first necessary to explain deflation further and to understand the conditions that lead to the paradigm shifts in technology in the first place.

  General deflation places a burden on debtors because as the value of money increases the cost of servicing existing debt also increases. General deflation benefits creditors as the currency used to pay creditors back is more expensive or worth more.   This naturally shifts capital to the payment of debt and away from investments.   Deflation reduces risk tolerance due to the incentive to pay off debt.   Stock market crashes in a relatively unencumbered economy as occurred in 1929 are the result of rapid increases in productivity leading to price deflation and the shifting of capital from equity markets to debt repayment.   The stock market crash of 1929 occurred because of the rapid introduction of labor saving devices such as the internal combustion engine, the telephone, and rural electrification into the farm sector during the period from about 1915 to 1930.   These developments led to rapid growth in productivity that caused an oversupply of agricultural products resulting in a rapid decline in the price of food.   The farmer could not sell his products at a high enough price to pay back the banks that loaned him the money to put in his crop or to buy his land. In fact, many farmers went into greater debt during this period to buy more land considering that it was much easier to farm the land with a tractor than with human labor or animal power thus compounding the problem. The drop in food prices led to farm foreclosures and a rapid decline in land values. Banks lost depositor's money and individuals as well as banks sold equities to make up the difference arising from the drop in land values. This resulted in a rapid drop in the price of equities. Unemployment ensued because of the loss of farm jobs and the decline in investments as investment capital decreased. As we have seen, in the first part of the twentieth century, agriculture made up at least 30% of the US economy so the effect was devastating. The effect of the rapid introduction of technology into the agrarian economy was civil unrest. The civil unrest manifested in calls for the government to restrict foreign importation of food products, i.e. for tariffs on food. The government responded and made things worse by subsidizing over production in the farm sector through the taxation of the non-farm industry and subsidies of farm production through the Smoot-Hawley Tariff. Corporate taxes went from 11% in 1929 to 15% in 1936, which is a 36% increase in the rate. The increase taxation in the non-farm industry slowed the growth of the non-farm sector which otherwise would have more rapidly absorbed many of those displaced from the farm. In addition, as we said the Smoot-Hawley tariff further aggravated the overproduction of the farming sector thereby prolonging the depression by many years. The Smoot-Hawley Tariff was largely responsible for the second economic downturn that occurred in 1936. At that time, the DJIA dropped 33% and unemployment went to almost 20%. Had the government not reduced corporate taxes and not interfered in the agrarian economy through tariffs, then the depression would have ended years sooner. The increase of industrial production as was occurring at the time would have reduced unemployment resulting in much greater wealth creation. Instead, during this period the US embarked on a series of laws and regulations which placed great encumbrances on the economy and which eventually led to the devastation of the economy in the 1970's.

Unions react to the influx of labor from the farm

The 1930's period also saw the rise of the labor unions as the migration of people coming to the city from the farm increased the supply of labor, which placed downward pressure on existing wages and threatened the jobs of many people as the government slowed industrial growth through increased taxation on corporations. The collapse of the equities market in 1929 also slowed investment in new industries further reducing the number of jobs. Of great concern to the unions was the migration of the Negro from the southern farms to the industrial northern cities. These people were the grandsons of the slaves that the

Northerners fought and died to free just 70 years earlier. This is one of the great ironies of history as the North, and the Nation in general, now was to pay dearly for the hubris of their abolitionist forefathers. The unions had a sympathetic ear with FDR and the Democrat Congress as union members voted Democrat, and the result was the Wagner Act of 1935. Through their work rules and seniority system, the unions effectively prevented the Negro from entering the factory floor or the trades in any significant numbers for at least 30 years or almost two generations. It was not until the number of Negros in the North increased sufficiently so that many Northern and some Southern politicians saw a reliable voting block that the Affirmative Action executive orders, and Civil Rights Legislation forced unions to start accepting Negros into their ranks by the 1970's. Still there are many unions, particularly among the construction trades, where there are very few Negros, but this has more to do with the low average intelligence of the Negro than with any legal or moral imperative. I will discuss the relationship between intelligence and job performance later.

Wagner Act and the Glass-Steagall Act encumber economy.

Besides the Social Security Act, two of the more egregious laws passed under FDR were the Glass-Steagall Act and the Wagner Act. The Glass-Steagall Act enacted in 1933 restricts banks from holding or selling stocks or loan money to someone to buy stocks. It legally separated the banks commercial transactions from investment type transactions. Even though a bank could still lend money to corporations, it could not directly buy the stock of those corporations. In other words, a bank could not have a direct ownership of a corporation to which it loaned money, which makes no economic sense. Although much controversy exists over the effectiveness of the Glass-Steagall Act in protecting depositors, it nevertheless encumbered the financial markets and interfered with commerce because it introduced conditions into contracts that otherwise would not be introduced by the parties to the contracts. Any transaction involves a contract executed in accordance with the freewill of the parties to the transaction. Whenever a third party, in this case the government, introduces himself into the transaction without the consent of the other parties and forces conditions to the transaction that the parties would not otherwise include then this act encumbers the transaction. Consequently, the transaction is much less productive than it would be otherwise. This is effectively what the Glass-Steagall Act did and it diminished wealth creation while the law was in effect. Congress repealed the Glass-Steagall Act in 1999 and its repeal did not create any problems in the financial markets. In fact, the Dow Jones Industrial Average (DJIA) market went from 9300 in 1999 to 13900 in 2007 a real gain in wealth of almost 50%. This gain happened despite interference in the economy by the Federal Reserve Bank in 2000 as I have previously discussed, and it points to the extent that the Glass-Steagall Act burdened the wealth creating capacity of the nation since its enactment.   Recall that the financial collapse occurring in 2008 was due to the government forcing banks to lend money to individuals (80% minorities) whom everyone knew could not pay back the money they borrowed.   This had nothing to do with the Glass-Steagall Act, which regulated the purchasing of stock by commercial banks.   Therefore, there is no connection between the repeal of the Glass-Steagall Act in 1999 and the collapse of the financial markets in 2008.   However, there is clear connection between the Community Reinvestment Act of 1979 (CRA) with Clinton's aggressive enforcement of it and the collapse of the financial markets in 2008.   Indeed the CRA was the cause of the collapse of the financial markets.

Before I discuss the Wagner Act, I cannot allow the interference in the economy by the Federal Reserve Bank in 2000 to go without additional comment.   The interference in the economy by the Federal Reserve Bank in 2000 was probably the most egregious act by the Federal Reserve to that point in time.   Despite historically low inflation at the time the Federal Reserve Chairman, Alan Greenspan took it upon himself to put a halt to a rapidly rising stock market by increasing interest rates to levels not justified by the level of inflation at the time or since.   He famously referred to the rapid growth in stock prices that occurred in the late 1990's as "irrational exuberance" as if it was even of any legal concern to him as Chairman of the Federal Reserve, which it was not. Greenspan's actions resulted in the markets collapsing in 2000 to less than half their value as interest rates increased from a prime rate of 7.75% in 1999 to 9.50% by the end of 2000.   This caused a 30% drop in the DJIA by September 2002.   By this time, the equity markets began to recover due once again to Greenspan dropping interest rates rapidly in 2001, so that by the end of 2001 the prime rate was 4.75%.   Figure 61 is a chart of the prime interest rate on a monthly basis beginning in 1949 and through 2012 and a twelve-month moving average of the CPI beginning in 1950.

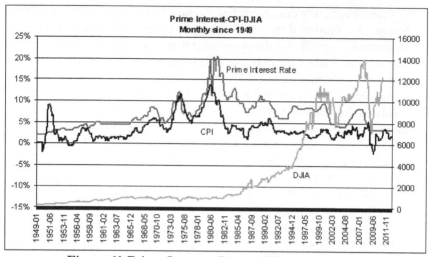

Figure 61-Prime Interest Rates, CPI and DJIA

Note that in general the prime rate exceeded the CPI throughout the years following the Korean War (1953) until 1974. Several significant events occurred in the period from 1966 to 1982 that almost destroyed the US economy and which continue to reverberate to this date. The events were all the result of extraneous government actions manifested in law and unrelated to protecting private property and enforcing contracts. The shock to the economy began with the build up to the Viet Nam War, which was the most politicized war in US history and made so by a leftist, envious, and godless media. The Viet Nam War was justified because communism as an ideology was a threat to private property and to halt the spread of this ideology is a proper act of a government whose purpose is the protection of private property. This was the first time that a significant and vocal minority of the US electorate given voice by a complicit and treasonous media desired the US to loose a war and purely for political gain for the treasonous political left. The build up of the war began in 1966, which was also the year that saw the passage of all the so-called Great Society legislation. This legislation opened the entitlement-spending spigot. Following the passage of Johnson's so-called Great Society legislation was the enforcement of the executive order on Affirmative Action issued by Kennedy in 1961 that further encumbered the economy by introducing more government coercion in the formation of contracts. The inevitable abrogation of the Bretton-Woods agreement followed in 1971, thereby eliminating the gold standard and creating the fiat currency. The increase taxation and reduction in productivity arising from the unprecedented encumbrances thrust onto the economy by the government and the increasing demands of the unproductive unions for unjustified wage and benefit increases during this period led predictably to a historically high inflation rate as shown by

262

the CPI curve in Figure 61. It also led to high unemployment and no wealth creation in the United States as evidenced by the flat or declining Dow Jones Industrial Average. Whatever productivity gains occurred during this period went toward overcoming inflation and not wealth creation. It was only with the deregulation of many industries, decline in the influence of unions and union membership, reduction in overall taxes and broadening of the tax base that occurred in the 1980's that enabled the economy to recover and to create wealth again. This is a formula, which works every time it is tried. The opposite also works every time the government tries it as well, which is unfortunately more often than not.

Monetary deflation is due to government reaction to economic deflation. Economic deflation arises from rapid increases in productivity due to the introduction of major technologies in the workplace as I have said. As a result, there is a rapid decline in employment with the potential for civil unrest in an encumbered economy. The government typically reacts to this by subsidizing productive industries thereby attempting to maintain or increase prices rather than letting prices decline in accordance with supply and demand. The subsidies are through government borrowing or taxes to purchase products and services thereby creating artificial demand to prop up prices and maintain high production or through tariffs that also raise prices and continue high levels of production. Since subsidies are to existing industry, there is a barrier to competition. Tariffs limit foreign competition. Therefore, even though margins are high there is no competition and thus prices become independent of supply and demand for goods and services. Otherwise, the high margins would attract new entrants as well as foreign entrants to the market. When subsidies end or when tariffs expire, margins drop and unemployment results as companies try to maintain margins through improved productivity. The result of government encumbrance on the economy is to prolong unemployment and aggravate a recession or a depression. It is only in an unencumbered economy that the disruptive effects of rapid gains in productivity mitigate through wealth creation and deflation is non-existent. In other words, government action creates the business cycle thereby weakening an economy and making the nation susceptible to calamity. Without government action as manifested through monetary policy or fiscal policy, which includes regulation, there would be no business cycle just the continuous creation of wealth interrupted only by the occasional and unpredictable natural calamity that will and does occur destroying wealth.

Economic deflation as opposed to monetary deflation is the result of rapid changes in supply or demand for goods and services. It is due to rapid gains in productivity and this is due to the introduction of major or paradigm shifting technologies. The railroads and telegraph of the middle 19th century led to deflation and ultimately the depression from 1873 to 1883, electricity and the internal combustion engine, and in particular rural electrification, and as I have shown mechanization of food production led to deflation of food prices and the Great Depression. The introduction of the computer, the internet, and the cell phone has resulted in tremendous gains in productivity that has contributed to the recession of 2008-2009 and continuing high unemployment, i.e. 2008 to the present. Although technically the economy is not currently (2014) in recession, i.e. no contraction in the GDP, it is as close to a recession as it can get. However, as I have said were it not for the economy encumbered by regulation, taxation, and coercion in the form of union contracts, then the gains in productivity would not have created the current recession but rather the wealth created by the gains in productivity would have resulted in greater investments leading to higher employment and greater real incomes. The current economic recession is more attributable to government action than at any other time in history. Note that I am using the term recession somewhat loosely to indicate negative or low growth in the GDP over the period from 2008 to the present. Had it not been for the government forcing banks to lend money to meet political and social ends rather than lending for economic ends beginning in the late 1990s then the current state of affairs, i.e. 2008 to the present, would not exist. The destruction of wealth engendered by the government's interference in the financial markets during the 1990's is unprecedented and the resulting collapse in the financial markets in 2008 rivals the destruction of wealth during WWII. The unprecedented coercion and levels of regulation introduced primarily into the financial markets, but also into the economy in general, began in the 1990's with Clinton's administration. It has created an economy that is relying increasingly on the store of wealth built up from the free market policies of President Ronald Reagan during the 1980's to sustain itself. There has been very little wealth creation after the collapse of the financial markets in 2008. The rise in the stock market since 2008 simply replaced what was lost at the time. Unlike previous recessions, the equity market rose at the expense of employment and a decline in median income. The restoral of values was limited to the market for equities and even here, the restoration was uneven. There has not been a restoration of values in the housing market or in other real estate values. This sector of the economy has yet to recover the wealth destroyed by the policies of the Democrats manifested in laws that interfere with the economy and the creation of wealth. The high level of unemployment is the result of companies taking advantage of new technology to improve productivity thereby improving margins despite the decline in economic activity as reflected in the low GDP growth rate and due solely to continuous government interference in the economy through taxes and regulations. The number of individuals employed as a percent of the total able-bodied work force dropped to a 35-year low in 2013 to a level of about 63% and it appears that it will continue to decline as the work force naturally increases and the number of opportunities decline with declining investment.   Although the stock market recovered from the shock of 2008-2009, its recovery was due in large part to the extraordinary and unprecedented liquidity introduced into the economy by the Federal Reserve Bank and manifested by prolonged and historically low interest rates.   The S&P 500 real earnings per share ratio based on one-year earnings at the end of 2008 was $71.19, rising to $88.27 by the end of 2012.   The increase in earnings was not due to increases in revenue as would be the case in a growing economy.   The inflation-adjusted revenue per share of the S&P 500 stocks dropped from the end of 2008 where it was $1,131.34 per share to $1110.97 per share by the end of 2012.   The revenue per share dropped by 1.84%, whereas the earnings per share increased 24%.   Additionally, real median income at the end of 2007 was $54,489.   By the end of 2011, real median income was $50,054 or 8.14% lower.   Since revenue per share dropped, then the increased earnings are due to rapid gains in productivity manifested in a large and continuing number of layoffs, a small number of new hires at wages and salaries lower than in the past, and a decline in the real median income or the employee expense.   This is the price paid by the US economy for the Federal Reserve Bank printing of money in an attempt to restore the value of assets it destroyed with the help of the godless Democrats and their policies built on envy.   It is the price the US economy is still paying as the government, under the Democrats continues to meddle in the economy for political gain.

It can truly be said that the great calamity has now arrived, engendered by envious and godless Democrats who we unfortunately appointed and elected to protect us.   Now the nation is living off its store of wealth accumulated since the halcyon era of Ronald Reagan in the 1980s as it struggles to keep inflation at bay with continuous gains in productivity and increasing numbers of unemployed with lower wages and salaries.   The sovereign in the person of the Democrat party has successfully satiated the godless and envious leftists and unionists as the nation moves closer to the calamity that is socialism and the destruction of wealth continues unabated.

Rapid gains in productivity create short-term oversupply of labor

Rapid gains in productivity resulting from paradigm shifts in technology always create a short-term oversupply of labor.   This oversupply persists until labor adjusts to the technology.   Then the technology creates new opportunities through new investments and generally at higher real wages than before adoption of the technology. Government policy that tries to fix the economy always makes it worse as in the post 2008 calamity.   Government either taxes industry, or borrows or prints money in order to accomplish its ends. When those ends go beyond protecting private property and enforcing contracts then government over-encumbers the economy. Taxing industry reduces productivity or the gains in productivity thereby reducing the wealth creating capacity of the nation, engendering inflation, and aggravating unemployment as any tax always discourages investment because it reduces the return on investment. Government borrowing and printing money reduces future wealth creating capacity by fomenting inflation, and sets the stage for even greater unemployment and civil unrest in the future. However if an economy is left alone, i.e. unencumbered by the government, the inherent gains in productivity engendered by technology lead to greater profits creating wealth and increasing investment. Increased investment results in greater demand for labor and capital. During times of economic deflation, resulting from overproduction, the ethical course of action for government is to allow unemployment to happen and not interfere with the labor force in any manner. This includes not enforcing union contracts and not providing unemployment compensation. In an overly encumbered economy, the reaction of the government to rapid increases in unemployment should be less regulation, less government debt, and lower taxes particularly lower corporate income taxes, and less government spending. The reaction of the Federal Reserve Bank must be to allow interest rates to respond to market conditions and insure liquidity is available but only to the extent that the economy is growing, i.e. increases in the money supply governed by the productivity of the economy. The money supply must track the growth of the private economy and not the growth of government. The payment of unemployment compensation or welfare is inherently unethical because it places a burden on wealth creation and prolongs unemployment. In an unencumbered, economy individual wealth overcomes calamity because only in an unencumbered economy does an individual create personal wealth. Government taxation and regulation undermines the creation of individual wealth. Thus, government largess sets the stage for civil unrest because it prevents the individual accumulation of wealth exposing individuals to calamity. Unemployment is a calamity for the individual and the individual must sustain himself through his store of wealth. An individual's inability to create wealth and thereby sustain a calamity is the direct result of government interference in the economy, i.e. coercion and regulation of commerce. It is for this reason that government must exist only to secure private property and enforce contracts. The burden by government on the wealth created by the individual, i.e. on the individual's productivity, reduces the ability of the individual to sustain a calamity and civil unrest ensues. As in the case of business cycles caused by government interference in the economy, so too is long-term individual unemployment and the ensuing poverty a result solely due to government interference in the economy.   It is for this reason that the US Founding Fathers and Framers of the Constitution only permitted white male landowners to vote.   Universal suffrage, i.e. allowing individuals to vote who do not contribute to the tax base, is the bane on wealth creation, and therefore on the ability of a nation to survive a calamity.   The history of the late nineteenth century and twentieth century has demonstrated this time, and time again, as universal suffrage has taken hold.

Universal suffrage

As I have indicated the current economic and political environment is the product of the Great Depression where the purpose of government turned from that of protector to that of benefactor.   As protector, the sovereign owed his allegiance to the individual and the individual owed his allegiance to the nation.   As the sovereign becomes benefactor, the individual owes his allegiance to the sovereign rather than the nation.   This is the welfare state aka socialism or communism.   To sustain itself the welfare state must be able to tax, or borrow, or print money at will.   If it cannot raise sufficient revenue by encumbering the economy the welfare state will arm itself and take the wealth of its neighbors by warring with them.   The income tax amendment added to the US Constitution in 1913 as the Sixteenth Amendment enabled the taxation of wealth creation by allowing the government to impose a graduated income tax based on the percentage of income rather than a head tax or direct tax that was the original intent of the Framers and codified in the Constitution.   A head tax is a fixed amount not a percentage and independent of income or wealth.   A direct tax or head tax is independent of the value of property, and independent of income, and the least burdensome on wealth creation.   An income tax is a great burden on wealth creation or productivity and a property tax or head tax is a burden on wealth.   The income tax set the stage for the welfare state ushered in at the first opportunity on the collapse of financial markets in 1929 and the government induced depression, which was the aftermath. As I said earlier, it was the rapid gains in farm productivity and rapid decline in the price of food that led to a drop in land values and foreclosures on farms.   The farm foreclosures in turn led to bank failures.   If left alone the free market would have corrected on its own because industry was absorbing much of the land and much of the labor freed up from the large gains in agriculture productivity.   However, the increase in income taxes and the imposition of tariffs on imported food, i.e. through the Smoot-Hawley Act, slowed economic growth in the industrial sector while creating even greater over production in the farm sector thereby further reducing food prices and causing land values to drop even more.   This prolonged the depression well into the 1930's and created much misery and poverty all of which were avoidable and unnecessary

In present times the combination of rapid gains in productivity in an encumbered economy, and the government induced collapse of the financial sector, which began in 1999 under specific and deliberate efforts of the godless Clinton and culminating in the collapse of financial markets in 2008, have undermined the wealth creating capacity of the US economy for years to come.   Given that the government since 2008 is meddling in the economy even more than in the past and encumbering it with unprecedented increases in regulations, taxes, profligate spending, and fiat money, then the number of unemployed will continue to increase, median income will continue to fall with civil unrest inevitable.

Summary of Section 1

In Section 1, I argued that the security of private property in the broadest sense is the motivating factor behind all economic activity. Private property secured by the government gives rise to wealth creation. In prosaic terms, the need to secure both space and time, i.e. through private property and through creation of wealth, drives man's economic activity.   The creation of wealth ensures the future security of private property so the creation of wealth is essential for survival.   Recall that I said that a man's life is private property and therein is the ethical and moral basis of wealth creation.   Productivity creates wealth so productivity, i.e. efficiency in the provision of goods and services is the sole ethical pursuit of man.   Efficiency manifests in profit ergo profit is the sole ethical pursuit of man.   It is also the only legitimate intellectual pursuit.   All human activity is ethical or unethical depending on whether or not it creates wealth i.e. profit, or creates life i.e. progeny.   An activity that fails to create wealth in all its manifestations or secure private property is unethical.   Man's actions that destroy private property or destroy wealth or the ability to create wealth are immoral, i.e. violate God's laws.   In other words, acts that fail to create or secure wealth are unethical and acts that destroy wealth or the ability to create wealth are immoral.

I went on to say that the creation of wealth engenders commerce through the exercise of freewill or liberty, which is the freedom to contract.   The freedom to contract therefore is essential to the creation of wealth.   Individuals of a nation appoint a sovereign for the purpose of securing private property and enforcing contracts.   There are risks associated with the sovereign.   The main risk is to liberty, which is the freedom to contract.   The more that the freedom to contract is abridged by the sovereign the less the wealth created.   A sovereign who does not fear God can act through his laws to undermine wealth creation and thereby threaten the security of private property.   A nation who does not fear God cannot survive because God proscribes envy and envy is the most destructive of all human passions.   Accordingly, a nation formed under God, and whose sovereign and populace fear God, will create wealth and prosper. A nation whose populace does not fear God will perish because such a nation will fail to create wealth and with envy consuming and destroying its wealth

I have presented two basic elements of a wealth creating economy thus far. These are the burden of the sovereign and the fear of God. The lighter the sovereign's burden and the greater and more ubiquitous the fear of God the more prosperous the economy and the wealthier the nation becomes. I will discuss in the next section, the purpose of the sovereign, the role of the passions in economics, and the fear of God as essential for the creation of wealth and the survival of the nation. I will introduce in more detail the third and final element essential for the creation of wealth. This is the average intelligence of the population. I will show that historically the greater the average intelligence as measured by the average IQ the more productive the economy and the wealthier the nation. A nation that lacks a high average IQ among its population will not be able to create wealth no matter the burden of the sovereign and no matter the fear of God.

Section 2. The Sovereign, the Passions, and God

In section 2, I present more detail about the purpose of the sovereign. Government is a coercive force essential for the securing of private property and the enforcement of contracts. Government is at the same time a burden on wealth creation and as such, government may act to reduce rather than increase the security of private property and wealth creation. Government also restricts the exercise of freewill thus undermining or restricting contract formation. A government through the laws it enacts has the potential to undermine wealth creation thereby leaving a nation more susceptible to calamity than would otherwise be the case. I will explore how this can come about. In any consideration of ethics and economics as is the instant case, human passions play a major role. The study of economics is a study of the aggregate behavior of individuals. The human passions play a role in human behavior, and therefore the human passions are a contributing factor in economic activity and the ethical behavior as well as the moral behavior of man. The basic human passions that affect economic decisions and influence ethical and moral behavior are fear, greed, envy, empathy, happiness, love, vanity, and hate. I will touch upon these basic passions in terms of their affect on economics and ethical behavior. I will also show how competition and self-interest serve to regulate all the passions but for envy, which is the only passion God specifically proscribes. Only the ubiquitous fear of God regulates man's envy. Without the fear of God, envy destroys man. Indeed envy was the first passion to manifest itself after Man's fall from Grace. Envy of God's favor caused Cain to kill his brother Abel and we see this act and its motivation play out repeatedly in man's history.

Human virtues do not create wealth nor do human vices destroy wealth

The human virtues include steadfastness; humility; faithfulness; loyalty; sacrifice; charity; and respect. While the virtues may exist in the mind and conscience of Man, they are not the ultimate determinate of Man's behavior. Acting virtuously is to act in one's self-interest and create wealth, i.e. acting virtually is not necessarily acting in accordance with the virtues. To the extent that the human virtues are altruistic in nature then they are contrary to the creation of wealth and therefore not virtuous. To the extent that the human virtues redound to self-interest then they enable wealth creation. Steadfastness for instance is a human virtue that serves a man's self-interest over the long run. Acting in accordance with the human virtues requires an act of will because it is contrary to self-interest, i.e. contrary to acting virtuously, which is to create wealth. It takes an act of will to be steadfast as it does to be loyal or charitable. The virtues arise out of the flawed Stoic notion that man's

270

will acting through man's reason can subdue his passions. This is an atheistic notion that precludes the existence of God and thus precludes the fear of God as necessary to restrain man's passions, i.e. his vices. Those that argue that man must behave in accordance with human virtue in order to live long and prosper assume that man's will acting through man's reason can overcome his passions. History and experience has shown otherwise. The virtues only marginally motivate or restrain a man. Man is either motivated, or restrained most deeply by the fear of God, the sovereign's power of eminent domain, and his own self-interest. There is no force to compel a man to act in accordance with the virtues other than his will. The fear of God manifests in obedience to God's Commandments and not in man's virtues. In other words, man's virtues do not compel man's obedience to God's Commandments only the fear of God can thus compel man.

Man's vices include envy, greed, gluttony, pride or hubris, lust, addiction of any form, arrogance, and vanity. Vices are expressions of man's self-interest and the vices of other men limit the vices of man except for envy, which only the fear of God restrains. For example, one man's greed limits the greed of another man through competition. Hubris leads to resentment, which is a form of envy and undermines contract formation thus limiting the ability to create wealth. The same is true of addiction, arrogance, lust, gluttony and vanity. Thus, the Stoic notion that the will can overcome the passions is applicable to all the vices except envy. Envy is the only vice that is not self-limiting nor is it limited by another man's envy. Envy is irrational and therefore not subject to a man's will acting through reason. Only by the fear of God does man eschew envy. To the extent that the fear of God restrains a man's envy then it is only to this extent that reason overcomes the passion. Without the fear of God, envy consumes man.

Man's virtues, as well as his vices other than greed, have little impact on his economic behavior, i.e. entering into contracts with others to create wealth for himself. I will treat man's virtues and vices in the same manner as I treat altruism, which is to regard both virtue and vice as against man's self-interest and destructive of wealth creation. A virtuous man is not wealthy because he is acting out of virtue; he is wealthy because he has created goods and services that ease the burden of his fellow man, and who in turn rewards him by exchanging a portion of his labor for whatever he created. Thus, a wealthy man is wealthy because he acted in accordance with his self-interest, i.e. acted virtuously. In other words, self-interest precedes all virtues. Similarly, a poor man is not poor because he is not acting through the virtues, but because he failed to ease the burden of his fellow man, and profit accordingly. A poor man is not virtuous and the reason he is not virtuous is he failed to create wealth. Hence, a poor man is a burden on wealth creation and subjects the nation to calamity. Governments create poor men because

271

the government encumbers the economy.   In the absence of the fear of God, poor men become envious and with universal suffrage enlist the sovereign power of eminent domain to satiate their envy.   The more the government taxes, regulates, and enforces union contracts the more poor men it creates, and the greater the burden on the economy.   The more secular the nation, i.e. the fewer individuals who do not fear God, the greater the likelihood that universal suffrage will bring forth a sovereign who will satiate the envy of the hoi polloi and destroy wealth by subjecting the nation to socialism and communism, that is to say calamity.

As I showed in the first section, the ethical purpose of government is the securing of private property and the enforcement of contracts.   Private property and the exercise of freewill or in other words the freedom to contract are essential for the creation of wealth. To fulfill its purpose the government must enact laws and impose taxes, which are also laws.   The enactment of laws and imposition of taxes places a burden on the liberty of the individuals to contract, and on the ability of the economy to create wealth.   When the government undertakes purposes unrelated to the protection of private property or the enforcement of contracts it unnecessarily and maliciously encumbers the economy and burdens the ability of the economy to create wealth. The further that the sovereign's reach extends beyond the securing of private property and the enforcement of contracts then the greater the encumbrance on the economy in terms of taxes, laws, and regulations with a concomitant reduction in the liberty to contract.   Accordingly, laws and taxes enacted and imposed by the sovereign, and not directed toward the original purpose of government are unethical, since they further burden an economy and the creation of wealth.   Such laws are also immoral because they expose the nation to calamity.   Thus, the sovereign jeopardizes his soul before God and risks rebellion before man when he acts to burden the economy beyond the need to protect private property and enforce contracts.

The tendency for a sovereign to undertake purposes further removed from the securing of property and the enforcement of contracts is inevitable and deterministic.   The primary determinant is the increasing wealth brought upon the nation through the absence of calamity.   As the wealth of a nation increases there is greater demand of the sovereign on that wealth, and the individuals comprising the nation are more willing to relinquish their productivity and their liberty for increasing the security provided by the sovereign.   Thus, there exists the tendency of individuals with wealth to seek greater accommodation with the sovereign's demands for more of the wealth of a nation.   This process eventually leads to the tyranny marking the end of a nation since it results in the end of private property and the freedom to contract at will to the chagrin of those that demanded greater security.   Tyranny leads to rebellion whereby private property reemerges, as it always must, but in different hands.   The process of wealth creation begins once again as individuals reorganize a new nation to secure private property and enforce laws and contracts.   The creation of wealth therefore contains the seeds of its destruction as well as the seeds of its reemergence.   The extent of the destruction and the timing of its reemergence relate to the store of intellectual capital, i.e. the average IQ of the nation's population.   The rising wealth of Rome provoked its envious northern neighbors who then posed a threat to the wealth of Rome, and resulted in the tyranny of the Caesars, as Romans were more willing to cede greater power to Caesar.   The Roman Republic became the Roman Empire.   Similarly, the wealth of ancient Athens provoked the envious Spartans into the Peloponnesian War in 431BC, with the defeat of Athens in 404BC.   In the case of Rome, the simultaneous decline in the intellectual capital that occurred through the intermingling of the Romans with the darker races that Rome conquered and enslaved resulted in Rome succumbing to the Caucasoid barbarians from the north, i.e. the Arian Visigoths.

The decline in the average IQ arising from the admixture of the Caucasian Romans with the dark and semi-dark Roman slaves suppressed the wealth creation of Western Man from the fall of Rome until the Renaissance.   With less wealth created, then the intermingling with the dark and semi-dark races slowed as the Europeans imported fewer of these people as slaves.   Over time, the intellectual capital inherent in the Caucasoid recovered thus spawning the Renaissance.   In fact, after the fall of Rome there were very few African slaves on the European Continent until the Portuguese started importing them in the 15th Century. In the case of Athens after their defeat by Sparta within a few years, the city recovered and reasserted its dominance because of the high average IQ of the Athenians.   The high average IQ of ancient Athens and the Roman Republic is obvious and manifested in the extent of the contribution to man's achievement by these civilizations.   Note that the threats to Rome and Athens were external threats and in both cases, the threat arose because of the envy that the wealth created by these civilizations engendered in others.   Clearly, envy was the human factor driving the barbarian enemies of the Romans and envy of Athens' growing wealth and influence among the other city-states provoked the Spartans to attack Athens.   Thus, fear of calamity and the other's envy are the reasons that nations establish sovereignties and must fear God. In modern times, there is less to fear from external threats as world armies and navies have been subdued at least for the time being except for those of the United States and the nuclear weapons the United States possesses.   The greater threat to a great nation such as the United States is internal as the nation continues to create wealth.   That threat is the same as threatened Rome, i.e. the envy of the populace arising as the internal enemies of the nation, who are the new barbarians, and who suppress the fear of God through their propaganda and denial and ridicule of God. These new barbarians are the godless liberals who have infiltrated education at all levels, government at all levels, and the mass media. These barbarians are the fifth column in the war against the enemies of private property, liberty, and the priority of the individual over the group. In other words they are the enemies of wealth creation and therefore of man. The threat of the envious manifests itself as socialism and communism.

The sovereign makes his will known through law

Law is the manifestation of government. The sovereign makes his will known through laws. The sovereign enacts laws as the means to fulfill his purpose and duty to the nation. However, the sovereign's will, and thus his duty, is to the protection of private property and the enforcement of contracts. The sovereign has no free will since his life and his soul is bound to the nation. By their nature, laws are coercive because they limit liberty to contract. All laws are an economic burden and a burden on wealth creation. Laws are ethical when they serve to protect private property, facilitate the enforcement of contracts, and limit the reach of the sovereign. Laws are unethical when they operate to reduce productivity, i.e. wealth creation, take private property without increasing security or enforce contracts that are exercised against the free will of one of the parties. Laws that are preferential or give one individual an advantage over another in the exercise of contracts are encumbrances to an economy and therefore unethical. Such laws introduce coercion in the formation of contracts. Laws placing restrictions or requirements in a contract contrary to the will of any of the parties are unethical as these laws place a burden on wealth creation and therefore make a nation susceptible to calamity. The Civil Rights Act is an example of an unethical law because it introduces coercion into the formation of contracts and the hiring of employees. Similarly, with the Executive Order on Affirmative Action, which compels terms in contracts that otherwise would not be included by the parties to the contract of their own freewill. Any contract formed against the will of the parties to the contract is unenforceable under Natural Law and common law. Laws that call upon the sovereign to enforce such contracts serve to encumber an economy, burden wealth creation, and weaken a nation.

Another example of an economically burdensome law is the Wagner Act of 1935 that I have mentioned before and that forced labor contracts on employers against their will. Both the Wagner Act and the Civil Rights Act have served to reduce the ability of the nation to withstand a calamity because these laws operate to reduce productivity, and to interfere with the liberty to contract thus reducing the creation of wealth. Repealing these laws would go a long way in restoring the wealth creating ability of the nation, as it existed at the end of the 19th Century. Repealing these laws will ensure the survival of the nation and the survival and well-being of all the individuals, i.e. the taxpaying citizens comprising the nation.

It is instructive to understand the conditions that gave rise to laws such as the Civil Rights Act and the Wagner Act because it supports the idea that in order for a nation to prosper and survive that nation must be a nation under God. In other words, the nation's citizens and the sovereign must fear God in order that the nation survive and prosper. The conditions that gave rise to the Civil Rights Act and the Wagner Act are rooted in the secularization of the nation. Secularization or godlessness engenders envy. The atheism of the early 20th century that gave rise to socialism and communism also was the ideology that underpinned the Wagner Act and the Civil Rights Act. Atheism eschews a fear of God and substitutes it with the fear of the State. Therefore, atheism calls for tyranny in order to achieve its political ends, which is the dominance of atheists over their fellow men. The creation of wealth is of secondary concern to atheists as is the well-being of man. Envy of their betters motivates atheists and they engender envy in others to meet their political ends else they would not be atheists. The combination of an encumbered economy, and unbridled envy engendered by atheists, motivated the Civil Rights Act and the Wagner Act. The encumbered economy resulted in high levels of general unemployment during the time of the Wagner Act, i.e. during the time of the Great Depression, and high levels of black unemployment at the time of the Civil Rights Act. The general decline in faith in God, and thus a decline in the fear of God, removed the moral prohibition against envy. This occurred despite the justification of the so-called civil rights movement in moral and religious terms. In fact, the acquiescence by the sovereign to the so-called civil rights movement was an unethical and immoral act in itself. The acquiescence of the sovereign to the so-called civil rights movement was unethical because it led to gross interference in the economy of the nation through suppression of liberty or freewill in contract formation. The Civil Rights Act banned discrimination in any form against a newly created protected class of individuals, the Negroid in particular, thereby forcing conditions into contracts that would otherwise not have existed. Discrimination is an act of freewill and freewill is the source of wealth creation. However now inherent in any contract between two or more parties are the requirements of the Civil Rights Law, to wit that neither party discriminates on the characteristics set forth in the law. Although this seems an innocuous condition to a contract, the insidiousness and wealth destruction of the law becomes apparent during enforcement. Under the law, almost anybody can invoke the Civil Rights Act to challenge any contract between any two parties whether or not the challenger is a party to the contract. Thus, a contract to construct a building is subject to challenge in a criminal and a civil proceeding under the Civil Rights Act by a person who was not hired to do work on the building even though that person was not a party to the contract. Similarly, an individual can challenge a hiring decision by a company in a civil and/or a criminal proceeding under the civil rights law and thereby force an employer to act against his will. The result of the Civil Rights Act and the affirmative action executive orders was an increase in the encumbrance of the economy leading to further reductions in productivity and thus reductions in wealth creation. This contributed to the destruction of the economy during the 1970's as the sovereign aggressively enforced civil rights legislation and the affirmative action orders. The enactment of these laws also gave rise to the welfare state with its permanent underclass and no wealth creation thus vindicating the notion that government unethical laws, regulation, and taxes create poor men. When people only feed on the teat of the government and defecate there is no wealth created. It was only through a supreme effort of will on the part of the sovereignty in the 1980's to overcome the damage done to the economy during the previous two decades by the Democrat party that enabled wealth creation to resume. The success of the 1980s aroused the envy inherent in the insidious and godless leftist ideologues. They persisted once again with their use of the instruments, and the institutions of government to damage the economy culminating first in the collapse of the stock market in 2000 and then in the 2008 collapse of the financial markets along with the stock market.

The sovereign

The individuals of a nation appoint or elect a sovereign solely for the purpose of protecting and securing private property, and enforcing contracts. For this purpose, the nation endows the sovereign with the power of eminent domain and the authority to adjudicate laws and contracts. The power of eminent domain is the power to take private property, which includes the taking of a life since life is also private property. The taking may or may not involve compensation. Since the sovereign can do no wrong in a moral sense, it is only through his grace as manifested through due process, i.e. law, that compensation is given. The exercise of the sovereign power of eminent domain is through due process. Due process is the law governing the taking of property including the taking of a life in whole or in part, that is imprisonment or conscription. Legally the sovereign power of eminent domain manifests itself in the criminal code in the form of punishment for offenses against the nation, i.e. violations of the nation's laws, or as a taking for public use, which includes conscription. Note that according to the Fifth Amendment of the United States Constitution the sovereign can only take property for "public use" and not for "public purpose"[5]. The Fifth

276

Amendment reads in part *"….nor shall private property be taken for public use, without just compensation."* Punishment for a criminal offense always involves the taking of private property in one form or another, i.e. life or property, which is the sovereign power of eminent domain. In the case of the execution of a man in accordance with due process, there is no compensation for the sovereign taking of a life. The adjudication of contracts is a function of the sovereign whose limits the sovereign may himself codify in a civil code. In other words, a sovereign may enact a civil code to govern torts and contracts such as between individuals, businesses, wills, and deeds and thereby guide the adjudication function. In any case, law in general is always an encumbrance to commerce. The Framers of the Constitution recognized the power of the sovereign to encumber an economy and it is the reason they originally adopted the Commerce Clause of the US Constitution. The Commerce Clause enabled Federal laws that forbade the placing of tariffs by the states on goods exchanged between the states. It limited the power of state governments. It was the original NAFTA agreement. In fact, the US Constitution limits the role of government in the economy and it limits the extent the government can infringe on the exercise of freewill in the formation of contracts. The US Constitution insured that coercion either by government or another party in the formation of contracts did not exist. It insures that nobody including the government can force a man to enter into a contract against his will or to include terms and conditions in a contract against the will of either party to the contract. Laws and regulations that require the inclusion of terms in a contract that neither party would have freely included undermine wealth creation and are unethical as well as unconstitutional. In enacting such laws, the sovereign inserts himself as an uninvited party to the contract and thereby abrogates his duty to adjudicate and enforce contracts. Accordingly, the government through such laws is failing in its fiduciary and sacred duty to protect and secure private property. In the process, the government is undermining the creation of wealth thereby threatening the survival of the nation in the event of calamity. The sovereign who enacts and enforces laws that threaten the survival of the nation abrogate the divine right of king accorded to the sovereign by God, thereby he jeopardizes his soul and invites rebellion.

The sovereign power of eminent domain manifests through the legislative, adjudicative, and executive functions performed by the sovereign. The function of legislation determines the conditions or boundaries of the sovereign power of eminent domain, the function of adjudication determines whether a violation of a contract or law has occurred, and the sovereign's function of execution or enforcement

---

[5] In a 5-4 decision the US Supreme Court in 2005 ruled in Kelo v. City of New London that the government can take private property for public purpose. This is another of the absurd rulings of the Supreme Court that is undermining private property.

punishes violators of the law and forces performance on contracts through his exercise of the sovereign power of eminent domain. While carrying out his duty the sovereign is himself immune and above the law. When the power of the sovereign embodies in a single individual that individual is the king or monarch. When the nation allocates the sovereign power of eminent domain to different persons elected by plebiscite then the sovereignty is a representative republic. Many of the acts that the sovereign commits are themselves unethical or immoral if committed by an individual other than the sovereign. The act of taking a life or taking property is otherwise immoral and unethical yet the sovereign is duty bound to perform such acts. This creates a moral and ethical dilemma vis-à-vis the soul of the sovereign, and this dilemma I will address next. That is, while the sovereign is above man's law as long as he is engaged in the protection of private property and enforcing contracts, is the sovereign above God's law?

The sovereign is above all law including Natural Law and God's Law

The sovereign power of eminent domain is the power to take life and property. This includes the power to tax. The taking of life and property by another is in general illegal, unethical and immoral as the taking of life and property by another is a destruction of wealth creation in all its manifestations. Nevertheless, this power is necessary for the sovereign to carry out his duty to protect private property and enforce contracts. Since the sovereign can do no wrong in an ethical or moral sense, the question arises as to the state of the soul of the sovereign. The soul is not private property but rather it belongs to God. God therefore disposes of souls according to His will as manifested in the Ten Commandments. By this reasoning therefore, why would an individual who fears God want to be king and protector and by extension a soldier? Why would a God fearing man jeopardize his soul through the acts of a king or a soldier? I am using the word king to mean any man in service to the nation including soldiers who must kill and destroy the enemies of the nation. This creates a conundrum for the king or soldier vis-à-vis the king's, or the soldier's soul. The conundrum exists only for those who are themselves moral, i.e. for those who fear God. Those that do not fear God are by definition immoral even though they may profess love of man who is the creation of God and Whom they deny. The only way that a God fearing individual would relinquish his private property, i.e. his life to the nation is if there was a God. An immoral or unethical and godless individual would not face such a dilemma since the taking of life and property is of no consequence in his unbelief other than legal, and the sovereign is immune from any such legal consequences. Without the existence of the soul, the sovereign has a license to take life and property and to enact and adjudicate laws that undermine wealth

278

creation and redound to the material or political benefits of the sovereign at the risk of weakening the nation. Therefore, the soul must exist otherwise no nation would exist. As the soul must exist, God must exist since the soul belongs only to God. The power of eminent domain is therefore a power accorded to the sovereign not by man but by God. The power to take property and life is a divine right, as it is a right accorded to the sovereign not by man but by God as the soul exists and belongs to God. The soul of the king is disposed by God according to the acts of the individual while he was not king otherwise the soul of the king would be punished by God because he violates God's sanctions while king, i.e. murder and theft. An oath or vow to God and before Man to protect and defend the nation is the point where the new sovereign acquires the divine right of king. The divine right of king is the taking of life and property in accordance with due process without fear of God's reprisal taken on the soul of the king. The divine right of king extends to those in service to the king. God holds harmless a soldier engaging in combat on behalf of the sovereign and his nation and he is immune from punishment of his soul. This must be the case otherwise who but the godless would be a soldier or a king. The king and the soldier seek to protect private property and life, which God ordained to be immortal. The king and the soldier are acting in accordance with the will of God and therefore they are subject to the divine right of king. . A nation therefore formed under God secures the soul of the king and the soldier. A nation whose citizens fear God is essential for the suppression of envy. Envy is the most destructive of the human passions. God's proscription against envy is the only force securing the nation from the ravages of envy. The fact that Western Civilization survives and continues to create wealth is a testament to the existence of God and Western man's fear of God.

Taxation is a manifestation of the sovereign power of eminent domain

Taxation is a manifestation of the sovereign power of eminent domain granted to the sovereign by plebiscite or taken by the sovereign to fulfill his purpose. It is a power of eminent domain because it is a taking of private property, i.e. income and wealth through force or threat of force. There are four basic types of taxes – a head tax which is a fixed amount and not a percentage, an income tax which is generally a progressive rate on incomes, a tax on transactions or sales tax which is generally a non-progressive rate, and a property tax that include taxes on inventory held. The head tax is an equal tax amount – not a percentage - on all individuals or citizens regardless of income or wealth. The head tax was the original individual tax established by the Framers and the only individual tax authorized by the US Constitution until the adoption of the 16th Amendment in 1913. A head tax is the only tax that treats each individual equally under the law.   Besides the head tax Congress was also authorized to collect duties and establish tariffs.   Tariffs are a form of transaction tax as is a sales tax.   In other words, the government collects tariffs only when an exchange of money for goods or services occurs. Property taxes whether they are a fixed amount or a percentage of property value are a tax on wealth whereas income taxes are a tax on wealth creation and not wealth.   Income taxes are a burden on productivity and therefore on wealth creation.   Property taxes are a burden on assets and they add to the fixed cost of an enterprise. Property taxes increase the break-even point of an enterprise making it more expensive to conduct commerce and making it easier to go out of business.   Property taxes are thus an encumbrance to commerce.   An individual or business must pay a property tax regardless whether an individual has an income or business earns a profit.   The sovereign takes private property at the point of a gun in the event the property tax is not paid.   This is an exercise of the sovereign power of eminent domain to which no individual has recourse but through rebellion.   Transaction taxes include sales taxes, tariffs, and value added taxes.   Transaction taxes tend to reduce profit margins and destroy wealth creation whereas property taxes destroy accumulated wealth, i.e. cash.   Taxes, in general reduce incentive because they reduce the expectations arising out of creativity and productivity, i.e. they reduce the expected return on investment.   Since income taxes are a burden on productivity, they are inflationary.   Prices increase in an economy where regulation and taxation create barriers to competition and reduce productivity.   While prices increase, margins or profits do not.   This causes investors to expect higher returns on investment thus hindering investment in general. The steady rise in the inflation rate since WW II directly correlates with the increase in the size of government in terms of Federal outlays. Figure 62 is a scatter plot comparing the CPI level and total nominal Federal outlays between 1948 and 2008.

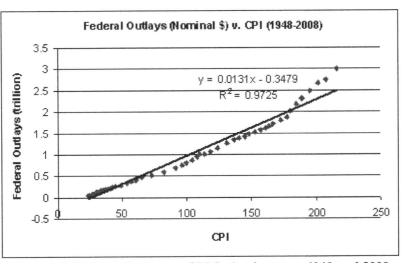

Figure 62-Federal Outlays v. CPI Index between 1948 and 2008

Note that the CPI level correlates almost perfectly with total Federal outlays between 1948 and 2008. Some may say that government spending simply kept pace with inflation, I say that government spending is the cause of inflation since WWII. To prove this point note that there is practically no correlation between government spending and the CPI between 1920 and 1939. (See Figure 63) The reason for this is the paradigm shift in technology that occurred over this period particularly in the farm sector of the economy with the introduction of the tractor, the automobile, the telephone and electricity. These technologies caused an explosion in farm productivity that overwhelmed any inflation caused by government spending, which was much smaller in terms of the total GDP during this period. Consequently, there is a low correlation between government spending and the CPI during this period.

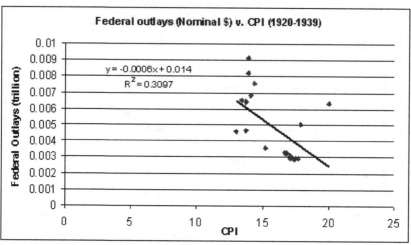

Figure 63-Federal Outlays v. CPI between 1920 and 1939

The same situation exists currently, i.e. a low correlation between government spending and CPI. Figure 64 below is a scatter plot of total Federal spending versus CPI between 2008 and 2013. The low correlation between Federal spending and CPI during this period mirrors the low correlation between 1920 and 1939 and is once again due to paradigm shifts in technology resulting in a rapid increase in productivity. These technologies include the computer, the cell phone, and the Internet whose benefits corporations and individuals exploited in great earnest following the collapse of the financial markets in 2008. During both these periods, i.e. between 1920 and 1939 (specifically between 1929 and 1939), and between 2008 and 2013, the result was an increase in unemployment and civil unrest. Also during both these periods, there was an increase in government regulations, taxation, and coercion over previous periods. Government's increased interference in the economy stifled investment and economic growth thus exacerbating and prolonging the unemployment arising from the rapid gains in productivity. The muted inflation between 2008 and 2013 was at the expense of both employment and a reduction in median income arising out of productivity gains.

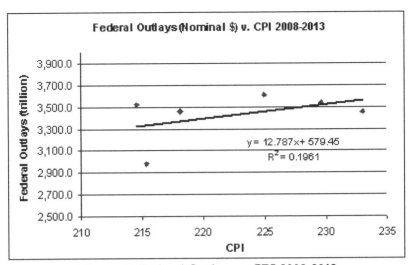

Figure 64-Federal Outlays v. CPI 2008-2012

These two periods contrast with economic conditions during the 1980's and after the low growth, and high inflation of the 1970's.   After 1980, there was a significant increase in the growth rate of productivity.   The productivity growth was due in large part to the reduction in the marginal tax rates and broadening of the tax base that occurred under the highly successful Reagan Administration.   During the 1980s and early 1990s, the real GDP grew on the average at 3.6% annually.   Despite the increase in productivity, unemployment was not a problem because investment in new goods and services were undertaken.   Investors were willing to take greater risks in a rapidly growing economy as evidenced by the large number of IPO's or Initial Public Offerings that occurred during the 1980s and 1990s.   As a result, employment grew quickly enough to absorb the new entrants to the labor force arising from the growth in population.

Besides the effects on productivity and wealth, taxes also introduce uncertainty into economic decisions as they are subject to the whims of politicians.   Income taxes tend to affect investment decisions in a negative way.   Tax incentives result from political rather than economic goals consequently they go towards subsidizing unproductive industry.   Investments in so-called green technology are the result of expected returns bolstered by tax subsidies or coercion in one form or another.   Once the government eliminates subsidies, the investment is generally non-performing and many resources expended for no economic gain, i.e. no wealth creation.   Taxes and government coercion in general cause investors to demand increased return on investment and tend to increase interest rates.

The head tax is the most equitable of taxes and the most ethical

The sovereign imposes duties and tariffs for political rather than economic reasons and they are a form of tax incentive to unproductive industries, i.e. they keep unproductive industries unproductive and consequently duties and tariffs are harmful to wealth creation.   No economic reason exists to justify duties and tariffs.   The original purpose of duties and tariffs was to raise revenue for the government and equally applied to all foreign traded goods.   Tariffs applied to productive industries also result in damage to the economy, as I pointed out in the last section when I spoke about deflation and the effect of the Smoot-Hawley Tariff.   Similarly, the sales tax adds to the cost of a good or service thereby affecting the demand for the good or service.   A sales tax is a tax on productivity because it is out of the profit of the enterprise. Of the different types of taxes, only the head tax is inherently equal because everyone pays the same absolute amount regardless of wealth or income.   A head tax is similar to the property tax since it is a tax on an individual's life, which I said is private property.   Accordingly, the head tax is least destructive of wealth creation but it is nevertheless a destruction of wealth.   Since a head tax is equally distributed, it affects more those with low incomes and little wealth than those with higher income.   In a nation where universal plebiscite selects a sovereign, a head tax will tend to mute calls for more government spending and increased taxation.   In other words, it mutes the legal manifestation of envy, which is the real and only purpose of unequal taxation.   All other taxes are inherently unequal and consequently they are a heavier burden on wealth creation than is the head tax.   All types of taxation, including the head tax are unethical since they threaten the survival of the nation. Unequal taxation is inherently immoral since it involves a taking of private property, i.e. cash from an individual against his will solely to satiate envy.   Thus when the sovereign imposes equal taxes on the individuals comprising the nation for the sole purpose of protecting private property and enforcing contracts he is acting in accordance with the divine right of king.   Just as in the case when the sovereign executes a man or has a man executed the sovereign has not committed murder so, in the case of equal taxes, the sovereign has not committed theft.   Thus, execution is not murder and equal taxation is not theft as these acts are in accordance with the divine right of king.   On the other hand, a sovereign who imposes taxes whether equal or progressive to redistribute wealth or to seek power over the nation beyond the power accorded him to protect private property and enforce contracts such a sovereign jeopardizes his soul before God and risks rebellion and punishment before man.   Such a sovereign does not fear God or man and is sure to destroy the nation as well as destroy himself and condemn his soul.

As I said taxes in general are a burden on wealth and wealth creation, accordingly taxes encumber an economy.   The more unequal or the less equally distributed the tax burden the greater is the encumbrance to the economy. Thus, a sovereign who imposes unequal taxes is abrogating the divine right of king. The divine right of king redounds to the sovereign's soul whose laws apply equally to all. Tax laws that demand more from one man than from another are not laws that apply equally to all men. The sovereign that imposes such laws acts as an individual and not as sovereign, accordingly such a sovereign becomes ripe for rebellion and jeopardizes his soul. The head tax is the least burdensome on wealth creation and the closest to an ethical tax. The other types of taxation are inherently unequal and therefore are a greater burden on wealth creation and these taxes are unethical for this reason. The burden on wealth creation extends to the uncertainty added to the return on investment by inconsistent tax policy. The uncertainty inherent in taxes tends to increase the expected return on investment and tends to drive interest rates higher further burdening wealth creation. Taxes therefore are unethical because they are an encumbrance on the economy and the greater the inequality engendered by the tax law the greater the encumbrance. In other words the more progressive a tax is then the greater the inequality and the greater the encumbrance. When the tax burden becomes so great that it makes the nation vulnerable to calamity in terms of the destruction of private property and the ability to create wealth then the sovereign who imposed the taxes leading to the destruction of wealth must abdicate his position or the nation must rebel to survive. The nation then must reorganize to the original purpose originally created to fulfill, i.e. the securing of private property and the enforcement of contracts. The American Revolution inspired by God-fearing men and the French Revolution inspired by atheists are the quintessential examples of a nation rebelling and overthrowing an over burdensome sovereign. In the former the result was a wealth creating economy in the latter an even more burdensome sovereign and a permanently weakened nation.

Similar to unequal taxation are laws forcing terms into contracts not otherwise included by the parties to the contract. These are unethical laws because they are an encumbrance to commerce and therefore an encumbrance to the economy. Laws in general are coercive because they place a limit or boundary on the individual's exercise of freewill, i.e. his liberty to contract. This is the reason that a sovereign must direct all laws only toward the protection of private property and the enforcement of contracts. Laws directed toward other purposes place an unnecessary and therefore unethical burden on wealth creation because they limit the exercise of freewill. The exercise of freewill manifests itself in the execution of contracts. A contract is enforceable only when all the parties to the contract become parties of their own freewill. Terms entered into a contract that must be included by law restrict the exercise of freewill of the parties to the contract. Such terms effectively make the government a party to the contract against the will of the other parties. At the same time that the sovereign becomes one of the parties to the contract through his law, he is the adjudicator to the contract. In other words, the sovereign is both a party to the contract and the adjudicator of the contract. Thus, a sovereign can force the abrogation of a contract between parties against their will. For example if a contract is executed between two parties that includes a legal requirement to hire certain classes of individuals and if the party whose legal obligation is to hire these individuals fails to do so then the contract can be abrogated by the sovereign for this reason alone. This is even if the actual parties to the contract are performing in all other respects and in the process creating wealth. The creation of wealth is paramount in any economic activity, and the sovereign's interference undermines the creation of wealth and therefore his interference is unethical. It is also immoral because undermining wealth creation subjects the nation to calamity. Laws that call for such interference in contracts are unethical and immoral notwithstanding the divine right of king.

A contract with the sovereign is unenforceable since the sovereign is both a party to the contract and the adjudicator to the contract. If the sovereign chooses not to honor his contract, the other party has no recourse but to accept its loss. In other words, a party to a contract with the sovereign cannot sue the sovereign absent his leave or permission. The legal principle or theory is that the sovereign is one in the same as the individuals of the nation and an individual cannot sue himself nor can he contract with himself.

Exchange of property always involves a contract

When I use the term contract, I mean the term in the broadest sense possible. Any exchange of private property for consideration involves a contract. Buying a dress for instance involves an exchange of money for a good. This exchange takes place because the two parties, i.e. the buyer and the seller have agreed to the price thus establishing an agreement or a contract between them. The exchange of money for the dress is a partial execution of the contract. The agreement may also include terms to return the dress for a full refund or even a partial refund for a specified time. The contract or agreement executes fully when the specified time is exhausted. A sales tax is a law that imposes additional terms on the agreement against the will of the buyer or seller. The additional terms manifest themselves as added cost to the item thus affecting both the supply of dresses and the demand for the dress. In a competitive market, the added costs are borne by both the buyer and the seller. The sales tax effectively imposes the will of the sovereign on the parties to the contract, i.e. the buyer and seller, and against their will. A sales tax therefore is unethical because it undermines profit and wealth creation thereby increasing the vulnerability of an economy to a calamity.

Since the sovereign can do no wrong and acts in accordance with divine right of king, the imposition of a sales tax is of no consequence to the sovereign other than rebellion arising out of his failure to secure private property and enforce contracts.   However, the sovereign jeopardizes his soul when he acts to burden wealth creation beyond that required to protect private property and enforce laws and contracts.   The ultimate determinant of the limits to the sovereign's power of eminent domain is the threat of rebellion or rebellion.   Absent rebellion, the only limit to the power of eminent domain is the limit imposed by the sovereign himself.   This is true regardless of the form of government, i.e. a monarchy or a constitutional republic.   A godless sovereign knows no limit or even acknowledges a limit and therefore a godless sovereign eventually falls to rebellion or civil war.

Constitutional Laws

The sovereign's law encumbers an individual's freewill and liberty to contract.   A nation must tolerate a certain encumbrance of freewill to gain security of life and property, and to facilitate the enforcement of contracts.   Constitutional laws are laws that limit or encumber the freewill of the sovereign.   To the extent that the freewill of the sovereign is limited then the less is the burden on wealth creation.   A constitution that effectively limits the freewill of the sovereign in relation to the individuals that comprise the nation is an attribution of God.   A nation formed under God has a sovereign and a populace who fear God.   A sovereign can do no ethical or moral wrong only when he acts in accordance with his duty as set forth in the laws he enacts.   His duty is to protect life and property and enforce contracts.   A sovereign may perform otherwise immoral and unethical acts with no consequences to his person or soul as long as he acts in accordance with his duty and in accordance with the law that he enacts.   In this sense, the sovereign is above all law and not accountable to God or man.   A Constitution is a manifestation of the will of the individuals that comprise the nation and it precedes the sovereign in all matters.   A Constitution therefore is a set of ethical laws because it limits the freewill of the sovereign and lessens the burden on wealth creation in order to secure a nation against calamity. Indeed the Constitution is the sovereign.   When a sovereign, whose life and property the individuals comprising the nation hold in common, does not fear God and goes against the will of God then he jeopardizes his soul and his person.   When a sovereign goes against the Constitution, he jeopardizes his sovereignty, as the individuals who created the nation for their protection and security demand the obedience of the sovereign to the Constitution.   The United States Constitution Article 2 Section 4 provides for the removal of the President, Vice President and all Civil Officers that comprise the sovereignty through a process called impeachment.   Given the sovereign can do no legal, ethical and moral wrong and given that the sovereign who is also the prosecutor and adjudicator of all individuals, then it is necessary to remove the person who is the sovereign from office before he can be indicted, tried and convicted of any crime, i.e. any violation of law. The sovereign can only remove himself from office and thus subject himself to trial. In the case of the US Constitution under Article 1 Section 2, the power of impeachment resides with the Legislative Branch and in the House of Representatives, which is the sovereign. Impeachment is therefore the means by which the person, who is the executive, legislator, or adjudicator and has the power of eminent domain, has this power taken from him thus enabling the sovereignty to prosecute the person who was once sovereign. Impeachment is the legal process that abrogates the divine right of king. The Article of Impeachment is the only law enacted only by the House of Representatives not requiring the approval of the Senate or the signature of the President. Once impeached an elected official is subject to prosecution under criminal or civil law, however he remains in office until and if the Senate acts on the article or articles of impeachment and votes to remove the elected official from office. The Senate vote is not conviction for a crime but the final legal step in the process of removal. Thus under the US Constitution it is possible for a convicted felon to remain in elected office until the end of his term. This was the case with Bill Clinton, impeached by the House, and found guilty of lying under oath, causing him to undergo punishment by losing his license to practice law. Clinton's impeachment abrogates the divine right of kings from the moment of impeachment. This was clear since he underwent his punishment. The question remains as to whether Clinton simply agreed to accept the punishment and not challenge it as he could have on the basis that until the Senate removed him from office he remained sovereign and the court could not punish him for any act without his permission. In the absence of any challenge to the court by Clinton then it remains questionable whether all of Clinton's actions both personal and official after his impeachment are subject to God's law and man's law regardless whether the Senate removed him from office. Indeed the absence of any court challenge is effectively his tacit permission for his punishment. Nevertheless, a sitting president underwent punishment under the law as if he was not sovereign. The failure of the Senate to remove Clinton from office is not an acquittal because the Senate was not trying and could not try him for a crime since the Senate is not an adjudicating body. The Senate's failure to remove Clinton from office did not restore his sovereignty, which the House of Representatives took from him by the Articles of Impeachment. These Articles of Impeachment although couched in terms of a House resolution nevertheless remain law under the Constitution. The only way for Clinton to have his impeachment overturned and his sovereignty reinstated is for the House to repeal the

Article of Impeachment, which the House has never done.   Accordingly, the prosecutor tried Clinton after the Senate failed to remove him from office and the court punished him with the loss of his license to practice law either because he was no longer sovereign even though he was still in office or because he tacitly gave permission for his punishment to proceed.   With the latter, Clinton avoided a determination by the court whether he was legally capable of enacting and enforcing the laws.   He also avoided the moral question i.e. the disposition of his soul for acts that absent the divine right of king are immoral.   Clinton's impeachment occurred on December 19, 1998.   From December 19, 1998, until he left office on January 20, 2000, Clinton was not sovereign because he remained impeached regardless of the Senate's failure to remove him from office.   During this period his vice president was the sovereign and not Clinton.   Accordingly, a legal question remains as to the constitutionality of any law signed by Clinton including treaties, or any executive action enacted by him, or of any pardons that he made during this period.   As Clinton was no longer sovereign and therefore not accorded the divine right of king, he knowingly jeopardized his soul before God for his actions after his impeachment.   In any case, the US Constitution provides for rebellion, i.e. impeachment and removal from office, if the sovereign fails to protect private property and enforce laws and contracts or for almost any reason whatsoever.   One other point here is that just like any other law Articles of Impeachment are subject to Judicial Review.   Although this has never happened it is possible for an impeached sitting president to ask the Supreme Court to have the impeachment declared unconstitutional on the grounds there was no *"treason, bribery, or other high crimes and misdemeanors"* committed.   Clinton never did this, nor was his punishment ever challenged on the basis that he was still sovereign because the Senate failed to remove him from office.   I contend he was not sovereign because the House never repealed the Articles of Impeachment and it remains law. This is more likely the reason that he never challenged his punishment and not necessarily because he gave tacit permission for his punishment although this is the legal effect of his lack of action.

Duty of sovereign

The duty of the sovereign remains the same whether the sovereign imposes himself by military force upon a nation or freely selected.   The British Rule of India that spanned almost 90 years is an example of a sovereignty imposed by one nation upon another.   Both Britain and India benefitted economically from this.   Britain protected and secured India while India provided valuable resources to the British, and served as a market for British goods.   Britain introduced India to British Law with private property as its basis.   This alone was sufficient to create great wealth.   British technology such as the railroad, telegraph and agricultural innovations, which included private property rights, helped to make India a prosperous country until the years following WWI. After WWI India's productivity as measured by the per capita GDP declined significantly (Figure 65), while at the same time the per capita tax burden increased. A general famine, i.e. a natural calamity is part of the reason that caused the decline in productivity during this period as measured by the amount of famine relief doled out by the government. (See Figure 66) This is an example of stored wealth used as a hedge against calamity. Had it not been for British technology and governance it is likely the effect of the famine would have been much worse than it actually was. To help pay for the famine and to recover their cost the British increased taxes. The increased taxes burdened the economy and reduced productivity thus having the affect of aggravating the destruction of wealth caused by the famine. Figure 67 is a graph of the ratio of GDP to tax burden. In other words, the increase in taxes had the opposite of the intended consequences as is always the case when government bureaucrats do not understand economics. The British after World War I were themselves set on a socialist course so the British at the time did what socialists always do and that is took to taxing their colonies to take their wealth, rather than reducing the tax burden to create wealth. World War II merely interrupted the British march to socialism. British socialism returned after the war when the Labor Party ousted Winston Churchill as Prime Minister, despite Churchill's contribution to the war effort and his prescience leading up to the war, thus effectively saving Britain from German occupation. Clearly, the British socialist preferred German socialism to Churchill's wealth creating capitalism else they would not have ousted him as Prime Minister immediately after the war. While on a national or political basis Britain prevailed over Germany, on an economic basis both Britain and Germany became socialist states after the war, thanks in large part to the United States providing military security. Thus, National Socialism prevailed after World War II and Germany ended up dominating the European economy as well as its politics after all. The fact that Britain, Germany and the other European countries had practically no military budget after World War II helped them sustain socialist economies for a time. This is now ending, as many of the European countries are experiencing recession, unsustainable sovereign debt, high unemployment, high taxes, and civil unrest, the hallmarks of socialist states.

Britain's increasing tax burden on the Indian populace set the stage for civil unrest that culminated in Indian independence after WWII. Thus, while the imposition of a foreign sovereign, Britain, secured and protected private property and enforced contracts, the nation of India overthrew that sovereign when the sovereign's tax burden reduced productivity and wealth creation. Nevertheless, had it not been for the British introduction of private property laws, and advanced technology

290

into the subcontinent of India that nation would not have prospered as it did. Britain, or at least the Britain of the 19th Century, changed the trajectory of India's economy and made it a much wealthier nation than it otherwise would have been. India was a grateful colony at that time and they displayed this gratitude by accepting Queen Victoria as Empress of India in 1858. It was only after British rule severely encumbered the economy through high taxation and regulation characteristic of a socialist sovereign that it was overthrown and deservedly so.

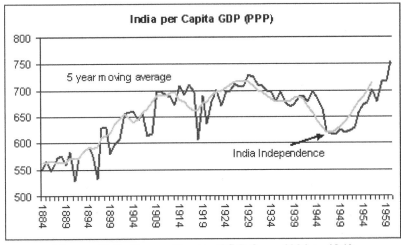

Figure 65-India per Capita GDP from 1884 to 1960

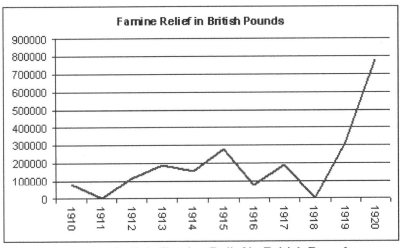

Figure 66- India's Famine Relief in British Pounds

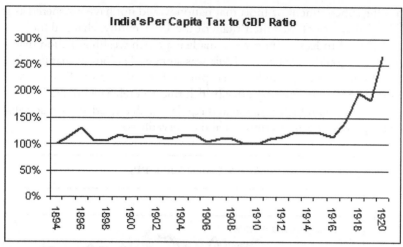

Figure 67-India change in per capita tax to GDP ratio

Inflation measures the degree a sovereign encumbers an economy

Failure to secure private property or enforce contracts efficiently always leads to rebellion in one form or another.   I have spoken of the burden that taxes, laws and regulations impose on wealth creation. Since taxes and regulations are the result of laws enacted by the sovereign, we can refer to law in general as a burden on wealth creation.   A Constitution is law that limits the freewill of the sovereign.   When I speak of law as a burden on wealth creation, I am referring to law that limits the freewill of the individual to contract and not law that limits the freewill of the sovereign.   The burden of law manifests itself in two ways. First as I said laws limit the exercise of the freewill of the individual to contract and secondly laws tax the fruits of labor or wealth creation. Law that requires terms in a contract that otherwise would not be included through an act of freewill is law that encumbers an economy. An encumbered economy is one where the price of a good or service is independent of supply and demand for goods and services.   Monetary inflation characterizes such an economy.   Monetary inflation therefore is a measure of the degree that a sovereign encumbers an economy.   High inflation means that the sovereign is severely overburdening the economy and the economy is not creating wealth but destroying wealth creation or the ability to create wealth.   Such an economy is bound to collapse in the sense that it will fail to secure individuals against calamity and rebellion or civil war will ensue to remedy the situation.   Germany's Weimar Republic and the present situation in Venezuela as well as Argentina are three of many examples where inflation has resulted in or will result in the overthrow of the sovereign.   In many cases, the overthrow of a sovereign is a violent act that may lead to civil war.   The collapse of the Weimar Republic was relatively non-violent.   The overthrow of the Venezuelan government will probably be violent and the overthrow of the Argentine government probably less so.

As I have shown productivity growth offsets inflation. Figure 68 is a graph of the relative level of the CPI and relative level of productivity in per capita GDP measured in Purchasing Power Parity (PPP) and benchmarked to 1890. The time period covered is from 1948 or after World War II to 2010. The reason for this is that World War II distorted the GDP due to unproductive government spending that was the result of borrowing and printing of a great deal of money. As I have indicated, the government-spending component of the GDP does not reflect wealth creation because it relies on taxing the productivity of the other three components. The growth in the private component almost equals the growth of the government spending components of the GDP after World War II so for purposes of this analysis I used the total GDP after 1948. Note that prior to 1972, the slope of the trend line curve was 0.11% for the per capita GDP and after 1972 the slope of the trend line curve for the CPI increases to 0.53% or almost five times greater. This indicates that the government encumbered the economy by a factor of 5 times greater beginning in 1972 due to the abrogation of the Bretton-Woods agreement, Civil Rights legislation, expansion of government entitlement spending, aggressive enforcement of affirmative action, government regulation in the form of the EPA and the expansion of other regulations.

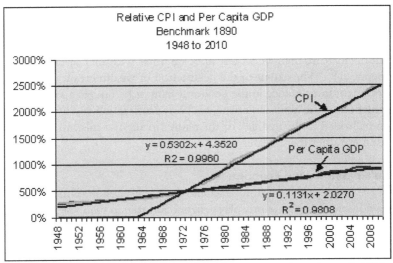

Figure 68 – Relative CPI and Per Capita GDP – benchmark 1890 – 1948 to 2010

Before 1972, the productivity growth rate matched the inflation rate. Since the inflation rate includes the offset of productivity then the growth in productivity created great wealth. After 1972, the inflation rate increased almost five times faster than the growth in productivity and it continues on the average to this day. This means that the economy is creating little wealth and most of the improvements in productivity have gone to expand government thus weakening the economy and the nation since 1972. The expansion in government is in the increase in government outlays (Figure 20 above), which are not all included in the GDP. The inflation rate slowed and productivity increased briefly during the 1980s. However, there was still a high level of government spending during the 1980s but it was for rebuilding a military and defensive infrastructure with which the enemy of private property, i.e. the communists and atheists of the USSR could not compete, and which led to their capitulation and the end of the Cold War. Nevertheless, if inflation continued along the productivity slope as it had before 1972 then the economy would have created great wealth.

In order to measure the amount of wealth created absent the interference of the government in the economy I extended the inflation rate from 1972 at the same rate as before 1972. I then adjusted the per capita GDP by the ratio of the extended inflation rate and the actual inflation rate at each point. The result is that the per capita GDP would be $107,705 instead of $30,491 or over 3.5 times more in 2010. If the government did not undertake the unprecedented taxation, and regulations that it did during the 1960's under Johnson and then under Carter in the 1970's we would all be over 3.5 times wealthier than we are now. Earlier I had shown that if the Federal government did not interfere in the economy since 1929 or at least if total taxes, i.e. Federal receipts remained at the 1929 level and the money invested in the private economy instead, then we would all be 80 times wealthier by 2012 (See Appendix 1). The extent of the destruction of wealth creation by government interference in the economy cannot be understated. The destruction of the ability to create wealth is accelerating and it will eventually lead to the inability of the nation to survive calamity as it consumes rather than creates wealth.

Man's passions and economics

A discussion of ethics and morals is a discussion of man's behavior and man's passions play a significant role in man's behavior. An economy is the interplay of individuals on both a rational level and emotional, which is to say irrational, level. Man's passions most at play in an economy are fear, greed, envy, empathy, happiness, love, vanity, and hate. I will discuss fear, greed, envy and happiness first.

At the most basic level it is fear of the future that gives rise to wealth creation. As I have said, wealth is a hedge against calamity. When or where a calamity will occur is unknown and rational individuals will build up a store or wealth in order to sustain themselves in times of calamity.   In the absence of calamity, the greater store or wealth eases the burden of life as I discussed in the first section.   Easing the burden of life yields happiness, therefore wealth in the absence of calamity engenders happiness.   Happiness is the absence or at least the mitigation of fear.   The creation of wealth depends on the security of private property and the enforcement of contracts.   Fear of the unknown also gives rise to the need to secure private property and enforce contracts. Fear of the future and the unknown is the reason and motivation for appointing or electing a sovereign.

Greed is a rational and an insatiable desire for more of something and a force of life, i.e. the need for man to extend himself beyond the grave.   Left uncontested greed becomes destructive of wealth.   Envy is also destructive of wealth because it leads to irrational behavior, as it is itself irrational.   Fear is a rational and natural response to uncertainty.   The creation of wealth is a rational act in a man's response to fear of the unknown and a response to man's insatiable desire to extend his ego beyond the grave.   When envy replaces fear as the dominant emotion in man there is no wealth created and destruction of existing wealth occurs.   Envy replaces fear when a nation's economy creates great wealth and the nation's citizens eschew God and do not fear God.   The difference between greed and envy as destroyers of wealth is that in an unencumbered economy, competition contests greed.   In other words, one man's greed contests another man's greed through competition.   Greed in an unencumbered economy i.e. an economy free of regulation, taxation and other means of coercion drives wealth creation through competition.   Greed therefore is self-regulating in an unencumbered economy.   Attempts to regulate greed by the government invariably eliminate competition in the marketplace, and rather than regulating greed, regulation promotes greed, which then results in the destruction of wealth.   Indeed this is what happened when the government interfered in the mortgage market through the Community Reinvestment Act.   The lending of money to individuals with no required down payment and with no verification of the ability to pay for the loan effectively created an infinite supply of buyers in the market.   Thus the sub-prime market was born.   This created great demand for a limited supply of houses.   Greedy homeowners kept increasing the price they were willing to sell their houses because buyers were able to get the loans they needed no matter the price.   Thus, the price of all houses kept increasing and builders were building more houses and increasingly expensive houses.   This created the bubble in housing prices and the housing market.   This continued until the sub-prime buyers could not afford to pay back their loans thus causing housing prices to plummet and banks to loose trillions of dollars of assets. Without the competition for mortgages, the greed of the homeowners prevailed and the result was great destruction of wealth.   Had there been competition for mortgages, housing prices would not have increased and the building of new homes done at a sustainable pace. The competition for mortgages happens by requiring significant down payments or in other words requiring borrowers to put upfront equity into the home. Aggravating the situation were accounting regulations that forced banks to mark down an entire class of assets when a few of the assets lost value. This was the "mark to market rule" implemented under the Sarbanes-Oxley Act of 2002. Ostensibly Sarbanes-Oxley Act was passed to help prevent accounting fraud but instead it amplified the financial calamity that the government under the godless Clinton caused with aggressive enforcement of the CRA. Once again, the government made matters worse by interfering in the economy.

Unlike the competition that regulates greed, envy has no control mechanism in the economy because it engenders irrational behavior. Therefore, envy, unlike the other human passions, is uncontrollable by man's reason and man's will, which puts the lie to Stoicism. If envy cannot be controlled or regulated by man's will then it must be controlled or regulated by God else wealth will be constantly destroyed and thus Man becomes susceptible to calamity and fails to achieve immortality as ordained by God. Indeed the passion of envy is the temporal mechanism to punish Man for his failure to acknowledge God and God's Law. Thus, atheists fall prey to envy and Man suffers accordingly unless Man purges atheism from his mind and heart. Note the difference between greed and envy. Greed is the desire to have more of something and therefore rational. Envy is the desire to keep another from having what he has including more of what he has and therefore irrational. Envy is not taking something from another to make it your own – this is theft. Envy satiates only by the destruction of its object, which is other man's wealth or his ability to have his wealth. Thus, Cain murdered his brother Abel out of his envy of .God's favor not to receive God's favor.

The following is another example of how competition regulates greed and how government regulation unleashes greed to the detriment of the economy. Consider the owner of the only gas station in a God fearing town. He will charge the maximum price for a gallon of gasoline because he knows that there is no competition. The only limit to the price is the willingness of the consumer to pay the price. The gasoline therefore goes to whoever pays the highest price and that is the price of the gasoline to everyone. Assuming that the wholesale cost of gasoline is low because there is ample supply then the gas station owner is making a large profit at retail as consumers bid up the price they are willing to pay. The large profit attracts other investors, because they are as greedy as the gas station owner is, and they too desire large profits. Note the new investors are not envious because God proscribes envy. If they were envious they would find a way to shut down the gas station not compete with it. That is they would look for alternative forms of energy and obtain subsidies by a godless government who they elected to satiate their envy. Since this is a God fearing and unencumbered free market and there is opportunity for them to create wealth, these new investors build a second gas station near the first. This causes the retail price of gasoline to go down because the second gas station must lower its price to attract customers. In this manner, the retail price of gasoline approaches the wholesale price. As long as the town is not growing, and the demand for gasoline stays constant then the retail price of gasoline remains near the wholesale price. The lower price causes margins to become smaller for both gas stations. This prevents other investors from entering the market. In order to boast margins and recover their investment the gas station owners must improve productivity. They can do this by reducing their expenses by operating more efficiently or by increasing revenues in other ways. Thus, one gas station decides to add automobile repairs to the services it offers and the other decides to add a grocery store. Competition has not only controlled the greedy owners and reduced the retail price of gasoline thus benefitting consumers, but has forced these owners to provide other services that add value to the town by satisfying some of the other needs of the consumers. In the process, the enterprises created opportunities for others by offering employment in retail and automobile repair thus creating wealth for themselves and the burden of life eased for the owners of the gas stations and for the town who benefit from the additional services.

Consider now the Environmental Protection Agency arbitrarily decides that in order to avoid ground contamination, all gas stations must be located at least 50 miles apart so local zoning codes must be revised to include this provision. This means that the owners of one of the gas stations must relocate 50 miles away. Now the greedy owner of the remaining station will increase the price of gas until it equals the cost and time associated with going to the competition 50 miles away. The remaining gas station no longer has to be productive by offering the additional services that it offered, which now provides less profit than the sale of gasoline. The gas station owners fired the retail employees and automobile mechanics. Now the remaining gas station owner became wealthier at the expense of his customers, not because he was any more productive or efficient but because the government made it impossible for competition to enter the market. The town lost additional services provided by the gas station owner thus increasing their burden through increases in the price of fuel as well as in services lost. As a result the overall wealth creation declined in the town although the gas station owner became wealthier, the expenses of everyone else increased in proportion making them less wealthy or consuming their wealth. In this manner, government changed the dynamics of the economy in this small town from one of economic growth, i.e. wealth creation for all, to a zero sum economy where one man gets wealthy at the expense of others

Prior to the government interfering in the local economy the improvements in the efficiency and productivity of the gas station owners created wealth manifested as investment in the grocery store and the repair shop.   After the government interfered, the economy became a zero sum game, i.e. the gas station owner became wealthy at the expense of the towns people.   There was no wealth created just wealth redistributed to the gas station owner.   This of course created the potential for envy in the town's people.   Since the town is a God fearing town, the populace does not act on the envy.   The next step by the government would be to pass laws that take God out of the public discourse and introduce godless intellectuals into the education system and other institutions who rail against the bigotry of religion and ridicule the existence of God and of man's soul.   Thus, atheism takes hold among the population of the town and the fear of God no longer limits man's envy.   The wealth of the gas station owner now engenders envy among the population.   Envy manifests itself at the ballot box.   The population elects a sovereign who will satiate the envy through the sovereign power of eminent domain.   The sovereign enacts laws that take the wealth of the gas station owner.   The government takes the wealth of the gas station owner through punishing taxes or confiscation because he has unjustly taken money from the citizens by "gouging" them and thus making an "unjust profit".   The government satiated the envy of the populace by taking the wealth of the gas station owner, and did not need to redistribute the wealth back to the town's people.   It was enough to deprive the owner of the gas station his wealth to satiate the envy of the town's people.   Eventually the gas station owner shuts down the gas station and people have to drive 50 miles to get their gas, placing an even greater burden on their lives, but this did not matter to the now godless and envious town's people.   Just as it did not matter to Cain that God's favor would not redound to him upon the death of his brother Abel.   It was enough to satiate Cain's envy merely to deny Abel God's favor by the hand of Cain, i.e. the murder of Abel.   Cain's envy was such that he would ask of God in Genesis 4:9 "Am I my brother's keeper?" to which God gave no reply.   Eventually envy consumes the remaining wealth of the town, and the town empties and disappears as the population becomes increasingly poor and miserable.   As it was for Cain, the suffering of the now godless population did not matter to them as long as the object of their envy no longer existed.   This is the reason that communist economies create no wealth despite the high IQ of the population.

Some may argue that the loss of the town in this manner is worth the environmental calamity that would have otherwise befallen the town. This argument is specious on several levels.   Apart from the fact there was little likelihood such a calamity would occur is the fact that a town with great wealth could easily overcome this calamity and continue to

298

thrive. Recall the purpose of wealth is as a hedge against calamity. In the absence of calamity, wealth eases the burden of life. Thus if the EPA is wrong, as it is generally wrong, then the individuals in the town would have been better off without the government interfering in the economy and no worse off if the calamity envisioned by the EPA actually occurred. As it turns out the EPA's regulations caused and thus made certain the calamity it ostensibly, but actually never, intended to avoid, i.e. the disappearance of the town.

After fear then comes greed and envy to govern an economy and ultimately determine the form and power of the sovereign. Greed and envy are different passions as I had explained previously. Greed is the insatiable desire for more of something including more of life leading to immortality. Envy on the other hand is the desire that another not have his possessions including even his life and his immortality. While unfettered greed and envy are both destructive of wealth, greed as I have shown is self-regulating in an unencumbered economy because it is rational, while God proscribes envy and the fear of God must regulate envy because envy is irrational. Therefore, besides the protection of private property and the enforcement of contracts a nation formed under God is necessary to regulate envy. The belief in God and the existence of God therefore is pivotal to the creation of wealth. Without God, wealth creation is unsustainable because sooner, or later, envy takes hold and replaces fear, and then wealth and the ability to create wealth destroyed. In any wealth creating economy, there is going to be disparity in wealth and without the fear of God, this disparity will engender envy. In an encumbered economy with a godless populace, competition also provokes envy. God regulates envy through his Commandments to Man. God's Commandment reads that *"You shall not covet your neighbor's house; you shall not covet your neighbor's wife, nor his male servant, nor his female servant, nor his ox, nor his donkey, nor anything that is your neighbor's."* In the Biblical account of Creation, envy was the second sin committed by man after disobedience to God. Cain's envy of Abel who obtained and possessed God's favor motivated Cain slaying his brother Abel. This is the basis of the Commandment proscribing envy. The Bible at the onset in Genesis sets the stage for the Ten Commandments by first describing the consequences of actions proscribed later by the Commandments as introduced to Man after the Exodus and written in stone. The killing of Abel by his brother Cain led to the destruction of the wealth that Abel possessed, which was God's favor. It also led to Cain's banishment from the land God gave him and the end of his seed within one generation. Thus, envy destroys not only the wealth and property of the man envied but also the wealth and property of the man who envies in accordance with the will of God.

There is no Commandment proscribing greed because greed is self-regulating. Greed exists apart from the existence of another man;

envy only exists with the existence of the other man, and threatens the existence of both. The ancients clearly understood man much better than do many moderns. Envy arises out of the flawed belief that life is a zero sum game. Communists and socialist economies are zero sum games and therefore they thrive on man's envy of his fellow man. In the zero sum game of life the reason that one man has wealth is because he took it unjustly from another man using guile or force. It assumes wealth not created, but simply unjustly and immorally redistributed. Envy gives rise to the notion of "social justice". When one invokes the notion of "social justice", he is really invoking his envy and his godlessness. However, in order for envy and thus "social justice" to take hold in an economy the first requirement is the denial of the existence of God and God's Commandments. If God does not exist, then envy takes root in man's heart. It is the reason for Marxism's infamous tenet *"religion is the opiate of the people"*. The "opiate" is the proscription against envy, which is the passion that Marxism and socialism must unleash in order to subjugate or eliminate the other man's wealth and property. A nation under God proscribes envy through fear of the disposition of the soul. Without God, there is no soul and without a soul, envy is unleashed. Envy always results in the destruction of wealth and the elimination of private property, which includes the elimination of life as life is private property. God's existence is essential for the creation of wealth and the creation of wealth is the hedge against calamity. In this sense, God enables man to survive a calamity, so giving thanks to God for the creation of wealth is justified, as is His existence. Therefore, individuals must form a nation under God or, in other words, a nation's individuals must fear God or else the nation will not survive. Accordingly, the sovereign must fear God and the laws of the sovereign, and the adjudication of the laws must be consistent with the Commandments of God and the Word of God for a nation to survive, sustain itself and prosper.

Other passions that affect human behavior and, therefore an economy are empathy, love and hate. These are lesser emotions than are fear, greed, envy and happiness in terms of the impact that they have on an economy. These emotions are self-regulating at the level of the individual. No external force is necessary to regulate these emotions. To have empathy or to display empathy is to "feel the others pain" or to "walk in another's shoes". Empathy is akin to altruism, which is sacrificing oneself for the good of the whole, or for the benefit of another. Empathy and altruism are antithetical to wealth creation because they call forth actions that result in non-profitable exchanges of goods and services. Any exchange of good or service that is non-profitable destroys wealth and is therefore unethical. Actions based on empathy, or altruism, reduce the capacity of a nation to withstand calamity, as these actions do not create wealth. Accordingly, such actions are unethical yet they occur because altruism satisfies a man's vanity, i.e. his ego.   Love and hate are the more complex passions because they manifest themselves in a variety of ways.   Love for instance manifests as love of parents, love of brother, love of a wife, love of country, love of man, love of God, love of self, etc.   The differences between the different kinds of love are subtle and it is difficult to quantify in any way the effect of love on an economy.   In a sense, love is also an altruistic behavior because it rarely profits.   Similarly with hate, that is hate is a complex passion difficult to quantify its effect on an economy.   Accordingly, I will say that these passions are amoral.   To the extent that love and hate cause irrational economic decisions or acts then these passions undermine wealth creation and thus are unethical.   Wealth is a product of man's intellect and man's reason and to the extent passions interfere with man's reason and result in irrational acts then it is to this extent that the creation of wealth is subdued or wealth destroyed.   A nation full of love is just as destructive of wealth as is a nation full of hate.

The admonishment to "love thy neighbor as thyself" or "do undo others as you would have others do unto you" are not really ends but rather means to an end.   Behaving according to these admonishments assures that one will not violate the Commandment proscribing envy.   From another perspective, these admonishments closely relate to empathy and altruism in that they involve a measure of self-sacrifice.   In a sense, therefore empathy and altruism are antithetical to envy.   The admonishments are actually a restatement of the Commandment proscribing envy but couched in terms that appear to place the burden on man's freewill and not on the fear of God.   So in order to have a godless nation the individuals comprising the nation must themselves violate Natural Law by acting with empathy and by behaving altruistically.   This is the philosophy of the Stoics, which taught that man's reason and his freewill can subdue the passions.   This is the case for all of man's passions save for envy because envy is irrational and therefore uncontrollable by man's reason and man's will.   Only the fear of God compels man's obedience to the Ten Commandments and His proscription against envy.   Fear of God and not reason compels man's obedience to the Ten Commandments.   A nation whose populace does not fear God, but rather rely on the Stoic imperative, will not survive calamity since empathy and altruism are also antithetical to greed and greed in an unencumbered economy is essential for the creation of wealth.

Security in space and in time relies on reason

I spoke of how human passions underlie human behavior and how fear, which is the basic human passion causes or gives rise to the need for security of private property essential for the creation of wealth. In this context, one's life is private property.   In other words, fear gives rise to the need to secure one's life in addition to the need to secure tangible and intangible property. Reason is the process by which an individual undertakes security. The need for security has two aspects. There is security in property, i.e. security in space and security in the future, i.e. security in time. First is security in space, achieved in a rational manner by the appointment or election of a sovereign on whom the individuals comprising the nation bestow the power of eminent domain. Second is security in time, achieved through the creation of wealth. The creation of wealth also relies on rational behavior. The security of private property is one prerequisite to the creation of wealth. The second prerequisite to the creation of wealth is freewill in contracting, therefore the nation bestows on the sovereign the function of adjudication. Adjudication relies on the sovereign power of eminent domain to compel performance of contracts. Without the sovereign's power of eminent domain, adjudication of contracts is meaningless.

Reason as manifested in the sovereign's power of eminent domain and the adjudication of contracts gives rise to the means to overcome fear of the present, .i.e. security in space, and the future, i.e. security in time. The creation of a nation under God is a rational response to the emotion of fear, i.e. fear of another's envy and fear of the disposition of the soul. A rational person secures his life and property through the creation of store or wealth. The creation of wealth is the only hedge against calamity.

Envy destroys life

As I have said besides greed, the other human passion that most threatens human survival is envy. Envy is not simply the desire for another's possessions. It is the desire that another man not have his possessions. When one man envies another man for his wife, it is not because he desires the other man's wife but rather he desires to deny to the other man his wife. Desiring another man's wife to be his is to lust and acting on lust is theft since a man's wife is his possession and it is trespass as the marriage unit is private property in a moral sense as ordained by God and in a legal sense under sovereign law. Whereas greed is a man's desire for greater wealth, envy is the negative of greed as it is the desire that the other man not have his wealth. If one entertains the flawed notion that an economy is a zero sum game then greed and envy conflate. This is the reason that many minds fail to distinguish between greed and envy. Wealth manifests in private property. Therefore, the only way to deny the other man his wealth, i.e. his gift from God is to take his life. God bestowed his favor on Abel and had no favor for Cain. Thus, Cain murdered his brother not out of his desire for God's favor because this was not possible and he knew it was not possible, but rather out of desire to deny Abel God's favor. This desire is irrational and therefore destructive of wealth creation. One cannot use reason to overcome envy, as he can to overcome fear and this is why Stoicism fails to sustain a nation.   Envy can easily overtake a nation originally formed to overcome fear of the future and of the unknown.   Envy overtakes a nation when there is significant disparity in the accumulation of wealth along with the secularization of the nation. Significant disparity in the creation of wealth only occurs in an encumbered economy because an encumbered economy suppresses opportunity.   An unencumbered economy provides opportunity thus the disparity in incomes motivate the creation of wealth reducing the disparity.   As I said if an economy is overly taxed, regulated and unionized, it is less capable of growing and creating wealth.   Productivity gains that are continuously taking place lead to unemployment in an encumbered economy.   High levels of unemployment lead to civil unrest and absent the fear of God engender envy as wealth disparity grows between the employed and unemployed.   Fear of God is the only means to rein in envy.   With the envious come the threat to the existence of private property and the threat to the creation of wealth, thereby increasing the nation's vulnerability to calamity.   History is replete with examples of the results of envy and the encumbered economy that it gives rise to.

The former Soviet Union was a nation built on a secular communist ideology that had at its core teaching the non-existence of God, the elimination of private property, and the subjugation of individual freewill.   In the Soviet Union, the sovereign was in total control of the economy, owned the means of production and all property, and individuals could not exercise their freewill through contracts.   Each man worked for the state and not for himself, accordingly there was little wealth created.   The Soviet Union was a return to feudalism with one important difference, the lack of the fear of God.   Feudalism lasted for hundreds of years because man feared God and despite the fact that the system created no wealth.   Feudalism engendered no envy in man despite the lack of opportunity and the encumbrance to the economy that it wrought.   The USSR lasted only 70 years and created little wealth. The abandonment of God under the communists allowed envy to take hold resulting in the overthrow of the landed gentry who were the economic engine of the Russian Empire up until the beginning of the twentieth century.   The reorganization of the important agricultural sector under the godless communist sovereign led to shortages of food where there once was plenty.   There was very little wealth created since the State redistributed the fruits of labor to unproductive ends. Eventually the nation collapsed as it became increasingly incapable of defending itself or sustaining itself.   Had it not been for fear of the military and nuclear power of the United States, the USSR would have overrun Europe to take their wealth.   This is what communist and socialist nations must do to sustain themselves.

China is another example where attempts at centrally controlling the agrarian economy failed leaving in the wake of the attempt millions of dead.   China has freed up its economy considerably in the last 30 years and the results are that wealth creation has resumed so its immediate future is increasingly secure.   Not coincidently, there is also a rise in faith in God in China as well, as this is necessary to rein in envy. Realizing this, the Chinese government is trying to suppress faith in God because communism relies on envy to keep in power.   China has also changed its laws to allow a form of property ownership where the Chinese government owns the land but individuals may own any structures on the land.   This is a middle ground between feudalism and a true capitalism based on private property.   Apart from this small concession to a capitalist economy, the Chinese communists continue to have contempt for private property.   This contempt extends to intellectual property such as patents and copyrights.   As long as China remains a godless communist state, it will eventually collapse despite its concessions to private property and wealth creation that this concession has engendered.   However, China's command economy is not able to support the huge population migration occurring from the rural areas to the urban areas in China.   Civil unrest is brewing in China and the collapse of China's communists will be much more violent than in the case of the USSR.   Its repercussions will be much more widely felt particularly in the United States.   One reason for this is the deep dependency the US economy has to the low labor costs and resulting high productivity of the Chinese.   Chinese productivity has helped to keep US inflation low during a critical time following the collapse of the financial sector in 2008 and the subsequent massive injection of fiat money into the US economy by the Federal Reserve Bank.   This has placed strains on the Chinese economy and these strains are beginning to show, as Chinese economic growth slows in 2014 and their own inflation starts to accelerate along with their interest rates.   Nevertheless, China is on a course of militarization because it will try to sustain itself by conquering its neighbors for their wealth.   It will ally itself with North Korea for this purpose.   It is clear that the Pacific will eventually become a cauldron of death thus belying its name.

History teaches above all that Man is predisposed to fear God since Man is aware of the destructiveness of envy.   Accordingly, as the history of Western Man is a history of wealth creation then God must exist and he is the source of that wealth.   Therefore, the prerequisite to the creation of wealth is fear of God as much as it is the sovereign's security of private property and enforcement of contracts, and the average intelligence of the nation's populace.

Encumbering an economy is unethical

Earlier I posed two ethical questions that I intended to answer. The first question was whether it is ethical for the sovereign to encumber an economy. From all that I have said up to now the answer is obvious, which is that it is unethical for the sovereign to encumber an economy unless the encumbrance directly increases the security of private property or facilitates the enforcement of contracts. An encumbered economy is an economy in which the sovereign introduces laws that interfere with the formation of contracts, i.e. the freedom to contract. These laws include taxes and regulations that add terms and conditions to contracts not in accordance with the freewill of the parties to a contract. Keep in mind that any economic transaction involves a contract where the parties agree to a price and to terms. The purchase of a package of gum is an economic transaction and involves a contract albeit an unwritten contract. The terms added to a contract by law interfere with supply and demand of the good or service and thereby affect the price of a good or service independent of the actual or underlying supply and demand. The more onerous the laws the greater the encumbrance and the less able the economy is to create wealth. Gains in productivity go towards overcoming the inflation engendered by the encumbered economy instead of creating wealth. The result is unemployment. Unemployment along with inflation is a measure of the degree a sovereign encumbers an economy. The greater the unemployment the more encumbered the economy and the less wealth created. Gains in productivity in an unencumbered economy do not result in unemployment because gains in productivity create wealth in an unencumbered economy. Wealth seeks to create more wealth through new investment. The new investment creates opportunities that counteract the labor displacements resulting from gains in productivity. Opportunity also suppresses envy as man now seeks to emulate the one that he would otherwise envy, as man is more predisposed to act rationally than irrationally. Acting rationally increases the chances of survival, acting irrationally reduces the chances of survival. As long as there is a high probability for success then opportunity suppresses envy along with the fear of God. A paradigm shift in technology results in rapid gains in productivity. This was the case of the internal combustion engine, and its introduction into the agricultural sector in the first part of the twentieth century resulting in short-term unemployment even in a relatively unencumbered economy. This brings us to the resolution of the next ethical question that is, whether or not gains in productivity should be undertaken if they knowingly result in high levels of unemployment? This question has two facets that I will address shortly.

Gains in productivity are ethical in an unencumbered economy

The second question that I set upon to solve is whether it is ethical to implement improvements to productivity that result in unemployment. This question assumes that there is a choice in improving productivity in the first place. Gains in productivity, undertaken in an unencumbered economy, result in little net unemployment. An unencumbered economy is free from taxation, regulation, and unions with wages set by the marketplace rather than through coercion. As gains in productivity takes place, a general increase in wealth occurs or in other words, the economy grows. Growth in the economy means additional investments made, and these investments place a demand on labor as well as on capital. The answer to the question about whether gains in productivity are ethical is yes gains in productivity are ethical because they result in the creation of wealth. A rapid gain in productivity in an unencumbered economy does lead to short-term unemployment. However, as I said earlier all rapid gains in productivity are always due to paradigm shifts in technology. The example that I used was the tractor replacing the horse drawn plow resulting in overproduction in the farm sector and causing an increase in unemployment in the farm sector in the first part of the twentieth century. The industry that gave rise to the tractor was growing at a rate faster than the displacement of labor in the farm sector and this at first absorbed the surplus labor. It was only after the government began to encumber the economy through higher taxes on corporations and through tariffs to support farm prices that unemployment rose to unprecedented levels.

Government infrastructure projects burden wealth creation

Up to now, my main argument has been that the only purposes of government are to secure private property and enforce contracts. To fulfill these purposes the government employs a military force to protect private property against foreign enemies, a police force to protect private property against criminals, and judges to adjudicate contracts and laws. A government through its legislative function creates the laws enforced by the police, and adjudicated by judges. All other functions that the government chooses to engage in and which add to taxes and reduce the liberty of contracting unnecessarily burden wealth creation, because these functions take the fruits of labor from the nation and apply them to unproductive ends. Keep in mind that any function that the government engages in is only through enactment of law. Thus, the law becomes the focus of that which contributes to the security of private property and the enforcement of contracts. Laws that do not contribute directly to the security of private property or the enforcement of contracts are laws that overburden an economy. One example of this is the government's role in the building of national and local infrastructure. The building of the infrastructure is through the passing of laws by the sovereign. These laws fund the building of the infrastructure through higher taxes. The national and local infrastructure includes roads, airports, docks and parks as well as water and sewer systems. The building of roads by a sovereign throughout history was not for engendering commerce, rather roads made the marching of armies more efficient. In other words, governments built roads to defend a nation, i.e. protecting private property for the creation of wealth. The Romans famously built good roads to make it easier to administer and secure its provinces and collect tribute from the populations that Rome subjugated. To the extent that the roads also engendered commerce then they added to the general wealth of the local populations and in turn to the wealth of Rome. The engendering and promotion of commerce was not the primary reason Rome built roads. Once conquering a foreign nation, Rome served as its sovereign protector and the conquered nation generally prospered because Roman law and Roman armies secured private property and her ministers adjudicated Roman law and contracts. In return, the conquered nation paid tribute to Rome. Thus came into being Pax Romana, i.e. the Peace of Rome, and it lasted for hundreds of years and created much wealth. Similarly with the German Autobahn which was built to enable the German military easily to cross Germany. The United States Congress authorized the construction of the Interstate Highway System under the auspices of national defense. The United States built the Interstate Highway System to enable the rapid evacuation of cities during times of war or other calamity and to move military assets easily within the nation. As in the case of Rome and Germany, commerce was not the legal reason the United States government funded and built the Interstate Highway System. Prior to the Interstate Highway System, the States funded many roads that crossed multiple counties within a state by borrowing the money and collecting tolls to pay back the debt. The Ohio Turnpike is one such example where the State of Ohio completed its construction at the time the building of Interstate Highway System had begun in 1955. The sale of bonds offered through a commission independent of the government of the State of Ohio funded the building of the Ohio Turnpike. The revenue from the tolls went to the payment of the bonds and the maintenance of the road. No revenue flowed to the State of Ohio. On the other hand, the building of the nation's roadway infrastructure was to fulfill one of the duties of the sovereign, which is the protection and security of private property. To the extent that the building of infrastructure does not facilitate the protection of private property, it is an unnecessary burden on wealth creation, and therefore the building of such infrastructure is unethical. On this basis, many of the other types of infrastructures currently under the domain of the sovereign should instead be in private hands so that they may become productive assets and generate a profit thus creating wealth. This includes airports, docks, parks, as well as water and sewer systems.   The nation is sacrificing the creation of great wealth by allowing the construction and maintenance of infrastructure in the sovereign's domain.   This sacrifice of wealth is weakening the nation and increasingly subjecting it to calamity.

Public education burdens wealth creation and is therefore unethical

Since the sole purpose of a nation's sovereign is the protection of private property and the enforcement of contract, it becomes difficult to justify burdening wealth creation for the purpose of public education. It is the epitome of credulity to argue that public education protects private property and enables the enforcement of contracts.   Nor is it credible to argue that a democracy or even a representative republic requires an educated populace in order to function.   Such an argument presupposes universal suffrage, which I have shown is ultimately destructive of wealth.   Education is a means to secure the future.   The education of an individual is wealth creation only to the extent that the education improves the productivity of the individual.   Education for any other purpose is vanity and vanity is destructive of wealth creation. An individual who acts out of vanity is not acting in his self-interest rather he acts to engender the envy of others.   Such an individual is invariably an atheist.   An atheist is one who is unable to conceive of anyone greater than he is himself.   An individual who fears God cannot act out of vanity.   As education is a source of wealth creation, it cannot by definition or in fact fall in the domain of the sovereign.   Education is cultivating an individual life just as planting seed is cultivating land.   It is no coincidence that the word "culture" is related to the verb to cultivate which relates to planting seed.   An education and the planting of seed on private property secure for the individual both the present and the future in the event of a calamity.   The purpose of government is to protect life and private property for the purpose of cultivation, i.e. the creation of wealth.   It is not and cannot be the purpose of government to plant the seed or to educate the individual as such a purpose burdens wealth creation.   Cultivation or education is for the owner of the private property, i.e. the owner of the land or the owner of his life, i.e. the individual to accomplish.   To the extent that the sovereign cultivates any property then the individual looses his freedom to engage in commerce, and this diminishes wealth creation.   In other words, public education undermines education as a commercial transaction, which would otherwise create wealth instead of consume wealth.   Therefore, laws funding public education are unethical because these laws burden wealth creation without increasing the security of private property.   Individuals buy and sell an education just as they buy and sell other commodities. Supply and demand for education determines the price of education in an unencumbered economy and competition improves the quality and productivity of education in the same way that competition improves the quality and productivity of all goods and services. An investment in education is an investment made by the individual for the purpose of cultivating his life or the life of his progeny and thereby securing his future through his progeny. If an individual invests in an education, he will expect a return on the investment thus his education will be productive or wealth creating and not for vanity, which destroys wealth. All publically funded education including higher education, which gets much of its funding from government, is replete with vanity and therefore destructive of wealth and wealth creation.

Obtaining an education is like planting seed on private property because in both cases, the product or outcome is wealth creation and wealth creation is a hedge against calamity and in the absence of calamity wealth eases the burden of life. Carrying the planting of seed analogy a step further, the productivity or the amount of wealth created for the same seed planted depends on the fecundity of the land. The more fertile the land then the greater is the yield. Similarly with education, which is to say the more fertile the mind, or in other words, the greater the intellectual capacity or the higher the IQ, the greater the yield in comparison to a lower IQ with exposure to the same education. It is intuitively obvious that an individual with a high IQ will benefit more from the same education as one with a low IQ. The creation of wealth or the return on investment in an education, relates directly to the intellectual capacity inherent in the particular individual, and in the nation's population in general. It is for this reason that education is a commodity, which goes to the highest bidder in an unencumbered economy, and the highest bidder is the one who will benefit the most, i.e. the one with the highest IQ. This increases the productivity of education and adds to wealth creation, which benefits the nation in general.

Publically funded education in a nation consisting of a homogenous race of either God-fearing Caucasoid or God-fearing Mongoloid is not as great a burden on wealth creation as it is in a nation that is more racially heterogeneous or a homogenous race of Negroid or mixed-race race individuals. The educational outcome is nearly as productive as individually and privately funded education in a homogeneous Caucasoid or Mongoloid nation. In other words, a public education or an education funded through tax revenue is almost as productive as a privately funded education when the population is 100% Caucasoid or 100% Mongoloid. However, in a nation more racially heterogeneous or a homogeneous race of Negroid or mixed-race individuals and with universal suffrage, public funding of education is a great burden on wealth creation offering no return even if the Negroid or mixed-race individuals are God-fearing. These statements are borne out when one compares the academic performance of United States suburban school districts that are nearly 100% Caucasoid with the nearly 80%

Negroid and mixed race urban school districts within any given State. The States are responsible for setting the education standards for all students and thus within a given State all students are exposed to the same curriculum regardless of school district.   The evidence is clear that the Negroid and mixed race students consistently and significantly underperform their Caucasoid counterparts not only between districts that are dominant in one race or the other, but also between races within districts.   I present specific data on the differences in academic performance in the following pages.   For now let me say that since public funding of education in racially homogenous Western nations does less to encumber the economy than public funding of education in a racially heterogeneous nation, which greatly encumbers the economy, the general rule must be that publically funded education is unethical. Consequently, education cannot be a function of the sovereign because it undermines the creation of wealth, particularly in a racially heterogeneous nation without contributing to the protection of private property or enforcement of contracts.

I have previously mentioned the government actions during the 1960's and 1970's that encumbered the economy included the civil rights legislation, affirmative action executive orders, Medicare, Medicaid, and welfare legislation, the EPA, OSHA, and the abrogation of the Bretton-Woods Agreement.   In addition, there were decisions by the Supreme Court in 1971 and 1974 forcing the busing of children to schools away from their neighborhoods in order to achieve racially "balanced" schools. The flawed reasoning behind this decision was that racially separate education facilities as existed throughout the nation was an inherently unequal system of education.   This was despite the fact that the States have always set standards for all schools and the fact that the separate facilities arose from disparity in wealth creation, which is a function of intellectual capacity in any case.   Presumably, this fictional inequality in education was the reason that the Negroid underperformed academically in comparison to the Caucasoid, which it was not.   Tragically, history has shown how flawed this reasoning was, and continues to be, as this decision resulted in much destruction of wealth, engendering of much poverty, and set in motion much unnecessary misery for many individuals. Forced busing increased the cost and reduced the quality of all education in a vain attempt made by pandering politicians and pandering educators to bring the naturally intellectually inferior Negroid to a higher level of academic achievement.   Forced busing resulted in people moving out of cities and into suburbs thus forcing housing and transportation costs to increase at a rapid rate.   In order to cover these costs married women who were mothers started to join the workforce in large numbers during the 1970s.   The affirmative action executive orders and civil rights legislation forced companies to hire women and minorities in part at the expense of the white male.   White male labor participation rate has declined from 82.6% in 1960 to 73.7% in 2008 and it is one reason that inflation in the economy persists. Figure 69 shows how the labor participation rate of white women increased very quickly by 1970 and continued to increase for the next 30 years. The rapid increase of women in the workforce occurred in large part to pay for the cost of moving to the suburbs, increases in taxes, increases in the cost of educating their children, and increasing transportation costs resulting primarily from the forced busing of children. It was common to hear complaints at the time that the woman went to work only to have her pay go to the higher taxes and very little to savings or wealth creation. School districts spent billions of tax dollars to satisfy court decisions and orders based on flawed principles that went counter to common sense and hundreds of years of experience with attempting to educate the Negroid. The entering of married white women into the workforce was the means that families improved their productivity as it became necessary to offset the accelerating inflation of the 1970s. The increase cost of educating children was due in large part to many families sending their children to parochial and private schools to avoid the government's heavy hand in forcing their children to attend schools the parents or the children did not want to attend and against the will of the parents. Simply stated there was justifiable fear on the part of parents that racial integration of the schools would lead to interracial mixing, i.e. miscegenation with the production of lower IQ offspring as indeed did happen. Enforcement of the executive orders on affirmative action facilitated the mixing of the races by creating a class of Negroid that earned more money than justified by his IQ and at the expense of the Caucasoid. Thus there was a mixing of the races that otherwise would not have occurred resulting in offspring of lower average IQ to the detriment of the economy and to the future ability of the nation to create wealth. Affirmative action, civil rights legislation, and court ordered racial integration of schools were the modern equivalent of the Edict of Caracalla. This was the beginning of the decline in the ability of the standard-bearer of Western Civilization, i.e. the United States, to sustain itself in the face of calamity.

In addition to the aforementioned acts of the Federal Government, the large number of relatively unproductive women into the workforce arising from forced busing added to the inflationary pressures that resulted in the destruction of wealth creation during the 1970's as manifested in unprecedented inflation rates followed by unprecedented interest rates.

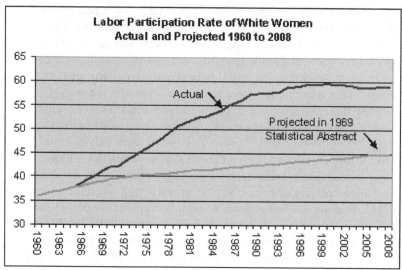

Figure 69 – Labor Participation Rate of White Women Actual and Projected from 1960 to 2008

Figure 69 also shows the projected level of women participation in the work force made by the Bureau of Labor Statistics in 1969. In 1969, the BLS had projected the labor participation rate for white women to be 39.6% in 1970, 40.4% in 1975, and 41.1% in 1980. The actual participation rate in 1980 was 51.2% or 25% greater than projected just 10 years earlier. It is clear that the Federal government failed to foresee the negative effects of its policies on the economy as is always the case. It is a failure that continues to persist and will continue to persist. Projecting the BLS estimate of the rate of growth of white women in the work force and comparing it to the actual rate of growth shows the extent to which not only the economy changed but also the extent to which the culture changed since the halcyon years of the1950s and the early 1960s.

Keep in mind that these changes to the national economy all contributed to the destruction of wealth that the economy otherwise would have created had the government not interfered in the economy and the culture of the nation. The amount of wealth that the economy would have created is 80 times greater than the wealth actually created since 1929. (See Appendix 1) Forced busing leading to the influx of relatively unproductive white women into the workforce with the displacement of the white male contributed significantly to the destruction of wealth that the economy otherwise would have created.

Destroying wealth by educating those that cannot be educated

Educating individuals who by nature lack the ability to be educated destroys wealth because it provides no return on the money expended. This is the case ever since government forced school racial desegregation occurred and the nation expended increasing amounts of wealth to educate Negroid children who the government and the educational establishment knew did not possess the intellectual ability to benefit from the education. Yet the government and the educational establishment, which was highly unionized and supported by tax dollars, continued to deceive the taxpayers to achieve undeserving economic benefits for themselves. In this way, the government continued the process of alienation from the taxpayer and the individuals of whom its establishment and its creation was to protect and to secure. In many cases, the deception went so far as to falsify the test scores of the Negroid in order to derive bonuses from the taxpayer. Nevertheless, driven by universal suffrage and a godless egalitarian ideology the government passed laws that went beyond the legitimate scope or intention of government. These laws included taxes including property, sales, and income taxes as well as regulations that forced greater costs for the public schools. The rise of issuance of municipal bonds is partly attributable to the provision of so-called free public education. Teacher's unions purchased much of this debt thus providing even more incentive on the part of the education establishment to continue the deception and subterfuge. This government debt further burdens wealth creation for no rational purpose as none can exist.

Various Federally mandated programs such as Title I, school meals, special education classes, mandated curriculums, and establishing minimum standards increased the cost of public education faster than the rate of inflation. The teacher unions have contributed to the exponential growth in the cost of education through collective bargaining by mandating small class sizes, introducing work rules requiring the hiring of more teachers, administrators and aides, as well as meaningless certifications in the union contracts thus placing significant barriers to competition in the labor market for teachers. Figure 70 illustrates the exponential growth of education spending by Federal, state and local governments in 2005 constant dollars between 1929 and 2012. The annual compound rate of growth is 4.78%. This compares to an annual compound growth rate of 3.23% for the CPI. Per capita spending on education increased at a compound rate of 3.60%, which is faster than inflation – see Figure 71.

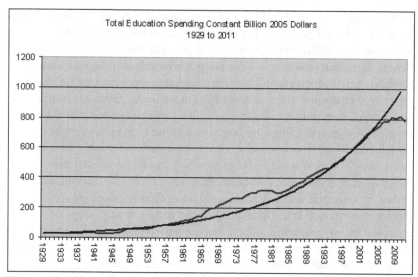

Figure 70 – Total Education Spending in 2005 Dollars – 1929 to 2011

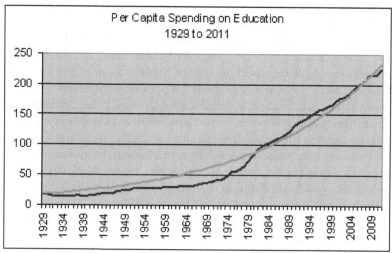

Figure 71 – Per Capita Spending on Education - 1929 to 2011

The fact that per capita government spending on education has grown faster than inflation means that education spending is a major contributor to inflation and that other spending had to be scaled back to cover education spending.   The total spending on education between 1966 and 2011 in 2005 constant dollars has been almost $22 trillion. This does not include government funding of higher education, which also increased tremendously after 1966 and which also contributed to the inflation rate.   By comparison, from 1900 to 1965, the total spending was $2.5 trillion in constant dollars or about ten percent of the amount

314

spent between 1966 and 2011.

Figure 72 charts education spending and population from 1900 to 1965. The average rate of growth between education expenditures in constant dollars and population is 1.07 as seen from the slope of the trend line through the graph. This means that education expenditures grew at an average rate that was 7% greater than the growth of population. While still inflationary this rate of spending resulted in a high level of education because most of the money went toward educating the highly productive Caucasoid male. Figure 73 graphs education expenditures and population from 1966 to 2012. There are two curves on this graph. The curve labeled actual and its associated trend line shows that education expenditures since 1966 have grown 5.5 times faster than the population. The curve labeled projected is an extrapolation of the trend line from the previous 65 years.

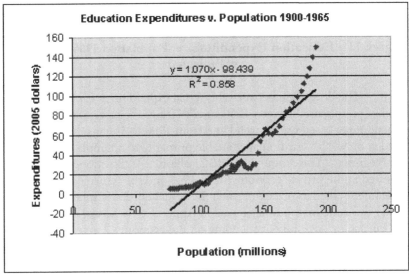

Figure 72 – Education expenditures v. Population 1900 to 1965

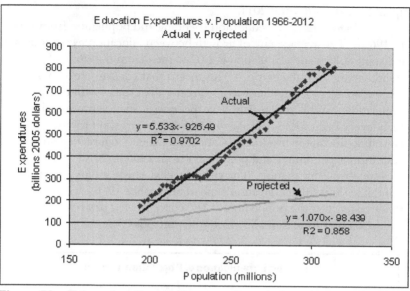

Figure 73 – Education Expenditures v. Population 1966-2012 Actual v. Projected

The difference between the actual expenditures for the same level of population between 1966 and 2012 and the extrapolated expenditures based on the trend line from 1900 to 1965 is the additional burden on wealth creation attributable primarily to attempts at educating the Negroid. This amounts to $13.7 trillion. If this money instead invested in the private economy since 1966 and the return on the investment taken into account then the actual burden is much greater. Using the same method that I used in Appendix 1 whereby I determined the burden of government spending on the economy, I invested the annual difference in 10 year Aaa rated corporate bonds at the annual interest rate for each year since 1966. At the end of each 10-year period, I reinvested the principle and interest at the rate for that year. This method yielded an additional annual burden of $82 trillion in 2005 constant dollars by 2012. This is five times the current annual GDP.

Figure 74 shows the effect of forced busing on the ratio of children enrolled in private schools to total enrollment. As forced busing became widespread, beginning in the 1970s and into the 1980s parents increasingly sent their children to private schools. This was a significant factor in adding to the total cost of education. Local and State governments realized the folly of forced busing by the 1990s and the tremendous cost associated with it. Thus, local authorities petitioned the Federal government to relieve the local school districts from the mandates to integrate. By the end of the 1990's school districts no longer bused children to achieve integration. By then the school districts in most large cities, i.e. the urban areas were predominantly composed of Negroid children and the suburbs were predominantly Caucasoid, as were most Catholic and other religious schools. In other words, despite the trillions of dollars wasted in attempting to integrate the Negroid and Caucasoid in the public school system segregation returned within two generations and remains with us. This time the segregation was along legal boundaries and not between areas within a school district. The low average intelligence of the Negro manifested itself in a sharp decline in graduation rates and academic performance in schools that once were effective and relatively efficient in the education of children. The low average intelligence of the Negro also manifested itself in increasing problems with school discipline, and increasing crime as these behaviors directly correlate with low intelligence. These factors added more costs to education in general as the government and the education establishment attempted one program after another to improve the academic performance of the Negroid and all in vain.

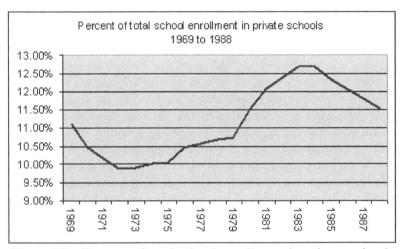

Figure 74 – Percent of total school enrollment in private schools 1969 to 1988

All these mostly vain and self-serving efforts caused the real cost per student in the public education system to increase from $3861 per year in 1970 to $7302 per year in 1996 using 1999 constant dollars. A public school student starting in 1970 cost $59,652 in constant 1999 dollars to educate after 12 years whereas a public school student starting in 1984 cost $85,351 in constant 1999 dollars to educate. To determine whether these costs add value to the economy, I will calculate the property tax paid by a married couple who are both high school graduates, employed and own a house. In order to recover the cost of the education in terms of property taxes I will assume that 1% of the price of a home goes toward property taxes every year. This is close to the national average.

A married couple that graduated from high school in 1996 and started working in 1998 would have a combined income of about $49,000 per year ($26,000 for the male and $13,000 for his wife). At this income level, the couple can afford a home of about $150,000 in 1998 or about 3 times their combined gross income. This will generate a property tax of $1500 per year. The total cost by the public to educate the 1996 graduating couple was over $170,000. Assuming no inflation then it will take 113 years for this couple to reimburse the cost of their education in terms of the property taxes they pay. In other words, it is now virtually impossible to recover the money spent on public education in terms of gains in wealth. It is the reason that public education continues to increase faster than the rate of inflation and that it contributes to the inflation rate. Thus, the high cost of educating individuals destroys wealth and it is one of the reasons that the nation is not 80 times wealthier as it could be without the excessive burden of all government since 1929. This alone is an argument for eliminating public education, eliminating the property tax supporting public education, and leaving the education of children to their parents and the competitive private market with no tax dollars used to support education.

At this point, somebody always says what about children with no parents or only one parent. Children with no parents are orphans and therefore wards of the state. Children are property and the purpose of the state is to protect private property. In this case, the state plays the role of parent, but this does not mean that the state needs an education system. Orphans can be educated in a private school in the competitive market just like anyone else. The widespread existence of the single parent is a recent phenomenon, and related directly to the interference of the government in the economy. The high divorce rate and out of wedlock births are the result of economic pressures on individuals arising from demands of the encumbered economy to increase individual productivity and output. Government interference in the economy creates single parents and orphans in the first place. In a God-fearing nation, it makes no difference whether the Church or the State cares for the orphans. The education of a child is an investment in the wealth of a nation only as long as the child has the intellectual capacity to benefit from the education. Otherwise, the attempt to educate a child beyond his capacity to learn, i.e. his IQ is vanity, and vanity is a burden on wealth creation.

Intelligence and Education

The purpose of education is to provide a literate and educated citizen to enable his ability to create wealth and potentially serve in the protection of private property and the enforcement of laws and contracts. This does not mean that an education be publically funded although this has been the case since the start of the second millennium AD. An education funded by the public in one form or another has existed since the Middle Ages in Europe. A characteristic of public education in Western Nations during the second millennium AD is the racial homogeneity of the population, i.e. the populations were of the Caucasian Race and directed to the male. This means that the average IQ of the population was 100 with a standard deviation of 15. Many well-documented sources exist that confirm this statistic including IQ tests as well as performance on school achievement tests, college entrance examinations, and armed forces qualifying tests. The average IQ of a homogeneous racial population is an immutable fact of nature. It has not varied over the historical record. I will provide some examples of this shortly. At the average IQ level of the Caucasoid, a publically funded education provided a return to the economy as is evident from the great wealth that Europe amassed during the second millennium AD. In the case of Europe and later in the United States, the high level of intelligence in the Caucasian population provided a return on the money expended on public education comparable to the return an individually funded education provided. This is apart from any consideration regarding an educated populace and its importance to a democracy or republic. While this is important, it is secondary to the cost of education and the manner by which individuals fund education, i.e. through taxation or through the free market. When I speak of publically funded education in Europe up until the 20th Century, I am including religious schools as well. This is because local towns in Europe offset some of the costs of religious schools through taxes. During the 20th Century, major funding for religious schools became private although the sovereign continued to provide some level of support. At the same time, public education became increasingly secularized, and this secularization contributed to the rise of atheism or godlessness among the population. As I have shown, atheism with universal suffrage always leads to socialism, and to communism, and ultimately to the destruction of private property, which is the source of wealth creation. Insofar as the sovereign controls public education and it serves the purposes of the sovereign, and to the extent that the sovereign seeks to rule rather than protect private property and enforce contracts, then it is to this extent that public education enables the destruction of private property, which is wealth, and of wealth creation.

The lesson of the later part of the twentieth century is that public education can quickly become a much greater burden on wealth creation in even a moderately racially heterogeneous populated nation such as the United States with approximately 12% Negroid. Besides the fact that government spending of any sort is destructive of the wealth creating ability of the economy, the most significant factor in the greater burden of public education is the knowingly flawed assumption on the part of United States education system bureaucrats that all students are inherently equally capable of learning. This sort of self-serving radical egalitarianism is not limited to those bureaucrats overseeing the United States public education system. Most overseers of the public education systems in other Western nations have also adopted the self-serving egalitarian ideology. Given this knowingly flawed ideology and to hide its self-serving motives, the public educational establishment, i.e. the sovereign, has invented other factors to explain the natural and inheritable lack of the ability to learn among the Negroid population. The factors or rather excuses are other than, and different from the genetic, i.e. racial makeup of the individual. These excuses include low socio-economic status, poor family values, poor cultural values, racism, lack of relevance in the curriculum, emotional makeup and other such non-sense factors. These factors are actually a product of low IQ so the use of these factors to justify more programs forms a circular argument. Unlike the inherently and naturally low average IQ of the Negroid, these factors are subject to self-serving programs masquerading as solutions, and resulting in increasing expenditures and waste of public funds. Despite the $22 trillions of dollars expended over at least three generations at government programs in large part and in a vain attempt to overcome the natural inability of the average Negroid to achieve at the same academic level as the Caucasoid or Mongoloid yet these programs have all failed miserably and predictably so. In the process there was, and continuous to be, much wealth destruction and an increasing secularization of the nation as much of the money and effort spent on education now goes toward legal fees to eliminate God from the curriculum. Much of the money also goes toward propaganda campaigns promoting miscegenation among the young, and thus reducing the average IQ of future generations further reducing the ability of the economy to create wealth. The idea behind the promotion of miscegenation is the elimination of the Negroid through the biological mixing with the Caucasoid and Mongoloid. Unfortunately, as I come to show the offspring of miscegenation lowers the nation's ability to create wealth and thus increases the nation's susceptibility to calamity. This was true for Egypt, Rome, and Portugal as these empires collapsed because they mixed with the darker races and thus were unable to produce men of genius essential for the material advancement of mankind.

Several obvious examples exist that illustrate the veracity of these statements. I will focus on Ohio's Public School System to show that despite the $13 trillion in additional spending over the last 65 years or since 1966, on primary and secondary education by the nation there is practically no improvement in the academic performance of the average Negroid. The reason for this is that the average IQ of the American Negroid is about 85 or about 1 standard deviation below the Caucasoid on the Caucasoid distribution. The standard deviation (SD) of the

American Negroid IQ distribution is 12.

      Table 6 below is a summary of the 12th grade math proficiency scores for Ohio public school students for the 2012-13 school year.   I selected the mathematics proficiency scores because mathematic ability correlates the closest to IQ as is well known by educators and psychometricians.

2012-13		freq dist		Average		St. Dev.	
IQ Level		**Black**	**White**	**Black**	**White**	**Black**	**White**
61.33	Math % Limited Level	0.244	0.064	14.965	3.925	127.677	95.704
76.33	Math % Basic Level	0.248	0.114	18.930	8.702	15.380	63.871
91.33	Math % Proficient Level	0.320	0.303	29.226	27.673	16.245	22.776
106.33	Math % Accelerated Level	0.115	0.222	12.228	23.605	56.294	8.895
121.33	Math % Advanced Level	0.073	0.293	8.857	35.550	100.613	133.306
136.33	Math % Advanced Plus Level	0.000	0.004	0.000	0.545	0.000	5.279
Average IQ and standard deviation				84.205	100.000	17.782	18.161

Table 6 – Black and White Average IQ and Standard Deviation derived from State of Ohio Math Proficiency Testing

The frequency distribution for black and white students performing at each of the six levels is as determined by the state from the raw scores. I determined the IQ level represented by each of the levels by setting the average IQ of the white cohort to 100 and assuming that one standard deviation separated each of the levels on the white distribution of intelligence, which is 15 points.   The State of Ohio did not identify what set of scores made up each of the levels on their web site.   I made the initial assumption that the math-%proficient level was equal to an IQ of 100 and each level separated by 15 points.   In other words, I assumed that an individual with an IQ of 100 tests at the math-proficient level or that he is proficient in math.   Using the goal seek function in Excel, I varied the math-%proficient level until the white IQ score was 100. This reset each of the categories to the values shown.   Thus, the math-%proficient level became an average IQ of 91.33.   Each of the other categories was 1 SD away or 15 points.   With the average white IQ set to 100, the average black IQ is 84 based on the results of the proficiency test.   The standard deviation of the white score is 18 for this cohort making the one SD point 82 on the white distribution.   In this instance, the black IQ is a little less than one standard deviation from the average white IQ.   One reason for this is that there are probably many blacks that score below the math-%limited level category but are included in that category.   Taking this into account then the average black IQ is about one standard deviation lower than the average white IQ based on the results of the State of Ohio Proficiency testing of 12th grade students. Note also that the white SD is 18.1 whereas the black SD is 17.8.   The narrower distribution means that black IQ cluster more around its mean than white IQ. The narrower distribution and the lower IQ also mean that there are very few, if any blacks with an IQ of 140 or better. In a population of over 12 million blacks statistically there are fewer than 9500 who may have an IQ higher than 140 assuming an average IQ of 85 and an SD of 12. In the same population of whites there are statistically more than 135,000 who may have an IQ higher than 140 assuming an average IQ of 100 and an SD of 15.

The enactment of the No Child Left Behind Law (NCLB) in 2001 mandated standardized testing and established minimum scores on these standardized tests for graduation as well as for teacher and administration evaluation. While the NCLB Law added slightly to the burden of the public school system, it nevertheless exposed and confirmed the folly of trying to educate the Negroid. It also tied teacher and administrator pay to the performance of their students. This created a conundrum for the education establishment because they knew that teachers and schools most affected by the law are those with a disproportionate number of the Negroid in their populations. Accordingly, school systems along with the teacher's unions took steps to minimize the impact of the law on teachers and administrators and their pay. These steps included reducing the rigor of the tests themselves and lowering the threshold for passing the tests. In some cases, there was actual cheating and fraud on the part of teachers and administrators and this in all likelihood is continuing considering the temptation of the financial benefits. The cheating and fraud includes correcting the answers of black students to the questions on the tests by teachers and administrators. The Atlanta School System is one recent scandal where the school superintendent, principles, and teachers all changed answers on tests to enable higher scores on the tests by black students. This resulted in higher pay and bonuses for those involved and it took place over several years. It is needless to say, we cannot draw conclusions from the testing of Atlanta's schoolchildren because of the corruption of the administrators and teachers. Other more subtle methods used to mitigate the effects of the NCLB law on teacher and administrator pay is to control the ratio of blacks and whites in any particular school. A school with 90% white students will invariably perform better than a school with 90% black students. Such mixing is limited to local school districts and in cases where a local school district has very few blacks or very few whites this strategy is not workable, so teacher's unions and cooperative administrators employ other strategies including and not limited to the kind of cheating that we saw in Atlanta.

Knowing that the average IQ of whites is 100 with an SD of 15 and the average IQ of blacks is 85 with an SD of 12 enables one to determine the extent of the corruption of the public school system if such corruption exists or when such corruption occurs. In other words if aggregate test results indicate that the black population has an average IQ that is much higher than 85 then there is a high probability that the test results are being manipulated by the administrators and teachers or in other words that fraud and cheating is going on.

Table 7 is the actual result of the 2012-13 - 12th grade math proficiency test submitted by the State of Ohio as required under the NCLB law. This is the same table used earlier to derive the average IQ and SD of the Black and White populations taking the test

2012-13		Black	White	Average Black	Average White	St. Dev. Black	St. Dev. White
70	Math % Limited Level	0.244	0.064	17.080	4.480	127.677	95.704
85	Math % Basic Level	0.248	0.114	21.080	9.690	15.380	63.871
100	Math % Proficient Level	0.320	0.303	32.000	30.300	16.245	22.776
115	Math % Accelerated Level	0.115	0.222	13.225	25.530	56.294	8.895
130	Math % Advanced Level	0.073	0.293	9.490	38.090	100.613	133.306
145	Math % Advanced Plus Level	0.000	0.004	0.000	0.580	0.000	5.279
				92.875	108.670	17.782	18.161

Table 7 – State of Ohio 12th Grade Math Proficiency test results

Once again, I assigned 100 to the math-% proficient level and varied the other levels by 15 points as shown in the table. Performing the analysis in this manner results in the average IQ of the black as 92.9 and the average IQ of the white is 108.7. This makes it appear that in the case of Ohio the average IQs of both black and white students is much higher than the natural IQ levels. However, this is not the case since the difference between the two scores remains one SD. The real meaning of these scores is that the education bureaucrats lowered the standard to enable more blacks to pass the test. In the process, the average IQ of the white also appeared to increase since lowering the standards also enabled more whites to score higher than they otherwise would have under a more rigorous test. A more rigorous test would enable a comparison of the proficiency level with earlier generations of students and their true level of education in comparison to their earlier peers.

Other states have done the same sort of thing. South Carolina for example has a test called the Longitudinal High School Assessment Program test. The latest results for the test show that 95% of the white population passed and 89% of the black population passed. On the surface, it appears that South Carolina is doing an excellent job in educating all its youth. In reality, it is doing the same or maybe a worse job than it did in the past. In order to achieve 89% pass rate for blacks we would have to design the test so that with an IQ of 85 and SD of 12 the number of students failing would be 11%. Statistically this would result in 2.4% failure for whites. In other words setting the standard to enable 89% of blacks to pass would result in about 97.6% of whites passing which is close to the actual number of 95%. In fact, given the difference I would argue that more blacks are passing than should pass or the education bureaucrats are suppressing the white scores in some fashion. Note that these results all assume a normal distribution, which is a reasonable assumption based on historical evidence and experience.

On the other hand, if we wanted 90% of whites to pass we would design the test such that with an average IQ of 100 the number of students failing would be 10%. In this case, the number of black students passing would be 64%. In other words adjusting the test to increase the passing rate of the black student to almost 90% from 64% only increases the white passing rate from 90% to 95%. So now, it appears the blacks are "catching up" and it gives the flawed impression that the public school system is accomplishing its goal when in fact it is failing and wasting trillions of dollars in the process.

I have spoken throughout this book about an unencumbered economy, i.e. a laissez-faire economy as the ideal environment for the creation of wealth. A sovereign burdens an economy by enacting laws that require the wealth creating entities in an economy, i.e. individuals and corporations, to include terms and conditions to a contract that the parties to the contract would not include of their own freewill. The explicit terms and conditions may or may not be in the contract but as long as they are enshrined in law, these terms and conditions might as well be in the contracts explicitly. These additional terms and conditions derive primarily from tax laws, specific industry regulations, labor laws, and civil rights laws including affirmative action executive orders. Taxes include income taxes; capital gains taxes; taxes on dividends; tariffs; sales taxes, and property taxes. Included in the income tax are taxes related to social security, Medicare, and taxes on corporate profits and dividends. Included in regulations are environmental regulations, OSHA, Endangered Species Act, ADA (American Disability Act) regulations, unemployment compensation laws, and workers compensation laws. These laws burden wealth creation and to the extent that they do not serve to protect private property and facilitate the enforcement of laws and contracts these laws unnecessarily burden wealth creation. These and similar such laws weaken an economy making it more vulnerable to calamity. As I had shown in Appendix 1, the burden of government taxes and regulations on wealth creation is to reduce the economy to one-eightieth of its potential since 1929. Thus the nation would be 80 times wealthier in real terms were it not for the government undertaking functions that go beyond protecting private property and enforcing laws and contracts since 1929.

Some may argue that regulations like OSHA and the EPA are necessary to protect life and property but this is only true when the sovereign holds property and is negligent in the protection of life. Recall that the sovereign's divine right of king secures the soul of the sovereign only in the course of his duty to protect private property where he must act in accordance with the law that he enacts.   Where there is private property, such laws are redundant as existing laws barring trespass of property and negligence accomplish the same ends.   Trespass is a criminal violation of private property and therefore subject to remedies under the sovereign's laws.   Spoiling of a stream or a lake by one individual reduces the wealth or wealth creation of others who rely on the stream or lake.   Thus, the spoiler is trespassing on the property of others and those that are affected are entitled to the protection of the sovereign under laws securing private property.   As one remedy, the sovereign exercises the power of eminent domain to take the property of the spoiler and force the spoiler under law to compensate for his trespass.   There is no need to enact any new laws that accomplish the same end as that accomplished with existing property law.   Similarly, with negligence wherein an employer trespasses on the life of an employee when he neglects to provide a safe work environment or at least provides a warning to the employee of hazardous work.   Such extraneous laws as the EPA and OSHA burden the creation of wealth without adding to the security of private property.   Even where the sovereign is the spoiler of the lake or stream, laws that permit the prosecution of the sovereign by individuals are all that are necessary to remedy the trespass by the sovereign.   Although in the case where the sovereign holds land, environmental laws do no harm to the economy as they encumber the sovereign and not individuals.   However if trespass by the sovereign is necessary for the protection of private property then there is no remedy under law for the affected individuals other than compensation if allowed by the sovereign under due process.

A nation formed under God is necessary for the survival of the nation

A nation formed under God is necessary for the survival of the nation through the creation of wealth.   The attribution to God accounts for the soul of the sovereign and the souls of soldiers that serve to protect private property and enforce contracts.   The attribution to God is also to regulate envy as God proscribes envy and only the fear of God controls envy.   When I speak of envy in the context of an economy, I am referring to laws motivated by envy and enacted by the sovereign to encumber an economy.   In a constitutional republic with universal suffrage and no fear of God, envy eventually manifests as socialism with a gradual destruction of wealth and a weakening of the economy and the nation.   Socialism is a linking of the sovereign with the economy through laws whereby the laws take the wealth of individuals and introduce terms and conditions into contracts that deliberately increase costs and thus encumber the formation of contracts and the creation of wealth.   Socialism destroys wealth and wealth creation ostensibly through redistribution and it eventually leads to civil war or rebellion.

Note that redistribution of wealth is not the object of socialism, nor the passion for socialism. Redistribution is merely a means to an end and the end is the destruction of another's wealth and his ability to create wealth. Thus, a godless constitutional republic with universal suffrage will always end in civil war and great destruction of life and property.

In a monarchy, envy manifests itself through rebellion. The French Revolution is the earliest modern example of envy's manifestation and the destructive power of envy. Increasing taxation of the population by the sovereign to sustain failed foreign adventures providing no monetary return to the nation encumbered commerce and increased the wealth disparity between the aristocracy and the hoi polloi. Thus, the population was ripe for the invocation of envy by the godless. As in all such rebellions, it was first necessary to inoculate the nation against God's proscription against envy by denying the existence of God. The French Revolution was as much an action against God as it was against the sovereign. The leaders and promoters of the French Revolution were all atheists and egotists. Atheists are by nature egotists, as they cannot conceive of anyone greater than them. Without the fear of God, all sin was possible. Thus, the Reign of Terror ensued with the murder of 50,000 innocents, and wealth destroyed. The French Revolution led to the rise of the atheist and egotist Napoleon who crowned himself emperor in a symbolic and spiritual break of the sovereign with God. The ensuing Napoleonic Wars were the most devastating and murderous in Europe up to that time and it took decades for Europe to recover even partially from Napoleon's madness and the madness and irrationality of the French Revolution. Nevertheless, the French Revolution and its philosophical underpinning, the so-called Enlightenment, planted the intellectual seeds for the subsequent secularization and socialism of Europe. The wars that followed the secularization and socialism of European nations in the Twentieth Century rivaled the Black Death in the destruction of humanity such is the destructiveness of envy manifest through universal suffrage. Actions of individuals, whether sovereign or not, and motivated by envy and leading to the taking of life and/or property are punishable by both God and man as they are murder and theft. Laws engendered by envy and manifested through universal suffrage bring the sovereign's power of eminent domain to bear and lead to socialism and the destruction of wealth thereby weakening an economy and a nation making it vulnerable to calamity. Therefore, a nation formed under God is necessary in order to account for the soul of the sovereign, proscribe envy, and instill the fear of God into the sovereign. Without the fear of God, a sovereign will take for himself that for which the nation appoints him to protect and defend, i.e. the lives and property of the citizens.

Summary of Section 2

Government through the law is a coercive force essential for the securing of private property and the enforcement of contract. Government is at the same time a burden on wealth creation and as such, government may act to reduce rather than increase the security of private property and wealth creation. Government through the law also restricts the exercise of individual freewill undermining contract formation. A government through the laws it enacts and the contracts it enforces has the potential to undermine wealth creation leaving a nation more susceptible to calamity than would otherwise be the case. I explored how this can come about. I showed that when the sovereign enacts laws not directed to the protection of private property and the enforcement of contracts then he harms the nation's ability to create wealth and sustain a calamity.

I also discussed the role that human passions play in an economy. The study of economics is a study of the aggregate behavior of individuals and human passion to a large degree plays a role in human behavior. Therefore, the passions are a contributing factor in economic activity and ethical behavior. The basic human passions that affect economic decisions and influence ethical behavior are fear, greed, envy, empathy, happiness, vanity, love and hate. I touched upon these basic human passions in terms of their effect on economics and ethical behavior. I showed how competition and self-interest serve to regulate greed and how competition is the engine of wealth creation. I also showed that the fear of God is necessary to proscribe envy, which is the most irrational and most wealth destructive of the human passions.

Section 3.   The Future of Mankind

Ethical and Moral Behavior

In section three, I will discuss ethical and moral behavior in light of wealth creation.   In this section, I will focus on how the other of God's Commandment to wit bearing false witness, i.e. dishonesty, misrepresentation, deception, and corruption encumber an economy and lead to the destruction of wealth and wealth creation thereby undermining the ability of an economy to withstand calamity.   While it may seem obvious to most readers that these behaviors are destructive of wealth there are those who subscribe to the flawed labor theory of value and to the idea of a zero sum economy who conflate these behaviors with making a profit or creating wealth.   To those that subscribe to the labor theory of value and to a zero sum economy, a man's profit is not a measure of how well the man meets the needs of other men but rather it is a measure of the extent of a man's dishonesty, prevarication, mendacity, and deception.   Profit to these simple minds is the rich getting richer at the expense of the poor.   Thus, profit is not a noble or worthy goal because it is necessary for survival but rather a manifestation of dishonesty, misrepresentation, and deception.   Therefore, man must shun profit, and mankind must ostracize those who espouse profit.   To these simple minds, altruism and charity are noble motivators of human behavior.   In a godless populace, envy is the source of such thinking, and this thinking has led to the destruction of wealth and to all the poverty, war, and misery that has occurred since the 18th Century and beginning with the Enlightenment and its manifestation in the French Revolution.

To many misguided individuals, a nation under God is a nation whose sovereigns and whose individuals obey the Commandment you shalt not bear false witness.   Thus, dishonesty, misrepresentation and deception are sins and profit is the wages of sin or so goes the thinking. The truth of course is very different and the truth is that profit is wealth creation through the satisfaction of the needs of men, and necessary for the survival and immortality of man as ordained by God.   Regarding profit with contempt is the hallmark of envy and the hallmark of socialism and communism.

There is a distinction between simple puffery and outright deception.   By puffery, I am referring to flattering, often exaggerated, praise and publicity, especially when used for promotional purposes. Competition regulates such behavior.   Where the sovereign encumbers an economy through regulations and taxes thereby placing barriers to competition, then puffery becomes deception because there are no competitive limits to it other than the fear of God.   Indeed, the government overburdening of the economy and atheism makes liars of all.

A good example of how the government makes liars of all is the so-called green energy movement that includes such technologies as the electric car, windmills, and solar energy. Government subsidy and promotion of green energy technology and the vilification of conventional technologies such as coal, oil, and nuclear has distorted the energy marketplace leading to wasteful investments in these so-called green technologies. None of these technologies has ever provided a return on investment and none ever will because basic physical principles prevent these technologies from competing with conventional and traditional energy sources at almost any level of application. Yet because of the heavy government subsidies and promotion, the competition from suppliers of conventional energy sources is effectively barred. Thus scarce capital and scarce resources are employed which do not and cannot create wealth. This is a reduction in productivity in a major sector of the economy overcome only through gains in productivity in other sectors. Government interference in the energy sector of the economy enables deception to flourish with the resulting destruction of wealth that deception engenders. Thus, we see the collapse of many companies engaged in the so-called green energy industry resulting in the loss of billions of dollars of wealth. The loss of wealth always weakens a nation and the more capital resources investors expend on green technology the poorer the nation becomes and the more susceptible to calamity

There are different sources of emotional motivation for human behavior embodied in capitalism, socialism and communism. Thus, the economic system is a determinant of the culture of a nation as is the culture of a nation in turn the determinant of the economic system and ultimately the survival of the nation. Changing the culture will change the economic system and changing the economic system will change the culture. The agent of change is the sovereign at least in the short term and potentially in the long term as the government shills in the media spoon-feed the deception to an increasingly unsophisticated electorate. An unsophisticated, poorly educated and thus gullible electorate arises from universal suffrage and a decline in the average IQ of the voting population. Introducing more Negroid and mixed-race individuals into the voting population reduces the average IQ of the voting population thus enabling the destruction of wealth through deception to take place.

Capitalism is the description of an economy where an individual pursuing his own self-interest satisfies the needs of others. In the process of individuals satisfying their self-interest, they create wealth. Capitalism requires the sovereign to provide for the security of private property and for the enforcement of contracts. Under a capitalist economy, the sovereign owes his allegiance and his duty to the individuals who appointed him to protect their private property and enforce their contracts. As long as the sovereign and the populace fears God and have faith in God then capitalism is a wealth creating economy because God proscribes envy. The fear of God and the opportunity inherent in a wealth creating economy hold envy at bay. A wealth creating economy creates disparity in wealth that in a godless capitalist nation engenders envy. Encumbering an economy by the sovereign limits opportunity and secularizing a nation by the sovereign gives rise to envy which leads to socialism and destruction of wealth. A wealth creating economy therefore requires three elements; (1)a nation that fears God, (2)a population with a high average IQ, and (3)a sovereign who protects private property, enforces contracts and does not overly burden the economy to accomplish these ends.

Individuals whether highly intelligent or not, but motivated by envy, will always espouse and promote a socialist economy. Such misguided individuals rely on the labor theory of value and assume a zero sum economy. Profit is the moral equivalence of theft to a socialist and therein in part is the source of their envy. Socialists espouse the atheism of Stoicism and of the Enlightenment, which make the flawed argument that man's reason acting through his will controls his passions and thus there is no need for God or no need to fear God or have faith in God in order that man live in peace. Just the opposite is true. Socialists through their ego and their hubris either ignore or fail to see that irrational envy is their motivator. Atheism is always a prerequisite for a socialist economy to emerge. Atheism enables envy as a means to motivate men to destructive ends by eliminating the "opiate of the people", i.e. faith in God who proscribes envy as well as murder, and bearing false witness. Socialists undertake to satisfy the needs of men as they see those needs through the actions of the sovereign as manifested in law, as well as through the sovereign's coercion, and intimidation. In a godless nation, the greatest need is the need to satiate envy. This need is primal and just as in the case of Cain and Abel it overwhelms the love of brothers and the need to survive. Under socialism, individuals owe their allegiance to the sovereign because he is the means to that end. Failure to show allegiance to the sovereign or to abide by the socialist altruistic manifesto is treason and punishable accordingly. The protection of private property, including the protection of individual life, and the enforcement of laws and contracts are not the primary purpose of the socialist sovereign. The primary purpose of the socialist sovereign is to satisfy the "common good" as he or the people by plebiscite define the "common good". Thus in a godless socialist economy the plebiscite is not only the means of selecting the sovereign but also the arbiter of morality. The "people" decide right or wrong and not God. At times, the sovereign can overturn the people when their will does not suit his purpose, which is the satiation of envy. A step toward socialism was taken by the US Supreme Court decision in Kelo v. City of New London, 545 U.S. 469 (2005) wherein they deliberately twisted the intent of the takings clause of the Fifth Amendment of the US Constitution to mean that the government can take property for "public purpose" in addition to "public use". "Public purpose" is another way of saying "common good". In the case of Kelo, the City of New London Connecticut forcibly took land from one citizen and gave it to a developer in order that he could build tax revenue producing structures. The developer would also profit from the taking of the private property and the original owner from whom the City took the property received only the compensation dictated by the City. The main purpose of the socialist sovereign is not to protect private property but to serve man or so he claims. Under a socialist system, it becomes necessary to exercise the sovereign power of eminent domain to take private property for the "common good" as defined by the sovereign. The methods used by the socialist sovereign to satisfy the needs of men are antithetical to private property and the exercise of freewill thus there is no wealth creation in a socialist economy. A socialist sovereignty relies on flawed humanistic, i.e. atheistic, or Stoic notions of the nature of man to enact laws governing the behavior of individuals. Altruism and charity are the most admired and promoted behaviors to socialists and since altruism and charity are counter to Natural Law and God's law they must be constantly reinforced by the socialist sovereign. Thus, constant vigil manifested as spying or monitoring, is necessary on the part of the sovereign to ensure that the citizens are sufficiently altruistic and work more for the "common good" than in their self-interest. Men are not naturally predisposed to altruistic behavior, and a socialist sovereign must expend much energy to force individuals to act altruistically, and to maintain an altruistic nation. It is the reason socialist nations are also police states and have high rates of taxation. Rather than the fear of God to control envy, socialists rely instead in eliminating the source of envy, which is economic inequality among the hoi polloi. Taxes are the means to force economic equality. The populace of course must not envy the sovereign as he has the power to take life and property with no recourse on his person. Thus, the fear of the sovereign replaces the fear of God. Unlike the fear of God, man can overcome the fear of the sovereign through rebellion because the fear of the sovereign cannot overcome man's envy of the sovereign. Hence, socialism always ends with the destruction of wealth and rebellion and for the same reason that it came to exist in the first place that is envy of the wealthy, now replaced with envy of the sovereign. Without the fear of God, man is constantly warring with man or in Thomas Hobbes words without the fear of God man exists in a state of "*war of all against all*".

Communism is an extreme form of socialism in which there is no private property or individual freewill in the formation of contracts. Under communism, the sovereign owns all means of production. Since private property does not exist, the communist sovereign serves only the "common good" or the "people" and not the individual. In a communist economy, the individual does not exist either in a legal or ethical sense. In a communist economy, there is no such thing as moral or immoral behavior since God does not exist. There is only behavior that is legal, illegal, ethical, or unethical. Legal behavior is in accordance with law and ethical behavior is in accordance with altruism. Thus, making a profit may not be against the law but it is unethical in a communist economy.

Both socialism and communism sow the seeds of their own destruction because they rely on false notions of human nature, i.e. that man is naturally altruistic, empathetic, kind, and generous when history and man's nature shows he is not. Feelings of altruism, empathy, kindness, and generosity do not come naturally to man. If these feelings or emotions did come naturally, then man would not survive but obviously, he survives. The continued existence of man and the creation of wealth is evidence that altruism, empathy, kindness, and generosity are not natural attributes of man's nature but rather only come about through an act of will. Man is kind or generous because he wills himself to be kind or act kindly or generously, or a man is empathetic or altruistic because he wills himself to be empathetic or to be altruistic. If he can will himself to act kindly then he can also will himself to act unkindly. Without the fear of God, the latter is more likely than the former and indeed this has been the case throughout history.

On the other hand, a man cannot will himself to be greedy or envious. These passions come natural to man. As I have said all along, greed drives man to survive and create wealth. Greed can also destroy man because it provides the temptation to deceive and lie, and thus sin. The greed of one man controls or regulates the greed of another through the mechanism of competition. Competition can only regulate greed in an unencumbered economy. When the sovereign encumbers the economy then the greed of men is unleashed and destruction of wealth ensues, as men in the absence of competition now become economic sovereigns, i.e. monopolies. By monopoly, I mean an entity that has no fear of competition and can thus set prices strictly on demand for its product or service with no concern about competition increasing the supply of his product or service. The Standard Oil Company was not a monopoly because it feared competition since the price of kerosene dropped the more efficient Standard Oil was in its production, refining and distribution. If it had no fear of competition, i.e. if it was a true monopoly, the price of kerosene would have increased and not decreased, as Standard Oil grew larger by acquiring its rivals. Had Standard Oil become greedy and increase the price of kerosene thus increasing its margin then other investors would have entered the industry to compete with Standard Oil, but the company held competition at bay by keeping its prices low thus benefiting consumers. This is the essence of capitalism. Yet in the process, the owners of Standard Oil Company became very wealthy. This wealth in the midst of the emerging atheism at the time engendered envy, particularly the envy of the political and intellectual classes. This gave rise to sovereign laws that eventually dismembered Standard Oil and set the stage for the dismemberment and destruction of future wealth as well.

Capitalism or a wealth creating economy is the natural state of man whereas socialism and communism are unnatural states of man. Thus, it takes more energy and effort, and thus a greater burden on the economy on the part of the sovereign to sustain a socialist or communist economy than it does to sustain a wealth creating economy. A constant state of revolution and thus increasing consumption of wealth is not necessary for a wealth creating economy as it is for a socialist or communist economy.

The individual as an actor in the wealth creating economy

Ethical behavior is any behavior directed toward the creation of wealth because the creation of wealth is essential for survival as it is the only hedge against calamity. An individual can take on three different roles within a wealth creating economy. Each role has associated with it distinct ethical behaviors. The first role is the individual acting on his own behalf or representing himself before others, next the individual acting on the behalf or at the behest of others, i.e. as agent, and finally the individual as sovereign or soldier. Each role has its own set of ethical codes as well as legal codes by which the actor must conform in order to create wealth or enable the creation of wealth.

An individual acting on his own must act in his self-interest in order to create wealth. The individual acting on his own behalf owes allegiance to himself only, and he must be true to himself and to others in order that he profit from his actions. Accordingly, he cannot act altruistically and at the same time be true to himself. An individual acting on behalf of a corporation or on behalf of others in a position of trust must act in the interest of the corporation or in the interest of his clients in order to create wealth. This does not mean that an individual acting on the behalf of others must do so in an altruistic sense, rather he does so only when the interests of the individual actor who is the agent are the same as or parallel to the interest of the corporation or his client. An individual actor who is in a position of trust vis-à-vis a corporation secures by contract. Any act by the individual actor violating the terms of the contract, i.e. breach of the contract, encumbers the creation of wealth and therefore it is an unethical as well as an illegal act. A breach of contract is only illegal if it violates civil or criminal codes enacted by the sovereign. If there are no civil codes proscribing a breach of contract then a breach of contract is merely a matter between the parties adjudicated by petition to the sovereign. A sovereign or soldier is an individual who acts on behalf of the nation and whose purpose is the protection of private property and enforcement of contracts. A sovereign cannot create wealth he can only take the wealth of others. A sovereign has the power of eminent domain and the authority to adjudicate laws and contracts. Acts by the sovereign, i.e. laws directed toward the protection of private property and the enforcement of contracts are acts enabling the creation of wealth and these acts are ethical even though the acts may themselves encumber an economy in general. Acts of the sovereign not directed toward the protection of private property and enforcement of contracts are unethical because they overburden the creation of wealth.

Ethical behavior for the individual actor

Individual ethical behavior manifests through the exercise of individual freewill in contracts. This is an individual pursuing his self-interest and engaging in commerce. Ethical behavior consists in honoring the terms and conditions of contracts and engaging truthfully and honestly in commercial transactions. This does not mean that the cost of a good or service be disclosed in relation to the price and against the will of the seller. Only supply and demand for a good or service determines the price of a good or service in an unencumbered economy. The cost to produce or create a good or service is of no relevance and should be of no relevance in the market place for the good or service. Commercial transactions in accordance with individual freewill are ethical because they engender the creation of wealth. Commercial transactions must take place within an unencumbered economy in order to maximize the creation of wealth. Individuals exercising their freewill and pursuing their own self-interest in an unencumbered economy creates the greatest wealth for the greatest number and provides the greatest hedge against calamity. In the absence of calamity, the individual or corporate creation of wealth eases the burden of life.

Ethical behavior for the agent

Corporate behavior manifests through the actions of the officers or agents of the corporation. Accordingly, the officers of a corporation have a fiduciary duty to the owners of the corporation. The officers of a corporation are in a position of trust secured under law by contract and thus enforceable by the sovereign power of eminent domain. An officer of a corporation must act at all times to benefit the corporation. As an officer of a corporation is also an employee of the corporation he also acts in his own self-interest, however he cannot act against the interest of the corporation. Where a conflict of interest arises, the officer of a corporation must yield his self-interest, just as in the case of a sovereign who also must yield his self-interest upon becoming sovereign. To the extent that an officer is also a stockholder then an officer also benefits himself through his actions.   An officer of a corporation is analogous to a sovereign wherein the life of the sovereign is common to the nation, so too the life of the corporate officer is common to the corporation.   Any action by the officer that violates his fiduciary duty is a violation of trust. Acts that are a violation of trust amount to an encumbrance on the economy because such acts go against the will of the owners of the corporation.   Such acts undermine the creation of wealth and hence they are unethical.   A corporation that fails to make increasing profits, or makes no profit or in other words fails to create wealth, is an encumbrance to an economy and therefore it must and will cease to exist.

Ethical behavior for the sovereign
In the case of the sovereign, the sovereign can do no wrong when engaged in the protection of private property and the enforcement of contracts.   A sovereign is in a position of trust within a nation. When the sovereign acts in violation of his trust, then his acts encumber an economy and undermine the creation of wealth.   Therein is the unethical behavior.   A sovereign who uses the power of eminent domain to take from the nation that which he was appointed to protect, i.e. life and private property, for purposes that are not directly related to the protection of private property is violating his position of trust. Accordingly, the sovereign acts to encumber an economy and suppress the creation of wealth and thus his acts are unethical.   Since the soul of the sovereign, as the soul of each individual, belongs to God then sovereign acts of eminent domain, i.e. the taking of life and property, which otherwise would be done through the invocation of the divine right of kings are immoral when such acts fail to protect private property and instead destroy wealth.   God disposes the soul of the sovereign of the nation formed under God, but also of a godless nation, depending on the acts of the sovereign during his reign.   This is because God exists regardless whether the nation or sovereign acknowledges His existence. If his acts are immoral then God disposes the soul of the sovereign accordingly.   A sovereign whose acts and laws encumber an economy causing the prices of goods and services to be independent of the actual or underlying supply and demand, and who creates high levels of unemployment is ripe for rebellion.   A sovereign encumbers an economy through the power of eminent domain when he enacts laws and regulations that undermine the formation of contracts.   He also encumbers an economy by enforcing unenforceable contracts. Unenforceable contracts are contracts whereby coercion causes one or more of the parties to execute the contract against their individual freewill. An example of such contracts is a labor contract wherein the labor union forces the corporation to execute the contract under the threat of a strike, which amounts to financial loss.   The fact that the unions also suffer losses during a strike is immaterial because there they act in accordance

with their freewill. A lockout is a rarely used coercion by a corporation to impose financial loss on the union and its members in order to arrive at terms more favorable to the corporation. This would not be necessary if the law did not enforce coercive union contracts in the first place. Therefore, lockouts are ethical since they are a form of corporate self-defense against the unethical coercion of unions and thus consistent with Natural Law.

The selection or appointment of the sovereign is critical to the survival of an economy and of a nation. A sovereign has one power, the power of eminent domain. Accordingly, a sovereign who fears God limits the exercise of the power of eminent domain. The sovereign power of eminent domain directed to the protection of private property and the enforcement of contracts is moral and ethical. The sovereign who fears God acts in accordance with the purposes for which the nation appoints or elects the sovereign. A man who would be sovereign and who fears God will not tempt fate and risk his soul by seeking office through appeals to envy because God proscribes envy. In order to obtain his appointment or election a man who would be sovereign must profess fear of God and faith in God. Those that oppose the man who would be sovereign because he professes fear of God and faith in God act to encumber the economy and act to undermine the creation of wealth and thus the survival of the nation under God. A nation and an economy can only survive when formed under God and with God's Commandments as the basis of law. The fear of God secures the soul of the sovereign and ensures envy does not emerge to undermine and destroy wealth. A nation formed under God means a nation whose populace and sovereign fears God and it is the fear of God that informs the laws and actions of the sovereign. A man who would be sovereign must appeal to liberty. Liberty is the exercise of freewill by the individuals in all commercial transactions. It does not mean the exercise of freewill where the acts of freewill are against the law and contrary to the will of God. Keep in mind that a sovereign can only secure and protect private property when individuals cede some of their liberty. A sovereign who appeals to liberty and who professes a fear of God will adjudicate contracts and the law in accordance with God's law and consistent with the creation of wealth. On the other hand, a sovereign that enforces contracts made against the freewill of one of the parties undermines an economy. Labor contracts are examples of such contracts as I have already stated. Corporations execute labor contracts under threat of a strike; accordingly, such contracts go against the freewill of the corporation as embodied in the officer of the corporation. Enforcement of such contracts by the sovereign encumbers an economy and suppresses the creation of wealth, which is the only hedge against calamity.

Unethical behavior is behavior that encumbers the exercise of freewill in the execution of contracts.   The parties to a contract or any commercial transaction enter into such a contract or transaction with their own freewill.   The terms and conditions of the contract or transaction must be clear and understood by all parties in order that they may ascend to the contract or transaction of their own freewill.   To the extent that there is coercion involved in the execution of a contract then the contract is an encumbrance to the economy and therefore unenforceable.   In the case of individuals, acting each on their own behalf and according to their freewill such coercion is by government. A tax added to a sale transaction is a form of coercion because it is a cost forced upon the buyer and the seller by the sovereign.   The sovereign is inserting himself as a party to the transaction against the will of the buyer and the seller.   To the extent that the tax affects the price of good or service sold then it is to this extent that the price is independent of supply and demand for the good or service.   Thus, the tax encumbers the economy and less wealth created thereby making the economy and the nation more vulnerable to calamity.

Considering that the sovereign is the adjudicator of contracts, he has behaved unethically by also becoming a party to a contract through the laws he enacts and taxes he imposes, and which he may eventually adjudicate.   The sovereign has thus engaged in a taking of private property through his power of eminent domain for purposes that do not relate to the protection of private property or the enforcement of contracts.   One can make the argument that the tax thus collected is for the legitimate purpose of government.   This argument is specious because not all individuals equally pay the tax or the amount of tax, since the sales tax is typically a percentage of the price of the goods and services sold.   Since the sovereign exists to protect the life and property and enforce contracts for all the individuals that are citizens of the nation, then all the individuals must contribute an equal amount to the sovereign's treasury or else the tax overly encumbers the economy suppressing the creation of wealth.   Thus, it is not only the level of taxation but also its unequal distribution that encumbers an economy. A high level of taxation that is unequally distributed is more of an encumbrance as a low level of taxation equally distributed.   All taxes burden and encumber an economy; however, some types are more burdensome and encumber an economy more than other types.   The least burdensome tax is the head tax.   A head tax is determined by dividing the total expense of government by the total citizen population. Non-citizens must also pay the head tax while in the nation that protects them.   Failure to pay the head tax is a violation of law and punishable by the sovereign power of eminent domain, i.e. a taking of property.   As the population increases then the tax burden of each individual decreases, assuming government spending remains constant as it should.   If the burden of government increases as population increases then there is no need for government.   The original purpose of government was to enable the efficient protection of private property and enforce contracts. This original purpose is defeated if the individual burden of government increases in proportion with population rather than in inverse proportion with population.

Corruption is particularly insidious unethical behavior

Corruption is a particularly insidious type of unethical behavior because it involves a willful disregard of fiduciary duty.   Corruption always involves an individual who acts on behalf of another i.e. an agent or the sovereign and it is an act of freewill.   There are two instances where corruption can occur and these are as an officer of a corporation and as the sovereign.   In one way or another corruption involves bearing false witness and therefore it is a violation of God's Commandment and it is punishable by God through the disposition of the soul.   Corruption is betrayal of trust.   Corruption encumbers an economy because it involves acts that take private property against the will of the owners of that property.   Any act done against the will of others suppresses the creation of wealth and subjects an economy to calamity.   A corrupt corporate officer will act in his own self-interest at the expense of those that have placed their trust in him to act in their interest.   A corrupt corporate officer therefore destroys wealth and this makes his acts unethical and punishable by man.   The same is true about a corrupt sovereign.   A nation and God endows the sovereign with the power of eminent domain for the protection of private property and enforcement of contracts.   A sovereign who undertakes the exercise of his powers for his own interest rather than the interests of the nation is corrupt and ripe for rebellion and therein is his corporal punishment by man.   Failing in his duty to protect private property such a sovereign abrogates the divine right of kings and jeopardizes his soul before God.   Acts of corruption by a corporate officer or other agent are ethical, legal and moral violations. Acts of corruption by the sovereign are ethical and moral violations since the sovereign can do no wrong in a legal sense.   Thus, a corrupt sovereign is punishable by rebellion and his soul punishable under God's law.

Throughout this book, I have emphasized that the exercise of freewill is essential to the creation of wealth.   Freewill in the context of a wealth creating economy is unencumbered action or inaction by the individual.   This means that an individual enjoys the freedom to contract, which is the freedom to exchange private property, or the freedom not to contract.   As long as the freedom to exchange private property is unencumbered then the actual exchange that takes place is the measure of the actual value of the private property exchanged.   This value is independent of the cost to create or improve the property.   Acts of freewill however can also destroy wealth and this is the reason that there must be limits to the exercise of individual freewill. Limits to the exercise of freewill are essential for the protection of private property and the enforcement of contracts. The sovereign imposes such limits through law and enforces the law through the power of eminent domain. God imposes limits to acts of freewill through his Commandments and the disposition of the soul. The purpose of God's Ten Commandments is to facilitate the creation of wealth in order to protect and shield a man from calamity both physical and spiritual. In this way, Man remains immortal as God ordained Man to be.

Acts of freewill engendered by envy are subject to the Commandments of God as is envy also subject to the Commandment of God. Contracts themselves also impose limits to freewill. Contracts rely on the self-discipline of the individual, and in the absence of self-discipline then the sovereign imposes limits to freewill through the adjudication of contracts and the sovereign power of eminent domain. Competition in an unencumbered economy also limits the exercise of freewill arising from greed. Acts of freewill therefore are ethical or unethical depending on whether or not they engender the creation of wealth within the limits imposed by God and by sovereign law. In all cases where acts of freewill destroy the ability to create wealth or destroy wealth they are inherently unethical, whether performed by an individual, an individual acting on behalf of another or an individual acting as sovereign. In the case of sovereign, the power of eminent domain is a license to destroy individual wealth including taking an individual life to secure wealth in general and therein is the divine power of kings.

True noble behavior is behavior that is directed to the creation of wealth because the creation of wealth is a hedge against calamity and therefore essential for survival and perpetuation of the individual. Altruism manifested as the sacrifice of one's life or a portion of one's life for another is faux noble behavior. By a portion of one's life, I mean a portion of an individual's time or labor or a portion of one's wealth. Superficially and naively, such a sacrifice appears to be a one-way transaction based on empathy or charity. Altruism when manifested as charity however engenders gratitude in a God fearing man who is the beneficiary of the charity, and gratitude is a form of debt so while it appears as a one-way transaction in fact it is not. Accordingly, the failure to pay the debt is a loss of wealth whether that debt is through an act of charity or not. Acts of charity therefore are accumulations of debt and failure to pay back the debt is a loss of wealth and consequently a reduction of the ability of the individual who acts charitably to survive a calamity. Unrequited charity therefore is unethical and to the extent that it destroys the life and property of the benefactor, unrequited charity is immoral as well.

The Wealth Creating Economy – a summary

Before I discuss socialism and communism in more detail, I would like to summarize what I have presented thus far. The economy that I have described is a wealth creating economy. A wealth creating economy has the highest probability of withstanding any given calamity when compared to an encumbered and a godless capitalism, and especially when compared to socialism or communism. Socialism and communism as manifestations of man's envy are in fact calamities in themselves. The wealth creating economy comes into existence to mitigate fear of the future. It has naturally evolved from a God fearing feudal economy where all property including the life of the serfs is in the hands of the sovereign lord who is the protector. England's economy is the quintessential example of the evolution of a wealth creating economy from a feudal economy. This evolution to a wealth creating economy occurred with the emergence of private property secured by the sovereign. A wealth creating economy is an unencumbered economy that engenders optimism in individuals and optimism promotes investment and continuous wealth creation. The optimism is due to the opportunity or potential for the individual creation of individual wealth as engendered by the experience of others. Private property and the exercise of individual freewill through contract are the two basic principles that give rise to such an economy, which is an economy of free enterprise. In a wealth creating economy, competition regulates greed. The individuals comprising a wealth creating economy naturally form a nation under God and appoint or elect a sovereign to protect them. The existence of opportunity, the fear of God and faith in God suppress envy and replace envy with the desire to emulate the creation of wealth through opportunity and optimism. Thus in a God fearing wealth creating economy there is a desire to emulate others, which is greed, and not to deny others what they have, which is envy. An example is the American British Colonies at the time of their independence. The nation the Americans formed arose through rebellion whereby they overthrew the existing sovereign by force as the existing sovereign overburdened them through regulations and taxation. The new sovereignty took the form of a constitutional republic under God. In a nation formed under God, the fear of God and opportunity holds envy at bay thereby enabling the continuous creation of wealth. Thus, the new nation created great wealth achieving world power status within 100 years after its independence while at the same time contributing myriad innovations and inventions that furthered the material and thus economic progress of mankind.

God anoints the sovereign with the divine right of king, i.e. God holds the king's soul harmless for his acts as sovereign, and by extension God also holds the soul of the soldier harmless. The sovereign's only duty to the nation is to protect private property and adjudicate laws and contracts. To perform this duty the nation accords to the sovereign the power of eminent domain, which is the power to take life and property. The sovereign who fears God acts morally and ethically in exercising the power of eminent domain, i.e. by means of due process. The fear of God as well as the preservation of opportunity must guide and inform the laws enacted by the sovereign in a wealth creating economy. As the sovereign exercises the power of eminent domain, he necessarily encumbers the economy. The exercise of the sovereign power of eminent domain manifests in laws, which include taxation, and regulations. The power of eminent domain is absolute as it necessarily involves the taking of life and property against the will of the individual with no recourse for the individual but rebellion.

The less encumbered an economy the greater the wealth created. In a wealth creating economy, only supply and demand of goods and services determines the price of a good or service and there is no monetary inflation or monetary deflation. Rapid gains in productivity arising from paradigm shifts in technology do not lead to unemployment in a wealth creating economy only to the creation of more wealth. The economy must continuously create wealth or the economy and the nation will fall to calamity, which is great poverty, and destruction of life and property. Productivity or the ability to produce goods and services efficiently from increasingly scarce resources must continuously increase to create wealth. The source of gains in productivity is technology, which is the product of human genius. When human genius fails then gains in productivity cease and wealth creation also ceases thus an economy and a nation fails. Failure is the inability of a nation to survive a calamity. This is the experience of the ancient Greeks and Romans as well as many modern European nations such as Portugal and modern Greece. The failure to produce human genius arises from the admixture of the less intelligent dark skinned races of mankind with the Caucasian Race. Human genius only exists in the Caucasian Race and it manifests in the dominance of Western Civilization in both the ancient and the modern world. .

The greatest calamity that can befall a wealth creating economy is a godless sovereign who encumbers the economy in order to remain in power thus returning to a wealth destroying feudal state. To encumber an economy the sovereign must first engender envy in the population and this he accomplishes by eliminating the fear of God from the population. If God does not exist then there is no fear of God therefore envy is unleashed and the sovereign becomes the means by which the envious satiate their passion. Thus, we see the Reign of Terror, the Holocaust, the Stalin Purges, the emaciation of the Ukraine, the Chinese Cultural Revolution, the Cuban Revolution, and on and on. These events have two things in common, a godless sovereign, and an envious populace who desired the destruction of those that were their economic betters more than they desired the things their economic betters owned. Just as Cain desired the destruction of his brother Abel more than he desired what Abel owned which was the favor of God. The destruction of Abel meant more to Cain than did God's favor or the love of his brother and honor of his parents and such is the power of envy.

Ethical behavior is any behavior that leads to the creation of wealth

Up to now, I have presented a view of ethics focused on the creation of wealth as the aim of all human activity. I have defined ethical behavior as behavior directed toward the creation of wealth. I called this view of an economy the wealth creating economy. Unethical behavior therefore is behavior directed to undermining the creation of wealth or leading to the destruction of wealth. The actual destruction of wealth or the ability to create wealth is immoral behavior and therefore subject to God's judgment. I have defined wealth as the hedge against calamity and necessary for the survival of the individual and the nation. Private property and the unencumbered exercise of individual freewill in the formation of contracts are necessary for the creation of wealth. Private property can only exist if secured through force or the threat of force, and the exercise of individual freewill in contract formation can only take place if there is no coercion. A nation under God, i.e. a nation whose individuals and sovereign fear God and have faith in God, protects private property and secures the exercise of individual freewill in the formation of contracts. The nation appoints or elects a sovereign and endows him with the powers of eminent domain to protect private property and enforce contracts. Thus, with an exchange of some private property and some loss in liberty then the nation obtains protection and security enabling the creation of wealth, i.e. the hedge against calamity. In the absence of calamity, wealth eases the burden of life. This is the basic view regarding God and wealth that I have advanced thus far. In this view, there is also the assumption that the nation is comprised of individuals with an average IQ around 100, which are mainly nations whose majority populations are pure Caucasoid or pure Mongoloid. I refer to this view of a nation and its economy as the wealth creating view. However, there are other views that I would like to briefly address and contrast with the present view. These are the views of capitalism, socialism and communism. Each of these views relies on a unique understanding of the aim of human activity i.e. the greatest good for the greatest number in the case of capitalism or the greatest good for the average number in the case of socialism and communism. As I will show, none of these views accounts for human activity directed to the creation of wealth as a hedge against calamity and therefore these views lack an ethical or moral basis. It is the creation of wealth as a hedge against calamity that I argue is the ethical and moral basis for all human activity and the formation of a nation under God is essential for that purpose.

The fear of God distinguishes a wealth creating economy from capitalism

Capitalism as an economic philosophy argues that the aim of all human activity is utilitarian, i.e. the greatest good for the greatest number, achieved through individuals pursuing their own their self-interest. The view that the aim of all human activity is to create wealth is most consistent with capitalism. Capitalism sees individual happiness as an end in itself while I argue that happiness is the absence of fear or at least the mitigation of fear. Happiness is not an end in itself but a product or an outcome of the true end of capitalism, which is the creation of wealth. The creation of wealth is an ethical and moral pursuit and therefore meaningful. When an individual fears God, he acts to mitigate that fear, thus he does not sin and he keeps God's Commandments. Under capitalism's view, the purpose of wealth is to engender happiness, however I argue that the purpose of wealth is to overcome fear and it is the absence of fear that is happiness. These are two fundamentally different views of the proper purpose and aim of human activity as each gives rise to a different motivation. Capitalism as an economic system is comfortable in a secular or godless context because it is amoral or at least it has evolved from a wealth creating economic philosophy in the last 100 years to become amoral, thus happiness or even hedonism has become the aim or end of capitalism to many minds. Accordingly, we see much behavior in a secular capitalist economy that is harmful to the protection of private property and the exercise of individual freewill. In particular, there is an engendering of envy in a highly encumbered secular capitalist economy, wherein a large wealth gap exists among politically equal individuals, i.e. where universal suffrage exists. The fear of God distinguishes a wealth creating economy from a secular capitalist economy. The fear of God operates in two arenas in a wealth creating economy, the proscription of envy, and the minimization of encumbrances, i.e. laws imposed by the sovereign.

The overriding dictum in a modern secular capitalism is for an individual not to harm another individual while the former individual pursues his happiness, which conflates with self-interest. Presumably, only the sovereign punishes or makes whole any harm done by one individual to another and there is no moral component to the harm done only the legal component enforced by the sovereign. This is a flawed view because it precludes the existence of God. The atheist and influential philosopher John Stuart Mill who was also an advocate of universal suffrage espoused the view that any act is ethical or moral as long as it does no harm to another. Such a godless view engenders man's envy, which is a cause of calamity in the form of socialism or communism. Although capitalism accounts for man's greed through the mechanism of competition, its dictum, i.e. do no harm to another as espoused by Mill, fails to account or regulate man's envy. The fallacy in this dictum is that there is no passion to compel man to do no harm to another. In fact, just the opposite is true, as history and experience has shown repeatedly. Mill's dictum does not regulate the passion of envy, only the fear of God and faith in God can rein in envy. As shown throughout this book man's envy is proscribed by God and in a godless nation with a capitalist economy, man's envy engenders the destruction of wealth. Therefore, the weakness in the encumbered and secular, i.e. Stoic capitalist view of the purpose of human activity is that it fails to account for man's envy. Envy gives rise to the view that the aim of human activity is to achieve the greatest good for the average number. This view manifests in socialism and communism. Socialism and communism are modern godless feudal economies and not natural states of man rather these economic systems spring from an immoral, godless, and Stoic capitalism. Socialism and communism differ from ancient feudalism in their atheism. Thus, feudalism lasted for centuries whereas historically socialist and communist nations collapse after two or three generations because these socialist and communist nations destroy wealth and invariably run out of other people's money.

Under a capitalist economy, the sovereign owes duty or allegiance to the individuals who appointed or elected him. As in the case with a wealth creating economy, the sovereign in a capitalist economy protects private property and enforces contracts. In order for a capitalist economy to achieve the greatest good for the greatest number, the sovereign cannot be over burdensome. This means that taxes are low and applied uniformly and there is minimal regulation as well as no enforcement of coercive contracts. Coercive contracts are contracts that are executed which contain terms and conditions against the freewill of one or more of the parties. Labor contracts with employers are coercive contracts and the enforcement of such contracts by the sovereign encumbers an economy. When individuals form a nation under God to secure a capitalist economy, then the nation becomes a wealth-creating nation of the sort that I have been describing. This was the United States after the American Revolution. When a nation is a secular, i.e. godless nation and attempts to secure a capitalist economy then that nation engenders envy amongst the individuals and the economy eventually becomes socialist, which is destructive of wealth creation. This was the aftermath of the French Revolution with the rise of Napoleon as Napoleon sought the wealth of Europe to appease the envy of the French populace. A socialist economy will either fail by succumbing to a calamity or become communist, which is a calamity. For France Napoleon was the calamity. After Napoleon, France increasingly became a capitalist economy with the protection of private property now embodied in the Declaration of the Rights of Man.

Although France remained more secular than were her neighbors.   After World War II, France, like the rest of Europe including Britain resumed her march to socialism, which began in the later part of the 19th Century. Once a nation and an economy become communist then the nation and the economy will fail whether there is any other calamity or not because a communist economy results in the continuous destruction of wealth.   A communist economy is itself the calamity.   This was the example of Russia after the Tsars.   Many European nations have become increasingly godless, i.e. Stoic following World War II and thus their economies have become socialist as the sovereign tries to appease envy by redistribution and thus the destruction of wealth.   The economically and intellectually weaker nations such as Greece and Portugal are unlikely to survive as independent nations soon as they find it increasingly difficult to sustain their welfare spending.   Rebellion is brewing in Europe and eventually there will be war as nations begin to arm themselves in order to steal from their neighbors to sustain their socialism.

A capitalist economy most aligns with a wealth creating economy however, its tolerance for a secular sovereign as well as its tendency to be generally tolerant of godlessness in all its forms makes it susceptible to envy and therein lays its weakness.   God proscribes envy.   Absent God then envy replaces fear as the nationally dominant human passion and socialism and eventually communism emerges.   Socialism and communism are the economic systems that satiate envy and envy is only satiated through the deliberate destruction of the wealth of the individual envied.   A secular capitalism leads to socialism, or worse yet communism, which is the inability of the economy to create wealth. The inability to create wealth subjects the economy and the nation to calamity.   In order for a capitalist economy to survive, it must exist as a nation under God and reject or even punish tolerance of godlessness in all its forms, and the sovereign must fear God and profess his dedication to liberty, i.e. the freedom to contract.   To a God fearing sovereign the profession of liberty is sufficient because only a God fearing sovereign does not bear false witness.   In other words in order for a capitalist economy and thus a nation to survive it must be a wealth creating economy.

The case for socialism stems from envy and not fear

The case for socialism stems from envy and not fear.   The socialist's view is that the goal of human activity or an economy is the greatest good for the average number achieved through individual altruism brought about forcibly by the state, i.e. through laws and the sovereign power of eminent domain.   The greatest good for the average number translates to material equality for all except for the sovereign who is the benefactor and therefore worthy of exaltation.   Socialism relies on the flawed notions of egalitarianism and Stoicism wherein all men are equal in all aspects and chance or corruption in some manner accounts for the differences in wealth. Those espousing socialism believe the source of civil unrest to be the difference in individual wealth brought about by chance or corruption, which to a socialist is how capitalism works. Thus by eliminating or mitigating the difference in wealth through law, i.e. through force, then there will be peace, harmony, and happiness, i.e. nirvana. Nirvana is the return to the Garden of Eden that God denied Man. Socialism therefore is a defiance of God and that is the reason it will always fail with the destruction of those that espouse and subscribe to it. Socialists believe that an economy is a zero sum game so that one individual always profits at the expense of another. The purpose of the socialist and Stoic sovereign is to remedy this condition and by so doing mitigate envy. They believe that since the total wealth of a nation is a fixed amount then with fewer individuals around each individual will have more of that wealth. Socialists make the self-serving argument that the Earth is a finite planet and the Earth's resources are limited therefore there are only so many people that the Earth's resources can support. This argument is analogous to the labor theory of value, and consistent with the view that the economy is a zero sum game. Thus the fewer the number of individuals then the wealthier and happier they will each be and the more likely mankind will survive and the closer to nirvana will he be. Thus, population control is an imperative of socialists because the fewer individuals the better for all, or at least for the remaining chosen few. These flawed notions are at the root of the Malthusian and Keynesian Economics as well as Marxism. Unlike the purpose of the sovereign in a capitalist or wealth creating economy, the purpose of the sovereign in a socialist economy is to remedy the difference in wealth and reduce the likelihood that the difference will reemerge by eliminating the opportunity to create wealth, which includes the opportunity to bring forth progeny. Thus, socialists and communists encourage and promote abortion and other means of population control particularly for the less intelligent races. In this respect they are somewhat justified. To a socialist war is a means of population control and therefore it is to be encouraged and entered into with great zeal. Woodrow Wilson provoked the German's by ignoring their warnings when they declared the seas around the United Kingdom to be a war-zone. Wilson deliberately failed to place a moratorium on Americans traveling overseas during a time of war although he could have done so. Had he done so then Americans would travel at their own risk and not be subject to the protection of the United States. Thus, events like the sinking of the Lusitania would not have been an act of war and create the excuse of going to war. The sinking of the Lusitania with the loss of 128 Americans on board provided the excuse that Wilson needed to murder more people by entering the war. At the time, Germany was on the verge of winning and ending the conflict. Had Germany won World War I we would have seen a unified Europe and there would not have been a World War II, although German socialism, which engendered the war may have still led to later conflict. Indeed Europe as well as Britain continued on their march toward socialism after WWI ended in any case. Similarly, FDR refused to sell oil to Japan on the pretext that they invaded Manchuria thus provoking Japan to attack the United States and leading to more deaths. FDR revealed his true motives for provoking the Japanese and entering World War II when he refused to interrupt the Holocaust when told about it and had the ability to do it. His true motive is the elimination of populations as is the true motive and objective of all socialism and communism. Thus, we see among the compliant media and educational establishment the elevation of Wilson, FDR, and Stalin, Mao, Castro and other socialist murders to almost god-like status. The only reason that the media and educational establishment publicly vilify the National Socialist Hitler is because he lost the war. I am sure however that in their hearts many socialists admire Hitler and seek out to this day individuals who can emulate the scope of his accomplishments, i.e. the efficient elimination of large numbers of people.

Besides elimination of the hoi polloi, socialists also believe altruism is the means to remedy wealth inequality and thus remove the reason for envy by satiating the envy in the Stoic sense. John Rawls, the Harvard philosopher put forth such an idea in his overrated and flawed tome "The Theory of Justice". The mechanism used to achieve material equality is termed "social justice", which is one of the common misnomers or euphemisms used by socialist to disguise their true intentions. The method is actually social injustice. Altruism is acting to benefit another materially with little or no benefit in return including the gratitude of the beneficiary. In other words, it is self-imposed slavery. Altruism is antithetical to the creation of wealth and therefore the sovereign must impose altruism, as it does not arise from fear of the unknown, i.e. it does not arise from Natural Law. Fear of the unknown manifested in self-interest or self-preservation is the motivation for the creation of wealth. Altruism has as its economic basis the labor theory of value which is the flawed notion that the price of a good or service must be equal to the labor that goes into producing the good or providing the service. The labor theory of value ignores supply and demand as the determinant of price. The labor theory of value eschews ownership of private property. Since the value of a good or service is only in the labor to produce the good or service then private property can have no value. Eschewing private property means eschewing an individual's life and indeed this is the case in socialist and communist economies. Altruism also underpins the flawed notion that usury and profit are unethical as well as immoral. Envy engenders altruism because the envious view altruism as the source of redemption for the object of their envy, i.e. the wealthy. If only everybody acted for the "common good" instead of their own self-interest then there would not be any wealthy or any poor since everybody would possess the same things at the same time and thus envy would not exist. An altruistic nation therefore does not require the fear of God to rein in envy and thus Stoicism and atheism would prevail in such a nation. Recall that the Stoics believed that man's reason acting through his will, i.e. in Nietzsche's terms this is the "will to power" and the "will to power" can control man's passions. So goes the theory.

However, altruism is not a natural state of man, so the sovereign must impose it on men through force. In the world of John Rawls, the "invisible hand" of Adam Smith's capitalism becomes the visible fist of "social justice". Altruism manifests in the forced redistribution of wealth, which takes place absent rebellion only if there is an absence of fear including absence of the fear of God. The absence of fear only exists in wealthy and godless nations so altruism must first have as its basis wealth and godlessness, i.e. atheism, and second altruism requires means to impose it on men. Under an altruistic economy the sovereign serves a different purpose than he does under an economy that exists to create wealth, i.e. he is the benefactor to all or the provider of all, and not the protector of individual life and property. Individual life and private property exist only through the grace of the sovereign as benefactor or provider, and the sovereign apportions all life and property as he sees fit. Thus we have terms as "rights of the people", the "common good", or the 'public good", or "fairness to all", or "separation of church and state", or "equality for all", or "social justice" appearing in the lexicon of the socialist and in public discourse. These terms also appear in judicial documents and court briefs as the socialist sovereign relies on these terms, and not on God's law or Natural Law to adjudicate contracts, as well as to enact and to enforce his laws imposing social justice. Socialism erroneously precludes the existence of calamity but it also erroneously precludes fear and in particular the fear of God. Socialism only arises after long periods of wealth creation, the absence of major calamity, and the accumulation of great wealth. Once a nation realizes that it has sufficient store or wealth and calamities are few, and far between the population becomes lulled into believing they have conquered nature and in particular man's nature. There arises a temptation among the populace in a capitalist economy to abandon the nation under God, to become more tolerant and adopt the sovereign as benefactor rather than protector. Socialism therefore cannot exist in Hobbes' primitive or natural state because socialism requires a preexisting store of wealth, but in Hobbes' primitive or natural state, there is no store of wealth. In an economy founded on envy, as all socialists economies are, the individuals have a duty to the sovereign who must take on the role of benefactor. In an economy founded on fear including the fear of God, i.e. an economy for the creation of wealth, the sovereign is protector and not benefactor. In an economy founded on envy the sovereign power of eminent domain exists primarily to serve the "common good" or "public good" and not for the protection of private property. A socialist economy suppresses the exercise of freewill as freewill threatens the sovereign's authority and creates wealth, so there is little contract formation. The creation and accumulation of wealth threatens the socialist sovereign as it serves as a catalyst for rebellion. Consequently, adjudication directs toward the enforcement of criminal law and less toward the enforcement of civil law. Acting in one's self-interest, or in other words profiting from ones enterprise is a crime or nearly a crime in a socialist state. In a socialist economy private property and life exists through the grace of the sovereign and not through the grace of God. The absence or denial of God is essential for a socialist nation to come into existence since God proscribes envy and envy is the foundation of socialism. A nation begun as a nation under God, i.e. with faith in God and for the purpose of protecting private property and enforcing contracts must first abandon its faith in God before it becomes a socialist state. Socialism and the fear of God are mutually exclusive, as one cannot exist with the other. Historically this has been the case. An economy founded on fear, and which creates wealth and a nation under God must always precede an economy founded on envy and a nation devoid of a faith in God or fear of God. Because wealth is the hedge against calamity, a nation that creates no wealth will eventually fail since calamity is inevitable. An economy founded on envy, i.e. a socialist economy must fail and historically all such economies have indeed failed and have been replaced by an economy founded on fear including the fear of God, and the creation of wealth. Socialism as an economic system is therefore fundamentally unethical as it is unstable since it fails to create wealth thus subjecting the nation to calamity.

A communist economy relies on envy

A communist economy also relies on envy. Unlike socialism communism springs from a feudal economy or evolves from a socialist economy. All it takes to convert from a feudal economy to a communist economy is to eliminate the fear of God and replace it with the fear of the state. This is the history of the USSR in the first decades of the twentieth century. Therefore, for a nation to become communist it must first abandon its faith in God because God proscribes envy. In this regard, communism is similar to socialism. Where socialism tolerates some private property and some exercise of individual freewill in contracting, communism is the complete elimination of private property, and no exercise of individual freewill exists, i.e. contracting between individuals does not exist. All property including the life of the individuals is in common and belongs to the sovereign. This is also true of property rights in inventions or patents. Under the old Soviet Union, all inventions belonged to the state, and the inventor had no ownership in his ideas. It is little wonder that no inventions of any great significance came out of the old Soviet Union despite the high average IQ of the Russians. The same is true of Communist China. The Communist Chinese to this very day do not respect the rights of foreign patents and copyrights for this reason. Foreign patent and copyright infringement is a daily occurrence in Communist China. Contrast this with the Nationalist Chinese of Taiwan who are very wealthy and respect all private property and who themselves have many patents. The same is true of the Japanese and the South Koreans. In a communist nation, the sovereign goes from mere benefactor as in a socialist economy to the provider of all goods and services. The sovereign owns all the means of production including the lives of the individuals comprising the nation. Accordingly, he can dispose of them as he pleases with no recourse to the citizens but rebellion. Under communism, the individuals stop being individuals and now become "the people" or "the masses", or the "hoi polloi". Also under communism, the value of the labor that produces the goods or provides the services is the sole determinant of the price of goods and services. The state sets prices and they are independent of supply and demand, accordingly the state determines both the supply and the demand for goods and services. The state determines the goods made, and services provided as well as the quantity of goods and services. The state however has a more difficult task in controlling the quality of goods and services because there is no competition. Accordingly, the communist nations are notorious for the poor quality of their goods and services. Under communism, an economy creates no wealth and therefore it is unable to withstand a calamity. Hence, a communist economy must fail and always does fail. A failed economy is an economy that does not create wealth and succumbs to calamity. It fails to meet the basic needs of the individuals comprising the nation originally formed to secure the economy. This is borne out historically. All communist and atheistic economies have indeed failed. In some cases, the failure is catastrophic as in the case of the German National Socialists or NAZI. As with a socialist economy, a communist economy can only come into being from an economy that is creating wealth or directly from a feudal economy. In other words, a communist economy cannot exist in a primitive or natural state because its foundation is envy and not fear, thus it cannot create wealth it can only consume wealth. Communism is nothing more than a return to a feudal economy with the only difference being the sovereign feared God under feudalism and protected his serfs. The communist sovereign does not fear God so he is not compelled to protect individuals. To the communist sovereign individuals are expendable and individuals exist to serve the state. This was the case with the USSR, Germany under National Socialism, and currently under

Communist China, Cuba, and North Korea among others.

Under a communist economy, the sovereign is provider or in other words, he is as a god and feared as a god. Sustenance and favors all come from the sovereign and just as they come from the sovereign, the sovereign can take them and more. Communism is essentially a centrally planned economy without regard to supply and demand but based instead on the sovereign's invariably flawed opinion on the needs of the nation. Prices of goods and services are set by the state as are wages and salaries and these quantities are independent of supply and demand. In order for a communist economy to be sustainable for any period, the sovereign must appeal continuously to altruism in order to meet the needs of the nation. This appeal manifests in meaningless slogans such as for the "good of the people" or the "common good". As envy is the foundation passion of a communist economy, and there is no wealth creation, the sovereign must instead create enemies, which continuously engender envy. These enemies are typically neighbor nations or even easily identifiable individuals within a nation who are not part of the ruling class as in the case of the Jews in Germany under National Socialism. Accordingly, a communist sovereign must continuously attack and take wealth from his neighbors or the easily identifiably elements of his population in order to sustain himself. A communist economy must feed on its neighbors since it creates no wealth. Communist revolutions are and must be never ending and admittedly so. A communist nation inevitably engenders fear in its neighbors, thus giving rise to wealth creation in the neighbor nations. Ironically, the existence of a communist state creates more wealth in its neighboring states enabling the neighboring states to protect themselves from the aggression of the communist state. Finally, the communist state collapses from its inability to feed on its neighbors by warring with them. A communist state thus contains the seed of its own collapse. This is exactly the fate of the old Soviet Union as the United States grew wealthier in order to protect itself and Western Europe while the Soviet Union grew poorer as it tried to assert itself but could not in the face of the might of the US military, which arose from the wealth creation of the United States. This was a deliberate strategy undertaken by the United States after World War II and known as containment. It came to fruition under President Reagan with the collapse of the USSR in 1989.

The divine right of king does not extend to a sovereign who fails to secure private property, and God disposes the soul of the sovereign of a communist or socialist state accordingly. Recall the role of the sovereign in a socialist economy is benefactor, i.e. a distributor or re-distributor of goods and services, while the role of sovereign in a communist economy is provider or producer of goods and services. Socialist and communist sovereignties are not protectors of private property. Thus, they create no wealth and subject their nations to calamity threatening the immortality of the human race as ordained by God. God therefore, condemns the soul of the communist or socialist sovereign and by extension, the soldier of a communist or socialist state as they have sinned before God by failing to secure the immortality of man through the creation of wealth. A communist and socialist nation thus condemns their sons and the souls of their sons while they seek the destruction of the wealth of others, just as Cain condemned himself and his progeny through the envy and murder of his brother.

At this point, it is significant to note the difference between a God fearing capitalist nation conquering and subjugating another nation and thus imposing its sovereignty and a godless socialist nation conquering and subjugating another nation and imposing its sovereignty. God does not condemn a capitalist nation subjugating and colonizing another nation because such colonization redounds to the benefit of mankind. The greater nation conquered the lesser nation because the lesser nation failed to create sufficient wealth to enable it to secure itself from calamity. The process of colonization and subjugation remedies that condition. If it does not then the nation is once again subject to calamity. God condemns a communist nation conquering and subjugating another nation because the conquest is to take the wealth of the weaker nation not to create wealth. This is the example of National Socialist Germany and of Imperial Japan. It would also be the story of North Korea, were it not for the intervention of the United States.

Truth and Beauty

In my introduction, I said that truth and beauty inexorably bind with wealth creation. When I speak of truth, I mean not only the truth of facts but also the truth of ideas. Facts relate to indisputable events or acts occurring in the past. Facts are also verifiable physical principles or laws. Accordingly, a fact is true because it is indisputable. A fact is absolute only when it comes from God. Thus, it is an absolute fact that the Ten Commandments exist to judge a man's soul whether men acknowledge them or not. A disputed fact is an opinion or a belief. Proof is necessary for an opinion to become fact. A fact contradicting an opinion will render the opinion as not true. If no fact can contradict the opinion then the opinion is not necessarily true, but a fact supporting an opinion makes the opinion true. A belief is an unshakeable opinion, i.e. individuals take ideas to be true even if facts contradict the belief. There is always tremendous destruction of wealth and impoverishment of the nation when beliefs fail to comport with the facts, i.e. when beliefs manifest in laws despite facts that contradict beliefs. For instance, many minds take the belief to be true that all men are equal in all aspects despite the existence of facts that prove it to be otherwise. Accordingly, legislatures pass anti-discrimination laws that interfere with contracts on the belief that individuals discriminate on characteristics other than physical or mental ability necessary for the creation of wealth. Thus, we have the spectacle of the Negroid entering professions mandated by law where he cannot possibly perform due to his naturally low level of intelligence. Facts form the basis of the adjudication of laws and contracts, and the prosecution of lawbreakers. The fact or stipulation of an event or an act determines whether the event or act is legal or illegal in a criminal proceeding. Similarly, the fact or stipulation of an event or act determines whether a contract breach has occurred in a civil proceeding. If the event or act is a fact then it is true.

For example, one can say that Columbus discovered America in 1492 is a fact. However, this fact is disputable. The dispute arises from the meaning of the word "discovered". America always existed so Columbus could not discover something that already existed. The fact that Columbus made America's existence known to Europe in 1492 is the truth. On the other hand, Pythagoras actually discovered the Pythagorean Theorem. The Theorem of Pythagoras is a mathematical algorithm whose manifestations exist in the mind of God. Mathematical algorithms exist only in the human mind, whereas a continent exists apart from the mind of man although it exists in the mind of God. The revelation of the Theorem of Pythagoras is indeed a discovery, while Columbus made America's existence known to the European mind.

Truth therefore exists in degrees or measures of fact. The measure of truth is the attention to detail about the fact or facts comprising the truth. The greater the detail in a statement of fact, then the higher the degree of truth contained within the statement and the more closely aligned is the statement to reality. The attention to detail that an individual demonstrates in his work and behavior aligns with the intelligence of the individual. The extent of detail within the institutions of a nation aligns with the intellectual capital or the highest intellectual capacity of a nation. Attention to detail in the study of mathematics, the composition of a piece of music or painting, the design of a bridge or building all reflect on the intelligence of the individuals comprising the nation. A measure of the genius of an individual is the degree of the attention to detail expressed in his work or acts. The greater the attention to detail in a man's work, then the closer the work is to the truth and the greater the genius.

Truth in art is in its attention to the detail of the object or idea that the art is rendering. Beauty in art or in any other product of the hand and mind of a man is the degree to which the attention to detail depicts that which is pleasing to the senses. Abstraction in any form is by definition something that is not pleasing to the senses and therefore ugly. Abstraction means away from reality or away from truth.

Man can direct his genius to the destruction of wealth

Man can direct his genius to the destruction of wealth as he can to the creation of wealth. Envy and greed direct man's genius. Robespierre, Napoleon, Hitler, Pol Pot, Mao, Castro, and Stalin are some of the most obvious and historically recent examples of the destructive power of man's genius directed by envy. Pol Pot, Mao, Castro, and Stalin were more enablers of the evil genius of others through their ruthlessness than they themselves were geniuses. The only factor that prevents man from directing his genius to the destruction of wealth is the fear of God. The risk inherent in a secular capitalist nation is the rise of men of evil genius engendered by envy. Once a nation's economy becomes a socialist economy then men of evil genius have indeed risen and calamity has befallen the nation. Men with evil genius seek to substitute themselves for God in the hearts and conscience of others. Evil genius manifests in politics more so than in any other area of human activity, although such men exist in philosophy, art, literature, religion, law, and science. Even the mundane profession of journalism has its men of evil genius. H.L. Mencken an influential journalist and atheist during the first part of the twentieth century was one such man. Mencken was an admirer of Friedrich Nietzsche, himself an atheist who probably did more than anyone else did to place much of Western Civilization on a secular and ultimately wealth destructive course. Mencken's writing promoted and popularized the atheism of Nietzsche thus setting the stage for the mass murder and wealth destruction of the first half of the twentieth century. The idea that God is dead is the single most wealth destroying idea to take hold in the twentieth century. Similarly, with Walter Duranty another journalist who also was an atheist and who had no compunction about lying, as most atheists are not compelled to be truthful since they deny the existence of God. Duranty lied about the mass murder of millions of people by Stalin during the purges of the 1920s and 1930s. His lies won him the Pulitzer Prize and encouraged the acts of Stalin thus paving the way for Hitler to accomplish the same thing by fiat. Hitler saw that the world did not object nor even express outrage at Stalin's purges and thus he correctly reasoned that there would be no objection to his purges. Duranty was as much responsible for the Holocaust as was Hitler. Duranty set the standard in terms of lying for most journalists up until even this day. Men of evil genius cultivate the envy inherent in their fellow man to enable them to control and subjugate him. Thus we have a Karl Marx for instance who first dismisses religion as the "opiate of the people" setting the stage for the revolution of the envious proletariat against the object of their envy the "decadent" bourgeoisie. The unspeakable horror and the enormous and unprecedented destruction of wealth unleashed by the atheistic philosophers of the middle eighteenth and early twentieth century is a testament to the power of envy among the godless.

The fact that God proscribes envy is an ancient testament to the utter destructiveness of this single passion. In a sense envy in man is the real consequence of man's fall from Grace and a continuous reminder of the existence of God. A nation, whose individuals and sovereign fear God, minimizes the risk associated with man's evil genius. The fear of God among the American populace served to mute the evil genius of Woodrow Wilson and FDR who sought to institutionalize envy, for example, in comparison to their more expressive likeminded contemporaries such as Lenin, Hitler and Stalin. The latter are the true inheritors of the French Revolution and its horrors. Nevertheless, Wilson, FDR, and their fellow ideologues, known as "the Progressives" managed to set in motion a secular government in the United States that quickly set itself apart from the nation's God-fearing individuals. Thus, there came into being the misguided and warped notion of "separation of Church and State" sanctioned under the FDR appointed Supreme Court, and earlier cynically manifested in the token fine of $100 against the teaching of evolution by John Scopes in the famous Tennessee v. John Scopes trial of 1925. The notoriety of the Scopes Trial, and the trivialization and mocking of the Biblical account of Creation that took place before the public during the trial, helped to usher in the secularization of the nation. Public schools have faithfully taught the theory of evolution as the legitimate explanation for the appearance of man on the earth since the 1930s, thus giving rise to generations of atheists. The result has been a decline in the fear of God and a faith in God among the United States population with the concomitant tendency among the populace to look to the sovereign as not only the taker of life and property, which is the proper and wealth-enabling role, but also as the provider or giver of life and property. Since the Second World War, the Federal government has relentlessly driven secularization of the nation by promoting and supporting atheistic groups and individuals through laws and court rulings. Groups such as the government funded ACLU, Planned Parenthood, the National Education Association, and others have fought hard to eliminate the faith in God and the fear of God from the public discourse and replace Him with the Stoic wealth destroying humanistic shibboleths of equalitarianism and altruism. The rise of the non-profit corporation, tax supported public television and radio, and various atheistic philanthropic funds, have helped to fuel and sustain the flawed notions of equalitarianism and altruism. The result of their efforts is beginning to bear fruit as atheism, and envy is on the rise with the destruction of wealth and wealth creation accelerating as a result. The election of Democrats is the manifestation of the atheism and envy that grips the nation.

In a wealth creating economy, the closer the individuals' intellectual alignment to reality i.e. the higher the IQ, then the greater the wealth created by the economy. In other words, the closer to the truth that an economy functions then the wealthier it becomes.   The further away from the truth the less wealth created by the economy.   By reality, I mean ethical, moral and physical reality not the so-called reality arising from the interactions between individuals other than those interactions arising under contract and through marriage.   Any so-called reality that contradicts God's Commandments or the Laws of Nature is a corruption of the truth and therefore undermines the creation of wealth.   Thus, homosexual relationships, which have no possibility of progeny, are a corruption of the truth of God in the creation of man and woman.   So are all interracial relationships with the Negroid, which all have a high probability of low IQ offspring and significantly reduce the likelihood of genius.

Since a corruption of the truth undermines the creation of wealth, a corruption of the truth is unethical and if the corruption of the truth also contradicts God's Commandments, it is immoral as well.   The corruption of the truth is most insidious when such corruption manifests in law.   Laws govern and place limits on the freewill of individuals comprising the nation.   When the sovereign enacts laws contrary to the truth then such laws inevitably lead to unintended consequences and thus undermine the creation of wealth.   The Wagner Act of 1939, which I mentioned earlier is an example of a law that is contrary to the truth in that it goes against the Laws of Nature, i.e. the law of self-interest and the law of self-preservation.   The Wagner Act enables the Federal Government to enforce so-called labor contracts that are contracts between a labor union and a company.   Labor contracts introduce the idea of "collective bargaining" which ostensibly enables the negotiation of wages and benefits of the union members with the company.   However, the negotiation is invariably one sided and wages and benefits are dictated by the union under the threat of a strike which in many cases leads to a company going out of business.   Thus a union labor contract violates the Laws of Nature because it is exercised under the threat of force and therefore against the will of the owners and managers of the company, i.e. against the self-interests of the company.   While the intention of union labor contracts is to improve the wages and benefits of union members, the unintended consequence is the decline of industry, a decline in benefits and wages, and a decline in total employment.   This is indeed the result of the Wagner Act since its enactment in 1935 as the Act compromises the potential wealth creation arising from the industry of individuals.   The Wagner Act is a significant contributor to the fact that the 2012 GDP is only one-eightieth of what it could have been had government not interfered in the economy since 1929.   Thus, the Wagner Act compromised the truth as manifested in the freewill and self-interest of the individual and the result is a significant decline in the creation of wealth.   In a sense, the Wagner Act was a taking by the government of the freewill of individuals to contract and the result of the taking of individual freewill is a reduction in the creation of wealth and a lowering in the ability of a nation to withstand calamity.

Other laws that corrupt the truth and effectively take the freewill of the individual to contract impoverish and weaken the nation include most of the so-called environmental protection laws, endangered species act, affirmative action, The Civil Rights Act, tax laws, and all such laws that unnecessarily restrict the freedom to contract. Thus, truth is inexorably bound to the creation of wealth and its corruption inexorably bound to the destruction of wealth.

Beauty and wealth

The Greek word for beauty is κάλλος, which is also the word for "good". The ancient Greeks associated beauty with good as the same word described both aspects of an act, a person, or thing. Truth is also good and as beauty is good so too beauty is truth; quoting Keats from his aptly named Ode on a Grecian Urn – *"Beauty is truth, truth beauty"*. Beauty is the quality of an act, person, or thing that engenders a feeling of attraction or well-being and is pleasing to the senses. The act of creating wealth is beautiful because wealth engenders a feeling of well-being to the creator since it secures his future from calamity. Hence, profit is beautiful. Although in a secular economy profit also arises from evil genius and to the degree that it does speaks to the degree of the corruption of truth and the eventual elimination of the ability to create profit and hence the destruction of the economy. Profit arising from the corruption of truth contains the seed of its own destruction. Thus, the profit arising from the creation of abstract art or profit arising from the application of green-energy is profit arising from the corruption of truth and such profit is akin to thievery. Beauty is an attribute of wealth and wealth creation in a God fearing economy where no corruption of truth exists. The wealthier a God fearing nation becomes then the more beautiful its institutions and its sentient manifestations, i.e. the more beautiful its art, its music, its literature, and its architecture. It is obvious that wealthy nations contain greater beauty than poor nations. It is also indisputable that wealthy nations produce beautiful art, music, literature and architecture. Greece and Rome for example, created great wealth and great beauty and while they were not Christian nations, they were not atheists. Much of beauty within these disciplines is a beauty of form characterized by symmetry and attention to detail. Symmetry and attention to detail are also characteristics of a high degree of intellectual capital, i.e. high IQ. Beauty binds to wealth through the intellect. A high level of intellectual capital within a nation produces a high level of beauty and a high level of wealth. Just as beauty is a product of the wealth of a nation, it is also a harbinger of its future in the sense that a decline in the beauty inherent in a nation's institutions and sentient manifestations portends a decline in the intellectual capital of the nation.

This eventually leads to an inability to create wealth thus making a nation susceptible to calamity. The decline of the Roman Empire followed an accompanying decline in the frequency of notable art as shown by the following timeline.

800 B.C.	600 B.C.	500 B.C.	400 B.C.	300 B.C.	200 B.C.	100 B.C.	0-100 A.D.	100 A.D.	200 A.D.	300 A.D.	400 A.D.	500 A.D.
The first primitive cottages on the Palatine.	560 v. Chr. The temples of Diana, Fortuna and Mater Matuta are build.	497 Temple of Saturnus is build.	387 The city walls of Rome are rebuilt.	Blossom-time of the Roman firm earthwork-industries.	200 The Greek art is brought to Rome.	78 Tabularium.	Augustus executes a build a program for Rome.	112 Consecoration of the Forum of Tajanus.	216 The Thermae of Caracalla are build in Rome, in	The bow of Constantine.	Mosaics in churces in Ravenna.	537-560 The Hagia Sophia in Constantinople is rebuilded.
Rockgraves in Caere.	Servius Tullius builds city walls.	493 Temple of Ceres is build.	312 The Via Appia and the Aqua Appia are built.	221 Cirus Flaminius build.	184 The Basilica Porcia is build on the Roman Empire.	55 The Theater of Pompeius is build.	79 Consecoration of the Colosseum.	118-128 The Parthenon is rebuilded.	Church buildings program in Rome, Jerusalem and Constantinople.			
The Forum Romanum is build; first permanent buildings of store in Rome.	Temple of Jupiter Capitolinus is build.	484 Temple of Castor is build.			179 The Basilica Aemilia and the Port Aemilius are build.	46 The Forum of Caesar is build.		126-134 Villa Hadriana, Tivoli.	271 Aurelianus builds city-walls around Rome.			
	509 Etruskian grave-paintings.	431 Temple of Apollo is build.			120 The Fortuna temple in Praeneste is build.	21 The bow of Augustus is build.						
						19 The Thermae of Agrippina are build.						
						17 The Theater of Marcellus is build.						
						2 The Forum of Augustus is build.						

Note that as the decline of the Roman Empire progressed, the amount of notable art declined. Similarly, with Roman literature, as shown below the decline of the empire also saw a decline in notable literature.

800 B.C.	600 B.C.	500 B.C.	400 B.C.	300 B.C.	200 B.C.	100 B.C.	0-100 A.D.	100 A.D.	200 A.D.	300 A.D.	400 A.D.	500 A.D.
	600 Oldest Latin inscriptions.	451 The Twelve Tables with Roman laws.		Important politician from this time: Appius Claudius Caecus.	Important playwrights from this time: Terentius and Accius.	Important lawyers and philosopher from this time: Cicero.	Important orator from this time: Seneca the Older.	Important poet from this time: Juvenalis.	Important lawyes from this time: Papinianus.	Important poets from this time: Ausonius and Claudianus.	404 Hieronymus translates the Old Testament into latin.	Important philosopher from this time: Boethius.
				Important playwright and poets from this time: Livius Andronicus, Naevius, Plautus, Ennius, Statius, Caecilius and Pacuvius.	Important historians from this time: L. Carpurnius Piso and Caelius Antipater.	Important historian from this time: Caesar.	Important poets historia from this time: Persius, Lucanus and Martialis.	Important poets historia from this time: this time: Suetonius. Ulpianus and	Important christian authors from this time: Ambrosius, Hieronymus and Augustinus.	Important historian from this time: Orosius.	Important historian and statesmin from this time: Cassiodorus.
					Important poets and philosopher from this time: Lucretius.	Important biologist from this time: Apuleius.	Important christian author from this time: Tertullianus.		Important orator from this time: Symmachus.	Important menof learning from this time: Servius and Macrobius. 429 Codex Theodosianus.	
				Important historian and men of learning from this time: Cato.	Important lawyers and politician from this time: C. Gracchus, L. Crassus and Q. Hortensius.	Important letter-writer from this time: Plinius the Younger.				Important poet from this time: Sidorius Apollinaris.	
					Important poets from this time: Catullus, Vergilius, Horatius, Tibullus, Propertius and Ovidius.	Important historian from this time: Tacitus.					

Note that Christianity helped to sustain Latin literature after the decline of Rome. Nevertheless, the decline in the frequency of notable literature occurred with the decline of the Roman Empire that began in 300AD. The decline in the frequency of notable art and literature occurred despite the increasing likelihood of extant art and literature with time. In other words, the decline is more profound than shown in the charts since the further back in time we go the fewer examples of notable art and literature that survive. The decline in the frequency of notable art and literature is a direct result of the decline in the intellectual capacity of the population. The increasingly mixed race population that comprised the declining centuries of the Roman Empire failed to produce

358

sufficient numbers of men of genius necessary to sustain the Empire, and to produce notable art and literature. This was the real underlying cause of the fall of the Roman Empire and it is the reason that all great nations and empires fail up until the modern era, i.e. after 1800. The inability of the Romans to produce genius is due to the admixture of the Romans with their less intelligent slaves who were of the dark race and mixed-races. The admixing had the effect of reducing the probability of men of genius in the population and thus the number of men of genius. Consequently, the Romans became susceptible to invasion from the north where admixture of the Caucasoid with the less intelligent races was nonexistent. The more intelligent northern Caucasoid Europeans, the Arian Visigoths, easily overtook the intellectually diminished Romans within 200 years after the Edict of Caracalla. The Edict of Caracalla of 212 AD granting Roman citizenship to all free men and women in the Roman Empire regardless of lineage, i.e. race, caused and hastened the decline of the Roman Empire. This was equivalent to our modern universal suffrage, which began in pre-Revolution France and manifested in the 15th and 19th Amendments of the United States Constitution. Caracalla was himself of mixed race ancestry having a Berber heritage. Unlike the Roman Emperors that preceded Caracalla, including Julius Caesar, Augustus, and Marcus Aurelius who distinguished themselves intellectually, Caracalla and his father Septimius Severus, whose name gave us the word "severe", and who lived up to his moniker, did little to distinguish themselves other than through the use of brute force - no attention to detail here. The reason for the Edict of Caracalla was to increase the tax base and to increase the population of available soldiers for the Roman army. It was a simple-minded approach to solve the problem of administering the Empire. This edict effectively eliminated any heretical proscriptions to the mixing with slaves and former slaves whose offspring now had rights and privileges once reserved to the Caucasoid Romans. The Edict of Caracalla accelerated the admixture and further reduced the probability of engendering men of genius in the population. The decline in the frequency of art and literature, which are indicative of that which is beautiful and indicative of wealth, followed the Edict of Caracalla. The Edict of Caracalla took place at a time of great monetary inflation in the Roman Empire and it had philosophical underpinnings embodied in the teachings of the Stoics who taught that all men are equal much like the so-called progressive ideology of the present time. The effect of the admixture between the darker races and the Caucasoid Roman was a lowering in the productive capacity of Rome that manifested itself in the inflation of its currency. Part of the reason for the lowering in the productive capacity was the increased tax burden brought upon by the demands of the government for more of the fruits of the labor of the Roman citizen. An interesting story from the time of Severus succinctly described the mixing of the races in Rome. During his campaign in British Caledonia, Severus' wife, Julia Domna, criticized the sexual morals of the British Caledonian women to the wife of Caledonian chief Argentocoxos. The wife of Argentocoxos replied, *"We fulfill the demands of nature in a much better way than do you Roman women; for we consort openly with the best men, whereas you let yourselves be debauched in secret by the vilest"*. It is needless to say, that the intellectually diminished Romans under Severus failed to take Caledonia and retreated back to Hadrian's Wall.

In order for significant admixture of races to occur there must be a change in the perception of beauty since beauty is a main factor in the attractiveness between a man and a woman particularly where the man an woman have high IQ's. The beauty of the woman correlates directly with her IQ and all women are attracted to men who display a high intelligence. Changes in perception of beauty indeed occurred and continue to occur. The prevailing philosophical outlook regarding the nature of man determines the perception of beauty and thus the comeliness of a mate at least among those with a high average IQ, i.e. 100.

During the period of the Roman Republic from the founding of Rome in the eighth century BC until the time of Marcus Aurelius, Romans regarded themselves correctly as intellectually superior to those they conquered, and they were indeed, otherwise they would not have succeeded in creating the greatest empire the world had known at the time. They were justified in thinking and believing in this manner as their art, literature, language, architecture, law, and engineering was far superior in the scope and attention to detail to those they conquered other than the Greeks from whom they descended and whose traditions they continued. Their concept of beauty as inherited from their Greek precursors manifested itself in appealing and satisfying, i.e. beautiful, forms that served to perpetuate the high level of intelligence in the Roman population as well as display their high intellect to the world. Roman art, literature, music and other intellectual accomplishments set the standard for beauty which governed the mating of men and women, and which led in turn to progeny of genius. Manliness and womanly beauty appear in the art of early Rome, which depicted idealized and anatomically detailed forms of men and women much akin even superior to that of their Greek precursors. Similarly, in the architecture of Rome there was great attention to detail and a desire to create perfection and symmetry in form and the Romans succeeded in doing so. Thus, beauty enabled the continuous creation of wealth by sustaining and perpetuating human genius in the population as the mating of individuals based on the beauty of the individuals was the means by which Rome produced men of genius. A change in the concept of beauty to be other than which gives rise to genius will of course lead to a decline in the production of genius and a rise in mediocrity in the population. Egalitarian ideas about the nature of Man drive such changes in the concept of beauty. If all men and women are beautiful, then there is no distinction nor can there be distinction made leading to the production of genius, however genius is a product of the inequality of men. Thus, cultural or general notions of beauty are critical to the creation of wealth, the emergence of progeny of genius, and thus the survival and perpetuation of a nation and of mankind as ordained by God.

Art and Economics

"Supreme art is a traditional statement of certain heroic and religious truth, passed on from age to age, modified by individual genius, but never abandoned." - William Butler Yeats

Beauty in art reflects the wealth creating ability of a nation that is the manifestation of the genius inherent in the population of a nation. The decline in beauty or the redefinition of beauty away from the quality of an act or thing that engenders a feeling of attraction or well-being reflects the destruction of a nation's wealth creating ability, i.e. the paucity of genius or at the very least the corruption of genius. Ugliness is the opposite of beauty. Ugliness engenders a feeling of revulsion or ill-being. When artists create things that are ugly and call or present the thing created as beautiful, or when there is greater value placed or given to something that is ugly than to something that is beautiful, then there is a conscious attempt at corrupting the truth by the artist and by the patron. Corruption of the truth is the means of abrogating the fear of God among the populace by those who seek to engender envy, i.e. by evil genius. The quintessential early twentieth century artist is the atheist and avowed communist, Pablo Picasso who was one of the founders of the Cubist movement. The Cubist movement is characterized by a distortion of reality yet it is touted by its proponents as just the opposite and somehow a greater reality, i.e. a greater beauty or greater truth. This is typical of those that espouse the atheistic ideologies socialism and communism. Atheists characterize reality or truth in terms that are the opposite of perceived or sentient reality, which is an exaggeration and distortion of reality or truth. An atheist is under the flawed and misguided notion that since there is no such thing as sin or the existence of the soul then lying is amoral. A lie to an atheist can only have political or legal ramifications accordingly there is an unconscious or even conscious political cost/benefit calculation done when an atheist lies. I say political because atheists typically lack the intelligence to perform an economic cost/benefit analysis. Thus, to an atheist truth is relative and not absolute. A man who fears God will not lie, as truth is an absolute good and lying is a sin or an absolute evil. An atheist is intellectually incapable of conceiving of anyone higher than himself. He is the ultimate self-centered egotist and rather than acting in his own self-interest he tends to behave altruistically and empathetically, which is destructive of wealth. It is for this reason that atheists seek sponsors.

Thus, Picasso, a purveyor of lies through his abstract art distorting reality and thereby distorting truth, promotes atheism in order to unleash man's envy and to achieve a communist economy, which the egalitarian atheist regards as nirvana. While Picasso himself became wealthy in the process of purveying lies though the distortion of reality in his art, the godless ideology he promoted resulted in the slaughter of millions of individuals and the enormous destruction of wealth. Had Picasso and other similar artists adhered to the truth at the time, and their art reflected reality and promoted the fear of God, it is possible atheism, and its handmaiden envy, may not have emerged thus sparing many lives and creating great wealth. Given Picasso's talent it is no doubt that had he painted beauty rather than ugliness he would have become equally if not more wealthy. His art appealed to atheists rather than to those who feared God and he became a cause célèbre as demanded by his ego. Why did Picasso not paint things of beauty and instead resort to abstractions that promoted godlessness? Technological innovation and change drove Picasso and similar artists to engage in abstraction in the arts and thereby abstraction in the truth. The invention of photography, which was the ability to capture true images, caused artists to seek ways to distinguish themselves from the technology. Abstract art and the resulting corruption of truth was the result.

Photography effectively improved the productivity of the artist in two ways. First, there was less skill required to render images of reality thus increasing the supply of those who produced portraits and other realistic pictures as demanded by the market. Second, as the supply of photographers increased the price of producing images dropped precipitously. Photography improved productivity in the image making industry, which up to the time of this invention was a manual and expensive process. Up until the emergence of the photographic camera, the artist was the craftsman whose skill captured reality and his success depended on how well he was able to render reality, i.e. his attention to detail. The great artists of the Renaissance were great in their attention to detail, i.e. in their renderings being closest to the absolute truth. While many of the scenes depicted were fantasy, the depiction of men and women remained realistic and idealized in the manner of the Greeks and Romans. Accordingly, the artists of the Renaissance were men of genius and sought after because of their genius, i.e. their ability to render physical reality in detail. As the case in all significant technological progress, the invention of photography was a paradigm shift in technology that threatened the existence of a category of labor through improvement in productivity. Artists responded by creating art that the camera could not easily replicate other than by photographing and copying it. Thus, abstract art or more accurately distortion art was born and a certain patronage emerged that supported and promoted this art form. The patronage tended to be atheists, i.e. humanists, socialists and communists as the art form promoted their ideology of non-truth and the abstraction and distortion of reality.   Picasso's first and lifelong patron was Gertrude Stein a homosexual, self-proclaimed and self-appointed intellectual and fellow atheist.   Stein's envy of white men who she correctly regarded as the crucible of genius in the human race inspired her homosexuality.   In Freudian terms, Stein was the quintessential penis-envying feminist, i.e. a female with an unresolved Electra complex, and thus sought to alienate man from God to spite her sex, i.e. the fact that she was born a woman and not a man.   Her support of abstractions from reality, which includes her writings, art, as well as her homosexuality were the means to that end.

Photography's impact on the arts was not limited to abstraction of the visual arts in all its forms it also introduced a form of abstraction in the literary and musical arts.   In literature, there emerged the nonsensical James Joyce "Ulysses" and "Finnegan's Wake" with its endless sentences euphemistically called "stream of conscious" writing.   Included in this group are the writings of the aforementioned Gertrude Stein.   In music, there is the emergence of such cacophonic composers as Schoenberg with his unpleasant sounding, but mathematically consistent, 12 tonal technique.   Clearly, there was no beauty in Schoenberg's music. Although Schoenberg professed himself Jewish, he did not hesitate to convert to Christianity when he thought it a political advantage.   His conversion from Judaism to Christianity and back to Judaism belies his essential atheism.   James Joyce was similarly ambivalent about his Catholicism.

Patrons, who desired the secularization of humanity as the precursor to its elimination or at least its diminution, elevated these atheists and others like them in the public arena.   Keep in mind that atheists believe that "overpopulation" is the bane of humanity and there were and still are many very wealthy individuals that continue to believe this nonsense.   Margaret Sanger the abortionist and founder of Planned Parenthood also emerged at the same time as Picasso and others.   She too was an atheist and communist and befriended many of the artists and writers of the early twentieth century and many befriended her as well. Too many people spoil the view - this is the mantra of humanism.   Thus, atheists promote and encourage anything that can reduce the population. In this regard, they were successful as humanity suffered by its own hand its greatest devastation in history during the first half of the twentieth century.   Atheism gave rise to the devastation of the first half of the twentieth century and not the devastation that gave rise to atheism, as some would lead you to believe.   Alienation of man from God was the cause of the death and destruction of the first half of the twentieth century and not the result or effect of the death and destruction. Gertrude Stein's "lost generation" was the result of her atheism and not the other way around.

A paradigm shift in technology (the photographic camera) resulted in improvements in productivity (rendering of reality) that led to a shift in the art created by the most talented artists from art depicting reality to art depicting the abstraction or rather distortion of reality and thus distortion of beauty and of truth.   Ironically, photography also served to make abstract art widely available amplifying its influence on the public psyche and on the psyche of many pseudo-intellectuals.   The abstractions and distortions in art led in turn to a general decline in the creation of beauty and a change in the definition of beauty away from absolute standards of beauty to relative standards or even no standards. Art that men once considered ugly men now hail as beautiful, and truly beautiful art men now called ugly, or at least not as worthy or valuable as the ugly art.   When ugliness and falsehood replaces beauty and truth, as is the case with the Cubist movement then man's psyche replaces the fear of God with the fear of Man himself.   With no God, man is compelled to obey only sovereign law and Natural Law.   Since no sovereign law can exist to rein in man's envy and Natural Law cannot rein in man's passions then a godless nation is susceptible to man's envy.   Such nations become socialist and communist economies ending invariably in the destruction of wealth including the destruction of man himself.   This is the lesson of the fate of nations in the twentieth century and if the lesson is not learned then it is the fate of nations in the twenty first century as well.

Ironically, while artists initially felt threatened by photography because it enabled the rendering of reality with great ease and efficiency, the invention served to make the work of artists much more widely known by larger numbers of individuals than before the invention. Photography served to communicate the abstract godless art arising out of its invention to the population in general.   This hastened the secularization of nations and set the stage for the socialist and communist economies with the concomitant destruction of wealth and the murder of millions of individuals as witnessed in the first half of the twentieth century.

The cautionary lesson for the current times is to be wary of the subtle shifts in the depiction of beauty in all the arts because these shifts portend the corruption of truth and the indoctrination into atheism or godlessness.   Corruption of truth and indoctrination into atheism is the intention of any art depicting homosexuality in a sympathetic light or in a light normalizing this behavior or its manifestations.   It is also the intention of juxtaposing blond and beautiful Caucasoid women and Negroid or mixed-race men in media to promote miscegenation. Corruption of truth manifests in the media depiction of women in the traditional roles of men, or men in roles of women.   It is also the intention of media depicting dysfunctional families and relationships such as homosexual, multiracial, unwed parents, single parents as normal or even exalted human conditions and relationships when in a God fearing reality they are not.

A particularly insidious, evil, and subtle means of undermining the existence of God and thereby the belief and faith in God is to cast images of men and women differently than God created man and woman to be. God first created man, and then woman to be his helper. It was not until man's fall from God's Grace that woman became the bearer and thereby the nourisher and sustainer of man's progeny, i.e. life. Thus, any image of a woman nourishing the child is a symbol of God's existence and a reminder of Man's fall from Grace. The atheists and Stoics apply equalitarianism to the differences between men and women to undermine the belief in God. To the atheist and Stoic, there is no difference between men and woman science and the law cannot overcome including even biological. The woman, whose biological destiny is the bearer of children and thereby the sustainer and nourisher of life is symbolically portrayed in various venues and roles as one who deals in death. Thus, we see a rush to select women as coroners, to have them speak of war, to participate in war, and to announce the death of others. The distorted symbolism extends to women as pallbearer in which the woman who God ordained to bear life into the world now symbolically bears the dead out of the world. If God ordained different roles of men and women, then undermining or reversing these roles also undermines the belief and faith in God. The idea here is that if men and woman do not differ in any respect at least symbolically then there is no God since God created man and woman to be separate physically, emotionally, and spiritually. The less men and women depicted as different the farther from God man becomes. Homosexuality and other dysfunctional behaviors become elevated in the media and in political discourse to appear as normal and thus through symbols undermine the belief in God moving the populace to envy. These and other methods atheists use to undermine the belief and faith in God and thus instill envy in the individual in order to acquire power over the economy and over the nation. The power they seek is the sovereign power of eminent domain, i.e. the ability to take life and property with no legal consequences to themselves. Thus, the atheist becomes God who in their egotistical view had the audacity to punish Man's disobedience by expelling him forever from the Garden of Eden, i.e. immortality. In this manner the atheist achieves nirvana which is fewer people populating their planet.

Only the light of day can defeat those that wish to corrupt truth and drive the fear of God from the heart of man. This is what I now give to my readers and with it, they and their children will shun the godless and all their shibboleths, and thus prosper and create great wealth.

The Great Error of Western Philosophy

There is however, an alternative view underlying the prevailing and traditional attitude about the non-equality of men and classical ideas of beauty, which were the hallmarks of Western Civilization up to the 20th Century. This alternative view is the idea that all men are equal in all respects, an idea first put forward by the Stoics but not widely accepted by sovereigns from antiquity to the 19th Century. Whenever the sovereign accepts Stoicism, as with Marcus Aurelius, then calamity followed. Stoics argued that all men including slaves are equal because they are all products of nature and thus cannot be otherwise. The Stoics arose in opposition to Plato who argued that only a few men were capable or were worthy of knowing the truth. It was these men, the Philosopher Rulers, who Plato placed as the sovereign leaders of nations in 'The Republic'. Plato's philosophy dominated the thinking of Ancient Greece and Rome. The democracy of Ancient Athens and the early republic of Rome consisted only of the intellectual male elites of these nations and modeled after Plato's Republic in this sense. Thus, these nations were Platonist in nature, i.e. characterized as Platonic. Stoicism however began to dominate Western philosophy, and Plato's influence diminished as the admixture of the races occurred and with the admixture, the decline in the number of geniuses produced as consequence. The Roman Emperor Marcus Aurelius was a Stoic and Stoics lived in Rome as well as Ancient Greece. The Stoic idea that all men are equal became manifest in law with the Edict of Caracalla thirty-one years after the death of Marcus Aurelius. The Edict of Caracalla marked the beginning of the decline of the Roman Empire and the beginning of the dominance of Stoicism in Western Philosophy further manifested in the philosophies of the Enlightenment over a millennium later. In the generations following the elevation of Stoicism to Roman law, there came a decline in the intellectual capacity, i.e. average IQ of the Roman population as the admixture with the darker peoples increased. With the decline in IQ came the inability of the Romans to withstand invasions and to sustain their empire. Prior to Caracalla there was some intermingling with the dark skin slaves but the offspring were not citizens of Rome and they did not enjoy the privileges of the Roman citizen thus there were social, cultural, legal, and economic barriers to increasing miscegenation among the Romans with the less intelligent dark races. After the Edict of Caracalla, the intermingling of the Caucasoid Roman with the Negroid and mixed race slaves accelerated. Within 70 years or about 3 to 4 generations after Caracalla, the Emperor Diocletian divides the Empire in two, an Eastern Empire whose capital was Constantinople and a Western Empire whose capital was Rome. This was a tacit acknowledgement that Western Civilization as embodied in the Roman Empire was now incapable of managing itself. This incapacity I attribute directly to the decline in the number of men of genius in the population, which is the direct result of the increased admixture of the Caucasoid and Negroid and mixed race peoples since the Edict of Caracalla. The current populations of southern Europe with their darker complexions and dark curly hair are the product of the admixture of the later Romans with the Negroid and mixed race slave.

The other Stoic notion is that reason can overcome emotion through the action of man's will. Thus, envy, anger, greed, fear, love, hate and the other passions are subject to man's reason and man's will. The fallacy with this idea, and with most philosophical notions about the nature of man, is that it presumes that all men are intellectually equal so human nature and intellectual capacity is homogeneous in the human population. Reason and the will can overcome the passions in men with the intelligence to reason and with the will to subject their passions to reason save the passion of envy. However, this is not possible in men who lack the intelligence to reason and/or lack the will to subject their passions to reason. It is this egalitarian view that is the most damaging to the creation of wealth and therefore the ability of a nation to survive calamity. The inability of philosophers after Plato to make a clear distinction in the intellectual capacity of the different races of man is the greatest error of Western philosophy up until the present time. This error portends once again the decline of Western Civilization, as it did during the time of the Roman Empire with Marcus Aurelius. After Rome, it took almost an entire millennium for the high intellectual capacity necessary for human progress and achievement to replenish. The high intellectual capacity inherent in the Caucasoid replenished itself because there was an absence of slavery and a halted importation of African and Middle Eastern mixed race populations on the European Continent and in particular Northern Europe. Although the Moors occupied the Iberian peninsula after the fall of Rome there was little admixture and the Christians successfully ejected the Moor by the end of the fifteenth century. The religious differences between the Christians and the Muslim Moor effectively prevented any significant admixture that would have otherwise corrupted the emerging intellectual capability of the Caucasoid European. This lack of admixture with the other races enabled the reemergence of men of genius on the European Continent as manifested in the Renaissance with a return to the teachings and accomplishments of the ancient Greek and Roman intellectuals. This continued the advancement and achievements of Western Civilization interrupted by Stoicism and its early consequences.

The epistemology of the word Moor is very telling. The word derives from the Greek word Μαυρος which means not only dark or black but also dim, as in dim witted, and given the superior intellect of the Ancient Greek mind, the attribution is accurate. Clearly, the Greeks were cognizant of the lower intelligence of the Negroid and all mixed race individuals. While the Stoic idea that reason can overcome emotion through an act of will is true of the highly intelligent Greeks and their early Roman heirs for all passions except for the passion of envy, this was not the case with the Negroid. Only the fear of God compels man's reason to rein in the passion of envy through the Tenth Commandment. Plato's notion of the intellectual superiority of some men over others created great wealth in ancient Athens and Rome. Without the fear of God, envy emerged periodically in the ancient world and destroyed wealth. The Peloponnesian War was the result of Sparta's envy of the wealth and influence of Athens. In the case of the ancient Greeks and Romans, it was economic opportunity that held envy somewhat at bay but without the fear of God envy periodically remerged to destroy wealth and weaken these nations. The Greeks in particular with their widely scattered city-states were prone to rivalry engendered by envy. The later Romans did not suffer the same internal rivalries as did the Greeks defeated the Greeks. In a sense the defeat and colonization of Greece by Rome is an early lesson about the destructiveness of envy. The early Greeks and Romans were clearly not atheists since they spoke of the soul but their concept of the soul did not altogether preclude envy from emerging. The Stoic notion that all men, regardless of race are intellectually equal, and that they are equally capable of applying reason to rein in their emotions through an act of will is the single most destructive idea in the now more cosmopolitan Western Civilization. It is the great error of philosophy. This Stoic notion manifested itself in universal suffrage during the later part of the 19th Century and early 20th Century, which as I have shown led to socialist economies thus undermining the creation of wealth and leading to wars, death and destruction of wealth. Just as the Edict of Caracalla marked the beginning of the decline of the Roman Empire, universal suffrage marks the beginning of the decline of Western Civilization. Universal suffrage is the modern equivalent of the Edict of Caracalla. With the decline of Western Civilization comes the inability of the human race to withstand calamity.

The ebb and flow of Western Civilization including its ancient precursors beginning with Ancient Egypt in terms of its manifest contributions to man's achievements is correlated directly with the extent of the Negroid admixture within the population of the great Western nations. The greater the admixture then the less the contribution of a particular nation to wealth, and the less wealth that is created and thus the more likely the nation will succumb to calamity. A historically recent example is the nation of Portugal, which had the largest empire in the world in terms of area during the fifteenth through the nineteenth centuries. Portugal continued to hold on to some colonies into the 20th Century, but the Portuguese empire effectively ended by the beginning of the 20th Century. Portugal was incapable of managing its empire due to a decline in the ability of the population to produce an adequate number of men of sufficient intellectual capacity to enable the management of the empire.   According to Arthur Kemp in his seminal work "The March of the Titans – A History of the White Race", Portugal imported huge numbers of black slaves during the sixteenth century.   Official estimates place the black slave population at 10% of the total population in Lisbon by 1550.   The need for the black slaves arose out of the Portuguese practice of sending their men out to help conquer and hold colonies rather than settle the colonies themselves, which was the practice of the English and to a lesser degree the Spaniards and French.   Due to a lack of laws restricting miscegenation by the Portuguese, the black population practically disappeared over time, as they were completely absorbed into the general population.   Migration from Portugal's African colonies added to the racial mixing of the population particularly during the 20th Century.   The decline of the Portuguese Empire followed the intermixing of the races.   Nations such as Spain and other European countries that were less inclined to mix with the Negroid and had miscegenation laws did not suffer the same rapid decline.   Today Portugal is the poorest nation that makes up the European Union and it is in financial trouble with its creditors.   Thus, the Portuguese essentially accepted the Stoic notion of equality of the races thus undergoing admixture only to find they are unable to sustain their empire and their nation.

It is easy to show mathematically the detrimental effect on the emergence of genius in a population due to mixing with the Negroid. The average and standard deviation of the Caucasian IQ is 100 and 15 respectively, and the average and standard deviation of the Negroid IQ (in the US) is 85 and 12 respectively.   If every Negroid mated with every Caucasian in a population of 12 million with each leading to a mixed race paired population of 12 million then the average of the offspring of this mixed race population is 92.5 and the standard deviation is 13.5.   Note that the admixture produced a population whose average IQ was half the distance of the IQ between original populations.   More significantly, the standard deviation is also half the distance between the standard deviations (SD) of the original populations.   The value of the SD assumes that the admixture was selective based on IQ.   In other words, individuals with the relatively corresponding IQ's within their respective populations mated.   Thus, a person within the 90 – 92 percentile range in the Caucasoid population mated with a person within the 90 – 92 percentile range in the Negroid population.   Assuming that an IQ over 150 is genius, then the original 12 million Caucasoid populations would have produced 5149 men of genius, and the Negroid population would have produced no men of genius.   The admixture produces statistically 123 individuals of genius.   In other words mixing with the American Negroid race reduces the probability of men of genius in this population of 12 million by almost 98%.   This is devastating to an unencumbered economy and a calamity to an encumbered economy.   In the case of

Portugal the influx of Sub-Saharan slaves whose average IQ was about 69 and standard deviation about 9 and the subsequent mixing resulted in a world empire becoming a third-world country in the short span of 300 years. This decline occurred with only 10% of the initial population Negroid but it was sufficient to lower both the average IQ and SD of Portugal to eliminate effectively any men of genius. The current average IQ of Portugal is 95, which is second to Greece and Ireland as the lowest IQ of any European Nation. Greece and Ireland have average IQs of 92. Considering that Portugal was most recently once a world power the fall of its empire is striking and had it not started off with a high average IQ for its population then the admixture would have been even more devastating and closer to that of Greece and Ireland. All these nations are having difficulties managing their affairs and are constantly seeking aid from the more intelligent and thus more productive Germans as well as the other Northern European nations to sustain their socialist economies.

Becoming Sovereign

The sovereign comes into existence in one of two ways either by plebiscite or by imposition. If the individuals comprising the nation select the sovereign, then they are the source of the sovereign's power of eminent domain accordingly obedience to the sovereign is generally voluntary and by tacit agreement. The form of government, i.e. monarchy or constitutional republic matters little in terms of the economy of the nation as long as the sovereign only engages in protecting private property and enforcement of contracts and does not over burden the economy with taxes, coercive laws, or onerous regulations. The only substantive difference between the two basic forms of government is in the manner that a revolt occurs. A monarchy is subject to rebellion wherein individuals take up arms against the sovereign. A constitutional republic is inclined toward civil war wherein individuals take up arms against each other. In a rebellion, the populace is in conflict with the military or in a coup d'état; the military joins the populace. In a civil war, the military often splits in its loyalties. The American Revolution was a rebellion wherein the colonies fought the sovereign's soldiers. The French Revolution also was a rebellion except the military with officers indoctrinated by the humanism and atheism of the Enlightenment for the most part joined the rebels. Napoleon was one such officer. This accounts for the French Revolution's success in overthrowing the monarchy. The American War between the States was a civil war and the military split in its loyalties. Robert E. Lee the southern general was a union general who fought for the South after the South seceded from the Union. Rebellion or civil war always leads to a change in the economic and political trajectory of the nation in addition to the manner of its governance. The American Revolution led to a change in the form of government, i.e. from monarchy to constitutional republic formed under God and giving rise to about 80 years of relative peace and stability, except for a short interruption during the War of 1812, until the War Between the States. The American Revolution led to a nation formed under God and its Declaration of Independence drew inspiration from the individualism of John Locke who was one of the few philosophers of the Enlightenment who feared God. The American Revolution also came on the heels of the First Great Awakening, which was a revival in religious thought that the Enlightenment undermined. The American Colonies first rebelled against the atheism of the Enlightenment before they rebelled against their sovereign. The French Revolution also led to a constitutional republic but its reliance on the ideals of the Enlightenment and the denial of God gave rise to Napoleon's tyranny. Napoleon's aggression resulted in death and destruction in the first part of the 19th Century in France and Europe. Following the American War Between the States there was great wealth created in the United States that enabled it quickly to surpass France as a world power. After Napoleon Bonaparte, France never recovered her former world status as a great power as the nation continued on a godless path flirting with socialism even until this day. Paris during the early part of the twentieth century was notorious as a city of atheists, sexual deviants such as homosexuals, socialists, and communists. It served as the crucible for the godless egalitarian ideas later used by tyrants such as Stalin, Hitler, Mao, Pol Pot, and Castro to justify the murder of millions of people and the destruction of great wealth.

The second way by which sovereignty comes about is through imposition. When one nation dominates another by conquering or otherwise subjugating another by force then those dominated are obligated to obedience; thus the conquering nation imposes its sovereign against the will of the individuals comprising the conquered or otherwise subjugated nation. The Romans subjugated the Hebrew Nation by force and the Jews were obligated to pay tribute or taxes to the Romans. The amount paid far exceeded the protection of private property or enforcement of laws and contracts that their imposed sovereign provided in return. The Jews rebelled against their imposed sovereign loosing much of their treasure as well as their nation, and not gaining their independence as a nation for two millennia thereafter and only after the sacrifice of millions of their brethren. Throughout history, the imposition of sovereignty, i.e. the conquering of one nation by another, is the most common means of establishing or growing a nation. Clearly, despite their professed belief in God, the Jews were obviously unable to create sufficient wealth to prevent the calamity that befell them which was the Roman Army. This was only due to the far superior intellectual capacity of the Romans, who created great wealth. The Jewish migration to the European Continent following their expulsion from

Palestine and the subsequent mixing, primarily with the highly intelligent Germanic peoples, enabled Judaism to emerge as one of the Great Religions of the world. The Ashkenazi Jew is a descendant of the admixture of the Jews of the Diaspora and the German people and this is the reason for the high IQ of the Ashkenazi Jew. Essentially the Germans adopted the clannishness of the Jewish religion more than they bred with the Jews themselves and became Jewish. This resulted in an inbreeding based on religion and directed to the creation of high IQ individuals but at the expense of health problems that tended to shorten the life of the Ashkenazi Jew.

Regardless of the means by which sovereignty comes into existence, as long as the sovereign secures private property, enforces laws and contracts, and does so with minimal encumbrance, i.e. low taxes, minimum regulation, efficient spending, and a stable currency, then the nation will create wealth and prosper. India whose colonization by Great Britain I discussed earlier is an example of a beneficial imposition of sovereignty that lasted for over 200 years including under the auspices of the British East India Tea Company. A nation that also fears God will overcome the envy that arises as the wealth of a nation increases and this secures a nation from the tyranny of the envious, i.e. socialism and communism.

God and Sovereignty

Without the fear of God, man's envy is easily provoked and the wealth of a nation destroyed. History has shown this to be the case. Examples include the French Revolution, the Russian Revolution, pre-WWII Germany, and other nations where socialism, communism and other godless sovereignties that take the wealth of some and give it to the many who then consume it thus destroying wealth. In all these instances, godlessness in the sovereignty and a manifest tendency toward atheism in the general populace was a prerequisite to the destruction of great wealth leading to poverty and death. The French Revolution was as much a rebellion against the Catholic Church, i.e. God as it was a rebellion against the landed aristocracy. The Russian Revolution over 100 years later was an overthrow of the Eastern Orthodox Church as well as the Czar. The writings and philosophy of Karl Marx, the quintessential socialist clown, succinctly displayed and espoused the godlessness of socialism and communism when he spoke of religion as the "opiate of the people". By this, he meant religion dulls envy, the passion socialist tyranny requires to motivate the populace into action and to sustain itself. The great irony with Marx is that while he arrogantly presumes to tell all of us how to live our lives he was unable to support and provide for his family. His family lived in continuous poverty and only three of his seven children lived to adulthood. Marx died a pauper with only a handful of people attending his funeral. In keeping with the leftist desire and propensity to rewrite history and hide truth, the English communist party erected his bust as a monument at his gravesite in 1954. Adam Smith, who wrote "The Wealth of Nations" on the other hand was highly successful and died a wealthy man. The fact that Marx's ideology continues as a legitimate course of study in colleges and universities is proof both of the lack of understanding of even the most basic economics by most academicians and the deliberate and calculated corruption of higher education by the atheism of the so-called Enlightenment since the beginning of the 20th Century.

Where there is economic freedom and the fear of God, i.e. where an unencumbered wealth creating economy exists, then opportunity exists and envy held at bay, as all the passions of a rational man are satiated through his material achievement in the creation of wealth and the fear of God. In the absence of calamity, wealth eases the burden of life and enables the creation of more wealth thus expanding opportunity, which helps hold envy at bay even among the godless. The sovereign enables the creation of wealth by efficiently protecting and securing private property and enforcing contracts. The creation of wealth is an uneven process that leads to variability in wealth creation that often spans generations. As variability in the natural environment exists, there is also variance in the intellectual and physical ability of a nation's individuals and thus variability in the creation of wealth. Thus, each individual is able to withstand calamity to varying degrees. The fear of God sustains a nation as God proscribes the envy arising from the variability in wealth creation, i.e. from the variability in man and nature. In the absence of actual opportunity, i.e. in an encumbered economy and in the absence of the fear of God, and faith in God then envy takes root and the destruction of wealth will ensue. A nation that does not fear God or lacks faith in God, and with an encumbered economy, where there is universal suffrage, and whose majority populace is intellectually incapable of continuously creating wealth becomes a totalitarian socialist or communist nation with the destruction of wealth ending in great poverty and death.

To avoid catastrophe and create wealth a nation's sovereign must inculcate the fear of God in the populace, and limit suffrage only to those who bear the burden of the sovereign. Whether a nation espouses or establishes a particular religion or allows freedom of religion is actually irrelevant to the creation of wealth. The fear of God and God's proscription against envy as it relates to the disposition of the soul is the essential element necessary to achieve and grow prosperity in a highly intelligent populace. Whether the fear of God comingles with the sovereign's power of eminent domain is not essential to the creation of wealth. The English sovereign is also the head of the Anglican Church but this is not essential to inculcate the fear of God and a faith in God in the populace. The United States supports religious freedom and the vast majority of its populace fear God, and has faith in God, and it creates great wealth. Although where there is little freedom of religion then the sovereign performs his duty to protect private property and enforce contracts less efficiently, since he must now also enforce the tenets of the faith using more resources than he otherwise would. Thus, a state religion enforced by the sovereign unnecessarily burdens and encumbers an economy and is unethical since it affects the creation of wealth more than were the fear of God left to the individual's conscience to resolve. How a man resolves the fear of God and his faith in God determines his fate and the fate of a nation regardless of the establishment or existence of an organized Christian church. To the extent that an organized Christian church makes known God, and performs the Christian sacraments then it is to this extent that it serves a purpose and it is therefore worthy of support by individuals who are so predisposed. However, as I indicated any third party could perform a sacrament such as a baptism or marriage as long as the act is in the Christian Tradition as found in the KJV. The KJV is the first English translation of the Bible, and thus the least imbued with modernism and therefore the least corrupted with egalitarianism even with some of the translation irregularities that I mentioned earlier and thus closer to God's Word.

The duty of the God fearing sovereign therefore is the inculcation of the fear of God in the populace all of whom are naturally inclined toward a belief in, and a fear of God. It takes great effort to remove the fear of God but little effort to instill such fear into a naturally receptive heart as is true of Man. This is because the future is unknown and this gives rise to men's fears. It takes continuous effort and therefore more energy to drive men from God than it does to bring men to God. It is the reason that communists speak of their ideology as a never-ending revolution. Castro, Mao, Stalin all dressed as revolutionaries with their fatigues and spoke of revolution all their lives for good reason. These atheists needed to work or rather fight continuously and expend resources and energy to remove the fear of God, and the faith in God from the heart of men. They did this by attempting to control future events. Since Man's propensity is to fear the future because it is unknown and therefore to fear God, then the way to overcome the fear of God is to plan the future. Planning the future theoretically eliminates fear of the unknown and thereby eliminates the fear of God. If everyman knows where his next meal is coming from, and that his person will be always safe and secure then he does not need to fear God. Thus, we have the spectacle of centrally planned economies governing everything from the prices of goods and services to the production of those goods and services. In this manner, the arrogant atheists believe they eliminate disparity of wealth and suppress the source of man's envy. Ergo there is no need to fear God and thus the atheists restore man back into the Garden of Eden in defiance of God who forbade man's return to the Garden of Eden. History has proven that the planning of an economy always fails to secure a nation against calamity because the planners themselves cannot know the future nor can they control future events. This is apart from the fact that merely planning the future does not secure the future. There is still the task of implementing those plans and the only method is through force in centrally planned economies. The inability to foresee the future and the use of force to meet arbitrary goals secure the failure of any centrally planned economy.

An individual accomplishes the same objectives by creating great wealth. That is an individual with great wealth secures for himself his safety and his security and thus tends not to fear God or have faith in God. When the wealthy do not fear God or have faith then neither will the populace and they will succumb to the temptation of atheists engendering envy. Great wealth gives rise to calls for greater security from the sovereign and the sovereign makes greater demands on the liberty and wealth of the populace leading to the very calamity that wealthy individuals sought to avoid which is the destruction of wealth. Without the fear of God or faith in God, government destroys wealth regardless of the form of government.

The future of Mankind

Given all the aforesaid, then the fate of mankind is predictable and extrapolated from the present with great certainty. As I have demonstrated throughout this book, there are three principles that completely explain man's past history. Just as these principles explain man's past history these same principles enable the prediction of man's fate. These principles are:

1. The fear of God
2. The average level and variance of human intelligence
3. The burden of the sovereign

The degree to which these factors are present or absent in nations determines the level of wealth creation, which is the hedge against calamity and the ability to survive calamity. In the absence of calamity, wealth eases the burden of life. The fear of God suppresses envy in a wealth creating economy. A capitalist economy relies on the existence of private property and liberty in contracting and it creates disparities in wealth. In the absence of the fear of God, and faith in God, the disparity in wealth engenders envy within the population. The level and variance of intelligence, i.e. the IQ and SD of a population determines productivity, which is the efficiency and rate of wealth creation. The burden of the sovereign is the wealth creating ability sacrificed by individuals to the sovereign for him to protect private property and enforce contracts. The burden of the sovereign determines the degree of encumbrance of the economy, and the level of opportunity available for the individual to overcome his disparity in wealth. A nation whose populace does not fear God and creates great wealth will lapse into socialism and communism, which are the political and economic manifestations of envy. The sovereign then takes for himself that for which the citizens appointed or elected him to protect i.e. life and property. Socialism is the form of government where the sovereign acts as benefactor more than as protector, i.e. he takes from the wealthy few and gives to the many who consume the wealth, thus encumbering the economy. Socialism tolerates a certain level of private property necessary to tax the wealth produced by those with private property. Communism is the form of government where the sovereign is the provider and neither protects private property or enforces contracts thus completely suppressing the creation of wealth. Both socialism and communism result from the unfettered envy of godless individuals. The aggregate fear of God ultimately determines the prosperity and survival of a nation of productive, i.e. intelligent individuals. The less intelligent the population the less that the fear of God is a determinant in its survival since the less intelligent the population the less wealth the nation creates. Thus, there are nations whose populations are God fearing or appear as God fearing yet fail to create wealth. Such nations exist in Sub-Sahara Africa. A nation that fails to generate sufficient wealth to overcome calamity will eventually succumb to calamity regardless of the fear of God or faith in God.

The continuous creation of wealth is the only determinant of the survival of a nation and of mankind in general. Mankind's survival depends on the existence of many wealth-creating nations, i.e. nations that successfully exploit the natural resources including labor within their boundaries. The existence of many nations also ensures that the sovereign faces temporal competition apart from the spiritual fear of God. In the competition of nations, the wealthiest nations are naturally God fearing, least burdened by the sovereign, and most productive, i.e. intelligent, accordingly such nations rightfully dominate the others economically and militarily. Wealthy and God-fearing nations are the least aggressive since they would have the most to lose in any attempts to overtake other nations. Since fear and not envy motivate wealthy and God-fearing nations then they are the most rational. Such nations prefer trade to war. The European nations are examples where no single nation dominated throughout history and their history is one of constant warfare. It was not until the United States achieved military and economic dominance over the European and Asian nations that the world enjoyed unprecedented peace and prosperity. The United States was also the most God-fearing, had the least encumbered economy, and a high average IQ as more than 80% of the population was Caucasoid. Indeed, if the United States were 100% Caucasoid and God fearing, it would have created even greater wealth and there would not have been wars, pollution or poverty.

Nations that do not fear God and are productive, i.e. of high intelligence, but whose sovereign burdens the economy thus limiting opportunity eventually fall into socialism. The envious populace of such nations calls on the sovereign to take on the role of benefactor and to redistribute wealth thus destroying wealth. Universal suffrage is the source of the calls on the sovereign by the godless envious individuals within a nation to remedy disparities in wealth. Such was the case with Germany in the later part of the 19th Century as I discussed earlier. It is not coincidental that the rise in German socialism under Kaiser Wilhelm II occurred at the same time German intellectuals turned to atheism. German atheists during the 19th Century that influenced the populace included Friedrich Nietzsche, Ludwig Feuerbach, Friedrich Engels, Karl Marx and others. These so-called intellectuals embraced the corrupt Stoic ideals of the Enlightenment and admired the French Revolution, which came with the murder of thousands of the French aristocracy. The violent expulsion of the French aristocracy had a profound effect on the monarchies and aristocracy of the other European nations. The overthrow of the French monarchy ignited the Napoleonic wars and accelerated the arming of Europe. To appease their growing godless and envious populations, European nations including the new German nation also embarked on a socialist course, which eventually led to World War I. The economic motivation for German socialism was to stem the tide of young Germans leaving for the United States, atheism provided the philosophical motivation and served to engender envy in the population as wealth grew, and the French Revolution provided the Prussian monarchy's political motivation for socialism, i.e. to become benefactor and thus avoid rebellion. All this considered then it is no coincidence that Germany was the crucible of Marxism and the catalyst of World War I.

Clearly, mankind is now entering a new dark age. This is evident from the following:

1) Current level of secularization and atheism concomitant with the rise of envy in increasingly wealthy nations;

2) The increasing burden of the sovereign arising from envy in these same nations and manifested in socialism with its redistribution and destruction of wealth;

3) Increasing miscegenation with the Negroid with the accompanying decline in the average intelligence of nations and narrowing of its variance.

This new Dark Age will witness destruction of wealth, massive poverty, great death and a declining population that ultimately may be irreversible. We are already seeing declining populations, as many European nations, as well as wealthy non-European nations such as Japan, are facing birthrates lower than death rates. The total fertility rate (TFR) in the European Union is 1.59, a TFR of 2.1 is necessary for the population to sustain itself. Japan's TFR is 1.39. Demographers expect Japan's population to decline precipitously in the next 30 years. Along with the decline in population is a decline in the total wealth created. Japan's declining birth rate has led to the decline in Japan's GDP growth as shown in Figure 75, although the per capita GDP is still rising as the population goes down illustrating the tremendous productivity and the store of wealth of the Japanese. Clearly, Japan as a nation is living now on the wealth created and stored in the 50 years after World War II.

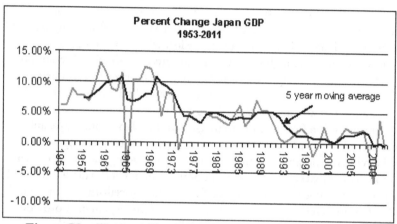

Figure 75 – Percent Change in Japan's GDP – 1953 to 2011

As I have said, God proscribes envy and it is the fear of God and faith in God that enables the creation of wealth. The Japanese depict envy as the Shinto god called Iki-Ryo. Iki-Ryo is the god of anger and envy, which harms the soul. Iki-Ryo is simultaneously the soul that exists apart from the corporal body. Thus in Japanese tradition, envy harms the soul and in this manner, God proscribes envy. To the extent that the Japanese feared God, the Japanese economy grew at one of the fastest rates in the world. Between 1964 and 1995, the real GDP grew at a constant average rate of 12.6 trillion yen a year. This rate of growth has since slowed so that between 1996 and 2011 it grew unevenly at the average rate of 4.2 trillion yen a year or about 33% of the rate between 1964 and 1995. See Figures 76 and 77 below

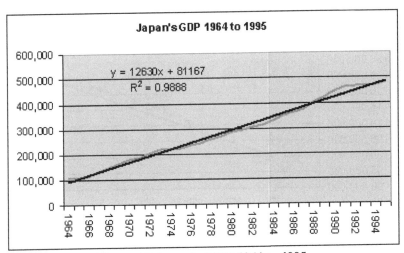

Figure 76-Japan's GDP 1964 to 1995

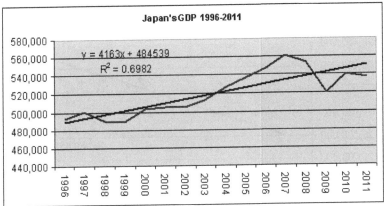

Figure 77 – Japan's GDP 1996 to 2011

This decline is largely attributable to the decline in the rate of population growth, which, in turn, is attributable to the increase secularization of the Japanese. Secularization always brings with it the destruction of wealth creation, in the case of Japan, the ability to create progeny at a rate high enough to grow the population. Figure 78 illustrates the high positive correlation ($R^2 = 0.93$) between the growth in Japan's GDP and the population growth between 1964 and 1995. On the other hand, the correlation between Japan's population growth and per capita GDP after1995 was less certain ($R^2 = 0.56$) as the population growth leveled off and the aging of Japan accelerated.(see Figure 79) The greater uncertainty of the Japanese economy is due to the population decline. This uncertainty will continue to increase as the population declines. Thus, Japan's survival as a nation is also uncertain.

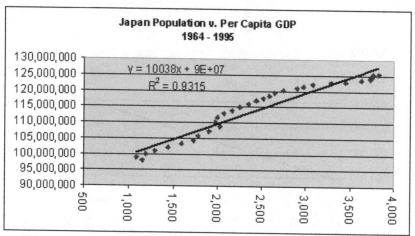

Figure 78 – Japan population v. per capita GDP 1964 to 1995

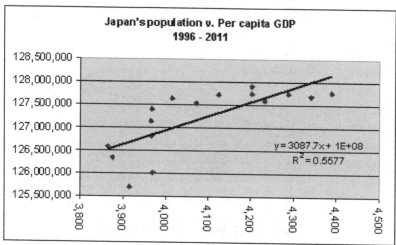

Figure 79 – Japan's population versus per capita GDP 1996 to 2011

The Japanese for the most part are increasingly secular in their beliefs, and rather than rely on envy's harm to the soul, i.e. the fear of God, as the means to suppress the manifestation of envy, the highly intelligent Japanese have succumbed to Stoicism, which fails to suppress envy. The move toward Stoicism is the first step towards atheism in highly intelligent nations. In the case of Japan, Stoicism, or the idea that man's reason and man's will overcome envy and the other passions, creates a culture that tolerates failure. If the government can enable everyone to be equally economically successful by subsidizing those that fail then the economic disparity that would otherwise engender envy disappears. So goes the flawed Stoic reasoning. The price for this ideology is a non-optimal economy as the Japanese place increasing emphasis on cooperation and a minimization of differences in individual wealth rather than on competition, profit, and the creation of wealth. Predictably, even though the Japanese are individually highly productive, their productivity is not creating wealth as their fear of engendering envy among a now godless populace is consuming their productivity with the government encumbering the economy to maintain unproductive enterprises. The institutionalization of Stoicism is the cause of Japan's economic demise or at the very least its economic malaise. Given that progeny are also wealth, i.e. a hedge against calamity, Stoicism and its handmaiden atheism is also the reason for the decline in the birth rate in Japan. As is currently happening in the Western Nations, Japan is becoming increasingly secular and godless consequently it has been on a socialist path as it has ceased creating progeny and ceased creating significant wealth since the 1990's. Japan's population growth has begun to level off, and now projected by demographers to be on the decline. The rate of population increase turned negative in 2005 for the first time since 1945 and remained at zero growth until 2008 where it turned increasingly negative through 2009. The result has been economic stagnation with the GDP growth essentially flat since 2000. Consequently and predictably, Japan is succumbing to calamity as they become increasingly secular and Stoic, i.e. atheistic, resulting in the dwindling of their population. The dwindling and aging of Japan's population along with the decline in the creation of wealth makes them vulnerable to attack from their envious and for the present their more militarily powerful neighbors. Communist China and communist North Korea in particular eye Japanese wealth with great envy. The United States has been Japan's protector but it has decided to consume its wealth and it too is on an atheistic and socialist path thus consuming its wealth. Consequently, the United States is increasingly less capable militarily to protect Japan as well as itself. Japan will eventually succumb to the Chinese and North Koreans who need Japan's wealth to sustain their atheistic nations and communist economies just as socialist Germany under the National Socialists needed the wealth and lives of their neighbors and their own Jewish population to sustain their socialist economy. The danger is that given the increasing weakening of the United States military then it is increasingly likely that the United States will resort to nuclear weapons in defense of Japan, Taiwan or South Korea. This will create calamity of unimaginable proportions and will hasten the decline of the human race. Armageddon will be the Western Pacific and not the Eastern Mediterranean and the first shot already fired in Hiroshima 70 years ago.

Like Japan, European nations are also becoming increasingly secular and atheistic. European governments are taking on the role of benefactors rather than protectors of life and property so the demise of these nations is also easily predictable and inevitable. The demise will manifest itself in the most militarily powerful of the socialist's states subjugating the others. This state is now Russia. However, there is a third force at work in many Western Nations, and in particular in the United States, just as insidious and destructive of wealth creation as atheism and the burden of government. This is the decline in the average intelligence of the population resulting from unbridled miscegenation with the Negroid Race. Legal attempts to elevate the Negroid to a status that his intellect does not entitle him, promotes and encourages miscegenation. Miscegenation with the Negroid serves to reduce the probability of genius in the population thus threatening the future survival of the nation as the decline of genius leads to a decline in wealth creation. Legally elevating the economic status of the unproductive and intellectually inferior Negroid reduces the nation's productivity. This reduces the creation of wealth and thus subsidizing the elevation of the Negroid becomes a burden on wealth creation. The decline in the average intelligence of a population has occurred in the past as I indicated earlier when I spoke of the decline of the Roman Empire, and historically more recently the rapid decline of the Portuguese Empire. To these two I can add the Ancient Egyptian Empire. The decline of these empires is directly the result of the admixture of the Caucasoid populations of each of these empires with the Negroid and mixed race peoples that they conquered and enslaved or in the case of the Egyptians with whom they traded. While the biological mixing of the races in the United States has not been significant since after the War Between the States because of the legal, moral, social and economic barriers to such mixing, these barriers are quickly disappearing. The Civil Rights Act, Affirmative Action, and the repeal of anti-miscegenation laws eliminated the legal and economic barriers to miscegenation. The economic barriers have fallen by government forcing employers through Affirmative Action and Civil Rights prosecutions to hire the unqualified and unproductive Negroid into relatively high paid positions. In much the same way that the Edict of Caracalla enabled and accelerated the mixing of the races in the Roman Empire, these modern edicts from the sovereign have enabled and are accelerating the mixing of the races in the United States since the 1970's. The aforementioned laws enabled a reduction in the normal disparity in earnings that would otherwise serve as an economic barrier to the mixing of the more intelligent Caucasoid with the Negroid.

Affirmative Action in particular has led to the hiring of fewer Caucasoid who are in most cases more qualified intellectually than the Negroid hired in their stead. This has reduced or distorted Caucasoid mating based on social and economic stratification, as the average income of the Caucasoid is less than the average income of the Negroid who is at the same or lower IQ level. The encumbering of the economy has accelerated this process, as the economy is approaching a zero sum economy.   Table 8 and Table 9 below list several professions based on the minimum IQs to maintain the required proficiency in the profession. The employment numbers are from the 2013 United States Statistical Abstract.   The IQ values by profession are from various sources.   The resulting effect of Affirmative Action enacted in the 1960s is to have large overrepresentation of the Negroid in higher IQ occupations, i.e. occupations with greater income potential.

Tables 8 and 9 apply the IQ and SD of the Caucasoid population or 100 and 15 respectively, and the IQ and SD of the Negroid population or 85 and 12, respectively to the relative populations for each occupation to determine if the Negroid under represents or over represents each occupation based on IQ.   For example, in the case of cashiers there are 3,254,000 of them in 2013.   An average IQ of 93.8 or greater is necessary for a cashier to be effective.   (Note that I am assuming the average of the population for each of the occupations and not one SD below the average.   The reason for this is first to establish a minimum level of competency and second to allow for the fact that no SD was determined for each population distribution within a specific occupation). The total number of Caucasoid employed in the US is 97,152,075, and the number having an IQ of 93.8 or greater for a cashier is 64,151,341 in 2013.   The total number of Negroid employed is 16,120,048 and the number having an IQ of 93.8 or greater to be a cashier is 3,734,654 in 2013.   Based on IQ, the ratio of Negroid to Caucasoid that could be cashiers is 5.82%.   The actual ratio is 33.4%.   Thus, the Negroid over represents the cashier occupation based on minimum ability to perform the job by 574%.   Were it not for the fact that employers have invested heavily in the last 30 years to mechanize the job of cashier with bar code readers and computerized point of sale terminals, the overrepresentation of the Negroid would have severely affected productivity.   The same is true for all the other professions shown as over represented.   Of the 78 occupations shown, 7 or about 9% under represent the Negroid while 91% significantly over represent the Negroid based on IQ.

	Total	Theoretical Possible			Actual - 2013 Statistical Abstract			Relative Black	Occupation
	employed	White	Black	Ratio	White	Black	Ratio	Represented	Minimum IQ
		Avg 100, SD 15	Avg 85, SD 12					>1 over	
Total, 16 years and over	143,929,000				97,152,075	16,120,048		<1 under	
Farmers	929,000	61,990,866	3,376,334	5.45%	876,976	6,503	0.74%	13.61%	94.7
Tool makers	53,000	60,524,410	3,149,119	5.20%	49,608	477	0.96%	18.48%	95.3
Sheet metal workers	113,000	75,619,302	6,210,583	8.21%	86,784	2,486	2.86%	34.88%	88.5
Veterinarians	87,000	47,542,611	1,606,970	3.38%	78,474	1,305	1.66%	49.20%	100.4
Bricklayers	130,000	71,997,086	5,309,383	7.37%	73,060	3,250	4.45%	60.32%	90.3
Lumberjacks	67,000	92,312,611	12,743,714	13.80%	56,615	5,762	10.18%	73.72%	75.3
Carpenters	1,164,000	77,677,534	6,782,354	8.73%	767,076	62,856	8.19%	93.85%	87.4
Roofers	203,000	74,047,392	5,803,974	7.84%	88,305	8,526	9.66%	123.18%	89.3
Fine artists	194,000	30,203,467	499,304	1.65%	169,750	3,492	2.06%	124.44%	107.4
Waiter/bartenders	417,000	57,538,191	2,723,439	4.73%	327,762	22,935	7.00%	147.84%	96.5
Sales representatives	1,319,000	44,449,670	1,342,499	3.02%	1,084,218	55,398	5.11%	169.17%	101.6
Electricians	730,000	64,624,485	3,817,065	5.91%	534,360	54,750	10.25%	173.47%	93.6
Carpet and tile installers	142,000	59,288,146	2,967,058	5.00%	68,018	6,106	8.98%	179.38%	95.8
Commercial airline pilots	135,000	34,435,571	693,485	2.01%	119,340	4,590	3.85%	190.98%	105.6
Construction workers	1,536,000	72,621,901	5,456,009	7.51%	721,920	104,448	14.47%	192.58%	90
Welders	575,000	66,719,451	4,199,995	6.30%	377,775	46,575	12.33%	195.85%	92.7
Industrial machine repairers	437,000	42,401,104	1,185,295	2.80%	346,541	20,102	5.80%	207.51%	102.4
Mechanical engineers	327,000	32,292,020	589,884	1.83%	10,791	4.27%	233.70%	106.5
Photographers	180,000	46,509,920	1,514,885	3.26%	145,260	11,520	7.93%	243.49%	100.8
Waiter/bartenders	2,124,000	57,538,191	2,723,439	4.73%	1,401,840	172,044	12.27%	259.29%	96.5
Firefighters	306,000	62,233,330	3,415,119	5.49%	242,964	34,884	14.36%	261.64%	94.6
Plumbers	553,000	55,515,000	2,461,235	4.43%	376,593	43,687	11.60%	261.66%	97.3
Real estate agents	769,000	34,194,879	681,293	1.99%	615,220	32,298	5.25%	263.50%	105.7
Automobile mechanics	863,000	69,197,564	4,693,508	6.78%	542,827	98,382	18.12%	267.21%	91.6
Sales representatives	432,000	44,449,670	1,342,499	3.02%	339,984	27,648	8.13%	269.25%	101.6
Dental hygienists	184,000	34,676,863	705,853	2.04%	154,560	8,832	5.71%	280.73%	105.5
Dietitians	110,000	69,418,040	4,739,682	6.83%	79,200	16,060	20.28%	296.99%	91.5
Painters	517,000	59,288,146	2,967,058	5.00%	229,548	36,190	15.77%	315.03%	95.8
Truck drivers	3,252,000	71,364,137	5,164,367	7.24%	2,065,020	497,556	24.09%	332.95%	90.6
Broadcast technicians	99,000	48,059,279	1,654,517	3.44%	70,686	8,118	11.48%	333.60%	100.2
Railroad conductors	50,000	71,786,999	5,260,862	7.33%	35,750	8,850	24.76%	337.80%	90.4
Civil engineers	360,000	38,361,751	913,568	2.38%	281,880	23,040	8.17%	343.22%	104
Psychologists	186,000	23,913,634	282,118	1.18%	158,658	6,696	4.22%	357.74%	110.3
Butchers	323,000	82,809,838	8,434,951	10.19%	126,939	47,804	37.66%	369.72%	84.3
Telephone installer/repairers	183,000	61,015,388	3,223,805	5.28%	124,440	24,705	19.85%	375.75%	95.1
Electrical engineers	300,000	29,069,119	454,167	1.56%	209,100	12,600	6.03%	385.68%	107.9
Architects	2,806,000	32,292,020	589,884	1.83%	2,124,142	154,330	7.27%	397.74%	106.5
Insurance agents	602,000	38,112,613	898,367	2.36%	455,112	43,946	9.66%	409.65%	104.1
Stockbrokers	278,000	29,294,439	462,912	1.58%	224,902	14,734	6.55%	414.59%	107.8
Child care workers	1,230,000	60,278,146	3,112,174	5.16%	750,300	162,360	21.64%	419.12%	95.4
Engineering technicians	365,000	41,891,461	1,148,285	2.74%	262,800	30,295	11.53%	420.55%	102.6
Bank Tellers	369,000	54,240,240	2,306,153	4.25%	231,363	41,697	18.02%	423.88%	97.8
Janitors	2,275,000	78,572,643	7,046,026	8.97%	1,078,350	418,600	38.82%	432.88%	86.9
Biologists	112,000	17,539,217	135,183	0.77%	84,672	2,912	3.44%	446.21%	113.7
Retail salespersons	3,230,000	51,157,996	1,961,367	3.83%	2,189,940	377,910	17.26%	450.10%	99
Data entry clerks	307,000	58,790,324	2,896,106	4.93%	207,532	46,357	22.34%	453.44%	96
Cooks	1,988,000	71,997,086	5,309,383	7.37%	898,576	304,164	33.85%	459.01%	90.3

Table 8 – Relative Negroid occupation representation based on minimum IQ of occupation – sorted by percent overrepresented

Continued on next page

Occupation	Total employed	Theoretical Possible White Avg 100, SD 15	Theoretical Possible Black Avg 85, SD 12	Ratio	Actual - 2013 Statistical Abstract White	Actual - 2013 Statistical Abstract Black	Ratio	Relative Black Represented >1 over <1 under	Occupation Minimum IQ
Secretary	2,922,000	40,622,692	1,059,645	2.61%	2,247,018	271,746	12.09%	463.62%	103.1
Physical therapists	224,000	30,203,467	499,304	1.65%	175,392	14,560	8.30%	502.16%	107.4
Accountants	1,814,000	38,112,613	898,367	2.36%	1,309,708	156,004	11.91%	505.33%	104.1
Computer programmers	489,000	38,112,613	898,367	2.36%	330,075	39,609	12.00%	509.09%	104.1
Receptionists	1,326,000	46,509,920	1,514,885	3.26%	873,834	145,860	16.69%	512.48%	100.8
Dentists	183,000	23,913,634	282,118	1.18%	137,250	8,601	6.27%	531.19%	110.3
Communications equipment mechanics	285,000	48,059,279	1,654,517	3.44%	194,655	37,050	19.03%	552.88%	100.2
Pharmacists	277,000	27,295,586	389,042	1.43%	188,914	14,958	7.92%	555.53%	108.7
Jewelers	54,000	40,369,941	1,042,571	2.58%	33,696	4,968	14.74%	570.89%	103.2
Cashiers	3,254,000	64,151,341	3,734,654	5.82%	1,753,906	585,720	33.40%	573.64%	93.8
Insulation installers	50,000	63,913,784	3,693,823	5.78%	23,300	7,800	33.48%	579.24%	93.9
Registered nurses	2,892,000	36,136,687	783,839	2.17%	2,169,000	303,660	14.00%	645.43%	104.9
Lawyers	1,092,000	16,210,343	112,505	0.69%	934,752	45,864	4.91%	706.96%	114.5
Police officers	697,000	42,146,141	1,166,678	2.77%	474,657	98,974	20.85%	753.27%	102.5
Teachers	3,038,000	28,620,857	437,090	1.53%	2,393,944	285,572	11.93%	781.11%	108.1
Mail carriers	75,000	50,900,127	1,934,363	3.80%	43,725	13,425	30.70%	807.91%	99.1
Clergy	410,000	26,860,513	374,047	1.39%	319,800	37,310	11.67%	837.79%	108.9
Taxi drivers	338,000	64,860,055	3,858,642	5.95%	166,634	83,486	50.10%	842.16%	93.5
Authors	209,000	15,257,490	97,770	0.64%	180,576	10,032	5.56%	866.97%	115.1
Bus drivers	582,000	62,233,330	3,415,119	5.49%	329,994	158,886	48.15%	877.40%	94.6
Chemists	121,000	23,913,634	282,118	1.18%	84,700	8,833	10.43%	883.97%	110.3
Security guards	858,000	61,260,082	3,261,543	5.32%	449,592	227,370	50.57%	949.88%	95
Licensed practical nurses	558,000	55,005,934	2,398,391	4.36%	329,778	140,616	42.64%	977.92%	97.5
Maids	1,401,000	56,022,845	2,525,161	4.51%	472,137	235,368	49.85%	1106.00%	97.1
Librarians	194,000	16,048,923	109,920	0.68%	165,094	14,938	9.05%	1321.08%	114.6
Computer systems analysts	534,000	21,919,919	228,934	1.04%	342,294	50,730	14.82%	1419.04%	111.3
College professors	1,313,000	14,045,499	80,794	0.58%	975,559	89,284	9.15%	1591.03%	115.9
Social workers	727,000	35,891,993	770,383	2.15%	448,559	159,213	35.49%	1653.67%	105
Statisticians	72,000	21,725,855	224,124	1.03%	43,344	8,208	18.94%	1835.68%	111.4
Physicians	934,000	12,487,651	61,746	0.49%	636,988	59,776	9.38%	1897.88%	117
Barbers	127,000	58,290,728	2,826,230	4.85%	40,767	43,815	107.48%	2216.70%	96.2

Table 9 – Relative Negroid occupation representation based on minimum IQ of occupation – sorted by percent overrepresented

It is instructive to note which occupations under represent the Negro and the amount of under representation. Table 10 is a list of some of the occupations that under represent the Negroid. Note that these occupations are highly unionized. In other words, the unions have effectively discriminated against the Negroid because many Negroid are intellectually qualified for these occupations, yet are not in these occupations. In other words, some of the unions, in particular the trade unions, have for many years effectively prevented the Negroid from entering occupations that they otherwise could perform. This is an argument for emphasizing vocational training for the Negroid rather than academic training, which has proven to be an expensive experiment and an abject failure. Unions however have lobbied for the Negroid to have management jobs many of which require post secondary education, thus displacing the Caucasoid manager with the less intellectually capable and easily manipulated Negroid manager. Barack Obama is the quintessential example of the incompetent manager manipulated by the unions for their unearned benefit at the great cost of the Nation's ability to create wealth and overcome calamity.

Occupation	%under	IQ
Farmers	13.61%	94.7
Tool makers	18.48%	95.3
Sheet metal workers	34.88%	88.5
Veterinarians	49.20%	100.4
Bricklayers	60.32%	90.3
Lumberjacks	73.72%	75.3
Carpenters	93.85%	87.4

Table 10 – Occupations under represented by the Negroid based on IQ

The total Negroid over representation in United States occupations is about 374% when considering those occupations where over representation exists. In other words, almost 3.75 times more Negroid are in occupations than their IQ would otherwise qualify them. Table 11 shows occupations where the Negroid significantly over represents.

Occupation	%over	IQ
Maids	1106.00%	97.1
Librarians	1321.08%	114.6
Computer systems analysts	1419.04%	111.3
College professors	1591.03%	115.9
Social workers	1653.67%	105
Statisticians	1835.68%	111.4
Physicians	1897.88%	117
Barbers	2216.70%	96.2

Table 11 – Occupations significantly over represented by the Negroid based on IQ

The over representation is a burden on productivity and a reduction in wealth creation.   The over representation of the Negroid in occupations based on their IQ is akin to a tax because it reduces the average productivity of the occupation.   The reduced productivity leads to monetary inflation.   Offsetting the lowered productivity is mechanization of the processes inherent in some of the occupations. However, this mechanization requires investment that otherwise may not have been needed.   For instance in the case of statisticians there are computer programs that now perform many of the calculations that required skilled manual manipulation in the past.   Thus, individuals with lower IQs than in the past can perform some of the work that statisticians traditionally do but without actually understanding what they do. The physician job has similarly been somewhat mechanized as well thus enabling less qualified individuals to enter the field. Nevertheless, while mechanization has enabled the Negroid to enter into a profession that he is otherwise not intellectually capable of fulfilling, the mechanization has gone to overcoming his lower productivity and not toward creation of wealth. Thus, for example we have inflation in medical cost that has consistently exceeded the general rate of inflation.

Most colleges and universities cooperate in populating occupations requiring a high IQ with the unqualified Negroid by granting the academically unqualified Negroid degrees to meet political rather than academic ends. The result has been a significant decline in the ability of the economy to create wealth thus jeopardizing the future well-being and survival of the nation. Once again, Obama is the quintessential example of the unqualified manager clearly given an unearned and undeserving passing grade by some of the more prestigious universities in the nation. The most telling evidence of this is the refusal by Obama to submit his college transcripts or any other records that would shed light on his accomplishments. Even if he did submit his records, the obvious disconnect between his miserable performance on the job and any possible respectable college record would be clear.

The inheritance of intelligence

Some misguided readers may dispute the fact of inheritability of intelligence of a population and that the race of a population's progenitors determines the average intelligence of a population independent of any environmental considerations. Keep in mind that I am referring to the average intelligence of a population not to the intelligence of any particular individual. While the intelligence of an individual is also due solely to the intelligence of the parents that in turn is a function of the racial makeup of the parents, this is not what I am setting out to prove. To prove the general inheritability of intelligence, I will use empirical data about the average intelligence of two populations and then simulate the random mixing of these populations to determine the resultant average IQ and SD. I will then compare this result with the actual average IQ and SD of the mixed population. If the results compare then the conclusion is that intelligence is 100% inherited, if they do not then intelligence is due to factors other than genetics.

The average IQ of a Sub-Sahara nation such as Nigeria is 69 with an assumed standard deviation (SD) of nine. With a greater than nine SD, we would be seeing many mentally dysfunctional individuals in African nations but we do not see this. In other words while the average IQ is low the individual Sub-Saharan African is still able to manage his affairs and survive albeit poorly. However, while able to manage his individual affairs he is unable to manage the affairs of his nation.   Managing the affairs of a nation requires a higher IQ than the Sub-Saharan Negroid is naturally not able to generate.   Thus, the IQ of the majority of the Sub-Saharan Negroid clusters around the mean and an SD of nine is justified.   Despite their low IQ, the Sub-Saharan Negroid is still able to survive although with very little creation of wealth and thus with great difficulty.   The nation of Nigeria is about 98% Negroid so the average IQ and SD is that of the Negroid from this nation.   Nigeria was the source for about 40% of the slaves brought to the United States. Other nations like Cameron, Northern Angola and Ghana supplied another 40%.   These nations have average IQ's of 64, 68, and 71 respectively.   Given this data I will assume that the average IQ of the Negroid slave when imported into the United States in the early part of the 19th Century was 68 with an SD of nine.   If we assume this as the average IQ and SD of the Negroid slave population imported into the US prior to the War Between the States, then the admixture with the Caucasoid will produce a mixed race population with an average IQ half-way between 68 and 100 which is 84.   This compares with 85, the current accepted average of the American Negroid.

The SD of the mixed race population is a function of the way that the mixing occurred.   Table 12 is a simple example of the effect of mixing populations with the same average value and different variances. Following is a brief explanation.

			Variance	Average
Population 1	0	100	100	50
Population 2	20	80	60	50
Mixture 1	10	90	80	50
Mixture 2	60	40	20	50

Table 12 – Mixing of two populations with the same average and different variances

Population 1 and population 2 each consist of two values whose average is 50 but whose variance or difference is 100 and 60 respectively. Mixture 1 is the combination of corresponding low and high values thus Mixture 1 has 2 values, 10 ((20+0)/2) and 90 ((100+80)/2), where each are the average of the corresponding high values of Population 1 and Population 2.   The resulting average of Mixture 1 is 50 and the variance is 80 (90-10=80).   Mixture 2 is the combination of the cross mixing of values, i.e. (100+20)/2 = 60 and (0+80)/2 = 40.   The average of Mixture 2 is also 50 but the variance or difference is 20.   Thus, the mixing of two populations with the same averages results in a population with the same average regardless of the way the populations mix. However, the resulting variance is always narrower than the highest variance of the original populations and it can be narrower than the lowest variance of the original populations. The latter depends on the way the populations are mixed and the value of the lesser variance. If the lesser variance of the original two populations is small enough, then the mixture variance will not be less than the original population variances but it will still be between the variance of the original populations.

This result is true for all values of the populations. The same is also true if the populations are random variables with a normal distribution. Thus knowing the averages of two populations and their variances enables one to predict the same statistics resulting from the mixing of these populations as well as the manner of mixing. In the case of the mixing of the Negroid and Caucasoid races the average IQ of the mixed population should be 85 and assuming that the mixture is with corresponding IQs, i.e. with higher IQs mating with each other and lower IQs also mating with each other, then the SD of the mixed population should be 12. This is the average of the sum of the two SD's. This is indeed the case. The conclusion here is there was a good deal of discrimination in terms of intelligence at the time the bulk of the mixing of the races occurred in the United States. In general, the Caucasoid consistently mated with the more intelligent Negroid whenever such mating occurred. If the mating consistently occurred with a less intelligent Negroid then the SD of the mixed population would have been three, which is the average of the difference between the SDs of the two populations. If random mating occurred, then the SD of the mixed population would have been about 7.5 or the average of the extreme values. Clearly, the Caucasoid male dominated the mating process and discriminated by intelligence, otherwise there would have been a smaller SD for the resulting mixed race population. Anecdotal evidence supports this conclusion as well. Specifically it appears that the Caucasoid male master mixed with the house Negroid female slave. Typically, the house Negroid female was of higher intelligence than was her field counterpart, because housework and child rearing was more complex and it required a more intelligent individual that the Caucasoid mistress could train without much difficulty. On the other hand mixing of the Caucasoid female with the Negroid male was very rare given the social mores and law at the time that heavily punished such alliances.

The other consideration then is the role of discrimination in mating based on intelligence has within the existing Caucasoid, and within the American Negroid mixed race populations. Within any given population, the tendency is for individuals with the same intelligence level to mate. If this were not true than the SD of the population would narrow over time and in the case of the Caucasoid there would be fewer geniuses created however, this is clearly not the case. In the case of the Negroid or mixed race populations a non-discriminating or random mating also would lower the SD over time, and produce fewer individuals at the higher end of their respective distributions. In the case of the American Negroid, which is about 20% Caucasian in terms of blood typing the SD has remained constant since after the War Between the States. Thus, there appears to be a strong tendency even within the American mixed race Negroid to mate with those of equal intelligence within the race. It appears that for the most part the mixed race American Negroid has avoided mixing with their pure race counterparts otherwise we would be seeing a lower IQ among the mixed race American Negroid. Simultaneously, mixed race or pure race Negroid mixing with Caucasoid has not occurred in significant numbers after the War Between the States due to the factors I mentioned earlier. The tendency to mate with individuals of equal intelligence within a race manifests itself in societal stratification based on relative wealth or in other words on the relative ability to provide a hedge against calamity and in the absence of calamity to ease the burden of life. That is wealthier individuals within a race tend to be more intelligent and tend to socialize amongst themselves and thus mate among themselves. This is true regardless of race. Social mores, customs and social institutions naturally arise within an economy to ensure that the highest intelligence within a given race is preserved. These same social mores, customs, and social institutions also serve as effective barriers to miscegenation. Thus, the so-called discrimination against the Negroid, including school segregation, existing in the South as well as in the North until the 1960s effectively prevented any significant mixing of the races since after the War Between the States thus maintaining the ability of the Caucasian Race to generate genius in the five generations after the War. The devastation wrought on the South by the War effectively barred any further mixing of the races. The genius emerging after the War Between the States led to tremendous innovations and advancements in science and technology beginning in the later part of the 19th Century and extending into the 20th Century. It enabled man landing on the moon and inventions that revolutionized the manufacturing and service industries. The effect of de facto and de jure anti-miscegenation was a tremendous gain in productivity and the concomitant creation of wealth.

Social mores, customs, and social institutions comprise the culture of the nation. Thus, the culture of the nation is a reflection of the level of intelligence in a nation. As I have shown when discussing the decline of the Roman Empire, a decline in the culture in terms of the quantity and quality, i.e. beauty, of the art and literature generated indicates and is a harbinger of a decline in the general level of intelligence in a nation. Consequently, there is a lowering of the probability for genius to emerge and engender the creation of wealth.

It is clear that some mixing of the Caucasoid and Negroid occurred at a level of only a single generation since more such mixing would lead to a higher IQ level and narrower SD among the American mixed race Negroid. The fact that the American Negroid by blood type whereby the American Negroid is about 20% Caucasoid corroborates the single generational mixing. Had significant mixing occurred in later generations the American Negroid blood type and IQ would have been closer to the Caucasoid and the average IQ and SD of the United States population in general would have been lower with fewer geniuses in the population. As it was, there was undoubtedly some reduction in the ability to create wealth as some mixing did occur. Considering the importation of slaves accelerated after the invention of the cotton gin in 1794, and that the War Between the States took place sixty five years later then at the most, two or possibly three generations of slaves were born under slavery. Thus, there was little opportunity for more than one generation of mixing. The War Between the States effectively halted any further significant mixing of the Caucasoid with the Negroid in the United States beyond one generation and until recent times. Had additional generational mixing taken place with the Caucasoid on any significant scale then the average IQ of the American Negroid would be 92 and assuming the intellectual discrimination in the selection of mates the SD would be 13.5. This however is not the case. In fact, there appears a clear tendency on the part of the mixed race first generation American Negroid to mix only with their kind – i.e. the lighter skinned Negroid rather than the darker skinned Negroid. Thus, the American Negroid actually consists of two separate sub-races, which are the virtually pure Negroid with IQ of about 68 and the mixed race Negroid with an IQ of about 85. The average IQ of the combined Negroid and mixed race Negroid is probably about 82 taking into account the relative populations. The reason that the lower number does not appear in some of the academic testing is there is a cutoff that treats test scores below the 70 percentile as within the 70 percentile. This tends to raise the apparent average IQ of the population as based on test results and therefore provides an upward bias in the average IQ and a skewing of the distribution of the IQ's of the American Negroid as measured by academic proficiency testing.

There are certain tradeoffs in smaller populations attempting to maintain or improve their average intelligence through inbreeding. Europe's aristocracy for instance suffered from diseases such as hemophilia, which was a direct consequence of mating with close relatives. While such mating maintained the high average IQ of the aristocracy, it came at a price in terms of the physical health of some of the progeny, which affects the lifespan of the progeny and thereby jeopardizes the continuation of the sub-group. Another example is the Ashkenazi Jew whose strong tendency to mate with those of high intelligence within a relatively genetically homogeneous population has resulted in many debilitating diseases that are unique to this population.

The Caucasoid Ashkenazi Jew has the highest average IQ of any world sub-population at 113, or almost one SD higher on the Caucasoid distribution.   Unlike national cultures, which tend to determine the social mores and institutions that effectively governed the mating of individuals, the mating of Ashkenazi Jew is strictly on religious principles that transcend national cultures.   The Ashkenazi Jew is of Germanic descent that originally converted to Judaism from the time of the Diaspora of the Roman Empire as the means of perpetuating and sustaining the high intellect of the indigenous Germanic peoples at the time and independent of nation states.   The Ashkenazi Jew is man's genius successfully sustaining itself through the fear of God and faith in God.

The Ashkenazi Jew and their health problems and the other health problems arising from populations of high intelligence attempting to sustain themselves is an indication of the biological limit to human intelligence.   In other words, man's ability to comprehend the universe and God is biologically limited.   This biological limit to intelligence seems to imply a limit to human existence since it is only through growth in intellect, i.e. the increasing ability to comprehend nature and God that enables man to progress and sustain himself.   Yet, paradoxically God ordained man to be immortal and thus he must continue to propagate, i.e. create wealth to fulfill the will of God.   If there were no limit in the growth of human intelligence then man would eventually become God, and hence reenter the Garden of Eden and become immortal once again, which is against the revealed will of God.   Thus, the biological limit to the intellect is a consequence of man's disobedience to God, and it insures that man will never be God nor ever again enter the Garden of Eden.   The growth in human intellect has manifested in continuous gains in productivity and the creation of wealth.   This must continue and it can only continue if human genius comes into being.   Thus, God has ordained the continuation of human genius, and its willful destruction as takes place with miscegenation is acting against the will of God.

From all that I have said thus far it is clear that the future of humanity, i.e. its ability to survive calamity is a function of the average IQ of humanity.   Keeping this in mind, I turn our attention to the course and future of humanity.   I begin by calculating the current world's average IQ as being 91.8 with an SD of 17.2.   I did this calculation using Lynn and Vanhanen's values of the average IQ of nations.   I made some assumptions of the SD for specific ranges of IQ as shown in Table 13.

IQ	SD	
59-79	9	
80-89	12	
90-102	15	
100-108	12	Asian

Table 13 – Standard deviation assumptions for specific ranges of IQ

Note that I used a standard deviation of 12 for Asian IQs in the range 100 to 108. The reason for this is that it is clear that the Mongoloid has not generated sufficient number of geniuses historically for its cultures and economies to dominate world culture and economy as has the Caucasoid since the dawn of history. The dominate world language, literature, art, music, religion, science, mathematics, and technology originated with the Caucasoid and continues to originate with the Caucasoid. This is Western Civilization. The Mongoloid has tremendous ability to learn, apply, and emulate the ideas and inventions created and discovered by the Caucasoid but they have not contributed nearly to the depth and scope of human achievement as has the Caucasoid. I believe that the reason for this is the narrower range of intelligence manifested in the Mongoloid Race. This is despite US data, which indicates an SD of 15 that I believe biased due to US Mongoloid populations not representative of the Mongoloid population in general.

The total number of nations in my calculation was 187 representing over 99.999% of the world population. Taking into account the variation in population growth rates in each nation I made a projection of the changes in the world IQ and SD for each of 5 years into the future. I summarize this projection in Table 14 below.

Year	IQ	SD	Population	%Change from 2014	IQ>140	%Change from 2014	%Population
2014	91.8	17.2	7,069,383,281		17,856,194		0.2526%
2019	91.4	17.2	7,467,060,447	5.63%	17,810,449	-0.26%	0.2385%
2024	91.0	17.2	7,900,212,546	11.75%	17,725,575	-0.73%	0.2244%
2029	90.6	17.2	8,372,811,610	18.44%	17,597,760	-1.45%	0.2102%
2034	90.2	17.2	8,889,367,703	25.74%	17,423,241	-2.42%	0.1960%
2039	89.8	17.2	9,455,012,779	33.75%	17,198,394	-3.68%	0.1819%
2044	89.4	17.2	10,075,599,186	42.52%	16,919,865	-5.24%	0.1679%

Table 14 – Projected Change in World average IQ and population

This table shows that the world's average IQ is declining while its population is growing as growth in the high IQ nations recedes, and growth in the low IQ nations increases. Within 30 years, the worlds average IQ will have dropped to 89.4 from 91.8 currently while the SD stays relatively constant. The result is that there is a statistical drop in the number of individuals with IQ's greater than 140 at the same time that population is increasing. By 2044, the population is over 10 billion or 42% greater than it is today while the number of individuals with IQs over 140 goes from about 17.9 million to 16.9 million or down by 5.24%. In other words, statistically the number of individuals with IQ over 140 goes from 0.25% of the population to 0.17% of the population. This does not bode well for future gains in productivity or the creation of wealth. In fact, it appears that instead of creating wealth, mankind will be consuming the wealth created to this point. Since the continuous creation of wealth is man's hedge against calamity then its consumption invites calamity. Indeed this will be the case if man maintains the current course. Increasing secularization engendering envy; increasing miscegenation with the Negroid race and mixed-race populations thereby reducing the average IQ of the productive nations; the increasing burden of the sovereign of wealthy nations manifested in socialist and communist economies, and declining birth rates among the Caucasoid are the causes of declining wealth creation that invite calamity.

The fear of God and faith in God along with the return of beauty to the cultural and social institutions; laws barring miscegenation; and return of the proper role of the sovereign will enable man to once again create wealth and enable him to survive calamity. Failure of the productive nations to embody these principles will result in much destruction, poverty and death in the future as it has in the past. Nevertheless, it is the will of God that man is immortal. Thus, mankind will eventually begin to create genius but only after the elimination of miscegenation with the Negroid and mixed race populations as occurred after the fall of the Roman Empire. In the meantime, we are entering a new Dark Age that will take centuries to overcome.

God and Science

Science is a wealth creating manifestation of man's genius. It is the process of discovery of the mind of God since all that exists can only exist in the mind of God. The discoveries of science are not to affirm the existence of God but rather the existence of God affirms the discoveries of science. Hence, any claims of scientists that do not comport with the Biblical account of Creation or of the Biblical account of man's nature cannot be true. Scientists propagating such claims are clearly attempting to advance atheism and in the process unwittingly or even willingly undermine the creation of wealth and thus bring about the destruction of mankind. I say willingly undermine the creation of wealth because all men are subject to envy and those that do not fear God are the most envious of all.

Unfortunately, there are individuals of high intelligence who have great difficulty with acknowledging the existence of God. It is an apparent paradox of high intelligence that while it is closer to God it tends to doubt the existence of God. Yet one must question whether those that express doubt in the existence of God are indeed of high intelligence or simply possessed of a large ego masquerading as intelligence to the uninitiated.   Notable men, i.e. men who have distinguished themselves before other men can be divided into two categories, men of words and men of numbers.   Those that have advanced human achievement, i.e. created wealth, are generally the men of numbers, while those that have held back human achievement, i.e. destroyed wealth are men of words.   Aristotle, Pythagoras, Euclid, Ptolemy, Copernicus, Galileo, Euler, Newton, Descartes, Adam Smith, Bohr, Einstein, Fermi and others of similar accomplishments were men of numbers and they were men who also feared God.   Unlike words, the manipulation of numbers instills a discipline on the mind that requires a high level of intelligence to master.   Typically, an individual's IQ most closely correlates with his mathematical ability than with his verbal ability. The history of the SAT math test and its high correlation with IQ at least prior to 1995 is evidence of the fact that mathematical ability most closely correlates with general IQ.   After 1995, there was a re-centering of the SAT as well as greater weight given to the verbal results in a vain attempt to make it appear the Negroid and the female were on an equal par with the Caucasoid male.   These attempts failed but the attempts skewed the results after 1995 in terms of the correlation with actual IQ.   This is the reason that Mensa, the society of individuals with IQ greater than 98% of the population does not accept post 1995 IQ SAT scores as a qualification for membership in the society.   Thus, claims that men of words are geniuses are not necessarily legitimate claims of high IQ.

One example will serve to make my case.   In the most concise explanation of the workings of an economy to that time, Adam Smith's Wealth of Nations written in 1776 is replete with specific references to the price of goods and labor during his lifetime.   His analysis of an economy using detailed economic data available at the time served to overcome the prevailing economic theory of the time, which was mercantilism.   Mercantilism was an economic system that was akin to the 19th century socialism and communism which followed its demise. It assumed that economics was a zero sum game just as socialism and communism assumes.   Mercantilism argued for the supremacy of the sovereign in the economic life of the nation as does socialism and communism.   High tariffs and the accumulation of gold by the sovereign rather than free trade characterized mercantilism whose object was the impoverishment of a nation's neighbors by selling goods and services for gold while at the same time placing tariffs on his goods and services.   This system created much tension between nations during the 17th and 18th Century and led to many wars.   Adam Smith's numbers introduced free trade and no tariffs as the defining relationship between nations.   This idea helped to unleash great wealth creation driven by free trade beginning in the 19th Century in those nations that adopted Adam

Smith's concepts.

Karl Marx on the other hand was a man of words.   His Das Capital contained reference to simplistic monetary transactions with assumptions that caused his calculations to produce predetermined results. For example, Marx first assumed that the value of a good is in the labor to produce it and then he set about showing this to be the case by making the absurd argument that the capital to produce it is equal to zero.   The following is an excerpt from Marx's Das Capital that illustrates the non-sense of his ideas.

"First we will take the case of a spinning mill containing 10,000 mule spindles, spinning No. 32 yarn from American cotton, and producing 1 lb. of yarn weekly per spindle. We assume the waste to be 6%: under these circumstances 10,600 lbs. of cotton are consumed weekly, of which 600 lbs. go to waste. The price of the cotton in April, 1871, was 7 3/4d. per lb.; the raw material therefore costs in round numbers £342. The 10,000 spindles, including preparation-machinery, and motive power, cost, we will assume, £1 per spindle, amounting to a total of £10,000. The wear and tear we put at 10%, or £1,000 yearly = £20 weekly. The rent of the building we suppose to be £300 a year, or £6 a week. Coal consumed (for 100 horse-power indicated, at 4 lbs. of coal per horse-power per hour during 60 hours, and inclusive of that consumed in heating the mill), 11 tons a week at 8s. 6 d. a ton, amounts to about £4 1/2 a week: gas, £1 a week, oil, &c., £4 1/2 a week. Total cost of the above auxiliary materials, £10 weekly. Therefore the constant portion of the value of the week's product is £378. Wages amount to £52 a week. The price of the yarn is 12 1/4d. per. lb. which gives for the value of 10,000 lbs. the sum of £510. The surplus-value is therefore in this case £510 - £430 = £80. We put the constant part of the value of the product = 0, as it plays no part in the creation of value. There remains £132 as the weekly value created, which = £52 var. + £80 surpl. The rate of surplus-value is therefore 80/52 = 153 11/13%. In a working-day of 10 hours with average labour the result is: necessary labour = 3 31/33 hours, and surplus-labour = 6 2/33"
Referring to the underlined portion here Marx simply ignores the £378 capital and non-labor expenses or constant portion that he refers to as the constant part of the product.   He arbitrarily sets this value to zero because he claims that the capital and non-labor expenses used to produce the yarn do not add "value" to the yarn.   The market price of the yarn (£510) less the total expenses (£430) is the surplus value or the profit (£80).   The weekly value created is therefore the surplus value and the weekly labor (£52) that went into the production of the yarn or £132. Thus in a given 10 hour day, we have necessary labor = 3 31/33 hours, needed to produce the yarn according to Marx, and surplus labor = 6 2/33hours, which is essentially the labor wasted, and which only benefits the owners of the mill and not society in general.   Thus, Marx concludes that the surplus value, i.e. profit is due only to the "exploitation" of labor. Marx also conveniently neglects to say how the price of the yarn came to be £510, which is the important and substantive economic and philosophical point, and not the labor that went into the production of

the yarn, which is meaningless and irrelevant in all aspects. This is typical of the kind of analysis Keynesians perform. They assume the price is arbitrarily set failing to realize that the competition for the good or service sets the price of a good or service not the labor or capital that goes into it. In other words, Marx proves nothing as he simply makes a *circulus in probando* (circular argument), starting from the flawed notion of the labor theory of value and simply assigning a meaningless quantity to it, i.e. necessary-labor. Yet so-called intellectuals take this absurdity seriously and continue to subscribe to this nonsense and to propagate it. John Maynard Keynes was an adherent to the Marxist ideology and he argued that government spending helps an economy when in fact it is just the opposite. His arguments comported with the political class's agenda and gave intellectual cover to the government's wealth destroying acts at the time. It is a characteristic of Marxists to espouse ideas counter to common sense, and maybe because they are egotists disguising themselves as geniuses or intellectuals and helped along the way by similar men. Marxists have mastered the absurdity in order to distinguish their ideas from the truth thus satisfying their ego. It is little wonder that Marxists promote abstract art, unconventional literature, cacophonic music, and ugliness in man. In other words, Marxists are simply bold face liars with big egos and low IQs, which is the same definition of an atheist. In Das Kapital, Marx's assumptions predetermined the outcome of his analysis. Marx's words unleashed nothing but poverty, misery and death. Marx, the man of words gave rise to calamity, and the man of numbers, Adam Smith, gave rise to great wealth. Along with Marx are such notable atheists as Fredrick Nietzsche, Voltaire, Rousseau, and others whom I have previously mentioned. These men have few numbers in their writings and they have enabled calamity by promulgating their atheism to unsuspecting and gullible populations. These and other atheists have contributed little to ease mankind's burden and their words have done much to increase his burden and shorten his life, which by the way is their objective.

Recall that it was irrational envy causing Cain to murder his brother, not to win the favor of God but to deny Abel, i.e. to spite Abel and his progeny the fruits of God's favor. God saw Cain's envy in his countenance. Indeed as God denies Cain His blessing God warns Cain by saying "οὐκ ἐὰν ὀρθῶς προσενέγκῃς ὀρθῶς δὲ μὴ διέλῃς ἥμαρτες ἡσύχασον πρὸς σὲ ἡ ἀποστροφὴ αὐτοῦ καὶ σὺ ἄρξεις αὐτοῦ", or in KJV *"If thou doest well, shalt thou not be accepted? and if thou doest not well, sin lieth at the door. And unto thee shall be his desire, and thou shalt rule over him."* My interpretation is different *"If you do not proceed on the true path, and the true path you do not travel, sins will be upon you that you cannot escape, and you will rule over sin."* Which is to say that once Cain yields to his envy it will consume him and his progeny. Cain and his progeny disappeared from the sight of God and of man within two generations. This is the lesson of the account of

Cain and Abel and indeed envy has consumed man whenever the fear of God departs Man's heart. Cain did not fear God and he murdered his brother out of envy. This is the story of the nineteenth and twentieth century.

Discoveries by science, i.e. primarily men of numbers, have served to reinforce the Biblical account of Creation. The Big Bang Theory of the creation of the universe comports with the Biblical account of Creation, i.e. its spontaneous creation out of the void. The fact that the Caucasoid with his high IQ appears suddenly in the anthropological record with no direct precursor in Europe also comports with the Biblical account of the creation of Man, i.e. Man's spontaneous Creation by God. However, the theory of evolution or at least the anthropological adaptation of evolution claims that all man including European man, i.e. the Caucasoid, came out of Africa. The assumption inherent in the theory that man evolved from lower animal forms in Sub-Sahara Africa is that humanoids have a common primal ancestor. Some later form of this ancestor eventually made his way to Europe to give rise to the Caucasoid and then east to Asia to give rise to the Mongoloid. The ancestor that remained in Sub-Sahara Africa became the Negroid. Given the fact that there is no fossil record of pre-homo sapiens in Europe, other than the Neanderthal a more intellectually advanced being than any of the pre-homo sapiens species found in sub-Sahara Africa then the idea of a common ancestor to explain the existence of all of mankind is not credible. The sudden existence of the Neanderthal is sufficient to dispel the notion of a common ancestor. To argue that man first evolved as Homo sapiens and then migrated north is to attribute a very rapid rise in the size and capacity of the human brain that the slow process of evolution through natural selection cannot accomplish. Adding to this is the evidence on the significant difference in IQ between two extant great Races of man, i.e. the Caucasoid, the Mongoloid and the third, i.e. the Negroid. This difference belies any common ancestor at least between the Negroid and the other two races. If indeed a common ancestor existed then the Negroid would have a much higher IQ than he does because evolution would have occurred at the same rate in Europe and sub-Sahara Africa. There is no evidence to show that human intellect evolves at varying rates nor is there any reason that it would. On the other hand, the proximity of the Caucasoid IQ and the Mongoloid IQ point to a common ancestor whereas the large distance between the IQ of these two Races and the Negroid begs for a separate ancestor for the Negroid. Given the plethora of fossilized pre-human species found in Sub Sahara Africa and the general ape-like morphology of the Negroid along with his low IQ, then it is likely that the Negroid evolved from the extant fossilized pre-human species and in turn from the lower animals that God created as set forth in the Biblical account of Creation. Indeed the Neanderthal with his low intelligence may have been the failed attempt at further evolution of the Negroid. Peking man and Java man may also have been failed attempts at further evolution of the Negroid.   Given the spontaneous and sudden appearance of the Caucasoid on the European Continent and his high IQ with his concomitant ability to conceive of God, then it is clear that God created the Caucasoid as set forth in the Biblical account of the spontaneous Creation of man.   The Caucasoid was thus the immediate precursor of the Mongoloid through limited natural selection.   When properly interpreted the Biblical account of the Creation of the Universe and the Creation of Man comports with modern science now more so than at any other time in history.   Hence, science has reinforced and continuous to reinforce the existence of God and the fact that He created the Universe and created Man in his own Image.   The more that man discovers about the universe the more secure is the Biblical account of Creation

Other more esoteric and subtle scientific evidence that supports the Biblical account of the Creation include the asymmetry in the standard model of particle physics, the arrow of time, and the limit to the speed of light.   In the former is the fact that unlike the electron and neutron, the proton does not decay into simpler particles by emitting radiation.   This means that the Universe will never collapse on itself and then begin anew.   The arrow of time is the fact that time is irreversible or in other words, one can never visit the past.   The limit to the speed of light is also the physical limit to man's intellectual ability.   These ideas are consistent with the Big Bang Theory of the creation of the universe, which is fundamentally asymmetrical and inconsistent with the Steady State Theory.   The Steady State Theory of the Universe is the discredited idea that the Universe oscillates and that eventually it will collapse and begin anew.   The Steady State Theory assumes that time is reversible, that it is possible to go faster than light, and that the standard model of particle physics is ultimately symmetrical.   The Steady State Theory precludes God as the Creator because a universe that oscillates does not require a prime mover whereas a universe that started spontaneously presupposes a prime mover as the cause.

Atheists cannot abide the Big Bang Theory because it threatens their unbelief and their agenda for a godless nirvana, i.e. a return to the Garden of Eden in defiance of God, which is a socialist one-world government with limited population consisting of only other self-centered atheists like themselves.   To an atheist the existence of God means their eternal damnation and they know it.   Accordingly, atheists have been desperately trying to revive the Steady State Theory by positing such absurd notions as dark matter and energy, the Higgs boson and gravity waves.   None of these entities exists, but this has not stopped the atheists from spending billions of tax dollars to "prove" their existence nonetheless.   The most egregious and most expensive of the efforts to revive the Steady State Theory of the Universe is the search for the Higgs boson. The Higgs boson has taken on mystical proportions among the atheists who have dubbed it the "god particle" and whose discovery will pave the way for the return of the theory of a Steady State Universe. The European Organization for Nuclear Research or CERN wasted about $6 billion in construction costs and $5.5 billion annually to build and operate the Large Hadron Collider (LHC) to hunt for the Higgs boson. Completed in 2011, the LHC has been plagued with many fundamental and structural problems causing its shut down repeatedly during its testing and operation and adding considerably to its cost. Despite claims of the "discovery" of the Higgs boson in 2012, no one has independently repeated and confirmed the experimental results. Conveniently, the LHC shut down for two years immediately after the "discovery" of the Higgs boson. The shutdown began on February 14, 2013 and in all likelihood given the large operating budget and the frequent breakdowns it will remain shut down forever. Ironically, and fittingly the same socialists that funded this new Tower of Babel cannot afford to operate it because socialism does not create the wealth needed to fund its operation. Because of its socialism, Europe is becoming increasingly less able to sustain itself. The EU will no doubt soon cancel joint unproductive projects such as this. Thus, there will never be independent confirmation of the "discovery", as the atheists desire not to have it independently confirmed in any case. The same individuals at CERN also claimed to have discovered neutrinos that travelled faster than the speed of light, which of course would mean that time is reversible. However, they recanted that claim when independent observers questioned the results. The obvious political agenda and the desire and eagerness to produce results after the expenditure of so many resources and wealth to build this boondoggle is first of all a testament to the ineptitude, bias, and narrow mindedness of the atheists running and promoting this program. The LHC is also a frightening example of the extent and expense to which atheists and socialists will go to disprove the existence of God. This is reason enough to doubt and ridicule the results apart from the fact they go counter to known truths as revealed to man by God in the Biblical account of Creation. Even if the Higgs boson exists, which it does not, the decay of a proton has never happened and until observed, which it never will be, the Big Bang Theory remains unchallenged, as it must be since it is true.

Attempts to find life on other planets is also an atheistic pursuit. It is obviously impossible for life in any form to exist on other planets because such life is not in the Biblical account of Creation. The process of searching for something that does not exist is simply a way to reinforce continuously the flawed assumption that God does not exist. To the extent that the sovereign expends tax money and intellectual capacity on these inherently flawed ventures then it is to this extent that the burden of the sovereign increases and wealth destroyed for no good reason other than to perpetuate and engender godlessness. Unless such ventures are necessary for the protection of private property and the enforcement of laws and contracts then they are not legitimate functions of the sovereign. Unless these ventures have as their clear and unambiguous object a profit then they are unethical. The only way that these ventures can become legitimate and ethical pursuits of science, is through private funding aimed at creating wealth. In the absence of such funding, they are the pursuits of vain men seeking to justify their atheism and inculcate atheism in others at taxpayer expense and nothing more.

Science therefore has the potential for economic good or ill but in a different sense than traditionally thought. Traditionally the economic good and ill of science is in terms of its application. Hence, we have discoveries of science such as the splitting of the uranium atom, which can produce weapons of massive wealth destruction and at the same time provide a source of cheap energy to power wealth creation. However, my meaning is different from this traditional meaning of good and ill. Since the Enlightenment, which sought to replace the fear of God with Stoicism and the fear of the state, science has become a tool of the atheist and his bedfellow the socialist. To the extent that atheists and socialists rely on science for their nefarious ends then it is to this extent that science becomes corrupt and poses a bigger threat to humanity than does the ill applications of any of its discoveries including that of nuclear weapons. Atheists and socialists use science to claim that God does not exist in order to remove the fear of God from the heart of man. They are the modern day Stoics imbued by radical egalitarianism, and driven by hubris, and their ego to believe erroneously that man's reason and man's will can control man's passions. In so believing, their intent is to unleash the passion of envy in every man to impose socialism on a population and be thus sovereign over all or in the German "*über alles*", and in keeping with the spirit of Nietzsche's "will to power". This is exactly the strategy of the French Revolutionaries, the German National Socialists, the Russian Communists, and other such atheistic and ultimately murderous political movements. It is a strategy continuing to this very day using science as a means to this end.

Other wealth destroying ideas promulgated by the atheists include such non-sense as "manmade global warming" aka "manmade climate change" and so-called "green energy". Ideas such as these intend to show to an uninitiated and gullible population that man and not God controls the earth's weather and climate furthering their desire to remove the fear of God from the hearts of man. Thus, when so-called scientists trumpet "discoveries" that if true would cast doubt on the existence of God there is every reason to doubt the veracity of their words and dismiss the discovery claimed as so much propaganda, which it is. The same is true of many so-called scientific facts based on sampling of populations, which defy common sense born of experience, and not repeated and confirmed by others.   Such samplings are easy to manipulate in order to achieve the desired results.   Since atheists do not fear God they have no qualms against lying, so neither trust the atheists trumpeting results based on sampling of populations nor rely on their results.   Maintaining this posture vis-à-vis modern science while fearing God will ensure the creation of wealth and secure the nation against calamity otherwise relying on such propaganda will result in disaster and death will surely follow as it has in the past so it will in the future.

The destiny of a nation

The destiny of a nation or in other words the ability of a nation to survive calamity embodies in the passions and intellect of the individuals, and the burden of the sovereign.   A nation where the individuals fear God, the average IQ of the population is relatively high, and whose sovereign protects private property and enforces contracts with little burden on the economy will achieve a natural control over their passions and create wealth.   Such nations are destined to survive as long as they remain fearful of God.   This was the state of the US in the 19th Century and immediately after World War II and during the Reagan Administration.   It was also Britain in the 18th and 19th Century.

An atheistic or Stoic nation with a high average IQ will always succumb to socialism and communism as the means to rein in the passions and thus fail to create wealth.   This is the old USSR, modern China, modern Europe and Japan.   Socialist and communist nations gradually sink into poverty as they consume their wealth and become increasingly unable to withstand calamity.   To avoid or delay this fate these nations will devote more of their resources to militarization in order to take wealth from their neighbors.   Just as the French under Napoleon, the Germans under Kaiser Wilhelm II and then the NAZIs, the USSR under the Communists, the Japanese in the early 20th Century, and on and on.   These same nations are the core of the next world war unless they significantly reduce the sovereign's burden on their respective economies, abandon Stoicism, and return to God.

It is obvious that a nation with a population with low average IQ will fail to create wealth regardless of its ability to rein in the passions through the fear of God.   Invariably tyrants who burden the economy lead nations with low average IQ's.   This is the case for most post-colonial African, Latin American, and most Middle Eastern nations. These nations are constantly in the throes of calamity with shortened life spans, great poverty, fearful lives, and misery.   The only salvation for such nations is colonization by the formerly wealthy and God-fearing Christian Nations should these nations change their course.   This was true in the past and it is still true.

Summary and Conclusion

I began this book posing two questions that have vexed me ever since my youth. The first question is "What becomes of the soul of a soldier when he kills another man in war with another nation?" The second question is "Are efforts to improve productivity which then lead to unemployment ethical?" Answering these two questions led me to examine such seemingly unrelated subjects as the existence of God, the aim of wealth, the role of private property and freewill in wealth creation, the proper role of government in an economy, and government's burden on wealth creation. I also discussed the role of the human passions and human intellect in the destruction and creation of wealth. I introduced the idea of a wealth creating economy, which is simply capitalism augmented by the fear of God. I contrasted a wealth creating economy with socialist and communist economies and showed how a wealth creating economy survives while socialist and communist economies fail to create wealth and eventually succumb to calamity. A calamity is the destruction of wealth, which is the destruction of life and property. I showed historically how this has been the case and how it will always continue to be the case. I defined a successful economy as one that can survive any calamity, and in the absence of calamity, a successful economy eases the burden of life. I showed that the only possible successful economy is the wealth creating economy. The three elements of a wealth creating economy are the fear of God, the intellectual capital inherent in the population, and the light burden of the sovereign. The degree to which these elements are present in the economy determines whether the economy is indeed a wealth creating economy, a capitalist economy, a socialist economy, or a communist economy. These factors are subject to the will of men. Men will themselves fearful of God or will themselves atheists. They will themselves the burden of the sovereign through the system of government. Men will themselves the average IQ of the population through laws and social mores limiting or promoting miscegenation with the dark races. Thus, the fate of man in terms of his individual suffering, and the fate of his individual soul are in his own hands. However, God foreordained Man's immortality and the immortality of man's soul. In other words, Man's fate and man's soul are no longer predestined and need not be predestined. Just as the creation of the Universe is a conception in the Mind of God that is eternal, so also the creation of each soul is a conception in the Mind of God that is eternal. Thus, each conception of man is a spiritual and physical reenactment of the Creation of the Universe and thus the soul of man is eternal in space and time as the Universe is eternal in space and time. Each individual therefore is an eternal Universe unto himself ordained and blessed by God at his conception.

I discussed the idea of private property and its significance in the creation of wealth, and its role in ethical and moral considerations. Along with private property is the exercise of freewill in contracting, which is liberty. Liberty engenders the exchange of private property through contract and thereby gives rise to commerce. I discussed the nature and purpose of wealth and its relationship to ethics and morality. The creation of wealth is essential to survival. Ethical behavior therefore is behavior directed to the creation of wealth. Wealth creation occurs through gains in productivity and so productivity is essential to survival. Rapid gain in productivity in an encumbered economy is a source of civil unrest because it engenders unemployment. This is not the case in an unencumbered economy where rapid gain in productivity creates wealth with little disruption in employment. Individuals undertake a contract through the exercise of freewill, which is liberty, the basis of wealth creation. The freedom to contract is free enterprise. Government is a coercive force essential for the securing of private property and the enforcement of contracts. Government is at the same time a burden on wealth creation and as such, government may act to reduce rather than increase the security of private property. Government also restricts the exercise of freewill, i.e. liberty that undermines contract formation. A government therefore has the potential to undermine wealth creation by taking private property and restricting liberty leaving a nation more susceptible to calamity than would otherwise be the case.

In any consideration of economics, human passions play a major role. The study of economics is a study of the aggregate behavior of individuals. Human passion plays a role in human behavior to a large degree and is a contributing factor to wealth creation and consequently to ethical and moral behavior. The basic human passions that affect economic decisions and influence ethical behavior are fear, greed, envy, empathy, happiness, vanity, love and hate. I discussed these basic human passions in terms of their effect on economics and ethical behavior. I showed that competition and self-interest serve to regulate human passions and in particular greed. However, only the fear of God suppresses envy, which is the most destructive of the passions. I discussed ethical behavior in light of the disruptions caused by rapid gains in productivity. I concluded that ethical behavior is behavior directed toward maximizing the creation of wealth through the exercise of freewill in contracting. Finally, I discussed how the creation of wealth and its ethical and moral aspects is an improvement over secular capitalism, socialism and communism in securing the survival of mankind. In other words, the human need to secure private property and create wealth manifested in the burden of government, the fear of God, and the average intelligence of the population are better predictors of the future survival, and condition of mankind than are the theories about human motivation embodied in capitalism, socialism and communism.

To Critics

Given the prevailing culture and its misplaced emphasis on multiculturalism and egalitarianism then it is not very difficult to anticipate the criticism to this work. My response to the criticism is simple and it focuses on the facts that I have presented to support my conclusions. Critics have only three paths. They must either, present a verifiable set of facts contradicting the facts I presented, or introduce a new set of verifiable facts leading to different conclusions, or accept the given facts and deduce a different conclusion. Otherwise, my conclusions remain valid and ultimately deterministic of the consequences of man's behavior and decisions. That is if man is godless then his godlessness will engender envy and envy will result in the destruction of wealth exposing him to calamity. If man of his own volition engages in miscegenation with the dark and semi-dark races then he will reduce his ability to create wealth also exposing man to calamity. A sovereign who overburdens an economy destroys wealth creation and subjects his nation to calamity.

The fear of God, the intelligence of citizens, and the burden of sovereignty are the only factors that determine the rise and fall of nations and no other. Each of these factors arises out of Man's will. Thus, Man is the ultimate determinate of his fate and not nature.

Appendix 1

Determining the Burden of Government

Reinvestment of Federal Government Outlays and State and Local Spending

In determining the government's burden on the economy and therefore the reduction in the wealth created, I begin by asking the question "What if there was no government?" This includes no local, state or federal government. If there were no government then all the money that government received from the taxpayers would go to other purposes or to other investments. Next to government treasury securities, the most conservative investment is corporate bonds. Thus, I perform my analysis by investing all government receipts for each of the years since 1930 in Moody's Aaa 10-year corporate bonds at the average rate in the year that the government spent the money. At the end of each 10-year period, I reinvested the interest and principle at the rate for the year that the bond expired. I used 1929 constant dollars to keep from earning interest on inflated dollars. I calculated 1929 dollars by using the GDP deflator whose value in 1929 is 0.0991. The GDP deflator is from *Table 1.1.9. Implicit Price Deflators for Gross Domestic Product* generated by the US Bureau of Economic Analysis. Dividing this number by each of the values in the subsequent years and multiplying this ratio by the nominal receipts in each year yields that year's receipts in terms of 1929 constant dollars. In 2012, the nominal government receipts were $4259.2 billion. In terms of 1929 constant dollars, the government receipts were $401.78 billion. I obtained total government nominal receipts including Federal, State and Local expenditures from *Table 3.1.-Government Current Receipts and Expenditures* from the US Bureau of Economic Analysis.

The result of investing all government receipts in the private economy is a total return of $166 trillion in 2012 in 1929 constant dollars. The GDP in 2012 in 1929 constant dollars is $1.6 trillion. In other words with no local, state or federal government and all taxes invested in the private economy since 1929 the nation would be over 100 times wealthier than it is now. This wealth would have eliminated all poverty, pollution and crime. Instead, we have much poverty, pollution and crime because of government. This is the true burden of government. However, we do need government to protect private property and enforce the law and contracts. Obviously, the government was able to perform these functions in 1929 with revenue of $10.4 billion in constant 1929 dollars, so it is reasonable to assume that this amount is all the government needs to provide these functions. Any amount greater than $10.4 billion is overburdening the economy beyond its basic functions and therefore reducing the amount of wealth created. Assuming that all the revenue between 1941 and 1945 went to fighting World War II, then maintaining government spending at 1929 levels would have resulted in a total return of $124 trillion in 2012 in constant 1929 dollars. This means that the nation would be 80 times wealthier than it is now and the government would have protected private property and enforced contracts as well as fought a major war.

The following is a portion of the spreadsheet that I used to make these calculations.

Year		Moody's 0	Aaa	Gov Receipts 1929 dollars	Sum	Total GDP 1929 dollars	0	1	2	3	4	5	6	7	8	9	0	1	2
1919		5.49%	5.49%																
1920		6.12%	6.12%																
1921		5.97%	5.97%																
1922		5.10%	5.10%																
1923		5.12%	5.12%																
1924		5.00%	5.00%																
1925		4.88%	4.88%																
1926		4.73%	4.73%				0	1	2	3	4	5	6	7	8	9	0	1	2
1927		4.57%	4.57%																
1928		4.55%	4.55%																
1929		4.73%	4.73%	10.50	10	105													
1930	0	4.55%	4.55%	10.38	10	96	10												
1931	1	4.58%	4.58%	10.06	21	90	11	10											
1932	2	5.01%	5.01%	10.74	33	78	11	11	11										
1933	3	4.49%	4.49%	11.59	46	77	12	11	11	12									
1934	4	4.00%	4.00%	12.39	60	85	12	12	12	12	12								
1935	5	3.60%	3.60%	13.14	76	93	13	12	12	12	13	13	13						
1936	6	3.24%	3.24%	14.72	94	105	14	13	13	13	13	14	15						
1937	7	3.26%	3.26%	16.95	115	110	14	13	14	14	14	14	15	17					
1938	8	3.19%	3.19%	16.96	137	107	15	14	14	14	14	15	16	18	17				
1939	9	3.01%	3.01%	17.49	160	115	15	14	15	15	15	15	16	18	18	17			
1940	0	2.84%	2.84%	20.20	184	125	16	15	15	15	15	16	17	19	18	18	20		
1941	1	2.77%	2.77%	27.13	216	148	16	15	16	16	16	16	17	20	19	19	21	27	
1942	2	2.83%	2.83%	32.96	255	175	17	16	16	16	16	16	17	20	19	19	21	28	33
1943	3	2.73%	2.73%	48.10	310	205	17	16	17	17	17	17	18	20	20	19	22	29	34
1944	4	2.72%	2.72%	48.76	367	222	18	17	17	17	17	17	18	21	20	20	23	29	35
1945	5	2.62%	2.62%	49.44	427	220	18	17	18	18	18	18	19	21	21	20	23	30	36
1946	6	2.53%	2.53%	42.93	482	194	19	17	18	18	18	18	19	22	21	21	24	31	37
1947	7	2.61%	2.61%	42.54	537	192	19	18	19	19	19	19	20	22	22	22	25	32	38
1948	8	2.82%	2.82%	41.31	593	200	20	18	19	19	19	19	20	23	22	22	25	33	39
1949	9	2.66%	2.66%	39.05	648	199	20	19	20	20	20	20	21	23	23	23	26	34	40
1950	0	2.62%	2.62%	47.58	717	216	21	19	21	20	20	20	21	24	24	24	27	35	41
1951	1	2.86%	2.86%	55.07	796	234	22	20	21	21	21	21	22	25	25	25	27	36	42
1952	2	2.96%	2.96%	57.11	879	243	22	21	22	22	21	21	23	26	26	26	28	37	44
1953	3	3.20%	3.20%	59.28	966	254	23	21	22	22	22	22	24	27	27	27	29	38	45
1954	4	2.90%	2.90%	55.56	1053	253	23	22	23	23	23	23	25	28	28	28	30	39	46
1955	5	3.05%	3.05%	61.50	1148	271	24	22	24	24	23	23	25	29	29	29	30	40	48
1956	6	3.36%	3.36%	64.02	1249	277	25	23	25	25	24	24	26	31	30	31	31	41	49
1957	7	3.89%	3.89%	65.35	1355	283	25	24	25	25	25	25	27	32	31	32	32	42	51
1958	8	3.79%	3.79%	62.98	1462	281	26	24	26	26	25	26	28	33	32	33	33	44	52
1959	9	4.38%	4.38%	70.32	1580	300	27	25	27	27	26	26	29	34	34	35	34	46	54
1960	0	4.41%	4.41%	75.82	1736	308	28	26	28	28	27	28	30	36	36	37	35	47	56
1961	1	4.35%	4.35%	77.57	1900	315	29	27	29	29	29	29	32	38	38	40	37	49	58
1962	2	4.33%	4.33%	82.99	2078	335	30	29	30	30	31	30	34	40	40	43	38	51	61
1963	3	4.26%	4.26%	88.41	2270	349	32	30	32	32	31	32	35	42	43	46	40	53	64
1964	4	4.41%	4.41%	89.44	2472	370	33	31	33	33	33	33	37	45	45	49	42	55	66
1965	5	4.49%	4.49%	95.08	2689	394	34	32	35	35	34	34	39	47	48	52	44	58	69
1966	6	5.13%	5.13%	104.01	2926	419	36	34	36	36	35	36	41	50	51	56	46	60	72

Reinvested all Government Receipts in 1929 constant dollars

Year		Moody's 0 Aaa	Aaa	Gov Receipts 1929 dollars	Sum	Total GDP 1929 dollars													
1967	7	5.51%	5.51%	108.48	3179	431	37	35	38	38	37	38	43	53	54	60	48	63	75
1968	8	6.18%	6.18%	120.51	3458	452	39	37	39	39	39	39	45	56	58	64	50	66	79
1969	9	7.03%	7.03%	129.17	3761	486	41	38	41	41	40	41	48	59	61	69	52	69	82
1970	0	8.04%	8.04%	124.09	4197	467	44	41	44	44	44	45	52	63	66	76	56	74	88
1971	1	7.39%	7.39%	124.87	4669	483	48	44	47	47	48	49	56	68	72	83	61	79	94
1972	2	7.21%	7.21%	136.82	5192	508	52	48	50	51	52	53	61	74	79	91	65	86	101
1973	3	7.44%	7.44%	145.95	5766	537	56	51	54	55	56	58	66	80	85	100	71	91	108
1974	4	8.57%	8.57%	148.23	6389	534	60	55	58	59	61	63	72	86	93	109	76	98	116
1975	5	8.83%	8.83%	139.10	7054	533	65	59	62	63	66	68	78	93	101	120	82	105	124
1976	6	8.43%	8.43%	151.03	7787	562	70	63	67	68	72	74	84	101	110	131	89	113	133
1977	7	8.02%	8.02%	159.59	8591	597	76	68	71	73	78	81	91	109	119	144	96	121	143
1978	8	8.73%	8.73%	169.82	9470	620	82	73	77	78	86	88	99	117	130	158	104	130	153
1979	9	9.63%	9.63%	177.10	10432	640	89	78	82	84	92	96	107	127	141	173	112	140	164
1980	0	11.94%	11.94%	178.08	11774	638	99	89	93	94	104	107	117	139	155	189	126	160	187
1981	1	14.17%	14.17%	187.20	13281	655	111	102	106	106	117	119	127	152	170	208	141	182	213
1982	2	13.79%	13.79%	180.47	14960	642	124	117	121	118	132	132	139	166	186	225	158	208	242
1983	3	12.04%	12.04%	184.92	16840	672	139	133	138	133	148	147	151	181	204	246	176	238	276
1984	4	12.71%	12.71%	198.71	18955	721	156	152	157	149	167	164	165	198	224	269	197	271	314
1985	5	11.37%	11.37%	210.19	21329	751	174	174	178	166	188	183	180	217	246	294	221	310	357
1986	6	9.02%	9.02%	218.86	23989	778	195	198	203	186	212	203	196	237	270	321	247	353	406
1987	7	9.38%	9.38%	232.22	26969	805	218	226	231	209	239	227	214	260	298	351	277	404	462
1988	8	9.71%	9.71%	240.33	30301	838	244	268	262	234	270	252	233	284	325	383	310	461	526
1989	9	9.26%	9.26%	250.44	34030	869	274	295	299	262	299	281	254	311	356	419	347	526	598
1990	0	9.32%	9.32%	253.52	36921	886	299	321	323	281	328	302	273	333	380	448	379	572	647
1991	1	8.77%	8.77%	252.54	40041	885	327	349	349	302	354	325	293	357	404	480	415	622	700
1992	2	8.14%	8.14%	258.83	43416	917	357	379	378	323	383	350	315	383	431	514	453	677	757
1993	3	7.22%	7.22%	267.07	47064	942	391	413	408	347	413	377	338	411	459	550	496	736	818
1994	4	7.96%	7.96%	280.80	51011	980	427	449	442	372	446	405	363	441	489	589	542	801	885
1995	5	7.59%	7.59%	291.37	55281	1007	467	488	478	399	481	436	390	473	521	630	592	871	957
1996	6	7.37%	7.37%	307.32	59901	1045	511	531	517	427	520	469	418	507	555	674	648	947	1035
1997	7	7.26%	7.26%	324.60	64902	1092	558	578	559	458	561	505	449	544	591	722	708	1031	1119
1998	8	6.53%	6.53%	342.74	70314	1140	610	628	604	491	606	543	482	584	630	773	774	1121	1210
1999	9	7.04%	7.04%	359.16	76164	1196	667	683	653	527	654	584	518	626	671	827	846	1219	1309
2000	0	7.62%	7.62%	378.96	81154	1245	718	732	696	557	691	615	547	661	709	871	910	1306	1394
2001	1	7.08%	7.08%	368.71	86446	1256	773	784	741	588	730	647	577	697	748	917	980	1398	1484
2002	2	6.49%	6.49%	345.52	92046	1279	831	839	789	621	771	681	610	736	791	966	1054	1497	1580
2003	3	5.67%	5.67%	347.41	97994	1314	895	899	840	657	814	716	644	777	835	1017	1135	1603	1683
2004	4	5.63%	5.63%	362.84	104325	1364	963	962	895	694	860	754	680	820	882	1071	1221	1716	1792
2005	5	6.24%	6.24%	394.46	111077	1410	1036	1030	953	733	909	794	718	866	932	1128	1314	1836	1908
2006	6	5.59%	5.59%	418.04	118269	1448	1115	1103	1014	775	960	835	758	914	984	1188	1414	1968	2032
2007	7	5.56%	5.56%	427.64	125913	1474	1200	1181	1080	819	1014	879	800	965	1040	1251	1522	2107	2164
2008	8	5.63%	5.63%	403.62	134006	1469	1292	1265	1150	865	1071	926	845	1019	1098	1317	1638	2257	2305
2009	9	5.31%	5.31%	365.61	142560	1429	1390	1354	1225	914	1131	973	892	1075	1160	1387	1763	2416	2454
2010	0	4.94%	4.94%	380.20	160222	1464	1459	1417	1270	966	1196	1024	942	1135	1226	1461	1850	2529	2544
2011	1	4.64%	4.64%	391.03	168292	1491	1531	1483	1317	1021	1262	1078	994	1198	1294	1539	1942	2646	2639
2012	2	3.67%	3.67%	401.78	166788	1532	1607	1562	1365	1079	1333	1136	1060	1266	1367	1620	2037	2769	2734

Reinvested all Government Receipts in 1929 constant dollars (cont'd)

Appendix 2

Non-random processes effect on statistical measurements

There are at least two measures of location or central tendency, the median and the mean in any random sample of a large population. If the data is from a random or non-deterministic process then the mean and median are equal to each other. This is easy to show using the formula for a normal distribution assuming that the mean is zero and the standard deviation is one and integrating the normal function from the mean to positive infinity yields 0.5. In other words, 50% of the values in a random distribution lie above the mean and 50% lie below the mean, thus the mean equals the median,

$$\mu := 0$$
$$\sigma := 1$$

$$f(x) := \frac{1 \cdot e^{\frac{-(x-\mu)^2}{2 \cdot \sigma^2}}}{\sqrt{2 \cdot \pi \cdot \sigma}}$$

$$\int_0^\infty f(x) \, dx \rightarrow \frac{1}{2}$$

This is also true of a random sample of a normal distribution. However if the sample is not large enough then there will emerge a difference between the mean and the median arising from measurement error. The greater the standard deviation of the original population then the greater will be the difference between the sample mean and the sample median. The closer that the absolute difference between the sample mean and the sample median to the sample standard deviation then the more likely that the process is a random process. The farther apart the sample mean and the sample median in terms of the sample standard deviation then the more likely there are underlying non-random processes at work.

An example will illustrate this concept. Utilizing the Data Analysis Tool of EXCEL I generated 1000 values of a single random variable that is normally distributed with $\mu = 4$ and $\sigma = 1$. The calculated sample mean
m = 3.9576 and a sample s = 1.0049 and the sample median = 3.9500. The absolute difference between the sample mean and the sample median is .0076. In terms of the sample standard deviation this is .0075 SD or well within one SD. This value implies that the process generating the set of 1000 values is likely a random process. Figure 80 is the distribution of the values of the normal random variable. Overlaid is

the theoretical normal distribution with the given the sample mean and the sample standard deviation. From the shape of the curves, it is obvious that the date is randomly distributed. In this example, I assumed that the random variable is the number of wage earners within the specified wage increment.

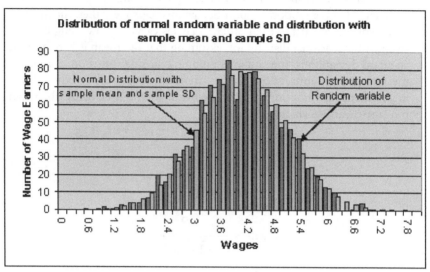

Figure 80 Distribution of normal random variable

If we now introduce a deterministic process into the data set then the shape of the distribution will change and the sample mean and the sample median have a wider variance in terms of the sample standard deviation. Figure 81 is the underlying deterministic process that I introduced into the values of the random value. This added 500 values to the original data set of 1000 values. The deterministic process is $y = x^{0.5}$ or the number of wage earners earning a specific wage rate is equal to the square root of the wage rate.

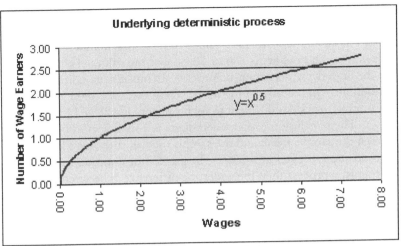

Figure 81 Underlying deterministic process

The result of the underlying deterministic process to the shape of the distribution is in Figure 82.

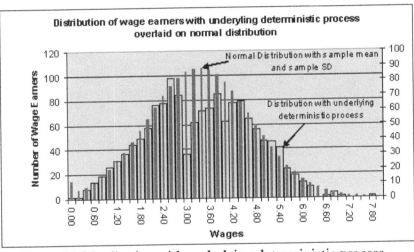

Figure 82 Distribution with underlying deterministic process

Figure 82 shows the distribution of wage earners with the underlying deterministic process. The sample mean for this distribution is 3.2457 and the sample median is 3.2659. The absolute difference is .0202 or 0.0150 SD. This is almost twice the distance in terms of the standard deviation when we introduce the underlying deterministic process.

Besides the size of the difference between the sample mean and the sample median, another method I use to indicate the difference between the curves is to take the difference between the number of values in each category of wage for the normal distribution with sample mean and sample standard deviation and the sample distribution. In the case of Figure 82 there are 1501 values and the total number of values different in each category is 306 or 20.14% of the values of the process with the underlying deterministic process are outside the normal distribution. In the case of Figure 80 where there are 1000 values, the total number of values different in each category is 121 or 12.13%.

The conclusion is that where there is a significant difference between the sample mean and the sample median then there are deterministic processes at work. The greater the contribution of the deterministic process then the wider the difference is between the mean and the median.

Bibliography

Title	Author	Published	Notes
A History of the American People	Paul Johnson	1999	
An Inquiry into the Nature and Causes of the Wealth of Nations	Adam Smith	1776	
Constitution of the United States of America		1788	
History of the Peloponnesian War	Thucydides	c.450 BC	Hobbes Translation
Human accomplishment : the pursuit of excellence in the arts and sciences, 800 B.C. to 1950	Charles Murray	2003	
Iphigenia in Aulis	Euripides	c.406 BC	
Leviathan ; Or, The Matter, Form, and Power of a Commonwealth Ecclesiastical and Civil	Thomas Hobbes	1651	Restored in 1885
Macbeth	William Shakespeare	1600	
March of the Titans - A History of the White Race	Arthur Kemp	2013	marchofthetitans.com
Race Differences in Intelligence - An Evolutionary Analysis	Richard Lynn	2006	
Race, Evolution, and Behavior: A Life History Perspective	J. Philippe Rushton	2000	
The Articles of Confederation		1781	
The Bell Curve : Intelligence and class structure in American life	Richard J. Herrnstein and Charles Murray	1994	
The Bible - King James Version			
The Declaration of Independence		1776	

Bibliography

Title	Author	Published	Notes
The Federalist Papers	Alexander Hamilton, James Madison, John Jay	1788	
The g Factor: The Science of Mental Ability (Human Evolution, Behavior, and Intelligence)	Arthur R. Jensen	1998	
The Histories	Herodotus	1890	Translated George Campbell MaCauley
The Iliad	Homer	c.1194 BC	
The Prince	Niccolò Machiavelli	1532	
The Road to Serfdom	Fredrick Hayek	1943	
The Tragedy of Othello, the Moor of Venice	William Shakespeare	1603	

Index

10th Amendment, 59, 221

14th Amendment, 128

16th Amendment, 46, 76, 128, 148, 161, 166, 238, 267, 280

17th Amendment, 46, 76, 128, 149

19th Amendment, 46, 76, 128, 149, 161, 359

Abel, 14, 22, 26, 32, 42, 214, 216, 218, 270, 296, 298, 299, 302, 330, 342, 397

abortion, 126, 138, 346

Abraham, 14, 15, 16, 26, 74, 163, 198

abstract art, 29, 357, 362, 364, 397

Adam Smith, 213, 348, 373, 395, 397, 413

Address of South Carolina, 75

admixture, 61, 143, 273, 341, 359, 360, 366, 367, 368, 369, 372, 382, 388

affirmative action, 57, 122, 224, 225, 229, 246, 260, 262, 274, 276, 293, 310, 324, 357, 382

Africa, 143, 196, 217, 376, 398

Agamemnon, 14, 17, 26, 218

Agricultural Credits Act, 93

Akron, 122, 160, 201

Alan Greenspan, 54, 118, 127, 192, 251, 261

altruism, 35, 36, 39, 40, 63, 154, 159, 163, 181, 198, 199, 271, 300, 301, 328, 331, 332, 339, 345, 347, 348, 351, 355

altruistic, 35, 36, 37, 63, 158, 270, 301, 330, 332, 333, 348

angels, 26

anti-Semitism, 171

apostasy, 164

Argentocoxos, 360

Aristotle, 159, 195, 395

arrow of time, 399

art, 29, 50, 54, 101, 124, 198, 204, 232, 257, 353, 354, 357, 358, 360, 361, 362, 364, 390, 393, 397

article of impeachment, 288

Ashkenazi Jew, 372, 391, 392

AT&T, 27, 45, 132, 133, 221

atheism, 22, 35, 37, 126, 127, 128, 138, 149, 164, 171, 198, 210, 211, 213, 216, 218, 219, 239, 275, 296, 298, 319, 328, 330, 333, 344, 348, 354, 362, 363, 364, 370, 372, 377, 380, 382, 394, 397, 401

atheist, 126, 138, 171, 198, 213, 215, 218, 238, 308, 326, 343, 354, 361, 363, 365, 397, 399, 401

Athenians, 25, 67, 273

Athens, 25, 273, 366, 368

Baal, 15, 25, 27

bank failures, 49, 50, 51, 52, 53, 55, 81, 88, 92, 93, 168, 182, 257, 267

bankruptcy, 122, 126, 174, 222, 236

baptism, 17, 18, 20, 138, 374

Barney Frank, 253

beauty, 28, 29, 352, 353, 357, 360, 361, 363, 364, 366, 390, 394

betray, 22, 23

betrayal, 22, 23, 154, 159, 212, 338

Big Bang Theory, 398, 399

Bill of Attainder, 41, 59

Bismarck, 199, 218

bonds, 78, 81, 86, 106, 110, 119, 225, 235, 307, 313, 316, 406

Bretton-Woods Agreement, 82, 89, 101, 104, 114, 122, 123, 126, 184, 310

burden of government, 58, 97, 120, 121, 122, 165, 316, 324, 338, 382, 404, 406

business cycles, 46, 266

Cain, 14, 22, 26, 32, 33, 42, 214, 216, 218, 270, 296, 298, 299, 302, 330, 342, 352, 397

calamity, 15, 22, 24, 25, 26, 27, 29, 30, 33, 34, 35, 37, 38, 39, 41, 46, 52, 56, 57, 58, 59, 61, 62, 64, 67, 68, 69, 70, 71, 72, 73, 74, 77, 78, 97, 100, 101, 107, 110, 121, 122, 125, 127, 129, 131, 132, 133, 137, 139, 140, 142, 143, 145, 148, 149, 152, 159, 160,☐ 161, 163, 168, 169, 170, 171, 172, 175, 176, 190, 191, 193, 194, 195, 197, 200, 201, 217, 219, 222, 230, 233, 236, 239, 241, 249, 251, 254, 255, 256, 263,

265, 270, 271, 272, 273, 274, 277, 285, 286, 287, 290, 292, 294, 296, 298, 300, 301, 302, 303, 307, 308, 309, 311, 320, 324, 326, 327, 328, 329, 333, 334, 336, 337, 338, 339, 340, 341, 342, 343, 344, 345, 348, 350, 352, 354, 357, 366, 367, 368, 369, 371, 373, 375, 381, 385, 390, 392, 394, 397, 402, 403, 404, 405

capital efficiency, 173

capitalist, 29, 63, 206, 304, 329, 343, 344, 345, 346, 348, 352, 354, 375, 403

Caracalla, 311, 359, 366, 368, 382

Carter, 113, 126, 191, 224, 229, 247, 252, 294

Castro, 347, 354, 371, 374

Caucasian, 26, 29, 143, 196, 217, 273, 319, 341, 369, 390

Caucasoid, 128, 143, 145, 195, 206, 217, 273, 309, 310, 315, 317, 319, 320, 342, 359, 364, 366, 367, 369, 376, 382, 383, 385, 388, 389, 390, 392, 393, 394, 395, 398

CDO
  Collaterized Debt Obligations, 117

cell phone, 53, 192, 221, 251, 264, 282

chained dollars, 103, 105, 107, 183

charity, 36, 37, 38, 39, 63, 72, 219, 270, 328, 331, 339

China, 80, 84, 102, 167, 171, 177, 209, 236, 304, 350, 381, 402

Christ, 18, 19, 22, 26

Christian, 12, 19, 22, 23, 33, 38, 64, 195, 357, 374, 402

Christianity, 18, 19, 24, 30, 196, 358, 363

Chrysler, 222

church, 19, 23, 64, 96, 164, 194, 195, 210, 318, 348, 355, 372, 373

Churchill, Winston, 89, 290

circumcision, 14, 15, 17, 18, 20

civil rights, 106, 112, 122, 184, 225, 246, 260, 274, 275, 293, 310, 324, 357, 382

civil war, 21, 30, 59, 72, 73, 76, 132, 148, 155, 156, 160, 162, 163, 191, 228, 256, 287, 292, 325, 370

Clayton Anti-Trust Act, 46

Clinton, William Jefferson, 117, 177, 181, 222, 242, 250, 251, 252, 255, 261, 264, 268, 288, 296

coercion, 46, 47, 55, 78, 111, 113, 117, 150, 159, 173, 175, 193, 194, 195, 196, 197, 200, 201, 206, 219, 255, 262, 264, 266, 274, 277, 282, 283, 295, 306, 330, 335, 337, 342

coined money, 87, 226, 239

coining of money, 91

collective bargaining, 159, 184, 188, 201, 202, 204, 219, 313, 356

colonization, 33, 34, 62, 143, 207, 352, 368, 372, 402

Commandments, 12, 13, 15, 16, 18, 19, 20, 21, 24, 29, 32, 34, 37, 43, 60, 63, 137, 147, 155, 164, 171, 210, 216, 271, 278, 299, 300, 301, 336, 339, 343, 352, 356

common law, 58, 111, 154, 201, 209, 219, 225, 274

communism, 14, 19, 60, 63, 107, 140, 153, 156, 157, 163, 181, 195, 197, 199, 214, 262, 267, 272, 274, 275, 304, 319, 328, 329, 331, 332, 333, 340, 342, 343, 345, 347, 349, 351, 361, 372, 376, 395, 402, 404

communist, 19, 24, 33, 35, 41, 64, 65, 157, 167, 200, 209, 225, 298, 303, 304, 332, 333, 344, 347, 349, 351, 352, 361, 363, 364, 373, 381, 394, 402, 403

computers, 185, 221

conception, 65, 66, 137, 138, 152, 403

Congress, 41, 53, 75, 81, 88, 103, 114, 148, 181, 219, 226, 235, 238, 250, 252, 257, 260, 280, 307

constitution, 162, 168, 287

Constitution, 41, 45, 59, 75, 94, 128, 147, 149, 162, 213, 220, 267, 276, 280, 287, 292, 331, 359, 413

constitutional laws, 287

continuous improvement, 173

contract, 20, 21, 22, 24, 27, 28, 30, 31, 34, 35, 37, 38, 40, 41, 43, 47, 48, 56, 57, 58, 59, 61, 69, 70, 71, 72, 76, 77, 78, 87, 94, 97, 101, 111, 113, 118, 120, 121, 122, 128,

129, 132, 133, 136, 137, 147, 149, 151, 153, 155, 156, 158, 159, 160, 161, 162, 165, 168, 170, 175, 176, 184, 185, 189, 193, 194, 197, 200, 201, 202, 204, 206, 207, 209, 213, 219, 221, 222, 223, 225, 236, 237, 255, 260, 262, 264, 266, 268, 270, 271, 272, 274, 275, 276, 278, 284, 285, 286, 287, 290, 292, 295, 299, 302, 303, 304, 305, 306, 308, 310, 313, 318, 324, 325, 327, 329, 330, 331, 333, 334, 335, 336, 337, 338, 339, 340, 341, 342, 344, 345, 348, 352, 356, 357, 370, 371, 372, 373, 374, 375, 401, 402, 404, 406

copyright, 65, 150, 209, 304, 350

corruption, 29, 176, 220, 222, 322, 328, 338, 346, 356, 357, 361, 364, 373

cost per student, 317

cotton, 74, 75, 76, 391, 396

court, 59, 126, 153, 219, 277, 288, 311, 330, 348, 355

covet, 37, 299

CPI
  Consumer Price Index, 54, 82, 83, 84, 85, 86, 93, 94, 99, 100, 104, 106, 110, 111, 115, 120, 121, 173, 240, 245, 261, 262, 280, 281, 282, 283, 293, 313

CRA
  Community Reinvestment Act, 117, 122, 243, 251, 252, 261, 295

creation, 20, 21, 22, 24, 27, 28, 29, 33, 35, 36, 37, 38, 39, 41, 42, 46, 47, 53, 55, 56, 57, 58, 60, 61, 62, 63, 64, 66, 68, 69, 70, 71, 72, 73, 76, 77, 78, 79, 81, 82, 84, 85, 86, 87, 96, 97, 99, 101, 104, 106, 107, 108, 109, 113, 114, 119, 122, 123, 126, 127, 128, 129, 131, 132, 133, 137, 139, 140, 142, 147, 148, 149, 150, 152, 154, 155, 156, 158, 159, 160, 161, 162, 163, 165, 168, 169, 170, 171, 173, 174, 175, 176, 181, 182, 184, 190, 191, 193, 194, 195, 197, 200, 201, 204, 205, 209, 212, 216, 217, 218, 219, 221, 223, 225, 226, 227, 229, 232, 233, 234, 236, 237, 239, 241, 245, 247, 249, 250, 255, 259, 260, 263, 264, 266, 267, 268, 269, 270, 271, 272, 273, 274, 275, 277, 278, 280, 283, 284, 285, 286, 287, 290, 292, 293, 294, 295, 297, 299, 300, 301, 302, 303, 304, 306, 307, 308, 309, 311, 313, 316, 318, 319, 324, 325, 327, 328, 331, 332, 333, 334, 335, 336, 337, 338, 339, 340, 341, 342, 343, 344, 347, 349, 351, 352, 353, 354, 356, 357, 360, 364, 367, 368, 372, 373, 375, 376, 378, 379, 381, 382, 387, 388, 390, 392, 394, 395, 396, 398, 399, 401, 402, 403, 404

Creation, 14, 16, 37, 39, 63, 64, 79, 152, 299, 355, 394, 398, 399, 400, 403

crime, 120, 288, 317, 349, 406

Crucifixion, 18, 20

Cubist movement, 361, 364

current expenditures, 99

Darwinism, 215

debt, 48, 78, 80, 81, 82, 83, 85, 105, 106, 109, 115, 117, 123, 124, 128, 136, 148, 165, 173, 183, 190, 193, 194, 196, 202, 203, 204, 207, 208, 210, 215, 224, 225, 226, 228, 229, 231, 232, 233, 234, 235, 239, 240, 244, 254, 258, 266, 290, 307, 313, 339

deception, 155, 313, 328, 329

deed, 14, 65, 149, 151

democracy, 32, 73, 162, 308, 319, 366

Democrat, 95, 113, 117, 181, 193, 222, 226, 251, 252, 260, 265, 276

depression, 46, 52, 53, 55, 76, 88, 90, 93, 94, 95, 103, 105, 108, 118, 165, 167, 182, 192, 226, 227, 257, 258, 259, 263, 264, 267, 275

depression of 1873, 88

depression of 1929, 167

Detroit, 122, 160, 201

Diaspora, 20, 372, 392

Divine right of king, 30, 31, 34, 36, 39, 70, 73, 137, 138, 139, 150, 155, 157, 160, 162, 163, 201, 277, 279, 284, 285, 286, 287, 288, 324, 335, 338, 340, 351

417

Dow Jones Indusrial Average, 95, 115, 231, 251, 259, 260, 261, 262

Dust Bowl, 93, 95, 167

duty, 35, 36, 39, 40, 41, 137, 149, 153, 154, 155, 156, 158, 159, 160, 200, 274, 277, 278, 287, 289, 324, 329, 334, 338, 340, 344, 348, 374

economic deflation, 105, 230, 257, 263, 266

economic inflation, 86, 91, 95, 105, 106, 115, 120, 173, 190, 227, 229, 230, 233, 245, 255, 256

Edict of Caracalla, 311, 359, 366, 368, 382

Edward VI, 95, 97, 255

efficiency, 45, 46, 132, 133, 172, 173, 175, 205, 219, 223, 247, 257, 268, 298, 364, 375

egalitarianism, 214, 218, 220, 320, 346, 374, 401, 405

ego, 38, 295, 301, 330, 362, 395, 397, 401

email, 185, 187, 189

eminent domain, 21, 22, 30, 32, 34, 35, 37, 40, 41, 48, 59, 67, 68, 71, 73, 75, 76, 86, 88, 97, 128, 136, 137, 147, 151, 155, 159, 162, 168, 197, 199, 215, 218, 271, 272, 276, 277, 278, 279, 287, 288, 298, 302, 325, 326, 331, 334, 335, 336, 337, 338, 339, 341, 342, 345, 349, 365, 370, 373

emotion, 295, 302, 367

empathy, 60, 63, 270, 294, 300, 301, 327, 332, 339, 404

employment, 27, 45, 55, 58, 59, 83, 84, 94, 114, 116, 117, 149, 154, 155, 165, 171, 175, 191, 201, 203, 204, 207, 224, 230, 232, 237, 239, 246, 247, 248, 249, 250, 252, 253, 257, 263, 264, 282, 283, 297, 356, 383, 404

employment at will, 59, 154, 207

Enclosure Laws, 96, 140, 142, 147, 205, 206, 209

encumbered economy, 27, 28, 38, 42, 43, 46, 56, 57, 67, 130, 131, 132, 139, 160, 165, 173, 181, 193, 202, 205, 227, 230, 232, 239, 241, 263, 266, 268, 275, 292, 299, 303, 305, 318, 369, 373, 376, 404

energy, 26, 134, 169, 200, 224, 296, 329, 331, 333, 357, 374, 399, 401

engineers, 45

Enlightenment, 31, 35, 147, 149, 164, 193, 196, 212, 213, 214, 215, 220, 326, 328, 330, 366, 370, 373, 377, 401

environmentalism, 224

envy, 12, 14, 15, 20, 21, 22, 23, 24, 30, 31, 33, 35, 39, 41, 42, 43, 56, 57, 60, 63, 89, 113, 126, 127, 128, 129, 130, 131, 132, 147, 149, 153, 155, 156, 157, 162, 163, 164, 167, 168, 171, 181, 192, 198, 200, 208, 209, 211, 213, 214, 215, 216, 218, 219, 223, 224, 226, 229, 234, 237, 239, 253, 256, 265, 268, 270, 271, 272, 273, 275, 279, 284, 294, 295, 296, 298, 299, 300, 301, 302, 303, 304, 305, 308, 325, 326, 327, 328, 330, 333, 336, 339, 340, 341, 343, 344, 345, 347, 348, 349, 351, 352, 354, 361, 363, 364, 365, 367, 368, 372, 373, 374, 375, 376, 377, 378, 380, 394, 397, 401, 404, 405

Envy, 14, 30, 36, 56, 60, 113, 127, 130, 147, 155, 156, 162, 181, 198, 211, 215, 270, 271, 275, 279, 295, 296, 298, 299, 300, 302, 344, 347, 354

EPA

Environmetal Protection Agency, 293, 299, 310, 324

Epicureans, 159

equality, 129, 130, 147, 199, 212, 331, 345, 347, 348, 366, 369

equity, 31, 77, 99, 115, 116, 118, 153, 168, 169, 174, 191, 231, 232, 233, 235, 237, 238, 244, 251, 254, 258, 261, 264, 296

ethical, 28, 32, 34, 42, 43, 45, 53, 55, 58, 60, 62, 63, 68, 70, 137, 150, 152, 153, 154, 155, 156, 157, 158, 159, 160, 174, 176, 193, 195, 197, 200, 201, 223, 238, 255, 258, 266, 268, 270, 272, 274, 278, 284, 285, 287, 305, 306, 327, 328, 332, 333,

334, 336, 338, 339, 342, 343, 356,
401, 403, 404
ethical behavior, 58, 60, 159, 255,
270, 327, 332, 333, 334, 342, 404
Europe, 33, 35, 61, 88, 91, 92, 94,
102, 115, 143, 147, 148, 164, 172,
183, 194, 195, 205, 207, 208, 210,
211, 214, 216, 239, 258, 273, 290,
303, 319, 326, 341, 344, 347, 351,
353, 359, 367, 369, 370, 371, 376,
377, 381, 391, 398, 400, 402
evil, 15, 18, 39, 156, 218, 354, 357,
361, 365
exchange rates, 80, 91, 112, 166,
183, 229
exectuive, 122, 128, 224, 246, 274
Fannie Mae
    Federal National Mortgage
        Association, 105, 234, 251,
        253
FDIC
    Federal Deposit Insurance
        Corporation, 53, 55, 93, 168,
        188, 238
FDR
    Franklyn Delano Roosevelt, 52,
        53, 90, 93, 94, 95, 103, 167,
        220, 258, 260, 347, 355
fear, 15, 16, 20, 21, 22, 24, 30, 31,
    34, 35, 36, 37, 39, 41, 43, 52, 56,
    60, 61, 62, 64, 70, 73, 77, 96, 113,
    128, 129, 130, 131, 132, 138, 140,
    145, 147, 155, 156, 157, 161, 162,
    163, 164, 168, 170, 184, 192, 194,
    198, 200, 209, 211, 213, 214, 215,
    216, 226, 250, 253, 255, 256,
    268, 269, 270, 271, 272, 273, 275,
    278, 284, 287, 294, 295, 298, 299,
    300, 301, 302, 303, 304, 305, 311,
    325, 326, 327, 328, 330, 332, 336,
    340, 341, 342, 343, 344, 345, 347,
    348, 349, 351, 354, 361, 364, 365,
    367, 368, 372, 373, 374, 375, 376,
    377, 378, 380, 392, 394, 398, 401,
    402, 403, 404, 405
fear of God, 20, 21, 22, 24, 30, 31,
    35, 36, 37, 39, 43, 56, 60, 61, 63,
    64, 96, 113, 129, 130, 131, 132,
    138, 140, 145, 147, 156, 157, 163,
    164, 170, 184, 192, 194, 198, 200,

211, 213, 214, 215, 216, 269, 270,
271, 272, 274, 275, 279, 298, 299,
301, 303, 304, 305, 325, 326, 327,
328, 330, 331, 332, 336, 340, 341,
343, 344, 348, 349, 354, 361, 364,
365, 368, 372, 373, 374, 375, 376,
378, 380, 392, 394, 398, 401, 402,
403, 404, 405
Federal outlays, 110, 183, 280, 281,
282, 283
Federal receipts, 294
Federal Reserve Bank, 46, 49, 50,
51, 52, 54, 56, 81, 83, 84, 85, 93,
102, 105, 106, 114, 115, 116, 118,
123, 124, 127, 128, 130, 149, 166,
183, 186, 190, 192, 193, 202, 225,
228, 229, 232, 234, 235, 237, 238,
239, 240, 243, 244, 246, 250, 251,
252, 254, 260, 261, 265, 266, 304
feudalism, 110, 140, 147, 148, 164,
184, 194, 206, 211, 214, 303, 304,
340, 341, 344, 349
fiat currency, 104, 105, 110, 113,
123, 126, 177, 183, 184, 192, 224,
229, 234, 235, 262
fiat money, 83, 105, 115, 226, 235,
239, 244, 268, 304
fiber optics, 53, 184, 192, 221
fiduciary, 153, 158, 277, 334, 338
FOMC
    Federal Open Market
        Committee, 81, 114, 225, 235
food prices, 52, 91, 92, 93, 94, 105,
111, 183, 207, 258, 259, 264, 267
Fordney–McCumber Tariff, 166,
182
fractional banking, 46, 48, 49, 55,
87, 236, 237
France, 60, 155, 164, 207, 213, 214,
215, 344, 359, 371
Freddie Mac
    Federal Home Loan Mortgage
        Corporation, 105, 234, 251,
        253
Fredrich Nietzche, 171, 215, 220,
348, 354, 377, 397, 401
free will, 17, 154, 274
French Revolution, 22, 31, 33, 35,
60, 149, 155, 164, 171, 207, 208,

213, 214, 215, 285, 326, 328, 344, 355, 370, 372, 377, 401

functions of the sovereign, 71, 151, 162, 401

GDP

Gross Domestic Product, 79, 80, 81, 98, 99, 100, 101, 103, 106, 107, 108, 109, 110, 116, 119, 120, 121, 122, 125, 134, 135, 143, 144, 145, 146, 161, 176, 177, 178, 190, 210, 217, 227, 232, 240, 241, 242, 243, 245, 246, 248, 249, 254, 255, 264, 281, 283, 290, 291, 292, 293, 294,□ 316, 356, 378, 379, 380, 381, 406

GDP deflator, 246, 406

genius, 14, 29, 45, 61, 96, 97, 143, 200, 206, 241, 258, 320, 341, 353, 354, 356, 357, 359, 360, 361, 362, 367, 369, 382, 390, 392, 394

Germany, 52, 60, 90, 95, 148, 170, 171, 182, 199, 207, 213, 214, 215, 216, 217, 220, 254, 290, 292, 307, 346, 350, 351, 352, 372, 377, 381

Gertrude Stein, 363

Glass-Steagall, 53, 260

God, 1, 12, 13, 15, 16, 17, 18, 19, 20, 21, 22, 23, 24, 26, 29, 30, 31, 33, 34, 35, 36, 37, 38, 39, 41, 42, 43, 56, 57, 60, 61, 62, 63, 64, 65, 66, 67, 69, 70, 71, 73, 77, 96, 113, 127, 128, 129, 130, 131, 132, 137, 138, 139, 141, 143, 145, 147, 149, 150, 152, 155, 157, 158, 160, 162, 163, 164, 168, 170, 171, 192, 194, 195, 196, 197, 198, 199, 201, 208, 209, 211, 213, 214, 215, 216, 218, 219, 226, 253, 255, 256, 268, 269, 270, 271, 272, 273, 275, 277, 278, 284, 285, 287, 295, 296, 298, 299, 300, 301, 302, 303, 304, 305, 308, 309, 318, 320, 325, 326, 327, 328, 330, 332, 335, 336, 338, 339, 340, 341, 342, 343, 344, 345, 346, 348, 349, 351, 352, 353, 354, 356, 357, 361, 363, 364, 365, 368, 371, 372, 373, 374, 375, 376, 377, 378, 380, 392, 394, 397, 398, 399, 400, 401, 402, 403, 404

godless sovereign, 35, 43, 162, 168, 170, 226, 234, 253, 287, 341, 372

gold standard, 51, 80, 82, 86, 88, 89, 91, 94, 101, 104, 112, 113, 115, 120, 123, 128, 166, 177, 192, 224, 234, 246, 262

Golden Rule, 29, 36, 37

gratitude, 39, 291, 339, 347

Great Britain, 75, 91, 217, 372

Great Depression, 52, 55, 76, 93, 95, 118, 182, 226, 256, 258, 264, 267, 275

Great Society, 112, 262

greed, 21, 33, 35, 60, 128, 181, 222, 224, 270, 271, 294, 295, 296, 299, 300, 301, 302, 327, 332, 339, 340, 343, 354, 367, 404

greed and envy conflate, 302

Greeks, 14, 25, 341, 357, 360, 362, 367

green energy, 329, 401

H.L. Mencken, 354

Haiti, 72, 177

happiness, 60, 149, 159, 270, 294, 295, 300, 327, 343, 346, 404

hate, 35, 60, 270, 294, 300, 327, 367, 404

head tax, 128, 147, 175, 267, 279, 284, 285, 337

Hebrew, 15, 17, 25, 371

Hebrews, 15, 16, 17, 18, 20, 23, 25

hedge against calamity, 22, 26, 29, 35, 56, 58, 77, 100, 137, 168, 172, 175, 194, 197, 290, 294, 299, 300, 302, 309, 333, 334, 336, 339, 342, 349, 375, 381, 390, 394

Henry VII, 95, 96, 101, 255

Herbert Hoover, 92, 93

Higgs boson, 399

Hitler, 90, 95, 167, 347, 354, 371

Hobbes, 70, 72, 157, 331, 348, 413

Hollywood, 95

homosexual, 29, 253, 356, 363, 365

human sacrifice, 14, 15, 16, 17, 24, 25, 57, 126

IBM, 132, 133

Iki-Ryo, 378

impeachment, 163, 287

income distribution, 131

India, 33, 74, 76, 209, 289, 291, 292, 372

inflation, 52, 54, 55, 79, 80, 81, 82, 83, 84, 85, 86, 88, 90, 94, 95, 98, 99, 101, 102, 104, 105, 106, 109, 110, 111, 113, 114, 115, 117, 118, 119, 120, 122, 123, 124, 125, 127, 134, 164, 170, 173, 174, 180, 181, 183, 184, 185, 189, 190, 191, 193, 197, 211, 221, 224, 225, 226, 227, 228, 230, 232, 233, 234, 236, 237, 239, 240, 242, 243, 244, 245, 246, 248, 249, 250, 251, 253, 254, 255, 256, 261, 262, 265, 266, 280, 281, 282, 283, 292, 293, 294, 304, 305, 311, 313, 314, 318, 341, 359, 387

inheritance, 140, 149, 387

inheritance of intelligence, 387

intellectual capital, 24, 43, 61, 102, 129, 140, 143, 169, 170, 181, 194, 196, 201, 209, 217, 273, 353, 357, 403

intelligence, 43, 60, 61, 71, 143, 169, 181, 195, 217, 260, 269, 304, 317, 318, 319, 321, 353, 360, 361, 367, 375, 377, 382, 387, 389, 390, 391, 392, 393, 394, 398, 404, 405, 413, 414

interest, 19, 23, 29, 35, 36, 37, 38, 40, 47, 48, 50, 51, 54, 56, 60, 62, 63, 80, 81, 87, 90, 97, 99, 100, 102, 109, 110, 111, 114, 115, 118, 119, 123, 124, 125, 127, 130, 152, 154, 155, 156, 157, 158, 159, 166, 172, 173, 174, 177, 179, 186, 190, 192, 193, 194, 195, 196, 198, 200, 202, 203, 204, 205, 224, 225, 231, 232, 234, 235, 236, 237, 238, 244, 251, 252, 254, 261, 262, 265, 266, 270, 271, 283, 285, 304, 308, 311, 316, 327, 329, 331, 333, 334, 338, 343, 348, 349, 356, 361, 404, 406

internet, 53, 184, 185, 186, 187, 192, 221, 251, 264, 282

IQ, 24, 43, 61, 129, 140, 143, 144, 145, 146, 155, 169, 194, 200, 205, 209, 217, 269, 273, 298, 309, 311, 318, 319, 320, 321, 322, 323, 324, 329, 330, 342, 350, 355, 357, 360, 366, 369, 372, 375, 376, 382, 383, 384, 385, 386, 387, 389, 390, 391, 392, 393, 395, 398, 402, 403

irrational, 35, 60, 153, 181, 191, 199, 229, 261, 271, 294, 295, 296, 299, 301, 302, 327, 330, 397

irrational exuberance, 261

Isaac, 15, 16, 26

Islam, 195

J.P. Morgan, 237

James Joyce, 363

Janet Reno, 117, 252

Japan, 43, 80, 90, 145, 146, 167, 171, 177, 178, 217, 236, 239, 347, 352, 377, 378, 379, 380, 381, 402

Jean-Jacques Rousseau, 31, 213

Jesus, 18, 19, 22, 23, 26, 27, 38

Jew, 19, 20, 171, 363, 371, 381, 392

John D. Rockefeller, 88, 205

John Locke, 212, 213, 371

John Maynard Keynes, 103, 397

John Stuart Mill, 213, 215, 343

Johnson, Lyndon Baines, 112, 123, 126, 191, 228, 247, 262, 294, 413

Judaism, 18, 19, 363, 372, 392

Judas, 22, 23, 30

judicial, 58, 138, 151, 162, 289, 348

justice, 30, 31, 40, 213, 300, 347, 348

Kaiser Wilhelm II, 199, 218, 377, 402

Kant, 215

Kelo v. City of New London, 277, 331

killing, 12, 13, 24, 25, 32, 65, 66, 67, 299

king, 13, 14, 15, 16, 20, 21, 25, 26, 30, 34, 36, 39, 40, 42, 60, 62, 70, 71, 72, 73, 76, 138, 139, 150, 154, 155, 157, 160, 162, 163, 164, 201, 212, 218, 277, 278, 284, 285, 286, 287, 289, 324, 340, 351, 413

Labor theory of value, 195, 196, 198, 199, 214, 328, 330, 346, 347, 397

labor union, 58, 113, 122, 159, 201, 207, 219, 259, 335, 356

laissez-faire, 130, 165, 324

law, 12, 20, 21, 29, 30, 32, 34, 36, 38, 40, 41, 43, 46, 53, 55, 56, 57, 58, 59, 66, 69, 70, 71, 72, 73, 76,

78, 87, 96, 98, 101, 122, 123, 128, 130, 132, 138, 139, 140, 142, 147, 149, 151, 152, 153, 156, 157, 159, 160, 164, 165, 168, 177, 184, 193, 194, 195,□ 200, 202, 205, 206, 209, 215, 223, 225, 226, 256, 259, 260, 264, 268, 270, 272, 273, 274, 275, 276, 279, 285, 287, 290, 292, 298, 300, 304, 305, 306, 308, 313, 318, 324, 325, 326, 327, 330, 333, 334, 335, 336, 337, 340, 343, 345, 348, 352, 355, 356, 357, 369, 370, 371, 372, 382, 394, 401, 403

layoffs ethical, 28, 201

legal, 13, 32, 34, 36, 40, 42, 43, 48, 58, 62, 63, 66, 67, 68, 70, 87, 89, 104, 105, 127, 136, 152, 153, 154, 159, 164, 174, 183, 191, 195, 209, 212, 221, 222, 234, 237, 247, 251, 260, 261, 278, 284, 286, 287, 302, 307, 317, 320, 332, 333, 338, 343, 353, 361, 365, 366, 382

legislative, 138, 151, 162, 277, 288, 306

liberty, 40, 41, 58, 61, 69, 70, 72, 76, 78, 129, 147, 160, 161, 162, 164, 168, 194, 215, 217, 268, 272, 274, 275, 285, 287, 306, 336, 342, 345, 375, 404

life as private property, 136

Lincoln, 74, 88, 92, 163

Lincoln, Abraham, 74, 88, 92, 163

love, 22, 23, 35, 36, 37, 60, 216, 270, 278, 294, 300, 301, 327, 330, 342, 367, 404

love of man, 22, 35, 36, 278, 301

loyalty, 23, 154, 155, 158, 159, 270

Luddites, 208

Lyndon Johnson, 112, 228

Lynn and Vanhanen, 392

Maiden Lane LLC, 105

Malthus, 142, 143, 146

Malthusian, 143, 145, 211, 217, 346

Manchuria, 171, 347

manmade global warming, 401

man's law, 347, 354, 371, 374

Margaret Sanger, 363

marriage, 18, 66, 69, 136, 138, 139, 152, 158, 302, 356, 374

Marx, 214, 215, 354, 372, 377, 396

Marxism, 196, 215, 300, 346, 377

materialism, 215, 216

mean income, 130, 132

median income, 83, 117, 130, 132, 191, 232, 242, 245, 253, 264, 268, 282

Mensa, 395

minimum wage, 59, 122, 159, 202

Minotaur, 25

miscegenation, 29, 200, 311, 320, 364, 366, 369, 377, 382, 390, 392, 394, 403, 405

mixed-race, 195, 309, 329, 359, 364, 394

Moloch, 15, 17, 25

monarchy, 71, 73, 76, 155, 162, 163, 208, 287, 326, 370, 377

monetary deflation, 189, 225, 226, 256, 257, 263, 341

monetary inflation, 91, 95, 104, 105, 106, 111, 120, 173, 174, 189, 190, 191, 225, 226, 227, 229, 230, 232, 233, 234, 244, 245, 254, 255, 292, 341, 359, 386

monetizing debt, 82, 240

money, 28, 38, 39, 47, 48, 49, 51, 52, 77, 79, 80, 81, 83, 85, 87, 88, 89, 90, 93, 94, 95, 97, 100, 101, 103, 104, 105, 107, 108, 109, 111, 112, 114, 115, 116, 119, 120, 123, 124, 127, 128, 130, 133, 136, 153, 154, 166, 168, 172, 173, 174, 175, 177, 185, 186, 188, 189, 190, 193, 194, 195, 196, 197, 198, 204, 222, 224, 225, 229, 230, 234, 235, 236, 237, 238, 239, 240, 243, 246, 249, 250, 252, 254, 255, 257, 258, 260, 264, 266, 267, 268, 280, 286, 293, 294, 295, 298, 304, 307, 311, 312, 315, 316, 318, 319, 320, 344, 400, 406

money supply, 49, 88, 90, 94, 104, 105, 112, 114, 130, 191, 225, 239, 240, 243, 266

Mongoloid, 145, 217, 309, 320, 342, 393, 398

monopoly, 88, 125, 187, 188, 223, 332

Moors, 195, 367

moral, 12, 13, 28, 30, 32, 34, 35, 36, 40, 42, 43, 45, 48, 58, 60, 62, 63,

65, 66, 67, 68, 70, 137, 150, 153, 154, 155, 156, 157, 158, 160, 174, 193, 195, 197, 200, 201, 223, 228, 229, 255, 260, 268, 270, 275, 276, 278, 287, 302, 328, 330, 332, 336, 338, 342, 343, 356, 382, 404

moral equivalence of war, 228, 229

moral philosophy, 28, 30, 33, 43, 153

moral standards, 28

Morrill Tariff, 74, 92, 163

mortgage backed securities, 105, 115

MBS, 105, 234

multifactor productivity, 134

murder, 12, 13, 14, 16, 20, 26, 30, 32, 33, 35, 36, 39, 42, 43, 65, 66, 71, 113, 156, 164, 214, 279, 284, 298, 326, 330, 346, 352, 354, 364, 371, 377, 397

music, 29, 65, 103, 353, 357, 360, 363, 393, 397

Napoleon, 155, 164, 214, 216, 326, 344, 354, 370, 402

Napoleonic Wars, 155, 215, 326

nation under God, 21, 56, 57, 62, 275, 300, 302, 328, 336, 340, 342, 344, 345, 348

National Socialists, 41, 52, 89, 350, 381, 401

Natural Law, 29, 33, 35, 36, 43, 62, 63, 64, 138, 157, 158, 159, 199, 219, 274, 278, 301, 331, 336, 347, 348, 364

Negroid, 126, 143, 144, 146, 196, 206, 217, 252, 275, 309, 310, 313, 316, 317, 319, 320, 322, 329, 353, 356, 364, 366, 367, 368, 369, 377, 382, 383, 384, 385, 386, 387, 388, 389, 390, 394, 395, 398

New Covenant, 17, 18, 19, 20, 23, 198

New Testament, 17, 139

No Child Left Behind, 322, 323

Noah, 15, 16, 17, 198

nominal dollars, 80, 92, 109, 165

nominal wealth, 80

non-profit corporation, 152, 355

normal distribution, 131, 324, 389, 409, 410, 412

North Korea, 167, 177, 304, 351, 352, 381

obligation, 20, 35, 36, 40, 59, 62, 153, 155, 156, 174, 239, 286

Old Covenant, 20, 22

Old Testament, 14, 15, 17, 18, 19, 22, 23, 24, 25

operational efficiency, 173, 175

orphan, 36

orphans, 139, 318

OSHA
Occupational Safety and Health Administration, 122, 225, 310, 324

overpopulation, 139, 140, 148, 363

paradigm shifts in technology, 206, 250, 258, 265, 282, 306, 341

parliament, 73, 75, 96, 162

passion, 14, 18, 21, 30, 32, 38, 60, 77, 113, 156, 157, 181, 198, 216, 226, 270, 271, 296, 300, 301, 302, 326, 327, 341, 344, 345, 351, 355, 367, 368, 372, 401, 404

patent, 65, 78, 150, 206, 209, 210, 304, 350

Peloponnesian War, 273, 368, 413

philosophy, 28, 30, 32, 43, 62, 63, 153, 216, 301, 343, 354, 366, 367, 368, 372

photography, 362, 363, 364

Picasso, 361, 363

pleasure, 17, 159

plebiscite, 19, 32, 76, 162, 163, 278, 279, 284, 330, 370

Pol-Pot, 113

poor, 26, 36, 62, 70, 77, 131, 198, 206, 219, 228, 271, 276, 298, 320, 328, 348, 350, 357

Portugal, 196, 273, 320, 341, 345, 368, 370, 382

PPP
Purchasing Power Parity, 134, 210, 217, 293

president, 93, 107, 123, 126, 167, 191, 222, 229, 238, 247, 251, 253, 254, 264, 287, 351

price controls, 123, 184, 189

price elasticity, 180

price of gold, 89, 90, 94, 112, 114, 120, 123, 125, 183

prime interest rate, 110, 124, 173, 251, 261

private property, 12, 21, 24, 29, 30, 31, 32, 34, 35, 36, 37, 38, 39, 40, 41, 42, 43, 56, 57, 58, 61, 62, 63, 64, 65, 66, 67, 68, 69, 70, 71, 72, 73, 76, 77, 78, 87, 94, 96, 97, 99, 107, 113, 120, 121, 128, 129, 131, 133, 136, 137, 140, 147, 149, 150, 151, 152, 153, 154, 155, 156, 157, 160, 161, 162, 164, 165, 168, 170, 176, 184, 189, 192, 194, 197, 199, 200, 205, 206, 209, 211, 213, 217, 218, 222, 225, 226, 236, 255, 256, 262, 266, 268, 270, 272, 274, 276, 277, 278, 279, 284, 285, 286, 289, 292, 294, 295, 299, 300, 301, 302, 303, 304, 305, 306, 308, 309, 310, 318, 324, 325, 327, 329, 330, 331, 334, 335, 336, 337, 338, 340, 342, 343, 344, 347, 348, 349, 351, 370, 371, 372, 373, 374, 375, 401, 402, 403, 404, 406

productivity, 27, 42, 45, 46, 52, 53, 55, 57, 58, 60, 61, 62, 79, 81, 83, 84, 85, 86, 90, 92, 93, 94, 96, 101, 102, 106, 107, 110, 113, 115, 116, 117, 119, 120, 124, 125, 127, 128, 130, 132, 133, 134, 139, 140, 142, 143, 160, 165, 171, 172, 174, 175, 177, 182, 184, 185, 186, 188, 189, 190, 191, 192, 193, 195, 197, 201, 204, 205, 206, 210, 211, 216, 217, 221, 222, 223, 225, 227, 228, 229, 230, 232, 233, 236, 239, 240, 241, 242, 244, 245, 246, 247, 248, 249, 250, 253, 254, 255, 256, 257, 258, 262, 263, 265, 267, 268, 272, 274, 276, 280, 281, 282, 283, 284, 290, 293, 297, 298, 303, 304, 305, 306, 308, 309, 311, 318, 329, 341, 362, 364, 375, 378, 381, 382, 383, 386, 390, 392, 394, 403, 404

proficiency, 321, 323, 383, 391

profit, 27, 28, 33, 42, 46, 47, 49, 58, 62, 64, 77, 79, 89, 98, 101, 108, 132, 152, 153, 157, 158, 165, 173, 174, 175, 176, 190, 193, 195, 196, 197, 199, 204, 220, 223, 230, 233, 234, 235, 236, 237, 238, 239, 241, 247, 255, 268, 271, 280, 284, 286, 296, 297, 298, 307, 328, 330, 332, 333, 335, 347, 355, 357, 381, 396, 401

progeny, 14, 15, 16, 17, 18, 20, 24, 25, 26, 29, 33, 35, 37, 57, 69, 77, 137, 139, 142, 143, 149, 153, 154, 218, 268, 309, 346, 352, 356, 360, 365, 379, 381, 391, 397

Progressive, 220

Prohibition, 92

property held in common, 67, 68, 69, 78, 98, 141, 154

public education, 57, 98, 308, 309, 313, 317, 319

punishment, 15, 31, 67, 151, 161, 276, 279, 284, 288, 338

Quantitative Easing QE3, 83, 105, 115, 235, 243, 244

race, 29, 129, 143, 171, 196, 206, 217, 309, 319, 329, 341, 352, 358, 363, 364, 366, 367, 369, 381, 382, 387, 388, 389, 391, 393, 394, 413

railroads, 86, 263

rational, 43, 60, 174, 181, 294, 295, 296, 299, 302, 313, 373, 376

rationing, 184, 190, 228, 233

Rawls, John, 347, 348

Reagan, Ronald, 107, 126, 181, 191, 221, 222, 229, 251, 252, 254, 264, 265, 283, 351, 402

real dollars, 107, 109, 211

real wealth, 53, 99, 195, 228, 249

rebellion, 21, 30, 32, 33, 37, 41, 59, 67, 68, 70, 71, 72, 73, 76, 97, 119, 132, 150, 155, 156, 157, 160, 162, 163, 168, 170, 176, 191, 201, 207, 208, 211, 212, 215, 216, 218, 234, 249, 256, 272, 277, 280, 284, 285, 287, 289, 292, 325, 326, 331, 335, 338, 340, 341, 345, 348, 350, 370, 372, 377

regulation, 28, 46, 47, 53, 54, 55, 57, 69, 94, 103, 107, 112, 117, 119, 122, 125, 130, 139, 165, 173, 175, 177, 193, 196, 200, 206, 216, 230, 233, 234, 246, 247, 249, 255, 258, 263, 264, 266, 276, 280, 291, 293, 295, 296, 306, 344, 372

Reign of Terror, 31, 164, 213, 214, 215, 326, 341

Renaissance, 61, 143, 194, 195, 206, 273, 362, 367

republic, 17, 32, 35, 60, 71, 72, 73, 76, 144, 145, 151, 155, 162, 163, 215, 273, 278, 287, 292, 308, 319, 325, 340, 360, 366, 370

Republican, 165, 235, 252

resentment, 39, 271

responsibility, 35, 95, 238, 253

Resurrection, 19, 23, 26, 27

Roman Empire, 17, 61, 68, 87, 143, 194, 195, 273, 307, 320, 357, 358, 360, 366, 367, 368, 382, 390, 392, 394

Sarbanes-Oxley Act of 2002, 296

Satan, 15

Schoenberg, 363

Schopenhauer, 215

science, 143, 354, 365, 390, 393, 394, 398, 401, 402, 414

security, 20, 35, 40, 41, 56, 57, 59, 66, 72, 77, 78, 86, 98, 101, 109, 123, 128, 140, 145, 160, 161, 164, 165, 176, 200, 207, 214, 216, 218, 237, 246, 260, 268, 270, 272, 274, 287, 290, 295, 301, 302, 304, 305, 306, 308, 324, 325, 327, 329, 342, 375, 404

seigniorage, 95

self-interest, 19, 29, 35, 36, 37, 38, 40, 60, 62, 63, 152, 154, 156, 157, 158, 198, 270, 271, 308, 327, 329, 331, 333, 334, 338, 343, 347, 349, 356, 361, 404

serf, 110

Shakespeare, 142, 196, 413, 414

slavery, 34, 74, 76, 140, 347, 367, 391

social contract, 40, 41

social justice, 300, 347, 348

Social Security Act
SSA, 260

socialism, 14, 19, 40, 60, 63, 103, 126, 140, 153, 156, 157, 163, 167, 171, 181, 194, 197, 199, 207, 210, 214, 216, 218, 224, 265, 267, 272, 274, 275, 290, 300, 319, 325, 326, 328, 329, 330, 331, 332, 333, 340, 342, 343, 345, 348, 349, 351, 361, 371, 372, 376, 377,☐ 395, 400, 401, 402, 404

socialist, 19, 24, 33, 35, 41, 52, 64, 90, 96, 127, 130, 157, 167, 170, 177, 189, 194, 200, 207, 209, 215, 216, 221, 234, 290, 300, 303, 330, 333, 344, 345, 347, 348, 350, 351, 352, 354, 364, 368, 370, 372, 373, 377, 381, 382, 394, 399, 401, 402, 403

soldier, 12, 13, 14, 20, 35, 36, 42, 63, 68, 154, 163, 201, 278, 333, 334, 340, 352, 403

Soul, 12, 42, 157

South Korea, 167, 350, 381

sovereign law, 43, 151, 159, 302, 333, 339, 364

Sparta, 273, 368

Spartans, 25, 273

speed of light, 399, 400

sperm whale oil, 205

stagflation, 224, 225

Stalin, 341, 347, 354, 371, 374

standard deviation
SD, 43, 61, 132, 319, 320, 321, 322, 323, 369, 375, 383, 387, 388, 389, 391, 392, 393, 409, 410, 411, 412

Standard Oil Company, 88, 205, 332

Stoic, 22, 213, 214, 220, 229, 270, 271, 301, 331, 344, 345, 346, 347, 355, 365, 366, 367, 369, 377, 380, 402

Stoicism, 22, 35, 126, 127, 149, 213, 214, 296, 303, 330, 346, 348, 366, 367, 380, 401, 402

Stoics, 32, 213, 301, 348, 359, 365, 366, 401

subprime mortgage market, 117, 192

suicide, 22, 23, 36, 43, 67

supply and demand, 49, 86, 122, 172, 173, 178, 179, 180, 181, 187, 190, 193, 226, 227, 230, 233, 234, 245, 255, 256, 257, 263, 292, 305, 308, 334, 335, 337, 341, 347, 350, 351

Supreme Court, 59, 126, 220, 277, 289, 310, 330, 355

tariff, 41, 52, 73, 74, 75, 76, 92, 93, 94, 101, 122, 125, 163, 166, 167, 182, 189, 192, 199, 207, 233, 234, 256, 258, 259, 263, 267, 277, 280, 284, 306, 324, 395

tax, 38, 41, 42, 46, 47, 53, 55, 58, 69, 72, 73, 75, 76, 77, 80, 81, 88, 95, 97, 100, 112, 116, 120, 122, 123, 125, 126, 128, 133, 147, 149, 161, 165, 170, 174, 175, 177, 181, 182, 184, 189, 192, 195, 199, 204, 206, 208, 211, 212, 216, 221, 224, 226, 229, 233, 236, 238, 239, 247, 250, 253, 254, 256, 258, 259, 263, 264, 265, 267, 268, 272, 276, 278, 279, 283, 284, 286, 290, 292, 294, 298, 305, 306, 309, 311, 313, 317, 319, 324, 328, 331, 337, 344, 355, 357, 359, 370, 371, 372, 376, 386, 399, 400, 406

taxation, 28, 34, 38, 42, 46, 47, 53, 55, 69, 75, 78, 85, 94, 96, 97, 101, 103, 107, 108, 110, 117, 122, 130, 139, 147, 162, 165, 170, 173, 175, 177, 193, 200, 206, 207, 209, 216, 230, 233, 234, 237, 244, 246, 247, 249, 254, 255, 258, 259, 262, 264, 266, 267, 279,☐ 282, 284, 285, 291, 294, 295, 306, 319, 326, 331, 337, 340, 341

technology, 27, 122, 127, 141, 186, 188, 192, 205, 206, 207, 211, 217, 221, 230, 250, 251, 257, 259, 264, 265, 281, 282, 283, 289, 305, 306, 329, 341, 362, 364, 390, 393

Ten Commandments, 13, 15, 16, 19, 20, 21, 29, 36, 43, 63, 156, 278, 299, 301, 339, 352

The Golden Rule, 36

The March of the Titans, 369

The Wealth of Nations, 373

theft, 34, 42, 43, 65, 66, 137, 279, 284, 296, 302, 326, 330

Theory of Justice, 347

Thomas Aquinas, 195

Thomas Hobbes, 70, 157, 331, 413

tolerance, 64, 213, 232, 258, 345

total government outlays, 109

Treaty of Versaille, 52, 170

truth, 28, 29, 39, 67, 100, 101, 158, 253, 328, 352, 353, 355, 356, 357, 361, 362, 364, 365, 366, 373, 397

Turk, 196

tyranny, 73, 76, 129, 132, 155, 163, 168, 189, 272, 275, 371, 372

uncertainty, 87, 118, 129, 145, 204, 230, 283, 285, 295, 379

unemployment, 27, 42, 46, 52, 56, 57, 58, 84, 94, 98, 100, 118, 127, 139, 142, 165, 182, 190, 191, 193, 201, 202, 204, 206, 207, 208, 211, 221, 224, 225, 230, 232, 233, 236, 237, 239, 244, 245, 249, 254, 257, 259, 263, 264, 266, 275, 282, 283, 290, 303, 305, 306, 324,☐ 335, 341, 403, 404

union, 57, 58, 60, 64, 74, 75, 111, 112, 125, 133, 147, 155, 157, 159, 173, 183, 184, 188, 195, 196, 201, 202, 205, 210, 219, 221, 222, 223, 224, 225, 229, 246, 247, 250, 253, 260, 263, 264, 266, 272, 303, 313, 336, 350, 351, 356, 369, 370, 378

United Cooper Company, 237

United States Postal Service USPS, 184, 185, 186, 187, 188, 189, 223

United States Statistical Abstract, 383

universal suffrage, 46, 76, 92, 113, 126, 127, 128, 130, 132, 137, 149, 161, 162, 163, 210, 211, 212, 213, 214, 215, 216, 218, 226, 237, 267, 272, 308, 309, 313, 319, 325, 326, 329, 343, 359, 368, 373, 377

US Bureau of Economic Analysis BEA, 99, 106, 406

USSR Soviet Union, 60, 64, 113, 133, 155, 157, 182, 199, 209, 225, 294, 303, 304, 349, 351, 402

usury laws, 193, 194, 195

vanity, 38, 60, 270, 271, 294, 301, 308, 318, 327, 404

variation in wealth, 129, 132

vengeance, 30, 31, 151

vices, 270, 271, 328

Vietnam War, 12, 112, 246

virtues, 213, 270, 271

Voltaire, 31, 213, 397

Wagner Act of 1935, 59, 122, 201, 260, 274

Walter Duranty, 354

war, 12, 20, 21, 34, 36, 46, 59, 62, 68, 70, 72, 73, 74, 75, 76, 78, 86, 87, 88, 89, 90, 91, 92, 94, 105, 106, 108, 112, 119, 120, 123, 125, 130, 132, 148, 155, 156, 157, 160, 162, 163, 165, 167, 170, 182, 189, 191, 198, 199, 201, 208, 209, 212, 215, 216, 218, 223, 225, 227, 228, 230, 233, 237, 246, 254, 256, 262, 273, 274, 287, 290, 292, 293, 294, 307, 318, 326, 328, 331, 345, 346, 351, 355, 365, 368, 370, 376, 377, 378, 382, 388, 390, 391, 402, 403, 407

War between the States, 73, 163, 370

war of all against all, 70, 72, 157, 331

War on Poverty, 106, 112, 246

Warren Harding, 165, 167

wealth, 1, 12, 14, 19, 20, 21, 22, 24, 25, 26, 27, 28, 29, 31, 32, 33, 34, 35, 36, 37, 38, 39, 40, 41, 42, 43, 45, 46, 47, 48, 53, 55, 56, 57, 58, 59, 60, 61, 62, 63, 64, 66, 67, 68, 69, 70, 71, 72, 73, 74, 76, 77, 78, 79, 80, 81, 84, 85, 87, 89, 91, 94, 95, 96,☐ 97, 98, 99, 100, 101, 103, 104, 105, 106, 107, 108, 110, 113, 115, 117, 118, 119, 120, 121, 122, 123, 125, 126, 128, 129, 131, 132, 133, 137, 139, 140, 142, 145, 146, 147, 148, 149, 150, 152, 154, 155, 156, 157, 158, 159, 160, 162, 163, 164, 165, 166, 167,☐ 168, 169, 170, 171, 172, 173, 174, 175, 176, 177, 180, 181, 182, 184, 189, 190, 191, 193, 194, 195, 197, 199, 200, 201, 204, 205, 206, 208, 209, 211, 212, 213, 214, 215, 216, 217, 218, 219, 222, 223, 225, 226, 227, 229, 230, 232, 233, 234, 236, 237, 239, 240, 241, 245, 247, 249, 250, 251, 252, 253, 254, 255, 259, 260, 263, 264, 265, 266, 267, 268, 269, 270, 271, 272, 273, 274, 275, 277, 278, 279, 283, 284, 285, 286, 287, 289, 292, 293, 294, 295, 296, 297, 298, 299, 300, 301, 302, 303, 304, 305, 306, 308, 309, 310, 311, 312, 316, 318, 319, 324, 325, 326, 327, 328, 329, 331, 332, 333, 334, 335, 336, 337, 338, 339, 340, 341, 342, 343, 344, 345, 346, 347, 348, 350, 351, 352, 354, 355, 356, 357, 359, 360, 361, 364, 365, 367, 368, 371, 372, 373, 374, 375, 376, 377, 378, 379, 381, 382, 385, 386, 387, 388, 390, 391, 392, 394, 395, 397, 400, 401, 402, 403, 404, 405, 406, 413

wealth creation, 21, 22, 27, 28, 29, 33, 35, 37, 38, 41, 42, 45, 46, 47, 53, 55, 56, 57, 58, 60, 61, 62, 63, 64, 68, 69, 70, 72, 73, 76, 77, 78, 79, 81, 84, 87, 96, 97, 99, 100, 101, 104, 105, 106, 107, 108, 109, 113, 114, 119, 122, 123, 126, 127, 128, 129, 132, 133, 137, 139, 140, 142, 147, 149, 150, 152, 154, 155, 159, 160, 161, 162, 163, 165, 168, 169, 170, 171, 173, 174, 175, 176, 181, 182, 184, 190, 193, 194, 197, 199, 200, 201, 204, 209, 217, 218, 219, 222, 223, 225, 226, 227, 229, 232, 233, 234, 236, 237, 239, 241, 245, 247, 250, 255, 256, 259, 260, 263, 264, 266, 267, 268, 270, 271, 273, 274, 275, 277, 278, 280, 283, 284, 285, 286, 287, 290, 292, 293, 294, 295, 297, 299, 300, 302, 304, 306, 308, 309, 310, 311, 313, 316, 318, 319, 324, 325, 327, 328, 331, 340, 341, 344, 348, 351, 352, 355, 356, 357, 373, 375, 379, 382, 386, 394, 395, 401, 403, 404, 405

Western Civilization, 19, 24, 143, 172, 194, 208, 209, 211, 279, 311, 341, 354, 366, 367, 368, 393

widow, 36, 212

William Butler Yeats, 361

women in the workforce, 311

Woodrow Wilson, 45, 161, 219, 346, 355

World War I, 88, 89, 90, 91, 94, 105, 108, 119, 120, 123, 125, 130, 148,

165, 167, 170, 182, 199, 201, 207,
210, 215, 216, 217, 223, 228, 254,
290, 293, 345, 347, 351, 377, 378,
402, 407
World War II, 89, 90, 94, 105, 108,
119, 120, 123, 125, 130, 167, 182,

201, 210, 215, 216, 223, 228, 264,
281, 290, 293, 345, 347, 351, 372,
378, 402, 407
Youngstown, 122, 160, 201

Made in the USA
Middletown, DE
21 October 2023

41176390R00239